THE CATHOLIC PRIEST IN THE UNITED STATES:

HISTORICAL INVESTIGATIONS

COMMITTEE ON PRIESTLY LIFE AND MINISTRY
of the
NATIONAL CONFERENCE OF CATHOLIC BISHOPS

Members

John Cardinal Krol
Archbishop of Philadelphia
Chairman

John Cardinal Carberry
Archbishop of Saint Louis

James V. Casey
Archbishop of Denver

Leo C. Byrne
Coadjutor Archbishop of
Saint Paul and Minneapolis

William W. Baum
Bishop of Springfield-Cape Girardeau

Alden J. Bell
Bishop of Sacramento

Ernest J. Primeau
Bishop of Manchester

Alexander M. Zaleski
Bishop of Lansing

Priest Consultants

Carl J. Armbruster, S.J.
Bellarmine School of Theology
Loyola University, Chicago

William A. Bachmann
Our Lady of Peace Church
Cleveland

John J. Egan
Archdiocese of Chicago
Senior Fellow
University of Notre Dame

John Tracy Ellis
University of San Francisco

Andrew M. Greeley
National Opinion Research Center
University of Chicago

Eugene C. Kennedy, M.M.
Loyola University, Chicago

Eugene H. Maly
Mount Saint Mary's Seminary
of the West
Cincinnati

The Catholic Priest in the United States:

Historical Investigations

Edited by

John Tracy Ellis

Chairman of the Subcommittee on History
of the
Committee on Priestly Life and Ministry
of the
National Conference of Catholic Bishops

SAINT JOHN'S UNIVERSITY PRESS
Collegeville, Minnesota
1971

In grateful and loving memory to
Paul J. Hallinan
1911–1968
Archbishop of Atlanta
who more than any other
single person was
responsible for these essays.

FOREWORD

The troubled state of human life throughout the world in the 1960's intensified the difficulties which normally attend the life and ministry of priests. As co-workers of bishops to whom Christ entrusted the message and ministry of reconciliation, priests are men of God among men; they are in the world but not of the world; they must conform the world to Christ and avoid conformation to the world; they are witnesses and dispensers of a life other than this earthly one; they must please God rather than men. Their mission is that of the Church — to unite men with God and with each other; their ministry — a never changing one, must be sensitive to the changes in the life and conditions of those whom they serve.

The Decree on the Ministry and Life of Priests of Vatican Council II acknowledging the difficulties experienced by priests as a result of the radical and rapid social and moral changes in contemporary life; affirms that the Holy Spirit is impelling "the Church to open new avenues of approach to the contemporary world and is also suggesting and fostering fitting adaptations in the ministry of priests." (n. 22)

The bishops of the United States were eager to learn the precise nature and dimensions of the difficulties experienced by priests as a result of the radical and rapid social and moral changes in contemporary life. The conciliar documents recommended the use of the findings of religious sociological and psychological surveys in adapting pastoral care to current needs (Bishops, n. 17; Church in World, n. 62). The stream of 'scientific' surveys which appeared after the Council increased rather than dispelled confusion. Some of the surveys were spotty and biased and geared to serve as instruments of propaganda.

At their meeting in April, 1967, the bishops authorized a complete, professional, and objective study of the life and ministry of priests. The study was entrusted to a committee of bishops, who were to develop plans for the study jointly with competent priests and laymen. The initial meeting of the Committee was held in Oak Park, Illinois, on December 16, 1967. At this meeting subcommittees for theology, liturgy, spirituality, history, sociology, psychology, ecumenism, and pastoral care were established. Each of these subcommittees was chaired by a priest, who in consultation with his respective episcopal moderator was to choose others of his own discipline to work with him. The full committee of the study held an average of two meetings a year since its inception at which progress reports were made and problems relating to their research and writing were discussed and resolved.

History helps us to know the past, to understand the present and to plan for the future. The history of the Catholic Church and of the priesthood in the United States is a glorious one. The last fifty years of this history is a record of incredible growth of the Church under the guidance of the Holy Spirit.

Through the period of unrestricted immigration, the Catholic population increased from an estimated 35,000 in 1789 to 17,000,000. The discriminatory restrictions introduced in 1921 and 1924 reduced the growth in the Catholic Church to a natural one — with insignificant accretion through immigration. Between 1920 and 1970 the Catholic population grew from 17,700,000 to 47,800,000 and the number of priests increased from 21 to 59 thousand, for an increase of 266% in population and 295% in the number of priests. The fifty-year increase approximates the total population of such countries as Spain and Poland and is five to seven times greater than the total population of such countries as Belgium, Austria, and Hungary. It is not unreasonable to conclude that under the guidance of the Holy Spirit, the growth of the Church in the United States is due in great measure to the zeal and diligence of the priests and of the religious.

The five essays that furnish the contents of this volume trace the history of select aspects of the American priesthood from the organization of the Church in the new Republic with the appointment (November, 1789) and episcopal ordination (August, 1790) of John Carroll as Bishop of Baltimore whose jurisdiction covered the entire United States, down to the present time. Since the experience of priests in colonial America, from the arrival in the 1520's of the first of their number on the soil of what would later become the United States to the age of Carroll and his contemporaries, was felt to have less relevance for American priests in the late twentieth century, it was agreed that it would be preferable to use the beginnings of organized Catholicism in the 1790's as a *terminus a quo* with the late 1960's serving as the *terminus ad quem*.

It is appropriate that the historians' work should precede that of the other subcommittees in order that the latter's reports may be afforded an ample background. The five essays contained in this book treat areas that are crucial to an understanding of the past of the priest in the United States as well as to an intelligent comprehension of his present status. The five topics chosen for treatment were: the priest's spiritual and intellectual formation, his relations to his bishop, his public image as reflected on the national scene, the relations of the numerous priests of religious orders and congregations to the bishops and to the diocesan clergy, and, finally, the role of the priest in the evolving patterns of the Church's social apostolate in theory and in practice.

Here, then, is the American Catholic priest presented through an historical perspective. Obviously, no two periods of American history or no two sets of circumstances which have encompassed the priests of this country have ever been identical. There have been similarities, however, that can serve as signposts, so to speak, even for so revolutionary an age as our own. If these essays demonstrate that the American Church has never encountered quite so severe a storm as that through which she is now passing, or that through which the Universal Church has passed in the centuries that have gone, they do reveal periods of strife and uncertainty that have tossed the barque of the Church of the United States to and fro as she proceeded on her pilgrim way. These periods of stress and tension date from the time when the Republic was young, a time that witnessed the unruly priests with whom Archbishop Carroll had to contend amid the abuses of lay trusteeism to the sometimes angry and impatient minority of priests who have broken from her obedience in the tumultuous years since Vatican Council II. Yet if the authors of these essays have been intent to set forth in the open and honest fashion that befits the canons of true historical scholarship the trials as well as the triumphs of the American priesthood over the 178 years that have intervened since Bishop Carroll ordained the first priest in May, 1793, their investigations have likewise made clear the love and loyalty of the great majority of priests for the Church and the regulations she had drawn up for their lives. In this sense the five historians whose essays are presented here have pursued their research and then cast their findings into narrative form in a consciousness of the truth expressed by the distinguished English priest historian, David Knowles, when he declared:

> So the historian, contemplating the lamentable weakness and catastrophes of men within the Church, whether in his own day or centuries ago, is able to realise that such things have been before and will be again, but that the light of the Holy Spirit, though now

and then dimmed and obscured by human weakness and malice, will shine forth again in due time. . . . [Thus] the historian will be able to say with Odysseus: 'Bear it, dear heart, for thou has borne ere now a worse blow than this.' [1]

JOHN CARDINAL KROL
Archbishop of Philadelphia
Chairman of the
Committee on Priestly Life and Ministry
of the
National Conference of Catholic Bishops

1. "The Need for Catholic Historical Scholarship," *Dublin Review*, CCXXXII (Summer, 1958), 124.

PREFACE

"The higher man rides on the shoulders of the past, the more likelihood that his perspective of the present will be clear." [1] I know of no more fitting way to introduce what should be said here than to quote those words from the late and lamented Archbishop of Atlanta, Paul J. Hallinan, who as its first episcopal moderator was responsible for the subcommittee on history of the bishops' Committee on Priestly Life and Ministry. Archbishop Hallinan was responsible as well for the selection of the subcommittee's chairman and for the original names of the four historians who were invited to write one or other of the essays in this book. There was no difficulty in agreeing on these names: Francis L. Broderick, Michael V. Gannon, James J. Hennesey, S.J., and Robert Trisco. At our first meeting in Oak Park, Illinois, on December 16, 1967, the archbishop was at pains to emphasize that there should be a lay historian working with the priests, and we were happy when Dr. Broderick, then Dean of Lawrence University, agreed to serve. Upon the latter's appointment as Chancellor of the University of Massachusetts, Boston, however, it became impossible for him to continue, and at that point Professor O'Brien of the College of the Holy Cross graciously consented to take up where Chancellor Broderick was compelled to sever his connection with the project.

Soon after the committee got underway a similar situation arose in regard to Father Hennesey who was named superior of the large Jesuit community at Fordham University, and when his new responsibility rendered it impossible for him to continue with us, Father John P. Marschall, C.S.V., then of Loyola University, Chicago, and later of the University of Nevada, with equal graciousness expressed his willingness to take over the assignment relating to the priests of the religious orders and congregations. Three and a half months after the Oak Park meeting Archbishop Hallinan died on March 27, 1968, and the subcommittee on history then had assigned as their episcopal moderator the Most Reverend Alden J. Bell, Bishop of Sacramento, to whom the historians are grateful for a ready compliance with every request made of him during the last three years. I like to think that Archbishop Hallinan would have been pleased with the essays in this book since they represent the finished product of the research and writing of the subcommittee that he brought into being in December, 1967.

To state that the American Catholic priesthood is at present passing through a grave crisis is to state the obvious. To say that the crisis among Catholic priests is worldwide is equally obvious, even though that fact does little to mitigate the conditions now prevalent among the priests of the United States. The American priesthood has offered no exception to the universal proposition enunciated by Pierre Teilhard de Chardin when he remarked that whatever one studied he was forced to the same conclusion, namely, "that everything is the sum of the past and that nothing is comprehensible except through its history." [2] Yet whatever benefits a knowledge of their own history might have bestowed on American priests, the present crisis finds them largely without enlightenment from that source. For in that regard they have shared the same training as the bishops, the religious, and the laity, all of whom have been taught little or nothing of their Church's past. Reflecting on this characteristic of the American Catholic community that has exercised so pervasive an influence on their thought and action, Garry Wills touched an Achille's heel when he declared:

> The barest acquaintance with history would have destroyed most Catholics' image of the church and of the Bible. . . . It was easier to pretend that the church had no past, only an eternal present. The church-then was just the same as the church-now; and we already knew the church-now, so we had nothing important to learn about the church-then. . . . Robbed of its past, the church existed in a present of precarious immediacy.[3]

So unaccustomed have American Catholics been to think and to speak in terms of an historical framework for their religious beliefs and for their Church as an institution, that less than a decade ago the application of terms like 'crisis' and 'revolution' to the huge and confident body that constituted the Catholic Church in this country would have been thought quite extreme if not somewhat eccentric. But the series of events that began to happen in their midst about the time that Pope John XXIII ascended the throne of Peter in October, 1958, and that has continued with seemingly ever accelerated speed to the present day, has left many Catholics, and especially priests, sufficiently shaken from their familiar and comfortable moorings that they no longer demur, as they would have done in the early 1950's, when they are told they are both witnesses to and participants in a revolution as profound as anything that the Church has experienced since the Protestant Reformation over 450 years ago, not excepting the violent changes that she was compelled to encounter when the French Revolution erupted and swept all before it in the years after 1789.

If the Catholic priest of the United States has found himself perplexed and bewildered by the apparent collapse of some of his stoutest supports in both Church and State, he cannot be blamed for his inability to understand fully the nature of the forces that have destroyed much of the world that he once knew. For it is no small part of the Church's present anguish that she is surrounded in every aspect of the secular and civil order in which she exists by a revolution as profound and mysterious as that that has unsettled man's religious life. When even so wise and experienced an observer as Walter Lippmann has been led to say, "I know of nobody, and I've heard of nobody, who has come anywhere near to understanding fully and practically this revolutionary condition," [4] the Catholic priest need feel no peculiar compunction about his failure to discover solutions for the well nigh unprecedented havoc that has swept his professional stability and vocational commitments into the whirlpool that seethes and churns so violently the society of which he is a part. In the priest's search for an identification of the principal factors that constitute what Lippmann has called "this revolutionary condition," a condition to which many features in ecclesiastical life at the present hour conform, the pattern of the past may lend some assistance. And here I know no better statement of these controlling factors, that at the same time says a lot about the situation for which the authors of the essays in this book have attempted to provide the antecedents, than that of Robert R. Palmer. In endeavoring to set the stage for the latter's notable two-volume work on the revolutionary generation of the late eighteenth century, he said:

> By a revolutionary situation is here meant one in which confidence in the justice or reasonableness of existing authority is undermined; where old loyalties fade, obligations are felt as impositions, law seems arbitrary, and respect for superiors is felt as a form of humiliation; where existing sources of prestige seem undeserved, hitherto accepted forms of wealth and income seem ill-gained, and government is sensed as distant, apart from the governed and not really 'representing' them. In such a situation the sense of community is lost, and the bond between social classes turns to jealousy and frustration. People of a kind formerly integrated begin to feel as outsiders, or those who have never been integrated begin to feel

left out. As a group of Sheffield workingmen demanded in 1794: 'What is the constitution to us if we are nothing to it?'

No community can flourish if such negative attitudes are widespread and long-lasting. The crisis is a crisis of community itself, political, economic, sociological, personal, psychological, and moral at the same time. Actual revolution need not follow, but it is in such situations that actual revolution does arise. Something must happen, if continuing deterioration is to be avoided; some new kind or basis of community must be formed.[5]

That 'something must happen,' all thoughtful men will, I think, agree if the present deteriorating condition among American Catholic priests is to be arrested and they are to regain once more a healthy and hopeful state. Precisely what that 'something' will be, no one can predict with certainty, and least of all should it be attempted by historians whose business it is to deal with facts not fantasies. Yet by reason of their special training, what historians can do better than others is to furnish as exact and complete a picture as possible of the evolving past. This picture, in turn, will then endeavor — and it is at best an endeavor — in the classical expression of Leopold von Ranke, to "show how things actually were" [*zeigen wie es eigentlich gewesen*]; and from the parallels offered by past and present situations some suggestion of what the future may hold in similar circumstances may emerge. That is what the five historians whose essays are published here have tried to do.

There are several qualifications and limitations that should be made clear in introducing the reader to the contents of the present volume. These essays do not constitute a history of the American Catholic priesthood. They represent rather an investigation of five distinct aspects of the priesthood as it has been lived in the American Church, five viewpoints or approaches, so to speak, to a very broad and highly varied spectrum that embraces in its totality much more than is found here. For example, the reader will find relatively little about the priest's pastoral and liturgical activities for the reason that special subcommittees of the Committee on Priestly Life and Ministry had been assigned those topics. This will likewise account for the absence of any detailed discussion of the priest in the sociological and psychological dimensions of his spiritual and professional life. It is to be hoped, however, that the historical essays will invite further probing and investigating and thus stimulate other studies on the priest as a leading personality in the Catholic community of this country. On the other hand, a conscious effort has been made to supply the *mise en scène* of the priest's secular background, for although the American priest could never be described in terms used by Denis W. Brogan of his French counterpart as "part of the national furniture," the priest like any other American has functioned in a real environment and not in a vacuum.

Religious history has long labored under a particularly heavy handicap. That handicap was induced and became fixed in the literary traditions of the late sixteenth century in consequence of the religious revolution when the historical polemics of the Lutheran Centuriators of Magdeburg prompted, in turn, the defensive and apologetic *Annales ecclesiastici* of Cardinal Caesar Baronius (1538–1607) and his successors. So deeply did this tradition color the thinking of men about Protestant and Catholic history that traces of it linger on here and there at this late date, and suspicions concerning the objective character of their own religious history are encountered among adherents of both the Catholic and Protestant Churches. The tradition persisted with a special venom and stubbornness among the English by whom it was carried to America and transmitted to their descendants here. An illustration of what is meant was afforded by the publication of the *History of England* by John Lingard, a diocesan priest. When Lingard sought to defend himself against his critics in a supplementary work, one of the leading religious journals of the time reacted by stating:

> We acknowledge that, on the first announcement of a History of England from the pen of a priest of the Roman Catholic faith, we did apprehend that neither the spirit of his religion nor the habits of his profession were calculated to prepare him for the composition of an impartial work.[6]

A word should, therefore, be said about the 'official' auspices under which this book came to be written. These essays were, indeed, commissioned by the American hierarchy, and all expenses incurred by the five essayists in their research, travel, and writing were generously paid by the bishops. Yet the authors worked with the utmost freedom, and with a single exception their labors proceeded entirely free of any attempt by a bishop or a diocesan official to censor, change, or modify what they had written. The exception has been noted in the essay on the priests of the religious orders and congregations where the writer states that of his requests made to six ordinaries of one region of the country to use their diocesan archives, only one, himself a trained historian, "granted unlimited access to official documents."[7]

The authors of this volume can say in the words of John Lingard, a priest historian whose pioneering efforts entitle him to an honored place in the historiography of the English-speaking world, "Through the work, I made it a rule to tell the truth whether it made for or against us." [8] At the same time they have not been beguiled by the delusion that they have written with absolute objectivity. No historian worthy of the name has ever written with absolute objectivity, whether it be von Ranke who reflected his deep attachment to the Lutheran Church or Ludwig von Pastor whose monumental *History of the Popes* with its manifold disclosures of scandals in the lives of high churchmen yet breathed the great Austrian historian's love for the Catholic Church. While the historians whose essays appear here have not, perhaps, been as explicit as Lingard was in declaring to a priest friend, "Whatever I have said or purposely omitted has been through the motive of serving religion," [9] they, nonetheless, own to their love of the Catholic priesthood and to their desire to render it a service by bringing to light hidden aspects of its American story. To pretend that this basic sympathy had not informed their narratives would be to speak and to act with less than the candor to which their readers are entitled. And in doing so they would add that they feel they have departed not a whit from the accepted canons of scientific history, for it has been their intent to write history and not to compile a soulless annal of the American priesthood.

In conclusion it remains to say only a word of thanks. As chairman of the subcommittee on history of the bishops' Committee on Priestly Life and Ministry the writer believes he can speak in the name of his four colleagues, as well as in his own name, in thanking Cardinal Krol, Bishop Bell, and the other episcopal members of the committee for the support that sustained them through a long and laborious assignment. He wishes as well to express his thanks to Father Edwin B. Ncill, Associate General Secretary of the National Conference of Catholic Bishops, for helping to clarify a number of procedural problems. And it is a particular pleasure to thank each of his four fellow historians for their patience in bearing with his repeated demands of one kind or another, and especially was this true of Monsignor Gannon and Father Trisco who were unfailing in their prompt responses to his numerous requests for their co-operation and assistance. As he comes to the end of this preface and realizes that it marks the end as well of a sometimes difficult yet always stimulating and profitable enterprise, he looks back in retrospect to an association that drew him closer to certain personal and professional friends as it opened the door first of acquaintanceship and then, hopefully, to a lasting friendship with others. In this he is reminded of an inscription which that distinguished historian of the Church, the late Monsignor Philip Hughes of the University of Notre Dame, entered in a gift copy of

Volume III of his splendid work, *The Reformation in England*, under the date of October 8, 1954, which read: *Haec est vera fraternitas*. It is, indeed, and I am grateful to one and all who made this scholarly voyage possible and who assisted in any way in bringing our common efforts safely into port.

John Tracy Ellis

San Francisco
January 16, 1971

1. "The American Bishops and the Vatican Councils," *Catholic Historical Review*, LI (October, 1965), 380.

2. *The Future of Man*. Translated by Norman Denny. New York and Evanston: Harper & Row, Publishers. 1964. p. 12.

3. "Memories of a Catholic Boyhood," *Esquire*, LXXV (February, 1971), 117.

4. "The Revolution No One Understands," San Francisco *Sunday Examiner and Chronicle*, June 9, 1968, p. 3.

5. *The Age of the Democratic Revolution. A Political History of Europe and America, 1760–1800. The Challenge*. Princeton: Princeton University Press. 1959. p. 21.

6. *Westminster Review*, VII (January, 1827), 187. The remark was occasioned by the appearance the previous year of Lingard's *A Vindication of Certain Passages in the Fourth and Fifth Volumes of the History of England*. 2nd ed. London, 1826.

7. Note 16, p. 414.

8. Lingard to John Kirk, Hornby, December 18, 1819, Donald F. Shea, *The English Ranke: John Lingard*. New York: Humanities Press, 1969. p. 26.

9. Same to same, December 18, 1819, *ibid.*, p. 27.

A NOTE ON THE CONTRIBUTORS

Monsignor Ellis, a priest of the Archdiocese of Washington, is professor of church history in the University of San Francisco and lecturer in church history in the Graduate Theological Union, Berkeley, California.

Father Trisco, a priest of the Archdiocese of Chicago, is associate professor of church history in the Catholic University of America, editor of the *Catholic Historical Review*, and secretary of the American Catholic Historical Association.

Monsignor Gannon, a priest of the Diocese of Saint Augustine, is pastor of Saint Augustine Church and associate professor of religion and history in the University of Florida at Gainesville.

Father Marschall, a priest of the Congregation of Saint Viator, is director of the Center for Religion and Life and lecturer in history in the University of Nevada at Reno.

Doctor O'Brien is associate professor of history in the College of the Holy Cross, Worcester, Massachusetts.

TABLE OF CONTENTS

THE CATHOLIC PRIEST IN THE UNITED STATES:

HISTORICAL INVESTIGATIONS

JOHN TRACY ELLIS

THE FORMATION OF THE AMERICAN PRIEST: AN HISTORICAL PERSPECTIVE

"Is it not a scandal that our students should find less resources in our seminaries than in any of the colleges of the University?" Such was the question asked by a writer in the August, 1831, issue of the *Annales de philosophie chrétienne* in defending himself against the attacks of certain critics of his recent contribution to that journal on the subject, "De l'Education Cléricale." [1] To read his reply with its emphasis on the century's pride in science, on the need for the seminaries to be abreast of contemporary thought while at the same time respecting the wisdom of the past, on the necessity for shortening the length of the seminary course, and to find the writer maintaining that it was the priest's mission to regenerate the world by his virtue and his learning, is to call to mind the oft-quoted French axiom, *plus ça change, plus c'est la même chose*!

A Problem With A Past

Discontent with the training of men for the priesthood has been — as it should remain — a constant refrain throughout the Church's history, for that education has frequently been at its worst when there appeared to be the most widespread satisfaction with it. It is doubtful, however, if any brief span of time in the Church's nearly 2,000 years of existence has witnessed more far-flung and revolutionary changes in the spiritual and intellectual formation of priests than have taken place in the present decade. These changes could be illustrated from a wide range of examples, but let two from the year 1966 suffice. November of that year marked the appointment of the American bishops' Committee on Priestly Formation, a group that has sponsored a scrutiny of the Church's commitment to seminary education in all sections of the United States. In that year too the first Catholic seminaries sought membership in the interdenominational American Association of Theological Schools in the United States and Canada, and by September, 1969, out of the AATS' total membership of 174 institutions thirty-nine were Catholic seminaries. Involved in these two events of 1966 was not only a serious effort for renewal and reform, but also a reaching out by the Catholic seminaries to other Americans of varying educational traditions in a way that would have been unthinkable twenty years ago.

It is to be hoped that the sweeping changes of the 1960's may by means of trial and error teach the responsible persons in a way that will have an enduring effect and render unnecessary a repetition of past mistakes. But in this regard the historical record is no more encouraging for churchmen connected with seminaries than it is for any other group of men. Henry Edward Manning, Archbishop of Westminster, put the point well nearly a century ago when he said, "History seems to some men to be written in vain; and the lessons of experience seldom outlive the first generation of those whom suffering has made wise." [2] Had it been otherwise, efforts during the 1960's to bring seminary education into contact with current realities would not need to have been nearly the unsettling and traumatic experience that some have found it to be. For, in fact, much of what has been said and written about the seminary since Vatican Council II has in no sense been strikingly new.

To cite a single example, in 1829 the Abbé Félicité de Lamennais counseled his fellow Catholics of France in terms that read like a commentary on the recent council's Decree on Priestly Formation promulgated on October 28, 1965. Lamennais urged his contemporaries not to be afraid to admit that theology, "so beautiful in itself, so engaging and vast," had become a lifeless subject the dryness of which repulsed students. "Cut from your course," he told the seminary authorities,

> many of the vain questions which tire them without results and which take away from them precious time which they could spend more usefully learning about things applicable to the century in which they live and in the world on which they must act. Everything has changed around you; ideas have taken and continue to take new directions; institutions, laws, morals, opinions, nothing resembles what our fathers saw. Of what use is the most intense zeal without knowledge of the society in whose midst it must perform. We must learn with another method and learn more; with another method, to understand better, in order not to fall behind those for whose guidance we are responsible. [3]

What was said by Lamennais in 1829, and two years later by the writer in the *Annales de philosophie chrétienne*, was not unrelated to the early history of the Church's seminaries in the United States.[4] Only thirty-eight years previous to the publication of Lamennais' book, seminary education under Catholic auspices had been begun in this country by a small band of French-born Sulpicians with the opening in October, 1791, of Saint Mary's Seminary in Baltimore. The story of this institution's severe struggles during its first decades of existence has been told before and needs no retelling here. Suffice it to say, the 115 students enrolled at Saint Mary's between 1791 and 1829, of whom fifty-two were ultimately ordained priests, were trained much along the lines of the system that their professors had known in France. In fact, according to one of the historians of the seminary, once the days of uncertainty had passed, "there was a distinct trend back to the conservatism, regularity and tradition of Paris." [5]

Following a visitation of the American houses in 1829 by Father Joseph Carrière, who was delegated by the Superior General of Saint Sulpice, a revised rule was put into effect at Saint Mary's. A sampling of that document not only affords one an insight into life at this mother seminary of the American Church in its early years, but it also suggests how remote are the seminaries of today from their prototype of 140 years ago. For example, it was prescribed that the students' morning prayer should last "thirty-seven minutes, comprising in that enough time for vocal prayer." Regulations pertaining to the retreat, which opened a new school year were retained, the rosary was to be recited at 6:45 P.M. on all days except walk days when it was said at 2:30 P.M., but the rule noted one change in the spiritual exercise when it stated, "The custom of going to the chapel at six o'clock in the evening for the Angelus will be suppressed." As for academic affairs, there was to be a class each day in both dogmatic and moral theology, and the customary examinations twice a year were to be re-established. The rule did not overlook practical matters such as the students' health, and as for their meals, at dinner they were to be given "a determined quantity of wine," while breakfast was to consist of bread, butter, and coffee, and they would be allowed "twelve minutes for this repast." [6]

A National Seminary?

If that Baltimore voice of 1829 sounds distinctly quaint and almost infinitely remote in 1971, another happening in the same city and the same year carries a ring that is all too familiar. Were one asked to state the single greatest weakness in Catholic seminary education both in the United States as well as in Europe and Latin America, the wanton dissipation of the Church's limited resources in a proliferation of small and feeble educational institutions would rank near the top of the list. True, the narrow and restricted intellectual range has likewise told heavily against superior education in the seminaries, but here as in other matters a remedy might have been found had there been a concentration in fewer institutions of size and strength. The causes for the multiplication of seminaries have, of course, varied, but many could be traced to the interpretation which churchmen since the late sixteenth century have put on the decree of the Council of Trent of July, 1563, which called for a seminary in every diocese wherever that was possible. Unfortunately, a literal interpretation of the conciliar legislation on this point was congenial to men whose intellectual horizons were already handicapped by a deep strain of provincialism and local pride, and they could usually cite as a warrant the Roman Curia's repeated inquiries of bishops concerning the need for a seminary in their dioceses. From the viewpoint of quality education the result was doomed to fail from the outset with both dioceses and religious communities struggling to have their own seminaries, regardless of their intellectual and material impoverishment.

The organized Church of the United States was scarcely a generation old before the traces of this influence appeared. More than a year in advance of the First Provincial Council of Baltimore in October, 1829, Benedict J. Fenwick, Bishop of Boston, attempted to rally his fellow bishops behind the idea of a central or national seminary to be in charge of the Sulpicians. James Whitfield, Archbishop of Baltimore, strongly seconded Fenwick's suggestion, and at first John England, Bishop of Charleston, agreed but later shifted his position. When the question was brought before the council, however, Benedict J. Flaget, Bishop of Bardstown, who had begun a seminary in Kentucky in 1811, led the opposition because of the expense and distance involved and the issue was thus killed for the time being. In the closing days of the council Archbishop Whitfield wrote Antoine Garnier, Superior General of Saint Sulpice, assuring him that he would do all in his power to further the Baltimore seminary, but he added, "the other bishops give but little hopes of their cooperation of rendering this a central seminary. They complain of want of money." [7]

A renewed attempt for a national seminary at Baltimore's Second Provincial Council of October, 1833, met with no more success than the first. Meanwhile the opening of small struggling seminaries continued apace in every section of the United States until by 1840 more than a dozen had been founded in the sixteen dioceses of that year with their total of 482 priests and approximately 660,000 Catholics, of whom more than 240,000 had arrived as immigrants only within the same decade.

There was not a really strong institution among these seminaries which were frequently located in remote spots that admitted no access to large centers of population, such as Saint Vincent de Paul Seminary at Donaldsonville, Louisiana, while they stretched for hundreds of miles apart from Dubuque, Iowa, in the west where the seminary begun in 1839 was in the house of Matthias Loras, the first bishop, to Lafargeville, New York, in the east where a few days after the opening in September, 1838, the rector, Father Francis Guth, described the scene for John Hughes, Coadjutor Bishop of New York, in terms that were typical of the period. He said:

> With the assistance of my two excellent colleagues, I have launched your small vessel with a most limited number of passengers — six young men and two boys. We hope to pick up some more travellers, or else we could not go far.[8]

It took no more than a year for it to become apparent that the seminary's future was at best a highly dubious one, and in informing Hughes that they had commenced classes the previous day "with a handful of children," Guth asked:

> Is it not a pity that for so few you should have such a burden and we so much labor and classes? We might be compared to a big stage-coach drawn by four horses, and no passengers.[9]

Most of the seminaries founded up to the mid-century and beyond had their own version of "no passengers," and the dioceses and religious communities that brought them into existence knew the same heavy drain on limited finances and manpower that the two false starts at Nyack and Lafargeville had cost the young Diocese of New York. Scarcely any of these institutions escaped the burden of conducting a boys' school of one kind or another in connection with the seminary, since the fees for the boys' tuition and board and room appeared to be the best means of securing the money to keep the seminary operating. Nor was there any notable difference in this regard between diocesan institutions and those of religious orders. For example, James Van de Velde, S.J., a future Bishop of Chicago, began his study of theology at Georgetown College in 1825, but nine years later at Saint Louis University where he served as minister, prefect of studies, professor of mathematics and Spanish, and for a time as treasurer, his course was still unfinished. It was little wonder that

Van de Velde should have asked John Roothaan, General of the Jesuits, "What is to be done in this scarcity of personnel when every one has on his hands all that he can possibly do?" [10] Reminiscing a generation later to Peter Beckx, Roothaan's successor as general, Father Ferdinand Coosemans, by that time provincial of the Missouri Province, threw light on more than one aspect of priestly training in these years when he wrote:

> All the time I have been in the Society I have been occupied with duties without having had a single year free for study. During the second year of my novitiate I repeated my Rhetoric. While still a novice I was sent to a college where, completely immersed in prefecting as also in teaching some four hours a day, I studied philosophy for the space of two years. This study amounted to little more than copying out Father Martin's notes; we had no printed text of philosophy. Fortunately I did not have much to forget when Father Martin's system was prohibited in the Society. [Martin had come under suspicion as an ontologist]. My study in moral was confined to Gury [Jean Pierre Gury, S.J. (1801–1866)] which I studied for a year and a half without having time to consult other authors; I was at the same time prefect of the students and professors. For one year only did I study Dogma, but I failed in my examination partly for lack of talent, partly because of the distractions occasioned by my prefecting and teaching. I was ordained priest that same year. Superiors no doubt did not forsee that I should one day find myself in my present position [of provincial].

The historian of the Jesuits of the Middle West concluded the citation of this letter with the comment, "Father Coosemans's experience was entirely typical." [11] And if these were the conditions that obtained in the Society of Jesus, the largest of the religious orders committed to the educational apostolate, it is not difficult to imagine how matters stood with the smaller and weaker religious congregations.

It was not that among both the bishops and religious superiors there were not men who showed an awareness of the weakness inherent in committing themselves to too many institutions with too few trained men and too little material resources to conduct them properly. For example, Bishop Fenwick of Boston told Francis Dzierozynski, the Jesuits' American superior, in 1830 that he had just dedicated two new churches, to which he added:

But *cui bono* when I have no priests to put in them. Oh what shall I do without a Seminary? In these degenerate days when you as well as all Bps of U. States are determined to act upon the maxim that charity begins at home.[12]

In like manner a few years later, Father John Hughes, future Bishop of New York, lamented to his former professor, Simon Bruté, recently elected to the new See of Vincennes:

With regard to any thing being done for the Education of clergymen, I despair of it, until the Bishops & Colleges or college shall understand each other, and themselves better. It is a subject on which there is too great a variety of opinion — and on which each Superior looks only to the boundaries of his own jurisdiction.[13]

Hughes had, indeed, put his finger on the prime cause of this folly, and during the next thirty years he led in the establishment of a seminary for the ecclesiastical Province of New York as well as giving strong support, once he learned the project was desired by Pope Pius IX, to the North American College in Rome. That the resources were inadequate for the seminaries would seem to be apparent from the repeated appeals in almost every national pastoral of the hierarchy from that of the single Bishop Carroll in May, 1792, to the lengthy letter of September, 1919, issued at the end of the hierarchy's first annual meeting. The appeal from the Third Provincial Council of Baltimore in April, 1837, was one of the strongest of all. In this instance the bishops stated:

In these United States, our fellow-citizens of various religious denominations, have numerous, large and well endowed theological schools, to which their yearly contributions are very considerable. Hitherto you have done little or nothing to aid our seminaries. Many of us have received for this purpose, moderate aid from the piety of our fellow catholics in France, in Austria, and in one or two instances from Ireland. The Holy See has also generously admitted some of our youths into the Urban College of the Propaganda at Rome, where they gratuitously receive their education and have their wants supplied. We strenuously exhort you to do your duty, by contributing to raise up a national clergy; exert ourselves [*sic*] to provide that your own sons should minister at your altars. In your several Dioceses you can co-operate, each of you with his proper prelate, for this most important object.[14]

In this as in all the Church's manifold activities the American Catholic laity ultimately acquired a worldwide reputation for extraordinary generosity, a fact of which the bishops took note in the pastoral letter of 1884 where they spoke of the "zealous liberality" by which the laity had enabled them to build and to support seminaries. And they added, "we are well assured that you will not be found wanting, should even greater efforts be necessary, to enable us to make the education and usefulness of the clergy as perfect as we desire." [15]

Nor were the laity found wanting in the years after 1884, but it was a pity that their generosity was not more evenly matched by the churchmen's economy and careful planning in the commitment to seminary education. It was not that they lacked papal sanction for such a policy. On the occasion of his golden jubilee as a priest Pope Pius XI issued an encyclical, *Ad Catholici Sacerdotii*, in December, 1935, in which he acknowledged the fact that it was impossible for every diocese to have its own seminary properly equipped for the training of future priests. Where this was the case the pontiff urged that the bishops of a region "should concentrate and unite their forces in a common Seminary, fully worthy of its high purpose. . . ." And he added that he had never let pass a chance to favor and encourage efforts of this kind. "Often, in fact," he said, "We have suggested and recommended them." [16] Pius XI's encyclical, however, was a reaction to a *fait accompli* rather than an exercise in creative leadership, and Roman directives continued to demand local seminaries down to the 1960's.

Like other directives of the Holy See with which bishops and religious superiors may not have been in full sympathy — for like most other men they have been quick to implement Roman suggestions that have confirmed their own views — the wise counsel of Piux XI brought about no noticeable change of policy in the United States. It would be gratifying to record that the situation which John Hughes had deplored in 1834 ceased soon thereafter, and that the multiplication of seminaries by both the diocesan and religious clergy was a phenomenon confined to the American Church's nascent years. On the contrary, this debilitating process continued down to the previous decade which opened on January 1, 1960, with a total of 525 Catholic seminaries in this country, both major and minor, of which ninety-six were maintained by the diocesan clergy and 429 by the religious congregations with an over-all total of 39,896 students. Fortunately, the trend was arrested during the 1960's, and the clustering of theological schools of different denominations in Berkeley,

Chicago, Rochester, Cambridge, and New York — to mention only the most widely publicized — offered promise of a much stronger theological training for future priests, to say nothing of other advantages to be derived from close association with one's peers.

Still another manifestation of a response to this situation was the theological coalition formed by some of the religious orders in the neighborhood of the Catholic University of America. Yet in view of the University's School of Sacred Theology for which, presumably, a number of these religious congregations were located in Washington in the first place, this coalition may, indeed, ultimately be seen as a backward step instead of an advance for theological training. Thus as the 1960's came to a close the rapid decline in vocations to the priesthood, set against a rising Catholic population, created many vexing problems for both bishops and religious superiors, not the least of which was the disposition of large and expensive seminary establishments for which there seemed to be no immediately foreseeable need.[17]

From Trent To Baltimore With the French

It is comparatively easy for the historian to treat the external aspects of priestly formation such as the enfeebling effect of an excessive number of seminaries of which we have been speaking. It is another matter to get beneath the surface and to analyze in a balanced and real way the subtle influences that have played upon the souls and minds of candidates for the priesthood as they made their way through the long period of schooling, and it should be said, to analyze these influences in a manner that will throw light on the American priest as he is known today. Difficult as that task may be, it must be attempted, and the starting point for seminaries as the modern Church has known them is the legislation of the Council of Trent, where for the first time laws of universal application for the Catholic world were centered on priests' education in anything like a systematic way.

What, briefly, did Trent provide in this regard? First, it should be noted that the council enacted only the bare outline in its decrees, which were fashioned in good measure after those drawn up by Cardinal Reginald Pole for the plenary council of English bishops over which he presided in December, 1555–January, 1556. At the outset, for example, the Tridentine legislation stated that all cathedral and metropolitan churches, "each according to its means and the extent of its diocese," should make provision for educating a certain number of boys in an institution that was to be "located near the said churches or in some other suitable place to be chosen by the bishop." Entrance requirements for students were few and very simple. They were to be at least twelve years of age, having been born of lawful wedlock, able to read and write, and possess a good moral character.

In their selection the "sons of the poor" were to be given preference, although sons of the wealthy classes were also to be received, "provided they be maintained at their own expense" and met the other requirements. It was left to the bishop to divide the students into as many classes as he thought proper according to their number, age, and "progress in ecclesiastical discipline," and to further their training in the last respect they were "forthwith and always" to wear the tonsure and clerical garb. As for their studies, the decree read:

> they shall study grammar, singing, ecclesiastical computation, and other useful arts; shall be instructed in Sacred Scripture, ecclesiastical books, the homilies of the saints, the manner of administering the sacraments, especially those things that seem adapted to the hearing of confessions, and the rites and ceremonies.

The students' spiritual training was for the most part covered in a single sentence that stated:

> The bishop shall see to it that they are present every day at the sacrifice of the mass, confess their sins at least once a month, receive the body of our Lord Jesus Christ in accordance with the directions of their confessor, and on festival days serve in the cathedral and other churches of the locality.[18]

Woefully delayed as Trent's action in behalf of clerical education had been, for a variety of reasons even the legislation of 1563 was long in being implemented throughout the Church. In France, rightly regarded as the principal birthplace of the modern seminary movement, for example, the crown's opposition prevented the Tridentine decrees from ever being officially promulgated, and only in 1615, more than a half-century after the close of the council, were these decrees "received" by the Assembly of the Clergy acting independently of the royal government. In the meantime the deplorable conditions that had obtained among many of the clergy since the late Middle Ages had gone from bad to worse, and Saint Vincent de Paul was heard to say on one occasion:

> The Church is going to ruin in many places on account of the evil life of her priests; it is they who are ruining and destroying

her . . . . and the depravity of the ecclesiastical state is the chief cause of the ruin of God's Church.[19]

Similar testimony could be cited from other pioneer architects of the seminary movement such as Vincent's contemporaries, the religious congregation founders Jean-Jacques Olier (Sulpicians), Pierre de Bérulle (Oratorians), and Jean-Marie Eudes (Eudists), all of whom figured prominently in shaping the Church's seminary system. It was understandable, therefore, that these men should have set as their primary goal a heightened moral standard in the lives of candidates for the priesthood and have settled for almost the minimum in their intellectual training.[20]

What, the reader may ask, has this to do with the formation of the American priest? Actually, it has a direct relationship to his formation, for with the single exception of the teaching of Vatican Council II on religious freedom, American theology has been derived entirely from Europe with the pedagogical methods in the Catholic seminaries following the European models as well as the thought patterns in philosophy and theology. So much has this been true that the President of the Catholic Theological Society of America devoted his presidential address in 1968 to an exhortation in behalf of originality of approach and an indictment of American Catholic theologians for their failure to think and to write creatively. *Inter alia* he said:

> The pressing need is the type of thing John Courtney Murray did so well in the area of religious freedom: to take for inspiration a critical American experience, face it with the totality of Catholic tradition, and come up with that paradox of all living theology: something at once genuinely Christian and radically new.[21]

For this reason the historian must treat the long range effects of policies such as those pursued by Vincent de Paul, Olier, and other seminary founders, policies that in the main were wonderfully helpful for the Church but likewise not without their unfortunate results in the intellectual order. Before these men had passed from the scene, ecclesiastical circles had already become embroiled in the bitter quarrels over Gallicanism and Jansenism during which little notable advance was made in either theological learning or methodology. The eighteenth century followed in due course with its spread of infidelity and the rationalism of the Enlightenment, as well as the controversies that centered around Febronianism and Josephinism which exhausted the time and energy of many men in both Church and State. Moreover, these controversies served to harden still more the excessive rigorism and defensive posture of Catholic theology as it had emerged from the Catholic or Counter Reformation of the late sixteenth century.[22]

Thus enfeebled in the intellectual aspects of their training, the Catholic clergy were ill prepared to offer impressive support of the Church *vis-à-vis* the forces that were directed against her. And when the initial blow of the French Revolution, the Civil Constitution of the Clergy, struck her in July, 1790, the abyss between the Church and the world widened perceptibly. At this point there ensued a quarter-century that ended with the final collapse of the Napoleonic Empire in June, 1815, during which the Church suffered the gravest series of trials she had known since the Protestants revolted from Rome nearly 300 years before. The Catholic seminary system in much of western Europe was virtually annihilated in this same quarter-century with effects that Edward Hales neatly summarized when, in mentioning the need for the restoration of the Society of Jesus, he stated:

> An equally essential need was to make provision for seminaries for the training of priests. The widespread closure of the seminaries, the hostility displayed by many of the revolutionary governments towards the pursuit of vocations, and the involvement of most of the young manhood of Europe in war had created by the year 1815 a general shortage of priests, especially acute in France, and had also had a most deleterious effect upon the quality of theological study.[23]

Such was the background out of which the Catholic seminary system of the United States was born, and the traces of the European movements and events sketched above were clearly discernible in every aspect of life in the new and struggling institutions wherein the impoverished Church of the young Republic sought to train her candidates for the priesthood.

That the widespread poverty of the Catholic community in both men and money was a gravely inhibiting factor in seminary education during most of the nineteenth century, there could be no doubt. For this reason the teaching seminarian was almost the rule in every part of the country up to and beyond the Civil War, so scarce were priests and so poor were most dioceses that they could not engage laymen for this work. For example, when John B. Purcell, Bishop of Cincinnati, was negotiating with the Jesuits to take over his college in

1840, the anxiety under which he was laboring was betrayed when he told their Missouri superior:

> For God's sake do not throw difficulties in the way and say wait, wait; for if you think fit to employ them, I can employ under your direction, as Teachers in the College, in Cincinnati, *twelve* seminarians. . . .[24]

In the sequel five or six seminarians continued to reside at Saint Francis Xavier College after it opened on November 3, 1840, while their classmates pursued their theological studies in the seminary newly begun in Brown County.[25] A similar situation obtained in most of the seminaries of the period. Thus Daniel Fisher, a New York seminarian who in 1852 had accepted the invitation of Bishop Joseph Cretin of Saint Paul to study for that diocese, found that his mission, as he told a New York friend, was teaching "the dirty little ragged Canadian and Irish boys" in the local Catholic school where he was sorely tried by "these impudent and insulting children of unthankful parents. . . ." It was little wonder that Fisher should have been uncertain about his future in the priesthood, for as he remarked, "Whenever I get time and my head ceases to ache, I study Theology — the Bishop told me the other day that he would ordain me in September; but whether he will ordain me priest or only Subdeacon I do not know." [26] Nor were the faculties of these seminaries in an improved position over that of the students.

Well beyond the mid-century the situation of many professors was not fundamentally different from that of Father John O'Hanlon who in 1851 was appointed to the seminary of the Archdiocese of Saint Louis at Carondolet, where in addition to serving as chaplain of the local convent of the Sisters of Saint Joseph and giving catechetical instructions to their students, he was the seminary's prefect of studies while teaching courses in English, logic, metaphysics, ethics, liturgy, ceremonies, and Scripture. "All this work," he stated in his memoirs, "left me hardly any spare time to study for my various classes; and, for necessary relaxation or exercise, there was little or no leisure." [27] Given the circumstances, O'Hanlon's remark would seem to have been something of an understatement.

Despite the growing number of seminaries, at no time in the nineteenth century, or even in the present century, was the Catholic Church able to recruit sufficient priestly vocations within her own community to satisfy the needs of the rapidly increasing population. The ideal, of course, was to have American candidates trained for the most part in American seminaries, and few would probably have disagreed with the strong plea voiced by one writer in October, 1860, for a native priesthood since, he said, "There is a kind of freemasonry among Americans that enables them to get along with one another, and understand each other's motives that does not exist between an American and a foreigner." [28] The result was that the Church was repeatedly compelled to seek priests abroad, and here France, Ireland, and Germany proved to be the best sources of men to supply religious services to the approximately 9,500,000 Catholic immigrants who entered this country between 1790 and 1920 to bring the total estimated Catholic population, at the opening of the decade that saw the first immigration restriction laws, to 19,828,000.

In considering the principal sources from which the American priesthood was drawn, and the type of spiritual and intellectual formation imparted, the following categories suggest themselves: 1) foreign-born and foreign-trained priests who came especially from France, Germany, and Ireland; 2) American-born students who were sent abroad to receive their ecclesiastical training; 3) American-born or foreign-born candidates who were educated at seminaries in the United States, which well into the twentieth century were often staffed by a large number of professors who had been born, educated, or both, in countries outside the United States.

As for the first group, during what historians of the United States call the early national period, it was the French who predominated. Thus the Sulpicians at their seminaries in and near Baltimore were mostly French-born, the first American to join the Society of Saint Sulpice being John Hickey of Fredericstown, Maryland, who was ordained a priest in 1814. Moreover, it was from French-born priests, who on the whole made admirable missionaries, that bishops were chosen for the American Church quite out of proportion to the number of French Catholic immigrants, a fact that was illustrated at the Second Plenary Council of Baltimore in October, 1866, where ten out of the forty-five bishops in attendance had been born in France. When confronted by the scarcity of vocations among American youths, a situation that obtained everywhere in these years, it was only natural that these French-born bishops should turn to their mother country which at the time was witnessing one of France's most flourishing missionary eras, to furnish their new dioceses with priests and seminarians willing to undertake a missionary apostolate in the United States.

For example, in the spring of 1835 the first Bishop of Vincennes,

Simon Bruté, confided to Joseph Rosati, Bishop of Saint Louis, that he saw no hope for his infant diocese except through recourse to France. "I have received from all sides the most pressing invitations," he said, "especially from my Bishop of Rennes and from a superior, who assures me very good priests, as well as other succor, if I will come in person." [29] As it turned out, Bruté was well repaid for his absence of a little over a year, for he returned to the United States in July, 1836, accompanied by eleven priests, two deacons, two subdeacons, three men in minor orders, and two other ecclesiastical students. [30] Long after Bishop Bruté had passed from the scene the scarcity of vocations among young Americans compelled bishops to continue enlisting help in Europe. The situation was exemplified in the Diocese of Detroit where Bishop Caspar H. Borgess entered upon his duties in the spring of 1870 to find eighty-eight priests of whom only six were native Americans, the others being divided among thirty-nine Belgians, twenty-one Germans, nine Irishmen, six Dutchmen, five Frenchmen, and two Poles. [31]

It is not easy for an historian of the priesthood to achieve the proper balance in his treatment of the factors that were most influential in moulding the seminarian and the priest, whether they completed their studies in Europe or in the United States. That the intellectual training of candidates both here and abroad often left much to be desired, was an acknowledged fact. Yet as one writer who recognized the deficiencies remarked, it should not be forgotten that in the inadequate American seminaries, "priestly character was moulded by daily intercourse with the self-sacrificing pioneer bishops and priests," [32] a genuine spiritual benefit that no thoughtful historian of the priesthood would wish to overlook or to discount. The difficulty in treating this subject is increased by the paucity of reliable evidence that enables one to speak with certainty on the various phases of seminary education. Difficult as it may be, however, it must be attempted. The best procedure, perhaps, is to summarize as well as possible the situation as it obtained in those countries that sent the largest number of men to the United States and then to sketch the general patterns of spiritual and intellectual formation as they were developed in American seminaries.

As has already been mentioned, in the early years of the American Church it was France that was the principal provider of priests and seminarians. At the very time that the Church in this country witnessed the close of what has been called the age of John Carroll with the death in December, 1815, of the founder of the American hierarchy and first Archbishop of Baltimore, the French Church was emerging from a quarter-century ordeal that left her with barely half the number of priests that had been there at the opening of the revolution in 1789, and most of these men were past middle age. The period known as the Restoration, however, witnessed a religious revival that not only marked the death of Gallicanism and the birth of a strong ultramontanist trend, but, too, vocations multiplied and new religious congregations were founded. Thus by the 1830's seminarians and priests were again in ample supply, and the spiritual tone and dutiful conduct of this new generation were markedly higher than had been true of the clergy of the *ancien régime*. Yet as a recent historian has said:

> their education prepared them badly for winning the minds of the young, or the respect of the intellectual world . . . . their priests, who came most often from peasant families, emerged from seminaries which were still poorly endowed in teachers and books and which deliberately insulated their charges from 'new ideas,' thus making it likely that they would henceforth be unable either to comprehend or to combat them.[33]

In an atmosphere of this kind seminarians who revealed a taste for intellectual pursuits, in other words, those who did not conform to the common pattern, were suspect by their superiors. The major emphasis in the seminaries was forming devout priests rather than men of learning, and at Issy, the Sulpicians' seminary near Paris, four hours were given over to intellectual work while the balance of the day was taken up with liturgical ceremonies, plain chant, visits to the Blessed Sacrament, benediction, recitation of the rosary, and other prayers.[34]

It was not surprising, therefore, that little or no disposition was found among the clergy to familiarize themselves with the latest developments in science and to confront the problems raised by these discoveries and by the rationalists and positivists who held such a commanding position in the most influential circles of national life. The Abbé Guillaume-René Meignan, professor of Scripture in the Sorbonne and future Archbishop of Tours and cardinal, one of the most open and scholarly clerical minds of the day, discovered this lack of intellectual concern in 1859 when he sought to alert French Catholics to the dangers for the Church in certain contemporary trends through a series of articles entitled "D'un mouvement antireligieux en France" published in *Le Correspondant*. The reception accorded Meignan's articles by the clergy was so unfriendly that he felt compelled to change his original plan and to conclude with an optimistic parallel between the crisis brought on in the Church of England by contemporary rationalism and the forceful resistance offered to this movement by French Catholicism.[35]

The contrasting emphasis in the French seminaries between the intellectual and the spiritual becomes apparent in an exchange of letters between Father Samuel Eccleston, Maryland-born convert, while he was in Paris making the solitude or novitiate as a candidate of the Society of Saint Sulpice and the French-born Sulpician Archbishop of Baltimore, Ambrose Maréchal. Eccleston stated that he regretted he found it impossible in Paris to fulfill one part of the program of studies that had been recommended to him by the Baltimore Sulpicians. "They will be much astonished as well as myself," he said, "on finding that there is no course in Canon Law in the seminary or even in Paris itself. . . ." He asked Maréchal's permission, therefore, to go on to Rome later for canon law. The archbishop's reply was revealing. He wrote:

> The principal object that ought before everything to occupy you during your sojourn at the Solitude, is to penetrate yourself well with the spirit of St. Sulpice; and be well persuaded, my Friend, that if you come here having imbibed all of that, this immense advantage will be for you & for the Church in the United States, infinitely preferable to all the knowledge that you can acquire during your sojourn in Europe; and as Theology is taught in the house you are living in profit by the lectures which are given there in that science. As for Canon Law, its use is so rare in this country, that I regard its study as a thing only secondary and ornamental.[36]

While giving Eccleston permission to proceed to Rome for canon law after he had concluded his stay in Paris, the archbishop added, "the grand object that the good of religion in this country demands that you have principally under your eyes, is sacred eloquence." He went on to say how eagerly the laity in both the cities and rural areas looked for good sermons; thus if a priest were to prepare himself carefully in homiletics, said Maréchal, he would,

> render to the Church of America an infinitely more important service than if he taught them the learned works of our most celebrated Theologians or the lessons in Canon Law contained in Barbosa, Fagnon, & Van Espen. . . .[37]

The matter of homiletics aside, it would not be difficult to see here a kind of early foreshadowing of the prominence later assigned in the American Church to canon law rather than to theology, a development that showed in the choice of bishops and religious superiors. And from that same emphasis there flowed the consequent legalism that characterized so much of the spirituality of both clergy and laity.

German and Irish Priests — Whence Had They Come?

If the training of the numerous missionaries who came to the United States from France during the nineteenth century had, generally speaking, more in common with the ideas of Archbishop Maréchal than it had with those expressed by Lamennais, the education of many of the German clergy had developed along other lines. Thanks to the initiative of Franz von Fürstenberg, Vicar General of the Diocese of Münster, reforms were introduced in the late eighteenth century that promoted a knowledge of the natural sciences, de-emphasized the classics, and gave German, the vernacular language, a more honored place in the curriculum. Moreover, the Catholic revival, so closely identified with the Romantic Movement, had as one of its most fruitful aspects the work of certain priest scholars such as Johann Michael Sailer and Johann Adam Möhler whose teaching represented a break with the decadent scholasticism of the period.

Sailer, Möhler, Joseph Görres, the lay historian, and Görres' disciples, Franz von Bäder and Johann Ignatz Döllinger, bore witness in university circles to the Catholic tradition in a way that was lacking in other countries. Consequently, the position established by these men at centers like the University of Tübingen and the University of Munich, prevented the virtually complete divorce of seminary training from university education that happened elsewhere. It would be an exaggeration, of course, to say that all the German missionary priests who came to this country were university trained men; but there was enough of that spirit in their background to distinguish many of them from their contemporaries who had been born and trained in countries like France and Ireland.

As for the Irish, who probably constituted the largest numerical group among the foreign-born clergy of the American Church, some had been educated on the continent in the Irish colleges of Spain, Portugal, France, and the Low Countries. For example, a number of Irish priests who saw service in Florida had finished their studies in Salamanca and Seville.[38] The majority, however, were trained at home once that again became a possibility with the British government's grant of 1795 that established Saint Patrick's College, Maynooth. Seminaries were also opened in Carlow, Kilkenny, Thurles, and other Irish towns, all of which in due time sent their quota of missionaries to the United States. Thus All Hallows College, established in 1842 in Dublin, had by 1961 alone furnished 1,076 priests and fourteen bishops to the American Church. It should occasion no surprise that a strong French influence should have pervaded some of these institutions since many of their early faculty members had been trained in the theological traditions of seventeenth and eighteenth-century France.

As the national seminary, Saint Patrick's College, Maynooth, was a special case in this as in many other aspects of Irish ecclesiastical life. Thus dogmatic theology was taught there by Louis A. Delahogue, emeritus professor of the Sorbonne, in the early years. At the outset of Maynooth's life an official ban on probabilism and other liberal interpretations in moral theology was issued by Cardinal Hyacinth Gerdil, Prefect of the Congregation de Propaganda Fide. In a letter of instruction to the trustees on July 10, 1796, Gerdil gave rather detailed directives, and a Maynooth official recalling the incident many years later characterized the Roman letter as "no homily on the text of the 'jugum suave,' " and he then added:

> Nor does it give the uncertain sound of a vague admonition to steer a safe middle course between the excessive laxity of some and the excessive rigour of others. It warns the Bishops of one danger only, the danger on the 'liberal' side, admonishing them merely to take heed that 'the excessive and wanton *liberality* of some in laying down the rules of morals' shall be so '*avoided*,' that 'the mildness and suavity of Evangelical charity *shall never be dissociated from that salutary severity which is characteristic of Christian teaching.*[39]

In an effort to guarantee that future priests should leave Saint Patrick's College with no taint of liberalism in their moral theology, Rome likewise gave instructions that the textbooks of Paul Gabriel Antoine, S.J. (d. 1743), one of the prime figures in the French school of rigid moralists, should be used, and to make doubly sure of its objective, Propaganda had a shipment of Antoine's volumes sent to Maynooth.

While all Irish institutions were probably not subject, in the same degree, to the rigorous scrutiny by the Propaganda as was true of the national seminary, given that an increasing number of their professors were trained at Maynooth as time went on, a similar spirit prevailed among these institutions. When one recalls how many priests had completed their theological training in Ireland before they came to this country, how the strange and often unfriendly circumstances surrounding their impoverished and unlettered immigrant flocks in the land of their adoption prompted the latter to seek counsel and guidance on all matters from their priests, and how commanding a position was quickly established over the entire Catholic community by those of Irish birth or descent, one can better comprehend the factors that played a lead in coloring the American Catholic psyche. If many of those of Irish birth or background in the United States continued for well over a century to display a strain of Jansenism in their thinking on moral issues such as problems connected with sex, as well as a healthy touch in the realm of Church-State relations of what in seventeenth-century France had come to be called Gallicanism, it was no mystery where the ideas had taken their rise. For as Newman said, when an idea, "whether real or not, is of a nature to arrest and possess the mind,

> [it] is carried forward into the public throng of men and draws attention, then it is not merely received passively in this or that form into many minds, but it becomes an active principle within them . . . . leading them to . . . . a propagation of it on every side.[40]

Americans At Louvain and Rome

When one turns to the type of spiritual and intellectual formation received by American-born young men who were sent abroad to study for the priesthood in Rome, Louvain, and Innsbruck one encounters many similarities to those already described. As for Rome, the first two Americans, Ralph Smith of Maryland and Felix Dougherty of Pennsylvania, arrived at the Urban College of Propaganda in January, 1788, to take up the two scholarships offered to John Carroll by the Prefect of the Congregation, Cardinal Leonardo Antonelli. Neither of these candidates persisted, but in the years that followed Americans continued to be sent to the Urban College at intervals, notably Martin J. Spalding of the Diocese of Bardstown who entered in 1830, was the first American to take a doctorate of theology at Rome (1834), and who died as Archbishop of Baltimore. James A. Corcoran and Patrick N. Lynch from the Diocese of Charleston were enrolled at the Urban College in 1833 and were both destined to distinguish themselves among the early Roman-trained Americans, the former as the leading theologian of the American Church in the years after the Civil War, and the latter as third Bishop of Charleston a post he occupied from 1858 to his death in 1882.

If the nineteenth century represented for Europe a major period of alienation from the Catholic faith, no small part of the blame was to be attributed to those responsible for the education of the clergy. The closed and suspicious attitude toward the world that prevailed in the seminaries was obviously an outgrowth of the blows sustained by the Church from the liberal philosophy of the Enlightenment, and its extreme expression during the quarter-century from the outbreak of the French Revolution in 1789 to the collapse of the Napoleonic system in 1815.

The churchmen's reaction was understandable but, nonetheless, unfortunate. For the paranoia, if that not be too strong a word, that took possession of the papacy and the Roman Curia in the period known as the Restoration, gave birth to a siege mentality that ultimately permeated much of the Catholic community. The door was shut, so to speak, on the currents of thought that were then sweeping through the intellectual centers and capturing the minds and imaginations of men with the scientists' exciting discoveries of facts hitherto unknown about man and his physical environment and the potentialities of future research, to say nothing of the new theories that revolutionized man's approach to his own origins, evolution, and ultimate destiny. One need mention only the names of Georg Wilhelm Hegel, Friedrich Schleirmacher, Auguste Comte, Charles Darwin, and Karl Marx to know what is meant.

Virtually all the extant evidence on the Roman seminaries from the years after 1815 to the era of Vatican Council II bears out their closed system of clerical education. For example, John Henry Newman arrived at the Urban College of Propaganda late in 1846 as a mature man of forty-five. That he was pleased at the prospect before him we know, for some weeks after reaching Rome he told his friend, Henry Wilberforce, "It is so wonderful to find myself here, in Propaganda — it is a kind of dream . . . . I was happy at Oriel, happier at Littlemore, as happy or happier still at Maryvale — and happiest here." Yet the new convert's personal happiness did not blind him to the weaknesses and defects he saw around him. It was an absurdity for Anglicans, he said, to suppose that the clergy of the Church of Rome were not absolute believers in the truth of their own system. "They are believers," he remarked, "so as to be bigots — their fault is that they generally cannot conceive how educated Englishmen can be Anglicans with a good conscience. . . ." [41]

The correspondence of Newman's time in Rome contained repeated references to both the method and the content of the courses he was following, as when he commented on one occasion, "We have thrown off today [November 11] — with 3 lectures — two in dogmatics and one in morals; and this seems to go on for five days in the week." [42] A short time later he informed another friend that James Robert Hope had warned him he would find little theology at Rome, to which Newman added, "a talk we had yesterday with one of the Jesuit fathers here shows we shall find little philosophy." This conversation had included a discussion of Greek studies at Propaganda which led Newman to inquire if the students learned Aristotle. "No," replied the Jesuit, "they did not," for neither Aristotle nor Saint Thomas Aquinas was in favor in Rome. "I asked," said Newman, "what philosophy they *did* adopt," only to receive the following answer:

> He said *none*. 'Odds and ends — whatever seems to them best — like St. Clement's Stromata. They have no philosophy. *Facts* are the great things, and nothing else. Exegesis, but not doctrine.[43]

Under these circumstances it was not strange that after some months of study and observation of the Roman scene Newman should have reached a conclusion which he confided to a close friend:

> you will not, cannot, get education here — not simply from the many objects there are to take you off your studies, but because you are not a boy. The lecturers are men quite up with their subject, but the course takes *four* years — if you don't stay that time, you only go through a part of it — and any how you go, lecture after lecture, to drawl through a few tedious pages — All this is quite necessary for boys, not for grown men. I seriously think (still in confidence) you will do as much sitting at home at Maryvale.[44]

Reports of a like character on the seminaries of Rome were not uncommon long after Newman had left Propaganda, even if the focus of criticism had in the meanwhile changed. For example, the future Canon William Barry found at the Roman College [Gregorian University] that history counted for little, everything in the teaching of dogma "was idea, was *a priori*, deductive and legal," and even though there was an admirable knowledge of Aristotelian methods, one would have to go elsewhere to experience anything of the great philosopher's inductive, experimental spirit. According to Barry, the intellectual climate had not changed since the days of Suarez (d. 1617), although one of the leading professors of the 1870's, Johannes Franzelin, S.J., spent considerable time refuting the condemned propositions of the nineteenth-century theologians, Anton Günther and Georg Hermes. Franzelin displayed an acquaintance with Scripture that was rare in a theologian, "though hardly ever touching on problems of criticism," and the German Jesuit appeared to Barry as one who was "completely unaffected by any modern influence," a man for whom time stood still, a distant figure who was to the students only a voice, "at the best a great light; but to the end a stranger." [45] A few years later Wilfrid Ward's impressions were not dissimilar. They were taught various philosophical positions as the "right view," he said, and if a student failed to find these convincing he was regarded as heterodox, to which Ward added:

> Thus philosophy which professed to prove the rational duty of accepting Theism and revelation was not really enforced by reason but by authority. It was really learnt by rote and by sheer memory.[46]

Such were the spirit and methodology that characterized the seminaries in the Eternal City to which young Americans went for their training during the years of the Restoration and on through the long reign of Pope Pius IX. To be sure, it was likewise a period that witnessed a distinct religious revival with the establishment of new religious congregations, a widening missionary zeal, ever-enlarging pilgrimages to shrines old and new, a heightening of popular devotions, and a notable rise in respect and veneration for the Holy See in the ultramontanist movement that after 1846 found its focal point in the warm personality of Pio Nono. While it was understandable that the latter's unhappy experience with the liberals in the first years of his reign should have thoroughly disillusioned him, it was regrettable that he should have shut himself away so completely from the currents of contemporary thought, an attitude that was also reflected in the thinking of his immediate entourage, and the Roman Curia in general.

The intellectual life of the Church, as determined by curial agencies like the Congregation of Studies, was thus deeply influenced by the movement of the *Risorgimento*. For the more the forces of the Italian nationalists and liberal revolutionaries pressed on the pope and his shrinking dominions in central Italy, the more intransigent did the pontiff become in his conservatism and the more did the ultramontane sentiment deepen among Catholics. Certain churchmen, reacting against the liberals' hostility, voiced their loyalty to the pontiff in a way that had reverberations in the seminaries and educational institutions of the Church. Thus Jean François Bertaud, Bishop of Tulle, on one occasion referred to Piux IX as "the Incarnate Word continuing Himself," and Gaspard Mermillod, Bishop of Lausanne and a future cardinal, went so far as to preach on the three incarnations of the Son of God, "in the womb of a virgin, in the Eucharist, and in the old man in the Vatican." [47]

When theologically bizarre opinions of this kind circulated without receiving the official repudiation that they merited, it should not surprise one to learn that such an atmosphere should have been conducive to extravagances at the highest level as well. Some of the eighty condemned propositions of the Syllabus of Errors of December, 1864, taken from various papal documents without any accompanying explanation of their context, could be read in this way. Theological learning could not flourish under these conditions, and it was no carping question when one historian, who treated the propositions of the Syllabus, asked:

> To what end was the pith of them circulated without any of the qualifying and restrictive interpretations of their context, and in a form necessitating considerable investigation to establish their relevance and purport? [48]

The theological refinement of their clergy was not, however, the main preoccupation of the American bishops; it was rather the pressing necessity of providing priests for the rapidly increasing immigrant flocks that assumed first rank as a problem for the Church in the United States early in the nineteenth century and that held that place well into the present century. From a Catholic population of around 195,000 in 1820, within a half-century the total had passed 4,500,000 with 1,683,791 immigrants from Ireland and 606,791 from the German lands, to mention only the two largest national groups that accounted for the over-all Catholic population level reached by 1870. The Church was quite literally a missionary enterprise at the time, and that was the over-riding consideration that colored every aspect of American Catholic development, including the education of the clergy.

This was no less so in regard to providing the opportunity for American candidates for the priesthood to study abroad. We have already seen the futile attempt to win collaboration among the bishops for the establishment of a national seminary in the 1820's and 1830's. The same fate would probably have overtaken plans for opening American seminaries outside the country had it not been for certain strong and persistent advocates. In fact, that was what happened in what was in all likelihood the first serious suggestion for a seminary in Europe in which men could be educated for the American missions. Bishop John B. Purcell of Cincinnati stated early in 1842 that it was "the constant desire" of Andreas Räss, Bishop of Strasbourg, to establish a seminary to train German missionaries for the United States in his diocese. "If two, or three American Prelates would unite in writing to him," Purcell told Bishop John Hughes of New York, "the means wd. soon be forthcoming — and if such a good work is not done, what shall become of our increasing German population? I would want ten more German priests just now." [49] Nothing came of Räss' idea either then or later and it had to await another fifteen years before an American establishment of this kind became a reality in Europe.

That reality was owed to the vision and energy with which a Kentucky-born prelate, Martin J. Spalding, Bishop of Louisville, and two natives of Belgium, Bishop Peter Paul Lefevere of Detroit and Father Peter Kindekens of the same diocese, conceived and propagated the idea of a seminary for the American missions in the immediate vicinity of the Catholic University of Louvain. While on a visit to Belgium in January, 1853, Spalding's imagination was fired with this idea, and in a discussion with Belgium's remarkable primate, Cardinal Engelbert Sterckx, Archbishop of Malines, the latter lent it his warm support. "A hundred young men educated at Louvain for the American missions!" Spalding's enthusiasm was running high as he communicated the prospect to Francis Patrick Kenrick, Archbishop of Baltimore, "Is not the thought enlivening?" [50]

It was, indeed, and it continued to enliven the mind of Spalding whose European travels suggested comparison of clerical education in the United States with what he had been observing, and that in a manner that was not flattering to the former. "Our studies in America are woefully below the European standard," he informed Kenrick, "and a few good missionaries educated in Belgium scattered through our various Dioceses would leaven the whole mass." [51] Needless to say, it took more than enthusiasm and good will to get the institution underway, but Spalding, Lefevere, and Kindekens succeeded in enlisting enough support to warrant opening the American College at Louvain in March, 1857. For the first half-century the students were largely Europeans who had volunteered for the missions in the United States, but from the beginning a few Americans were sent to avail themselves of Louvain's superior facilities, among whom was John Lancaster Spalding, nephew of the co-founder, who entered in 1859 and who later became the first Bishop of Peoria. Up to 1890 the college had sent 329 priests to the United States of whom nine were raised to the episcopacy, six Belgian-born men and one each born in Germany, Canada, and the United States. [52]

If the college at Louvain had come into existence by reason of

American initiative, the American college at Rome owed its origins principally to an Italian archbishop, Gaetano Bedini, Apostolic Nuncio to Brazil, who visited the United States on a special assignment in 1853–1854. A detailed report on Catholicism in this country that Bedini addressed to Cardinal Filippo Fransoni, Prefect of Propaganda, in July, 1854, contained a lengthy section devoted to the need for an institution in Rome where American candidates for the priesthood would be trained. Such an institution, Bedini thought, would assure the "Roman Catholic spirit" in both the clergy and laity of the United States, facilitate and encourage vocations, and offer candidates a more complete and solid education than they were then receiving at home. "I was present," he remarked, "at some examinations and scholastic excercises, or concursus, and I was not at all satisfied with the results." The preparation of future bishops furnished a further reason for such a school. "How else," asked Bedini, "will you prepare for the succession of as many Bishops as you now have in the United States?" And in revealing his deep sense of the *Romanità*, he added:

> The American facilities are positively not enough, and even if their number increases, no one can know whether they will leave something to be desired. Perhaps, none of them will be able to offer the same guarantee of success as one in Rome, the center of the Catholic World, where the means, the resources, the occasions for perfecting oneself in learning, in spirit and zeal abound. There is no doubt that the best priests now among the American Clergy are the ones who were educated at the Propaganda.[53]

As it turned out, Archbishop Bedini's idea found increasing application as time went on, for the defects of Roman education of which Newman and others had spoken to the contrary notwithstanding, the number of American bishops trained there grew steadily.

Thus in the half-century preceding the inauguration in November, 1966, of the National Conference of Catholic Bishops, roughly forty per cent of the more than 400 priests selected for the American hierarchy had been educated at Rome.[54] While the great majority of these Americans had been students of the seminary that Bedini had helped to bring into being, a lesser number from the United States attended the Capranica College, the Lateran Seminary, and other ecclesiastical schools in the Eternal City.

The proposal of an American seminary in Rome had no more

enthusiastic supporter than Pope Pius IX who early in 1855 told the American bishops, "We strongly desire . . . . that after mutual consultation and collaboration, you should set up, here in this venerable City of Ours, your own College for clerics from your own nation." [55] At first, however, the "mutual consultation" yielded such negative results as to warrant the historian of the college speaking in terms of the "uncertain response" to Pio Nono's letter. In fact, the bishops of the Provinces of Cincinnati and Saint Louis voted against the idea. John Hughes, Archbishop of New York, vehemently opposed it for a number of reasons among which was the impression that students would not receive at the Urban College of Propaganda, where it was intended they should take their classes, the kind of training that would fit them for the American missions. Hughes did not persist in his opposition, however, and before the college had become a reality his well-known erratic manner was revealed when he made a complete *volte face* and declared the project was "by all odds the most important measure that has been adopted since the appointment of the first Catholic bishop in the United States." [56]

Meanwhile the proposed seminary had found two steady supporters in Archbishop Kenrick of Baltimore, and Michael O'Connor, Bishop of Pittsburgh, who pushed the matter energetically with their fellow bishops. After Pius IX purchased an old Visitation monastery in the Via dell'Umiltà and turned it over to the American hierarchy there was hardly any likelihood of them turning back. Plans went forward and finally in December, 1859, the North American College was formally opened with twelve students representing eight dioceses of the United States with the Irish-born Bernard Smith, O.S.B., professor of theology in the Urban College, acting as pro-rector until the American bishops had agreed upon William G. McCloskey, a priest of the Diocese of Brooklyn, who took charge as permanent rector in March, 1860.

It is a commonplace in the history of American education that the migration of students from this country to Europe in the nineteenth century often resulted in the creation here of schools of thought modeled on European patterns once these students had completed their training and returned home. A case in point is history where men like Joseph G. Cogswell, George Bancroft, George Ticknor, Edward Everett, and others were able, after some initial setbacks, to exercise a deep influence in historical circles with new trends and methods such as the seminar that they had encountered during their years of study at one or another of the German universities. In only a very qualified sense could the same be said for the American clerics who had been trained at Louvain, Rome, Innsbruck, and other theological centers. While a good number of these priests returned to American dioceses to be appointed to seminary faculties by reason of their degrees in one of the ecclesiastical disciplines, they brought to these institutions nothing that was essentially new and original either in content or in method.

That this should have been the case was no reflection on the ability of these European-trained professors, since the seminary system throughout the Catholic world had long since become frozen in a mold that was universally believed to have been fixed at the Council of Trent. It was only the rare man whose intellectual curiosity prompted him to investigate Trent's legislation on seminaries for himself, and thus to become aware that what passed for the Tridentine seminary bore little resemblance to the decrees enacted by the conciliar fathers in 1563.

As for content, the Church's teaching in dogmatic and moral theology, in canon law and philosophy, was viewed as more or less static as well. It was quite exceptional, therefore, when a Catholic center of learning became the scene of an intellectual controversy such as happened at Louvain between Professor Casimir Ubaghs and his followers of the ontologico-traditionalist school and their adversaries who contended against each other in *La revue catholique* and the *Journal historique et littéraire*, their respective journals, until a decree of the Holy Office in September, 1861, censured Ubaghs' theories and caused the controversy gradually to become extinct.

The Trauma of the Closed Mind

While it was, and still is, the obligation of the Church's theological faculties to adhere to her defined doctrines, the story of seminary training both in the United States and in other countries gives ample evidence of the deleterious effects which narrow interpretations of official teaching have had on the intellectual development of the Catholic clergy. The point could be illustrated from the history of any American Catholic seminary, but let Saint Francis Seminary in Milwaukee serve as an example, simply because we know more about that institution, thanks to the highly informative history written by one of its professors.[57]

As is well known, Wisconsin was one of the principal areas of settlement for German immigrants in this country, and it was to be expected, therefore, that when the training of candidates for the priesthood was inaugurated in 1845 in the residence of the Swiss-born Martin J. Henni, first Bishop of Milwaukee, and long after the seminary had been located in 1856 at its present site, the professors and students should have been predominantly German by birth or background. Nor was this a passing phenomenon, for between 1850 and 1900 the net German Catholic immigration reached a total of 1,134,887, not to mention the additional thousands of German-speaking immigrants during the same years among the 42,289 Catholics from Switzerland and the 443,230 who came from Austria-Hungary. This immense immigrant population necessitated a steady supply of priests who spoke German. The fact that out of the total of 3,505 priests in the United States in 1869, one-third or 1,160 were of German birth, descent, or German-speaking was a tribute to the seriousness with which the Germans took their religious obligations at a time when the great majority of them were convinced that to lose their language meant to lose their faith. Moreover, they held to this percentage to the end of the century, having 2,863 of their number among the total of 8,992 priests in 1892.

Saint Francis Seminary was strongly influenced in its early years by developments at the Austrian seminaries of Innsbruck and Linz due to the number of its professors who had been educated there. Although men like Joseph Salzman, Frederick X. Katzer, Joseph Rainer, Simon Lebl, *et al.*, brought that kind of background, the proximity of these Austrian seminaries to the Universities of Innsbruck and Linz contributed nothing by way of a critical approach to the learning process at Milwaukee. On the contrary, the seminary historian remarked that throughout the nineteenth century "practically every course included apologetical material," and the emphasis given to various science courses was "chiefly on account of their value for apologetics."[58] Furthermore, since the professors were held responsible for instruction in several different fields, the result was an excessive number of hours of teaching which left them "little or no time to pursue specialties or indulge in writing."

From the beginning of classes in Henni's residence the curriculum followed the standard pattern of the period with the textbook in dogmatic theology being the very widely used work of Giovanni Perrone, S.J., *Compendium Dogmaticae Theologiae*, while moral theology was taught from the equally popular text of Jean-Pierre Gury, S.J., *Compendium Theologiae Moralis*. Both these authors were professors in the Roman College, and the choice of their textbooks indicated, according to Johnson, "an influence traceable to the theological faculty newly established in 1858 at the University of Innsbruck."[59] While both Perrone and Gury were able manualists, their textbooks, and the way in which the professors employed them, left little room for the expansion of the minds of students. Nor was there any departure at Saint Francis from the virtually universal Catholic practice of requiring students in the major seminary to attend twenty or more hours of class a week through three years of theology; it was only in 1910 that the fourth year was introduced at Milwaukee.

What has been said of the major seminary of Milwaukee could *mutatis mutandis* be said of all the theological schools of the American Church during the last century. It took the Thomistic revival initiated by Pope Leo XIII in 1879 to displace Perrone and Gury from their long established leadership as textbook writers, although here and there one heard of exceptions such as that found at Saint Mary's Seminary in Baltimore in January, 1875, by Canon Peter Benoit, President of Saint Joseph's College, Mill Hill, London. Benoit remarked that the Sulpicians were using for a moral theology text the popular work of the late Bishop of Le Mans, Jean-Baptiste Bouvier, *Institutiones Theologicae*, which had originally appeared in 1817 but had undergone a number of revisions to eliminate certain passages with Gallican overtones. In fact, so strongly had the textbooks of the Roman Jesuits established themselves in American seminaries that even the works of Francis Patrick Kenrick, then Bishop of Philadelphia, were making a relatively slow progress in spite of the recommendation they had received from the bishops of the Fifth Provincial Council of Baltimore in May, 1843. "The commendation to adopt the Theology [textbooks] which are my work," he told his brother over six months after the council, had not yet been issued by Samuel Eccleston, S.S., Archbishop of Baltimore, and at Mount Saint Mary's Seminary in Emmitsburg, he added, they were hesitating to adopt Kenrick's volumes lest "they appear to hurt the majesty of the city [Rome] by introducing the work of a stranger." [60]

Not infrequently the observations of foreign visitors who have been eye witnesses to a situation convey an understanding of its nature that one does not find elsewhere. Thus the Italian-born missionary, Samuel Mazzuchelli, O.P., in attempting in 1843 to describe the American Catholic scene for his fellow countrymen, stated that the seminaries were still in their infancy with some having only six to twelve students. "The major difficulty in the way of erecting these establishments," he said, "is the lack of funds to construct the necessary building and to support professors and clerics." [61] But the failure of the seminaries to achieve a higher goal was due to more than lack of money; it was due as well to the virtually complete absence of any attempt to venture beyond the approved interpretations of the standard authors in theologizing, so to speak, on the American Catholic experience. For that reason when Newman's *Essay on the Development of Christian Doctrine* came out late in 1845, embodying his famous theory of doctrinal development that won such wide acclaim in Vatican Council II, it was severely handled by most American bishops, theologians, and lay writers like Orestes Brownson. "I find here that the theory is utterly condemned," said Thomas F. Knox, the future Oratorian, writing to Newman while on a visit to the United States, "and the book is considered as of very dangerous tendencies & quite anti-Catholic." A further insight into the American Catholic mentality of the time was gained when Knox added:

> You must know that the scholastic form of doctrine is that which is in vogue here, and nothing but that. Petavius [Dionysius Petavius, S.J. (1583–1652), church historian and theologian], whom I mentioned, seemed to have but little favor in their eyes. They take their faith as they find it in the scholastics but of the early Fathers I sh^d imagine they knew, many of them, but little.[62]

Insofar as matters relating to the general interpretations and methods employed in the seminaries were concerned, the situation within the Catholic community of the United States, as observed by men like Mazzuchelli, Knox, and Benoit, remained substantially unchanged until the 1960's. Thus early in 1875 Benoit noted at Saint Mary's in Baltimore, "They have no ecclesiastical history. This seems to me a great defect." In that regard a better condition obtained in the seminaries of Louisville and Cincinnati where Benoit was a guest a few months later. Remarking that Perrone and Gury furnished the textbook material in dogma and moral classes at Louisville, he shed some light on the instructional methods of the period when he stated:

> The professors lecture & the students take notes. They follow Pabish's Alzog & intend to finish it in 3 years [Johann B. Alzog, *Manual of Universal Church History* translated by Francis J. Pabish and Thomas S. Byrne. (Cincinnati, 1874–1878)]. But they skip the dogmatical parts. The professor simply lectures on history, abridging some parts & enlarging on others, without any notes being taken by the students.[63]

Shortly thereafter Benoit met Pabish at Mount Saint Mary's of the West Seminary in Cincinnati where the latter was then rector, and in summarizing Pabish's comments on the church histories of Alzog and Joseph E. Darras, the English visitor remarked:

> He has two lessons a week of three quarters each, & the students prepare 12 pages each time. He contents himself with the summary about the Gnostics, on acc't of that sect being too complicated in its ramifications.[64]

If Pabish's method was not all that might have been desired, it was at least an improvement over what Benoit had observed at Baltimore where church history was not taught at all.

Baltimore's Early Councils

Meanwhile, what action was being taken in the official canonical gatherings of the American bishops in behalf of the spiritual and intellectual formation of their future priests? We have already mentioned their inability to reach agreement on a national seminary in the provincial councils of 1829 and 1833. Were one to judge by the total absence of seminary legislation in the five national councils held at Baltimore between 1837 and 1849, and the relatively few decrees devoted to that subject in the First (May, 1852) and Second (October, 1866) Plenary Councils, he would be inclined to conclude either that seminaries were not one of the bishops' major concerns, or that matters were proceeding so well in that aspect of ecclesiastical life that no laws were needed. At the plenary council of 1852, however, the single decree was forward-looking when it stated that bishops who were not able to have their own seminary should take counsel with their fellow prelates in such a way as to insure the establishment of at least one seminary in each ecclesiastical province.[65]

Fourteen years later the twelve decrees passed by the plenary council of 1866 were along lines that had been suggested by the Prefect of Propaganda, Cardinal Allesandro Barnabò.[66] Here for the first time the bishops attempted to legislate on the seminary curriculum. Having declared that it was desirable to have minor seminaries after the mind of Trent, it was stated that in these institutions there should be instruction in Latin, Greek, and the vernacular language, as well as courses in Gregorian chant, liturgy, and the history of the Bible and of the Church. In the major seminaries emphasis should be given to dogmatic and moral theology, canon law, Scripture, and sacred eloquence. Finally, in seminaries of a provincial character a more advanced Scripture course should be offered with at least a year of Hebrew, while in philosophy the various schools of thought should be explained, especially those of more recent date, with a view that the difficulties that these systems raised against the doctrine of the Church might be easily refuted [*facile refellantur*].[67]

The bishops passed several other decrees in 1866 relating to the education of the clergy that are worthy of mention. A lengthy paragraph was devoted to students' spiritual life in which seminary superiors were exhorted to be vigilant in seeing that their charges progressed in this aspect of their training. What would it profit, it was asked, if men excelled in learning and were deficient in "humility, chastity, and the other virtues," for as Pope Benedict XIV had said, it was preferable to have fewer priests of proven virtue than many who were not. Superiors should make certain, therefore, that the rules governing the students' spiritual life were carefully observed.[68]

Another decree stated that experience taught the risk often involved in admitting transfer students from other seminaries, men who were trying to escape severe discipline or who were motivated by a certain inconstancy and levity; for that reason no student should be received without testimonial letters from his bishop and the superiors of the seminary he had previously attended. And in whatever diocese or province there were numbers of Catholics who used the German language, it was proper that in the seminaries of those jurisdictions, German should be included in the curriculum.

Finally, it was at the Second Plenary Council that for the first time in a national gathering of the hierarchy there was raised the question of education on a university level for the American clergy. It was the idea of the two Spaldings, Martin J., Archbishop of Baltimore and the council's apostolic delegate, and John Lancaster, his priest nephew, who was home only about a year and a half from his European studies. As early as August, 1865, the archbishop had manifested his interest when he asked John Timon, Bishop of Buffalo, "Why should we not have a Catholic University? It would be a great thing, if we could only agree as to the location & arrangement." [69] Through the ensuing months and into the council itself he continued to urge the project, but the bishops' general lack of interest, plus the critical state of the finances of the North American College at Rome, combined to kill the prospect of a university.

In the end the chapter of the council's decrees entitled, "De Universitate Literarum Fundanda," paid tribute to the American seminaries at Rome and Louvain and to All Hallows College, Dublin, for what they had done by way of educating priests for the United States, but in regard to a university, it closed with no more than the adumbration of a distant hope when the decree stated:

Would that in this region it were permissible to have a great college or university which would embrace the advantages and the usefulness of all these colleges whether domestic or foreign; in which, namely, all the letters and sciences, both sacred and profane, could be taught! Whether or not the time for founding such a university has arrived, we leave it to the judgment of the Fathers, that they may examine the whole matter more maturely hereafter.[70]

Given the conservative and traditional approach of these conciliar directives — and the same could be said for those of the Third Plenary Council of 1884 — one would have no right to look to that source for any stimulation to original thinking by the professional theologians. In fairness to the bishops, however, it should be stated that, to speak only of the period before the Civil War, more was heard from prelates like Archbishop Carroll, Bishop John England of Charleston, and Archbishop Hughes of New York by way of a theology on Catholicism's unique American experience than was true of all the professors of theology in the seminaries combined. In that connection it should be mentioned that Bishop Francis Patrick Kenrick's three-volume *Theologia Moralis* (1841–1843) had been written explicitly for Americans and had incorporated many comparisons of canon and American civil law and custom. Likewise the attempts of Kenrick and his friend, Bishop Michael O'Connor, to change the Church's discipline in regard to married convert ministers could only have happened in a pluralistic environment such as obtained in this country.

Relations Between Church and State

These facts were the more noteworthy in that as far back as May, 1831, a perceptive foreign visitor, a Catholic layman, had immediately been struck upon his arrival in the United States with the country's religious aspect, and the longer he remained, he said, "the more I perceived the great political consequences resulting from this new state of things." His desire to discover the causes that lay behind this unusual phenomenon increasing from day to day, Alexis de Tocqueville in consequence interrogated many clergymen on the point. As a Catholic he had come into more intimate contact with priests than with other ministers of religion, and the implications for theology in the new American framework might, one would have thought, have prompted Catholic theologians to have engaged in research and writing on a topic that had deeply intrigued de Tocqueville. In regard to his acquaintance with American priests, he observed:

> To each of these men I expressed my astonishment and explained my doubts. I found that they differed upon matters of detail alone, and that they all attributed the peaceful dominion of religion in their country mainly to the separation of church and state. I do not hesitate to affirm that during my stay in America I did not meet a single individual, of the clergy or the laity, who was not of the same opinion on this point.[71]

More than a century passed, however, before an American Catholic theologian did justice to this subject when the series of incisive essays of John Courtney Murray, S.J., brought out in the late 1940's and the early 1950's the full significance for Catholicism of the separation of Church and State. In so doing he incurred the displeasure of certain powerful figures of the Roman Curia like Cardinal Alfredo Ottaviani; nonetheless, he laid the foundation, so to speak, for the Universal Church's adoption of the principles underlying the American arrangement in the Declaration of Religious Freedom of Vatican Council II promulgated by Pope Paul VI in December, 1965, a document of which Father Murray had been one of the principal authors.

Yet it would be a bit quixotic to expect that the theologians of the last century should venture in an imaginative way onto the terrain that as late as the 1950's proved too risky even for Father Murray.[72] There were too many danger signals, for example, Pope Leo XIII's encyclical, *Longinqua oceani*, addressed to the Church of the United States on January 6, 1895, where after giving high praise to American political institutions, he said:

> Yet, though all this is true, it would be very erroneous to draw the conclusion that in America is to be sought the type of the most desirable status of the Church, or that it would be universally lawful or expedient for State and Church to be, as in America, dissevered and divorced.[73]

In fact, up to the 1960's the intellectual climate within the Church was far too hostile for ideas of this kind to be discussed with any freedom. The point can be illustrated by reference to the years between the American bishops' first and third plenary councils, 1852–1844, a period that proved significant for educational developments relating to the Catholic clergy in more than one sense.

As the movement for Italian unification gained momentum during the 1860's and gradually closed in upon the Papal States, eliminating them entirely with the seizure of Rome in September, 1870, Pio Nono struck out more and more vehemently against the aggressors. "He became profoundly convinced," as Hubert Jedin remarked, "that a barrier must be erected to prevent the irruption of modern philosophical and political ideas into the very heart of the Church. . . ." [74] Obviously, in this struggle his only weapons were in the moral order, for it was apparent that his volunteer army was no match for the Italian nationalists, to say nothing of the French with whom they were secretly allied, nor for the Austrians whose power in the Italian peninsula could not even at that late date be entirely discounted.

To some the undulating waves of Italian politics may seem an oddly irrelevant factor to introduce in an essay on the formation of candidates for the American priesthood, but there was a connection. It sprang in part from Pius IX's conviction that his power to wield spiritual weapons in the form of excommunications and condemnations of doctrinal errors and the policies of civil governments, might still produce the effect that they once had on sovereigns in the distant past when much of western Europe was actively Catholic. Events were to prove him wrong in this supposition, but not before he had marshalled his forces and moved into battle with the world with armament such as *La Civiltà Cattolica*, the Jesuits' Roman journal begun in 1850, wherein the ultramontanist emphasis was a notable feature, the issuance of the Syllabus of Errors in 1864 which carried a strong condemnation of many trends of thought current at the time, and the definition six years later at Vatican Council I of papal infallibility, all of which helped to solidify the pope in his stance under the new banner of prisoner of the Vatican. On one occasion during his last years in reply to a question from Monsignor Vladimir Czacki about his desires concerning the policies of his successor, Piux IX remarked — as he likewise did to several others — that his successor might take inspiration from his attachment to the Church and his desire to do it good, to which he added, "as for the rest, all has changed around me; my system and my policy have had their day, but I am too old to change my course; this will be the work of my successor." [74a] Thus was the official Church kept at odds with the world until the passing of the aged pontiff in February, 1878, permitted his successor to inaugurate a more relaxed and realistic policy.

That these developments had relevance for what Americans were expected to teach and to emphasize soon became apparent. Archbishop Spalding, obviously embarrassed by certain passages in the encyclical, *Quanta cura,* of December 8, 1864, and the accompanying Syllabus of

Errors, which were clearly at variance with universally accepted concepts of American life, undertook the delicate task of writing a pastoral letter that would try to explain them to his people. Upon finishing the pastoral he designated certain persons at the Roman Curia to whom copies were to be given by his nephew who was in Rome at the time. He asked Father Spalding to see Cardinal Giacomo Antonelli, Secretary of State, and to ask for explanations of four specific propositions of the Syllabus which, he said, "will be construed here as condemning our system of religious toleration, so advantageous & so [word illegible] to Religion." He then added, "I fear these & some other propositions will furnish a pretext to the fanatics to persecute us, which they will probably do any how." [75] In fact, nearly twenty years after the Holy See's loss of Rome the intransigent attitude assumed in 1870 by Pius IX was still regarded as sacrosanct.

The editor of the *Catholic Mirror* of Baltimore discovered that when in an editorial of November 9, 1889, he ventured to speak for all American Catholics in saying it was not desired that there should be any interference with the present boundaries of the Kingdom of Italy. The prerogative of a secular ruler that formerly attached to the pope was, said the editor:

> neither essential nor indispensable to the spiritual authority or spiritual dominion of the Pope. The Holy Father, as Vicar of Christ and visible Head of the Church, has no absolute need for extensive territory wherein to wield the power and exercise the rule of an earthly kingdom.[76]

The reaction from Rome was immediate and sharp. As a consequence Cardinal Gibbons felt bound to rebuke the editor who, in turn, two weeks later carried a second editorial entitled "The Roman Question" which was a complete *volte face* from his original position with the official line now dictating a stern condemnation of the Italian government for having seized the Papal States. In this regard what was true of the teaching of bishops' pastoral letters and the Catholic press was *a fortiori* true of what was taught in the seminaries.

The Revival of Thomism

Previous to Pope Leo XIII's election to the papacy on February 20, 1878, he had manifested as Bishop of Perugia a keen interest in the teaching of Saint Thomas Aquinas. He was not on the chair of Peter very long before he launched an energetic campaign to revive Thomism throughout the Church, a goal that he outlined in an encyclical, *Aeterni patris*, of August 4, 1879, when he told the bishops of the Catholic world:

> We exhort you, Venerable Brethren, in all earnestness to restore the golden wisdom of St. Thomas, and to spread it far and wide for the defence and beauty of the Catholic faith, for the good of society, and for the advantage of all the sciences. . . . Let carefully selected teachers endeavor to implant the doctrine of Thomas Aquinas in the minds of students, and set forth clearly his solidity and excellence over others. Let the academies already founded or to be founded by you illustrate and defend this doctrine, and use it for the refutation of prevailing errors.[77]

And that this was no passing fancy of the new pope became evident from the practical directive that followed a year later in the apostolic letter, *Cum hoc sit*.

While scholasticism had, indeed, declined woefully during the eighteenth and nineteenth centuries and stood in need of fresh inspiration, it was apparent from Leo XIII's approach that he did not conceive philosophy as a system of thought at which one arrived after a process of reasoning, nor was there any indication in *Aeterni patris* that its author had taken cognizance of scholasticism's medieval pluralistic origins or of its history. To the pope it was rather an instrument of apologetics that was to be imposed by his authority, and it was not far off the mark, therefore, when Lorenzo Michelangelo Billia, one of the opponents of this attempted revival, characterized the new approach as "a system of philosophy by decree." [78]

As it turned out, there was a marked turn-over in the Roman seminaries with the opponents of the Thomistic revival dropped from the faculties to make way for the followers of the new dispensation. The Gregorian University, for example, lost five of its well known professors, including Domenico Palmieri, S.J., who had been on the faculty since 1861 and who was transferred in 1878 to Holland to teach Scripture, and in his place came Camillo Mazzella, S.J., whom Leo XIII made a cardinal eight years later. The same was true at the Urban College of Propaganda where Benedetto Lorenzelli was introduced to teach philosophy with the pope's favorite, Francesco Satolli, replacing Bernard Smith, O.S.B., who had been teaching dogmatic theology there since the early 1850's. Similar changes took place at the Appolinare and other Roman seminaries, and with the changes in personnel there came a change of textbooks as well.

Obviously, no such radical transformation could be brought about without arousing opposition, even allowing that the directives had emanated from the pope himself and his Jesuit brother, Giuseppe Pecci, Cardinal Prefect of the Congregation of Studies and Director of Rome's Academy of Saint Thomas. There were a number of professors who were not of a mind to comply, and the Rector of the North American College, Louis E. Hostlot, was not exaggerating when he told John M. Farley, the future archbishop and cardinal, "The Pope is meeting with a good deal of quiet, concealed opposition from many professors on account of his Thomist ideas. Several professors have been removed," to which Hostlot then added, "They all ask, 'a chi tocca dopo? C'è pericolo, ci vuol prudenza.' " ['Who will be hit next? It's dangerous: we must be careful.'] [79] Americans studying in Rome felt the changes, of course, and the new situation was described for Archbishop Gibbons of Baltimore by James M. Connelly, one of his students, when he wrote:

> . . . . As Your Grace is aware, scholasticism's star is now in the ascendent throughout the Eternal City. The majority of professors not bred up as Thomists have been forced to vacate their chairs in favor of the Neapolitan schools of philosophy and theology; whilst every tongue has learned to lisp the new slang phrase in Rome 'ut ait Sanctus Doctor' ['as the holy Doctor (Aquinas) says'].
>
> That the Propaganda should catch the infection we of the Alumni [i.e., students] would never have suspected one year ago. . . . How our eyes stared and our mouths stood agape, when the new professor of dogmas passed up to his pulpit with a real volume of St. Thomas under his arm, and laid it down with the exclamation that it would be our sole textbook. [80]

While it would be easy to find flaws in some of the methods by which the Thomistic revival had been introduced and pursued by Pope Leo XIII and his followers, there could be no question but that it was a distinct improvement over the intellectual stagnation that had permeated most of the Church's educational institutions since the waning of the fervor that had accompanied the founding of the new seminary system in the period after Trent. This was especially true of the two pontificates that had preceded that of Pope Leo [Gregory XVI and Pius IX, 1831–1878] when higher authority seemed to take cognizance of the scholarly endeavors of men in the ecclesiastical disciplines in only a negative way by warnings and condemnations that left little hope for real research and any positive advance. Pope Leo XIII, on the contrary, made a sincere effort to move forward and to meet the age in which he lived, even though the way he chose to do it was not free at times from the arbitrary use of authority.

The difference was illustrated by Leo's initiative in requesting Victor Dechamps, Archbishop of Malines, in December, 1880, to establish a special chair of Thomistic philosophy at Louvain. Moreover, when Désiré Mercier, the man chosen to inaugurate the course in October, 1882, encountered formidable opposition from Jean B. Abbeloos, Rector of the University, and others, the pope gave the young professor his strong personal backing. The result was the formal inauguration in November, 1889, of Louvain's Institut Supérieur de Philosophie, a development from which a considerable number of American students were to profit.[81] Actually, the latter had been put in a position to derive benefit from this advantage some years before when Father John De Neve, Rector of the American College at Louvain, announced in a circular letter of January, 1882, to the alumni at the time of the silver jubilee of the college that the best students would henceforth be attending the university. The news pleased none of the alumni more than Bishop Spalding of Peoria who told the rector:

> I am especially glad to see from your letter that the better sort of students will be permitted to follow the university course. This is undoubtedly very important, and was, as you know, a chief reason for founding the College at Louvain.[82]

In the same year that the Bishop of Peoria expressed gratification with developments at the Catholic University of Louvain, steps were taken to advance clerical education among the Protestants in the United States. One of the most frequently recurring refrains in the history of both the Protestant and Catholic branches of American Christianity has been criticism of the inadequate and unsatisfactory character of seminary education. A century ago, for example, Charles W. Eliot, a Unitarian, assumed the presidency of Harvard University, and after some years in that office he determined in 1882 to try to raise the standards of the Divinity School. Protestant institutions for both ecclesiastical and lay students had multiplied far beyond the point where they were able to offer sound education by reason of the competition between denominations, and as a recent historian has said, "continued bitterness . . . . had levied a heavy price on their energies and achievements." [83] Eliot's reform measures included the requirement of a bachelor of arts degree or its equivalent for entrance to the

Divinity School with a view, as he said, to making the bachelor of divinity degree "inaccessible except to men of thorough training. . . ." In closing his report to the Board of Overseers the Harvard president summarized his objectives in these words:

> The present dearth of able ministers, which is acknowledged in all Protestant denominations, will probably continue so long as young men of independent spirit and mental virility are repelled from the profession at the very threshold, as they are now. A partial remedy for this evil is likely to be found in the conduct of theological education at universities, or other centres of diversified intellectual activity, instead of in isolated denominational seminaries, and with the same academic freedom for teacher and pupil which is allowed in other great departments of study.[84]

The senseless and wasteful duplication of "isolated denominational seminaries" was all the more unfortunate when it was concentrated in a single denomination. For it had been a predominant weakness among the Catholics almost from the beginning where the fifty seminaries of 1868, including those for both the diocesan and religious clergy, had a combined student population of only 913. And that matters had not improved by the time the Church entered the twentieth century was clear when the year 1900 showed 109 Catholic seminaries with a total of 4,628 young men enrolled or an average of slightly more than forty-two students to each institution.[85] Nor, as we have seen, had the persistence of a few far-sighted leaders made headway in convincing the majority of the bishops that the resources of the Catholic community should be directed toward a strong national seminary.

Yet Martin Spalding for one had refused to abandon this ideal about which he repeatedly approached his fellow bishops as, for example, when in anticipation of the First Plenary Council he addressed two letters in a single week to John B. Purcell, Archbishop of Cincinnati, saying in the second, "I hope most sincerely that the project of a general theological seminary will succeed." [86] Purcell, in turn, seemed ready to move beyond a national seminary when in the same month he asked the council's apostolic delegate, Archbishop Kenrick of Baltimore, "Is it expedient and practicable to found a Catholic University? And if not, how shall we otherwise efficiently provide for the education of such clergy as the peculiar circumstances of this country require?" [87] As we know, the plenary councils of both 1852 and 1866 left Purcell's questions unanswered, and thus the successors of these bishops had to face them when early in the 1880's plans began to take shape for the hierarchy's third plenary assembly.

The Third Plenary Council

In preparation for the council the archbishops of the United States were for the first time summoned to confer in advance with the cardinals of the Congregation de Propaganda Fide. They were at Rome for four weeks in November–December, 1883, where the first topic at the initial session dealt with clerical education. Propaganda's recommendations, contained in a document entitled *Capita praecipua*, included summer villas for seminarians after the European model, major and minor seminaries for every diocese where that was possible, and a six-year course in the major seminary that allotted two years to philosophy and four to theology with all classes to be taught in Latin. After certain Americans had raised objections to some of these proposals — for example, to summer villas — the recommendations were revised and issued under the title of *Capita proposita*. Upon the archbishops' return to the United States they, in turn, submitted the *Capita proposita* to their fellow bishops with those of each ecclesiastical province made responsible for shaping a particular portion of the proposed laws for submission to the full hierarchy in council.[88]

Although the chapter on seminaries had been assigned to the bishops of the Province of Baltimore, the prelates of the Province of Milwaukee volunteered such ample comments on this subject that the views of the two groups figured in the final recommendations. While they differed over instituting summer villas for seminarians with Baltimore in favor and Milwaukee opposed to such, the two groups were in substantial agreement on the more important matters of the length and content of the seminary curriculum, with the midwesterners urging the need for uniformity throughout the country in order to safeguard academic excellence. The Baltimore prelates called for chairs of liturgy and sacred eloquence in those major seminaries where they were lacking, and specified that in minor seminaries instruction should be given in both the natural sciences and in those languages where local need would dictate as among immigrant settlements that used German, French, or one of the various Slavic tongues.

The principal difference within the Province of Milwaukee arose over the proposal of Thomas L. Grace, O.P., Bishop of Saint Paul, that the council undertake the establishment of a Catholic university. Michael Heiss, Archbishop of Milwaukee, on the contrary, maintained that the Holy See's wish was not for a national theological center but rather for strengthening the seminaries already in existence, an opinion which, he said, was shared by the bishops of the East. In the end they agreed that the council should appoint a committee of bishops to investigate the means available for founding a *seminarium principalissimum* for the American Church to promote higher philosophical and theological studies.[89]

If one were interested in gauging how far the norms for priestly formation had changed over the last eighty-five years he could scarcely find a better way by which to judge than to contrast the detailed prescriptions drawn up by the bishops in the Third Plenary Council of Baltimore which, incidentally, were largely confined to seminarians' intellectual rather than spiritual training, with the regulations — or the lack of them — that obtained in the Catholic seminaries of the late 1960's. It is a point that might profitably be kept in mind in what follows. The first working session of the council was convened in the *aula maxima* of Saint Mary's Seminary on November 7, 1884. The agenda or *Schema Decretorum* had been mailed to all the bishops about three weeks in advance of the opening, a brochure of nearly 100 closely printed pages that consisted of eleven major titles. The fifth title treated clerical education under the following headings: minor seminaries, major seminaries, *seminarium principale*, examinations of the junior clergy, and theological conferences.[90]

First, in regard to minor seminaries the Council of Trent was invoked on their usefulness and stress was laid on the need to raise their standards. As to the best means to accomplish that end, it was said that the course should not be less than six years in length, and the bishops then for the first time went into detail concerning the curriculum. Christian doctrine took first place among the subjects to be taught with instruction in English, at least one modern language, and Latin and Greek prescribed, the last in order to enable students to read the New Testament in the original as well as to familiarize themselves with the source materials on the ancient Church. Other subjects that should find a place in the curriculum were history — both sacred and profane with a special emphasis on the history of the United States — geography, physics, chemistry, geology, astronomy, Gregorian chant, liturgy, and bookkeeping. The *Schema Decretorum* likewise urged that a syllabus be prepared for each course under the supervision of the seminary director and with the approval of the bishop, and all institutions for training the clergy, both diocesan and religious, should be expected to follow them.

Although it was very much open to question if the standards of

the minor seminaries of the 1880's were even up to the modest requirements invoked in these schools in the 1960's, the authors of the 1884
proposals maintained that students who had been educated in colleges
for laymen were not to be considered as having fulfilled the training
prescribed by Trent. While allowance was made for exceptions, the
bishops were urged to see that those who had attended the *collegia
mixta* had their preparation accommodated as much as possible to the
norms of clerical education.

On many aspects of the proposed legislation there was general
agreement, but differences arose over such matters as the emphasis
given to Latin with Spalding of Peoria and Bernard J. McQuaid,
Bishop of Rochester, contending that Latin was stressed too much,
while Patrick J. Ryan, Archbishop of Philadelphia, and Bishops
Joseph Dwenger, C.PP.S., of Fort Wayne and William H. Gross,
C.SS.R., of Savannah held out for the original reading, a position that
won in the final vote. The suggestion of Thomas F. Hendricken,
Bishop of Providence, that students be compelled to take a course
in drawing to acquaint them with the fundamentals of architecture set
off a lively debate with his proposal winning by the narrow margin of
three votes, while the wish of Richard Gilmour, Bishop of Cleveland,
to have all students take a course in music met opposition from Bishop
John Ireland of Saint Paul and ended with the *Schema Decretorum's*
recommendation of practice in plain chant and a general cultivation
of the art of music being retained by a single vote.

The responsibility of seeing that students were prepared to meet
the entrance requirements of the major seminary also occupied the
bishops and the prolonged debate closed with agreement that a special
group bearing the title of synodal examiners should be appointed to
determine the students' fitness in this regard. And in an attempt to
insure uniformity in both the program of studies and in examinations,
James O'Connor, Vicar Apostolic of Nebraska, suggested that the
apostolic delegate appoint a committee of bishops to consult with the
authorities of the seminaries at Rome, Louvian, and Innsbruck, a
suggestion that carried, along with Spalding's amendment that one or
more priests should also be members of this committee.

Not unexpectedly, the *Schema Decretorum's* proposals for major
seminaries were twice as numerous as those for preparatory seminaries, but limitations of space will permit only a bare summary here
of the lengthy conciliar debates to which they gave rise. It was apparent
that in drawing up the preliminary draft the bishops and their theological advisers had leaned heavily on the legislation of European

councils beginning with Trent and including recent provincial councils held at Ravenna, Venice, Aix, Bordeaux, and Utrecht. Having stated the philosophy that motivated their establishment and the spirit that should prevail in houses intended to prepare men for the priesthood, separate decrees treated such subjects as those responsible for their erection and management from the bishop on through the rector, spiritual director, and professors, the spiritual life of the students, among others.

For example, it was said that the post of teacher in a seminary was of such importance that it should not be entrusted to a man who would view it as a temporary task; rather it should be assigned to those of a generous disposition, mature, and prudent men who were eager to devote themselves entirely to the "glory and increase of ecclesiastical knowledge," and who had the matter so much at heart that they would not permit themselves to be distracted by undertaking work outside the seminary. Under the heading of the students' spiritual life emphasis was placed on the development of priestly virtues, particularly those the defect of which is perceived in this age such as humility, obedience, and the respect owed to superiors. Students were to be on their guard against an "immoderate love of their own freedom" and a dislike for rules and regulations, for nothing, it was said, was more contrary than this defect to the sacredotal spirit.[91]

Reference has been made to the little flexibility allowed in seminary classrooms for originality and experiment in thought and expression by reason of the detailed directives that accompanied Leo XIII's revival of the teaching of Saint Thomas Aquinas. The Americans' unquestioning compliance with these directives was nowhere more in evidence than in the decrees on the curriculum of the major seminary. Here both the professors' lectures and the student disputations of the two years of philosophy and the four years of theology were to be conducted in Latin, with the textbooks for each course to be designated and to be approved by the bishop of the diocese. Nothing was more important and desirable, it was stated, than to comply religiously with the wishes of the encyclical, *Aeterni patris*, and for that reason, as the decree read, "we desire and we order that in teaching the philosophical and theological disciplines all professors follow studiously and faithfully in the footsteps of the Angelic Doctor. . . ."[92]

In this as in most of what pertained to the curriculum the original draft was accepted and became the final reading of the conciliar decrees as, for example, those on the individual subjects to be taught, the spirit of which can, perhaps, be conveyed by what was said about the history of the Church. The professor of ecclesiastical history was exhorted to aim at establishing the truth of history against the false knowledge that had passed as truth and, too, he should "show how much good for human society has been derived in all ages from ecclesiastical institutions." [93]

While the sources for the conciliar debates do not permit the historian to speak with the precision he might wish, for the most part the *Schema Decretorum's* draft legislation on major seminaries was found acceptable to the bishops. Exceptions related to the decrees on summer villas which were finally eliminated and to the six-year curriculum which was retained, but to meet the objection of several bishops from the Middle and Far West who had a shortage of priests, there was inserted the phrase, "unless necessity compels the Ordinary to adopt a shorter course in a particular case." The recommendation of several consulting theologians that ascetical theology be dropped from the curriculum was overruled by the objections of Bishops Gilmour, John Watterson of Columbus, and John J. Kain of Wheeling. Other proposals in regard to the course of studies that lost after some debate were the suggestion of Silas Chatard, Bishop of Vincennes, that Scripture be taught in Latin and Spalding's desire that debating societies be established in the seminaries.

The other means instituted by the council of 1884 for what would today be termed the continuing education of the clergy, met with virtually unanimous assent and occasioned only a few verbal changes. One was an annual examination for five years for newly ordained priests to help insure a spirit of study in their lives and to assist them in keeping abreast of developments in the ecclesiastical sciences. The second was a series of clergy conferences for both diocesan and religious priests who were engaged in the parochial ministry, which were normally to be held four times a year and in rural dioceses at least twice a year. Attendance at both the examinations and the conferences was made obligatory with the subject matter for the former and the papers and questions for the latter to be taken from dogmatic and moral theology, Scripture, canon law, and liturgy, with the young priests also made responsible for examination in the history of the Church.[94]

The junior clergy examinations and the clerical conferences were not, however, the council's most striking break with the past in what pertained to clerical education. That was embodied in four decrees headed, "De Seminario Principali," which after prolonged debate represented the bishops' final expression concerning a higher school of theology for the clergy. During the interval of fourteen years since the

Second Plenary Council several churchmen, disappointed that no action had been taken at that time, had maintained a steady campaign in behalf of a university for the American Church. Among the leaders in this endeavor were two converts, Thomas A. Becker, Bishop of Wilmington, and Isaac T. Hecker, C.S.P., founder of the Paulists, whose efforts were even outdone by John Lancaster Spalding who in 1877 had been named first Bishop of Peoria. Spalding was determined that the idea should not die, and that in spite of repeated discouragement and indifference experienced at the hands of his fellow bishops. When he succeeded in getting a young convert friend, Mary Gweldoline Caldwell, heiress to a large fortune, however, to promise that she would give $300,000 for such an institution, his hand was greatly strengthened. Moreover, Spalding's eloquent plea, "The Higher Education," preached on November 16 as one in the council's series of sermons, was a powerful stimulation for the hierarchy to move forward in this undertaking. As in previous public statements on the subject, the bishop paid tribute to the existing seminaries, but he then made perfectly clear the distinction between the ordinary seminary and what he had in mind when he said:

> . . . . the ecclesiastical seminary is not a school of intellectual culture, either here in America or elsewhere, and to imagine that it can become the instrument of intellectual culture is to cherish a delusion . . . . its methods are not such as one would choose who desires to open the mind, to give it breadth, flexibility, strength, refinement, and grace. Its text-books are written often in a barbarous style, the subjects are discussed in a dry and mechanical way, and the professor, wholly intent upon giving instruction, is frequently indifferent as to the manner in which it is imparted; or else not possessing himself a really cultivated intellect, he holds in slight esteem expansion and refinement of mind, looking upon it as at the best a mere ornament. I am not offering a criticism upon the ecclesiastical seminary, but am simply pointing to the plain fact that it is not a school of intellectual culture, and consequently, if its course were lengthened to five, to six, to eight, to ten years, its students would go forth to their work with a more thorough professional training, but not with more really cultivated minds.[95]

Bishop Spalding's sermon came about ten days in advance of the conciliar debate on the *seminarium principale*, a debate that was enlivened at one point by a heated exchange between Robert Fulton,

Provincial of the New York-Maryland Province of the Society of Jesus, and Thomas S. Byrne of Mount Saint Mary's Seminary of the West, Cincinnati, later Bishop of Nashville. Fulton maintained that university education did not suit the role of the diocesan clergy but was rather the work of the religious orders, a position to which Byrne voiced a prompt and strenuous objection. That the project enjoyed anything but unanimous support was evident when a motion by Bishop Tobias Mullen of Erie to have the entire chapter on the proposed university expunged or referred to the next plenary council gathered twenty-three votes. Yet in the end the opposition was defeated and the apostolic delegate was instructed to appoint a committee of bishops to undertake the work.[96] Thus was official sanction given for the establishment of the institution which opened in November, 1889, as a graduate school of theology for priests under the name of the Catholic University of America.

The Catholic University of America

The founding of the university in Washington was, to be sure, a step in the right direction, even if it would be some time before the institution was able to overcome certain initial handicaps that weighed heavily against its effectiveness. Thus well into the present century the academic achievements of the Catholic University of America were at best modest in character and few in number. It was a situation that lasted long after the student days of Father Terence Moore of the Archdiocese of Saint Paul who a year and a half after the university's inauguration described for President William Fortune of All Hallows College, his *alma mater*, the elaborate plans made for a public disputation. "Really when I heard this first announced," said Moore:

> and saw all the fuss they had about decorations etc. I was sure I would experience something extraordinary; but the fact of the matter is it was more like a fifteenth century performance than like a scene enacted in an enlivened and enlightened nineteenth century.[97]

To the lack of interest and financial support of so many of the bishops there was added an aloofness amounting in some instances to hostility on the part of large segments of the Catholic community. Many of the Germans, for example, felt it was largely an "Irish" undertaking, some leading Jesuits saw it as a threat to Georgetown University, certain highly placed conservatives, both clerical and lay, were alienated by the liberal views of the first rector, Bishop John J. Keane, and, finally, the overwhelming majority of the more than 12,000,000 Catholics of 1900 had neither the experience nor the hope of a university training. In all these categories there were, of course, exceptions who were friendly disposed, but the general policies of the respective groups were frequently determined by those of an opposite mind. When these factors were combined with the change that came over the Church's intellectual climate in the transition years between the two centuries, about which we shall speak in what follows, it was small wonder that the university was not able to advance the education of the American clergy to the degree and at the pace that some had probably anticipated.[98]

While the standards for priestly formation were such as to leave many dissatisfied as the century came to a close, there were not lacking perceptive Catholic critics who spoke and wrote of the seminaries in a highly constructive way. Nor was discontent confined to Catholic circles, for the American ethos had taken an even heavier toll among the Protestants where the national tendency toward the practical gained an early ascendancy that it long maintained. "The kind of practical Christianity which had its roots in the revivals," declared a Protestant survey of the historical background, "had little interest in theology as a direct expression of human faith in God and love of neighbor." And if the Catholics escaped the worst features of the influences these Protestant writers deplored, they were by no means free of what the latter had in mind when they stated:

> Theology as such was often subject to religious contempt. Empirical religion in the churches frequently joined hands with anti-intellectualism in equalitarian democracy . . . . insofar as ministers received a special preparation for carrying on their tasks, they were trained in practical work more than in theological disciplines.[99]

In that connection one is reminded of the advice given on one occasion to Thomas J. Shahan, Rector of the Catholic University of America, by Patrick W. Riordan, Archbishop of San Francisco and surely one of the most enlightened bishops of the American Church at the time, when he told him:

> I need not tell you that the spiritual part of the University training is not as it should be. The young students are not trained for the ministry such as they must exercise when they come back to their respective dioceses. Very few of them will ever be professors. Nearly all of them will be employed in the active ministry

of parish work, and for that reason they should be taught how to preach and how to conduct the services of our holy religion. Very little of this kind of instruction is now given to them.[100]

While one would not question that young priests should be instructed in homiletics and rubrics, one would have supposed that these exercises in the practical ministry would have been sufficiently well taken care of in the seminary and not be thought a proper part of their university studies.

One of the best means for facilitating the spiritual and intellectual formation of priests and seminarians are journals that enable them to keep *au courant* with the latest currents of religious thought, as well as to afford a medium for publication of the ideas of the minority whose talents and tastes prompt them to undertake writing themselves. Aside from *Brownson's Quarterly Review* (1844), there was little of this sort of thing available to the Catholic clergy until *Ave Maria* and the *Catholic World* appeared in 1865, with matters further improved by the establishment of the *American Catholic Quarterly Review* in 1876. In this regard the 1880's witnessed considerable advancement when clerics interested in history had at their disposal the *American Catholic Historical Researches* (1884) and the *Records of the American Catholic Historical Society of Philadelphia* and the *United States Catholic Historical Magazine*, both of which began in 1887. Of broader scope and more particularly addressed to priests and seminarians were the *Sacred Heart Review* (1888), the *American Ecclesiastical Review* (1889), and the *Homiletic and Pastoral Review* which started publication in the last year of the century.

Thanks to periodicals of this kind those interested in clerical education were able to become acquainted with the thinking of the best minds in the Church of the United States on seminary training. There was, for example, the *American Ecclesiastical Review's* series by John B. Hogan, S.S., Rector of Saint John's Seminary, Brighton, which opened in May, 1891, with an article entitled "The Curriculum," and which were later published in book form as *Clerical Studies*.[101] The extraordinary qualities of the Abbé Hogan, as he was affectionately called, were brought out after his death in a striking tribute from Austin Dowling, a former student and a future Archbishop of Saint Paul. The value to be derived from the writings of a man like Hogan was suggested when Dowling said his was "the rare gift of filling the student's mind with the unrest of inquiry. . . ." In his desire to make students think Hogan would often seem, as Dowling said, "to go to the very limit of daring in the vigor with which he plied us with objections," for as he added, "sure of his own faith, he had no fear of ours. . . ." The Sulpician's breadth of view, his youthful mind, and his tolerance for those in error were an unfailing source of surprise to seminarians who, according to Dowling, had been "hitherto resting content with the cogency of our syllogisms and the smartness of scholastic repartee. . . ." It was little wonder that the future archbishop should have concluded of such a man, "To have lived with him was a liberal education. To have been guided by him was an incomparable privilege. . . ." [102]

The Abbé Hogan's series of nearly forty articles during the 1890's in the *American Ecclesiastical Review* revealed the qualities of mind that gained the admiration of Dowling and many others, and when assembled in book form they constituted about as enlightened a commentary on the intellectual formation of the priest as one would find anywhere at that time. The point was exemplified in his treatment of Pope Leo XIII's encyclical on the revival of Thomism. Hogan was aware of the opposition that had been aroused in certain circles by the pope's directives that Thomism alone should inform the teaching of philosophy and theology. He proceeded, therefore, through a careful analysis of *Aeterni patris*, somewhat after the fashion in which Félix Dupanloup, Bishop of Orléans, had in 1865 published his brochure to quiet the critics of the Syllabus of Errors. In conclusion Hogan stated:

> Thus limited to its true meaning, the encyclical loses that seeming exclusiveness which made it objectionable to many, because they confined their attention to separate passages, and failed to grasp the spirit of the whole.[103]

Seminary education was a popular theme with contributors to Catholic journals during this period, a fact that likewise served to bring out the talents of a number of diocesan priests such as several professors at Saint Charles Borromeo Seminary of Philadelphia. For example, James A. Corcoran wrote commentaries on both *Aeterni patris* and the decrees of the Baltimore council of 1884 [104], while his colleague, James F. Loughlin, discussed the Catholic seminary system of the United States in a way that showed his annoyance with recent critics. "Without doubt," said Loughlin, "the severest, and, we must add, the most peevish and unreasonable critics of the priesthood are to be found among the Catholics themselves; nay, in the ranks of the clergy." [105] One of the "severest," although hardly the "most peevish" of these critics was Bishop McQuaid of Rochester who did not hesitate to level sharp strictures at his predecessors in the hierarchy for their neglect of seminaries. According to McQuaid, they had "placed in improvised Seminaries whatever seemingly suitable subjects came to hand," in institutions where, as McQuaid pictured them, "the buildings were wretched, the equipments no better; and the professors were inadequate in number and fitness for their task."

Under circumstances such as those described by Bishop McQuaid it was not surprising that priests who had been compelled to finish their studies in these seminaries should not have been, as he remarked, "over-grateful for the miserable pretence of instruction they received, while craving the highest and best to fit them for their Master's work." While matters had improved of late, the American Church had not yet reached a standard in this regard of which Catholics could be proud. "Our efforts in Seminary work," the bishop declared, "are still elementary in more ways than one." [106] Were one to supplement the blunt criticisms of the Bishop of Rochester with the book on seminaries of John Talbot Smith, a priest of the Archdiocese of New York, that had appeared the previous year, it would be easy to comprehend what painful reading it must have made for conservatives like Loughlin and those of a similar mind. Smith wrote with a forthrightness equal to McQuaid's, and one of his main points was made in a vigorous plea for central rather than diocesan seminaries, and that partly as a response to the marked tendency of current American social and political trends toward concentration of effort. "In planning new institutions or adopting new methods," said Smith:

> it is advisable to study the tastes and manners of the age, and rarely is it wise to run counter to them . . . The narrowness of diocesan seminaries is as certain and ineradicable as the narrowness of a country town.[107]

Unfortunately, voices such as those of John Talbot Smith sounded their warning in vain, and the dismal procession of numerous small and weak seminaries continued to appear in every part of the land through the ensuing decades. By 1912 the United States Commissioner of Education reported a total of 182 seminaries in the country of which only one-fourth had 10,000 or more volumes in their libraries, a value of $100,000 or above on their buildings and grounds, and endowments of $250,000, and just above a dozen of these 182 institutions had attained any university level or affiliation, namely, the theological schools at Harvard, Yale, Colgate, Washington, Oberlin, Chicago, Boston, Northwestern, Vanderbilt, Tufts, Augustana, the University of the South, and the Catholic University of America. Contrasting this seminary proliferation with the nation's medical schools which within three years had seen the closing of forty-seven inadequate institutions, one writer inquired:

> So the question arises: How many of our theological schools may well be dispensed with by consolidation or otherwise? I shall not hazard an exact estimate but I am confident that if their present number were largely reduced in the next few years it would be distinctly in the interest of religion.[108]

Needless to say, neither among the Protestants nor the Catholics did anything of the kind happen, and in the case of the latter the multiplication continued into the 1960's until the year 1966 found the Church of the United States sponsoring 607 of these institutions, including the major and minor seminaries for both the diocesan and religious clergy, with a total of 48,046 students.

At the time that Pope Leo XIII gave formal approval to the statutes of the Catholic University of America he suggested a form of joint action when he said:

> We exhort you all that you should take care to affiliate with your University your seminaries, colleges, and other Catholic institutions, according to the plan suggested in the Constitutions, in such a manner, however, as not to destroy their autonomy.[109]

Partly with a view to implementing this papal directive and partly in the hope of strengthening the seminaries, in 1897 the university's second rector, Thomas J. Conaty, decided to initiate action. At a meeting of the university trustees in October he sought and won authorization to summon a conference of seminary presidents.

Under the chairmanship of Monsignor Conaty the heads of ten seminaries met at Saint Joseph's Seminary, New York, on May 25, 1898, with five others having sent letters giving their approval for some form of collaboration. Conaty outlined the need for organization and stated that the first thing to be determined was the relationship between the seminaries and the university after which, it was hoped, certain academic standards might be agreed upon for all these institutions. One of the prime factors that had motivated the university rector from the beginning had been the need for remedying the university's experience of having so many priest students seek to matriculate in the School of Theology only to learn that they were unable to follow the courses without a loss of considerable time in fulfilling prerequisites. In an apparent endeavor to relate their common undertaking to the needs the Church then faced, Conaty told the seminary presidents:

> Our young cleric must be prepared to meet the issues of the hour — issues no longer between the true Church of Christ and the sects, but between revealed religion and all forms of agnosticism and false individualism. . . . He must also be prepared to enter into the field of social and economic reform. . . . The battle of the future is to be a philosophical battle, as well as scientific and historical. It will be a defence of the very foundations of belief. . . .[110]

The Educational Conference of Seminary Faculties

In the action of the New York meeting in voting to establish a permanent organization to which was given the name of the Educational Conference of Seminary Faculties, one could discern the first evidence of a dawning consciousness of the need for a formal professional approach to their work. Given that the American Association of Theological Schools, a predominantly Protestant organization up to the 1960's, was founded only in 1918, the Catholic seminary people were somewhat advanced in organizational structures. The fairly wide interest that marked the Catholics' first two annual meetings soon faded, however, and it was not until the university's third rector, Monsignor Denis J. O'Connell, proposed in 1904 that the seminary group join with those already formed for Catholic colleges and parochial schools that that interest was revived.

It was from a combination of the three that there was born the organization that ultimately came to be called the National Catholic Educational Association. Organizational details were worked out during the first combined annual meeting held in Saint Louis in July, 1904, and at the next meeting in New York in July, 1905, the seminary representatives devoted their three days to hearing and discussing a series of papers the nature of which could be gleaned from the following titles on the program: "On the Principles and Methods of Our Biblical Studies," by Simon Lebl of Saint Francis Seminary, Milwaukee; "The Study of Scripture in the Seminary," by James F. Driscoll of Saint Joseph's Seminary, New York; "The Teaching of Pedagogy in the Seminary," by Thomas E. Shields of the Catholic University of America; and "Charitable Work of Seminarians as a Preparation for the Work of the Ministry," by Anthony Viéban, S.S., of Saint Mary's Seminary, Baltimore. The report likewise stated that William C. Hoctor, C.M., of Saint John's Seminary, Brooklyn, had urged that something be done "to enable the students to acquire such knowledge as will enable them afterwards as priests to construct churches in accordance with the canons of sacred liturgy and architectural fitness." [111]

At the closing session on July 13 six resolutions were adopted by the seminary men in which certain aspects of priestly formation were singled out as deserving special emphasis in the curriculum, for example, catechetics and homiletics, with the suggestion that particular attention be given to pedagogical principles and methods in the courses of logic and psychology and the added note that seminaries had an obligation to direct students with an aptitude in these subjects to graduate work so as to fit them for the growing needs of the Church's elementary and secondary schools. Seminarians, it was also agreed, should be encouraged as far as their time allowed to visit hospitals, prisons, etc., and steps should be taken as well to equip them with a sufficient knowledge of ecclesiastical art and architecture to insure "that our churches may be constructed and adorned in accordance with proper liturgical and artistic ideals." [112]

Americanism

In a paper on the Catholic priest and his relationship to the American intellectual community since 1900 read at the historians' annual meeting in December, 1968, Michael V. Gannon of the University of Florida stated that until very recently there had been precious few instances of any inter-relationship since, as he remarked, "the history of those two entities during most of the last sixty-eight years is largely one of estrangement, if not hostility." [113] No one with any knowledge of this area will question the validity of Monsignor Gannon's conclusion, and it is of interest here because the causes that lay behind the situation he described relate directly to the present investigation, a matter he has discussed in detail in his essay in this book. For hardly had the first indications of a budding intellectual life among the Catholics begun to appear than its promise was suddenly overshadowed and snuffed out by certain movements within the Church herself. One was the flurry over the so-called heresy of Americanism which was condemned by Pope Leo XIII in his apostolic letter, *Testem benevolentiae*, of January, 1899.[114] Here in measured and temperate language the pontiff summarized what some — and they were mostly French churchmen — had characterized as heretical teaching among the American Catholics, prompted, as the critics had been, in part by a hurried translation of a popular biography of the founder of the Paulist Fathers. While the pope had been at pains not to accuse the Catholics of this country of holding the condemned ideas, the episode had a dampening effect on scholarly endeavor in American ecclesiastical circles. In that sense *Le Temps* of Paris, a paper that had shown a warm sympathy with the open and progressive thought of the so-called Americanizers in the Church of the United States, expressed an accurate editorial judgment. Stating that the condemnation would not surprise those who thought freely on these matters, the writer continued:

> But it will echo mournfully in the hearts of several young ecclesiastics who, despite many warnings, have believed these last years in the possibility of a 'renewal.' With this dream they associated the dream of a more profound and widespread social action and of an understanding between Catholicism on one side, and science and free research on the other. Apparently the wings of these dreams have been clipped.[115]

It took time before it became clear to all just how far 'wings had been clipped' in the American Church, but the series of events that had begun in June, 1895, with the dismissal of Monsignor O'Connell as Rector of the North American College and included the forced resignation of Bishop Keane as Rector of the Catholic University of America in September, 1896, were unmistakeable signs of a change of direction in the ecclesiastical winds. It was a change that boded ill for the advocates of an open and scholarly approach in intellectual affairs, and the new mood passed all down the line with a retrenchment that soon overtook as well the very modest gains that had been made up to that time in ecumenical matters. The latter fact was evident from Leo XIII's letter of September, 1895, to the American bishops, inspired by Archbishop Satolli, Apostolic Delegate to the United States, which forbade future Catholic participation in interfaith assemblies such as that in which the Catholics had shared at Chicago in September, 1893, in the World Parliament of Religions. The change in Satolli's early friendly disposition toward the progressive wing of the American hierarchy was a key factor after 1895, and when he returned to Rome the following year and was made a cardinal and Prefect of the Congregation of Studies, his hostility toward his former friends showed in more ways than one. For example, when the American archbishops' request for permission for the Christian Brothers to continue teaching Latin was denied in 1900, it was Satolli who had played a leading role in the decision. The Washington *Times* was not far off the mark, therefore, when they expressed regret that Satolli had of late "shown

anything but a friendly spirit to the land of his recent residence." And
the editorial writer then went on to draw an inference from the
Christian Brothers' case that was not unwarranted in the circumstances
and that carried unhappy implications for the spirit that the progressive
bishops had been trying to cultivate and sponsor with non-Catholic
Americans. The *Times* writer said:

> Whether justifiably or not, the action of the Vatican in the case of
> the Christian Brothers will create an impression that foreign
> interference with strictly American affairs and interests is not as
> impossible as the patriotic opinions and conduct of leading Ameri-
> can prelates have been gradually but effectively teaching the
> country to believe.[116]

Obviously, decisions of the Holy See relating to Catholic concerns
in the United States would not be regarded in the same light by the
Roman Curia and American journalists, and informed Catholics themselves would normally not see Rome's action as "foreign interference."
Yet the last years of the nineteenth century and the early years of the
present century witnessed more than the ordinary number of directives
from the Roman Curia that touched closely, and at times adversely,
on the intellectual life of American priests and the formation of
seminarians as future priests. To be sure, clear condemnations such as
those contained in *Testem benevolentiae* were more the exceptions
than the rule; but where harm was at times done in clerical circles
was in the creation of an atmosphere or climate of opinion that was
injurious to free inquiry and scholarly pursuits. The publication in 1896
of *Evolution and Dogma*[117] by Father John A. Zahm, C.S.C., furnished
an instance of what is meant. In his book Zahm attempted to reconcile
the Catholic profession of faith with the theories of evolution, and he
was sufficiently successful that the work won considerable attention
and was translated into several languages. Upon learning from what
he described as "unquestionable authority" that the Holy See was
opposed to the further distribution of his book, however, Zahm told
his Italian translator that he had ordered it withdrawn.[118] The priest-
scientist's humble submission to Rome's wishes did not, nonetheless,
change his opinion about evolution, for he remarked to one correspondent:

> My views may not be looked upon with favor by all in Rome. I
> do not expect so much and I really do not care for the approval
> of every one. But I know that every eminent man of science
> throughout Europe is in perfect sympathy with my views. I ven-

ture to say that the twentieth century will not be very old before nine out of every ten thinkers will be evolutionists as opposed to believers in special creation.[119]

The significance of the Zahm case for the present discussion was implied by Thomas F. O'Connor when he stated that Rome's disapproval of *Evolution and Dogma*, "marked the end of his [Zahm's] labors in this field. Thereafter he published nothing more on science or on the relations of science and religion."[120] Nor was the loss of John Zahm to scholarship an isolated instance in these years, with the consequence that the general content and quality of Catholic efforts in the ecclesiastical sciences were seriously lowered to the injury of all concerned.

The long reign of Pope Leo XIII, whose efforts in behalf of a revival of Thomism had an enduring influence on the spiritual and intellectual formation of the Catholic clergy throughout the world, came to a close on July 20, 1903. Two weeks later there was elected as his successor Giuseppe Sarto, Cardinal Patriarch of Venice, who took the name of Piux X. The first encyclical of the new reign, *E supremi apostolatus*, dated October 4, 1903, ranged over a wide spectrum of topics, among which were certain observations concerning the special obligations which bishops had to foster vocations to the priesthood, to give close attention to their seminaries, and to show a particular interest in young priests. The Catholic bishops of the world were exhorted to regard as their "first care" the forming of Christ in their priests, to exercise such a vigilance over the seminaries that, "All other tasks must yield to this one," for, said the pope, they should bear carefully in mind that "as a general rule the faithful will be such as are those whom you call to the priesthood." The new pontiff then stated:

> Furthermore, be most solicitous for young priests who have just left the seminary. From the bottom of Our heart We urge you to draw them often close to you, in order to enkindle them and inspire them so that they may aspire only after God and the salvation of souls.[121]

Here was a paternal mandate in the best sense of the term, a beginning that offered high hope for the new pontificate.

Modernism

Yet the generally positive and benign tone of *E supremi apostolatus* on matters relating to priestly formation had in less than four years given way to what was, perhaps, the harshest and most negative language employed by a papal encyclical in this century, with the possible exception of Pope Piux XI's ringing indictments of Fascism, Communism, and Naziism which appeared in the 1930's. The change had been heralded in a number of signals from the Roman Curia, the most important being the Holy Office's decree, *Lamentabili*, of July 3, 1907; but the full force of the new mood was reserved for the encyclical, *Pascendi Dominici gregis*, which was issued on the following September 8.

This is not the place to attempt an analysis of the Modernist Movement that occasioned the strong positions taken by the Holy See in 1907. Suffice it to say, the supreme authority's response to a series of tendencies in Catholic intellectual circles, especially in the Church's seminaries and institutions of higher learning, had been provoked by what were considered to be ideas seriously at variance with orthodox doctrine. Since the modernists had no common program or set of principles, and admittedly differed at times among themselves, the movement did not lend itself to precise definition. One of the key ideas that lay behind the modernists' efforts was their desire to bring the Church abreast of the latest research and scholarship in all branches of knowledge. For example, in seeking to have Catholics adopt a new attitude toward the Bible these men would have their coreligionists conform to the *avant-garde* positions taken by the leading non-Catholic biblical critics of the day.

The modernists were likewise inclined to reject what they regarded as the excessive intellectualism of scholastic philosophy and theology and to subordinate doctrine to practice. A number of them leaned, therefore, toward the pragmatism of Maurice Blondel and William James and the intuitionism of Henry Bergson. In other words, to the true modernist Christianity's essence was to be found in life and not in an intellectual system or a religious creed. History was viewed in a teleological sense in that they believed the historical process was revealed rather in its issue than in its origins, a view that led some of their number to a deep scepticism concerning the historical origins of Christianity. Symbol played an important role in the thinking of the modernists, for example, they contended that the Mass stood as a symbol of man's religious feeling which would endure whether or not Christ had ever instituted it at the Last Supper.[122]

The encyclical's most somber paragraphs were contained in the concluding section where the bishops were given practical instructions on how to proceed in their dioceses. If an administrative officer or a professor in a seminary or a Catholic university was found "in any way" to be tainted with "modernism" he was to be excluded "without compunction." Equal diligence "and severity" were to be used in examining and selecting candidates for the priesthood, the *imprimatur* and *nihil obstat* were to be employed on all books touching religious subjects, priest-editors of newspapers and periodicals were to be closely scrutinized for their policies, and for the future meetings or congresses of priests were not to be permitted "except on very rare occasions," since this was a favorite device of the modernists for propagating their views. The regulations issued in 1896 by the Congregation of Bishops and Regulars for both the diocesan and religious clergy of Italy on attending secular universities were henceforth to apply to all nations. Clerics were not in the future to be allowed to follow courses in secular universities where such courses were available in Catholic institutions. "Let the Bishops who form the Governing Board of such Catholic Institutes or Universities," said Pius X, "watch with all care that these Our commands be constantly observed." [123]

In each diocese a vigilance committee was to be set up for the purpose of extirpating error, removing teachers of unsound doctrine, etc., and the bishops were told that they were to report to the Holy See every three years on all the points contained in these instructions. The sweeping character of the encyclical as well as the general spirit that pervaded the document can, perhaps, be conveyed by the pontiff's words following his command that those tainted with "modernism" were to be removed from office "without compunction." At this point he declared:

> The same policy is to be adopted towards those who openly or secretly lend countenance to Modernism either by extolling the Modernists and excusing their culpable conduct, or by carping at scholasticism, and the Fathers, and the magisterium of the Church, or by refusing obedience to ecclesiastical authority in any of its depositaries; and towards those who show a love of novelty in history, archaeology, biblical exegesis; and finally towards those who neglect the sacred sciences or appear to prefer to them the secular. In all this question of studies, Venerable Brethren, you cannot be too watchful or too constant, but most of all in the choice of professors, for as a rule the students are modelled after the pattern of their masters. Strong in the consciousness of your duty, act always in this matter with prudence and with vigor.[124]

Our sole interest in *Pascendi Dominici gregis* and its sequel here is the bearing they had on the intellectual life of the American priests and on the lives of those preparing for the priesthood in the seminaries of the United States. While France, Italy, England, and Germany — roughly in that order — were the principal centers of the modernists, the American Church was not entirely free of all aspects of the movement, even if an unnamed writer was exaggerating when he said, "It is our frank opinion that the evils of which the Pontiff chiefly complains exist to a very large and dangerous extent in the United States." [125] The same writer conceded that there were few in this country who had made original contributions to the ecclesiastical sciences and that Americans still had to go to Europe for what he termed "the best part of our material." Yet an uneasy feeling was probably left in his readers' minds when without naming names he maintained, "We have not many such; but we have some who are thoroughly imbued with the notions which the Encyclical censures." [126] Four months later in the same journal Anthony Viéban, S.S., of Saint Mary's Seminary, Baltimore, wrote under the title, "Who Are the Modernists of the Encyclical?" [127] But Father Viéban dealt entirely with Europeans, and at the end of the same year Charles Warren Currier, C.SS.R., reviewed "modernism" during 1908 without mention of any American Catholics.[128]

Yet in the aftermath of *Pascendi Dominici gregis* and the papal directives to which it gave rise such as the *Motu proprio* of November 18, 1907, *Praestantia Scripturae*, on the authority carried by decisions of the Biblical Commission and the similar document of September 1, 1910, *Sacrorum antistitum*, that exacted the antimodernist oath of professors in seminaries and institutions of higher learning, the general commotion felt in the world's Catholic intellectual centers did not leave the Americans untouched. To say the least, a tense situation was created. Rumor was rife and suspicion widespread in Catholic ranks, and thus was the stage prepared for what in other circumstances Wilfrid Ward once described as a setting "in which misunderstanding acquires the heat of righteous wrath, and to listen to explanation is held to be giving ear to the tempter." [129] A good number of their European coreligionists would, of course, at the time have taken it for granted that "modernism" existed in the American Church, for ever since the uproar over Americanism a firm connection between the two had been fixed in their minds. In fact, as late as 1948, a leading Italian Catholic reference work ended its article on Americanism by stating, "indistinctly it contained in germ many errors which were afterward condemned by Pius X under the collective name of modernism." [130]

The climate of opinion in Catholic biblical and theological circles in 1971 is so vastly different from that of 1907, the year of the papal encyclical, that it must be difficult for some to see how both could find a place within the framework of the Church. True, certain positions taken by the modernists are now accepted by all informed Catholics — the non-Mosaic authorship of the Pentateuch is a case in point. Other attitudes, however, were undeniably harmful to all Christian theology whether it be Catholic, Orthodox, or Protestant. Among these were the modernists' teaching on immanentism, their denial of the possibility of certain knowledge of the supernatural, a position which leads to agnosticism, and the separation of historical knowledge from dogma. In regard to this kind of essential belief of the Christian tradition George Santayana's words written over a half-century ago still have validity. Agnostic though he was, his acute intelligence perceived the irreconcilability involved when he declared:

> In a frank supernaturalism, in a tight clericalism, not in a pleasant secularization, lies the sole hope of the church. Its sole dignity also lies there. It will not convert the world; it never did and it never could. It will remain a voice crying in the wilderness; but it will believe what it cries, and there will be some to listen to it in the future, as there have been many in the past. As to modernism, it is suicide. It is the last of those concessions to the spirit of the world which half-believers and doubleminded prophets have always been found making; but it is a mortal concession. It conceives everything; for it concedes that everything in Christianity, as Christians hold it, is an illusion.[131]

Obviously, it was and will always remain the right and duty of the Church's magisterium to safeguard the orthodoxy of her doctrines. But in the efforts to expose what turned out to be a tiny minority of Catholic scholars who held modernist opinions, the gravest excesses were committed against many innocent men.

The "integral Catholics," or integralists, as this party was called, not only had ready access to the highest authority, a right denied to their opponents, but they also enjoyed the active support of powerful curial figures such as Rafael Merry del Val, Cardinal Secretary of State, Gaetano De Lai, Cardinal Prefect of the Consistorial Congregation, and José Vives y Tuto, Cardinal Secretary of the Congregation of the Inquisition. It was the secret operations of Monsignor Humberto Benigni and his followers, working from their headquarters in the Vatican Secretariat of State, that enabled the integralists to instigate a witchhunt within ecclesiastical circles the like of which had not been seen in the Church since the days of the Inquisition. An idea of the atmosphere that pervaded the Eternal City at the time was conveyed by Father Giovanni Genocchi, M.S.C., when he told Baron Friedrich von Hügel in the autumn of 1906, "Rome is swarming with spies watching the Modernists. To be a friend to suspected people is a crime. Woe to the friends of [Romolo] Murri and other heretics!" [132]

The Aftermath of Pascendi Dominici gregis

Meanwhile what were the practical effects of all of this on the Catholics of the United States? To the vast majority of the estimated 16,363,000 American Catholics of 1910 the Modernist Movement meant little or nothing since most of them, without benefit of any superior education, pursued their religious life in a very simple manner quite oblivious of the exciting events that then preoccupied their bishops and clergy. But to the Catholics of this country who were engaged in education it was a different story. Professors at institutions like the Catholic University of America and those on seminary faculties, for example, had to take the anti-modernist oath, and dozens of other American priests became involved as members of vigilance committees commanded by the Holy See with a view to scrutinizing the circulation of ideas within their respective dioceses.

The fear and suspicion inculcated by these and other measures killed off what little creative scholarship existed in the Church of the United States at the time, a point best illustrated by the speedy demise of the most learned journal published to date under American Catholic auspices, the *New York Review*, which had first appeared in June, 1905, under the editorship of several professors of Saint Joseph's Seminary, Dunwoodie, the major seminary of the Archdiocese of New York. When the apostolic delegate, Archbishop Diomede Falconio, O.F.M., expressed misgivings concerning the doctrinal soundness of the *New York Review* to John M. Farley, Archbishop of New York, the latter ordered publication of the journal suspended with the issue of June, 1908.[133]

From the publication of *Pascendi Dominici gregis* to well beyond World War I, the issue of "modernism" continued to overshadow the Church's intellectual centers both here and abroad. As it turned out, less than a dozen American priests were investigated, more or less officially, on the score of their teaching, and in the case of several of these a simple interrogation by their superiors ended the matter. Such was true of Joseph Bruneau, S.S., of Saint Mary's Seminary, Baltimore, about whose views Cardinal Merry del Val made inquiry in March,

1910, after learning that both the *Civiltà Cattolica* and the *Osservatore Romano* had been severely critical of the errors found in Bruneau's French translation of *The Catholic Doctrine of the Atonement* by Henry N. Oxenham. On Merry del Val's instructions sent through Archbishop Falconio, the apostolic delegate, Cardinal Gibbons took up the question with Bruneau, the latter prepared a detailed statement of the circumstances surrounding his translation of the Oxenham book which Gibbons forwarded to the Holy See with a covering letter, and that was the last that was heard about the matter. [134]

A second case in which the Cardinal of Baltimore was involved was not solved so simply. Henry A. Poels, Dutch-born associate professor of Old Testament in the Catholic University of America, of which Gibbons was chancellor, found difficulty in accepting the Biblical Commission's decision of June, 1906, that Moses must be held to have been the main and inspired author of the Pentateuch. Although a trip to Rome in the summer of 1907 and an audience of Pius X was thought by the professor to have cleared his position with the ecclesiastical superiors, such was not the case and the matter dragged on until the spring of 1910 when the Board of Trustees of the university voted to terminate Father Poels' contract. The latter felt deeply aggrieved and before departing for the Netherlands he composed a lengthy privately printed brochure, *A Vindication of My Honor* (Washington, 1910), in which Gibbons and the Rector of the University, Thomas J. Shahan, were made to bear the principal blame. At this point Poels was lost to biblical scholarship, but the years before his death in 1948 were dedicated to an active apostolate in Catholic social movements in his native land that won him widespread esteem.[135]

It was not surprising that publication in the *New York Review* should have cast suspicion on a number of men, especially when it is remembered what the apostolic delegate thought of the journal — news of that kind travels rapidly in clerical circles — and, too, that the contributors' learned articles often touched on problems of biblical exegesis, probably the most sensitive of all the controverted areas to come under the scrutiny of the opponents of "modernism." James F. Driscoll and Francis E. Gigot, two of the editors of the *Review*, were in this category. Both were among the professors of Saint Joseph's Seminary, New York, who left the Sulpicians in 1906.

Driscoll, who had studied under Alfred Loisy at the Catholic Institute of Paris in the 1880's, had been the seminary rector since 1902. He did not long survive the extinction of the journal he had founded, however, for in July, 1909, he was suddenly removed from the rectorship when

Archbishop Farley, then at Rome, cabled his vicar general to announce the appointment of John P. Chidwick, Pastor of Saint Ambrose Church, as the new rector. Driscoll replaced Chidwick in the Manhattan pastorate and died in 1922 as Pastor of Saint Gabriel Church, New Rochelle.[136]

Like Driscoll, Gigot had been a student at the Catholic Institute of Paris and like his colleague he also had taken a liberal attitude in regard to biblical studies. That attitude was summarized in 1900 when Gigot quoted a passage from Hogan's *Clerical Studies* on Scripture in the seminary, remarked that several things were implied in Hogan's words, and then stated:

> In the first place, the time is gone when the questions involved in the higher criticism might be simply identified with rationalistic attacks upon the revealed word. Again, one can no longer afford to be ignorant of topics which, perhaps more than any others at present, engross the attention of the intellectual and religious world. . . . [137]

Even though Gigot spoke of the safeguards that needed to be used in handling scriptural problems, his position was too open and critical for the clerical mind represented by the integralists who had everything their own way in the days after the encyclical. In any case, Father Gigot remained on at Dunwoodie until his death in June, 1920, his last years showing a marked decline in the scholarly contributions he had made to the *New York Review* earlier in the century when both he and Driscoll were also writing numerous articles for the *Catholic Encyclopedia*.

One of the most enthusiastic supporters and earliest contributors to the *New York Review* was Cornelius C. Clifford who after twenty years as a Jesuit served in various posts as a diocesan priest following his resignation from the society in 1899. Clifford was appointed professor of metaphysics and church history in Immaculate Conception Seminary, South Orange, New Jersey, in 1907, but two years later he was removed to an obscure pastorate by John J. O'Connor, Bishop of Newark. The ostensible reason given was a recent decree of the Congregation of Religious forbidding ex-religious to hold teaching or administrative positions in seminaries, although Clifford and his friends felt there was more behind the sudden change than appeared on the surface.

During the years he had spent in England as a Jesuit, Clifford had come to know George Tyrrell, S.J., Baron von Hügel, Maude Petre, and others in their circle quite well and had continued to correspond with some of them. This sort of association, along with Clifford's articles and book reviews in the *New York Review*, were more than enough to arouse the suspicion of conservative churchmen about his orthodoxy. Yet he was never formally condemned, and from 1913 until shortly before his death in 1938 he went regularly from his parish at Whippany, New Jersey, to lecture in scholastic philosophy at Columbia University. It was during this period that he became a friend of Columbia's president, Nicholas Murray Butler, and of Dr. Alexis Carrel, the Nobel Prize winner of the Rockefeller Institute for Medical Research, both of whom were in attendance at his funeral.

Two other men of New York State whose ecclesiastical careers were destined nearly a quarter-century later to converge in San Francisco were also affected by the anti-modernist campaign, the one in a minor way, the other in a far more serious manner. They were Edward J. Hanna and John J. Mitty. After the latter's ordination in December, 1906, as a priest of the Archdiocese of New York he was sent for graduate work to the University of Munich. But his studies were interrupted when in November, 1908, his superior, Archbishop Farley, received a letter from Thomas F. Kennedy, Rector of the North American College in Rome, in which the latter stated that Cardinal Merry del Val, "says Munich is no place for young priests at this time." Moreover, Kennedy reported that Mitty and two others were said to be living outside a religious house and that they went around Munich "with turn down collars and red and white neckties," to which he added, "One attends lectures in a travelling cap." Less than a month thereafter Mitty informed Farley that they had booked passage for home. Thus were the graduate studies of a future Bishop of Salt Lake City and Archbishop of San Francisco rather abruptly terminated at the beginning of a new academic year.[138]

The Hanna case was both more serious and more complicated. Following an outstanding undergraduate theology course at Rome's Urban College of the Propaganda, Hanna was ordained a priest of the Diocese of Rochester in May, 1885. He spent an additional year in Rome and then returned to Rochester where he first taught in the minor seminary, Saint Andrew's, before he was transferred to Saint Bernard's Seminary in 1893 with the opening of the major seminary. Here he was professor of dogmatic theology while another former Roman student, Andrew J. Breen, three years Hanna's junior, served as professor of Scripture. As the historian of the Diocese of Rochester expressed it, "their personalities differed widely, and one fine day they were going to collide." [139] In addition to this teaching Hanna did some writing, including an article entitled "The Human Knowledge of Christ," which appeared in three installments in the *New York Review* in 1905–1906. The January, 1906, issue of the *American Journal of Theology* which was published under Protestant auspices, carried a brief article of his on "Some Recent Books on Catholic Theology," and he likewise contributed four or five articles to the *Catholic Encyclopedia*, the one on "Absolution" later being questioned at Rome.

Whatever internal differences there may have been among the faculty of Saint Bernard's Seminary, they remained largely a private affair until attention was focused on Hanna by the petition of Patrick W. Riordan, Archbishop of San Francisco, to have him named his coadjutor with the right of succession. Riordan inaugurated his effort in April, 1907, but only in November of that year did he become aware that the cause for the delay was due to his candidate's orthodoxy having been called in question at the Holy See. The story is too complicated to be told here in all its details. Suffice it to say, the doubts about Hanna's doctrinal soundness were leaked to the press and before long it was known on both sides of the Atlantic that he had been delated to Rome by one of his fellow professors.

The Bishop of Rochester, Bernard McQuaid, was not the type of man to allow a matter of this kind to go unresolved, so he summoned a meeting of the seminary faculty in which he asked that each man sign a prepared statement declaring that he had not sent any report on Hanna to the Holy See. Breen alone refused to sign, whereupon he resigned and prepared to depart, but not before he had published a lengthy statement in the Rochester *Democrat and Chronicle* of January 14, 1908, that was highly critical of both McQuaid and Hanna. With all the publicity attending the case it was hardly surprising that Rome should have postponed Hanna's appointment to the episcopacy. Only when Riordan pressed the matter a second time was the appointment made in October, 1912, when approval was given for Hanna as auxiliary bishop to Riordan but not coadjutor with the right of succession. It was not until nearly six months after Riordan's death that Edward Hanna was appointed third Archbishop of San Francisco.

To this point we have dealt solely with priests who were merely suspected of "modernism," for in no instance was it either admitted by the men involved or proven against them. There were three other priests of the period, however, who openly admitted their modernist views, left the Church, married, and in two of the three instances affiliated with other churches. They were: the Irish-born Thomas J. Mulvey who at the time he announced his resignation from the priesthood in July, 1908, was an assistant pastor at Saint Edward's Church, Brooklyn, New York; John R. Slattery, former superior of Saint Joseph's Society for Negro Missions, whose decision had been taken privately as early as January, 1904, but who did not make it publicly known until September, 1906, when his article, "How My Priesthood Dropped From Me," [140] appeared in *The Independent*, a weekly journal of opinion published under Protestant auspices; and William Laurence Sullivan, a Paulist, who like Mulvey had contributed to and supported the *New York Review*, and who announced in May, 1909, that he was resigning his pastorate of Saint Austin's Church, Austin, Texas.

The New York *Sun's* publication on July 18, 1908, of an interview with Mulvey in which he stated that his action was the culmination of extended thought prompted by Pope Piux X's encyclical, drew a comment the following day from Cardinal Gibbons in which he was quoted as having described Mulvey's departure as "the first defection from the Church on the grounds of modernism since the Pope's encyclical letter defining and attacking that heresy." [141]

The later careers of the three men varied considerably with Mulvey serving as superintendent of the First Presbyterian Church of Wenonah, New Jersey, until his death in 1952 without much more being heard of him on the national scene. On the other hand, Slattery (d. 1926) translated one of the volumes of the well known French modernist, Albert Houtin, as well as a book by Paul Sabatier, the French Protestant clergyman who wrote on Saint Francis of Assisi. But in the history of the movement Slattery is chiefly remembered for his article, "The Workings of Modernism," which came out three years after he had left the Catholic Church in the *American Journal of Theology*,[142] edited at the Divinity School of the University of Chicago. The last of the three, William L. Sullivan, became a Unitarian minister in 1912 and before his death in 1935 published *Letters to His Holiness Pope Pius X* (1910) which was followed the next year by a novel called *The Priest: A Tale of Modernism in New England*. It was nine years after he had died that there appeared the volume entitled *Under Orders. The Autobiography of William Laurence Sullivan*.[143]

If the treatment of "modernism" in the Church of the United States has dealt almost entirely with men and institutions along the Atlantic Coast, it has been due simply to the fact that the evidence for that region is more plentiful and available than for other sections of the country.

The scares created in the faculties of the major seminaries of Baltimore, Newark, New York, and Rochester, as well as in the School of Theology of the Catholic University of America, following upon the investigation of or suspicions concerning the doctrinal soundness of some of their number were, *mutatis mutandis*, reflected in the seminaries of the Middle West, the South, and the Far West if in a less obvious manner. Even men of an otherwise courageous character became timid and frightened when they observed how ruthlessly the integralists went about their task, not sparing even the highly placed.

Pietro Maffi, Cardinal Archbishop of Pisa and one of their victims, described the effects of this campaign for Cardinal De Lai when he alluded to the power exercised by the printed organs of the *Sodalitium Pianum*, the integralists' name for their elite corps, so to speak, a name by which they paid tribute to Saint Pius V, the uncompromising reformer of the years after the Council of Trent. Bishops had become increasingly divided against each other, said Maffi, and suspicion was growing everywhere, and he added, "instead of the bond of faith, a single newspaper becomes arbiter of the fate of a diocese!" [144]

When members of the hierarchy such as the Archbishop of Pisa, Cardinal Mariano Rampolla who had been Pope Leo XIII's Secretary of State, Eudoxe-Irenée Mignot, Archbishop of Albi, and others felt compelled to raise their voices in protest against the excesses being committed, it was hardly surprising that many university and seminary professors should have been frightened off from any further scholarly endeavors and reduced to a dull routine of adherence to traditional and accepted positions in Scripture, theology, and the other ecclesiastical sciences. Maffi unconsciously described the state of the Catholic academic community throughout the world when he attributed to the integralist campaign "a general feeling of mistrust, paralysis, inability to act. Of course, anyone who acts may make a mistake," he declared, "but since mistakes are pounced upon while good deeds go unnoticed, most people decide to play safe and do nothing!" [145]

Several years later the Archbishop of Albi addressed a letter to Domenico Ferrata, Cardinal Secretary of State to Pope Benedict XV, in which he forcefully and graphically expressed the plight to which Catholics engaged in intellectual pursuits had been reduced. Mignot's words have frequently been quoted, but they were so accurate a portrayal of the state of mind of many in those years that they warrant quotation *in extenso* in this context. He said:

> In this doctrinal reaction, have not some of the underlings gone a good deal too far? Have they not sometimes given an im-

pression of enmity to sincere and impartial research? There is
no doubt of this. And in consequence there is a real wave of
anger against authority among scholars and thinkers everywhere.
The Church has lost some of the prestige which was hers under
Leo XIII. Within the bosom of the Church, discouragement has
seized upon intellectual and social workers. Denounced, spied
upon, abused by the papers of the occult power [the *Sodalitium
Pianum*], held in suspicion by those who, deceived by false reports,
suspected the honesty of their intentions — they found their work
grown very difficult. Many a man withdrew once and for all
from the lists who might have won many a victory for the
Christian cause.

This sense of unrest has made itself most unfortunately evident
in many major seminaries, in religious houses of study and in
university centers. Upon this, testimony is unanimous: our young
men have lost the sacred passion for intellectual labor, and it is
very difficult for their professors to stimulate it. After the enthusiasm — the often feverish enthusiasm admittedly — for the
study of apologetics, exegesis, positive theology, philosophy and
sociology, the students are now satisfied with a dull flat study,
and theology of the handbook sort. Natural laziness has something to do with this, but many certainly think it the best way to
assure their future and further their personal ambition. The
perpetuation of this state of things will mean an inferior clergy,
more concerned with the externals of worship than with the
spiritual realities of interior religion — a clergy which will understand nothing of the intellectual and moral difficulties of the time,
or of the movement of ideas, and the Church will be the loser.
Such a clergy will stand motionless amidst a world on the
march, a world whose light they ought to be. Neither their minds
nor their hearts will be opened to those who are besieged by doubt,
and so much in need of them.[146]

It would be difficult to find anywhere a better description of the
general state of affairs that obtained within the Church in the period
leading up to and well beyond World War I. For Archbishop Mignot
not only included all the main features of the situation in his own time
but he prophetically forecast the main lines of development in the
future, even to the all too constant factor of ecclesiastical ambition
which played no minor role in hampering a viable intellectual life as
it had always done and as it probably will go on doing to the end of
time. True, the integralists received a decided check several weeks

after Mignot's letter to Cardinal Ferrata, for with the death of Pius X on August 20, 1914, and the election on the following September 3 of Giacomo della Chiesa, Cardinal Archbishop of Bologna, who had been a favorite target of the zealots, there ensued a marked change. As von Hügel remarked,[147] the very name taken by the new pontiff, Benedict XV, was itself a happy presage, for it had been 140 years since a new pope had chosen a name other than Gregory, Leo or Pius.

If there had been any who had doubted that the new pontificate would make a clean break with much of the spirit that had dominated the Church's immediate past, those doubts were laid to rest with the publication on November 1, 1914, of Pope Benedict's first encyclical, *Ad beatissimi*. Faced with the responsibility for guiding the Universal Church, and that in the midst of the tragedy of World War I which had already run three months, the pope's concerns in the encyclical went far beyond the theological differences about which we have been speaking. Yet he found space for a pointed warning to those factions who had caused him so much personal pain during his years in the Secretariat of State and the Archdiocese of Bologna, and this without in any way nullifying his predecessor's condemnation of "modernism" which, he said, "We now renew to the full." The success of any society, said Benedict XV, depended on the harmony of its members, and in this the Church was no different than other societies. And since the Church's enemies viewed dissension within her fold as an opportunity to be used against her, there was an added reason for laying down certain regulations to which he expected the Catholic community to conform, rules that were clearly aimed at the integralists even though they were not mentioned by name. For example, no private person was,

> either by the publication of books or journals, or by delivering discourses, publicly [to] assume the position of a master in the Church. . . . Concerning matters in which, since the Holy See has not pronounced judgment, saving faith and discipline, discussion may take place pro and contra, it is certainly lawful for everybody to say what he thinks and to uphold his opinion.

Catholics who engaged in controversy were exhorted to avoid all intemperate language in their differences with others, to maintain their own views freely, yes, but modestly, and the pontiff then admonished:

> let him not imagine he is justified in casting suspicion on the faith or discipline of those who hold a contrary opinion simply because they differ from him.[148]

Ad beatissimi came like a breath of fresh air for many in the Church, even if it was too late to overtake certain personal losses and if much of its salutary teaching went unheard amid the rising din and distraction of international warfare. As for the Church of the United States, there had been relatively little intellectual life for the integralists to stifle, and in this regard Slattery was not far off the mark when he cited with approval the remark attributed to Maria Joseph Albert Erhard, professor of church history in the recently erected Catholic faculty of theology in the University of Strasbourg, to the effect that there was "hardly a trace of intellectual activity in the Catholic Church of America." [149] Yet the foreshadowings of such had made their appearance in the period before 1908 among such men as those who had founded and had written for the *New York Review*, but with the extinction of that journal the light flickered and went out for nearly a half-century. It would be an exaggeration to say, of course, that every vestige of intellectual endeavor in the American Church had been snuffed out, as the continuance of the *American Ecclesiastical Review* and the *Homiletic and Pastoral Review* attested. But the highly conservative and circumspect policies of these journals helped to account in the final analysis for the very feeble over-all result.[150]

An Intellectual Reawakening

Only in the days after World War II did Catholic intellectual effort in the United States take on a really viable character, a development that was stimulated by such positive steps — to name only three examples of the increasing number of publications and research centers that served to heighten the prestige of American Catholics in scholarly circles as well as to broaden and deepen the education of their clergy — as the founding in February, 1940, of *Theological Studies*, the quarterly of the combined Jesuit theological faculties of this country; the establishment of the Franciscan Institute at Saint Bonaventure University in 1942 for research and publication; and two years later the same friars' Academy of American Franciscan History for a similar purpose in the field implied by its name.

In no single aspect of the ecclesiastical sciences, however, did the Catholics make more striking progress than in biblical studies where during the past quarter-century their scholarly productions have won international recognition. In this field the Americans furnished an admirable exemplification of a practical implementation of one of the principal aims of a papal encyclical, for the distinguished work they produced after the early 1940's had been a stated purpose of Pope

Pius XII's *Divino afflante Spiritu* of September, 1943, namely, to encourage biblical scholarship.

The historian of the American priesthood finds relatively little of national significance to record for the half-century from 1910 to the opening of the 1960's. True, with the steady growth of the Catholic community new seminaries were opened and older institutions were expanded, one of the most constant reasons for such being the hope of increasing the percentage of native priests in the Church of the United States. In this connection the Archdiocese of San Francisco's experience was typical of what was transpiring in many American sees. Thus in 1885 at the end of the nearly thirty-five year administration of Joseph S. Alemany, O.P., the Spanish-born first archbishop, there were eighty-eight priests in the jurisdiction of whom only four were native Americans, the vast majority, sixty-four, having been born in Ireland.

It was little wonder, then that Alemany's successor, Patrick W. Riordan, hoping to attract native vocations, should have set his heart on the building of a seminary. It entailed a long and hard struggle before Saint Patrick's Seminary was finally dedicated in August, 1898, and the early years gave slight relief from the strain with only a handful of students enrolled and an unfortunate rift in the faculty between the French-born and American Sulpicians who had been given charge of the institution. Yet Archbishop Riordan persisted, and he had the satisfaction of seeing the original student enrollment of twenty-eight begin to increase. In a spirit of high hope he reported in the autumn of 1912 to his brother, a Chicago pastor, that twenty new students were then at hand. Tempering his optimism, Riordan remarked, "Of course we shall lose a good many of them before they get through," but he added,

> it is encouraging to see vocations increasing year by year. When I came here, there were very few vocations to the priesthood, and, now in a few years if things continue as they are going, we shall be able to supply the Diocese with our own priests. It has been a long work, and a hard work, but what succeeds always gives pleasure.[151]

Meanwhile in other parts of the United States individual seminaries were experiencing both the success and the failure that characterize the vicissitudes of time. At Rochester, for example, the dream of Bishop McQuaid was finally realized in September, 1893, with the opening of Saint Bernard's Seminary with thirty-nine students. The pioneer faculty of eight had probably been as well or better trained than any American Catholic seminary faculty to date, for McQuaid had made a particular point of sending his prospective professors away for graduate study. A decade later, therefore, the Abbot-President of the English Congregation of Benedictines, Francis Aidan Gasquet, struck the right note when he wrote following a visit to the Rochester seminary:

> The secret of the undoubted success of St. Bernard's in great measure lies in the fact that Bishop McQuaid recognized the fact that the first essential in a seminary, of course after good discipline, was excellence of teaching. He consequently from the first has obtained the services of the best professors, and he has spent money lavishly in educating students likely to make good teachers in the best schools of France, Germany and Italy.[152]

On the occasion of the same visit to the United States in 1904 Gasquet preached the retreat for the students of Saint Paul Seminary which had opened in September, 1894, aided by a handsome gift from James J. Hill, President of the Great Northern Railroad. Here the English monk was especially impressed by the seminary library that John Ireland, Archbishop of Saint Paul, had assembled. "It has been his special care," said Gasquet, "to collect for the use of his professors and students books, new and old, that could help them in their studies," to which he added:

> It was a source of wonder to me to find already on the shelves almost every book of any value for the purpose he had in view. I tested the collection in various ways, by looking for works I hardly supposed could be found there, but in most instances they were in their places.[153]

Both the Rochester and Saint Paul seminaries acquired solid reputations, and as a consequence attracted students from a good many dioceses other than their own.

Meanwhile older institutions like Saint Mary's in Baltimore and Saint Francis in Milwaukee came to have an increasing influence in the American Church by reason of the number of students from outside their respective dioceses who received part or all of their training under their auspices. For example, between 1859 and 1892 most of the priestly candidates for the Archdiocese of Saint Louis were sent to Milwaukee. Saint Louis' seminary history was a rather checkered one with the opening, moving, and closing of institutions until a major seminary was once again opened in December, 1892, in an old Visitandine convent. In the eyes of the Abbé Félix Klein of the Catholic Institute of Paris who visited it in 1904 it was anything but a suitable location, and he made known the painful impression left on his mind to John J. Glennon, the new archbishop, who assured him that this state of things would not last. "Now that he has full authority," said Klein, "I am sure that one of the first uses he will make of it will be to remove his future priests from a lodging which is at best suitable for our poor dioceses of Europe." [154]

Two decades before the Abbé Klein visited the United States the first major seminary for New England's diocesan clergy to succeed and endure had been provided with the opening in September, 1884, of Saint John's Seminary, Brighton, in the Archdiocese of Boston with an initial student body of thirty-two of whom only four had not already studied in other institutions. Saint John's was placed in the charge of the Sulpicians by John J. Williams, Archbishop of Boston, who was an alumnus of Saint Sulpice in Paris. The seminary continued to show satisfactory progress under the Sulpicians, but in June, 1911, they were dismissed by Williams' successor, William H. O'Connell, who was intent on modelling his seminary after his own *alma mater* at Rome, the North American College, of which he had also been rector. The historians of the Brighton seminary concluded their account of this unhappy episode in American seminary history by saying:

> On the Sulpician side, a righteous reluctance to retire under fire, and the local Superior's actual lack of authority to annul the contract spontaneously, had preceded and delayed the final arrangement. In the end, pronounced bitterness on the one side and a sense of unwarranted persecution on the other were left to be crystalized in parties, both in the diocese and the province, which made very difficult the task assumed by the diocesan priests, who took over direction of the Seminary.[155]

Mention of these seminaries, the writer sincerely trusts, will in no way be interpreted as slighting the contributions made to the formation of numerous American Catholic priests by other institutions that have deserved well of the Church of the United States, for example, Mount Saint Mary's in Emmitsburg, Maryland, which traces its beginnings to 1808, Cincinnati's major seminary which Archbishop John B. Purcell, an Emmitsburg alumnus, named after his *alma mater*, a seminary where hundreds of priests of the Middle West had their formation, as well as the seminaries of large and important jurisdictions such as the Archdiocese of Philadelphia where Saint Charles

Borromeo's beginnings date back to 1832, or the much more recent Saint Mary of the Lake Seminary at Mundelein which has served the Archdiocese of Chicago since its opening in 1921. It is impossible to speak of all the country's seminaries for the diocesan and religious clergy in any detail, and the general account given in the preceding pages will, therefore, have to suffice. With that remark, and with a repetition of the statement that little of truly national significance in the Catholic seminary world of the United States happened between the aftermath of "modernism" and the last decade, we make the leap forward, so to speak, to the 1960's which, as a friendly non-Catholic critic has said, "undoubtedly has been the most tempestuous and exciting time in the history of American Catholicism as far as seminaries are concerned." [156]

The Turbulent 1960's and Vatican Council II

Obviously, there are numerous reasons that justify the description of the 1960's as "the most tempestuous and exciting time" in the history of Catholic seminary education both here and abroad. In what follows we shall endeavor to touch on all the principal factors involved, deliberately omitting, however, a detailed account. In this the writer has in mind to avoid a repetition of what has already become well known to those interested in the seminaries through the extensive literature assembled on this subject during the last ten years.[157] One of the reasons why attention has been directed in a particular way to the seminaries of late was implied by a set of figures published in 1967 by an agency of the Holy See.

Employing statistics gathered from forty-one countries for the years 1964 and 1965, it was revealed that although there had been between those two years an increase of 14,447,540 lay Catholics, the total number of priests, both diocesan and religious, was 313 less than the total reported for 1963.[158] The disproportion had been true from the beginning of that decade, and it is an ominous fact that this disproportion has steadily grown, and in no country, perhaps, has the widening gap between the number of lay Catholics and the number of priests been more stark than in the United States. This fact alone furnishes reason why those responsible for the welfare of the American Church will in all likelihood feel that they should keep their eyes centered in the years ahead on the problems that surround her seminaries.

In the numerous and searching critiques of the Catholic seminary system in recent years it is doubtful if there has been a more constantly recurring theme than the complaint about the seminaries' removal and aloofness from real life. As we shall see, it was a characteristic that showed quite varied ramifications in the evolution of these training schools for priests, and it, too, had its own history. For from the seminaries' beginnings there were those who insisted on the need that candidates for the priesthood had to maintain a degree of remoteness from the world lest they should be victimized by its contagion. There was, there is, and there always will be a certain validity to this position. Viewed historically, however, it was only one more manifestation of the virtually universal siege mentality that overtook Catholics in the wake of the Protestant Reformation and the counter measures to which the latter gave rise such as the Council of Trent, although this is not meant to deny the positive value for the Church's renewal in Trent's reform decrees.

Thus after some of the first seminaries had been located in the cities, there gradually developed a trend in the opposite direction. The establishment of these institutions in country districts, it was thought, would avoid the temptations and distractions of the large urban centers and would offer less of a hazard to deepening the spiritual life of the students. In time this became more or less the fixed pattern, and as late as 1885 it provided the principal reason in the mind of William Henry Elder, Archbishop of Cincinnati, for objecting to the city of Washington as a site for the Catholic University of America. Elder thought Washington might be a good place for the pursuit of the sciences but not for congregating ecclesiastical students. "The distractions of public affairs," he remarked to Michael A. Corrigan, Coadjutor Archbishop of New York,

> the intercourse with public men, — the gathering of unscrupulous men for their various interests from all parts of the country — the amusements — the social & convivial habits prevailing, appear to me very strong objections.[159]

Elder's view was the more remarkable when it is recalled that at that time the prospective university was intended to be primarily for ordained priests and not for seminarians.

In any case, the remoteness of American seminaries from the life of the world around them was not solely a matter of physical location; it related as well to their attitude toward such outside influences as accrediting agencies and professional philosophical and theological groups. Insofar as the first were concerned, the national or regional accreditation bodies, it was not until the 1950's that the stance inspired either by smugness or by naivete born of ignorance that prevailed in most Catholic seminary faculties began to dissipate.

The dawning consciousness of how much the exacting academic standards invoked by inspection teams of educational experts had done to improve the Catholic colleges and universities, was one reason for the change of attitude. Another was the realization of how the many students who dropped out of the seminaries were placed under an unnecessary handicap because the institution had failed to secure accreditation for its academic program. For by the end of the 1950's it had become evident to all but the most benighted among seminary administrators and teachers that the realities of American academic life were scarcely satisfied by the nominal affiliation of their seminary either with the Catholic University of America, or, for that matter, as a pontifical faculty with the Congregation of Seminaries and Universities as that division of the Roman Curia was then called.

By that time, in fact, a number of the more enterprising seminaries had sought and won approval from their respective regional accrediting agency, and they could speak, therefore, with first-hand knowledge of the highly revealing and helpful experience that accompanied the self-evaluation study that most of these agencies first demanded before they would undertake inspection of an institution. The results of such experience came through strongly at a joint session of the major and minor seminary departments of the National Catholic Educational Association held at Atlantic City in April, 1959.

On that occasion the seminary representatives were addressed by the late J. Cyril Dukehart, S.S., who had shortly before been appointed as secretary of the Association's seminary departments. Father Dukehart was candid in saying that up to that time he had been only feeling his way in his new post and trying to analyze the means by which his office might best serve the seminaries. He urged the hundred or more priest educators to have their seminaries affiliated with the Catholic University of America, and he added, "it is a duty of our seminaries to fit themselves and to apply for regional accreditation." [160]

It was gratifying to hear the representatives of one seminary after another at the Atlantic City meeting extol the benefits of accreditation and describe the advantages that their institution had derived from it, as well as to hear, in turn, others make inquiry of these men as to the proper procedure to be followed in seeking such accreditation. What impression was left on the minds of others in the audience, the writer does not know; but he has a distinct recollection of having left the meeting with a feeling that the seminaries of the American Church had that day taken a significant step forward. The fact that in the course of the intervening decade virtually every Catholic seminary of any size and importance has known this salutary procedure speaks well for them as institutions of learning. The nature of that procedure and its results have been described in the case of some, for example, Saint Meinrad Seminary which gained accreditation in March, 1961, from the North Central Association of Colleges and Secondary Schools.[161]

As for the relationship of the typical Catholic seminary of the United States with the professional groups or learned societies whose principal business it was to advance the cause of scholarship in one or other of the ecclesiastical sciences, it takes little imagination, historical or otherwise, to picture the state of affairs before the thaw induced by Vatican Council II. Specifically warned in Pius X's encyclical of 1907 against "modernism" about the dangers of assemblies of scholars even when the membership was exclusively Catholic, at least in name; held to the impression, by repeated official pronouncements such as Pope Pius XI's encyclical *Studiorum ducem*, of June 29, 1923, commemorating the sixth centennial of the canonization of Saint Thomas Aquinas, that Thomism and Thomism alone was acceptable doctrine in Catholic institutions; [162] subject to the same human weakness of laziness and mental sloth that play a role in the lives of all men; and, finally, thoroughly indoctrinated from childhood in the necessity for remaining aloof from contact with men of other religious persuasions lest their faith should be contaminated, American Catholic seminary faculties for the most part have shown no disposition, up to the previous decade, to affiliate with their respective professional groups.

Here was still one more manifestation of the ghetto's imprint, an imprint from which Catholics were at length liberated by the election in 1960 of one of their own as President of the United States and the action two years later of an ecumenical council. When, therefore, five Catholic major seminaries sought and were granted membership in the almost exclusively Protestant organization, the American Association of Theological Schools, at the latter's biennial meeting in 1966, it was understandable that one friendly Protestant observer should have remarked, "This step will merit watching in terms of results." [163] It will, indeed, and if the powerful impulse to imitation that has been a constant factor in shaping the policies of Catholic institutions is any criterion, the A.A.T.S. will probably find itself confronted with applications for membership from most of the Catholic seminaries of the land in the not too distant future. Certainly it will be another forward move, even if this professionalization falls somewhat short of the prediction made by the same Protestant writer when he declared, "If Roman Catholic theological education in the United States becomes truly professional, it will soon be in a good position to lead the entire Catholic world." [164]

Whether American Catholic theological education will in time lead the Catholic world is something that only time itself will tell. But that by the mid-1960's it was on the move there was no doubt, and one aspect of that movement was in the direction of the urban centers and their large universities. Like all the changes that have accompanied the Church's *aggiornamento* launched by Pope John XXIII, this change of scene for the training schools of the clergy has met with opposition from some conservative minds. Yet it is probably true to say that a majority have approved, for a good number of churchmen, as well as many of the highly educated laity, have sensed how imperative it is for the priests of the future to experience close contact with the world in which they are to exercise their ministry. They are aware, to be sure, that the change involves certain risks, but with Father Karl Rahner, S.J., they share the belief that certain situations call for the adoption of a "theology of risk." The distinguished German theologian explained what he meant when he said:

> The risk we are concerned with here does not consist, naturally, of an uncritical conformity with every tendency to innovation in the most widely differing areas of human existence. Risk here means simply the courage to come to new decisions drawn from the very being and mission of the Church, as an answer (positive or even negative!) to the present-day situation; it means relinquishing old, tried ways and risking untried paths, where the future historical outcome cannot be adequately foreseen.
>
> In this sense the courage to undertake risk is today an urgent necessity. The Church is living in a period of ever accelerating change, and the tempo for the most part does not depend on her: she must keep pace with this new situation. . . .[165]

Those who sponsored or supported the change of the seminaries' locale from a rural to an urban setting did so in the anticipation that the Church might thus help to bridge the chasm created during the modern age between herself and the secular society in which she lived. They hoped, too, that this policy would serve to bring the Good News of Christ and His saving mission into the midst of the secular universities which exercised so vast an influence on national life. In this way, it was hoped, at least a partial remedy might be offered for the lack of faculties of theology in the public universities and a supporting arm given to the predominantly Protestant theological faculties of the large private universities. In that connection the words of an international authority on Spanish literature and life, written a generation ago, are relevant here. Remarking that he was an alumnus of a university that had taught theology but had spent all of his adult life in another that had not, he could testify to the loss entailed for the state universities of Spain to be without faculties of theology. He then continued:

> But the worst sufferer is the Church; for her future ministers, instead of joining freely, at the most impressionable age, in the life of a University, are relegated to seminaries, completely cut off from lay thought and lay ideals, neither themselves leavening the academic world nor receiving from it that influence without which the priest is apt to become narrow in his interests, in his outlook upon life and in his judgments of his fellows. [166]

It was with a view both to achieving the objectives mentioned above and avoiding the effects that inevitably follow from the remoteness of seminaries from the centers of the nation's life, that there have come about of late changes in the location of Catholic seminaries that would have been unthinkable even in the 1950's. No more can be attempted here than to give a few general facts about several of these developing centers of theological activity.

One of the principal locations has been Berkeley, California, where five Protestant seminaries joined to establish in 1962 the Graduate Theological Union in the immediate neighborhood of the University of California with which close academic ties were established from the outset. The Dominican friars were the first Catholics to affiliate with the G.T.U., with the Franciscans transferring their theology students there from Santa Barbara in 1968, and Alma College, the house of theology for the California and Oregon Provinces of the Society of Jesus, arriving on the scene in the autumn of 1969. In the Middle West the Passionists, Franciscans, and Servites combined in 1968 to form a theologate neighboring the Divinity School of the University of Chicago and its affiliated Protestant seminaries.

Meanwhile on the Atlantic Coast the Boston Theological Institute located in Cambridge soon attracted Weston College, the Jesuits' New England house of theology, while the oldest of the American schools of the same order, Woodstock College at Woodstock, Maryland, prepared to transfer to New York to be in proximity to Union Theological Seminary, the Jewish Theological Seminary, and Columbia University. At all these centers — Berkeley, Chicago, Cambridge, and New York to mention only four of the most prominent clusters of this kind — the Catholic professors and students constituted a minority among the more numerous Protestant institutions previously assembled near the respective universities.[167] Not only did this trend among the Catholics satisfy a current view of American theological education, but it met with the highest approbation of their own Church as well, a fact that became apparent on June 27, 1968, when Cardinal Gabriel Garrone, Prefect of the Congregation for Christian Education, made public a set of directives for Catholic seminaries among which, he said, there should be featured,

> a strong effort to break isolation so that there will develop a closer collaboration between the various faculties of the ecclesiastical schools and between these schools and civil universities.[168]

It is a commonplace of contemporary ecclesiastical history that Vatican Council II, the four sessions of which ran from October, 1962, to December, 1965, has to date been the most decisive single influencing factor of the twentieth century for reform and renewal in the Church. While in the minds of many churchmen the final product of its debates on the priesthood, the Decree on Priestly Formation, promulgated by Pope Paul VI on October 28, 1965, left considerable to be desired, it was recognized by all that this document offered at least a beginning for renewal in the lives of the world's Catholic priests as well as in the seminaries that were training their successors. As was true of all the debates on the sixteen major documents that ultimately came from the council, the schema on priestly formation occasioned real differences between the bishops and at times even heated discussions.

The exchange of views between Cardinal Ernesto Ruffini, Archbishop of Palermo, and Cardinal Paul Emile Léger, Archbishop of Montreal, on November 14, 1964, concerning the place of Thomism in the seminary curriculum illustrated the point. Ruffini, strongly supported by Archbishop Dino Staffa, maintained that the schema had slighted Thomism, a system which, he said, had merited special commendation from eighty popes since the thirteenth century. Léger, on the other hand, contended that no single system should be designated as the "perennial philosophy" since historians had shown that there was not one scholastic system but many. The concept of a perennial philosophy likewise conflicted with the very nature of philosophy since, said the Archbishop of Montreal, it did not proceed from authority but from investigation into reality; moreover, it was dangerous to impose western philosophy on non-western seminarians.[169] As frequently happened in the council, the final wording of the text was something of a compromise, although it probably gave more emphasis to the position of Léger than to that of Ruffini. It was stated that while students should base themselves "on a philosophic heritage which is perennially valid," they should also:

> be conversant with contemporary philosophical investigations, especially those exercising special influence in their own country, and with recent scientific progress. [170]

It was in this fashion that the seven brief chapters of the Decree on Priestly Formation evolved from the conciliar debates, although it was a compliment to those who had drawn up the text that only forty-seven votes among the more than 2,000 bishops were cast against it.[171] It was a matter of prime importance that the first directive of the decree should have given the initiative for inaugurating programs of seminary reform and renewal into the hands of the national episcopal conferences. In this way, it was said, the laws of the Universal Church were to be adapted "to the special circumstances of time and place," and thus priestly formation would always answer "the pastoral needs of the area in which the ministry is to be exercised." [172] The chapters treated such topics as the need to foster priestly vocations, the programs of major seminaries which, in turn, entailed the revision of ecclesiastical studies, the promotion of the "strictly pastoral training" of future priests, with a final statement that the circumstances of contemporary society made it imperative that priestly training should not end with ordination but rather should be pursued after the seminary course had been completed.

In the widely used volume of Abbott and Gallagher containing the texts of the council documents each was preceded by an introduction written by a Catholic and was concluded with "a response" from one of the non-Catholic observers at the council. In his introduction to the Decree on Priestly Formation, Alexander Carter, Bishop of Sault Sainte Marie, was at pains to emphasize that, like all the texts, the lead and inspiration for that on priestly formation were to be sought in the council's Dogmatic Constitution on the Church and the Pastoral Constitution on the Church in the Modern World. Thus, he said, with the Church's "new awareness of her mission," it was evident that "training of a priest must undergo change. His training must be at once doctrinal and pastoral." And in conclusion Bishop Carter wisely cautioned in regard to this decree, "Do not look for a detailed plan." In other words, its general counsels were not intended as a blueprint for the solution of the seminaries' problems, but rather as a statement that suggested the spirit in which, as it was said, bishops, seminary faculties, both diocesan and religious priests, but "most of all the seminarians themselves must use their ingenuity and will and must respond to the grace of Christ to work out the solution." [173]

The response in this instance was written by Warren A. Quanbeck of the Lutheran Theological Seminary in Saint Paul. The reader who shared the theological perspective of the Reformation, he said, would find "many impressive features in this document." Particular mention was made of the decree's emphasis on Scripture so that with biblical themes at the center, "the other disciplines must be rethought in this light." The adaptation to local conditions and the bringing of the council's ecumenical climate into the educational process were commended, as were the stress put on the seminary's "genuine and deep formation of students" and the prescription of an historical approach to dogmatic theology. As for this last point, Professor Quanbeck believed that the council's desire to relate to the contemporary world would be advanced more "by taking this seriously than by anything else which could be mentioned."

On the negative side this observer noted the absence of any mention of "the freedom and dignity of the individual," as well as of the desirability of developing among priests the diversity of the Holy Spirit's gifts. He did not find gratifying the decree's repeated mention of the perennial character of the teaching of Thomas Aquinas, deplored the fact that "virtually nothing" had been said about the seminary library,[174] and thought that too little stress had been placed on the faculty and on the encouragement that should be given to experiment in education and to communication.

Discipline And Spiritual Formation

One chapter of the Decree on Priestly Formation deserves special treatment here. It was entitled "The Deepening of Spiritual Formation," and dealt with the molding of a priestly character in those destined for that state. It is comparatively easy for the historian to chronicle the external happenings in the evolution of the Church's training schools for her clergy. It is quite another and far more difficult task to write about the spiritual aspects of that training in distinction to the intellectual. For the most part the former lie hidden in the deep recesses of the individual seminarian's soul where there takes place the quiet and sustained dialogue between himself and the Holy Spirit. Obviously, this constitutes a much more delicate terrain for the outsider than does the clearly discernible areas of the seminary's curriculum, its discipline, and even the general spirit that pervades the institution.

On this subject the council's decree gave salutary guidance in a general way, for example, in stating that the seminarian should look for Christ in many places and in all the people to whom he would be sent, but especially in "the poor, the young, the sick, the sinful, and the unbelieving." Students for the priesthood, it was said, should be "thoroughly penetrated by the mystery of the Church," in a manner that would make real in their lives the saying of Saint Augustine, "A man possesses the Holy Spirit to the measure of his love for Christ's Church." [175]

While the decree warned seminarians and priests against the "very severe dangers" by which their chastity would be assailed in present day society, it dwelt at greater length on the need for them to develop maturity, emotional stability, and the art of making considered judgments on men and events. And here the bishops were at pains to stress the need to prize and cultivate the qualities which, they maintained, were so highly regarded by contemporary man, namely, "sincerity of heart, a constant concern for justice, fidelity to one's word, courtesy of manner, restraint, and kindliness in speech." As for seminary discipline, it was, of course, necessary, but the decree stated that those in authority should exercise it in such a way that the students would develop an internal attitude that accepted the discipline through "an act of personal conviction, that is, conscientiously and for supernatural reasons." [176]

Regarding the spiritual formation of students in American seminaries, in this as in all other aspects of Catholic life, the last decade has witnessed profound changes. The latter have come in response to the necessity of transforming the traditional patterns of spiritual exercises that — allowing for variations among the religious orders and congregations — were followed down to the beginning of the 1960's pretty much unchanged from that July day of 1791 when Father François Nagot, S.S., led his three Sulpician confrères and the five seminarians they had brought with them from France into the One Mile Tavern on what was then the outskirts of Baltimore to inaugurate Saint Mary's, and with it seminary training in this country.

As was to be expected, the approach of a particular seminary to the method of student spiritual formation was largely governed by those who happened to be in charge. Thus while the Benedictines held for the most part to the *Rule of Saint Benedict* and the principal commentaries on that notable treatise, so Jesuit scholastics were reared on the *Spiritual Exercises* of Saint Ignatius Loyola, students in seminaries conducted by the Vincentians heard more of the spirituality of Saint Vincent de Paul, and those in Sulpician houses were in an earlier period raised on the works of Louis Tronson, S.S. (d. 1700), such as *L'esprit d'un directeur des âmes ou maximes et pratiques de M. Olier touchant la direction* (1672) and *Examens particuliers sur divers sujets propres aux ecclésiastiques* (1680), which were replaced in the present century by the widely used *Precis de théologie ascétique et mystique* (1923) of Adolphe A. Tanquerey, S.S. (d. 1932), which was translated into many languages.

There have probably been few ways in which seminary life has altered more radically in this decade than in the rules governing students' spiritual formation, including the rigid regulation of their day from early morning until late at night that characterized practically all Catholic seminaries before 1960. From the previous practice of giving students little or no freedom to make decisions on their own, many seminaries have made a notable shift that has made the individual student personally responsible for his prayer life and for the use of his time. Closely linked to these changes has been the relocation, as previously mentioned, of a number of seminaries in the cities near urban universities where opportunity is afforded for student involvement in various phases of the pastoral ministry which is seen as another prime requisite of our time and which the rural areas in which these seminaries formerly existed could not provide.

Perhaps some idea of the extent of the change between the open and free atmosphere of these seminaries of the late 1960's and the distance they have travelled from their predecessors can be conveyed by noting the regime that was demanded at the Catholic University of America in the late 1880's, and that of students who were already ordained priests. They were expected to be present at the following religious exercises in common: a half-hour meditation each morning, an examination of conscience before the midday meal, a spiritual conference of a half-hour before the evening meal, night prayers, and on Sundays and feast days at public recitation of the breviary; on one day a week they were free to leave the campus.[177] That these rules should soon have engendered a spirit of rebellion was understandable, although the regime of most seminaries in the United States followed just such a pattern up to the recent past. The university's regulations were opposed by some of the priest-professors as well as by the students, and the seminarian of the 1970's would appreciate the sentiment of the German-born professor of philosophy, Joseph Pohle, when he said:

> I would propose to have the students themselves work out a code of rules by which they should be governed, and so give them back that feeling of personal freedom which is so essential and important an element of a free country and of an American citizen.[178]

If the "feeling of personal freedom" was a factor to be conjured with in dealing with young priests at the time that Pohle wrote, it was far more so with their counterparts and with seminarians in the late 1960's. And one of the clearest expressions of that feeling within the Catholic community has been the manner in which these clerics have set their own spiritual goals and pursued them with means and methods quite at variance with those advocated by traditional spiritual writers and seminary spiritual directors of the past. For example, the current emphasis on involvement with the world and its problems is in stark contrast to the monastic ideal of remoteness which down to the recent past continued to dominate seminary life. The same can be said for the present effort to confront the secular and to find in it something of merit, a value that some have termed "holy worldliness."

While there is, indeed, a single Christian holiness for those who espouse Jesus and His way of life, there is an almost infinite variety of ways of expressing and realizing that holiness in men's lives. For that reason the individual seminarian or priest's style of spirituality should not be condemned simply because it is different. As James A. Laubacher, S.S., has said, so long as that style or form really expresses, is faithful to, and adheres to "the permanent realities and values and truths of the one authentic Christian holiness," it should not only be tolerated but encouraged. "Personally," said Father Laubacher, "I am convinced that this new approach is valid." [179]

In fact, this approach is both old and new, for the enduring qualities that must necessarily be found in any authentic Christian holiness for the seminarian and priest were never, perhaps, more strikingly delineated in this century than in the famous pastoral letter, *Priests Among Men*, of Emmanuel Suhard, Cardinal Archbishop of Paris, signed on April 14, 1949, just six weeks before his death. In this extraordinary document there will be seen the adumbration if not the outright expression of many of the ideas pertaining to priestly spirituality that have circulated since Vatican Council II. The priest, said Suhard, must not limit his efforts to communicating God's gifts and word to men; he must go beyond that and make his own a concern for their salvation, even to the point where he feels the anguish of their redemption more keenly than they do. "And here lies the mystery of the priest," said the cardinal for,

> What he unites in himself is what tears him apart. At every moment of his life he must answer two callings and entirely satisfy each of them without ever sacrificing either. . . . . Transcendent yet incarnate; here is that same fundamental dualism which . . . constitutes the mystery of the Church and the paradox of Christian humanism.

As for what is today commonly spoken of as the priest's and the seminarian's involvement in the world's fate, be that fate for weal or for woe, the churchman who was responsible for the establishment of the *Mission de France* as well as for the forerunner of the worker priests in the *Mission de Paris*, earned a special right to be heard. On that point Cardinal Suhard declared:

> So it is fitting for priests to become witnesses again, not so much to convince people as to serve as a sign to them. It has been truly said, that to be a witness does not consist in engaging in propaganda, nor even in stirring people up, but in being a *living mystery*. It means to live in such a way that one's life would not make sense if God did not exist. To be a witness is much less a matter of external changes in one's way of living than of firm determination to establish a real community of destiny with the disinherited masses.[180]

The Uncertain Future

Yet it would be less than honest to pretend — if one may use an increasingly fatigued word — that the unstructured character of the students' spiritual life in the "new" seminaries, the relaxing of discipline, and the trek toward the cities, had been achieved without dissent. In fact, in some cases these changes met stout resistance not only from conservative minded churchmen but from laymen as well. The result was that as the 1960's came to a close there was hardly a seminary in the land that was altogether free of internal tension and turmoil, even if they did not witness the student protests such as occurred at Saint Charles Borromeo Seminary in Philadelphia and the threat of rebellion against authority as happened in March, 1966, at Saint John's Seminary, Brighton, to mention only two institutions where the situation became generally known through the press and the other news media.

Nor were the voices of those who questioned the wisdom of the changes always from the right wing of the hierarchy or seminary faculties. An occasional voice was likewise heard from outside the Church as, for example, that of Rabbi Arthur Hertzberg who came away from an institute held at Saint Meinrad Seminary in August, 1967, with a conviction that, he said, would doubtless put him "at some variance" with what he saw as the major thrust of liberal Catholic opinion at that time. Monasteries and convents, he observed, were "now seething with the desire to become more involved and less apart." The rabbi then described his own education at the Jewish Theological Seminary where close relations were maintained with the latter's neighbors on Morningside Heights, namely, Union Theological Seminary and Columbia University. "It is precisely from this perspective," said Hertzberg, that he felt there was something to be said for theological training "within a monastery, amidst a worshipping community." He then continued:

> The men of religion will find the world soon enough, for it beats insistently upon everybody. The question remains: what will they bring to the world out of the transforming power of their faith? . . .
>
> We are talking very much today of bringing religion into the world, but after that glittering proposition is stated I hear little agreement on what the message to be brought ought to be. I sat at St. Meinrad and wondered whether it would not be better for at least some men to make it their vocation to keep examining this world of ours while remaining strongly rooted in a community of worship and contemplation. . . .
>
> Religion and the world are, by their very nature, in tension. The urges to contemplation and action are the reflections of this tension in the lives of men. Precisely because we are all so busy in action, or in feeling guilty that we are not active enough, St. Meinrad reminded me that Moses was not always in the midst of affairs in the camp of the Jews. He was most useful to them and most transforming of them after he had ascended Mount Sinai and was alone with God for 40 days.[181]

The revolution that has swept over the world since the 1960's has brought in its wake the inevitable stress and strain to every phase of human affairs that are common to every revolution. As for the Catholic Church, in her history of nearly 2,000 years she has not seen a parallel to her present state since the Protestants left her fold over 450 years ago. Moreover, it is a condition that in all likelihood will continue into the indefinite future. To be sure, it does not make the most pleasant prospect for a young man who has given serious thought to becoming a priest. Yet if he feels bewildered by the turbulence that he observes all around him in both Church and State, he can take consolation in the realization that his bewilderment is a state of mind shared by virtually all the men of his time. Most Americans would agree that there are few wiser and more perceptive living observers of world affairs among their countrymen than Walter Lippmann, and yet he has said, "I know of nobody, and I've heard of nobody, who has come anywhere near to understanding fully and practically this revolutionary condition." [182]

Thinking solely of the Catholic Church, this revolution has produced results that are both good and bad insofar as the prospective seminarian is concerned. It would be absurd to try to list all those results here, but let the following suffice. First, the revolution has forced a quickening of the pace of maturity within the Catholic community with an accompanying openness and honesty that would have been quite impossible two decades ago. This maturing process has shown in a hundred different ways, for example, in the belief becoming more and more widespread in Catholic circles that for an age such as that of the late twentieth century the minor seminaries are no longer suited for the role that they once played in the life of the Church. As the educational level of the general Catholic population has risen, so has there receded the need for early decisions about a priestly vocation on the part of young men, and thus Douglas Woodruff remarked, "parents and teachers will naturally and rightly advise the postponement of so vital a decision." In 1949 a Catholic who would question the wisdom of the minor seminary would, to say the least, have met with the deep frowns of his coreligionists both clerical and lay; in 1971 the same man found an ever growing amount of opinion on his side.

The rising educational level of the Catholic community has, however, rendered the priestly vocation more difficult in another sense. The coming generations will almost certainly be as reluctant, if not more reluctant, than the present one to accept in the docile manner that was characteristic of their ancestors the authority of the Church's magisterium. The role of the priest will as a consequence be a more complicated one than that of his predecessors who were able to command unquestioned obedience. Douglas Woodruff put the point in these words:

The priesthood of tomorrow, like the episcopate of tomorrow, is likely to find itself sharing many of the experiences long painfully familiar to Protestant parsons and bishops, that they are listened to selectively, approved and commended by those who like what they say, and politely disregarded by those in the pews who withhold their assent on that point.

With the world's climate of opinion now running almost universally in favor of individual human freedom, personal responsibility, and liberty for each man and woman to do or not to do as their conscience dictates, Vatican Council II may have come, indeed, as Woodruff said, "just in time with its changes in the formation of the clergy, so that the Council's decisions, if they increase the difficulties, will also help to meet them." [183]

Meanwhile since the close of the ecumenical council in December, 1965, in most of the countries of the world the Catholics have proceeded at varying tempos with programs of seminary reform and renewal in the mind of the conciliar directive that responsibility for changes in the seminaries' spiritual regime, curricula, disciplinary rules, etc., would be assumed by the respective national conferences of bishops and shaped in accordance with local customs, conditions, and needs. In some countries, especially The Netherlands, Belgium, Germany, and France, bold experiments have been launched. To cite a single example, the German Diocese of Trier with over 1,860,000 Catholics, more than 1,250 diocesan priests, and some 200 or more seminarians undertook several experimental programs. Following upon the success of these programs Bernhard Stein, Bishop of Trier, announced in August, 1967, that henceforth the major seminary would divide the students' time as follows: the first year would be spent in the seminary where regular classes would be pursued; the second year the students would live in one or other of the towns of the diocese and do part-time parish work; the third year would be spent at one of the universities in the area; and in the fourth year the students would have the option of living either in the seminary or in town.[184]

To date the American Church has witnessed no such radical transformations as have taken place in a number of seminaries, old and new, in Europe like those at Trier, the Seminary of Pope John XXIII at Louvain, the Institut voor Europese Priesterhulp at Rothem in The Netherlands, and in the seminaries at Pontigny in France and in the German Diocese of Mainz. In Germany, in fact, the theology department of the seminary of the Archdiocese of Munich was closed entirely by Cardinal Julius Doepfner, Archbishop of Munich and President of the National Conference of German Bishops, who sent his students to the Catholic Faculty of Theology of the University of Munich.

Yet change is definitely in the air in the United States as well, and programs such as those introduced at Saint Mary's Seminary, Baltimore, at the Theological College and the School of Theology of the Catholic University of America, and at Saint Patrick's Seminary, Menlo Park, California, to mention only three institutions, may be expected to grow in the immediate future. The program inaugurated in 1969 at Saint Patrick's by James A. Laubacher, S.S., the rector, and his faculty has been generally so favorably received by the students that a considerable number of their counterparts elsewhere have sought to transfer from other seminaries to Menlo Park, even though the same program has drawn criticism from conservative minded pastors *et al.*, both within and outside the Archdiocese of San Francisco.

As previously mentioned, new programs have been inaugurated in a number of seminaries. Space will not permit a detailed treatment of any single one, but by way of illustration a few words may be added here on that begun in 1969 at Saint Patrick's Seminary. Based on the premise of a college education or its equivalent as a requirement for admission, the Menlo Park program has as its

> primary purpose . . . . to build upon that education through a variety of learning experiences, in such a way as to assure the candidate's theological, spiritual, professional and pastoral competence as a minister of God's Word, upon completion of his years in the theologate.

The seminary's spiritual life is organized on the small group principle with these small units used as the "particular center of focus," and with each group directed by personnel trained in group dynamics. "Counselling," it is said, "is an important part of the seminary life." The academic offerings are centered around a series of core subjects, electives, and directed reading projects with a gradual deepening in the major theological disciplines as the student moves from his first through his second and third years. The fourth and final year is designed to serve two main purposes: first, for the majority of students it constitutes a year of internship in a parish of their diocese as a practical introduction to the priesthood; secondly, for students of "special intellectual ability who should be encouraged to go on to higher studies," the fourth year may be devoted to graduate work and directed toward an advanced degree. In a broad sense the three chief areas of pastoral involvement in the fourth year will be parochial, institutional, and educational.[185] To one acquainted with the tightly structured, enclosed, and mass-oriented system of the seminaries before Vatican Council II, even so brief an outline as that given above for the Menlo Park program, the difference will be a notable one.

The spirit behind the changes so far brought about in American Catholic seminaries may be expected to deepen as time goes on and to occasion further changes as the bishops' Committee on Priestly Formation adds to its knowledge through continuing conferences of seminary administrators and faculty members and as they make a more serious effort to learn and to profit from the suggestions of the students themselves. The committee has already gathered a great amount of data such as that pertaining to the frequently revised theological curriculum issued in December, 1968. Here the general principles reflected post-conciliar thinking on these matters, a point that can be illustrated by the document's statement of what was termed "The Historical Dimension of Theological Study," where it was said:

> Modern man is characterized by a deeper consciousness of the historicity of human existence. This historical consciousness inevitably affects Catholic theology and causes a greater awareness of the historical dimension of every subject in the curriculum. In every course we must help the student develop a critical sense of history and an insight into the richness as well as the limitations of the varying cultural expressions of the Christian faith through the centuries. Paradoxically the modern student often appears disinterested in history, because he regards it as remote and irrelevant. He must be helped to see that the past conditions our present, and that present problems cannot be understood without knowing the past. To do this he must according to his ability grasp the critical methodology of history.
>
> In this emphasis two extremes are to be avoided: a) an emphasis on static immutability which seeks to explain away the fact of doctrinal development or to elevate one period of Church history as the model for all others; b) or, at the other extreme, an excessive relativism which would destroy continuity with the past and which would lose sight of the fact that Christianity is above all an historical religion.[186]

Historians of the Church will not be the only ones to rejoice in the anticipation of future priests who have been instructed in the spirit of this approach, an attitude which in one way or another all the documents of Vatican Council II were at pains to inculcate.

In the final analysis, however, the seminaries' success or failure in programs for reform and renewal will depend upon the flexibility that is maintained within these institutions. And not only flexibility but, too, the openness and honesty with which the seminary's problems are approached and analyzed with the over-all informing principle that a unity of religious faith in a seminary faculty and student body should never be equated with a conformity of conduct and style of living on the part of those who compose its personnel. In that regard the rector of the major seminary of the Diocese of Mainz, Bishop Josef Maria Reuss, was right when he declared:

> It would be a very poor system of education which would try to make candidates for the priesthood conform to a standard formula without taking into account their personality. One single norm is essential: disposition and behavior must conform to Jesus Christ. The candidate himself can only approach this norm by a slow growth on the lines of his own individuality, with his faults and shortcomings and with the help of God's grace.[187]

And that candidate can find no better or more universally approved norm for the molding of his priestly character in a way that will win him the maximum credibility of the men of his time than a strict adherence to what, historically speaking, have been esteemed in a special way by his fellow Americans, namely, the natural virtues of truthfulness and honesty that constitute the essence of personal integrity. Anything short of those qualities will be occasion for seminarians and priests being "turned off" regardless of their clerical status, for the men of the late twentieth century put a particularly high premium on genuinity and on being real in one's relations with their fellowmen. Pope Paul VI emphasized the point in his letter commemorating the fourth centennial of the Council of Trent's decree on seminaries when he said:

> Moreover, in his dealings with others the man who wants to bear witness before the world — with Christ and for Christ — to that truth which brings freedom, must be trained in the virtue of truth in word and action, and so must cultivate sincerity, loyalty, integrity, fidelity.[188]

Both here and abroad the immediate future of the Church's seminaries is a clouded one, with deep crises, as Denis E. Hurley, O.M.I.,

Archbishop of Durban, South Africa, has said, of relevance, celibacy, authority, and seminary training itself. "It is good for those in authority in the Church to know this," he said, "for though one cannot fairly expect them to remedy overnight all the seminaries' ills, their authority increases their responsibility, and it will be helpful for them to be prodded so they will not yield to the all too human impulse to shelve grave problems that require new efforts of thought and consultation." The Archbishop of Durban expressed a profound truth which touches the seminary system in a vital spot when he urged that ecclesiastical authorities, and those associated with them, reconcile themselves to the fact that there are problems that admit of no solution and questions that admit of no answers. Then in words that make a fitting conclusion for this essay on the formation of the American priest, he declared:

> Church authority will not solve this problem alone. There is no going back to the old idea that ready-made solutions can be handed down by authority. Authority's function is to set up the conditions in which a solution can be sought by the Church, that is, the community. In most cases there will be no final solution, only a continual attempt to adjust oneself to a perpetually evolving situation. This is certainly true of the methods of priestly training that will have to be fashioned in the near future to meet the crisis of relevance, loneliness and authority.[189]

1. S.F., "De l'Education Cléricale," *Annales de philosophie chrétienne*, III (Août, 1831), 123.
2. Quoted by Cardinal Arthur Hinsley in an address in 1941, John C. Heenan, *Cardinal Hinsley. A Memoir.* (London: Burns Oates & Washbourne Ltd. 1944). p. 110.
3. *Des Progrès de la Révolution et de la guerre contre l'Eglise.* 2nd ed. (Paris: De Berlin-Mandar et Devaux. 1829). pp. 276–277. The Jesuits, who were among Lamennais' stoutest opponents on many issues, were of the same mind on the sorry state of theological learning at the time. In the letter of 1832 of John Roothaan, General of the Society, issued in connection with the revised *Ratio studiorum*, he spoke of the decadence of the sacred scinces and he remarked, "In the higher studies scarcely anything solid is to be found. . . . everything has been reduced to a mountain of erudition which conceals an abyss of emptiness and vague uncertainties." Quoted by Robert G. North, S.J., *The General Who Rebuilt the Jesuits.* (Milwaukee: Bruce Publishing Company. 1944. p. 200). One of the leading historians of Catholic theology was of the same opinion. "The first years of the nineteenth century," he said, "were characterized by a profound decadence of theology: in Germany it was infected or stifled by the surrounding errors; in Italy and in Spain it vegetated without any luster

or radiance; in France ecclesiastical science was for all intents and purposes annihilated." Edgar Hocedez, S.J., *Histoire de la Théologie au XIXe Siècle.* I, *Décadence et Réveil de la Théologie, 1800–1831.* (Bruxelles: l'Edition Universelle, S.A. 1948). p. 13. Among the causes for this state of affairs Hocedez enumerated the suppression of the Jesuits and the destructive work of the French Revolution; but more important, he said, was the perversion of ideas of the period with rationalism and its offspring mentioned first and by a strange paradox it found an unconscious but active ally in Jansenism; thirdly, was the regalism then prevalent in the courts of Europe, and finally, among the causes adduced by Hocedez, was the almost universal disdain into which scholasticism had fallen. (*Ibid.,* pp. 14–21).

4. For a brief history of seminary education from the apostolic age to the present, see the writer's two chapters in James Michael Lee and Louis J. Putz, C.S.C., (Eds.), *Seminary Education in a Time of Change.* (Notre Dame: Fides Publishers, Inc. 1965). pp. 1–81.

5. Joseph W. Ruane, *The Beginnings of the Society of St. Sulpice in the United States, 1791–1829.* (Washington: The Catholic University of America Press. 1935). p. 204.

6. *Ibid.,* pp. 204–206. Needless to say, seminary discipline varied from place to place. For example, Father Luigi Gentili, missionary of the Institute of Charity in England, gave the first retreat that the seminarians of Prior Park College near Bath ever had, complete with rules for rigid silence, etc. In commenting on the experience to his confrère, Jean Loewenbruck, he remarked, "The face of the place is changed," and he then continued:

> Formerly, the best went once a month to the Sacraments, and not even that. The least fervent only went after a great lapse of time, others did not go for some years. Now on every Sunday and feast there are a great number of holy Communions: some go several times a week. We are now making the month of May with salutary results. Next week there will be celebrated Corpus Christi, and the Bishop has ordered that about sixty students will walk in cassock and cotta as we do in Italy. [Gentili to Lowenbruck, n.p., May 5, 1836, Claude Leetham, *Luigi Gentili. A Sower for the Second Spring.* (London: Burns & Oates. 1965). p. 70].

Herbert Vaughan who after 1872 was Bishop of Salford and later Cardinal Archbishop of Westminster, gave a good deal of thought to seminary training. What he said about discipline might, *mutatis mutandis,* have been said about American seminarians as well as English students for the priesthood. He confided to his diary that the "severe system of discipline, such as that used at the German College [Rome] and at St. Sulpice, I much doubt whether it would answer with Englishmen. We are naturally free; we care for our freedom more than any other nation. . . . English students should be guided without their knowing that they are guided. Let us transplant the Sulpician or German plant to England with enough earth to keep it alive, but then let it be planted in English soil and develop according to the genius of the country." J. G. Snead-Cox, *The Life of Cardinal Vaughan.* (London: Herbert and Daniel. 1910). I, 60.

7. Whitfield to Garnier, Baltimore, October 17, 1829, Archives of Saint Sulpice, Paris, Matthew Leo Panczyk, "James Whitfield, Fourth Archbishop of Baltimore. The Episcopal Years: 1828–1834," *Records of the American Catholic Historical Society of Philadelphia,* LXXV (December, 1964), 243. For the question of a national seminary at the Baltimore councils of 1829 and 1833, see this work and its continuation in *ibid.,* LXXVI (March, 1965), 21–53.

8. Guth to Hughes, Lafargeville, September 25, 1838, John R. G. Hassard, *Life of the Most Reverend John Hughes, First Archbishop of New York.* (New York: D. Appleton and Company. 1866). p. 191.

9. Same to same, Lafargeville, September, 1839, *ibid.* Saint Joseph's Seminary

which opened at Rose Hill c. 1840 with a slightly better prospect and continued there until supplanted by a provincial seminary of the same name at Troy, New York, in 1864, had its own severe problems. See Francis X. Curran, S.J., "Archbishop Hughes and the Jesuits. Fordham's Prologue," *Woodstock Letters,* XCVII (Winter, 1968), 5–56, and also Thomas F. O'Connor, "Pioneer Catholic Seminaries in New York," *New York History,* XXIV (April, 1943), 211–219.

10. Van de Velde to Roothaan, n.p., 1834, General Archives of the Jesuits, Rome, Gilbert J. Garraghan, S.J., *The Jesuits of the Middle United States.* (New York: American Press. 1938). I, 639.

11. Coosemans to Beckx, n.p., March 16, 1866, General Archives of the Jesuits, Rome, *ibid.,* I, 639–640.

12. Fenwick to Dzierozynski, Boston, October 1, 1830, Archives of the Archdiocese of Boston, photostat, Panczyk, *Records,* LXXVI (March, 1965), 43.

13. Hughes to Brutè, n.p., June 10, 1834, Archives of the Archdiocese of New York, copy, *ibid.*

14. Peter Guilday (Ed.), *The National Pastorals of the American Hierarchy, 1792–1919.* (Washington: National Catholic Welfare Council. 1923). p. 113.

15. *Ibid.,* p. 240. Directing their remarks to Catholics of wealth, the bishops described "As specially useful the founding of scholarships, either in their diocesan or provincial Seminaries, or in the American College in Rome, or elsewhere, as circumstances may suggest."

16. *The Catholic Priesthood, Encyclical Letter ("Ad Catholici Sacerdotii") of His Holiness, Pope Pius XI.* (Washington: National Catholic Welfare Conference. [1936]). pp. 44–45.

17. For example, in the annual report of the Congregation for Catholic Education made public early in 1967 it was stated that in forty-one countries there were 479,568,500 Catholics with a total of 346,685 priests which was 14,000,000 more Catholics and 313 less priests than those reported in 1963. *National Catholic Reporter,* February 22, 1967, p. 9.

18. [Henry] J. Schroder, O.P. (Trans. and Ed.), *Canons and Decrees of the Council of Trent. Original Text with English Translation.* (Saint Louis: B. Herder Book Company. 1941). pp. 175–176.

19. Quoted by Louis Abelly, *La Vie du Vénérable Serviteur de Dieu, Vincent de Paul.* (Paris: Lambert. 1664). Sect. I, 213.

20. See the chapter, "The Reform of the Clergy," Pierre Coste, C.M., *The Life & Works of Saint Vincent de Paul.* (London: Burns, Oates & Washbourne Ltd. 1934), I, 243–267, for a description of the scandalous conditions among the French clergy of the period. Coste stated that "considering their age and habits," Vincent de Paul regarded any attempt at reform of the older priests as "useless or superficial," and for that reason he concentrated his attention on the selection and preparation of younger men who showed a desire to become priests. I, 243.

21. Walter J. Burghardt, S.J., "Towards An American Theology," *American Ecclesiastical Review,* CLIX (September, 1968), 184.

22. For a good account of this period, see E. Preclin and E. Jarry, *Les luttes politiques et doctrinales aux XVIIe et XVIIIe siècles.* (Paris: Bloud & Gay, 1956), pp. 703–802. For a splendid brief account, see A. G. Dickens, *The Counter Reformation.* (New York: Harcourt, Brace & World, Inc. 1969).

23. *The Catholic Church in the Modern World.* (Garden City: Hanover House. 1958). p. 74. The shortage of good priests was a widespread phenomenon. For example, Paolo Leardi, Nuncio to Austria, told Cardinal Ercole Consalvi, Secretary of State to Pius VII, in a letter from Vienna on August 29, 1817, that the clergy of the Austrian Empire presented "a truly horrible aspect." Not only were they extremely scarce and unable to provide for the needs of the people, but the bishops were constantly hampered by the interference of the government, which, according

to Leardi, wished to perpetuate this "wretched condition." As for the clergy themselves, "their way of life," said the nuncio, "is generally without discipline, shameful, and scandalous. . . ." Alan Reinerman, "The Return of the Jesuits to the Austrian Empire and the Decline of Josephinism, 1820–1822," *Catholic Historical Review*, LII (October, 1966), 377.

24. Purcell to Peter Verhaegen, S.J., n. p., August 17, 1840, Garraghan, *op. cit.*, III, 167.

25. Francis Joseph Miller, *A History of the Athenaeum of Ohio, 1829–1960* (Ann Arbor: University Microfilms, Inc. 1966). p. 86.

26. Fisher to Arthur J. Donnelly, Saint Paul, 1852, "Letters of Daniel J. Fisher, A Seminarian in St. Paul," *Acta et Dicta*, I (July, 1907), 45–46.

27. *Life and Scenery in Missouri. Reminiscences of a Missionary Priest.* (Dublin: J. Duffy & Company Ltd. 1890). p. 228.

28. "Our Future Clergy: An Inquiry into Vocations to the Priesthood in the United States," *Brownson's Quarterly Review* [Third New York Series] I (October, 1860), 504. This article signed 'J.W.C.' was written by Jeremiah W. Cummings, Pastor of Saint Stephen's Church, New York City.

29. Bruté to Rosati, n.p., April 23, 1835, Mary Salesia Godecker, O.S.B., *Simon Bruté de Rémur, First Bishop of Vincennes.* (Saint Meinrad: Saint Meinrad Historical Essays. 1931). p. 241.

30. Bruté to 'Your Grace,' [Vincent Milde, Archbishop of Vienna], Rouen, May 30, 1836, *ibid.*, p. 274. In the same manner the Irish-born bishops in this country turned to Ireland for priests and seminarians as John England, Bishop of Charleston, told Cardinal Carlo Pedicini, in 1833, "I have lately been in Ireland, and have made arrangements with several bishops there by which I can hope for a sufficient number of good young men who aspire to the ecclesiastical state; but the means are wanting to place upon a solid basis a seminary for their education and for the education of those who will succeed them; as also for the establishment of a college, in which the youth of the country could receive a good education, and from the profits of which the expenses of the ecclesiastical seminary could be defrayed." England to Pedicini, Rome, 1833, copy, "Papers Relating to the Church in America from the Portfolios of the Irish College at Rome," *Records of the American Catholic Historical Society of Philadelphia*, VIII (1897), 322–323.

31. George Paré, *The Catholic Church in Detroit, 1701–1888.* (Detroit: Gabriel Richard Press. 1951). p. 530.

32. Anthony Viéban, S.S., "The Ecclesiastical Seminary," *Catholic Encyclopedia.* (New York: Encyclopedia Press. 1912), XIII, 698.

33. Paul A. Gagnon, *France Since 1789.* (New York: Harper & Row. 1964). p. 109.

34. Adrien Dansette, *Religious History of Modern France.* (New York: Herder and Herder. 1961). II, 6.

35. Roger Aubert, *Le pontificat de Pie IX, 1846–1878.* (Paris: Bloud & Gay. 1952). pp. 212–213.

36. Eccleston to Maréchal, Paris, n.d., Columba E. Halsey, O.S.B., "The Life of Samuel Eccleston, Fifth Archbishop of Baltimore, 1801–1851," *Records of the American Catholic Historical Society of Philadelphia*, LXXVI (June, 1965), 81.

37. Maréchal to Eccleston, Baltimore, February 12, 1826, *ibid.*, pp. 83–84.

38. Michael V. Gannon, *The Cross in the Sand. The Early Catholic Church in Florida, 1513–1870.* (Gainesville: University of Florida Press. 1965). pp. 89, 102 *et passim.*

39. Gerdil's letter was quoted by William J. Walsh, "The Alleged Gallicanism of Maynooth and of the Irish Clergy," *Dublin Review*, 3rd Series, XXXIV (April, 1880), 247.

40. *An Essay on the Development of Christian Doctrine.* Charles Frederick Harrold, (Ed.), (New York: Longmans, Green and Company, 1949). p. 34.

41. Newman to Henry Wilberforce, Rome, December 13, 1846, Charles Stephen Dessain, (Ed.), *The Letters and Diaries of John Henry Newman.* (London: Thomas Nelson and Sons Ltd. 1961). XI, 294–295.

42. Newman to Richard Stanton, Rome, November 6, 1846, *ibid.*, XI, 270.

43. Newmann to John D. Dalgairns, Rome, November 22, 1846, *ibid.*, XI, 279.

44. Newman to Richard Stanton, Rome, February 21, 1847, *ibid.*, XII, 48.

45. "Roman Memories," *Dublin Review*, CLXVII (October, 1920), 234–236.

46. Ward's unpublished memoir was quoted by his daughter, Maisie Ward, *The Wilfrid Wards and the Transition.* (New York: Sheed and Ward. 1934). p. 66.

47. Aubert, *op. cit.*, p. 303.

48. Norman Sykes, "Religion and the Relations of Churches and States," *New Cambridge Modern History.* (Cambridge: At the University Press, 1960). X, 93.

49. Purcell to Hughes, Cincinnati, January 24, 1842, John Tracy Ellis, *Essays in Seminary Education.* (Notre Dame: Fides Publishers, Inc. 1967). pp. 84–85.

50. Spalding to Kenrick, Malines, January 7, 1853, John D. Sauter, *The American College of Louvain, 1857–1898.* (Louvain: Publications Universitaires de Louvain. 1959). p. 19.

51. Spalding to Kenrick, Florence, March 6, 1853, *ibid.*, p. 19.

52. Sauter, *op. cit.*, pp. 113–114.

53. "The Nuncio's Report," Rome, July 12, 1854, James F. Connelly, *The Visit of Archbishop Gaetano Bedini to the United States of America, June 1853–February, 1854.* (Rome: Libreria Editrice dell'Università Gregoriana. 1960). p. 245.

54. John Tracy Ellis, "On Selecting Catholic Bishops for the United States," *The Critic*, XXVII (June–July, 1969), p. 47. On the same subject, see the writer's earlier article, "On Selecting American Bishops," *Commonweal*, LXXXV (March 10, 1967), 643–649.

55. Pius IX to the American bishops, Rome, January 1, 1855, Robert F. McNamara, *The American College in Rome, 1855–1955.* (Rochester: Christopher Press, Inc. 1956). pp. 16–17.

56. Hughes to Bernard Smith, New York, August 12, 1858, *ibid.*, p. 21.

57. Peter Leo Johnson, *Halcyon Days. Story of St. Francis Seminary, Milwaukee, 1856–1956.* (Milwaukee: Bruce Publishing Company, 1956). It was not surprising that an historian of theology in the period, 1831–1870, should have said of this country, "North America was rich in hopes; but its hour had not yet come to contribute to the progress of the theological and philosophical sciences." Hocedez, *op. cit.*, II, 198.

58. *Ibid.*, p. 225.

59. *Ibid.*, p. 226. Another textbook used in some of the so-called German seminaries was Matthias J. Scheeben, *Handbuch der katholischen Dogmatik.* 3 vols. (Freiburg, 1873–1882) translated by Joseph Wilhelm and Thomas B. Scannel in two volumes, *Manual of Catholic Theology.*

60. Kenrick to Peter Richard Kenrick, n.p. December 4, 1843, F.E.T. [Francis E. Tourscher, O.S.A.] Trans. and Ed., *The Kenrick-Frenaye Correspondence. . . , 1830–1862.* (Philadelphia: The Author. 1920). pp. 179–180.

61. Sisters Maria Michele Armato, O.P., and Mary Jeremy Finnegan, O.P. Trans. and Eds., *The Memoirs of Father Samuel Mazzuchelli, O.P.* (Chicago: Priory Press, 1967). p. 307.

62. Knox to Newman, Boston, September 22, 1846, John Tracy Ellis, Ed., "An English Visitor's Comments on the American Religious Scene, 1846," *Church History*, XXXVI (March, 1967), 6.

63. "Hasty Notes of a Journey to America. . . ," p. 256, photostat, Archives of the Society of Saint Joseph, Baltimore. The writer wishes to thank his friend, the Reverend Peter E. Hogan, S.S.J., for supplying a copy of this lengthy travelogue.

64. *Ibid.*, p. 291.

65. *Concilium Plenarium Totius Americae Septentrionalis Foederatae, Baltimori Habitum Anno 1852.* (Baltimore: John Murphy Company. 1853). p. 47.

66. *Concilii Plenarii Baltimorensis II. . . . . Acta et Decreta.* (Baltimore: John Murphy Company. 1868). p. xxvi. The full text of Barnabò's letter to Martin J. Spalding, Archbishop of Baltimore and Apostolic Delegate of the Council, Rome, January 31, 1866, is given here, pp. xxiv–xxviii.

67. *Ibid.*, p. 108.

68. *Ibid.*, p. 109.

69. Spalding to Timon, Baltimore, August 23, 1865, John Tracy Ellis, *The Formative Years of the Catholic University of America.* (Washington: American Catholic Historical Association. 1946). pp. 45–46.

70. *Concilii Plenarii Baltimorensis II. . . . . Acta et Decreta*, p. 228.

71. Phillips Bradley (Ed.), *Democracy in America by Alexis de Tocqueville.* (New York: Alfred A. Knopf. 1953). I, 308.

72. For a brief treatment of the tension in Catholic intellectual circles in the 1950's and early 1960's, see John Tracy Ellis, *A Commitment To Truth.* (Latrobe: Archabbey Press. 1966). pp. 50–54.

73. John J. Wynne, S.J. (Ed.), *The Great Encyclical Letters of Pope Leo XIII.* (New York: Benziger Brothers. 1903). p. 323.

74. *Ecumenical Councils of the Catholic Church. An Historical Outline.* (New York: Herder and Herder. 1960). pp. 188–189.

75. Martin J. Spalding to John Lancaster Spalding, Baltimore, February 20, 1865, John Tracy Ellis, "Some Student Letters of John Lancaster Spalding," *Catholic Historical Review*, XXIX (January, 1944). 536.

76. *Catholic Mirror* (Baltimore), November 9 and 23, 1889. For this episode, see John Tracy Ellis, *The Life of James Cardinal Gibbons, Archbishop of Baltimore, 1834–1921.* (Milwaukee: Bruce Publishing Company. 1952). II, 343–346.

77. Wynne, *op. cit.*, p. 56.

78. Roger Aubert, "Aspects Divers du Néo-Thomisme sous le Pontificat de Léon XIII," Giuseppe Rossini, (Ed.), *Aspetti della Cultura Cattolica nell'Età di Leone XIII. Atti del Convegno Tenuto a Bologna il 27–28–29 Dicembre 1960.* (Roma: Edizioni Cinque Lune). 1961. p. 150.

79. Hostlot to Farley, Palestrina, August 28, 1879, McNamara, *op. cit.*, p. 243.

80. Connelly to Gibbons, Rome, April 29, 1881, *ibid.*, p. 243.

81. The story of Mercier's early struggles at Louvain is told in considerable detail by Aubert, "Aspects Divers. . . . ," pp. 172–190.

82. Spalding to De Neve, n.p., n.d., J. Van der Heyden, *The Louvain American College, 1857–1907.* (Louvain: Fr. & R. Ceuterick. 1909). p. 174.

83. Hugh Hawkins, "Charles W. Eliot, University Reform, and Religious Faith in America, 1869–1909," *Mississippi Valley Historical Review*, LI (September, 1964), 201.

84. "President's Report for 1881–82 to the Board of Overseers," *Annual Reports of the President and Treasurer of Harvard College, 1881–82.* (Cambridge: University Press. John Wilson and Son. 1882). pp. 27, 29–30.

85. *Sadlier's Catholic Directory, Almanac, and Ordo.* (New York: D. & J. Sadlier & Company. 1868). p. 426; *Catholic Directory, Almanac and Clergy List — Quarterly for the Year of Our Lord 1900.* (Milwaukee: M. H. Wiltzius & Company. 1900). Insert following p. 820.

86. Spalding to Purcell, n.p., November 27, 1851, Miller, *op. cit.*, p. 118.

87. Purcell to Kenrick, n.p., November, 1851, *ibid.*

88. Francis P. Cassidy, "Catholic Education in the Third Plenary Council of Baltimore," *Catholic Historical Review*, XXXIV (October, 1948), 260–270, contains a summary of the Roman conferences.

89. *Ibid.*, pp. 270–273.

90. *Schema Decretorum Concilii Plenarii Baltimorensis Tertii.* (Baltimore: Privately printed by Foley Brothers. 1884). pp. 39–52.

91. *Ibid.*, pp. 44–45.

92. *Ibid.*, pp. 46–47. One American institution where by reason of the existing tradition the transition to Thomistic teaching was easily brought about was Saint Francis Seminary, Milwaukee, where, as mentioned above, the influence of the Innsbruck Jesuits was strong. Thus when Joseph Selinger of the Archdiocese of Saint Louis was loaned to Milwaukee as professor of dogmatic theology, a post he held for fourteen years, he came with the background of his Thomistic training at the Urban College of Propaganda under Francesco Satolli where he had earned his doctorate in 1887 and where Satolli thought highly enough of him to invite him to become a lecturer. Selinger adopted *Medulla Theologiae Dogmaticae*, an abridgement of the latter's three-volume *Theologiae Dogmaticae Compendium.* Johnson, *op. cit.*, p. 230.

93. *Ibid.*, p. 47.

94. *Acta et Decreta Concilii Plenarii Baltimorensis Tertii.* (Baltimore: John Murphy Company. 1886). pp. 95–98.

95. Spalding, *Means and Ends of Education.* (Chicago: A. C. McClurg and Company. 1895). pp. 212–213.

96. For a detailed treatment of the events that preceded the opening of this institution, see the writer's volume, *The Formative Years of the Catholic University of America.* (Washington: American Catholic Historical Association. 1946). Leopold Bushart, Provincial of the Jesuits' Missouri Province, was at pains to inform Archbishop Gibbons that Fulton's council speech had expressed his personal views, "and by no means the opinion of the Fathers of our Society as far as I have been able to ascertain." The Jesuits were not opposed to the education of the clergy, said Bushart; on the contrary, "we favor it and we shall do all in our power to promote it." As it turned out, Bushart's prediction that any measure adopted by the bishops toward that end, "will meet with the most cordial approval of our Society," did not prove an accurate one, for the new university experienced considerable opposition from a number of prominent Jesuits during its early years. Bushart to Gibbons, Baltimore, November 26, 1884, Ellis, *The Formative Years.* . . . pp. 107–108.

97. Moore to Fortune, Washington, March 14, 1891, Archives of All Hallows College, Dublin. The writer wishes to thank Father Kevin Condon, C.M., archivist of All Hallows College, for this and other materials taken from these archives.

98. Those interested in the history of clerical education will find a good deal of material in the volumes that covered the administration of the university's first three rectors: Patrick Henry Ahern, *The Catholic University of America, 1887–1896. The Rectorship of John J. Keane.* (Washington: The Catholic University of America Press. 1948); Peter E. Hogan, S.S.J., *The Catholic University of America, 1896–1903. The Rectorship of Thomas J. Conaty.* (Washington: The Catholic University of America Press. 1949); Colman J. Barry, O.S.B., *The Catholic University of America, 1903–1909. The Rectorship of Denis J. O'Connell.* (Washington: The Catholic University of America Press. 1950).

99. H. Richard Niebuhr, Daniel Day Williams, and James M. Gustafson, *The Advancement of Theological Education.* (New York: Harper & Brothers. 1957). p. 4.

100. Riordan to Shahan, San Francisco, September 18, 1909, Archives of the Archdiocese of San Francisco, copy. The writer wishes to thank his friend, Monsignor James P. Gaffey, for the generous loan of this letter and other materials from his manuscript biography of Archbishop Riordan.

101. IV (May, 1891), 342–349. The Hogan book was published by Marlier, Callanan & Company of Boston in 1898.

102. *A Garland of Affectionate Tributes.* (Boston: Privately printed. 1906). pp. 63–65.

103. "The Encyclical 'Aeterni Patris,' " *Clerical Studies,* p. 45. This was a slightly different version than the original article, "Clerical Studies. Philosophy," in the *American Ecclesiastical Review,* VI (February, 1892), 81–88, in which Hogan treated the encyclical.

104. "The Recent Encyclical Letter of Pope Leo XIII," *American Catholic Quarterly Review,* IV (October, 1879), 719–732; "The Decrees of the Third Plenary Council," *ibid.,* XI (April, 1886), 344–356.

105. "The Higher and Lower Education of the American Priesthood," *American Catholic Quarterly Review,* XV (January, 1890), 104.

106. "Our American Seminaries," *American Ecclesiastical Review,* XVI (May, 1897), 463.

107. *Our Seminaries. An Essay on Clerical Training.* (New York: William H. Young & Company. 1896). p. 54. Numerous examples could be cited to illustrate the validity of Smith's observation, but let the following suffice. In January, 1883, Saint Thomas Seminary was opened under the auspices of the Society of Mary near Mission San Jose, California, with the idea that it would serve the dioceses of the Far West. The superior, Father John Francis Regis Pestre, S.M., soon informed the Marist Superior General, Julien Favre, of how impossible the situation was. Mission San Jose was thirty-six miles from San Francisco which could be reached only after a three-hour journey, there were no more than five students, only one of whom was ready for theology, two professors had already abandoned the seminary for less frustrating tasks, the bishops of the region were too impoverished to lend assistance, and two of the suffragan bishops of the Province of San Francisco had adamantly opposed the seminary's establishment at Mission San Jose. "Here we are," said Pestre, "isolated from the rest of the world and reduced to a single province of San Francisco where two suffragans are against us." Pestre to Favre, San Jose, January 26, 1883, Gaffey, *op. cit.,* pp. 150–151. The unhappy results of a proliferation of seminaries where there was neither the financial resources or the trained personnel to sustain them properly were not confined to the American Catholics. Among the latter's coreligionists in England, for example, Henry Edward Manning, Archbishop of Westminster, had taken the lead in establishing separate institutions of which seven diocesan seminaries were founded between 1873 and 1891 with only two of these that survived, namely, Saint John's, Wonersh (Diocese of Southwark) and Saint Joseph's, Upholland (Diocese of Liverpool). David Milbourn, *A History of Ushaw College.* Durham: Ushaw Bookshop. 1964. pp. 263–264.

108. Anson Phelps Stokes, "University Schools of Religion," *Religious Education,* IX (August, 1914), 324.

109. Leo XIII to Cardinal Gibbons, Rome, March 7, 1889, *The Statutes of the Catholic University of America.* (Washington: The Catholic University of America. 1937). pp. 5–6.

110. "Educational Conference of Seminary Presidents," *Catholic University Bulletin,* IV (July, 1898), 401.

111. *Catholic Educational Association. Report of the Proceedings and Addresses of the Second Annual Meeting, New York, July 11, 12, and 13, 1905.* (Columbus: Secretary's Office. Published by the Association. [1905]), pp. 212–263, for the texts and discussion on these papers.

112. *Ibid.,* p. 212.

113. "The Priest and the United States Intellectual Community Since 1900," read at a joint session of the American Catholic Historical Association and the American Society of Church History, New York, December 29, 1968, p. 2. The writer wishes to thank Monsignor Gannon for his permission to quote from this unpublished paper.

114. The best work on Americanism is that of Thomas T. McAvoy, C.S.C., *The*

Great Crisis in American Catholic History, 1895–1900. (Chicago: Henry Regnery Company. 1957).

115. Quoted in Jean-Jacques D'Aoust, "The Reaction to Americanism in France," pp. 20–21, a paper read at the same session as that of the paper of Michael Gannon. The writer is grateful to Professor D'Aoust of Wells College for permission to quote from his paper.

116. "A Blow to Americanism," Washington *Times* [morning edition], January 3, 1900, p. 4.

117. Chicago: D. H. McBride and Company. 1896.

118. Thomas F. O'Connor, "John A. Zahm, C.S.C.: Scientist and Americanist," *The Americas*, VII (April, 1951), 444. O'Connor quoted this letter from Ernest C. Messenger, *Evolution and Theology.* (London: Burns and Oates and Washbourne Ltd. 1931), pp. 233–234, who gave no source for the original.

119. Zahm to Alfonso Golea, Notre Dame, May 16, 1899, *Literary Digest*, XIX (August 12, 1899), 200.

120. O'Connor, *op. cit.*, p. 445.

121. Vincent A. Yzermans (Ed.), *All Things in Christ. Encyclicals and Selected Documents of Saint Pius X.* (Westminster: Newman Press. 1954). pp. 8–9.

122. The best general account of the movement in English is Alec R. Vidler, *The Modernist Movement in the Roman Church. Its Origins & Outcome.* (Cambridge: At the University Press. 1934); the most recent extensive work, and probably the best in any language, is Emile Poulat, *Histoire dogma et critique dans la Crise Moderniste.* (Paris: Casterman. 1962). The present writer treated the aftermath of the encyclical briefly in *A Commitment To Truth.* (Latrobe: Archabbey Press. 1966). pp. 38–50. There is no scholarly account of the movement in print insofar as it related to the Church in the United States. For a definition of modernism, see that suggested under "Modernism," *New Catholic Encyclopedia.* (New York: McGraw-Hill Book Company. 1967). IX, 994–995.

123. Yzermans, *All Things in Christ*, p. 125.

124. *Ibid.*, pp. 124–125.

125. "Modernism in the Church in America," *Ecclesiastical Review*, XXXVIII (January, 1908), 2–3. Speaking of the young American Catholic man and woman this writer stated that those who had a strong and clearly defined notion of the principles of their faith, "owe it almost entirely to Irish traditions, or the habits of their parents to whom their religion is dear on many accounts," and as for those of German background, "it is the parish school. . . ." What saved the Catholic youth, beyond the above mentioned influences from "falling in with the modernist speculations is their absorption in the pursuit of material advancement." (p. 5).

126. *Ibid.*, p. 4.

127. *Ecclesiastical Review*, XXXVIII (May, 1908), 489–508.

128. "Modernism in the Past Year, A Review," *Ecclesiastical Review*, XXXIX (November, 1908), 465–472; (December, 1908) 618–627. Currier stated that the Board of Trustees of the Catholic University of America at a meeting on November 13, 1907, had "agreed in regarding 'Modernism' as a serious danger to the Church," and had instructed Cardinal Gibbons, Chancellor of the University, to write a letter to Pius X declaring "the adhesion of the University and its trustees to the Encyclical." (p. 619).

129. *The Life of John Henry Cardinal Newman.* (New York: Longmans, Green and Company. 1912), I, 160. Ward was speaking of the opposition that had arisen to Newman's work, *An Essay on the Development of Christian Doctrine*, published late in 1845.

130. Emmanuele Chiettini, O.F.M., "Americanismo," *Enciclopedia Cattolica.* (Città del Vaticano: Ente per l'Enciclopedia Cattolica a per il Libro Cattolico. 1948). I, 1056. Chiettini was professor of fundamental theology in the Antonianum in Rome. That the association of Americanism and modernism was widespread and

believed to have a more or less common unorthodox origin was unquestionable. For example, in counseling 'a young girl,' Columba Marmion, O.S.B., stated in a letter from the Abbey of Maredsous, October 27, 1919, *inter alia*:

I fear you have a false American view about doing good. You seem to feel that you can't show your love, or be useful unless by some *external* activity; & yet the absolute donation of self to Xt, so that He may dispose of us as *He pleases*, is above every other form of love & more useful to the Church than any form of human activity. Gisbert Ghysens, O.S.B., and Thomas Delforge, O.S.B., (Eds.), *The English Letters of Abbot Marmion, 1858–1923*. (Baltimore: Helicon Press, Inc. 1962). pp. 176–177.

131. *Winds of Doctrine*. (New York: Charles Scribner's Sons. 1913). pp. 56–57.

132. Genocchi to von Hügel, Rome, November 5, 1906, Michael de la Bedoyere, *The Life of Baron von Hügel*. (New York: Charles Scribner's Sons. 1951). pp. 181–182. For a brief account of the integralists' campaign, see Walter H. Peters, *The Life of Benedict XV*. (Milwaukee: Bruce Publishing Company. 1959). pp. 42–53. De la Bedoyere was mistaken in referring to Genocchi as a Dominican; he was a Missionary of the Sacred Heart.

133. Information contained in notes taken by George J. Bryan, C.SS.R., and given to the writer on September 20, 1958, from the Farley Papers, Archives of the Archdiocese of New York. There was likewise contained here the summary of a letter from Falconio's secretary, William F. Hughes, a priest of the Archdiocese of New York, dated Washington, January 4, 1909, in which Hughes stated that the delegate still thought there was a clique of modernists in New York, eight in fact, although he did not know their names! Falconio's eyes were said to be centered on Saint Joseph's Seminary and particularly on the ex-Sulpicians on the faculty. Five of the six Sulpician professors at Dunwoodie had left the Society of Saint Sulpice in January, 1906, over dissatisfaction with the Paris administration, especially with the latter's censorship of their writings. On this subject, see the communication, privately printed, of the American Sulpician superior, Edward R. Dyer, dated Baltimore, April 18, 1906, and entitled *To the Sulpicians of the Vicariate of the United States*, a copy of which was given to the writer by Lloyd P. McDonald, S.S., late provincial of the Sulpicians of the United States.

134. Ellis, *Gibbons*, II, 475–476.

135. *Ibid.*, II, 171–182.

136. Terrence F. X. O'Donnell, "The Influence of Modernism on the Catholic Church in the United States," p. 24. Father O'Donnell's study was done as a thesis for the master's degree at Saint Joseph's Seminary, Dunwoodie, New York, in 1963. The writer wishes to thank him for the very considerable data provided by this thesis and, too, his friend and former student, Peter E. Hogan, S.S.J., Archivist of the Society of Saint Joseph, Baltimore, who kindly supplied him with a copy of the O'Donnell work.

137. "The Study of Sacred Scripture in Theological Seminaries," *American Ecclesiastical Review*, XXIII (September, 1900), 234.

138. Kennedy to Farley, Rome, November 8, 1908, Archives of the Archdiocese of New York, I-11-K; Mitty to Farley, Rome, January 19, April 10, May 5, July 4, 1908, I-11-M; Mitty to Farley, Munich, October 10, November 20, and November 30, 1908, I-11-M. In the letter of November 30, Mitty told the archbishop, "I read your letter this morning and communicated its contents to my companions. We immediately went to the Hamburg American Office and booked for passage on the SS. Amerika, sailing December 11th and due in New York on December 20th." When the previous January, Falconio, the apostolic delegate, had reported the young New York priests as consorting with modernists in Rome [Falconio to Farley, Washington, January 15, 1908], Mitty explained to Archbishop Farley that they had once gone to confession to Father Giovanni Genocchi, M.S.C., to whom they had talked in New York and that after their confession Antonio Fogaz-

zaro, the Italian novelist charged with being a modernist, had come in, but the young Americans had left after two or three minutes. Mitty actually wrote 'Fogazzarino' but in all likelihood it was Fogazzaro who was meant. Mitty's companions in Rome and Munich were Francis X. Albert, Edwin J. Ryan, and Daniel W. Sheeran. [Mitty to Farley, Rome, January 19, 1908].

The writer wishes to thank a former student of his at Brown University, Regina B. Walsh, for these references from the Archives of the Archdiocese of New York which she used in her master's thesis at Brown, "Academic Freedom in American Catholic Higher Education during the Modernist Controversy," 1970.

139. Robert F. McNamara, "Archbishop Hanna, Rochesterian," *Rochester History*, XXV (April, 1963), 10.

140. LXI (September 6, 1906), 565–571.

141. New York *Times*, July 19, 1908, p. 10.

142. XIII (October, 1909), 555–574.

143. New York: Richard R. Smith. 1944. On Sullivan, see John Ratté, *Three Modernists. Alfred Loisy, George Tyrell, William L. Sullivan.* (New York: Sheed and Ward. 1967). pp. 259–336.

144. Maffi to De Lai, n.p., February 10, 1911, Carlo Falconi, *The Popes in the Twentieth Century. Leo XIII to John XXIII.* (Boston: Little, Brown and Company, 1968). p. 38.

145. *Ibid.*

146. Mignot to Ferrata, n.p., October, 1914, Nicolas Fontaine, *Saint Siège, Action française et Catholiques intégraux. Histoire critique avec documents.* (Paris: Librairie Universitaire. J. Gamber. 1928). p. 133. According to Gerald J. O'Brien, S.J., "Anti-Modernism: The Integralist Campaign," *Continuum*, III (Summer, 1965). 195, n. 34. Fontaine was a pseudonym for M. Canet, an official of the Quay d'Orsay who dealt with religious groups. The most recent extended work on modernism is that of Michele Ranchetti, *The Catholic Modernists: A Study of the Religious Reform Movement, 1864–1907.* (London: Oxford University Press. 1969); it has been severely criticized, however, by scholars, e.g., by Thomas Michael Loome in *The Tablet* (London), CCXXIV (January 24, 1970), 82.

147. Maisie Ward, *Insurrection Versus Resurrection.* (New York: Sheed and Ward. 1937). p. 331. Benedict XV was quoted as having told Cardinal Louis Billot, a strong sympathizer with *l'Action française*, that he wanted to hear no more talk about 'integrism.' (*ibid.*). The Ward work is especially rewarding for intellectual trends within the Church at this time.

148. "First Encyclical of Benedict XV," *Catholic Mind*, XII (December 22, 1914), 745–746.

149. Op. cit., p. 571. Slattery cited Johannes Kübel's *Geschichte des katholischen Modernismus* (Tübingen, 1909) as the source of the Ehrhard statement; he likewise remarked that Kübel had devoted only a few lines to the United States.

150. A very considerable amount of research and writing touching on this subject have been done in recent years. The following items may be of assistance to students who wish to do further reading. One of the best surveys of Catholic theological developments in the present century was that of Roger Aubert, "La Théologie Catholique au Milieu du XXᵉ Siècle," *La Revue Nouvelle*, XVII (Juin 15, 1953), 561–576, which continued through the successive issues to that of October 15, 1953. Aubert mentioned 114 French authors, twenty Germans, five Dutch or Flemish, and one Italian; but there were no references to any American or English theologian. Some years later in referring to the Aubert work, George H. Tavard stated that although the situation had remained largely unchanged, he was inclined to believe that since Vatican Council II the Germans had gained first place. Regarding the Americans he said, "The United States lagged behind, in spite of the valuable but very specialized productions of the Franciscan Institute and the distinguished contributions of *Theological Studies*." *The Pilgrim Church.* (New York:

Herder and Herder. 1967). p. 16. For a comparative study devoted mostly to Protestant authors, see Eric W. Gritsch, "European and American Theological Education: Appraisal and Comparison," *American Review* [Bologna], III (Spring, 1964), 44–55. On a wider spectrum than theology alone but definitely related to the ecclesiastical sciences, was the writer's *American Catholics and the Intellectual Life.* (Chicago: Heritage Foundation, 1956); and Thomas F. O'Dea, *American Catholic Dilemma: An Inquiry into the Intellectual Life.* (New York: Sheed and Ward, 1958). See also Gustave Weigel, S.J., "American Catholic Intellectualism: A Theologian's Reflections," *Review of Politics*, XIX (July, 1957), 275–307; Walter J. Burghardt, S.J., "The Intellectual Formation of the Future Priest," *Bulletin. National Catholic Educational Association*, LXI (August, 1964), 58–68, and the same writer's presidential address before the Catholic Theological Society of America, "Towards an American Theology," *American Ecclesiastical Review*, CLIX (September, 1968), 181–187.

151. Riordan to Daniel Riordan, San Francisco, September 13, 1912, copy. Archives of the Archdiocese of San Francisco, Gaffey, *op. cit.*, p. 164. Monsignor Gaffey added that the archbishop expressed the same sentiments to his brother three months before his death in a letter of September 29, 1914.

152. "Some Impressions of Catholic America," *Dublin Review*, CXXXVIII (April, 1906), 95. For Saint Bernard's, see also Robert F. McNamara, *The Diocese of Rochester, 1868–1968.* Rochester: Diocese of Rochester. 1968. pp. 160 ff.

153. Gasquet, *op. cit.*, p. 87.

154. *The Land of the Strenuous Life.* (Chicago: A. C. McClurg Company. 1905). p. 203. Actually, the last group of priests to be ordained from the old seminary were those on June 5, 1915; on the following September 14 the new Kenrick Seminary was opened at its present location.

155. John E. Sexton and Arthur J. Riley, *History of Saint John's Seminary, Brighton.* (Boston: Roman Catholic Archbishop of Boston. 1945). p. 143.

156. Walter D. Wagoner, *The Seminary. Protestant and Catholic.* (New York: Sheed and Ward. 1966). p. 68.

157. For full bibliographical data on both the history and the present state of Catholic seminaries in this country, see the footnotes in the writer's volume, *Essays in Seminary Education.* (Notre Dame: Fides Publishers, Inc. 1967). There is a certain justification for what Richard P. McBrien, professor of theology in Pope John XXIII National Seminary, stated in reviewing Jacques Duquesne's *A Church Without Priests?* (New York: Macmillan Company. 1969): "There is nothing in this book that has not already been said before (and perhaps too many books are falling too often into this category)." *Commonweal*, XC (July 11, 1969), 444.

158. *L'Attività della Santa Sede nel 1966.* (Città del Vaticano: Tipografia Poliglotta Vaticana [1967]), pp. 975–976. In 1960 the 5,426 priests, diocesan and religious, ordained in thirty-nine countries were forty-nine below the total for 1959, according to the report of the Congregation of Seminaries and Universities. *L'Attività della Santa Sede nel 1961*, pp. 262–264.

159. Elder to Corrigan, Cincinnati, March 20, 1885, Ellis, *The Formative Years of the Catholic University of America*, p. 135. Elder added, "The Jesuits can keep their young members out of these dangers; but secular Priests & Seminarians will be vastly more exposed. Even the Professors will have their serious dangers." Bishop Gilmour of Cleveland was of the same mind about Washington, as he told Archbishop Elder, "not only for the noise and bustle, but far more for the unhealthy atmosphere of a capital." Gilmour to Elder, Cleveland, March 24, 1885. *ibid.*

160. "Our Seminaries: Their Commitments and Resources," *Bulletin. National Catholic Educational Association*, LVI (August, 1959), 74.

161. Adrian Fuerst, O.S.B., and Polycarp Sherwood, O.S.B., "Academic Renewal in a School of Theology," *American Ecclesiastical Review*, CLI (November, 1964), 289–297. See also the unpublished doctoral dissertation of Campion E. Baer,

O.F.M.Cap., "The Development of Accreditation in American Catholic Seminaries, 1890–1961," University of Notre Dame, 1963.

162. Pius XI declared that the teachings of Saint Thomas, "with reference to the value of human thought are beyond all controversy." To avoid the errors that were a prime source of the evils of the present day it was necessary, said the pontiff, "religiously to hold fast, now as never before, to the teachings of the Angelic Doctor." Then directing his remarks particularly to "those professors who teach in Seminaries," he stated they should reflect upon and follow faithfully all the prescriptions of Leo XIII, Pius X, and of himself regarding Thomism, being thus convinced that "they will live up to all their obligations and fulfill Our wishes if after they themselves have come to a great love of the Angelic Doctor by long and assiduous study of his works, they communicate their own love of him to their pupils." James H. Ryan, (Trans. and Ed.), *The Encyclicals of Pius XI.* (Saint Louis: B. Herder Book Company. 1927). pp. 83, 92, and 94.

163. Wagoner, *op. cit.*, p. 106, n. 2.

164. *Ibid.*, p. 86.

165. "The Theology of Risk," *The Furrow*, XIX (May, 1968), 267.

166. E. Allison Peers, *Spain, the Church and the Orders.* (London: Eyre and Spottiswoode, 1939). p. 39.

167. See Walter D. Wagoner, "Seminary Clustering: The Way the Wind Blows," *American Ecclesiastical Review*, CLIX (December, 1968), 378–390.

168. New York *Times*, June 28, 1968, p. 3.

169. Floyd Anderson (Ed.), *Council Daybook. Vatican II. Session 3.* (Washington: National Catholic Welfare Conference. 1965). p. 264. For the full text, see William K. Leahy and Anthony T. Massimini, (Eds.), *Third Session Council Speeches of Vatican II.* (Glen Rock, New Jersey: Deus Books. Paulist Press. 1966). pp. 307–311.

170. Walter M. Abbott, S.J., and Joseph Gallagher (Eds.), *The Documents of Vatican II.* (New York: America Press. 1966). p. 450.

171. *Ibid.*, p. 435.

172. *Ibid.*, p. 438.

173. *Ibid.*, p. 436.

174. *Ibid.*, p. 460. Quanbeck added at this point, "It is rumored that not all bishops are poignantly aware of the importance of libraries, so some specifics on this topic could be helpful." In his encyclical, *Menti nostrae* of September 23, 1950, Pius XII spoke strongly about seminary libraries and their use, urging the bishops, "according to the splendid tradition of the Church," to restore dignity and efficiency to libraries under their jurisdiction. He then added:

> These libraries must not be neglected receptacles for books but living structures with a room for reference and reading. Above all, however, let them be up to date and enriched with works of every kind, especially those relating to the religious and social questions of our times, so that teachers, parish priests, and particularly young priests may find there the doctrine necessary for diffusing the truth of the Gospel and for fighting error. *Menti Nostrae. Apostolic Exhortation of Pope Pius XII to the Clergy of the Entire World on the Development of Holiness in Priestly Life.* (Washington: National Catholic Welfare Conference 1950). pp. 38–39.

Falconi's bias against Pius XII showed in a number of instances, for example, in connection with the clergy he said, "As for the priests, Pius XII did not even accord them the reforms relating to ecclesiastical studies about which his predecessors had been concerned." *op. cit.*, p. 286.

175. Abbott-Gallagher, *op. cit.*, p. 446.

176. *Ibid.*, p. 448. For the eloquent intervention in the council of Cardinal Albert Meyer, Archbishop of Chicago, on the need for candidates for the priesthood possessing the ordinary virtues that should identify every member of the people of

God, see Vincent A. Yzermans (Ed.), *American Participation in the Second Vatican Council.* (New York: Sheed and Ward. 1967). pp. 410–413.

177. Ahern, *The Catholic University of America. . . ,* p. 39.

178. *Ibid.,* p. 40, n. 19. There were deep differences on this matter between the faculty, the administration, and the trustees. Even so forthright a 'liberal' prelate as John Ireland, Archbishop of Saint Paul and a trustee of the university, told Bishop Keane, the rector: "If there are objectors, the ring leaders should be quietly asked to go home. The mass of students will soon settle down to the rule. . . . I sincerely trust that my students are not among the objectors. If they are, I will recall them at once, & replace them by worthier men." Ireland to Keane, Saint Paul, December 7, 1889, *ibid.,* p. 41, n. 19.

179. "The Spiritual Life of the Priest," a paper read at the study day of the Senate of Priests of the Archdiocese of San Francisco, San Francisco, March 2, 1969, p. 9.

180. *Priests Among Men.* Translated by Lucien Bégin, Carol Jackson, and Joseph Lamontagne, S.S.S. (Notre Dame: Fides Publishers, Inc. 1960), pp. 28 and 50.

181. "The Long View from St. Meinrad," *National Catholic Reporter,* September 20, 1967, p. 10. Martin E. Marty of the Divinity School of the University of Chicago, has also shown disagreement with certain trends among Catholics, for example, in an address to the fifth National Workshop for Christian Unity at Detroit, which he entitled, "A Protestant Critique of Extremism in Catholic Renewal," *National Catholic Reporter,* June 26, 1968, p. 5. More recently a Catholic writer who has generally been identified with the liberals expressed some misgivings along similar lines, especially as they related to the sisters' communities. See Michael Novak, "Where Did All the Spirit Go?" *Commonweal,* XV (September 5, 1969), 540–542.

182. "The Revolution No One Understands," San Francisco *Sunday Examiner and Chronicle,* June 9, 1968, p. 3.

183. "The Fathers Disperse and Reflect on Whence They Came," *The Tablet,* CCXIX (December 10, 1965), 1377.

184. *Delmarva Dialog* (Wilmington), August 4, 1967, p. 10.

185. *St. Patrick's Seminary Theologate. Catalog — 1969–1970.* (Menlo Park: Saint Patrick's Seminary. 1969), pp. 11–14.

186. "Theological Curriculum for the Priestly Candidate, fifth version, December 20, 1968, issued by the bishops' Commitee on Priestly Formation, p. 3 [Mimeographed].

187. Quoted in Willard F. Jabusch, "New Seminaries in Europe," *Commonweal,* LXXXV (October 7, 1966), 18.

188. *Summi Dei Verbum. Apostolic Letter of Pope Paul VI on Occasion of the Fourth Centenary of the Establishment of Seminaries by the Council of Trent, November 4, 1963.* Washington: National Catholic Welfare Conference. News Service. 1963. p. 13.

189. Introduction to *The Experience of Priesthood.* Edited by Brian Passman. (Wilkes-Barre: Dimension Books. 1968), p. xvi.

ROBERT TRISCO*

BISHOPS AND THEIR PRIESTS
IN THE UNITED STATES

Both by the nature of their calling and by the circumstances of their ministry the bishops and priests of the United States have from the beginning been forced to live and work in a close relationship. Whether the bishops regarded their priests as sons and younger brothers or as rivals and opponents, they had to rely on their co-operation; whether the priests regarded their bishops as fathers and elder brothers or as tyrants and oppressors, they had to depend on their direction. As members of the same family are bound together by indissoluble ties and yet are sometimes opposed to one another in certain respects, so too the head and the lower-ranking clergy of many an American diocese have at times disagreed and even quarreled among themselves without breaking the bonds of the sacred orders that they possessed in common. On some occasions their mutual antagonism even transcended diocesan boundaries and threatened to become almost a class struggle between the first and second orders of the hierarchy.

The history of such movements within the Church of the United States has never been traced beyond individual episodes, nor can a thorough study be attempted here. A connected account of the principal events on a national scale, nevertheless, may be useful to the bishops and priests of the present day who are seeking better ways of collaborating for the promotion of the Church's saving mission in this country.

In treating such a broad subject, one must try to restrict and categorize the available data if one expects to arrive at meaningful con-

*The writer wishes to express his gratitude to Reverend Monsignor John Tracy Ellis, the Reverend John P. Marschall, C.S.V., and Brother David Thomas Spalding, C.F.X., for the constructive criticisms that they gave him after reading a preliminary draft of this paper; to the following for the copies of primary sources that they generously furnished him: Monsignor Ellis, Brother David, the Reverend Henry J. Browne, the Reverend Jay Dolan, Reverend Monsignor James P. Gaffey, and the Reverend Henry A. Szarnicki; and to the Reverend Nelson Callahan and Professor Samuel J. Miller for the copies of their manuscripts of a series of articles on Eugene M. O'Callaghan and of a biography of Peter Richard Kenrick respectively that they kindly lent him.

111

clusions. On the one hand, the normal relations between bishops and their priests have been recorded in all the diocesan archives of the land and can be taken for granted. On the other hand, the various conflicts between them that have occurred in the past are too numerous to catalogue; even a partial list of such incidents would seem tedious and useless, because in many cases the causes of disputes were not disagreements over principles of ecclesiastical polity or law, but rather moral faults on one side or the other, clashes of personality, misunderstandings, and the other usual factors that often give rise to disharmony in human relations.

Instead of enumerating instances of discord and attempting to apportion blame, the purpose of this paper is to describe the successive efforts of bishops and priests to alter the laws and customs regulating their reciprocal relations. Their initiatives were for the most part directed to four goals: (1) giving the priests of a diocese a voice in the selection of their bishop; (2) giving them a share in his authority through the creation of a chapter of canons or a board of consultors; (3) giving them security of tenure by making them irremovable pastors; and (4) giving them the protection of strict judicial procedures in case they were accused of serious misdeeds. In a word, a prolonged effort was made to introduce the common law of the universal Church into the United States, where special arrangements had been permitted in the early days because of the missionary status of the Church.

Since to a certain extent all four of these objectives were interrelated, the movements to achieve them can conveniently be studied together. A chronological approach will show the steady development most clearly.

Part I: From the First Bishop to 1850

As far as the choosing of candidates for the episcopacy is concerned, the fact that the first bishop in the United States was elected by the clergy was never forgotten by subsequent generations of American priests.[1] This privilege had been requested by a committee of the clergy in a memorial that was sent to Pope Pius VI on March 12, 1788; they asked not only that an episcopal see be erected in the United States but also

> . . . that the election of the bishop, at least for the first time, be permitted to the priests who now duly exercise the religious ministry here and have the cure of souls. This being established, your most vigilant wisdom, Most Holy Father, after hearing the petitions of our priests of approved life and experience, and

considering the character of our government, will adopt some course by which future elections may be permanently conducted.[2]

The memorialists offered as their reason for these requests that the appointment and authority of any bishop might be "rendered as free as possible from suspicion and odium" to their countrymen.

The Congregation *de Propaganda Fide* (hereafter cited as Propaganda), which had immediate jurisdiction over the Church in the United States until 1908, decided to comply with the desires of the American clergy and recommended that the Pope, "on this first occasion at least," permit the priests exercising the care of souls to nominate the bishop. Pius VI having given his consent, the cardinal-prefect of the Congregation, Leonardo Antonelli, replied to the memorialists on July 12, 1788, that "His Holiness, as a special favor and for this time," had sanctioned such an election.[3] Accordingly, when the priests met in their third General Chapter at Whitemarsh, Maryland, in May, 1789, they proceeded to elect the existing superior of the missions, John Carroll, as the first bishop of the new see which they wished to have located at Baltimore.[4]

Then, seizing the opportunity provided by the Holy See's favorable disposition, they passed several resolutions designed to ensure the continuance of episcopal elections by the clergy. They proposed that all "the clergymen of the United States living within a convenient distance from the residence of the bishop" and approved for the administration of the sacraments during the three years immediately preceding "ought to concur in the election of the bishop"; these clergymen were to be divided into groups of six, each of which would choose two electors; whenever a vacancy occurred or a new see was to be established, the electors were to meet and vote for some clergyman within the diocese; on the first two ballots two-thirds of the votes of all the electors present were to be required for election, but only a majority thereafter. If it should ever be thought proper to appoint a coadjutor, the ordinary was to convoke the electors and could recommend candidates to them; then the electors would vote, and the bishop also would cast a ballot.[5]

Although the Chapter asked that this plan be confirmed by the Holy See, it was not mentioned again. In fact, it was implicitly rejected in the papal brief *Ex hac apostolicae*, by which the Diocese of Baltimore was erected and Carroll was appointed the first bishop, for it was twice stated there that the priests had been permitted to elect their bishop "for the first time only" and by a special concession, and it was also laid down that in all future vacancies the bishop would be chosen by the pope.[6] For this first time, however, Pius VI ratified the priests' election of Carroll; he was even pleased that the clergy had concurred with the choice that he had made when he had appointed Carroll superior of the missions in 1784.

When in 1791, the year following his episcopal consecration, Bishop Carroll convoked the first synod, he asked the priests whether, in their opinion, the extensive diocese should be divided or a coadjutor should be named. He was advised to recommend to the Holy See the creation of a second diocese with its seat at Philadelphia or New York. Writing afterwards to the Propaganda, Carroll in his own name as well as in that of the priests requested the privilege of electing the bishop of the new see or, if the Holy See preferred, the coadjutor of Baltimore. It had been proposed by the synod that a nominating committee of fifteen priests should be named; ten of them should be those who had served the longest on the missions and the other five should be chosen by the bishop. The cardinals of the Propaganda decided that in order to introduce and preserve uniform discipline at the beginning, the diocese should not be divided yet but that a coadjutor should be appointed. Cardinal Antonelli replied, however, that the privilege granted for the one occasion of Carroll's election could not be permitted a second time even though a direct appointment by Rome might be interpreted by the enemies of the Church in the young republic as a violation of the spirit of the Constitution. The prefect, nevertheless, informed Carroll:

> This Sacred Congregation, therefore, with the express sanction of His Holiness, enjoins Your Lordship to consult with the older and more prudent priests of the diocese and to propose any priest in the American mission whom you think fit and capable; the Holy Father will then appoint him coadjutor with all necessary and seasonable faculties.[7]

Bishop Carroll conducted the prescribed consultation of the clergy in the form of an election. The priest whom he personally favored, Lawrence Graessl, a native of Bavaria then laboring in Philadelphia, was chosen by his fellow priests in May, 1793. When the Propaganda received Carroll's report of the election, it proceeded to have Graessl formally appointed a titular bishop and coadjutor to Carroll, but before its letters and the papal bull were even composed, the candidate died, in October, 1793, of yellow fever contracted while he was ministering to the victims of an epidemic in Philadelphia. The following year

Carroll apprised the Propaganda of the election of Leonard Neale, Graessl's successor as pastor of St. Mary's Church in Philadelphia, and the Holy See promptly complied with the request; because of the troubled conditions in Europe, however, the bulls of appointment were not received in the United States for five years.

Not only a coadjutor was requested by Carroll in 1793 but also a cathedral chapter. He considered it "very opportune and almost necessary that some sort of ecclesiastical group be formed in which, during the vacancy of the see [if there were no coadjutor with the right of succession], the power of administering the diocese may reside." He understood that in those circumstances a group of priests large enough to constitute a cathedral chapter could not reside in any one place such as Baltimore, and for this reason he asked the Congregation to authorize him to appoint ten or twelve priests who were in charge of the principal congregations in the diocese as a chapter for the consultation of the bishop. This position, he said, should be enjoyed by their successors; in turn they would choose their dean, and when the see was vacant they could attend to whatever might be necessary for the spiritual rule of the flock.[8]

This petition was discussed in a general congregation of the Propaganda, and its decision was subsequently approved by the Pope. Carroll was then informed that the plan should be deferred until he might have a larger number of priests so that some of them, less charged with the care of souls, might be able to reside in the same place. In the meantime he was permitted to set up an honorary chapter, lacking jurisdiction, which would consist of those priests and pastors whom he might see fit to choose. To provide for the government of the diocese in case the bishop should die without any successor or coadjutor having been named, Pope Pius VI ordered an extension of the bull *Ex sublimi* (January 26, 1753) of Pope Benedict XIV by which Carroll could designate the vicar general to function in the place and with the authority of a cathedral chapter.[9] Carroll did not make use of the authorization to establish an honorary chapter, probably because he thought that such a body would serve no purpose. In any case, it does not seem that the kind of chapter envisioned by Carroll would have been given any real share in his authority during his lifetime.

In 1807, when the Propaganda at last decided to divide the Diocese of Baltimore, it asked Carroll to recommend candidates for the new sees. Apparently without consulting the clergy, he proposed priests for the new dioceses of Boston, Philadelphia, and Bardstown, and the Holy See, without consulting Carroll, chose an Irish Dominican living in Rome as the first bishop of New York.[10] Thus the privilege that the priests enjoyed at the end of the eighteenth century was not extended into the nineteenth.

The new hierarchy that came into existence in the early 1800's probably saw little reason for allowing priests any formal part in the choice of candidates for the episcopacy. The bishops, many of whom had come from France, were intent upon preventing the disruptive interference of the Irish hierarchy in episcopal nominations, and they feared that the clergy, many of whom had come from Ireland, might change the Anglo-American character of the Church in this country by electing one of their fellow countrymen. Individual priests, nevertheless, sometimes wrote to the Propaganda, recommending candidates for vacant or new sees.[11]

With respect to parochial rights and clerical punishments it is to be remembered that there were no parishes in the canonical sense of the term, but only missions in the United States, with the exception of the parish in New Orleans and later of some in California. Hence, there were no pastors properly so called, but only rectors. The title of ordination for priests, moreover, was that of the mission (*sub titulo missionis*). In most dioceses, furthermore, there were not enough priests trained in canon law to conduct regular trials such as the law required for the removal of pastors.

Throughout the nineteenth century vocations to the priesthood in the United States were so few that the bishops were obliged to obtain a large part of their clergy from Europe. While many of these foreign priests came to this country with the purest and highest motives, others left their native lands because of troubles due to their own failings or misdeeds. In the free air and open spaces of the United States, the unruly dispositions of some priests developed to the point of insubordination. Hence, many of the bishops felt themselves bound by the duties of their office to rule their dioceses with an iron rod. They insisted that the extraordinary situation of the Church in the United States, as compared with so-called Catholic countries of Europe, where the bishops' coercive authority was in many ways enforced by the State, demanded a greater concentration of power in their hands.

Archbishop Carroll's second successor, Ambrose Maréchal, nevertheless, renewed the request for a chapter of canons. In 1820 he asked the Propaganda for permission to establish a chapter of eight or ten priests who would have all the rights and privileges of cathedral canons but, in view of the duties that they would have to discharge in far-flung missions, would not be held to the obligation of residence at the cathedral or of the office in choir. This body would advise him in the administration of the archdiocese, and after his death it would elect a vicar capitular who could govern the archdiocese during the vacancy.

The consultor whose opinion the Propaganda first requested and then adopted, Abbot Mauro Cappellari (later Pope Gregory XVI), expressed his opposition to the archbishop's proposal. His reasons were embodied in the reply sent in May, 1821, in which Maréchal was reminded that the kind of chapter of which he conceived was quite contrary to canon law, because it would not only lack an endowment and prebends but also would not share in the authority to administer the archdiocese; the canons, moreover, would not be bound to residence or to choir. Since bishops could not depart from the sacred canons on their own authority, Maréchal was admonished that he could not institute this new form of chapter without the special permission of the Holy See.

The cardinals of the Propaganda, however, did not deem it expedient that such authorization should be granted him, because, in their minds, it was neither necessary nor opportune. It was not necessary for the purpose intended, because he could appoint a council of ecclesiastics without calling them canons and sufficient provision was already made for a vicar capitular. Nor was it opportune, because this institution would imply a substantial innovation in the canonical discipline regarding the form and constitution of cathedral chapters; furthermore, it would injure the rights of those who in the present state of affairs could have a share in the election of a vicar capitular but would be excluded once the chapter were erected.

Hence, the archbishop was told that the kind of chapter which he had proposed could by no means be approved. If he should be able to satisfy the canonical requirements for the erection of a chapter, however, the Congregation said that it would not hold him back.[12] The Propaganda also refused his other request, namely, that European priests who were accepted into American dioceses should be obliged to stay there even against their will. This restraint on foreign priests was finally decreed by the First Provincial Council of Baltimore.

Maréchal's friend and confidant, the Vicar Apostolic of the London District, Bishop William Poynter, wrote him that summer:

> I have endeavored to support your cause with Card. Fontana by the strongest arguments & observations that I could propose. I see that those Roman Canonists are too much attached to certain *accidental* formalities, to know how to make allowances for Countries where the Catholic Religion is not publicly adopted in all its external forms. I have made some strong observations to

them on this subject & have urged the propriety & advantage of your having a Chapter, which will add dignity to your clergy & be a great support to your Grace's authority.[13]

In the autumn Maréchal's agent or procurator in Rome, Robert Gradwell, rector of the English College, resumed his efforts to obtain authorization for a cathedral chapter in Baltimore,[14] but he achieved no success. As it turned out, the Church in England was to institute cathedral chapters of canons in 1852, after the hierarchy was restored there, while a majority of the later American bishops did not share Archbishop Maréchal's belief in their necessity.

A demand for pastors enjoying full canonical rights was voiced directly to the pope by the trustees of St. Mary's Church in Philadelphia after their pastor, the Dominican priest, William Vincent Harold, had been suspended by the bishop, Henry Conwell, at the end of a protracted dissension on April 3, 1827. The second resolution contained in their memorial to Pope Leo XII was worded as follows:

> (2) That Your Holiness be pleased to annul the abuse by which it is now sought to hold the Second Order of the Priesthood in a state of servitude, not to the Canons, not to any law, but to absolute masters; that you re-establish their rights and cause their titles to be permanent, according to the wisdom of the Canons; that you prescribe a mode of trial for them conformable to those Canons, and consistent with the laws of these United States. We ask this not only for the Pastors of the Church of St. Mary's, but for all other Churches, which do now, or may hereafter afford a competent subsistence to the Pastor.[15]

Although the Holy See later heeded another of the trustees' pleas by withdrawing Bishop Conwell's jurisdiction over his diocese and appointing a coadjutor to govern in his place, it did not see fit to remove one of the causes of the unrest by allowing or commanding the bishops to appoint irremovable pastors.

Father Harold had appealed from Bishop Conwell to the metropolitan of the province, and when Archbishop Maréchal rejected his appeal, the Dominican replied with acerbity. He rebuked the prelate for calling "this country a mere land of missions where the priest employed in the sacred ministry 'can be removed at any time,'" and for supposing that such a system, though admittedly "obvious to some inconveniences," was still "the best to promote the good of Religion in a country like this." Harold refuted the argument which Maréchal had put forth by alleging a parallel between the Catholic Church in the United States and in England, and he added:

It would be difficult to account for the predilection of Your Grace in favour of a system of rule so incompatible with the very nature of your own title, if one did not know how strange are the effects of uncontrolled power on whoever has once exercised it, let his natural benevolence and wisdom be ever so genuine. It is in the very nature of man, when once raised above the level of his fellow creatures, to imagine the short road of absolute power to be the best for attaining the ends of government. . .

It is painful to look forward to the sort of clergy which this unmitigated despotism must produce; destroying as it must every principle of honest candour in the breast of its victim, withering the moral feeling which renders reputation dearer than life. Such men would become fit for any purpose however wicked in the hands of a bishop, divested himself of every sensibility except the sensibilities belonging to the worst passions . . . I would only ask, with what effect the Catholic Religion can be inculcated by a clergy debased by servile fear and rendered utterly heartless by this necessity of humoring a man whom no law restrains? Can the Catholic people listen with docility to the moral principles inculcated by men who dare not act towards each other on the principles which they inculcated? What is to become of the rising generation who can see nothing, hear nothing of the church which is to lead them to heaven, that does not put it in the aspect of a despotic government in which if the virtue of one Bishop promises to fructify, it must be in defense of the system, whilst the madness of another may lay waste the flock of Christ with impunity? . . .[16]

The Bishop of Charleston, John England, thought that this case should be referred to a provincial council, and he expected this procedure to show "all concerned that there was a tribunal at home to repress the excess of *any* individuals." [17] In the absence of such a council it is impossible to ascertain whether or not it could have been settled in that way without the scandalous notoriety that actually ensued before Harold finally returned permanently to Ireland.

The bishops of the United States first discussed among themselves in a formal way the problem of their relations with their priests in the First Provincial Council of Baltimore, which was held in 1829. The first decree that they drafted read as follows:

Because on many occasions some people have questioned the right of the bishops in these United States to assign priests to any part of their dioceses and to recall them thence, as they judge best under God, we order and declare that all priests who reside in these dioceses, whether ordained or adopted into them, are bound by the promise made in ordination to obey the bishop when he orders them to go to any mission in the diocese, where he judges that the priest will receive sufficient and proper support and where the work is proportioned to his abilities and health. By this declaration we do not wish to make any changes in regard to those who possess parochial benefices, of whom, up to now, only one is known in these regions, namely, in New Orleans. . . .[18]

Some annotations were added to the decrees of the Council by the secretary, John B. Damphoux, S.S., when the draft was submitted to the Sacred Congregation *de Propaganda Fide* for approval. In explanation of this first decree it was said that the purpose was to prevent priests from leaving their missions at will, as sometimes happened to the great harm of souls, and from taking up others at their own initiative, or from remaining in their positions with the support of the laity against the will of the bishop who would deem it necessary to remove them.

Pursuing this object of stronger discipline, the fathers ordered in their second decree:

that every priest ordained for any diocese in this Province is bound by the force of the promise made in ordination to stay in that diocese and obey his bishop until such time as he shall be canonically dismissed.

The also ordained "that the same obligation binds every priest who is adopted into a diocese." [19] Father Damphoux commented that this provision was directed against priests who through fickleness might abandon the diocese at whose expense they were educated.

Having received the draft of the decrees, the Propaganda asked the Bishop of New York, John Dubois, to submit his opinion. Bishop Dubois, who had not attended the council, was in Rome at the time. He stated that the first three decrees had been drawn up to check those foreign priests whose character was marked by boldness and erratic behavior, and who had come to the new world in search of good places. The French-born bishop remarked that such undesirable priests came "mainly from Ireland," and he grouped them into three classes. In the first were the ignorant, with no hope of finding a good assignment in their homeland, and they caused much trouble. Secondly, there were those of clouded reputation, whose superiors had given them an *exeat* just to be rid of them; these needed cautious treatment in America. Finally, those who had fled their native land because of a ruined reputation should not, in Dubois's opinion, be accepted by any bishop. From his own bitter experience the Bishop of New York could speak with authority.[20]

In the meeting of the Sacred Congregation, Cardinal Pietro Caprano, the *ponens*, observed that the first decree intended to canonize the system by which the priests, as missionaries, performed their ministry at the will of the bishop. He objected, however, to the Council's deducing the movability of priests at the will of the bishop from the solemn promise of obedience made by priests at their ordination as if by that promise they were obliged to accept any mission that the bishop might assign to them within the diocese. The cardinal quoted Pope Benedict XIV's explanation of the ordination oath:

> Nor do we think that one should hold as a bare, empty formula that solemn promise of obedience and reverence which the priest makes in the hands of the ordaining bishop in keeping with the most hallowed custom of the Church, but rather we hold readily that the priest, by virtue of the same promise, is bound by this law, among others, that he should not leave the service of the church for which he was ordained without the permission of the bishop.[21]

Hence, as was stated in the Instruction subsequently issued by the Propaganda, the fathers of the council seemed to speak about that obedience in a stricter way than Benedict XIV had done. The Congregation, therefore, decided that the following words should be substituted: "We admonish the priests that mindful of the promise made at ordination, they refuse not to accept whatever mission the bishop may designate." [22] This change made the decree hortatory rather than mandatory as it had been in its original tenor. The American bishops amended the decree in the prescribed way; they could still insist on their right freely to appoint priests to missions and to transfer them but they could not base their claim to obedience so directly on the ordination oath.

Cardinal Caprano also brought to the attention of the Congregation a letter written in the closing hours of the council by Francis Patrick Kenrick, an Irish priest who had studied at the Propaganda's Urban College in Rome, had come to labor in Kentucky, was professor of theology at St. Thomas' Seminary, and was serving as the theologian of the Bishop of Bardstown, Benedict Joseph Flaget. Commenting on the council, Kenrick said that no decree had been made on the establishment of parishes (instead of missions), although Bishop England was of the private opinion that they should be established in order that the condition of religion might be stable and that the pastors might not be removed except for canonical causes. The other bishops, however, held the contrary opinion, especially the Archbishop of Baltimore, James Whitfield, who maintained that only faculties which could be revoked *ad libitum* should be granted to all priests. Hence, all priests enjoyed only delegated authority (with the sole exception of the pastor of New Orleans), and therefore the bishop at his will or according to the deserts of the priests or the circumstances could remove and transfer them without stating any reason. Kenrick added:

> Since the Protestants are wont to stir up ill-will against the Church among the people who are so fond of liberty and republican government by asserting that everything in the Church is managed tyrannically and arbitrarily, it seems right to me and likely to benefit our cause that the condition of pastors which is in force throughout the whole Church should be set up also in these States. It seems to me that the advice of Pope Benedict XIV on the use of extrajudicial suspension greatly favors the opinion of the Bishop of Charleston on preserving the system of trials in general. These two things, namely, the establishment of parishes and the system of trials, although distinct in themselves, are connected in these circumstances. For if parishes are not established, the bishops will continue, without any kind of trial, to withdraw faculties, as they say, without inflicting suspension. Thus no alternative is left to the priest but to depart from the diocese, if permission to leave is granted him. And his condition is worse than that of a suspended priest if permission to depart is denied him, and it could happen that an innocent priest would thus be deprived of every sacred office by the decision of the bishop and also of every means of support.[23]

As an example Kenrick cited the appeal made to the council by a priest of New York, John Farnan, who claimed that he had wrongly been suspended by his bishop.

The biographer of Bishop England and historian of the Councils of Baltimore, Peter Guilday, praised the First Provincial Council for its "efforts to create uniformity of Church law for the United States and to bring the American Church into closer union with the Holy See" and for its "sturdy reminder to malcontents among clergy and laity that the days of rebellion and disorder were passing." He added this observation:

> Had the bishops gone a step further and given the pastors a canonical status, as Dr. England earnestly urged in the private sessions of the Council, it would have brought much satisfaction to the clergy who realized their helpless position in case justice demanded an appeal to a higher ecclesiastical court. . . . Apart from this one door left open for the entrance of further disorder, the decrees of the Council, while rigid in many respects, were productive of immeasurable good to a Church which was then on the eve of a remarkable period of progress.[24]

Though aware of the difficulties, the Propaganda did not alter the decrees of the First Provincial Council of Baltimore in this respect.

In analyzing the causes which had impeded the progress of the Church in the United States for the previous decade, Bishop England wrote to the Propaganda in 1833 that the successors of Archbishop John Carroll in Baltimore had not been the best fitted for that position, and that many other nominations to bishoprics were not well received and did not turn out well. He intimated, "Although the priests have not yet spoken openly on this matter, nevertheless, it would be leading the Holy See into error to say that either the clergy or the great body of the laity is content with nominations procured privately." Bishop England also set forth another grievance of the clergy:

> Many priests complain that while the hierarchy is fully established in regard to Bishops, nothing has yet been done in regard to priests. They have only delegated jurisdiction which can be taken from them at the pleasure of the Bishops, and has frequently been so taken, without any chance for appeal, since no censure was inflicted. This power, up to a certain point, is absolutely required, as all confess; but many are of opinion that it would be well to form some parishes, and thus to give to the American Church a more perfect form, and to the older and more experienced among the clergy a more respectable standing.[25]

In the other provincial councils of Baltimore held during England's lifetime and after his death up to 1849, however, no measures were taken to remove these grounds for dissatisfaction. These first seven provincial councils of Baltimore in effect were national councils inasmuch as they legislated for the whole Church in the United States which made up only one province.

Between the Second and Third Provincial Councils of Baltimore the first episcopal council in the United States was created in the Diocese of Mobile. At Bishop Michael Portier's first synod, celebrated at Spring Hill, Alabama, in January, 1835, it was decreed that two priests appointed by the bishop together with the vicar general should constitute the episcopal council, should meet on the second Thursday of every month (whether the bishop was present or not) to discuss affairs pertaining to the welfare of the diocese, and should be invested with the faculties granted by law *"in pari casu"* (which probably meant that they should have some of the rights and duties of cathedral chapters).[26] Episcopal councils, or boards of consultors, nevertheless, did not become common, even in the large dioceses, until after the First Plenary Council of Baltimore.

In the same year as the First Provincial Council of Baltimore was held, the Propaganda approved a new method of choosing candidates for vacant sees in Ireland. Since many American clergymen later in the century were to regard this method as a model worthy of imitation in the United States, it should briefly be explained here. The plan was originally proposed to the Congregation by the Irish episcopate as a way of striking a balance between the higher and lower clergy in the choice of nominees. According to this method whenever a see became vacant the vicar capitular (or administrator if there was no cathedral chapter) informed the metropolitan (or the senior suffragan if the metropolitan see was vacant) of the death of the bishop and of his own election for the interim government of the diocese. The archbishop (or senior suffragan) then directed the vicar capitular (or administrator) to convoke all those who had a right to participate in drawing up the *terna* twenty days later. If a coadjutor was to be appointed, the bishop was to call the meeting.

On the appointed day the archbishop (or one of the suffragans delegated by him for this purpose) went to the place to preside over the voting. The body composing the *terna* consisted not only of the canons (if there was a chapter in the diocese) but also of all the parish priests (pastors). The necessary quorum consisted of one-fourth of those entitled to be present; however, absences had to be explained in order to preclude the danger of fraud. Each voter, after affirming under oath that he would act according to his mind and conscience without human calculation, wrote three names on the same ballot. After the votes were counted, the presiding prelate announced the names of the three candidates who had polled the largest number of votes. After the *procès-verbal* of the voting was composed and signed in duplicate one copy was sent immediately by the vicar capitular to the Holy See, and the other was kept by the archbishop.

Ten days later the metropolitan convoked his suffragans, read to them the *procès-verbal* of the voting, and requested their opinions of the three candidates. Their comments were written in a document which was then signed by all the comprovincials, sealed by the metropolitan, and sent to the Holy See. If the opinion of the bishops was not favorable to any of the candidates proposed by the lower clergy no other names could be substituted; in this case the pope would provide for the vacant see according to his own wisdom.[27] Although in practice the Holy See sometimes appointed a priest not included in the *terna* it could not easily act with such independence for lack of adequate information. In effect the part played by Rome in the choice of bishops for Irish sees was greatly reduced for many years after 1829.[28]

American Catholics also closely observed developments among their coreligionists in England. When Pope Pius IX restored the Catholic hierarchy in that country in 1850, many English priests expected to receive the rights of pastors, and a group of them sent to the Holy See a petition for the appointment of parish priests who would not be removable at the bishop's will; they also asked that the election of the bishop should rest with the priests of each diocese.[29] However, they were to be disappointed in these hopes.

The English diocesan chapters, consisting ordinarily of ten canons and a provost or dean, were, indeed, established along with the residential sees. When a bishop was to be named, the chapter was to meet under the presidency of the archbishop or senior bishop and by separate ballots to choose three candidates. The names were to be arranged in alphabetical order, and the list was then to be discussed by the bishops of the province who were to forward it to Rome with their comments on each candidate.[30]

At the First Provincial Council of Westminster held at St. Mary's College, Oscott, in July, 1852, the question of establishing canonical parishes was raised but action was deferred because the bishops believed that most of the missions were not yet established solidly enough to be made canonical parishes; the possibility, however, of later applying the ordinary law of the Church to England in this respect was left open.[31] As a compromise, which was declared in the acts to be a step toward the gradual introduction of the parochial system, it was decreed that some churches should be selected to be regarded as quasi-parishes *(ad instar paroeciarum)*; their rectors were to be permanently appointed, that is, they were to be declared irremovable except for some specified offenses. In the diocesan synod, moreover, the bishop was to choose priests of approved goodness to form a commission of investigation; a permanently appointed rector could not be definitively deposed until at least three of these five had examined the case and had given their counsel to the bishop.[32] The council did not determine the procedure, but it deputed a committee of bishops to draw up a proposal.

The priests who had previously petitioned the Pope now requested clearer regulations. In the following year Cardinal Nicholas Wiseman, Archbishop of Westminster, transmitted a suggested form of procedure to Rome and it was approved by the Propaganda. Although it did not provide for a judicial trial, it defined better the mode in which an investigation was to be conducted before a missionary rector could be removed from office.[33] The English priests were still not satisfied, however, for they wanted the parochial system in its entirety.

Part II: From the First Plenary Council to the Second

In 1852 the first plenary council in the United States was held at Baltimore under the presidency of Francis Patrick Kenrick, Archbishop of Baltimore, as apostolic delegate. It was then decreed that bishops should be exhorted, where it was possible, to choose priests suitable by reason of their age, knowledge, blameless life, and administrative ability, and to appoint them consultors; and afterwards to request their opinion when there was a need of it in the administration of the diocese. The fathers of the council also praised the custom, which existed in some places, of holding a meeting of the consultors at least once a month on a fixed day to discuss the affairs of the diocese.[34] This decree, it would seem, was enacted more for the purpose of procuring assistance to the bishops than of sharing their responsibility with their priests. In the fourth and fifth public congregations, held on Thursday and Friday afternoons, May 13 and 14, 1852, the theologians, in the presence of all the bishops and the superiors of religious orders, debated the expediency of appointing canonical pastors in these provinces.[35] Those theologians who took the affirmative side, however, failed to convince the bishops.

After the first plenary council the bishops entrusted the decrees and the petitions for the erection of new sees to the Bishop of Chicago, James Oliver Van de Velde, who was to take them to Rome and see to their final approval. The Prefect of the Propaganda, Cardinal Giacomo Fransoni, sent them for evaluation and criticism to the highly esteemed Jesuit theologian, Giovanni Perrone. Van de Velde also submitted his personal opinions, which in some respects were contrary to the decisions of the majority of the American hierarchy. He informed Perrone that the decree exhorting bishops to appoint consultors was designed to keep bishops informed of diocesan affairs as well as to guard against episcopal arbitrariness. Perrone suggested that the words "where it can be done" be inserted into the decree because he doubted the possibility of finding suitably gifted priests in all cases. Van de Velde also suggested as an addition to the decrees that priests should be appointed pastors in the canonical sense "where it can be done" in order to give them more stability and security, but Perrone merely advised that any arbitrary removal of a priest from a church be guarded against.[36] Hence, the First Plenary Council brought little personal or canonical satisfaction to the American priests.

After the Council Francis Patrick Kenrick wrote to his brother, Peter Richard, who was Archbishop of St. Louis, "For the present I think it is not advisable to plan the establishment of a Cathedral Chapter. It will surely be put off." He believed, however, that "a few priests, rectors of churches, or others holding office" in the archdiocese could be associated with the archbishop "as a counseling board according to the Law" (probably the civil law), "or in some other way constituted by a charter." Francis Patrick further advised his brother to consult a prudent lawyer and added, "Later on perhaps it may be well to erect a Chapter after the way of those erected in England, but in the meantime we must make provision for the security of the temporal goods of the church." He suggested that Peter Richard bring the matter "before a provincial council for full consideration in order to insure the approval of the Holy See." [37]

Later that year a priest of the Diocese of Pittsburgh who had traveled about discussing with his colleagues the question of their position vis-à-vis the bishops wrote to the respected old missionary Thomas Heyden:

> All the Priests with whom I conversed on my tour seem to feel the necessity of taking some step towards obtaining the rights of the clergy. But are at a loss to know the best means of obtaining this most desirable object. I have been told that the *Nuntio* [*sic*] *intimated* to some respectable clergymen of New York that something of this kind is in contemplation, and probably forms a part of the object of his mission. Be this as it may — Archbishop

Hughes has positively forbid [*sic*] any of his clergymen either to speak or write any thing on this subject.

The writer wondered what "the best or most prudent course" might be for the priests to pursue under these circumstances.[38] The American priests were to remain in this quandary for many years.

The nuncio of whom this priest wrote was Archbishop Gaetano Bedini, who had been sent by the Holy See in 1853 to visit the United States en route to his diplomatic post in Brazil. He was instructed to observe the condition of the Church in this country and to try to win the federal government's assent to the establishment of a nunciature in Washington. He traveled extensively and in several places barely escaped physical injury at the hands of rabid Know-Nothings and European revolutionary exiles. Returning to Rome, Bedini drew up a long report dated July 12, 1854, and submitted it to the Cardinal Secretary of State and to the Cardinal Prefect of the Propaganda. In treating of the relations between American bishops and priests, he wrote:

> . . . it is important to speak about the clergy's great depen-dence on the Bishops. Opinion is divided about this. It seems that the priests during their ministry do not have the full guarantee of security which Canon Law gives them, and their positions may be changed from one moment to the next. There are no parishes but missions, and so, the priests assigned to them find themselves in such a precarious position that they always fear an immediate change. Is this system expedient or not? I must confess that I thought it imprudent to give a decisive ruling on this. There are "pros" and "cons." [39]

After describing the three principal dangers to priests in America, Bedini continued:

> . . . it is difficult for a priest to work hard in his mission, to build churches and schools at great sacrifice, to obtain the good will of the parishioners and then suddenly to be transferred by the unexpected inclination of the Bishop. We cannot suppose that these transfers are the result of mere whim; on the contrary, they surely suggest a good which is more pressing and more lasting. But the priest always considers the possibility of a transfer and prepares himself beforehand by accumulating money so that he will be prepared for any eventuality, or he performs his duties carelessly. For these, detachment and zeal are precious qualities.

The lack of Chapters puts all the administration of the Diocese in the hands of the Bishops. Their priests therefore have no knowledge of the progress nor even of the resources of the Diocese. They only know that the Bishop controls what he is doing (if you pardon the terms) and so it causes them to fear his arbitrary power; and in that country more than others, this is the most horrible supposition. To tell the truth, though, there was no reason to think that any Bishop was guilty of this injurious supposition. They are all loved by their priests. . .

More than one ecclesiastic of high rank, speaking of this power of the Bishops without complaining of any abuses, showed the burning desire that the presence of a Nuncio, the Pontifical Representative in that vast country, would mitigate this power. This desire is so strong and so general among the American priests that if the Holy See would disregard it, it would lose their affection, which it now has.[40]

This desire for a papal representative residing in the United States, nevertheless, was not to be realized for four decades. It is apparent from the report that on his tour Bedini, as an impartial observer, spoke not only with bishops but also with priests.

In 1855 the provincial councils that were held in Baltimore and St. Louis advanced the legislation affecting priests. The Eighth Provincial Council of Baltimore, recalling the sixth decree of the First Plenary Council, exhorted bishops to increase the number of consultors to ten or twelve without obliging them to ask the opinion of each consultor on every matter even if it be important. They thought that it would be sufficient to refer each question to three or four consultors. The fathers of the council then stated:

> It will be the duty of all the consultors, however, after the death of the bishop, to make known in writing to the archbishop (or, if he has died, to the senior bishop) who each one thinks should be promoted to the vacant see. Let them also add the reasons for their opinion and any other information which may be useful to the bishops so that they may be able to recommend worthy priests to the Apostolic See.

They repeated that they did not wish to lay down any fixed law about either the number or the duties of the consultors, and especially not about the recommendations for the episcopate, but rather they left it "to the prudence and the conscience of each bishop." [41]

This decree had been proposed by a committee of which the Bishop of Pittsburgh, Michael O'Connor, was the spokesman. The rest of the fathers adopted it only after some discussion. The Bishop of Wheeling, Richard Vincent Whelan, recommended that the new consultors whom the bishop was to add to the existing body should be regarded as supernumerary, especially if they resided outside the see city, and that they should give their advice only in those cases in which the bishop might wish to consult them; when a vacancy occurred they could write to the archbishop, expressing their opinion about a suitable successor. The Bishop of Philadelphia, John Nepomucene Neumann, saw no need for additional consultors; he thought it would be enough for the existing three or four to send to the archbishop the names of those whom they wished to have recommended for the see. John McGill, the Bishop of Richmond, on the contrary, maintained that each priest of the diocese should be asked to express his opinion individually to the archbishop. In the end the decree was approved by the unanimous consent of the fathers.[42]

When the decrees of this Eighth Provincial Council were submitted to the Propaganda, they were handed over to a consultor for examination. He reported that in his judgment the proposed method of allowing the diocesan consultors to present their opinions of candidates for a vacant see would be most useful by reason of "the more exact knowledge which is ordinarily wont to be found in the lower clergy of the needs of the diocese as well as of the qualities which are particularly to be desired in the new bishop." He did not recommend, however, that the decree should be declared obligatory for all the bishops, especially for those outside the Province of Baltimore.[43] Following this advice, the cardinals of the Propaganda decided to leave it to the conscience and prudence of each bishop to allow the diocesan consultors to make the first proposal of candidates; they added that the bishops of the province should also take into consideration the candidates found on the list of the deceased bishop.[44] No other ecclesiastical province adopted this farsighted decree.

In the same year, 1855, the First Provincial Council of St. Louis enacted a decree determining a new procedure for the trials of priests accused of crimes. The bishops declared first: "Priests who by sentence of the ordinary have been forbidden to exercise the sacred ministry have no right to ask support from him because by their own fault they have rendered themselves incapable of working on the missions." [45] In order to remove all grounds for complaints, however, the bishops prescribed the form of trial which the ordinaries should observe in criminal cases of clerics or priests. According to the original tenor of the decree the ordinary or the vicar general delegated by him for this purpose was to choose two or three priests who were to assist him in judging an accused priest; at least one of them should (*debeat*) sustain the bishop's verdict, but if all of them disagreed with him, the case was to be referred to the metropolitan, who would weigh the reasons for the divergent opinions and give his own decision. If the case involved a subject of the metropolitan and all three consultors disagreed with him, it was to be referred to the senior suffragan bishop of the province, and his decision was to be final, without prejudice to the authority of the Holy See.[46]

After the decrees of this council had also been submitted to the Propaganda for confirmation, they were subjected to the scrutiny of the same consultor. In his opinion, the choice of the assistant judges (assessors) should not be simply left to the bishop but rather should be restricted to a certain group of persons who, by reason of the legitimate representation with which they were permanently invested, would be more acceptable, or at least not suspect, to the accused. Accordingly, he recommended that the bishop should normally choose his assessors from among the diocesan consultors, and that he should at first choose only two (in order to avoid the inconvenience of a tied vote); if the third assessor was excluded from the first judicial hearing it would also be unnecessary to say, as did the original decree, that at least one of the assessors had to support the judgment to be pronounced by the bishop or the vicar general — which, besides, would be odious to the accused. If both the assessors disagreed with the bishop in the first hearing, a third could be employed in a second hearing before the case would be referred to the metropolitan.

The consultor of the Propaganda also advocated an express mention of the presence of the notary or chancellor which was necessary for the legal composition of court records. Accordingly, he proposed the following revision of the decree: the bishop, or at his commission the vicar general, was to choose two of the bishop's consultors, and not always the same ones, who were to assist him in the presence of his notary in judging a priest accused of a crime; each was to have one vote, and either one could agree with the bishop; but if they both disagreed with him, he was to choose a third from among his consultors, and the case would be settled on the side with which the third consultor agreed. If, however, all three consultors should disagree with the bishop, then the case was to be referred to the metropolitan. Finally, the consultor suggested that the amended decree be extended to all the dioceses of the United States with the added injunction of raising the number of consultors to a level in keeping with the state of each diocese.[47]

Since the consultor's recommendation was espoused by the prefect, Cardinal Alessandro Barnabò,[48] it was also approved by the rest of the members of the Sacred Congregation.[49] Afterwards Barnabò explained to the Archbishop of St. Louis the reasons for the changes that had been made in the original wording. He also asked Kenrick to send copies of the revised decree to the other metropolitans of the United States, because the Congregation wished it to be recommended to them too. [5] Even with the improvements introduced by the Propaganda for the sake of justice and equity, however, the procedure was still so heavily weighted on the side of episcopal authority that it could hardly have been thought likely to redress the grievances of the clergy.

American priests became more and more dissatisfied with the way in which their bishops were chosen. For example, the Bishop of Hartford, Bernard O'Reilly, who was lost at sea in 1856, had continually fought with his clergy, and their quarrels had often been publicized in the newspapers. After his death an anonymous commentator wrote (in Italian) to the Propaganda:

> It seems to many that one of the principal reasons for this discord between bishops and priests in America is the manner in which bishops are named at present. The priests, being entirely excluded from any part in the naming of bishops, complain that the bishops, in naming new bishops, always choose those of their party, that they never pay attention to the qualities of the candidate; it is enough that he be a favorite. Thus old priests and good missionaries are governed by young bishops without much experience; hence, these bishops are never either respected or obeyed as they ought to be; hence the quarrels and often also the scandals with great harm to the Church.

This writer thought that the question of the naming of bishops in America had become more important and more intricate because of the growth of nativism, and he suggested that the time had come to grant the priests a share in the process.[51]

About the same time three pastors of the Diocese of Hartford presented their views on the choice of a new bishop to Archbishop Bedini, who had meanwhile become the secretary of the Propaganda. They criticized their deceased bishop for his ignorance and requested a scholar as his successor. After mentioning other faults, they continued:

. . . those petty [?] evils are not confined to our diocese alone. The case is the same in many other dioceses, especially in those lately formed in this country. To administer the highest offices in the church Priests have been appointed and consecrated who had always been regarded by their brethren as men of very moderate acquirements and of no extraordinary piety. In most cases the announcement of their elevation surprised the clergy they were thenceforward to govern. Each one thought himself to be as pious and as learned and as zealous as his ordinary and relied as much if not more upon his own opinion than upon the direction of authority, and therefore the necessary cooperation of the one with the other was not produced, causing as we have already intimated dissension and discontent. The cause of this misery may be traced to the irregular manner in which Bishops are appointed in this country. They are generally favorites of the appointing dignitary, favorites by reason of personal predilection or on account of their wealth, circumstances which weigh heavily in the consideration of the patron if we may judge by the selections which have recently been made to fill the episcopal sees recently erected in many parts of the country. We mention this matter not with the spirit of criticizing the conduct of Rome in its judgment, God forbid! but we only mean that perhaps necessary information may sometimes be withheld, information which if known might have induced the proper confirming authority to have acted otherwise. These are simply our own [?] conjectures.[52]

In reply Bedini praised their zeal for the prosperity and growth of the Catholic religion and promised to report to the Sacred Congregation what they had confidentially written him.[53] Hence, it is clear that the Propaganda did not listen only to the bishops.

A few months later the well-known Italian Dominican, Samuel Mazzuchelli, who by this time had been a missionary in the Middle West for twenty-nine years, informed Bedini that the Catholic newspapers had reported that Rome intended to change the manner of naming bishops for the Church in the United States. He pointed out that in this process the bishops did not ask the slightest advice of any priest, and he proceeded to describe the disadvantages of the existing method:

The Propaganda should not be surprised if matters of such importance, handled without a certain round [of inquiries], in such great secrecy, and often by a single head, are not in this

country as they could and should be. If the naming of bishops
were a part of the episcopal ministry, I would not have a word to
say. . . . For now I shall content myself with writing that the
episcopate is too high here and the clergy too low, and that a
newly ordained priest without experience and also without learning, in the eyes of the Church, has all the rights and is worth as
much as a priest with fifty years of laborious and useful ministry.
In my opinion, I see too much on one side and nothing at all on
the other — a sure cause of the clergy's indifference toward the
diocese. This contrast between the bishop and the clergy becomes
a little odious in a country where the republican political spirit
desires to see a little more republicanism also in the Church —
something that would make a better clergy in the United States.

Mazzuchelli offered to write "a little article on the naming of bishops
for this republic and the part that the clergy ought to have in it." [54]
Without explicitly accepting this offer, Bedini replied that he had
reflected on the observations sent him and would submit them to the
Sacred Congregation at the first opportunity. [55]

Here and there incidents occurred which illustrated the defects in
the existing method of choosing candidates for the episcopacy. In 1858
the Bishop of Pittsburgh, Michael O'Connor, desired a coadjutor because of his impaired health. The bishops of the province thereupon
submitted to the Propaganda a *terna* consisting of three brothers of
American prelates, namely, Edward Purcell, brother of the Archbishop
of Cincinnati, Benedict Spalding, brother of the Bishop of Louisville,
and James O'Connor, brother of the Bishop of Pittsburgh. Bishop
O'Connor recommended to the Congregation not his own brother,
whose name was third on the list, but rather Father Purcell.[56] Since
the bishop, however, had previously asked his consultors to send Archbishop Kenrick their opinions of Purcell, Spalding, and three priests of
the diocese, none of whose names appeared on the final *terna*, the
rumor was now spread that he was trying to have his brother appointed,
for the latter's name had been substituted for the other three. One of
these, therefore, Thomas Heyden, who had declined an appointment to
the See of Natchez many years previously, [57] now complained to his
old friend, the Archbishop of New York, John Hughes. The archbishop
replied that since Pittsburgh was not one of his suffragan sees,
this matter was none of his business but that Heyden might write to the
Propaganda; then he added:

The time is rapidly coming when by necessity of circumstances the Priesthood of this country will have as their rightful privilege the opportunity of making known to the Holy See their sense of duty and their wishes, under the guidance of a good conscience in regard to the Prelates who are to be appointed as successors of those who are now burthened with the Episcopacy.[58]

The Holy See subsequently named Edward Purcell, but he refused the appointment.

In the following spring Bishop O'Connor submitted his resignation to the Pope, but the prefect of the Propaganda was unwilling to let it be accepted. The cardinal-prefect recommended that O'Connor appoint a priest to take charge of the diocese for a while. Archbishop Kenrick, interpreting the prefect's mind, advised O'Connor to name his brother James vicar general and to hand the administration over to him.[59] Bishop O'Connor followed his metropolitan's advice and then sailed for Europe.

In his absence the inexperienced administrator through his lack of ability and use of severity irritated many priests of the diocese. When Michael O'Connor returned in 1860 he was so distressed by the attitude of the clergy that he again tendered his resignation and proposed three entirely different candidates to the Propaganda through Archbishop Kenrick. This step having become known, Heyden inquired about the proper role of the consultors in the choice of the new bishop. Michael O'Connor replied that the Eighth Provincial Council had not intended, or at least had not required, "that all or any names contemplated should be submitted to them, but merely that they should have an opportunity of suggesting any they thought fit." He said that he had gone beyond this requirement in 1858, notifying them of all the names he had in mind in order that they might be able to express their desire for any of those mentioned. He believed that the opinions then manifested were still valid, and he saw no reason for repeating "the course recommended by the Council." [60]

The clergy of Pittsburgh were not pleased with O'Connor's refusal to give the consultors another opportunity to present their views on the choice of his successor. Tobias Mullen, one of those whom he had suggested in 1858, commented in a letter to Heyden:

It is a curious thing if notwithstanding the decree on the subject our good Bishop can resign in favor of any one without consulting his Priests about the matter. . . We ought to have a Nuncio in this country who would from time to time furnish Rome with a correct report on the state of affairs. Were some arrangement of this kind made, such a case as ours could scarcely occur.[61]

As soon as Michael O'Connor's resignation was accepted by the Holy See, Archbishop Kenrick appointed James O'Connor administrator of the diocese and ordered him to submit to the consultors the three names proposed by the former bishop.[62] Although Kenrick directed that no other letter than the one containing the opinion of the majority of the consultors should be sent to him or to Rome, Bishop O'Connor told the clergy in the meantime that he did not consider it improper for any or all of them to write to the metropolitan, not only giving their opinions of the candidates on the *terna* but also suggesting others whom they might wish to be considered.[63]

Archbishop Kenrick was unwilling to let the privilege of recommending candidates be extended to all the priests of the diocese, but he directed the administrator to increase the number of consultors and to allow them to name additional candidates. After Bishop O'Connor had opened the floodgates, however, not even the metropolitan could prevent the rest of the priests of the diocese from taking advantage of the opportunity. Kenrick wrote him later, "It was not the intention of the council that all the clergy should be consulted, but they all poured in their letters, some of them repeatedly." [64] The bishops of the province considered the candidates proposed by the Pittsburgh clergy and even named one of them on their own *terna* (in first place), but in the end a Vincentian, unknown to most of the priests of the diocese, Michael Domenec, was appointed to the vacant see.

During this episode Louis Leitner, a German alumnus of the Urban College of the Propaganda, wrote to Archbishop Bedini, secretary of the Propaganda. Leitner had gone to Pittsburgh in 1846 but had departed almost immediately. He had been a professor of Scripture for several years at Mount St. Mary's Seminary in Emmitsburg and at this time was a pastor in the Diocese of Philadelphia. He called the Congregation's attention to the method of choosing bishops for the United States, which may have been wise, he admitted, at a time when the number of bishops, priests, and dioceses was small, but now needed to be altered to fit the new circumstances. Having established with various proofs his loyalty to episcopal government, Leitner explained how it sometimes happened that all or nearly all the priests of a diocese were opposed to the bishop:

> Suppose that the Diocese [*sic*] of New York becomes vacant. Two or three neighboring bishops, that is, 400 or 500 furlongs

[*stadii*] away, prepare to choose a successor for the diocese without being acquainted with the present circumstances and needs and without knowing the dispositions and the character of about a hundred priests whom they must govern. Every new bishop, deeming himself more Catholic, more zealous, more judicious than his predecessor, begins by making new rules and constitutions. One sets up what the other thought it good to knock down. The consequences are incalculable — disobedience, lack of respect for the episcopal character, satires in the public newspapers, discontent, and — believe me — even invective against the Propaganda and the Holy See. And who can put the whole blame on them if, seeing among themselves [priests] more worthy either by reason of labors sustained on the missions or by reason of their superior abilities, they see an entirely incompetent stranger put over them. I said "incompetent" because, seeing a large number of the individuals promoted to episcopal sees, I shall say, and I say it with the most profound conviction, that if they had been examined at Rome, a third of them would not have been admitted even to ordination, not a few would have been found lacking in common sense, so that by way of merits it seems that the bishop-electors, in giving successors to vacant sees, have sought no other qualification than that of the male sex.

Then after inveighing against the reluctance of bishops to listen to the advice of even their oldest priests, Leitner continued:

I know well that in the present circumstances it would be very dangerous to leave the election of bishops in the hands of priests. . . If the present system cannot be changed, at least those chosen should be obliged to go to Rome and to undergo an examination — at the expense of the bishop-electors, who will then be careful not to propose incompetent persons. If this appears excessive, let them oblige those chosen to undergo an examination here before persons delegated for the purpose and for each case by the Propaganda. Let there be given at least to the pastors, if not to the [whole] clergy of the diocese, if not the nomination, at least the privilege of accepting *per modum suasionis* to be limited by the Propaganda. Or if nothing else, let the bishop-electors be constrained to publish the names they have chosen two or three months before sending them to Rome, so that whoever may know something to their discredit may have time to make it known to the Propaganda. The sooner some reform is made in this regard, the better it will be for the Church in America.[65]

Certainly the Propaganda did not lack for information from eye-witnesses.

Moved by some unfortunate choices, the prefect of the Propaganda wrote to all the archbishops in the United States in 1859. He stated that notable defects had often occurred in the present system of recommending priests for the episcopate and that in spite of the Congregation's efforts to obtain adequate information about the candidates it happened not infrequently, as recent facts had proved, that men were proposed who lacked the necessary virtue or learning or spirit of self-denial and who knew nothing of the nature or needs of the dioceses over which they were to be set. He then asked each archbishop to consider the matter and to suggest in secret what he would judge necessary for the improvement of the system. [66]

Of the seven archbishops who replied, none recommended any participation of the dioceasan clergy in the procedure. Francis Patrick Kenrick suggested certain minor alterations but thought that the existing method should not be changed lightly, because it afforded an opportunity to gather the votes of the bishops and to explore the dispositions and desires of the clergy; apparently he was more interested in preserving the practice of his ecclesiastical province, which allowed a preliminary voice to the diocesan consultors, than in extending it to other provinces. [67] In any case, when the system was revised in 1861, provision was made for securing more accurate information about the candidates, but no specific functions were prescribed for the clergy of the diocese.

Meanwhile the request for cathedral chapters had again been urged by certain bishops. The initiative was taken this time by the Bishop of Santa Fe, John Baptist Lamy, who feared that priests who opposed him would not respect the authority of the priest whom he, before his death and by virtue of the faculties received from the Holy See, would appoint to govern the diocese during the vacancy, because the Mexicans were accustomed to see the vicar capitular elected according to the canons. Lamy's metropolitan, Archbishop Kenrick of St. Louis, not only endorsed his petition but also asked that cathedral chapters be erected in all, or at least in the principal, dioceses of the United States.

He buttressed his request with two arguments. First, the consultors of the bishops, not being recognized in canon law, were for that reason without any determined rights, while, on the contrary, canons of cathedrals had definite rights and really constituted the bishop's council. Secondly, the present state of the American dioceses seemed to require that the bishops in the management of temporal affairs be at the same time supported and to some extent limited by the chapters; this would help to remove the suspicion and odium that they incurred by acting alone and without any restraint.

Alluding, no doubt, to the Know-Nothing movement, Kenrick asserted that the administration of a diocese according to the common law of the Church would be more welcome and safe in the dangerous circumstances of that time: "If we were allowed, by means of a body of canons, to approximate more closely, so to speak, the feeling and legislation of this country, I believe that the unpopularity (*invidia*) which is now generated among non-Catholics (*apud exteros*) by the unlimited power of one man, as they say, would be diminished if we were to manage our affairs by means of a body, and the security of church property would also be better guaranteed." He also requested permission for the bishops to dispense the canons from the usual obligations, as was required by the condition of the American dioceses which lacked other benefices than those to which the care of souls was attached.[68]

The archivist of the Propaganda, who was asked to provide background for the cardinals, observed that although previous requests for cathedral chapters had been submitted by American bishops, none was marked by the peculiar circumstances adduced by the Bishop of Santa Fe. The archivist also pointed out that the Propaganda's main reason for not allowing the erection of cathedral chapters in the past had been that the canonical requirements could not be fulfilled and that in more recent times the Holy See had permitted exceptional arrangements for certain chapters, for example, in Canada, England, and some dioceses of Ireland. In regard to Kenrick's request the archivist emphasized the constant insistence of both the Propaganda and the American episcopate on uniformity of ecclesiastical discipline in all the provinces and dioceses of the United States. By quoting the decree (XXX) of the First Plenary Council in which it was said that a single norm for all the scattered dioceses could hardly be maintained otherwise than by discussion among all the bishops, he hinted that the matter of cathedral chapters could well be left to the Second Plenary Council, which was to be held ten years after the first, or four years from the time of his writing.[69] Evidently he convinced the cardinals that compliance with Lamy's and Kenrick's requests would not be consistent with this traditional policy, for when they considered the questions in a general congregation they decided that for the time being the erection of a cathedral chapter in Santa Fe or in St. Louis or in other dioceses of the United States was not expedient. [70]

When Archbishop Francis Patrick Kenrick revised his manual for seminarians and priests, *Theologia Moralis,* he advocated observance of the decree passed by his brother's provincial council. He stated quite candidly:

> In this country bishops are accustomed to "revoke the faculties" which they had granted to missionaries whenever they judge priests to be unworthy of their office; in this respect for the most part they do not observe the form of trial which, however, the Sacred Congregation *de Propaganda Fide* has signified should be observed hereafter when it approved the decree of the Council of St. Louis on criminal causes of clerics. Many distinguish this revocation of faculties from suspension.
>
> Many and serious reasons are alleged why bishops revoke faculties *ex informata conscientia.* . . . But to speak frankly, when no form of judicature is observed, occasions are given for disparaging the bishops as doing everything according to their own will; and by practically denying the remedy of appeal to the metropolitan, no other hope seems to be left to the accused except the undertaking of a journey to Rome.
>
> Hence, I think that the censure of suspension should normally be imposed after a duly conducted trial, as circumstances allow, so that the defendant may appeal to the metropolitan if he wishes, and by the metropolitan's judgment relief may be brought to the innocent if by chance the bishop has been deceived, or the accused may be confounded, so that it may be evident to all that he has been afforded another opportunity of vindicating himself. [71]

After this open admission by the Archbishop of Baltimore it would be difficult for the American prelates to deny that a problem existed.

Only one year later, in 1862, Orestes A. Brownson, the influential convert and apologist, trying to disavow the despotism imputed to the hierarchy by non-Catholics, had to refute a possible objection to his thesis by explaining the contemporary American situation. He admitted that the Church in the United States was "in an abnormal state," subject to the Propaganda as a missionary country, and he continued:

The canon law has not been generally introduced amongst us, and the power of the bishops is not restricted by its provisions. Each bishop is well-nigh absolute in his own diocese, and the freedom of the second order of the clergy has no security but in the will and conscience of the bishop. Their position, legally considered, is one of absolute dependence, and that dependence, instead of being mitigated, would seem to be, if possible, rendered more absolute by the canons and decrees of our own councils. The bishop can order a priest to any post he pleases, remove him when he pleases, and withdraw his faculties when he chooses, without being responsible to any one but to God, for he can do it without being obliged to assign any reason therefor, or convicted of violating any canon recognized as in force. A slight step in protection of the second order, we confess, has been taken in some provinces, but it is only a slight one, and we believe it is by no means recognized in all our provinces. We are far from saying or from insinuating that any bishop has ever abused his power, or ever will abuse it, but as long as he has despotic power, its influence will affect more or less unfavorably those subject to it, and we believe the spirit and tone of our clergy would be much elevated, their zeal increased, and their duties more cheerfully and energetically performed, if they had the protection they have in other countries where the canon law is in force. That the church approves the present order of things, we know is not true, because the very existence of canon law proves the contrary, and she evidently submits to it only as a present necessity, and as a provisional and temporary state of things. Of the necessity and advantage of it in the present state of things, we are not competent judges, and if we refer to the fact, it is solely to show our non-Catholic friends that they have no right to conclude from it any thing against our assertion that the government of the church is a government of law, not a government of persons, or of arbitrary will.[72]

The question of the relations between bishops and priests, therefore, appeared to be inescapable for any future national council.

The Second Plenary Council of the United States, which was held at Baltimore in 1866, was intended by the one who organized it and presided over it as apostolic delegate, Martin John Spalding, Archbishop of Baltimore, to provide a textbook of ecclesiastical legislation for the priests and seminarians of the country. In preparing the agenda for this council Archbishop Spalding in the autumn of 1865 solicited suggestions from his fellow bishops.[73] Archbishop Kenrick of St. Louis responded enumerating several topics which had been "suggested as of urgent necessity to be brought before the Council" at a meeting of bishops held on the day after the consecration of the new bishop of Nashville, Patrick A. Feehan. After the first two suggestions Kenrick set down these three:

> 3. The expediency of recognizing the inamovability of pastors, after a certain time during which, wither [?] as assistants or pastors, they may have been employed on the missions: say after ten years. By *inamovability* I understand non removal without a canonical cause duly established, or the consent of the party.

> 4. Experience has shown that for the want of the power to compel witnesses to attend and depose before the bishop and assessors against a priest, the form of trial as suggested by the Provincial Council of St. Louis, and recommended by the S. Congregation, cannot be always observed. It would be desirable if a course of proceedings conformable to our peculiar circumstances, and efficacious for the preservation of ecclesiastical discipline, were recommended by the Council and sanctioned by the Holy See. Thus would the complaints now so frequently made against our action in this matter be silenced. . .

> 5. A bishop ought to have a Chapter of Canons. They have them in England and Ireland. Why not have them here? We ought to adopt the practices which have the sanction of the Church in circumstances by no means essentially different from ours. At present too much power and too much responsibility are placed in the ordinary.[74]

The following spring, having been officially authorized by the Holy See to proceed, Spalding apportioned the topics among some of his fellow metropolitans. Kenrick promised to try to do what was expected of him and sketched the form that his ideas would take:

> I incline much to the introduction of the ecclesiastical system in its normal state, — parishes and parish priests, chapters and elections by chapters. I shall also propose that the Metropolitans be made delegates of the Apostolic See to take information and try bishops accused of crimes, the whole testimony and defense to be sent to Rome by a trustworthy priest, where the inculpated may appear and where the Holy Father will pronounce sentence.[75]

In his replies Spalding made no reference to these suggestions. Finally, in May, 1866, Kenrick submitted his draft of the parts assigned to him, expressing his "mortification at its smallness and unfitness to be placed among more full and worthier contributions." He added:

> Probably also I should apologize for the boldness of the changes I have proposed. The present mode of designating priests for the episcopate I regard as a failure; my experience has severely taught me the truth of a remark I once heard from a zealous priest; that the priests knew one another better than the bishops knew them. The impression is on my mind that in some communication from Rome, which possibly may be found in the Cathedral Archives of Baltimore, the mode suggested by me was mentioned in commendatory terms. . . . I say nothing about parish priests, because I could say nothing that you yourself did not already know. [76]

In reply Spalding praised Kenrick's "conciliatory exposition" as "admirably written," but he added:

> I trust you will, however, pardon me, if I offer some remarks on certain views taken by you, which, though well drawn out, are in my view, rather premature, & will not, I have reason to fear, meet the views of any considerable number of our Prelates. I refer chiefly to your plan for presenting candidates for the episcopacy, & to your idea in regard to parish priests.
> 1. The plan for presenting candidates, though Irish, is not in accordance with the General Catholic discipline, which embraces the chapter as a principal element; & as we propose to have chapters, it is inconsistent with our coming Church polity. Besides, as we have not parish priests, & cannot expect to have them, except *paullatim*, & for a considerable time to come, it is decidedly premature.
> 2. While I would favor the gradual creation of parish priests, beginning with the large cities, & legislating in that direction also for country districts — according to the plan of yr Vener. Brother [Francis Patrick] (Synod. Balto. 1853, can. 3) I would, with him, still maintain their *movability ad judicium Episcopi*; & I would deem it premature & probably disastrous in its consequences, to adopt *at once* the full parochial system, for which we are scarcely prepared. . . .
> . . .

5. In regard to presentation of Bishops, I would suggest this plan: First, rehearse & renew previous Baltimore Legislation; 2. Add the Instruction (No. 2) of Rome, printing the schedule of questions & qualifications *in Actis*, & requiring its being filled up, & duly attended to in the triennial Provincial Councils; 3. I would then add, instead of the Hibernian method, one which would approach to & tally with the erection of Chapters, i.e., a vote of presentation by the Consultors, or quasi-chapter, which should be sent to Rome with the regular Episcopal presentation. This I think would meet the views of the Bishops, & the approval of the Holy See. [77]

Kenrick, however, was not convinced; he dilated on these two points in another letter to Spalding toward the end of that month:

1. As to Parish Priests. I believe that there is no medium that will give satisfaction between our present system and that suggested by me. Where there is a Hierarchy it would appear that there should be parish-priests. There is a great deal of discontent among the clergy on this subject. . . Inamovibility except for crime, or with the consent of the priest, appears to be the only means of satisfying the great majority of the clergy; and this cannot be well secured to them, except by making them parish-priests. Perhaps ten instead of five years might remove the objection to the suggestion made by me; as some would think that the latter term was too short.

2. As to the nomination of bishops. Had I thought that we should have chapters, and that the Holy See would sanction the canonical mode of election by chapters, I would have proposed it; but I fear that Rome would not allow one or the other.

Kenrick pointed out that a chapter would elect a single person instead of nominating three candidates, and the bishops of the province would have no right to interfere with the election, although they could and should interfere to prevent the confirmation of a poor candidate. He added:

. . . but this is a voluntary act, i.e. not an official duty. I was under the impression that the Sacred Congregation intimated a wish that the Irish system should be adopted; but in this I was probably mistaken. The mode of designating bishops varies with difference of times and circumstances. The election by the Council would cause more dissatisfaction to those who are not of the Council than the present mode. . .[78]

Spalding found Kenrick's "second edition of material for the Council . . . very satisfying" except for the chapter on parish priests. Since Kenrick had not modified it, Spalding said that he himself might do so, for he thought that the system of parishes with irremovable pastors should be introduced only gradually. He was confident, however, that Rome would permit the establishment of canonical chapters in the form adopted in England and asserted by Bishop Thomas Grant of Southwark to be working well there. [79]

Since the draft of the decrees proposed by Kenrick has not been preserved, the extent of any subsequent revision cannot be ascertained. When Spalding thanked Kenrick for rewriting his *tituli*, he admitted that much had been added in Baltimore and several things had been "more or less modified, to make them tally" with the other decrees.[80]

In the final draft of the decrees, therefore, that was prepared by Spalding with the assistance of theologians and canonists and was discussed in the Second Plenary Council, it was not proposed to introduce the practice of appointing irremovable pastors. It was proposed, on the other hand, to establish cathedral chapters. The citation began thus:

> Since bishops, especially in these Provinces, are so burdened with work and strained by responsibilities for the administration of their dioceses both in spiritual and in temporal matters, that by themselves they are hardly capable of properly fulfilling the grave duties incumbent on them, it is necessary that they call to their aid priests conspicuous for their piety, zeal, prudence, and learning, who may help them by wise advice and willingly take on their own shoulders some of the heavy burden and solicitude of the bishops. By acting in this way, the second order of the priesthood will come to the relief of the first order, and by the common consent and approval of all the unity of administration will be strengthened, and everything will be accomplished more agreeably and surely unto the greater glory of God and the salvation of souls.[81]

Recalling the exhortation of the First Plenary Council regarding episcopal consultors the fathers in 1866 were to state, according to the draft, that the way had thus been prepared to set up in this country "that ancient and praiseworthy system of administration which has already been established almost everywhere in the Catholic world, and the chief functions of which are performed by cathedral chapters." Outstanding priests were to be chosen, therefore, who would be called canons and who would sing the divine office and assist the ordinaries in handling affairs. Then the words of the Council of Trent about chapters of canons were quoted, and their duties, rights, and privileges were set forth. It was admitted that many obstacles hindered the full introduction of the canon law pertaining to cathedral chapters, especially the greater distances between places and the smaller number of priests in relation to the needs of the faithful. Nevertheless, in order that everything pertaining to the normal government of the Church might at least gradually be introduced, the Holy See was to be petitioned for the faculty of establishing chapters in these provinces and of doing so according to the form permitted in England. Metropolitans were to set the chapters up as soon as possible; bishops were to be free to do so a little later and with fewer than ten canons if this smaller number should be found opportune in the provincial councils which were to be held after the decrees of the plenary council were approved by the Holy See. Finally, the entire instruction of the Propaganda sent to the bishops of England in 1852, which exempted canons from the obligation of residence and determined the mode of their election, was quoted *in toto*.[82]

Farther on in the draft of the decrees was a chapter on the choosing of bishops. The earlier methods of proposing candidates were reviewed, and were said not to have turned out so successfully when they were put into practice as to preclude often notable mistakes, for unsuitable or unworthy men had sometimes been recommended to the Holy See. The procedure had last been altered in 1859 but it still did not allow any participation of the priests. Hence, the fathers were said to believe that something should be changed in the system inasmuch as priests were excluded although they sometimes knew one another better than their ordinaries were thought to know them. Since in each diocese some priests were chosen to form the episcopal council, they were to be consulted about candidates; it was proposed that after a bishop would die or the see would become vacant in some other way and also when the ordinary would desire a coadjutor, these consultors were to be called together and given the opportunity of presenting candidates, or at least the names of the candidates chosen by the bishops were to be disclosed to them and their opinions were to be communicated to the Propaganda. Finally, it was stated that no inconvenience would be likely to follow from making the names public;

on the contrary, the result might be that the merits of the candidates would become better known, for according to the Roman Pontifical, what sometimes is not known by the majority is known by a few, and thus in a way also the opinion of the people would be sought in a matter that interests them greatly. In this manner, moreover, the way would very easily be prepared for the erection of cathedral chapters, and if the Holy See should approve it, many difficulties which then occurred in the selection of bishops would be removed.[83]

The following chapter was devoted to priests having the care of souls. Here it was declared quite desirable that in keeping with the custom of the universal Church pastors properly so called, such as existed in Catholic regions, should be appointed also in the churches of the American provinces, but the time did not allow that to be done. The mind of the fathers was said to be that little by little and insofar as circumstances would permit, the American practice should be made uniform with that of the universal Church. The Council was said to wish, therefore, that in all these provinces, especially in the larger cities where there were several churches, a certain district with exactly determined boundaries should be assigned to each church and that parochial or quasi-parochial rights should be granted to its rector. It was explicitly stated, however, that the bishops did not thereby intend to grant any rector the right of irremovability or to abrogate or in any way diminish the power which the bishop had from the practice accepted in these provinces to deprive any priest of his position or to transfer him to another place. But the bishops were to be advised and exhorted not to use this right of theirs except for serious reasons or without regard for a priest's deserts.[84]

The chapters on the choosing of bishops and the appointing of pastors were referred to a committee of seventeen theologians for consideration. This committee suggested that the priests making up the episcopal council declare their opinion of the merits or demerits of the candidates under secrecy; nine of the seventeen theologians would have required an oath of secrecy, and six thought a promise on their priestly faith sufficient. As far as publicizing the names of the candidates was concerned, six wanted to omit the reference to learning the opinion of the people who were so greatly affected, and nine others wanted to omit the entire paragraph lest in places where there were different nationalities occasion be given to prejudiced opinions or improper criticisms of the candidates. All the theologians of this committee agreed that it would not be fitting to divulge the names either to the people or to the clergy. With respect to the next chapter, the theologians not only recommended that some parishes be erected in the larger cities but also that their pastors be given the right of irremovability; and that in the other, quasi-parishes the pastors not be removed until the bishop had sought the advice of the episcopal council. Thus the theologians refused to endorse the draft decrees in their entirety.[85]

In the council the Archbishop of New York, John McCloskey, and the Bishop of Wheeling, Richard Vincent Whelan, argued in favor of omitting the paragraphs concerning the cathedral chapters. Being convinced that the time had not yet come for this step, a majority of the fathers voted for the proposed deletion.[86] Archbishop Spalding, nevertheless, was so eager to save this provision that in commenting privately to the Propaganda on the changes effected in the draft by the council, he said that this negative decision did not seem to him to stand in the way of leaving it to the discretion of the metropolitans and bishops to introduce the chapters little by little; hence, he recommended that the decree be retained but instead of saying "as soon as possible," the words "as soon as it may seem good to them in the Lord" be substituted.[87] When the cardinals of the Sacred Congregation came to vote on Spalding's observation, they decided against it.[88] Hence, the paragraphs concerning cathedral chapters were definitively deleted.

When the conciliar fathers deliberated on the proposed mode of choosing bishops, the Bishop of Savannah, Augustin Verot, and the Archbishop of New Orleans, John Mary Odin, recommended that the council omit the paragraph prescribing that the consultors be assembled and asked to state their opinions concerning candidates. Since only four votes supported this motion, the paragraph was approved. At the suggestion of Archbishops McCloskey and Purcell, however, the following paragraph, which recommended the publication of the names of episcopal candidates and acknowledged the desirability of cathedral chapters, was struck out.[89]

Presenting this question to the Congregation, Cardinal Teodolfo Mertel pointed out that although in various places the chapters or pastors might draw up a *terna* to be examined by the bishops who would then make the presentation to the Holy See, still it was to be borne in mind that it was always a question of moral bodies established in canonical form or of individuals canonically recognized as such, while in the present case it was a question of private counsellors of the bishops, chosen by the bishops according to their own judgment and in no way recognized in law; on the other hand, the same bishops were unwilling to have chapters. Cardinal Mertel also remarked that according to a prior directive of the Propaganda, the names of the candidates were to be kept secret to avoid arousing ambition, and this regulation would be meaningless if the proposal of the bishops were approved.[90] The cardinals responded negatively, therefore, to the question whether the bishops' original plan for hearing the opinion of the episcopal counsellors when candidates were to be proposed for vacant sees should be approved. Afterwards the corresponding modifications were made in the final decrees.[91]

The Second Plenary Council also re-enacted the first and second decrees of the First Provincial Council of Baltimore, the decree (VI) on consultors of the First Plenary Council, and the decree (VI) on clerical trials of the First Provincial Council of St. Louis.[92]

In a review of the published acts and decrees of the Second Plenary Council Isaac Hecker, the founder of the Paulists and a prolific writer, attempted to correct the impression that canon law did not oblige in the United States. In his opinion, "a more erroneous or mischievous idea could scarcely have been propagated." He admitted that some laws presupposing circumstances that did not exist in this country were on that account not applicable here, but he declared to be "simply monstrous" the proposition that canon law itself was not binding. He professed not to know "whom it would affect worse, the higher or the lower orders of the clergy," and on that hypothesis he asked, "On what does an aggrieved clergyman rely for the right of appeal?" Hecker hailed the volume "as the beginning of a new period in our American church, the period — *detur venia verbo* — of the reign of law." [93]

That the tensions within the Church were not yet evident to outsiders may be seen in an article entitled, "Our Roman Catholic Brethren," which the well-known biographer James Parton contributed to the *Atlantic Monthly* in 1868 for the enlightenment of his Protestant brethren. After describing Catholic worship, organization, and finances in New York with mixed admiration and condescension, this writer went on to assert:

> The archbishop, be it observed, is the almost absolute ruler of the priests of his province. He places them, removes them, suspends them, according to his own good will and pleasure, subject to the laws and usages of the church. There is no appeal against his decisions, except to Rome; and this resource is seldom within the compass of a priest. Rome is far away, and a priest appealing against the judgment of his superior must have a very

good case or a very good friend, in order to obtain a favorable judgment. . . . The instances are rare in which an American prelate has abused his power over the clergy, and I believe no priest has yet applied to Rome for the redress of a grievance.[94]

Protestants such as Parton were soon to be disabused of their roseate notion of the relations between bishops and priests in the United States.

Part III: Champions of Priests' Rights

Shortly after the publication of the decrees of the Second Plenary Council a movement for priests' rights was initiated in the *New York Freeman's Journal and Catholic Register*. This weekly was probably the Catholic newspaper most widely read throughout the country. Its circulation exceeded ten thousand, and priests were numerous among its subscribers, for at that time there was no journal specifically designed for the clergy. During this campaign the paper claimed that it had gained several hundred subscriptions from clergymen in addition to "the thousand and more of them" that were already patrons.[95] Since there were about 3,780 priests in the United States in 1870, it is likely that one out of every three received the weekly and even more read it; the ratio was undoubtedly higher among the diocesan priests than among the religious.

The *Freeman's Journal* was not a diocesan newspaper; it always sneered at the "official organs" of the bishops which merely echoed the voice of an individual who was not the editor and which ignored the important issues of the day. The *Freeman's Journal* was Catholic in its principles and interests, but independent of ecclesiastical authority.

The owner and editor of the *Freeman's Journal* since 1848 had been James Alphonsus McMaster, a convert from Presbyterianism and Episcopalianism and an ultramontane champion of Catholicism. Some of his fellow journalists likened him to Louis Veuillot, editor of *L'Univers*, and Orestes Brownson's son described McMaster as having "the same zeal and earnestness; the same rashness and imprudence, the same deference to papal, and want of respect for episcopal, authority"[96] as the Frenchman. Whenever McMaster espoused a cause, he promoted it with irrepressible courage and without regard for the consequences. He was well prepared to debate religious questions, for he had studied theology, and he also knew Latin and Greek as well as French.

On October 3, 1868, the *Freeman's Journal* carried a notice taken from the *Chicago Tribune* about "The Bishop of Chicago and His

Clergy." [97] Bishop James Duggan had peremptorily suspended and dismissed from the diocese several of his priests, among whom were the vicar-general, Dennis Dunn, the pastor of the cathedral parish, Joseph P. Roles, and the former president of the now closed University of St. Mary of the Lake, John McMullen; all three had been members of the bishop's council.[98] Included in the notice was the text of the curt letter in which Duggan had informed Roles on September 14, "I hereby announce to you that your faculties shall cease, and your connection with this diocese terminate on Monday next, the 21st inst." An editor's comment expressed regret that this and other pertinent documents had been given to the press, but since they had appeared in print, it added, "it would be a mockery of quietism for a paper such as ours to decline publishing them."

In the same issue McMaster launched a campaign for parochial rights with a long editorial under the heading, "Do Not Dioceses Suppose Parishes?" [99] To explain his unprecedented *démarche* he wrote that for some time he had "been informed on very high ec- clesiastical authority, that a certain degree of ventilation of some questions of general discipline among . . . Catholics, would be pro- ductive of good, if strictly controlled by respect for authority, and dictated by Catholic charity." He stated that he looked upon the dis- cussion of such questions with reluctance and preferred to avoid it, but he was persuaded that the time had come to speak of one question in spite of its delicacy, namely, "*Why* have we Dioceses, and Dioceses multiplying, and *not one Parish*, in all these States?" He assured his readers, "The 'unpleasantness' at Chicago is not the *cause* of our dealing with it, now. But, it is the *occasion*." When he had read "the splendid and inappreciable volume of the Acts and Decrees of the late Plenary Council of Baltimore, as emended at Rome," he had marked this "as one of the matters that invited attention."

Reviewing the titles under which priests were ordained in this country, he wondered why the ordinary title of benefice, or title to a church, was not used. He pointed out that there were quasi-parishes in New York that surpassed several dioceses in other parts of the country with respect to the number of the faithful, permanency of residence, supply of vocations, and amount of revenue, and he asked, "Is not the *parochial* relation as much a part of the permanent discipline of the Catholic Church as Dioceses are?" If those who are priests now may be bishops in the near future, "Why are they not worthy, now, to be *Parochi* — not *quasi* Parish Priests, but *real* Parish Priests?" He continued:

The *Priesthood* is one. What affects the honor, the consideration, or the permanency, of the Hierarchy of the second order,
affects the entire Hierarchy. It is *not* the law, nor the will, of the
Catholic Church, that the parochial priesthood shall exist only at
the *will* of their Prelates. If secular clergymen offend against the
law of the Church, or, irregularly, disobey their Bishops, they
are subject to discipline. But there is *no law*, nor meaning, of the
Catholic Church, that they shall be thrown, as pariahs, on the
world. No true gentleman, no matter how fervent a Catholic,
could consent or acquiesce without the deepest misgivings, to his
young son becoming a secular priest, if, after five or ten years of
faithful duty, the *possibility* can be foreseen that, on some difference of "views or sentiments," his Bishop may write him a
note, charging him with no fault in his sacerdotal functions, but
saying that his connection with the Diocese he belongs to has
ceased! It is true, and ought to be stated, that the exquisite tender-
ness and prudence of our revered Prelates have, in almost all
instances, rendered their absolute authority over the standing of
their priests easy, and pleasant. Nevertheless, it is an *arbitrary*
power, and not the *liberty* of law, provided by the general rule
of the Catholic Church.

McMaster was apprehensive of the kind of men who would thereafter become secular priests in this country. He remarked with satisfaction that the Holy See had refused the bishops' request for permission to ordain secular priests *sub titulo missionis* for twenty years
longer, and he hoped that it would "take note of the fact that the time
has come to establish, under all proper guards, parish rights, and
parish responsibilities." Otherwise he hoped that the same authority
would "reconsider whether Vicars Apostolic are not more suitable to
our present needs here, than Bishops." To draw this parallel was to
attack boldly the position of the bishops who wished to perpetuate
the existing system.

This daring editorial provoked an immediate response from many
of the readers. In the next issue McMaster said that he was gratified
by the tone of the letters he had received and that he had "not mis-
judged the sentiments of the second order in the Catholic Hierarchy."
He went on to reassure those who had cautioned him that not a word
would be published "to promote disquiet or a factious spirit," or that
could "offend the most sensible regard for the preservation of Catholic
peace and good order." He invited suggestions from bishops and

priests and promised to keep them as confidential as the writers might wish. "We will permit in our columns, no exciting discussions, nor undue haste for the grand end," he serenely stated.[100]

Meanwhile McMaster had been answered in the *Pittsburgh Catholic* by a defender of the existing system who used the pen name of "Placidus" to insinuate the impetuosity of his adversary. McMaster reprinted this piece in his next issue and replied in an editorial.[101] "Placidus" had imputed to McMaster the "avowed design" of revolutionizing, "if possible, the American Church, by agitating Parochial rights, and pastoral privileges." The undaunted editor's rejoinder was that if such a thing as the *"American* Church" existed, "apart from the common Communion of the Holy Roman, Apostolic, and Catholic Church, we would want to 'revolutionize' it." He continued, "We do desire to see the day when the grand work now carried forward gloriously by our revered Hierarchy, in America, may culminate in the *perfect organization* of the Catholic Church among us. This is to *plant*, to *build*, to *complete*, not to '*revolutionize.*'

"Placidus" had also rebuked the editor for his "singular oversight" in not finding in the decrees of the last council any provision for a wronged priest to vindicate his rights. McMaster replied that Decree 77 was "a *suggestion*, not a provision of law," which left "the whole matter *optional* with each Bishop." "If we are to suppose a Bishop forming a wrong judgment about the conduct of a priest, it is equally possible that the same Bishop may find that *non sibi videatur* to refer the case to a clerical judge of the matter — and all in the very best of faith on his part."

According to "Placidus," moreover, McMaster had erred in stating that there was not one parish in the United States, for there was one, as he could have seen in the "precious book." The editor peremptorily denied "the proposition of our Pittsburgh friend" and defiantly demanded, "Name it!"

"Placidus" had pointed out a third misstatement in McMaster's assertion about "the supplication of the Fathers of the Council regarding the *Titulus Missionis*," which actually was granted in substance while "the term of duration is only an accidental circumstance." McMaster contradicted him: "The very *essence* of their request belonged to the category of *time*. They asked for *twenty years*. This was what we rejoiced was refused."

Finally, "Placidus" had called McMaster's "a strong position to assume, a bold step to take, especially for a layman." Stung by this aspersion on his competence, the editor replied that it was a mistake to think "that a layman has not all the right to discuss these matters of public ecclesiastical law, that a clergyman has." He developed this thought thus:

> That is a nonsense. A layman *may* be erudite in these matters. It is just possible that some clergyman may *not* be sufficiently instructed to discuss them with advantage! It is a matter of *knowledge*, not of *ecclesiastical position*. An *ignorant,* or an *unscrupulous*, discussion, could not fail to do much harm — be it by layman or clergyman. If by the latter, *more* harm would come of it. In our columns it will be harmless, because the discussion shall be, wholly, *unauthoritative,* and *laic.*

McMaster concluded: "We despise and contemn all *mouse-like nibbling* at an important matter. When largely informed that this or that is important to be said, we love to *say it right out,* in big figures." He also promised to retract what he had said if he could be shown that he had exceeded his right.

"Placidus" returned to the fray in the *Pittsburgh Catholic*, and McMaster again reprinted the article in his own paper along with another editorial.[102] The anonymous opponent maintained that McMaster had "blundered" in calling the provision of the Second Plenary Council by which the grievances of a wronged priest might be righted a suggestion. The only thing left to the bishop's discretion, he contended, was whether the members of the judicial bench should be selected from the bishop's council (the consultors) or from the rest of the clergy. Obviously disconcerted, McMaster could only reply that if this was the accepted interpretation of the text, "would it not follow that it has been abided by. . . ?" He doubted that his friend meant to say that this was the case. Even if this was "the sense of the Plenary Council," the editor did not yet "find the *honor* of an accused priest protected."

The third and last exchange between the *Pittsburgh Catholic* and McMaster was published in November.[103] The Pennsylvania editor had expressed his pleasure "at the gentlemanly tone of the brief discussion" and his esteem for McMaster, but he warned that "zeal may very easily lead one into imprudence." He explained: "It is not meet that every subject should be discussed in public journals; the public is not the fitting tribunal before which to lay all questions; this time or that occasion may not always be the proper one for mooting certain points." McMaster concurred in deriving "so consoling a gratification" from the termination of the discussion, but he reiterated two "facts" which he believed resulted from it:

1st. It is *not*, in the judgment of the Vicar of Christ, expedient that the title of the priesthood, in this country, shall continue to be that of the "Mission" — completely subjecting them to the arbitrary disposition of the Bishops . . . . . *2nd.* It stands confessed, and declared, that there is need of action, at a very early day, to render the *status* of the second Order of the Hierarchy more stable, and dignified, in the eye of Catholic discipline, than it is at present.

Adverting to his fellow editor's admonition, McMaster asked what prudence was and defined it as meaning looking far off to an end to be obtained and consisting in looking up the means to secure the end. He declared the end he was seeking to be "the more perfect development of the Catholic Church in this country." He justified his course, asserting:

> A "multitude of prudent Presbyters" — some who have grown grey in the service of the Lord, and have never had any personal difficulties with their Bishops, *from observation*, assure us that it is *most prudent* in us to discuss this question. *Cowardice* is not prudence! *Procrastination* is not prudence! Leaving matters to take care of themselves is not prudence! These are *vices, opposed* to the virtue of prudence . . .
>
> . . . We consider it the line of true prudence to look ahead, for the coming generation, that they be not deprived of priests. In other times, and in other lands in our own times, the self-will of Bishops has rendered the yoke of the priesthood intolerable.

McMaster did not want to rely on "a succession of miracles" to preserve the prosperity of the Church in the United States.

One of the "prudent Presbyters" to whom McMaster alluded was probably William Wheeler, pastor of St. Patrick's Church in St. Louis, who had written to the editor in October:

> You write in your issue of the 17th, that instances are little known, if any at all, of priests suffering from the arbitrariness [?] of Bishops in our country. I can tell you from nearly a quarter of a century's experience here on the mission, as a pariah if you will, that they have suffered, and do suffer at present, in a manner that no priest in downtrodden Europe would be allowed to suffer. But why not ventilate it? Simply because we have no law in the case, and 2ly because it is contrary to the spirit of the sacerdotal order, to appeal from the ordinary to the people. Some

fifteen years ago, when the canonical status of the quasi-parish priest was ventilated, not by you but by other parties, I felt opposed to the movement, as I thought the status of the country did not call for it, but I think now that the time has come for the Church to take the girlish pants off of her priests and put on them men's breeches, and as canonical parish priests, give them the power to elect their own Bishops. The *valet de chambre* manner in which priests are nominated to the holy see for Bishop-riks [*sic*], as at present existing, is to me, truly, disgusting. It is true, we have had hard working, active and zealous priests nominated from time to time, but this was rather the exception. The rule always was, and is, that the obsequious wirepuller with influential ladies at his back, was and is sure to succeed rather than the hard-working zealous retiring priest. The *decreta concilii* gives you the *modus operandi, in modo publico*.[104]

Perhaps McMaster thought that another priest who had written to him, William Mahoney, of the Diocese of Green Bay, was also a prudent presbyter. The editor could not have known that his correspondent was speaking from personal experience when, after thanking him for his "articles in behalf of the rights of the priesthood in America," he said:

An humble priest as I am I have often deplored that so many priests were cast on the world to the great scandal of religion. I am convinced that many an unfortunate priest would have been saved from destruction if the justice and charity which the Church wishes to be shown them, had been shown them by their Bishops. The evils of which you complain will be remedied — better that it be done now, than when it may be attended with more serious consequences to religion. A priest in America has duties, hard, arduous duties but no rights whatever. A Negro has the right of trial if accused, a priest — none. He is at the mercy of his Bishop who we know but too well is often influenced by passion or prejudice. I need not say to you fear not for there is no mean alloy in your composition. You take the view of the matter the unerring Church of God takes of it — and therefore you are on the side of right, justice & truth. None but a layman can plead for the rights of the Priesthood in America, for if a Priest undertook it he would be speedily crushed.[105]

For the first month McMaster conducted the campaign single-handedly. He thought that it would be better for only a layman to discuss the question in his paper, for without the involvement of authority "there would be less solicitude about any danger of a heated, or disedifying, controversy." [106] In November, however, he published a letter from a priest which was to undo his original plan. By way of introduction he said that he did not feel at liberty to refuse this letter which came "from a tried and laborious Priest, honored by his Bishop, and living in the best ecclesiastical relations with him." McMaster also gave an explanation of the term "canon law" which was to be invoked so frequently; the reverend correspondent was advocating "not any one special code of laws, such as have existed in other times and lands, and under other circumstances," but merely "the substitution of fixed and approved *rules* and *ordinances* for the arbitrary will of an ecclesiastical Superior." The editor believed that the discussion of this matter among the priests themselves and with their bishops, even more than in the newspapers, would help to prepare the bishops for the deliberations expected in the Vatican Council.

The heralded letter to the editor, printed over the pseudonym of "Ecclesiasticus," was a long encomium of canon law. The writer pleaded that this law be introduced into the United States, for "in scarcely any diocese — perhaps not in one — in the land, is there a regularly constituted ecclesiastical tribunal to which a priest may appeal in case of disagreement between himself and his Ordinary." He could not always appeal to Rome, and even if he did, "the poor priest, pending the inquiry, may be crushed by the authority and, perhaps, imprudent zeal of his Ordinary." But if canon law were established, "the respective rights and duties of each would be sharply defined; and in case of difference, which would be almost impossible, there would exist a tribunal at home which could take cognizance of the difficulty and adjust it satisfactorily." "Ecclesiasticus" complained that the "late venerable Plenary Council at Baltimore has done nothing in the way of defining the mutual relations of priests and their prelates, but left the former subject to the arbitrary will of the latter." He rejected the excuse that this country should still be regarded as a missionary field, and he set forth the advantages to the bishops themselves in governing by law. He also expressed the fear that the children of that submissive generation, influenced by the recalcitrant spirit of the times, would not tolerate arbitrary rule. In conclusion he said that the fault probably lay with the priests for failing to urge the question.

Although "Ecclesiasticus" hinted that he might write again, no more letters appeared over this pen name in the *Freeman's Journal*. Instead in the following month there was published the first of what were to be a dozen letters from "Jus." McMaster did not let his readers know that "Ecclesiasticus" and "Jus" were the same person, Eugene M. O'Callaghan, an Irish-born priest of the Diocese of Cleveland.[107] Under neither pseudonym did O'Callaghan mention concrete instances of the abuses he deplored, but he alluded to troubles in his own diocese, where he was actually one of the leaders of a clerical faction bitterly opposed to Bishop Amadeus Rappe.[108] It is unlikely that McMaster, who had commended "Ecclesiasticus" for his good relations with his bishop, had more than a vague and partial knowledge of the impassioned controversy in Ohio.

After McMaster had published his first letter, O'Callaghan had thanked him and complimented him for intending "to continue to agitate the question." He was confident that the result would be good and in that case McMaster would have the credit, for the priest had looked in vain "for one other editor that would have the independence much less the ability to undertake the task," which he called a Herculean labor worse than the cleaning of the Augean stable. He continued:

> The status of the Church in America is intolerable and cannot long continue. If priests had independence and prudence enough "the views & sentiments" of Bishops would soon change on this subject: without sin or scandal they could make the regime of Bishops so burdensome to themselves (the Bishops) that these would soon fly to the Canons for relief. *Entre nous*, many of our priests have no independence and too much "prudence," i.e. that prudence that is ravished at a bishop's smile and trembles at his scowl. I verily believe I have received many more privileges from my Bishop than if I sneezed every time he took snuff, and yet he would sing Alleluia if I were out of the diocese. Of this I am perfectly aware, yet we are on very agreeable terms. Had I been afraid to speak I would have received many a rebuk[e]. Such is human nature, weakness evokes tyranny.
>
> I lose no opportunity of telling priests that they ought to discuss this question among themselves and urge it upon their bishops. If this were more generally done, their Lordships would lend a more willing ear: one poor priest is powerless before a bishop but a cause urged by many if legitimate would hardly be long ignored. Truly as you say must we be wise as serpents,

if not the innocence of the dove will not for many many years effect our purpose. We must use better and sterner logic than cooing to convince our bishops that the wisdom of the Church is superior to their individual wisdom.

It is miraculous how the Church endures and progresses with the human the worldly the selfish interests of even *Bishops* too frequently dragging her earthward. Would to God that things were different but we must hope for better. As you are according to your own declaration "beyond being spoiled" this little morsel of scandal will not damage you.

I will if possible next week send you another letter for publication but I think I must assume a new *nom de plume.* I have been more than suspected and although I do not care a straw personally, yet my persistence may injure other measures on the *topic* which may reveal themselves soon . . . . I am constantly employed even, if I may say it without boasting, without rest and have very little time left for public letter writing still *I promise to drop you an occasional epistle on this important subject if acceptable to you leaving to your judgment to clip and prune them as you may.*

O'Callaghan enclosed a gift of a hundred dollars "contributed on the spur of the moment" by fifteen priests in the diocese as "the feeble expression of their esteem." He added:

If you would not be scandalized at a malicious suggestion I would like you to *continue sending* the *Freeman* to those Rt. Rev. and Rt. worthy Bishops who refused to continue their subscriptions to the *Freeman.* Debit us and regard this as the pre-payment of their dues. Who knows that the reading over of your occasional articles on this subject may not move them to a better mind.[109]

After receiving such a letter, McMaster should have suspected that the writer would hardly be objective and fair in his treatment of the question, but like a typical crusader seeking support wherever he might find it, he accepted this radical ally without hesitation or investigation.

On December 12, 1868, therefore, the *Freeman's Journal* carried the first letter from "Jus." [110] The writer began by denouncing those who were always content with the existing state of things:

They call themselves *conservatives*, and scout the idea of change, but they should remember that while conservatism is a very praiseworthy quality, it may be abused; the Scribes and Pharisees of old were conservatives and would not tolerate a change, even by the introduction of a perfect law, to supersede an imperfect and preparatory law. Yet they erred. And may it not happen that the *conservative*s of to-day may err, who oppose the introduction of canon law to supply the place of the imperfect and preparatory Missionary system. The relation of the Missionary law to Canon law may, not inaptly, be compared to the relation existing between the old and the new law, the latter being in each case the perfection and fulfilment of the former.

In proper scholastic fashion "Jus" taught that conservatism could be grossly abused in two ways: by defect, it would run into anarchy and revolution, and by excess, it would dwindle "into old fogyism and fossility." He then presented a serious argument for the introduction of canon law as follows:

American Protestants, and even American Catholic laymen, have scarce a conception of the beauty and grandeur of Catholic discipline, in its full and perfect development. Intelligent and liberty-loving Protestants would then admire the wisdom and equity of her laws, as they now admire the beauty and sublimity of her music, her painting, her sculpture, and her architecture. Each of these has been the avenue through which many of the most gifted Protestants were led towards the Church, and finally *into it* to find rest in its bosom.

How much greater influence would not her salutary laws have upon the practical and liberty-loving American mind! . . . Every American should then admire the justice of the Church, her hatred of oppression, and her protection of the weak against the strong; and he should confess that her canons are the *beau ideal* of order and true liberty.

"Jus" contended that the present system of discipline was not that preferred by Rome and that, consequently, it was not disrespectful to *petition* the bishops to "conform to the desire of Rome." He boasted, ". . . we are with the Holy Father, *with the Head.*" Rome he supposed to be well informed as well as disinterested, while the bishops might be suspected of advocating that system which gave them "more advantage and more power." He claimed to have searched in vain through the acts and decrees of the Second Plenary Council "for even the *least right* granted to Priests"; he interpreted Number 125 as meaning, "*A priest has no right which a bishop is bound to respect.*" Hence, he recommended to the clergy "a respectful protest." At the end "Jus" suggested in view of the forthcoming ecumenical council that the priests "present a *petition* to the Holy Father, praying for the introduction of parishes among us, and for a discipline in accordance with the canons."

Later in the month McMaster wrote in an editorial that he had received from priests "a great many letters on this subject, and on matters immediately cognate." [111] One had exhorted him "to promote *blind* obedience, to Bishops, in place of seeking for *canonical* obedience." The editor scorned this writer as having no experience as a secular priest and as not knowing a hundredth part of what Mc-Master knew "of the damage to religion that has come of the present exceptional system of subjecting the secular clergy to the arbitrary rule of Bishops." On the other hand, he had received "several hundreds" of letters from priests assuring him that he was doing a good work for religion. Although many of these letters were written for publication, in most cases they dealt "in specifications of hardships in Dioceses given by name." McMaster believed that the time had not come for such publications, but he threatened, "if any attempt be made to defend the present very abnormal practice, . . . to pile in a host of well-selected instances to show the *wrong*, in *practice*, as well as on *theory*, of the rule of Bishops in Sees without any Priests in Parishes." He offered, however, to print any communications similar to those of "Ecclesiasticus" and "Jus," "conceived in the same spirit of public good, and executed with that style of ability."

Whatever the conception and style of the other letters that McMaster received may have been, he continued to publish only those of "Jus." Early in February, 1869, the letter took the form of a dialogue in which a bishop proposed reasons for the frequent removal of priests and the writer gave answers showing "the wisdom of the Church in establishing her Pastors *inamovable*." If a priest was found to be unworthy of his ministry, the canons would provide for the case in spite of his "right of inamovability." If another congregation needed his services, a priest could still not be removed against his will, for "the Church will not permit her ministers to be deprived without a crime." When the "Bishop" was made to insist, "But he can do more good elsewhere," "Jus" retorted sarcastically, "Some American *bishops* would do a great deal of good in China or Africa as *Vicars Apostolic* or simple priests, yet I suppose they do not accuse themselves of sin because they neglect to do all the good they might do."

Finally, the imaginary prelate was made to admit that he wished to remove the priest because he disliked him for personal reasons; then "Jus" could decry this as "the plea of a tyrant." He concluded that the canons could provide "for every necessary difficulty," and he asked why "this wise and time-honored legislation" should be excluded any longer "in order to give scope to the fickle and ephemeral whims of any man, even be he a bishop." In contrast be observed, "The Pope — although most grave theologians have advocated his personal infallibility — does not act toward the whole Church, nor any particular part of it, with the hundredth part of that absolutism with which some American bishops act in their respective dioceses." In pathetic terms he depicted the harm done by tearing a pastor away from his loving congregation and transferring him to a strange one, and he maintained that the "present system, just like divorce in the natural family, breaks up those spiritual relations" between the pastor and his flock and that their union should be permanent just as the union of the family is indissoluble.[112]

Drawing attention to this letter in an editorial, McMaster said that "Jus" had asked in a private note why other priests did not participate in the discussion. The editor was certain that they were not apathetic, and he invited them to put their sentiments in form for publication. He went on to remark that the question of ecclesiastical law was being considered by one of the congregations preparing work for the ecumenical council, and he advised the American clergy to make their needs and wishes known to this body. Individuals might be ignored, he admitted, but "a carefully matured memorial from any body of the clergy would command a far greater attention." He also warned that action should not be deferred until the council met, because its sessions might last "but for a few weeks." In jest he suggested that the bishops' councils "would be appropriate bodies to initiate such a work," or the ecclesiastical conferences (which were rarely held), or that some of the priests might consult together.[113]

"Jus" resumed his series at the end of February with a bombastic statement on the importance of leaving a priest in a position where he was content and doing well. Here he left the professed altruism and unselfishness of his motives open to question. If there were parishes, he declared,

> Each pastor would labor in season and out of season to build up his congregation, conscious that it was *his own*. It would be a monument of his zeal; he could enjoy it during life, and, if infirm, he would have a *just* title to his maintenance. There would be an

emulation in well-doing among fellow-pastors, and even coad-
jutors would be influenced by the same zeal, in the hope of being
soon rewarded with a parish.

"Jus" compared the present system in the American Church to the
"tenant-at-will" system in Ireland and to the slavery system in America
before the Civil War, in which "some slave-masters never disturbed
or sold their slaves," just as some bishops seldom or never exercised
their power, but "death or accident might deprive these slaves of their
masters," and thus end their happiness and protection. Rhetorically he
asked, "But how would our Most Rev. and Rt. Rev. Bishops relish
it if they, like priests, were ordered from place to place, without consulting their feelings or assigning a reason, and sometimes *on a moment's warning?*" He urged the priests, then, to "take prompt, speedy
and decisive action," praying Pope Pius IX, "the great reformer of
the Church, the Hildebrand of the nineteenth century, . . . to turn
a benignant eye upon America, the Land of Promise of the Catholic
Church, and . . . to grant to its faithful and zealous clergy a full
measure of ecclesiastical rights." "Jus" was confident that if "a true
representation of the condition of the American clergy be laid before
the coming Council, with some voice to state their wrongs and advocate
their rights," success would crown the issue. Apparently he did not
distinguish between the Pope and the council.[114]

Not to be impartial but to show the weakness of the other side, Mc-
Master published in the same issue a letter from "one of the old
priests," signing himself "Justitia," who thought that for the good of
religion it would be "better . . . for the clergy to remain in *statu
quo.*" This writer feared that if there were parishes, a bad priest
would "sometimes be obstinate and reckless and produce much
scandal." He predicted that a bishop would seldom abuse his authority,
and if he should, a good priest would always have his conscience. He
argued, moreover, "Now, surely, there is no degradation in a priest's
being removed from one place to another. But if a parish priest had
to be tried, and is condemned, there is degradation." He professed
to know nothing of the absolutism of any bishop but averred that if such
a thing existed, it could be remedied without parishes.

In his "comments" McMaster reminded "Justitia" that there had
been troubles in his own diocese, and advised looking to the future.
"This question cannot, and shall not, sleep. . . . It is false security
to say that the Archbishops and Bishops of our country cannot do
wrong." The editor concluded:

> We think that every objection that can be urged against a settled and *law-founded* order of the priesthood has been suggested to us, by kind correspondents. There is not *one* argument that can bear investigation. If there be one, let some one state it, not as a "doubt," but as a *reason*, and we will publish it.[115]

At this juncture a shocking incident occurred in Auburn, New York. The insubordinate and delinquent pastor, Thomas O'Flaherty, resisting his transfer to another town, provoked his adherents in the congregation to a scene of violence and defiance in the presence of the newly consecrated and first Bishop of Rochester, Bernard McQuaid.[116] As reports of the conflict spread throughout the country, Archbishop Spalding in a letter to the Archbishop of New York, John McCloskey, deplored the events in Auburn and continued:

> I have heard it stated on seemingly good authority that Dr. McG--n of St. Stephen's is the chief inspirer of those incendiary articles of McMaster on the rights of Parish priests, the fruits of which we are beginning to see. Can it be so? And if so, what remedy can be applied to check the evil? This is the question — & a most important one it is likely to be for all of us before long.
>
> There are four Statutes in the late Plenary Council, num. 123 to 126, clearly stating the status of the Pastoral clergy, and setting forth our wish to approach as fast as we prudently can to the normal state of the Church. Would it not be well to publish these, with comments, in our official organs, without, of course, entering into any controversy on the subject? Above all, would it not be advisable for the Bishops to agree among themselves to follow strictly the rule laid down in num. 126, & also in nums. 70, 71 & 77? The organizing of a regular Episcopal *Curia* or Court, & the advising with the Council on *all* matters of importance — especially removals or exchanges of the higher & older Pastors, would go far toward diminishing the odium now attaching to the Episcopal office; nor would this be a change, but only a carrying out of our own legislation. This can be best done in Provincial Councils, & we shall do it in ours, where there is probably less need of it than in some other Provinces; at least no outbreak of this kind is at all likely South of Penna.[117]

At least in his private correspondence, therefore, Spalding acknowledged the grounds for complaints and blamed his fellow bishops for not carrying out the conciliar decrees. Apparently he felt that he was personally being attacked by the repeated strictures on "his" plenary council.

In his reply McCloskey expressed surprise at Spalding's suspicion of Edward McGlynn; he admitted that the priest was "one of the advanced school," but defended him as "a very devoted & zealous priest, as well as a most docile & obedient one." The archbishop doubted that McGlynn could influence more than two or three of the pastors in New York, for he was unpopular with the rest, and his whole school was "falling more & more into disrepute." On the main issue McCloskey wrote:

O'Flaherty was one of the correspondents of McMaster. And it is well that the cases advocated by the Freeman's Journal should be tested in the person of one who is thoroughly without character or credit. Should be appeal to Rome, as he professes his determination to do, it will give us an opportunity of obtaining from the Cardinal [Prefect of the Propaganda] a decision on the *principles* involved. I am entirely of opinion that it is best to take no notice of McMaster in the papers under our control. Let McMaster alone & he will not fail to bring discredit upon this as he has done upon almost every other cause that he undertakes to advocate. His insolence and intemperance of language simply disgust the laity, & make more sensible clergymen, otherwise in sympathy with the progressionists [?], rather ashamed of the whole affair. The object is to bring a pressure to bear upon us which will force us to a change in our discipline, or failing in this, to attract thus the attention of the General Council, & bring about such legislation as will satisfy them. I do not see that any good would come from republishing in our papers the statutes of our Councils. These are very well known, but certain ones are dissatisfied with them — they want to bring us up to a Roman standard &c. There is no fear of their succeeding, & anything like a yielding on our parts or seeking to conciliate would in my judgment, be very unadvisable. Gregory XVI declared that very many of the gravest evils in the Italian Church was [*sic*] due to the law of immovability. How much more true is this of Spain, South America & the Spanish colonies &c. Good Catholics know & feel all this, and the second order of clergy have much more dread of this tyranny of Parish Priests than of Bishops, and as for the laity they complain much more of our leniency towards their Pastors than of our severity. There may be, of course, & are exceptional cases. It is undoubtedly proper that the Bishops should seek to carry out as far as practicable the statutes of the Councils. Yet an Episcopal Council is not always either a safeguard or corrective.

Thus the Archbishop of New York presented a full statement of the case for the defense, but it never reached the eyes of those who most needed to be convinced. He added in his letter to Spalding:

> I may mention that many anticipated that the question of Parish rights would be mooted at our synod. I myself rather expected it to be raised by some one of the clergy, & I left a fair opening for it, being prepared to meet it. Yet in view of the statutes of the Plenary Council to which I have called their attention, no one ventured to say a word. The late Archbp ceased holding synods because of the unpleasantness that had grown out of the attempt to agitate this point.[118]

McMaster was eager to disassociate himself from the "miserable disturbance" in Auburn, saying that the "proceeding was disreputable" and that Catholic sentiment would condemn it. He used the incident, however, to reinforce his own position:

> We can regret, at the same time, even for the personal feelings of the Bishop of the new Diocese of Rochester, that there has not been, of fixed law, some *court* of priests, by their position not under suspicion of Episcopal control, that could have examined the case. There may be reasons for forbidding a priest to officiate, that do not reflect on his moral character. . . . The people are no judges in matters of sacerdotal fitness. It is true that their *wishes*, and *affections*, may very wisely, be consulted, in appointing a pastor, or quasi-pastor. But, as to *fitness* for the Divine office, the laity make a grievous mistake when they meddle, against authority. But these excesses will always happen, to the scandal of religion, till there is a settled *law* in regard to the status of priests.[119]

In another editorial McMaster indignantly repudiated the charge made in the *Catholic Telegraph* of Cincinnati that the disturbance at Auburn was a "natural development" of the previous discussion in the *Freeman's Journal*. The Cincinnati editor had laid down the maxim, "Laymen and editors should mind their own business." McMaster agreed but insisted, "One of the greatest 'businesses' of editors, whether laymen or not; and of laymen, whether editors or not, relates — supposing these 'editors and laymen' to be Catholics — to having *effect* given to the *general* law of the Church, as declared at Rome." The New York editor also disputed the minor premise that "discipline in the Church was not the business of laymen and editors; if this meant that a code of discipline, such as the published decrees of the last council, was 'not a proper subject for examination and comment,' then," he flung back, "our Cincinnati *friend* has not learned the liberty and right of discussion encouraged by the Catholic Church." [120]

McMaster thought it necessary to remind his readers what "Jus" meant by canon law, for some labored under misconceptions:

> Those who oppose or, rather, *doubt*, whether it is timely to have Canon Law in this country, seem to us to consider Canon Law as a one fixed system; identical in all countries; full-fledged and unchangeable; which has been written down in certain tomes, of greater or lesser bulk, and which must be received as a whole, in a manner existing in every other country, or else will not exist at all. This is a wild conception of Canon Law, and one unsound in point of Catholic theology. We can well conceive the horror of a priest at the idea of having the Canon Law as it existed in Austria or Spain, being set forth as a law for this country. We can understand the objection to it, as it exists in Ireland.
>
> But, what *is* Canon Law?
>
> It is the *sum of laws declared by the authority of the Pope, for the spiritual good of the faithful.*[121]

Consistent with his ultramontane principles, McMaster seems to have held that the binding force of the decrees of provincial and plenary councils was derived solely from their approbation or confirmation by the Holy See. To illustrate his idea of "canon law," he explained that its establishment would not prevent alteration of the existing boundaries of parishes. He repeated, "The aim of Canon Law is not to hinder, but to expedite the common good of the faithful. Its establishment is not to shield the unworthy, but to protect justice." He was anxious to "correct the idea that the Canon Law is any one immutable set of rules for the spiritual government of the faithful, unchanged by time, or by circumstances of countries."

In the next issue the relentless editor answered the objection that the establishment of canon law would render it more difficult "for the people of a given congregation to get a scandalous-living priest removed." On the contrary, he replied, it would render it easier and would make the need for removal rarer.[122]

At the same time, "Jus" continued to contribute sententious articles on the status of the clergy, or of "the second order of the hierarchy," in the United States. In one he argued that although he believed that bishops have been commissioned by God to govern the Church, it did not follow that they could do no wrong or always governed wisely. He gave historical examples of their errors, failings, and scandals and concluded that "Priests or laymen ought not to follow their Bishops, except inasmuch as their Bishops follow Rome," but they refused to introduce parishes as the Pope wished; *ergo.*[123]

The next letter from "Jus" became, perhaps, the most notorious of all because of the crude play made therein on the words "suspension" and "hanging." The writer was becoming more audacious in his denunciations of the bishops, saying that perhaps in no other country of the world was there "exhibited such absolute and irresponsible autocracy on the part of the bishops." He criticized the Second Plenary Council for seeming "to mock the helplessness of the priest by telling him that *after* being hanged (suspended), the bishop who played the triple role of judge, jury and hangman may, if he choose, then grant him a trial." He paraphrased the existing law as follows:

> Hang a priest first; then, *if you wish*, try him *afterwards.* Hear it, ye priests of America! Your whole hope, and claim, and title to an impartial trial, no matter how innocent you may be, absolutely depends on the mere condescension of the bishop, and this only after you are hanged (suspended), "*Si Episcopo videatur.*"

"Jus" believed that even if the bishop would allow a trial after suspension, no jury would "declare in favor of the already degraded priest, even though innocent, and thereby pronounce the bishop a spiritual murderer who *hanged* an innocent priest," for a juryman who would do that would "put his own neck in the halter." Just as Henry VIII cowed his Parliament, so "may a bishop, who acts unjustly towards a priest, compel a jury to ratify his sentence and approve his acts."

"Jus," therefore, exhorted his clerical readers: "Arouse [*sic*], then, ye priests of America, and make use of the means that God has at present vouchsafed to correct this abhorrent system." After more inflammatory declamation, the demagogue suggested that "something be done to memorialize the Holy Father in our behalf," and he predicted that "a petition bearing the signatures of three thousand priests, praying for protection against the absolute and irresponsible will of individual bishops" would be granted in Rome. He promised, moreover, to propose a practical way of having such a memorial drafted and signed.[124]

At the same time a "Juvenis Sacerdos" attempted to explain the inactivity of the priests that McMaster had decried.[125] He offered this reason:

> It is, probably, that we are too fearful of offending "the powers that be." We have been so long accustomed to an abnormal condition of dependence, that we have contracted a certain habit of childlike timidity. Hence, though we are all very anxious, of course, to obtain and secure the establishment of Canon Law, which means *order*, we have not the courage to contribute, openly, our exertions to the desired effect. I speak now of individual exertion. It is generally apprehended, that any priest, becoming prominent in this matter, would be quickly snubbed for his presumptuousness, and, perhaps, censured, or removed from his comfortable, though precarious living, to some wilderness of exile.

The young priest thought that the remedy for this evil lay in a leader who would fearlessly advocate the clergy's rights. The priests would gather around him, and the bishops would "cheerfully accept" their common sentiment. The writer believed that the required leader was "Jus," and he suggested that a meeting of priests be called in New York.[126] No such concerted effort, however, was ever made.

So many readers of the *Freeman's Journal* complained about the unseemly pun on hanging and suspending, that the editor felt compelled to defend his contributor. He aggressively attributed their annoyance to "the peevish spirit of the eunuch," and he warned that "*tea-table politeness*" should not be "mistaken for the true type of Catholic obedience to *authority — properly* grounded." In McMaster's mind the argument of "Jus" was not that this or that bishop had used his power in an oppressive way but rather that the plan of episcopal government in the United States in its form and substance was abnormal in the Catholic Church and disruptive of the peace of the Catholic community. McMaster went so far as to say that it could be called tyranny, but he hastened to explain that according to the ancient usage of the word, a tyrant was one who acted with a power not based on law. His thesis was not that the abnormal power of bishops was abused but that it was liable to abuse, that the possession, not the exercise, of abnormal power created solitude.

Another objection to the "*approximation* to the regular system of Catholic order" was "the absence of well-trained *canonists* among the clergy." The editor's answer was, "*Demand* creates *supply.* . . . Let it be announced that three, or five, years hence, the system of conformity to law, as opposed to Episcopal good pleasure, is to prevail in any given Diocese, and it will be wonderful how many canonists, up to the mark, that Diocese will find." [127]

Using every available weapon, the militant editor next reprinted an article by Nicholas Wiseman entitled, "Ecclesiastical Organization," and originally published in the *Dublin Review* of August, 1842. It was basically a review of the volume of decrees of the first four Provincial Councils of Baltimore which had appeared that year. Writing before the restoration of the Catholic hierarchy in England, Wiseman advocated the ordinary form of church government.[128] In an editorial Mc-Master commented that Wiseman's "most valuable suggestion" was his "sagacious plan . . . for a careful sifting" of the ponderous tomes of canon law from Europe and a judicious selection of what was applicable to the changed times and circumstances of the United States. The editor denied that the bishops in general were opposed to the discussion in his paper. He admitted:

> It is true that most of our Prelates apprehend imprudence in a public discussion of the question. Were there a clerical journal published, say monthly, as we think there ought to be, in this country; in which these matters might be discussed — and some of those *ad clerum* published only in Latin — and were there *liberty* for the clergy without censure, to speak out boldly on all debateable [sic] questions, we would not use our columns for these discussions. The case is otherwise. It is only in a paper purely laic, and supported, as well for its political writings, by subscribers other than Catholic, as for its defence of Catholic faith and morals, that, in this country, at the present time, this discussion can be had.

He affirmed that it would not be much overstating what he knew to be true to say that nine-tenths of the priests felt the want of a system of law in the organization of the hierarchy.[129]

The next week the editor asserted that he had received "hundreds on hundreds . . . of letters from priests, who, not wishing to assume any responsibility for the *prudence* of *our* discussions," nevertheless, said "in substance that the existing *dispensation from ecclesiastical law* has outlived its time, in our older Dioceses, at least — and that its continuance is an *abuse.*" With these words he introduced another letter from "Jus," who upheld his right to convey unpleasant truths in "plain, unvarnished language." In particular he rationalized his play on the words "hang" and "suspend" thus: "As I would not wish to live under a political government under which every man may be hanged without a trial, so likewise I do not like to live under an ecclesiastical government under which every Priest may be suspended without a trial." Once again he implored the priests to bestir themselves "to bring the question at an early date before the coming Council," but he still presented no practical plan for achieving that object.[130]

"Jus" then lapsed into silence for two months. When he broke it, he merely delivered another theoretical disquisition on parochial rights. He asked why Protestants regarded the Church "as inimical to liberty and intelligence" and replied "that the abnormal relation of our Bishops to our priests and laity *seems* to justify the Protestant opinion." He continued:

> But were I to grant — which I am not willing to admit — that our American Bishops are despotic, it would by no means follow that the Catholic Church is despotic. Our difficulty is, that we are in a state of rapid transition, and we have almost grown to maturity while we are yet subject to a discipline suited to the infant state of the Church. . . .
>
> I do not assert that our Prelates are despotic; I merely say that their very position and the *dependent* condition of those who ought to advise them, *keep them in a fog.* Those worthy counselmen justify their *criminal* silence by the reflex principle that the Bishop *will* have his own way anyhow, and hence it is useless for them to advise him; and, besides, the Church, they say, is infallible, and all these mistakes will come right in the end. But they forget that the American Church is not infallible, and may go to the devil through their neglect. . . . .
>
> However, there remains the ugly fact of Bishops' arbitrariness, which is a stumbling block to Protestants on their way towards the Church. Preach to them about the Church's being the guardian of liberty, and they will laugh at you as long as they see a mitred Prelate play the absolute lord, spurn the prayers of his people and disregard their virtuous and pious wishes to be permitted

to enjoy the direction of a Priest who has won their love and confidence, and against whom there may be not a shadow of a charge. They will reply with a smile of pity: You eulogize the liberty of the Catholic Church while here in America the galling chains are chafing your very bones. We *do not inquire* how much liberty the Church grants her children in other countries, but we *do know* that their spiritual rulers do not allow them a very great measure here; therefore, before you ask us to become Catholics, Physician cure thyself. Such is the Protestant sentiment put into words, and every one must acknowledge that it has its prejudicial influence. But admitting the truth of all that is said, what follows? simply that our American bishops are arbitrary and rule without law — nothing more. . . .

Not only did this abnormal system, "Jus" affirmed, prevent Protestants from coming into the Church, but it was also driving Catholics out, for it gradually weakened "the faith of the shallow-minded and un-instructed Catholics," to whom the Church's enemies kept preaching law and liberty and pointing out the bishops' "high-handed acts of arbitrary will." Finally, the system fomented "dissatisfaction and discord in the Church" by offending "the very best and most practical Catholics." "Jus" professed his inability to understand why the bishops wished to perpetuate a system entailing this threefold evil.[131]

The *Freeman's Journal* carried two more letters from "Jus" that summer but then none for nearly three months. In the first of those two he quoted the decree of the Council of Trent on perpetual pastors and denied that the times had so changed as to justify the bishops in ignoring this urgent command. He also contended that the Pope regarded this decree as still expedient. For the bishops he drew a lesson: "Now if Bishops do not incline towards the spirit of a General Council, even when excused by circumstances from carrying out its letter, how can they expect that priests and laymen will reverence *their* commands? Bad example is contagious, even when given by Bishops . . ." Once again he reminded the priests of their duty to aid in making their case known at Rome and tauntingly said that if they were "too inert, or too pusilanimous [*sic*], or too sycophantic to manifest their desires," they deserved "the pity and prayers of the faithful." [132]

In some places this constant goading began to produce the intended effects. A priest in Wisconsin informed McMaster:

> At a meeting of the English speaking priests of the Dioces [*sic*] of Milwaukee, (I think about forty were present) held

during our Retreat last month, I introduced the question of our Parochial rights — and I am happy to say — everyone present — not a solitary exception — pledged themselves to do all they can to obtain that right.

You can reckon on us to a man. I found from speaking with the German Pastors that they are *nearly all* straight on the petition too.

The writer promised a hundred dollars toward the support of a representative at Rome.[133]

The other contribution of "Jus" published in the *Freeman's Journal* that summer occupied three and half columns of small print. It was an attempt to prove that the bishops were persisting in a system of government that was opposed to reason. "Jus" affirmed that arbitrary rule would "never succeed with subjects distinguished for intelligence, wisdom, and piety as are the subjects of Bishops." He blamed the bishops for disregarding the advice of their counsellors:

He has, indeed, counsellors *in nomine tantum*, but if he treat them as the pagans sometimes treated their gods — rebuke them if their decisions differ from his own, and spurn their deliberations to follow his own darling ideas — is it then to be wondered that the counsellors of a Bishop say: O, these councils are all a humbug and a farce; we and the Bishop understand each other, the Bishop never thinks of accepting our deliberate advice, hence we never think of deliberating; we are called in simply to say — *yes*, to whatever the Bishop proposes, and by doing this we save a double annoyance.

Heaping more obloquy on the bishops, "Jus" declaimed:

God almighty and infinite rules by law, not by arbitrary will; our Bishops, finite and fallible, rule by arbitrary will, not by law. As subjects of an All-wise and Omniscient God, we *have rights which he is bound to respect*, but as subjects of American Bishops, and their *equals* in knowledge, wisdom, and piety, '*We have no rights which they are bound to respect.*'

The result of such government must necessarily be "dissatisfaction, murmuring, confusion, and scandal, if not schism and heresy." Terminating the tedious diatribe, he said: "With *law* there is no class of subjects easier to govern than priests . . . But *without law* there is no class of subjects more difficult to govern and while they may not give scandal they can make the life of an arbitrary bishop miserable despite all his power." [134]

Early in August McMaster reprinted a report taken from the Baltimore *Catholic Mirror*, which in turn had taken it from the *Chicago Tribune*. This was an exposé of the financial disarray of the Diocese of Chicago, which was due to mismanagement. Although the editor feigned regret at "the republication of this document in the official organ of the ab-Legate of the Holy See, and Pro-Primate of the Catholic Church in America," he believed that it would be "mock squeamishness" in him not to pass the matter on to his readers. He obviously welcomed, however, the opportunity "to make use of the scandal already created," in this way: "The results of imposing Bishops on the Diocese of Chicago without regard to the will of the constituent clergy, has *three several times*, proved disastrous. Suppose, now, that *one* experiment be made in the way of *satisfying* the wishes of the clergy of the Diocese! " [135] Instead of developing the idea of consulting the clergy, however, McMaster re-emphasized the incongruity of "a thing *called* Catholic organization, composed of fifty Bishops, or more, *all inamovable*, with a clergy of many thousands, no one of whom holds his position except at the *will*, or, as has been too often proved, the whim, of some new and inexperienced Bishop." He was certain that this "preposterous blunder" would be remedied, and he asked the bishops opposed to giving tried and worthy priests tenure to advocate "for consistency's sake" the movability of all American bishops.[136]

In the middle of August McMaster recommended that the clergy of the United States have "at Rome a special representation of *clergymen devoted to the promotion of their cause*." Although many clerical correspondents had written to him, " 'Jus' *must* go," he told them that "Jus" could not go, deceptively suggesting that "Jus" had been burdened by his bishop with the administration of the diocese for the duration of the council. McMaster insisted, however, that someone or two, "already having good standing at Rome, and faultless with their local Ordinaries," ought to go, and he asked whether it would be possible to raise "the necessary amount to send these clergymen to Rome, and to keep them there, in a position corresponding to the importance of their mission." [137]

Apparently McMaster did not receive an immediate assurance, for he did not resume his proposal for a collection until November. Meanwhile he endeavored to convince the good priests who believed in the movement but were afraid of imprudences — he reckoned them as constituting twenty-nine per cent of the total — that they should dismiss their fears. He summarized the demands, answered objections, dispelled misconceptions, and expressed impatience — "Why is there so much trouble in understanding and accepting our position?" [138]

In November, on the editorial page, McMaster announced that the "Rev. E. M. O'Callaghan, of Youngstown, Ohio," had departed for Rome. He called him "one of the most beloved and respected priests" of the Diocese of Cleveland and said that he enjoyed the esteem of his brother priests, the affection and reverence of the laity, and the high regard of the non-Catholics of his city. He suggested that the purpose of the voyage of this "devout lover of Rome and of our Holy Father" was merely to "find strength and health of spirit in visiting the Eternal City at the time of the opening of the Council of the Vatican." [139] He did not hint, however, that O'Callaghan was really "Jus" or that he was going to Rome as the representative of the priests who desired the introduction of canon law (meaning concretely the irremovability of at least certain pastors and due process in clerical trials). Nor did McMaster reveal, though he must have known, that O'Callaghan had been suspended by Bishop Rappe. Having learned that O'Callaghan was operating a bank (the Home Building and Loan Company), the bishop transferred him to Lima, Ohio. The pastor protested that this sudden act was actually a demotion, and, refusing to accept the new assignment, he appealed to the metropolitan, Archbishop Purcell, who had already departed for the Council. Perhaps he expected a favorable hearing, because the archbishop operated a much larger bank of his own in Cincinnati. O'Callaghan obtained Rappe's permission to go to Rome in order to prosecute his appeal, and he set out on November 7. The editor probably did not know that O'Callaghan's further end was to effect the removal of Bishop Rappe.[140]

A fortnight later McMaster informed his readers that "in two months" there would be in Rome, "with the leave of the proper authority, in every case, an advocacy of the cause that has been pleaded in the *Freeman's Journal*." In view of the considerable expense involved, he suggested that those who were "equally convinced of the necessity of this movement" make "a moderate contribution" in order to balance the account. "With great reluctance, and on the advice of its convenience," he consented "to be the agent of such contributions," which he would forward to "a responsible party in Rome." At the same time he proposed "that priests convinced of its salutary effect . . . give their names, collectively or individually, to be signed to a dutiful 'Petition of Right' . . . to be presented, with every respect of prudence, to the Holy See." The petition would contain the following three propositions "with no word added":

I. That every priest who has, for *seven years*, been in charge of souls, without reproach, shall be inamovable, except for cause.

II. That no priest shall be punished, except by temporary suspension, unless on the sentence of the *Judices Causarum* of the Diocese.

III. That these *Judices Causarum* shall be nominated *singulatim*, by the Ordinary of the Diocese, each year, according to the provisions of the Council of Trent. But, as our Bishops have no "Chapters of Dioceses," that, as nearest to it, the Priests who have attained the position of inamovability except for cause, shall have the right, in Annual Synod, to *approve*, or *reject*, any of the Judices Causarum, named, one by one, by the Ordinary.

McMaster acknowledged his discomfort in taking part in such matters, and if he was "intruding on the sanctuary," he offered as his excuse "the expressed encouragement . . . of *over one thousand of the clergy* of the United States," although he admitted that not all of these were ready to commit themselves, for many of them feared that he would "go too far." To allay their anxiety he averred, "In regard to faith and ecclesiastical discipline, we are planted at the footstool of the Throne of the Vicar of Christ." [141] Thus after more than a year of desultory talk, a plan of action seemed to be emerging.

The editor's suggestion of a petition was seconded by a letter from "Jus" published at the same time. The main burden of this missive was to compare the missionary or infant stage of the Church to a time of persecution and warfare and to prove that such was no longer the case in the United States. He argued thus:

It would be monstrous to see a General, before he had conquered his right to the soil on which he stood, erect a splendid palace and enjoy all the luxuries of ease and peace, while his soldiers lived in tents, subject to all the vicissitudes of war. Strange as this may appear, it is the exact relation of Bishop and Priest in the present *status* of the Catholic Church in America. Our bishops live in palaces, have splendid cathedrals, enjoy inalienable revenues, and are in-a-movable, while their poor soldiers, the priests, who have borne the brunt of the battles with them, and exhausted themselves in the conflict, must live in *tents* — in the congregations they have spent themselves in building up — subject at any moment to be ordered away at the arbitrary command of their Bishop, even without the least subjective fault.

The conclusion to this fantastic, inflated comparison was, "If the General may enjoy a *palace*, let the poor Soldier possess the rough comforts of the barracks." [142]

During the following week McMaster received "many letters," [143] and in the next issue he announced, "We peremptorily withdraw the proposition to accept names to be signed to any 'Petition' whatever. There are obvious reasons for this." He did not, however, state any reasons; perhaps he feared that if the names were ever divulged, the signers would be exposed to retaliation from their irate bishops. Secondly, he stated that priests had suggested a contribution of ten dollars each; he gave notice that no sum exceeding that amount would be accepted, and he advised priests in poor missions not to contribute more than five dollars. He was certain that in this way all the expenses, including those for translating, copying, and printing in Rome, could be met, and he promised a strict accounting of monies received with an audit. Whatever might be left at the end would be at the disposal of the contributors — "to be returned to each, except as each may vote it to fit out an Episcopal belonging for 'Jus,' if it should happen that he is called to Rome, and comes back a Bishop!" [144] If McMaster intended that remark sincerely, he demonstrated his naïveté, and if he intended it facetiously, he manifested a strange sense of humor.

The extent of the response from the clergy to the combined appeal of McMaster and "Jus" cannot be determined. The editor never revealed how many priests contributed to the fund or how much they contributed in all.[145] He made only one more mention of the collection, just before the Council was opened,[146] and then never referred to the financial question again.

Though "Jus" had nothing new to say, he labored the issue in another letter on the unseemly contrast between fixed bishops and unsettled priests. It must have taxed his literary ingenuity to repeat the now trite ideas in different words and figures. He stressed the importance of sending to Rome someone who had the cause at heart: "He may not be a personage of great importance, yet his presence there may avail much . . . . It is not an imposing presence and lofty conversation, but the goodness of his cause that will recommend him." "Jus" pretended to leave to others the choice of this representative and the time and manner of his going.[147]

In commending this "well-reasoned letter of 'Jus'" to the attention of his readers, the editor again sought to calm their fear of any incitement of "hostility to the authority of Bishops" by assuring them that "Jus" was one who had "never had a note of censure passed on him, as to the excellence of his personal character." This was an unjustified equivocation, since suspension always supposes a moral fault. Alluding cryptically to O'Callaghan's banking activities, McMaster continued: "Great amounts of money have passed through his hands. He has accounted for it, to the last cent. In a position to have become rich, he is *poor*. We *know* it." [148]

As the council convened, McMaster kept the interest of the priests alive and their expectations high by reporting that he had received "some surprising, and unexpected, documents fortifying the cause." The vicar-general of an important diocese had declared that "a moderate and respectful petition" would have his signature and that of the entire body of the clergy in his diocese. Like an auctioneer the editor asked, "What other Diocese will second this movement?" He suggested "that the *best* way to go to work would be, in each Diocese, or district of a Diocese, supposed to have a Dean, to have a brief and simple petition drawn up, in Latin or French, as languages understood in Rome." He thought that only "agreement in *principles*" was required, and he offered to forward any such documents, presumably to "the messenger bearing the respectful representations of the Priesthood in the United States to Rome." [149]

In his first issue of 1870 McMaster gave, ostensibly for the benefit of hundreds of new subscribers, "a succinct statement of the *object* sought by this series of publications." Only his fourth (last) point had never been elaborated before:

> There is another thing that a multitude of most excellent ecclesiastics think necessary for the good government of Dioceses. It is that some plan be ordained by law, since the old canonical forms are inapplicable, for ascertaining the will of the clergy of a Diocese, in regard to the Bishop appointed. It is very certain that ignoring this, has not wrought well in America. Had the will of his immediate predecessor in office been heeded, the present Archbishop of Baltimore would not have been Bishop of Louisville. Let us stop here, and not tell other instances of mistake. The voice of the clergy of a Diocese ought not to be passed over, without an *organized* and *official* expression. Rome, alone, can give them this, in America. It is not necessary that this voice be always complied with. But the fact that it has been *heard*

and *weighed*, and that the status to speak as an organized Diocese has been created and considered, will be enough for all the good Priests, who — if they had been heard in some cases that have occurred — would have prevented some misfortunes that have happened.[150]

Meanwhile the American bishops attending the Vatican Council wondered who the clergy's representative in Rome was. Bishop McQuaid wrote to a priest in Rochester:

The probability is that the "Jus" people will get more than they bargained for when they come on as the Freeman tells us they are to do. In other words, they will find out that McMaster has been making fools of them. The general feeling is that many of the troubles of the Church have proceeded from that principle and the Council, with the experience of the past before them, is not likely to go back in her discipline. We have a Priest here from the Cleveland Diocese, who would have done better to have remained at home.[151]

McQuaid, however, did not recognize the priest from Cleveland, O'Callaghan, as the representative of the clergy.

In the latter part of January, McMaster with obvious distaste published a long letter to which he gave the prejudiced title, "Opposing Canon Law." In an editorial he recounted that he had received the letter a few weeks previously, and he deviously asserted that he had then concluded that the letter "was *devised* to do damage to the cause it professed to support." He named the writer as "Jos. A. Stephan, Pastor of the Orphan Asylum, and Congregation" in Rensselaer, Indiana. Recently he received a note from the Bishop of Fort Wayne, John H. Luers, asking why the letter had not been published and stating that it had been written with the bishop's "consent and approbation." McMaster alleged this episcopal endorsement as his "excuse for occupying our columns with what, otherwise, some might say, was a figure of chaff set up by us for the purpose of scattering it." The straw man was a stronger opponent than McMaster was disposed to admit, for the editor had to use four columns to refute Stephan's two columns and even then he left some of the objections unanswered.

The editor then proceeded to confound his correspondent point by point. Stephan thought it better that the clergy who desired a change should first deliberate about it among themselves in their conferences and synods and then lay the question before the bishops in their provincial councils; only when they failed in this way to obtain what they thought was due to their state should they appeal to the Holy See. McMaster replied that if conferences were established in local districts with deans presiding, such questions would be discussed, but, at present, deaneries existed in very few dioceses. "As for Diocesan Synods," he continued, "there will not be much opportunity for such discussion, if the opening address of the Ordinary reminds the priests that they have nothing to do with the legislation of the Diocese, except to carry out the system as it exists." The failure of the Second Plenary Council "to determine *as of right*, the position of a Priest in his Diocese . . . was the *occasion* of the commencement of this discussion in the *Freeman's Journal*," he reminded his adversary. Stephan, moreover, questioned the assumption that fixed bishops necessarily supposed irremovable pastors, because the former existed "from the very beginning; but centuries elapsed before Parishes were erected with inamovable Pastors." Bringing more theology into the discussion than earlier participants, Stephan contended:

> The Bishop alone is the only real pastor of the Diocese and all the congregations in it. Not the congregation with the Parish Priest, but the Bishop with the Diocese formed the unit. The priests, whether inamovable or otherwise, are his assistants and coadjutors . . . Now it is only natural that the Bishop should send his assistants where, in his judgment, he deems them most necessary, fit and useful to religion. It is not the length of time that constitutes the Pastor in the sense just mentioned, but the sending of him by his Bishop to take charge of a particular place or congregation in the Diocese . . . . It is not at all essential to his office that he be inamovable.

Stephan asserted that even in countries where the parish system prevailed, no one ordained for only seven years was made a pastor for life, and hardly anyone who had not been ordained for fifteen or twenty years. "Why then," he asked, "should there be such indecent haste of being appointed a Parish Priest?"

It was a peculiarity of McMaster's apologetics that he rejected as tainted with Protestantism or with Jansenism and Gallicanism any argument based on the practice of the early Church. The editor, therefore, derisively calling Stephan "Rev. Pastor of the Orphan Asylum, &c.," declined to respond to "such an appeal in the mouth of a Catholic priest." Betraying his impatience, he rambled on and on about the obligation of missionary priests to offer Masses for their congregations on days of obligation. Stephan, furthermore, had argued from the needs of the congregation, asserting that if a pastor in Europe were to lose his first fervor he could rely on assistants to supply his shortcomings, but in this country there were few assistants. McMaster abusively replied that if Stephan "knew even a little of the existing Canon Law, he would know the *remedies*, in the power of a Bishop, for the securing the due performance of all obligations of parochial functions," and he reverted to his favorite parallelism: "Do Bishops never cease to be as active in old age as they were in youth? Are we, therefore, to advocate having them sent to the beggars' hospital, when they have worn themselves out in the service of the Lord?" Then too, Stephan had denied another supposition of the editor and his disciples:

> To judge from the tone of the communications, one would suppose that our Priests were changed about at a wonderful rate. In reality, however, comparatively few transfers take place, and fewer still against the will of the respective Pastors. Our Bishops are glad to leave their Priests where they find them doing well, and where a change is made of well-deserving Priests, they are invariably appointed to more honorable and lucrative positions. The contrary is a rare occurrence.

McMaster simply scoffed at this assertion as due to ignorance: ". . . we have had a longer and wider observation than he has had. We have, even, shed tears over ruined vocations, and broken hearts."

Stephan had also reminded the readers that a form of trial for priests had been prescribed by conciliar decree and that the way to Rome was always open. In rebuttal the editor insisted that no bishop was bound to heed a priest's claim to a trial and that it was not "the *will of Rome*, that this way be trodden so often" as it had been in recent years. Finally, Stephan had expressed the opinion that most of the readers were tired of this controversy and it should cease, but if it had to continue, he hoped that it would at least be with the respect due by priests to their bishops. Furiously McMaster snapped back that if Stephan "had the handling of the hundred and more letters" that the editor received "every day," he would go away an astonished man. With a concluding display of bad temper McMaster wrote: "This controversy will cease when the Vicar of Christ has spoken! Our correspondent . . . does not need to give us advice about having the discussion in our columns conducted with all respect and reverence to ecclesiastical authority. *We* will attend to this. . ."[152] Apparently

McMaster had become so fanatical in his devotion to this cause that he was deaf to "Jus's" strident tones and could not answer Stephan with arguments much more substantial than invective and ridicule.

It was undoubtedly with satisfaction that McMaster published a fortnight later a letter from a priest who had labored on the missions for thirty years, as a quasi-pastor, without incurring the slightest censure. This anonymous writer rehashed the evils with which the present system was fraught. With maudlin eloquence he described the poor old priests who pine away and "die paupers and dependents, as they had no 'parochial rights.' " Piteously he asked, "Why do not some of our magnanimous Prelates stand forward to lead in this great work of reform?" [153]

In the next issue McMaster felt himself under constraint to publish a letter from an unnamed bishop, but he tried to offset the damage inflicted on his cause by giving a rebuttal in the editorial columns. The writer asked which canons required the adoption of the measures advocated by "Jus" and others. With a blush at the supposed episcopal ignorance the editor pointed to the Council of Trent and the Second Plenary Council of Baltimore. Secondly, the bishop wanted to know how parishes could be instituted before one of the essential conditions was satisfied, namely, a sufficient and permanent fund, or benefice, out of which the expenses could be defrayed. Replying *ad hominem*, McMaster observed that there had been "Dioceses made, with no provision of funds secured for the dignity becoming the Episcopate." As far as the territorial requirement of a parish was concerned, the bishop perceived a difficulty arising from the presence of different nationalities within the same congregation. McMaster's rejoinder was an insult: "Our correspondent — so much greater, and better, and holier, than we are, in matters of personal import — has not had, or taken, the time to understand, how *elastic* Canon Law is." Then, confusing nationalities with rites, the editor adduced the precedent of the simultaneous existence of different patriarchs in the same town in Asia Minor, and he argued by analogy: "there is no reason why, in Sees where there are tens of thousands of a nationality and language not that of the country, there should not be appointed, by the Holy See, *Vicars Apostolic*, for these nationalties." The bishop, furthermore, asked why length of service (seven years) should be the standard of qualification for permanent tenure rather than capacity and merit. Evading the question and denying the need for debating specific propositions at that point, McMaster insisted, "The clergy of these States want *nothing* but what is esteemed becoming to the dignity of the priesthood, in France, in Germany, in Belgium, in Ireland." Finally, the episcopal correspondent demanded:

> According to what right did the Priest, who has gone to Rome as the representative of those who have assisted him, leave his congregation, and upon what principle does he ignore his Ordinary, to whom he has sworn reverence and obedience, pass by the Propaganda, and even the Holy Father himself, to lay their case before the General Council, thus actually accusing our Bishops before any demands whatever have been presented to them?

Since O'Callaghan had been suspended, McMaster chose to reply enigmatically:

> 1. Neither has the Priest that has gone to Rome *"left* his congregation," nor is he absent from it without the consent of his Ordinary. We do not mean to say that the consent of an Ordinary would be necessary, were it a case of appeal, in a *casus* occurring between a Priest and his Ordinary. *Many* ways lead to Rome!
>
> 2. The Priest who has gone to Rome, as he goes by consent, does not "ignore his Ordinary."
>
> 3. The said Priest will, most certainly, *not* "pass by the Propaganda, and even the Holy Father."
>
> 4. The Priest that has gone to Rome providentially charged with the exposition of the cause of "Jus," if he is not *called* to the Council of the Vatican, is far too wise and modest a man to seek to obtrude on its attention a matter of *local dispensation* from Catholic discipline that, as we understand it, cannot — *because* local, come before the Council, at all.
>
> 5. Pleading for *Ecclesiastical Law* is not "accusing our Bishops." And, if accusations were to be made, the "Priest who has gone to Rome" knows too much of Canon Law to make such accusations before the Council. There are proper, and permanent, Tribunals, in Rome, for the hearing of such matters.
>
> 6. May not the thought be aroused, by the last paragraph of our venerated correspondent, as to how liable even excellent Bishops may be, when they act without the restraints of ecclesiastical law, to form rash judgments in regard to priests, and to believe, against them, most unfounded accusations?

After this exercise in equivocation and mental reservation McMaster was so irritated that he exclaimed, "We cannot help writing with some heat, when we discuss this subject, because it concerns what is most real, most intimate, most important, of all our earthly affairs." [154]

Meanwhile the American bishops at the council were still looking for the representative of the clergy. McMaster's special correspondent in Rome, William Browne, wrote him:

> I need not tell you every one here is not your friend. I have even heard it doubted if there was such a man as "Jus" and whether any priest has really been sent here to further the cause of Parochial Rights. There have been a good many guesses about "Jus" & the other priest also. As far as this question of Parochial Rights is concerned I do not think that there has been any attempt to hush it up, on the contrary I have heard that there have been allusions to it in the Council & that if all the Bishops were of the same opinion as those who made the allusions that the question as advocated by Jus & the N.Y. Freeman's Journal had but a very poor show of success.[155]

Bishop McQuaid also wrote about this time to his friend Michael A. Corrigan, vicar-general of the Diocese of Newark and administrator in the absence of the bishop as well as president of Seton Hall College:

> We are still waiting for the appearance of McMaster's champion of Priests' rights. No one can make out who he is; certainly he has not made himself known as such, or in that character to any in authority. My own suspicion based on good reasons leads me to think that I know him, and that he has been here, but not as McMaster described; that he has done no more than represent, when he found opportunity, the great agitation in the United States, but never putting himself forward as the representative of any body. His character was such that no one suspected him, nor did we until quite lately know that he had had trouble with his Bishop. As the trouble has been settled, it is probable that he will return to his Diocese and try to conceal his part in the agitation. There is a Priest here, O'Callaghan, of Cleveland Diocese, complaining of his Bishop, but he does not go beyond his own affair.[156]

Thus it seems that no finger of suspicion was pointed at O'Callaghan because he simply failed to represent the aggrieved American clergy.

Toward the end of February, O'Callaghan sent McMaster the last of the series by "Jus." In a covering letter he begged the editor not to speak of him any more as one who might be made a bishop, for not

only did he modestly disclaim any such ambitions but he also realistically understood that "the hope were to be foolish especially," as he
said, "after my irremissible sin of writing against those who have been
appointed by the Holy Ghost to govern the American Church and who
have such faith in his guidance as to scoff at the intermediation of any
law." [157] Before the letter from "Jus" was published, O'Callaghan
wrote McMaster again describing his relation to the American
bishops in Rome:

> Although my Metropolitan, the Archbishop of Cincinnati, al-
> ways treats me with much kindness, yet I know I am an object
> of dislike to a great many Bishops who know that I have come
> to appeal from the act of my Bishop in removing me without
> cause on my part.[158]

"The Parting Hail of 'Jus' " resounded in the *Freeman's Journal*
at the beginning of spring. It was another screed against the arbitrary
power of bishops and another apotheosis of law. In several ways he
demonstrated how law would benefit the bishops just as its absence
injured them. He also demolished what he understood to be "the
principal ground on which the advocates of the present status" stood,
that is, "that *Law* would protect the bad priest" by preventing the
bishop from punishing him; he declared: "It is an insult to American
Priests even to breathe this objection . . . . Let us hear no more of
this vile imputation that American Bishops need arbitrary power,
otherwise they could not govern their Priests." The essence of this
last message from "Jus" was found in the middle of the letter:

> The time has arrived when the new status shall be inaugurated,
> if the Priests of the United States desire it . . . . The most
> favorable accounts have been sent from Rome by the Priest
> who has undertaken to represent us there . . . . He states, upon
> authority not to be despised, that the whole question, whether we
> will or will not have Law instead of Arbitrary Government,
> now depends entirely upon ourselves . . . . The critical moment
> has come . . . Rome, ever accessible to justice, law, and reason,
> is ready to hear our complaints (or has already heard them) and
> IS ONLY WAITING TO GRANT OUR PETITIONS.

It is difficult to conceive of any foundation that O'Callaghan, even with
the most optimistic outlook, might have had for such an assurance.
It is also doubtful that he had any serious prospects of actually serving

as the clergy's agent. In spite of the unpropitious situation in Rome, nevertheless, he incited the priests to immediate action, as he continued:

> No representative at Rome, no matter what his wisdom or influence, can effect any good without petitions. This is the burden of our Representative's letters; *without a petition* we can effect *nothing,* or very little. *With a petition we can effect everything reasonable and desirable.* Should our Representative present himself *formally* before the Holy Father or the Propaganda de Fide [*sic*], he must go *armed,* taking with him a petition in which our wants, few and simple, are stated, and praying the Holy Father to hear and grant them. This petition must be signed by a *Majority of the Secular* Priests . . . .
>
> . . . Let no time be lost in forwarding this Petition, because those whose influence may be of the highest value to us may leave Rome before our Petition would reach thither . . . .

"Jus" tried to shame all the priests into signing the petition by saying that he did not expect or desire the signatures of the inert and selfish, much less of any bad priest. In a peroration to the whole series he denied that he had said anything that could reasonably offend or that he had been induced to write from personal grievances.[159] If "Jus" was not a hypocrite he was at least a poor judge of others' sensibilities and of his own motives.

The urgent appeal of "Jus" for signatures to a non-existent petition provoked a varied response from the American priests. Some ingenuously asked McMaster to attach their names to "the petition to Rome" or to "any petition that may be sent to Rome." Others inquired how the signatures should be forwarded or suggested ways, in which they could be collected.[160] It was obvious that through their inept leadership McMaster and "Jus" had created great confusion among the clergy. There is no reason to assume that McMaster ever assembled these signatures in one list or forwarded them to O'Callaghan in Rome. It seems rather that about this time the editor decided to abandon the campaign entirely.

It is not clear why McMaster suddenly ceased to agitate for parochial rights, but it is likely that he was influenced by a fear of episcopal condemnation. In March he received a letter from an anonymous friend signing himself "Sacerdos," who informed him that the newly consecrated Bishop of Alton, Peter J. Baltes, had issued a pastoral letter and had ordered it to be read from the pulpits or altars on the following Sunday. The priest enclosed a section of the pastoral entitled, "Anti-Catholic Press," which, in his judgment and in that of others with whom he had spoken, was "directly levelled against the *Freeman's Journal.*" He added, "I deem it but right to send it to you for the purpose of making such animadversions on it as you shall think fit." The section read:

> Whilst we earnestly recommend to you the support of the Catholic press, we do not wish to be understood as recommending those so-called papers which of late have erroneously considered themselves called to sow the seeds of discord between the Superior and inferior clergy, between the Roman Catholic Bishops of the United States and the Priests of their respective Dioceses. The course pursued by these papers can be productive of evil only to those who pursue such a course, and those who allow themselves to be duped by them. Let those editors, and those who support them, as well as the heads of families who bring those papers before their children, bear in mind that God is just and will mete out to them what they wish to mete to others. Though they boast of powerful support we have good reason for believing that their course will be short and will end in a manner detrimental to themselves. We forbid the circulation of these papers amongst the faithful of our Diocese.[161]

A little later another priest also wrote to McMaster about Bishop Baltes' pastoral. He quoted the same passage with some variation indicating that he translated it from the German version which he had found in a German-language newspaper, and he commented: "Now, dear Sir! You will admit that such language from a Bishop, tyrannical as it is, will have its influence on a certain number of priests. Yet I say, poor, indeed, must be the cause, which cannot bear a free discussion."[162] As it turned out, Bishop Baltes waited nine years before he condemned the *Freeman's Journal* by name.[163]

Whatever reasons he may have had, McMaster refrained from mentioning the topic again in his weekly until the end of the spring. Meanwhile many priests whose expectations he and "Jus" had raised to such heights became disillusioned with the lack of progress. One of them, after praising the editor lavishly in his letter, sharply called him "to task and to order for the rights of the priesthood:"

> Now, my dear McMaster, to speak plainly to you & with you, our cause has been lost; you have allowed the rights so ably defended and so clearly advocated by Jus & your noble self to go by default, to use a legal term. Now to come to the point with you &

to the matter at issue, I beg & request of you in the name of God and for the sake of our holy religion not to allow this matter to drop & die away. My suggestion and plan is to send circulars to all the priests of the United States to request they will now or never give and permit their names to be put or signed to a petition or document to be laid at the feet of the Holy Father. I and a few others will defray the expenses of the circulation & from thence to Rome. This only remains to make you a bold, fearless defender and the never failing champion of our rights.[164]

McMaster, however, was not moved by this desperate plea. He let three more weeks pass without uttering a word on the subject.

In the middle of June he reiterated the hope of having ecclesiastical law soon, but he also upheld episcopal authority, saying:

. . . because Bishops are set in the Catholic Church to govern the peoples committed to them it is obligatory on us, as Catholics, to recognize their authority, as direct, and immediate, in all ordinary cases. Now and then cases may occur, recognized by established law of the Church, and understood by all who will, with any wisdom, make the appeal, to higher authority, and finally, to the Holy See, the supreme and ultimate authority in the Catholic Church.

The editor asserted that his reason for stating this principle was "to guard the minds of the unwary against foolish, garulous [*sic*], and untenable propositions suggested to the faithful by incompetent writers in papers called Catholic." [165] Perhaps the reason was really a desire to placate Bishop Baltes and like-minded prelates. He never referred to "Jus" again, however, before the end of the council.

Only after the council was adjourned in the summer did McMaster briefly revive the discussion of "the establishment of a fixed system of law." Again he endeavored to remove the misunderstanding of some bishops who thought that he had wanted to introduce "the cumbersome fabric of a *jus canonicum vetus* if not *vetissimum*," a "superannuated system." He confessed no guilt in the affair:

No scandal, but rather the reverse, arose from that discussion, in our columns. That is a *fact* that we insist on having recognized. The *appeal to law, rendered the right exercise of law more emphatic, and potential.*

Meantime, from competent authority, we were advised that, *for the present*, the discussion, in the columns of a Journal, had gone far enough. It had aroused thought, reflection, consideration. It would not have been *good* that rights for the second order in the Hierarchy should have been *forced* from the Ordinaries of Dioceses. Such was never the intention of *"Jus"* nor of the *Freeman's Journal.* Our appeal was to the conscience of the Prelates, and to their respect for sacerdotal honor.

The kindliness, the Apostolic gentleness, of many of the Bishops, in private communications, has shown how surrounded with difficulties the true solution of this question is.

It would not be proper here, we think, to indicate the steps already taken, by some of the Bishops, to show their desire to make their clergy happy.

Such mild, humble language was not typical of the old warrior. His effort to reassure his clerical readers was equally unconvincing: "The *cause* is not dead, by any means. On the contrary, it has ceased to raise a ripple, of late, because it is in so healthy a condition of progress." He promised that when the right time would come, the discussion, if necessary, would be conducted "on a *higher* plane." His stoic advice was, *"Patience,* for the moment, is the highest wisdom." [166]

McMaster's patience was taxed beyond his ability to control it, however, when the rumor was spread that his paper had been censured by a bishop. He rejected this allegation with fierce indignation:

The *Freeman's Journal* has *not* been denounced, by any competent authority, high or low, in the Ecclesiastical Order. It has not merited any such denunciation, and, has not received it . . . *We* continue our pleading for the introduction of some *fixed law* in the large and populous Dioceses, and Ecclesiastical Provinces, of these States . . . .

. . . If the Bishops do not *like* it [the paper], we are sorry. As to the condemnation of it, without *cause* stated, *words* cited, etc., this is not the way law is executed in so perfect a community as the Catholic Church. [167]

McMaster may have been right about the legal procedure, but perhaps he feared a condemnation none the less. In any case, thereafter in regard to the question of canon law he followed his own advice of patience for the remaining sixteen years of his life.

Meanwhile O'Callaghan in Rome accomplished nothing for his fellow priests, although apparently he made some slight efforts. Bishop McQuaid wrote to a priest in Rochester:

No one here has been able to discover the representative of "Jus." We can only laugh at the tone of the Freeman. It is probable that when his agitation dies out that [*sic*] Bishops themselves will take up the matter and see what can be done, in justice to the interests of religion as well as of Priests. The matter only once came up in a meeting of the American Bishops and on that occasion the only difficulty in the way of giving it examination was McMaster's agitation.[168]

Apparently McQuaid was referring to the meeting held at the American College on December 22, 1869, at which the American bishops gathered in Rome for the council considered the question of irremovability and agreed to prepare a statement for the Propaganda's consideration; the project seems to have been abandoned thereafter.

In the spring of 1870 the Bishop of Fort Wayne, John Henry Luers, who had remained at home during the council, warned Archbishop Spalding against O'Callaghan. Not knowing that the priest was "Jus," he identified him only as the leader of the conspirators in the Diocese of Cleveland who were compassing the removal of Bishop Rappe. Luers asked Spalding to acquaint the cardinal prefect with the despicable methods employed by this group, for he feared that if these priests succeeded in their plans, no bishop in the country would be safe. He wrote: "There is a bad spirit among not a small portion of our clergy, and unless a check is put upon it by Rome and these priests who now agitate against Bp. Rappe receive a severe lesson, the Church in the U.S. will suffer." Luers admitted, however, that the American bishops should recognize that they could no longer act arbitrarily and should deal with their priests according to "reason, justice, and Canon law." [169]

Though Bishop Luers deplored O'Callaghan's objectives and methods, he conceded, in effect, that "Jus" was right in describing the unjust behavior of some bishops. A few months later he wrote to Cardinal Barnabò:

A great evil exists in some dioceses of this country and is the source of many complaints, because it causes the ruin of a good number of ecclesiastics.

When a priest has lost the good graces of his superiors or has been accused of a crime, it is not rare to see him deprived of his powers or functions, his only means of existence, and that without any previous form of inquiry. He is simply dismissed without being told what he must do to be restored in his functions, without even being given the hope of ever being rehabilitated, so that the poor ecclesiastic is left entirely at the mercy of his ordinary. Evidently the Holy See alone can remedy this abuse, and if I may express my opinion, the matter could be handled thus:

(1) All the ordinaries should be commanded to observe to the letter the decrees enacted by themselves in the councils confirmed by Rome.

(2) A form of simple and uniform procedure should be enjoined on them to judge, suspend, or interdict priests either suspected *ex informata conscientia* or accused publicly. In case of conviction a suitable penance should be imposed on them, and when it has been performed the ordinary should either rehabilitate them or provide for their existence. This, however, would not apply in the case where there was no hope of amendment.[170]

This advice probably arrived in Rome about the same time as another priest from the Diocese of Cleveland, Charles Evrard, Pastor of St. Alphonsus' Church in Norwalk, came to the support of O'Callaghan. Two years previously he had been reinstated in his parish by order of the Propaganda after having been transferred by Bishop Rappe to a poorer parish. Now he submitted an "Humble Pétition en faveur du Clergé secondaire aux États-Unis d'Amérique." After echoing the laments of "Jus" about the abnormal position of the American priests and the "absolute power" of the bishops, he asked:

Must this situation remain unremedied? Since the opening of the council, our thoughts and our hopes have been with Rome, and we have been awaiting an assuagement of our woes from the Propaganda. Deign to do something for such a zealous and hardworking class. I do not come to ask of Your Eminence either the establishment of *parishes* or *canonical irremovability* for the *pastors* of these parishes. Our desires are much more modest and come down to the following proposals:

(1) The present practice of changing priests *ad nutum* would be maintained only for the young priests during a period of probation (*un temps d'épreuve*) from five to ten years, determined by the Holy See.

(2) After the priests have honorably passed this time, they could not be changed *against their will* unless an ecclesiastical tribunal, formed *ad hoc*, would find the bishop's reasons sufficent. Before the judgment would be pronounced, the priest would have

full freedom to justify his conduct and to answer all the accusations brought against him.

(3) To offer every guarantee of impartiality, the ecclesiastical tribunal could be formed in the following manner: The bishop in synod would present a list of candidates larger than the number to be elected. The members taken from this list who would receive a majority of the votes would constitute the ecclesiastical tribunal.[171]

Even these reduced requests, however, failed at that time to evoke a favorable response from the Propaganda.

Evrard's aid notwithstanding, O'Callaghan, with his reputation clouded by Luers' denunciation, could not be an effective spokesman for the American clergy. He succeeded, nevertheless, in his more limited ambitions, for his suspension was lifted and his bishop was forced to resign. By that time, however, it was too late for him to promote the cause of parochial rights.[172] The priests of the United States could hardly have been more poorly represented at Rome even if there had been a chance of achieving anything through representation on that occasion in the first place. All that O'Callaghan and McMaster accomplished was to accentuate (not to create) the discontent of priests without being able to propose any feasible way of appeasing it.

A quarter of a century later O'Callaghan admitted in the *Freeman's Journal* that he was "Jus" and had gone to Rome in 1869 to forward the cause he had been advocating in that newspaper. He claimed that in Rome he had become "acquainted with a certain Italian bishop, . . . the bosom friend of Pius IX and who was afterward raised to the Cardinalate." O'Callaghan had rendered him "important service" and thus "became quite intimate with him"; during his visits he "again and again spoke of the abnormal condition of the Church in America," and he assumed that his friend related his pleadings to the Pope. He also boasted that he had found in Rome "an old friend, an official of another great order of the Church, who held high office in one of the most important Congregations of the Church."[173] Perhaps these "influential patrons" aided him in his own case, but he could not point to any success that they might have helped him to achieve for the priests of the United States.

Even though the First Vatican Council was terminated before disciplinary questions could be considered, they had not been overlooked in the preparatory stages. In a questionnaire presented by Cardinal Prospero Caterini, prefect of the Sacred Congregation of the

Council, to the bishops who were in Rome for the canonization of some saints on the eighteenth centenary of the martyrdom of SS. Peter and Paul, it was asked whether the number of cases should be increased in which pastors could be deprived of their right to their churches and whether a simpler procedure for effecting such deprivations, *salva iustitia*, should be instituted; it was also asked how the Tridentine decree on suspension *ex informata conscientia* should be executed.[174] Four American prelates, namely, Archbishops Spalding of Baltimore and Purcell of Cincinnati, and Bishops William Henry Elder of Natchez and Thomas L. Grace of St. Paul, were present. According to the summary of the replies, the majority of the bishops were in favor of facilitating the removal of pastors "in order that these shepherds of souls may be all the more held within their office and may not fall into any excesses." With respect to the decree of the Council of Trent, the bishops unanimously affirmed that their extraordinary power to suspend priests could not be abolished or restricted but should not be used frequently; some said they never used it, and many others said they used it only very rarely and in emergencies. Archbishop Spalding, the only American mentioned in the summary of these sections, was quoted as having replied that at least the spirit of the Tridentine decree should be observed, but the letter only as far as possible.[175] The tendency of these replies seems to have been contrary to the position of McMaster and "Jus," who advocated more stability for pastors and more formality in clerical trials. Since, however, the European bishops and the American publicists were approaching the problem from opposite extremes, they might have come together on a mutually acceptable middle ground.

In 1869 Archbishop Spalding submitted to the preparatory commission in Rome a more detailed statement on the irremovability of pastors. He believed before God that this right should be restricted rather than enlarged because of the most grave abuses to which it often gave rise. In the United States, where it did not exist, he explained, a pastor who gave public scandal could easily be removed, to the great benefit of religion. He continued:

> Since this is well known to both the pastors and the Catholic people, the pastors are wont to be careful not to fall into serious sin, and once a scandal has arisen, the people spontaneously call to the ordinary for the removal of the pastor. But if the pastors were irremovable, it would be difficult to remove those who gave scandal — perhaps only after a canonical trial, or even a civil

trial, which would aggravate the scandal itself, much to the detriment of religion. In the Spanish and Portuguese colonies which adjoin us, in both North and South America, such alas! is not the case. There even the most scandalous pastors can hardly be removed, even if they have concubines, as, unfortunately, not infrequently happens, especially in tropical regions. On the one hand, these pastors claim the right of irremovability, and when the ordinary threatens or attempts a canonical trial for their expulsion, they appeal to the civil governor, who usually supports the cause of a scandalous priest against his bishop, claiming the right of intervening from the privileges which, according to his wrong interpretation, follow from the union of the Church with the State.[176]

Since there was no union of Church and State in this country, the archbishop does not seem to have been entirely logical in objecting to the irremovability of pastors in the United States. In any event, the minds of the American and European bishops as expressed during the preparatory phase make it seem unlikely that the ecumenical council would have satisfied the demands of the American priests even if it had reconvened in the autumn of 1870.

Part IV: After the First Vatican Council

During the 1870's individual bishops and priests came into conflict with increasing frequency, and both turned to Rome for support. In 1873 the Bishop of Natchez, William Henry Elder, inquired whether a priest who had rendered himself unworthy of exercising the sacred ministry was left without the title of the mission, under which he was ordained, and whether the ordinary was bound to provide for his sustenance. The Propaganda replied that if the bishop first warned the priest, as long as the latter persisted in his evil way of life and showed no sign of sincere repentance and reform, the bishop was not obliged to support him. In a private letter, however, Bishop Elder was advised not to make that declaration until he had urged the priest with fatherly and repeated admonitions to amend his ways but in vain, and until he had obtained certain proof, even outside of a trial, of the priest's crimes and his public loss of reputation such as could be submitted to the Sacred Congregation in case of an appeal. The Propaganda also decided that this answer should be communicated not only to the bishop presenting the question but also to all the prelates dependent on that Congregation. It followed from this reply that even if a priest by his own fault had made himself incapable of holding an ecclesiastical office, he was not immediately to be deprived of all means of support but only after he had demonstrated his contumacy. The bishop was still to furnish him with a decent livelihood even though the bishop was justified in removing him from his church unless the priest stubbornly refused to follow the advice.[177] This decision, exhibiting the Propaganda's patience and sympathy with the priests, would seem to have softened the decree of the First Provincial Council of St. Louis and the Second Plenary Council of Baltimore declaring that priests who had been forbidden to exercise the sacred ministry had no right to request support from the bishop. The decision, however, does not seem to have been widely known among the priests and was not cited by writers on the subject in the decades immediately following.

The well-known canonist, Sebastian B. Smith, of the Diocese of Newark, published his *Notes on the Second Plenary Council of Baltimore* in the following year.[178] In this work he did not hesitate to point out the conciliar decrees which were not being fully or universally observed by the bishops. He called most opportune the recommendations of the First Plenary Council regarding the bishop's councillors or consultors which were repeated in 1866, and he admitted that most, if not all, of the bishops had their councils. But he suggested that this seeming compliance was specious by adding: "Yet we venture to ask, does it [the council] exist generally also in reality, or merely in name? Are its members formally consulted or called together at stated times?"[179] Speaking of the manner of choosing bishops, he showed in a brief historical review that "the priests of the respective dioceses have, from the very beginning of Christianity to the present day, been recognized in the common law of the Church as the original and ordinary electors of bishops," and he supposed it to be "in accordance with the wish of the Holy See, that this right should be exercised by the priests in America."[180] Remarking that candidates for American sees were merely presented by the bishops by way of recommendation or supplication without any implied obligation being imposed on the Pope, he said:

> This would seem to be an additional argument in favor of allowing the clergy a share in this counsel-giving nomination. Who, as a general rule, know better the faults or the virtues and other good qualifications of priests considered worthy of promotion, than their fellow-priests?

Besides, it would always remain the privilege of the bishops of the province to accept or reject the choice of the clergy.[181]

He concluded, therefore:

In the opinion of eminent men, and also according to the instructions of the Holy See, it would be desirable, as well as conformable to the general discipline of the Church, that the second order of the hierarchy, that is, the priests, should have a voice in the election of bishops.[182]

In a section on "Immovability of Parish Priests," Smith adverted to the accusation made against some bishops —

that when charges were brought against a priest, bishops adopted a system of espionage to discover the truth of the allegations made against them, not even informing the accused of these imputations, and then either removing or suspending the priest without having given him any opportunity of self-defence.[183]

Smith did not assert that such a state of things actually existed, but he showed from the life of Demetrius A. Gallitzin that it could occur, and he contrasted it with the attitude of Martin J. Spalding toward his priests. He seems to have agreed with the late archbishop that the institution of irremovable pastors should be introduced gradually. He called the movableness of pastors a grievance which was "itself the result of an evil . . . far graver than the former," that is, "the total absence or want of any fixed and canonical mode of appointing and promoting pastors." [184]

With respect to the mode of judicial preceedings in the United States, Smith wrote:

. . . Although bishops in this country may not always be able to follow the canonical mode of procedure in the strictest sense of the term, yet it is incumbent on them, according to the decrees both of provincial and national councils, to adhere to the normal judiciary form of the Church, and but rarely to admit of exceptions to this rule.[185]

Applying this principle to the practice of suspension *ex informata conscientia*, Smith quoted the reasons that Francis Patrick Kenrick had set down in his *Theologia Moralis* to explain why bishops revoke priests' faculties without assigning any reason or without due process of law, but he asserted that Kenrick had exaggerated the reasons "for this abnormal and extraordinary manner of proceedings," which, nevertheless, was "so universally adopted by the American episcopate." He commented: "It seems no longer to be the exception, as canon law would have it: it has become emphatically the rule followed by the bishops of this country."[186] Then he quoted with approval the cautions uttered by Kenrick, and concluded:

> The bishops of America, consequently, are bound to observe the decree of the Council of St. Louis, which is sanctioned by the Holy See, and which provides for a fair trial. . . . so that the defendant or accused ecclesiastic may have a chance of defending himself, and, if need be, of appealing to the metropolitan.
>
> As long as the above decree is not enforced and complied with by the prelates of this country, every priest must be simply at the mercy or caprice of his bishop, and, practically speaking, little if any protection against slander and injustice is left him.[187]

Smith thought that it was hardly surprising that some priests in such circumstances had had recourse to civil courts, and he believed that the most effective way of preventing ecclesiastical matters from being carried before lay judges was to conform to the wise provisions of ecclesiastical law. He dismissed all objections to the contrary as being "of little weight when compared with the pernicious effects of judicatories *ex informata conscientia*."[188]

A few years later Smith published an article on "Cathedral Chapters as Adapted to the United States."[189] Here he summarized the origin and history of chapters, described their structure and functions, and contrasted them with the bishops' councils or quasi-chapters recommended by the Second Plenary Council. Then he asked, "Would it be feasible to institute chapters in this country on the model of those in Ireland or England?" In the latter country the canons had no prebends or benefices but were pastors or professors living in various parts of the diocese; they were excused from the obligation of residing near the cathedral and of reciting the divine office in choir. Accordingly, he concluded that with the permission of the Holy See, which could readily be obtained, "chapters, as they exist in England, could easily be introduced into nearly every diocese of the United States."[190]

In 1878 the Bishop of Ardagh, George Conroy, who had been sent to Canada as a temporary apostolic delegate by the Holy See, was directed to visit the United States as well. After an extensive tour he wrote for the Propaganda a long report on the state of the Church in this country. He stressed the importance that the American prelates attached to skill in managing finances when they both recommended candidates for the episcopacy and appointed pastors. He said that in order to safeguard the property of the Church, a bishop felt obliged to choose a priest capable of collecting money successfully; but if it should become clear from experience that a pastor was unable or unwilling to raise enough funds not only to support himself but also to pay the current interest, the bishop deemed it necessary to deprive him of his parish and to transfer him to another post. To this practice Conroy attributed the frequent complaints about the arbitrary procedure of the bishops. When a bishop found that a particular priest was adept at raising money, he was easily induced to transfer him to another parish in which the finances were in a bad state. Hence, it happened at least now and then that an outstanding and zealous pastor was rewarded by being deprived of his parish and being sent to an inferior one carrying an enormous debt.[191]

Bishop Conroy had been asked by the cardinal-prefect of the Propaganda to study the opportuneness of establishing an apostolic delegation in the United States. Accordingly, he discussed this question with as many bishops and priests as he chanced to meet. From their remarks he concluded that the sending of a delegate would not encounter any serious opposition on any side and would even be welcomed with joy by the clergy in general and by some bishops; he admitted that the other bishops did not like the idea but would not resist; only three bishops considered the establishment of a delegation to be necessary.[192]

Then the Irish observer proceeded to describe "the ever increasing discord between the bishops and the priests" over the rights of pastors. He was careful to state that the priests had not rebelled against episcopal authority or unduly displayed their ill-temper by their actions, except in some very rare cases. He had noticed, nevertheless, "a certain rumbling [*sordo*] discontent among the clergy which could easily open the door to some serious scandal." The visitor reduced to two headings the complaints raised by the priests.[193]

In the first place, Conroy reported, the priests complained about the manner in which candidates for the episcopacy were chosen:

> With regard to the first complaint, it must be observed that the clergy do not condemn the method prescribed by the Holy See concerning the nomination of a bishop, but rather the manner in which this method is carried out in practice by the bishops. According to them, the bishops do not take the trouble either to seek the best candidates or seriously to inform themselves of the quality and habits of the candidates who are proposed. The protection of some influential bishop is sufficient to make the

choice fall upon whoever possesses it, and this protection is generally the reward for services rendered to the bishop by the candidate, or at least an act of personal friendship and not a testimonial to singular merit on his part. And since the bishops observe secrecy regarding the terna that they have proposed to the Holy See, any communication of information about the demerits of the candidate if he should have any is rendered impossible. And even in the case that some priest through an obligation of conscience went to the bishops in order to reveal some defect in the candidate, these do not want to listen to him, heedless of what the *Pontificale Romano* says, that *quod nonnumquam ignoratur a paucis scitur a pluribus.* Hence, it has sometimes happened that even after the receipt of the Papal Brief and even up to the very eve of the day fixed for his consecration, the bishop-elect was forced to withdraw. Another very grave inconvenience in this matter also comes to pass which deserves consideration. The secrecy observed by the bishops regarding the proposed terna is *a fortiori* maintained at Rome; it happens, consequently, that it is impossible to communicate even to the Holy See information on the character of the candidates, even in the case that such information would be necessary for the good of souls. In order to understand how pernicious the result of the present manner of selecting bishops is, it is enough, so the priests say, to cast a glance at the American episcopate! Of the total number of sixty-eight bishops, there are hardly *ten* distinguished for talent of any kind. The others hardly reach a decent mediocrity, and in theological knowledge they do not reach even mediocrity! It should not cause surprise, therefore, that the clergy has begun to lose the respect due to the episcopacy. This is true of the clergy in almost every part of the United States.

It seems to me that these complaints, though too harsh in form, are not unreasonable in their basis. For the peace of the Church, for the decorum of the episcopate, for the benefit of souls I am of opinion that it would be good to broaden the range of the persons from whom the Holy See receives information on the priests proposed for the episcopal office. Moreover, I am of opinion that this can be done without at all abandoning the system in use at present, which allows a deliberative vote only to the bishops in the choice of the terna. I am quite far from believing that it would be good to introduce into America the Irish system which allows the pastors a deliberative vote; however, I am convinced that it would be an excellent move to grant the American pastors a consultative vote when the bishops are about to draw up a terna. If the Holy See would issue an instruction commanding that at the death of a bishop or in the case of a vacancy for whatever reason, the pastors of the vacant diocese would have to send to the archbishop or to the senior suffragan, within twenty days, a letter in which each of them would communicate *coram Domino* the names of the three priests whom he judges to be the most suitable for the government of the vacant see, the bishops would be able to proceed with greater assurance to deliberate upon the terna to be proposed, serious errors regarding the persons themselves would be avoided, and a legitimate satisfaction would be given to the American clergy. The archbishop or the senior suffragan would have to be obliged to send to the Sacred Congregation, as an integral part of the procès verbal of the bishops' deliberation, a summary of the letters sent to him by the pastors of the diocese. If to these two distinct sources of information there would be added also the analogous report of an apostolic delegate, nothing more complete could be desired. I have questioned several archbishops and bishops of the United States about this modification of the present system, and I have found that they all indicated their satisfaction with it. Indeed, to my great pleasure, I learned that in the Diocese of Baltimore the pastors have enjoyed a consultative voice from the time of that great prelate, Archbishop Kenrick; and I should say that I have not found in the United States a clergy more content or a diocese more prudently governed than that of Baltimore.[194]

The other main complaint of the priests that Conroy treated in his report was that the bishops took little or no account of canon law when they exercised their authority:

Regarding the second complaint raised by the clergy against the bishops, it is unfortunately true that not only the bishops but even the priests very often do not care about the provisions of canon law. Indeed, it can be said that the same [Second Plenary] Council of Baltimore is by this time *tanquam non esset*. During my journey in the United States which lasted more than three months, I often heard some bishop appeal to the decrees of Baltimore when there was occasion to punish some priest, and I heard many priests appeal to other decrees of the same synod to defend themselves against the abuse of power by some bishop;

but rarely did I find among bishops or priests anyone who wished to make use of the provisions of the synod, taken in their entirety, as rules for his government either of the diocese or of the parish. However that may be, it is evident that the American clergy is very irritated against the bishops because of the use which they make of the right accorded to them by the Synod of Baltimore of changing pastors, that is, *ad nutum*, from one parish to another. The numerous recourses which are made against the American bishops in this matter are more than sufficient proof of this fact. To tell the truth, a conflict on this ground was inevitable, the respective claims of the bishops and of the pastors being so incompatible. The bishop interpreted the Synod of Baltimore in a way that removed from the pastor all right to permanence in his parish and made him a mere vicar of the bishop. The pastor, on the contrary, especially for the past five years, while conceding to the bishop that the pastor is removable *ad nutum*, insists upon the bishop's obligation of not removing him from his parish *sine causa*. This serious dissension is further fomented by some occasional causes. Many of these priests who have taken their appeals to the Holy See have returned victorious to their parishes; and since some of them were anything but respectable in their lives, their triumph aroused the indignation of the bishops, even against the Holy See. Some pastors claim every right for themselves [reading uncertain here] while to their wretched flocks no right is granted; but perhaps it will be true that to attack the bishops means to defend the Church. But in my opinion, if immediate steps are not taken to give us such instructions as will be able to set up a practical rule to follow in the cases of priestly scandals, there will not remain in the country at the end of two generations as much religion as would suffice to reward us for our present efforts. So one bishop; let us now listen to a most respectable priest who writes to me in this way on May 25: "We shall not have peace in this country until the relations between bishops and priests shall be established and made clear according to the norms of the provisions of canon law, which is desired so much by all of us. Today priests have no rights at all; they can be chased from their posts at whim while the bishops exercise a veritable tyranny over them." From these two extracts from letters it is easy to understand how divided the minds are at present, and how much everyone wants a clear and precise rule on the canonical position that the American pastors occupy.[195]

Since one of the priests whom Bishop Conroy visited was his former schoolmate, Richard L. Burtsell, pastor of the Church of the Epiphany in New York, who was soon to become prominent in the struggle for the rights of the clergy, it is not surprising that the delegate showed more sympathy for the priests than for the bishops in his report.[196]

It is unlikely that Bishop Conroy's report was submitted early enough to influence the Propaganda in its next action regarding the trials of clerics. The only recourse of priests who claimed, rightly or wrongly, that they had been mistreated by their bishops was to appeal to the Holy See. The Propaganda learned by experience that the established order of trials was not entirely capable of preventing complaints on the part of those punished. For it often happened that priests who were condemned at trials conducted in that way and were removed especially from the office of missionary rector complained about their bishops and frequently also appealed to Rome. Not rarely the result was that many things and especially necessary data were found to be lacking in the records transmitted, and thus serious doubts often arose as to whether credence should be given or denied to the documents presented in these cases.

In 1878, therefore, the Sacred Congregation decided to seek "a remedy for these troubles and thus to provide for justice, in order that innocent clerics might not be punished unjustly nor those guilty of some crime escape from the deserved punishment because of a less correct form of trials." The Propaganda thought that it would achieve this end if it ordered the observance of all the sacred canons regarding ecclesiastical trials, but it recognized that this was not possible in the United States. Hence, it decided to prescribe a method by which at least those criminal investigations might be carefully conducted which were deemed absolutely necessary before a punishment could be inflicted. The Propaganda, therefore, with the approval of Leo XIII decreed that each bishop in the United States should, in a diocesan synod to be convoked as soon as possible, select five, or, if so many were not available because of peculiar circumstances, at least three priests among the most upright and, if possible, those trained in canon law; these were to form a judicial council or commission of investigation with one of the members as chairman or president. If for some serious reason a diocesan synod could not be held immediately, five or three ecclesiastics were to be appointed by the bishop. The main duty of this commission was to examine criminal and disciplinary cases of priests and other clerics according to the rules given in the same Instruction, and to furnish aid to the bishop in deciding them. The members of the commission were to endeavor to obtain testimony from witnesses and to find out from the accused everything that might be necessary to arrive at the truth and that might supply certain or sufficiently strong arguments to pronounce a just decision. No rector of a mission could be removed from his office unless at least three members of the commission were deputed to investigate the case and the bishop listened to their advice. The elected members of the commission were to remain in office until the next diocesan synod would be held and then they would be either confirmed in office or replaced. If any of the members should die or resign in the meantime, the bishop was to appoint a substitute outside a synod. Finally, the Propaganda laid down fourteen rules of procedure for the commission.[197]

Some of the American bishops were not pleased with this new legislation, for they had not been consulted by the Propaganda. The same was true of some priests but for a different reason; the Bishop of Newark, Michael A. Corrigan, wrote to his friend, Bishop McQuaid, "It is said the clergy are not too well satisfied with it, as they think that great notoriety will now follow necessarily all such trials, and that failings cannot be covered up as in the past." [198] The practical question also arose whether a bishop was obliged to consult the commission of investigation before transferring any rector from one mission to another against the will of the latter. According to Bishop McQuaid, who went to Rome in the autumn of 1878 for his *ad limina* visit, the question had already been decided in the affirmative and the letter containing this answer was written but had not yet been sent to the American bishops. McQuaid, who feared neither his own priests nor his fellow bishops nor the curial officials, thought that the new legislation "would inflict very great injury on the Church in this country." [199] Hence, he begged that the matter be reconsidered or at least that the American bishops be consulted before a final decision should be made. Bishop Corrigan wrote to James Gibbons, Archbishop of Baltimore:

> He has protested very strongly against the sweeping accusations made against us [bishops], — especially that our "arbitrary" conduct makes Priests bewail their ordination, — anxious to escape the country as from a prison, and makes Parents refuse to permit their sons to study for the Priesthood.[200]

McQuaid aroused the apprehension also of Cardinal Henry Manning, Archbishop of Westminster, and Bishop W. J. H. Clifford of Clifton, who were also in Rome, by pointing out that the same law would apply to the English hierarchy. Before he could obtain an answer from the

Propaganda, McQuaid was struck down by typhus for twenty-four days. Meanwhile the anxious Bishop of Newark wrote to the Bishop of Cleveland, Richard Gilmour:

> . . . I hope that they [the Propaganda] will not force us [bishops] to consider every Priest now in charge of a mission as a missionary Rector, — no matter how short a time has elapsed since his ordination. Would not this be worse than Canon Law? [201]

The Propaganda finally issued the response desired by McQuaid and most of the other American bishops. It reminded them, however, not to transfer unwilling priests from one mission to another without a serious and reasonable motive. It also clarified the way in which the members of the investigatory commission were to be chosen in the diocesan synod; they were not to be elected by the clergy but rather to be named by the bishop after he had heard the advice of the clergy which he could afterwards reject for reasons known to him alone. Outside a synod the bishop could choose the members by himself, but he was counseled to hear the opinion of the rest of the commission; he was not obliged to follow it. The finding of the commission, moreover, was always consultative; the final sentence was reserved to the bishop. The proceedings of the inquiry, however, and the opinion of the commission were always to be inserted into the record of the trial. The Propaganda also made clear that the bishops had not been deprived of their extraordinary faculty of proceeding to suspension *ex informata conscientia* whenever they might judge the reasons most grave and canonical or might decide in an emergency that some provision must be made for the salvation of souls even without receiving advice. Finally, the Propaganda assured every rector of the right to bring another priest, approved by the bishop, along to the investigation before the commission for the purpose of either simply assisting him or presenting his observations and defense.[202]

Since the Propaganda thus vindicated the bishops, it was not surprising that McQuaid could extol the outcome as "so grand a victory for the American Church." Although he boasted that the cardinals and other officials of the Congregation "had never heard an American bishop talk to them just as I did," he admitted modestly that "it was Cardinal Manning's powerful influence which made the Cardinals revise their first decision and arrive at the present conclusion." [203] When Corrigan received this letter, he joyfully communicated the news to Gilmour, saying that "the old decree restricting episcopal powers and practically entrusting the care of the Diocese to 'the coroners' " had been re-versed.[204] After McQuaid had returned to Rochester, Corrigan in-formed him confidentially that "the *Instructio* had its genesis from the suggestion of Mgr. of Indianapolis." Corrigan said that Bishop Francis Silas Chatard had drawn up a memorial for Cardinal Simeoni or Franchi with his own comments, for example, the clause requiring the preservation of the papers in the episcopal archives. "Other sug-gestions," Corrigan added, "were disregarded." [205]

The publication of the official response, however, was delayed. Cor-rigan reported to McQuaid what he had learned from his Roman agent, Miss Ella B. Edes: "Mgr. Agnozzi was still holding back the ex-planation of the Instruction, — unwilling, it seems, that any part of the former document should be set aside." He continued:

> Advocates — Priests only — to be first approved by the Ordi-nary, — and then permitted to defend a brother Priest, *all* cases of the past to be ruled by the Instruction, no matter *when* they occurred, and not by the Second Plenary Council. This is the sum and substance of the news.[206]

When the responses were finally promulgated and McQuaid read them, he commented to Corrigan: "The 'Instructio' as explained is not the great thing that some disaffected priests looked for. Fixity of Tenure and immunity of discipline were what they wanted. Bishops and people were to have no rights as against their claims." [207] And to Gilmour he wrote: "All we have to do now is to hold Rome to the 'Instructio,' to this letter of explanation, and to the Second Plenary Council of Baltimore. We shall have to make a little more definite what may be considered *justa et rationabilis causa* for a transference." He believed that after this precedent Rome would take its cue from the bishops if the latter would "only condescend to enlighten and guide the authorities in Rome in charge of church affairs in America." [208] McQuaid never let his episcopal colleagues forget that he had, "by bold officiousness, staved off a great calamity for the American Church." [209]

Bishop McQuaid's attitude was shared by his fellow prelates. An example may be seen in the advice that Archbishop Gibbons gave a few years later to Archbishop Elder, who was preparing the Fourth Provincial Council of Cincinnati:

> Under the heading "disciplina Ecclesiastica," the relations of Bishops & priests, I would advise you to assert the broad principle that priests, even Rectors may be removed without trial by the

Bishops from one place to another whenever in his judgment the interests of religion call for such a removal (the Bishop of course in all cases acting with prudence & discretion) . . . . We cannot too much insist on the rights of Bishops on this point, as they are so often called in question, & the exercise of this right is essential to the discipline of the Church . . . .

In view of recent experiences I think the H. See will be disposed to sustain the action of Bishops in a forcible removal from one place to another & in withdrawal of faculties, if the Bishops are careful to preserve in writing the charges on which they have acted, or when they can state the grounds on which they have decided ex informata conscientia.

Although we are not obliged, I think it is desireable whenever the nature of the offense will admit of it, to give Pastors of mature years a trial before degrading them to an inferior place. It is well to have the clergy sustain an action when practicable . . . .[210]

The Council, however, made no reference to this topic in its decrees.

When the Instruction of 1878 was issued, a priest who had been ordained for the Archdiocese of Baltimore in 1860 but had been deprived of all his faculties there [211] and then had practiced the sacred ministry in Wisconsin, William Mahoney by name, had already begun to write a book which he published anonymously in 1883 under the title, *Jura Sacerdotum Vindicata, The Rights of the Clergy Vindicated; or, A Plea for Canon Law in the United States.*[212] In these 381 pages be begged the hierarchy "in the name of hundreds, if not of thousands of the clergy of the United States, to remedy the evil" which he described at length, namely, "that of priests being uncanonically dismissed from their dioceses and thrown helplessly on the world." [213] In his opinion it was

in consequence of this very abuse, and of the insecurity in general of the clergy as to their rights, that a spirit of estrangement has arisen of late years among many of them and their bishops, and is apparently gaining strength.[214]

The remedy that he prescribed was "the conscientious observance of the wise and salutary laws of the Church, made for the mutual welfare of the hierarchy of the first and second order," [215] particularly of the decrees of the Second Plenary Council of Baltimore, and the Instruction of 1878. Developing his presentation, he asserted, "To no one, among the hierarchy of either the first or second order, has she [the Church] ever entrusted absolute, much less arbitrary power;"[216] for bishops as well as for the pope and the humblest of the clergy and laity "LAW rules supreme." [217] Canon Law "is the only sure and safe guide of action for all possessed of ecclesiastical authority." [218] In spite of these lofty principles, he declared,

> The exceptional, or rather the anomalous and uncanonical form of ecclesiastical government, as it has been, alas, but too often administered in the United States, especially as regards the relationship of the bishop with his clergy, beyond a doubt has approached the absolute; nay, has often been none other than the arbitrary and sometimes capricious will of one man . . . . "Ego sum jus canonicum," are the words that fell from the lips of a bishop of the United States, yet living, to show the extent of his power, and the folly of resisting his will. In fact, "I am the bishop," is the only and *ultima ratio* that some prelates in the United States have sometimes given for their acts, how incomprehensible soever they were in themselves, or opposed to the spirit and letter of the Canon Law of the Church.[219]

The author maintained that the "anomalous condition of ecclesiastical government" was "conspicuously made manifest" in the cases of priests who for a "fault of frailty or surprise, certainly not of malice," "without admonition, warning, citation or trial," were dismissed from their dioceses and made helpless outcasts on the world.[220] In such banishment, exile, and social death he perceived no proportion between the punishment and the crime, or between the draconian treatment of weak and erring priests and the leninet attitude toward notorious apostates. He feared that little relief would be brought by the Instruction of 1878 alone, for since the Plenary Council of 1866, he said,

> I doubt very much if throughout the length and breadth of the United States, there has been one canonical trial and one canonical punishment of an erring clergyman . . . . From present appearances it looks as if the "Instructio," like the Council of Baltimore, would be "put on the shelf." [221]

As consequences of this neglect of the law the writer pointed out "discord, dissatisfaction and confusion." [222] If a bishop's sentence was unjust, "the only hope of redress heretofore has been a journey to Rome, for an appeal to the Metropolitan or Senior Bishop was not in order, as a bishop's sentence in the United States has generally been

ex informata conscientia, which allows recourse only to the Holy See."
Few priests, however, he averred, had the means to undertake such a
journey, and many lacked the courage.[223]

Mahoney believed that the United States should no longer be considered a purely missionary country and therefore all the "laws of
ecclesiastical discipline observed throughout the Church should be
gradually introduced," [224] and he argued from several indications
that Rome too desired "that Canon Law, as far as possible and practicable, should be introduced and observed in the United States, especially
as regards the bishop's relation with his clergy." [225] He affirmed that
the clergy of the United States longed to be under "the aegis of the
benign, just, and merciful discipline of the Church of Rome." [226]

In deploring the denial of protection and clemency to erring priests,
he admitted a legitimate exception only in a case of contumacy, which,
however, "necessarily supposes the existence of ecclesiastical
courts." [227] With maudlin eloquence he depicted the sad fate of a
priest abandoned by his bishop and driven into exile, and he accused
many unnamed bishops of violating the statute (No. 122) of the
Second Plenary Council of Baltimore and the decree of the Ecumenical
Council of Trent (Sess. XIII, cap. 1, de Refor.) which he interpreted
as forbidding this practice. It was also prohibited by the laws of both
charity and justice. The resultant scandals and disorders, in his judgment, were more imputable to the bishop than to the priest. He laid
down the rule, ". . . in no case and for no fault how grave soever,
is a bishop justified in abandoning an erring priest, if he is pen-
itent . . ." [228] A priest thrown out of his diocese is generally forced
either to beg or to engage in secular pursuits, but both these ways of
gaining a living are positively forbidden to priests. On the contrary, the
Church has legislated, in prescribing a title of ordination, that every
priest who submits to her discipline should receive a *congrua perpetua-
que sustentatio.*

Mahoney warned the bishops that the insecurity of priests in the
existing unsettled state of ecclesiastical discipline was calculated to
give occasion to avarice. He contended that by contumacy alone does
a priest forfeit his right to a becoming subsistence, notwithstanding
the contrary decree of the Second Plenary Council (No. 77), which
he considered to be opposed "to the spirit and letter of the highest and
most venerable authorities in the Church" [229] and therefore untenable
and unjustifiable. He insisted that this solicitude for delinquent priests
was necessary for the honor and dignity of the priesthood. Verbosely
he extolled the benign spirit of Rome toward the clergy as manifested

in numerous decisions, and this he contrasted with the "pharisaical spirit" of many contemporaries and with the conduct of many bishops.[230]

After a wordy "recapitulation" Mahoney proceeded to show how a priest accused of any fault ought to be treated — that he should be canonically tried and, if found guilty, canonically punished. He accumulated a large number of sources ranging from Innocent III to the Instruction of 1878 and described the procedures for trials *ex notorio*, summary trials, and sentences of suspension *ex informata conscientia* (which last he did not wish to see employed except in cases of occult crimes not susceptible to canonical investigation), as well as the quasi-judicial investigation prescribed by the Propaganda a few years before. It seemed to him that the faithful observance of the provisions of this Instruction would be "the first step towards the introduction of Canon Law into our land." [231] Adding a chapter on canonical punishments, Mahoney asserted that in the United States deposition and degradation, which by law were intended only for heinous crimes, were frequently inflicted on delinquent clergymen "not formally . . . but practically and to all intents and purposes . . . for ordinary faults." [232] Although, according to the author, "Rome is eminently just, and in matters of justice has no respect of persons," still she does not wish to oblige everyone seeking justice to cross the ocean, but rather "the Church wishes her tribunals of justice to exist in every part of the Church, with the right of appeal to Rome, the supreme and ultimate tribunal for the settlement of all ecclesiastical matters." [233] On the contrary, uncanonical proceedings, he reminded his readers, had sometimes culminated "in seeking redress in civil courts, to the great disedification of the people, and to the scandal and dishonor of religion." [234] He advocated that an erring priest, instead of being immediately transferred to another post, "be retired to the quiet of some religious monastery, or ecclesiastical Home for one year or more, to recover the health of his soul . . . . If his infirmity is radical, or incurable, he ought to be left in the hospital altogether, or in other words, be kept permanently in holy retirement." [235]

In order that existing and future ecclesiastical law might be enforced throughout the vast and growing country, Mahoney affirmed that an apostolic delegate, like a new Esdras, was absolutely necessary "for a few years, until [uniform] ecclesiastical discipline has been firmly and securely established";[236] only then might another plenary council for which Mahoney suggested the agenda (including "a more satisfactory method of appointing bishops," such as the one used in Ireland, where the clergy had a voice in the selection, or "cathedral chapters like those which exist in England"),[237] be held profitably. In conclusion, protesting his loyalty to and respect for the hierarchy, he fervently implored the bishops to remedy the evils of uncanonical treatment of the clergy by establishing canon law in the United States.

Shortly before the book was published, Mahoney informed the Archbishop of Baltimore, James Gibbons, that he had directed the publisher to send him a copy. He described the book as the result chiefly of his leisure at the Trappist monastery in Gethsemani, Kentucky, where he had been sent to make a retreat originally limited to three months but extended by Gibbons to three years. With pointed irony he wrote:

> I present to you the labor of these years & the satisfaction of knowing that you efficaciously contributed to the production of the work by giving me time to study up the matter and write it out. I pray Your Grace to use your exalted position to abolish forever the evil I have brought to the attention of the American hierarchy & to bring law & order into the ecclesiastical regimen of this land.[238]

A fortnight later Archbishop Corrigan, who had received through the mail a prospectus of the book, wrote to Gibbons that the publisher, James Sheehy, had recently met one of his priests, John Farley, and had mentioned that "Archbishop Gibbons had sanctioned, verbally, the author's design." Corrigan wished Gibbons to know how Sheehy was using his name in this connection. The coadjutor added that he knew nothing whatever of the work itself or of its author, noted that no imprimatur had been given or requested, and reported that Sheehy intended "to send a copy to the Pope, and on receipt of his approbation, the author will then drop his incognito and reveal his identity." [239] In reply Gibbons told Corrigan who the author was and that he had been deprived of his faculties by three successive archbishops of Baltimore. Gibbons proceeded to say: "So far from sanctioning or permitting such a publication, I was absolutely ignorant of the author, & even of the work till within the last few days, & when I heard of its author I had reason to believe that he would pour on my own head the vials of his wrath." Gibbons offered to write to the publisher a repudiation of his alleged approval of the book.[240]

Upon receipt of this letter, as Corrigan later wrote to Gibbons,

> Mgr. Quinn called on Mr. Sheehy and informed him that he had undoubted authority for knowing that you had *not* spoken of Rev.

Mr. Mahony's [*sic*] forthcoming book with the sense alleged by him. Mgr. Quinn further called attention to the fact that the publishing of such a book, in contravention of the Council of Baltimore, was a serious matter. The Publisher expressed his willingness to permit Fr. Quinn to see the proofs, but *refused* to consent to make any correction that might be deemed necessary.

He also reiterated the previous statement that your encouragement of Mr. Mahony's [*sic*] essay only fell short of a *formal* and *open* approbation. Mgr. Quinn ended by saying that if the book was published, Mr. Sheehy himself must take the consequences.

I think it is hardly worth while for you to take the trouble to write Mr. Sheehy. He knows perfectly well that you disapprove of the book.

I may add that Mr. Mahony [*sic*] has written a most impertinent letter to the Cardinal, taking Fr. Farley to task for presuming to ask Mr. Sheehy if there were any Ecclesiastical Sanction to this new book in Canon Law. The Cardinal of course took no notice of the letter, further than to direct Fr. Farley to enclose it to Abp. Heiss.[241]

Two days later Corrigan wrote Gibbons that he had to do Mahoney the justice of reporting that the author had just sent Cardinal McCloskey a second letter, "intended seemingly as a sort of apology for the first, and stating that he was so stung by the *unwarrantable* interference of Fr. Farley that he had given way to his feelings: that his own 'beloved and amiable Archbishop' had not insisted on an 'Imprimatur' (the book being printed elsewhere)." The cardinal ordered that this "second effusion" also be sent to Archbishop Heiss.[242]

A long and hostile review of the book, signed with the pen name of "Clericus" and written in the form of a letter to the editor, was soon published in the *Freeman's Journal,* beginning on the front page.[243] The anonymous critic indicated nothing praiseworthy in the entire work. In his opinion, Mahoney's thesis that "an unworthy clergyman, provided he avoid the sin of contumacy, has an inalienable right of support from his Bishop" was "in direct contradiction to the teaching expressly sanctioned by the Holy See in approving the First Provincial Council of St. Louis," the adoption of which was also prescribed by the Holy See so that "our prelates, obedient to the voice of authority, could not but enact the same law for the whole country in the Second Plenary Council." "Clericus" asserted that Mahoney's error resulted "from his confounding our missionary rectors with canonical parish priests, and other beneficed clergy," while actually in this country "the obligations of the Ordinary and of rectors or assistants are based on" the implied mutual contract *"Do ut des."* "Clericus" accused Mahoney of using irrelevant or even garbled sources and of lacking any authority at all for his position on suspensions *ex informata conscientia.* Making the attack personal, the reviewer remarked, ". . . with regard to this penalty, the author betrays the dread the burnt child has of the fire." Finally, "Clericus" ridiculed Mahoney's treatment of the question of the imprimatur "as a further specimen of sublime ignorance." He concluded his critique with the abusive comment, "Would that 'A. R. C. P.' had made his studies before rushing into print! Would that he had also taken a theme proportionate to his powers . . . !" "Clericus" never admitted the desirability of introducing the law of the universal Church into the United States.

Severely stung by this total condemnation of his book, Mahoney sent McMaster an answer through his publisher and also wrote him directly over his own signature:

> . . . I hope in honor to yourself & justice to me you will insert my defence or answer to him ["Clericus"]. Without reason or the most remote provocation he attacks my personal character by base & unmanly & unchristian & unclerical innuendos. . . It is but another phase of the petty persecution my book has suffered in the ignoble efforts to prevent its publication. My *learned* & venerable Metropolitan [Michael Heiss] is aware that I published the book. Thru its very nature it was useless for me to ask an imprimatur which besides was not required . . . .
>
> The book . . . will help to bring *law* & *order* into the ecclesiastical regimen of this country, something which if I mistake not you yourself have been advocating for years back & which Rome desires . . . . I & many priests whom you esteem very much would be sorry to see the old war horse McMaster place himself in a false position in this matter thru the influence of "Clericus" or any other kid gloved gentleman who would subvert the laws of the Church for centuries & substitute his paltry wisdom for her divine inspirations.[244]

In spite of this urgent appeal to his love of "fair play & justice," McMaster did not publish Mahoney's defense.[245] It seems that in thus refusing to revive the old controversy, he was following the direction of the coadjutor archbishop of New York.[246]

Mahoney had been informed by Sheehy that Gibbons "had written to the N. Y. authorities denouncing and condemning" his "humble work" before Gibbons had even seen it and even though Mahoney had assured him "that it was in all things orthodox and conformable to Catholic & Roman teaching." Mahoney was "pained beyond expression" to hear that Gibbons, furthermore, had "volunteered to denounce its poor, humble author." The latter in turn denounced the "unmanly, unconstitutional & uncatholic proceedings" of the New York authorities (Cardinal McCloskey excluded). He warned Gibbons that his publisher would have "recourse to the law to protect himself in his rights so shamelessly outraged in defiance of the laws of the United States and of the Catholic Church," and thus the "farce" would be exposed to the public through the civil courts. Reversing Corrigan's approach while professing "a true & sincere friendship" for Gibbons, Mahoney deplored the ignoble use made of the archbishop's name to besmirch the author, and he begged Gibbons not to let himself be "mixed up with so bad a cause." [247] Apparently having received no reply, Mahoney wrote to Baltimore again, lamenting the "short sighted, if not unjust & most imprudent manner" in which the officials of New York had acted. He asserted that he had informed Archbishop Heiss, who had approved his reasons for not requesting the imprimatur, and that the archbishop had said "they acted most foolishly in N. Y. in condemning & trying to suppress a book they knew nothing about." Then he directed his rage to the "dastardly letter" of "Clericus," conjecturing, "Many suppose 'Clericus' is Dr. Corrigan & for that reason McMaster refused to insert my letter & others in answer to him." [248] He was probably not far from being right.

A little later Gibbons remarked in a letter to Corrigan: "Rev. Mr. Mahony [*sic*] will not let me alone. He is very angry with the criticism which appeared in the Freeman's Journal, & suspects either you or myself of being the author. It is an excellent article, whoever wrote it." [249] Pretending innocence, Corrigan wrote to Gibbons: "Wm. Mahoney, I am told, has been writing fierce letters to the Freeman's Journal but so abusive that they could not be admitted to its columns." [250] Consequently, the controversy subsided.

In the preface of his book Mahoney had announced:

> I may, possibly, if there is much demand for my humble work, issue another edition of it; and will do so, if urged thereto by those whose judgment and piety convince me that my work is serviceable to Holy Church, and if the proceeds of the present edition enables me to do so.[251]

Apparently he received the desired assurance and support, for he published a second and enlarged edition two years later and even admitted his authorship by placing his name on the title page.[252]

Shortly after the publication of Mahoney's first edition the pastor of the Church of Our Lady of Hope in Hoboken, New Jersey, Patrick Corrigan, put out a pamphlet entitled, "Episcopal Nominations. Do the Interests of the Church in the United States Require that Priests Should Have the Power of Nominating the Bishops?" [253] At the very beginning the author stated his position by answering the question affirmatively; at least "a certain qualified number" of priests should have that power.[254] He believed, however, that the bishops themselves could hardly be expected to take the initiative and that they should be informed "of the real wants of the Church in all parts of the country"; the best way of bringing this knowledge to them would be to ascertain the opinions of the priests; for this purpose a "proper organization" with branches in all the dioceses might be necessary. He recognized the first obstacle to be overcome, saying: "The whole matter rests with the Bishops, *for it is certain* Rome *will grant this power to Priests, if the* Bishops *think* it for the best interests of the Church in this country." [255] Corrigan thought that this concession to priests would strengthen the Church by securing the co-operation of a majority of the clergy and consequently of the laity and that it would "put an end to the many causes of discontent" arising within the Church by securing the promotion of "men of experience on the mission" who would be thoroughly acquainted with the priests and the people.[256]

Corrigan stated that he was moved to write this pamphlet by the observation that he had made during a European tour in 1882. Beholding "the deplorable state of religion in Italy, France, and Spain," he resolved to forewarn his fellow American Catholics lest they come to be oppressed by similar evils. In the first part of the pamphlet he tried to depict in dark colors "the sad condition of the Church" in those so-called Catholic countries and to explain the causes of it. He attributed the Church's lack of influence over the masses mainly to the reluctance of certain conservative ecclesiastics to tolerate a greater measure of political democracy and ultimately to the close union of Church and State which left the nomination of bishops under the control of the government. In the second part he analyzed some of the causes of uneasiness in this country such as the financial mismanagement of some bishops and their failure to render public accounts, as well as attempts at "imprudent legislation" forbidding the attendance of Catholic children at public schools under spiritual penalties. He declared that the remedy for these difficulties consisted in revising the system of nominating bishops so that experienced pastors and men of proven administrative ability might be chosen. He added: ". . . to make a man a Bishop in this country who has never been on his mission, is a cruelty to the man himself, if he feels his inability, and it is also a great injustice to the Church. He may be a great theologian, or a great saint, but he is certainly not qualified to be a Bishop without a thorough acquaintance with the diocese and the priests of the diocese." [257] In Corrigan's opinion the priests of a diocese were the ones most qualified to choose the best men for the episcopacy, while "bishops are often unable, owing to circumstances, to decide whether certain persons have the requisite qualities." He would, however, have restricted this power to rectors of churches or even to those rectors who had served a number of years. He was confident that scandals and disorders during the election could be prevented by appropriate regulations, as in Ireland, and that the nominees selected by the priests of the diocese should be subject to the veto of the bishops of the province. Asking himself whether bitter feelings of nationalities would arise, he replied that they would be much less intense than those currently engendered, but if such a question was raised, the bishop should be an American, that is, one "who has been in the country from his youth and who has been thoroughly identified with the spirit of the country." [258]

Setting forth the alleged defects of the present system, Corrigan revealed his antagonism against the German-American Catholics. He asserted that the pertinent decrees of the Second Plenary Council were not observed in many parts of the country and that even many of the restraints placed on the mode of selecting men for bishoprics were made to yield to the personal preferences of individuals; he concluded, therefore, that new legislation was necessary to render such abuses impossible and that another plenary council should be held. In that eventuality, the priests of the country should present a request for the right to nominate bishops. He was sure that neither the bishops nor Rome would be displeased by such a suggestion. He even hazarded the argument that "in the event of a revolution in our form of government, some efforts might be made by a new power to get control of this very power [of nominating bishops], to the injury of the Church"; if the priests posssessed the power, the civil authority would be less likely to attempt to seize it.[259]

Striking out at Ella B. Edes, he deplored the fact that "the laity and the priests, and the very Bishops themselves, of the great American Church *have to depend upon the enterprise of a pious lady convert at Rome for the first authentic information of the appointment of the Bishops for this country.*" [260] He blamed not Rome but the bishops for the failure to have either an American representative in Rome or a delegate in the United States. With his characteristic admiration for the American ethos he pointed out "the fact that in our present mode of appointing Bishops we ignore without apparent reason the fundamental doctrine of the land — the principle of self-government." [261] He predicted that, with the remedy that he proposed, the Church would retain its firm hold on the laity.

Since Corrigan published this tract without an imprimatur, he exposed himself to disciplinary action. Within a few weeks of its publication his bishop, Winand Wigger, ordered him to withdraw the pamphlet from circulation. Aside from the lack of permission, the bishop considered the pamphlet to be "calculated to do an immense amount of harm." [262] The editor of *Ave Maria*, Daniel C. Hudson, C.S.C., on the contrary, commended the pamphlet to the attentive perusal of his brother-priests and hoped that it might secure the attention of the bishops also. He found it "full of good thoughts forcibly expressed," and he observed, "Appearing at a time when the Archbishops of the country are about to assemble in Rome, and when there is prospect of a Plenary Council for the United States, it seems to us most timely." [263] Bishop Wigger then wrote to Father Hudson, expressing his displeasure at the favorable notice that the latter had given to the pamphlet; the bishop objected to Corrigan's views on schools, the question of Church and State, the ability and honesty of American priests, and the condition of the Church in France, Italy, and Spain; he said nothing, however, on the main issue of allowing priests to participate in the choice of their bishops.[264]

In compliance with his bishop's demand, Father Corrigan withdrew the edition. The former Bishop of Newark, Michael A. Corrigan, wrote to McQuaid:

> Father Corrigan has made his submission to the Bishop and, in compliance with an absolute order, has suppressed the stereotype edition, — and the plates were broken up by the Publisher in the Bishop's presence. But the latter has since informed me privately that he had reason to believe that the pamphlet has been passed over to a Protestant firm by Sullivan and so the poison will spread.
>
> F. Corrigan, of course, has had me in mind many a time in

writing. I have seen him only once since his return from Europe, and then he called to ventilate his views on Episcopal nominations. I imagined it was in view of the Prov. Synod then about to be held; not a word was breathed of any possible publication.[265]

A month later Archbishop Corrigan informed McQuaid:

F. Corrigan is still trying to obtain Episcopal Sanction for a revised edition of his pamphlet, but without success. He says he has been offered $4,000 for it and that, by some formality, the copyright has passed out of his hands.[266]

It might have been foreseen that a man of the author's temperament would not meekly resign himself to his bishop's intervention.

It was probably with Father Corrigan, among others, in mind that Archbishop Corrigan, Bishops McQuaid and Wigger, and the other bishops who assembled in the Fourth Provincial Council of New York during the next month enacted a decree stating that notwithstanding repeated prohibitions, books dealing with religion and divine worship continued to be published without the proper authorization of the ordinaries; they again demanded, therefore, that any writings treating of religion to be published by Catholics be submitted to the diocesan censors for examination and that permission to publish be granted by the bishop only after the examiners would have testified that there was nothing contrary to faith or morals in the writing.[267] Since the decrees of this council were not promulgated, however, until 1886, Father Corrigan was not deterred by them in his next move.

In spite of the suppression of his pamphlet, Father Corrigan put out another the following May under the title, "What the Catholic Church Most Needs in the United States, or, The Voice of the Priests in the Election of the Bishops."[268] Aiming a blow at the Coadjutor Archbishop of New York and the Bishop of Newark, the author professed that the suppression had been a great surprise not only to himself "but to all the Clergy of the land, for the brochure had been printed and published in the City of New York, and without the slightest objection on the part of the Cardinal [John McCloskey], who alone had any right to interfere with publications of his own city."[269] He asserted:

. . . The denial of this right of a Priest to discuss in a proper manner a question of vital importance to the Church, and not directly treating of faith or morals, without having previously obtained a formal license to do so, is a thing unknown in this country, and calculated to excite alarm in the minds of those who are most anxious for the future of the Church in America. Hence, though I regarded the action of the Bishop of Newark *as merely local, and in no way expressing the sentiments of the other Bishops of this land*, most of whom are in favor of giving, at least, some say to the Clergy in the choosing of Bishops, still, lest his action should be taken as a *precedent*, and perhaps as a *salutary warning against future reference to this matter by other* Priests, I felt it my duty to the Church in this country, and to the Priests in particular, to protest while I rendered obedience.[270]

The intrepid writer stated that his declining to request a formal license to publish the first pamphlet indicated no lack of respect for ecclesiastical authority but that he wished to save his own bishop, "only lately consecrated, from annoyance on the part of the other members of the American Episcopacy, who *would naturally blame one of their youngest brethren for formally sanctioning a movement that aimed at depriving them of their present unlimited power*." [271] Corrigan asserted that Bishop Wigger was in favor of giving this power to the clergy, but in any case it was an open question which he had a right to discuss without asking anyone's permission. He candidly admitted that it would have been foolish for him to ask it.

Father Corrigan then repeated his comments on ecclesiastical finances and clarified his remarks on the school question. He was of the opinion, however, that the real objection to his first pamphlet was directed against his proposals regarding episcopal nominations. In response he boasted that "one of the most eminent Cardinals of Rome," to whose judgment he had referred the question of the orthodoxy of the pamphlet, praised the good spirit of the author and found no fault with his orthodoxy; rather, the cardinal "blamed the 'violence' of the suppression of the work." [272] He charged that some, probably meaning Archbishop Corrigan, had employed other means than the open ones of his own ordinary to lessen the influence of the pamphlet in Rome. On the other hand, he still believed that "many of the most leading members of the Episcopacy [were] in favor of giving the Clergy some say in the choosing of Bishops." [273] According to the author, the "reception of the pamphlet by the Clergy and laity was most enthusiastic," as evidenced by the "hundreds of letters" that he received from all parts of the country.[274] Recognizing the futility of the course that he had previously proposed, however, he now suggested that the priests themselves by prudent and united action might obtain from Rome what the bishops in the forthcoming plenary council might hesitate to request. Hence, he recommended a "petition from a few of the representative Pastors of Baltimore, Philadelphia, New York, Brooklyn, Boston and Chicago," [275] requesting a vote for the priests in episcopal elections.

After this prolix introduction Corrigan launched into his new treatise, which was "intended to show the Priests that they have a right to this power by the laws and practice of the Church, and that it is their own fault if they fail to obtain it in this country." [276] To prove this thesis, he attempted to trace the history of episcopal elections from apostolic times, accounting for past interference with the right of the clergy. He urged his adversaries to recognize "that arguments drawn from the fact that the Church in past ages withheld or limited this power of the Priests, are very poor indeed when applied to the present day and especially to the Priests of this country." [277] He expressed the hope that a change in the mode of selecting bishops would not consist "merely in giving the few members of a Chapter a voice," for in this way "the great masses of the Priests" would not be represented but rather would be irritated.[278] In the light of these ancient testimonies he could claim:

> . . . we are not introducing revolutionary principles into the Church, we are not trying to Americanize the Church by advancing democratic demands on the part of the Priests hitherto unheard of, and that would tend to destroy the Church of America.[279]

Still he pleaded that the Church should anticipate the wish of the American people by harmonizing her laws with the instincts of the country whenever possible: "The cry for *representation* is heard all over the world: why not hearken to it, when it is in harmony with the fundamental laws of the Church . . . ?" [280]

Returning to the subject of a "papal delegate," he said that Rome had been preparing to send such a representative but then had been dissuaded by the American archbishops who were in Rome the previous autumn; from this episode (really connected with the choice of a delegate to preside at the Third Plenary Council) he drew another argument in support of his proposal: "This action of the archbishops seems to strengthen the demands of the Clergy, who claim that the Church in this country is so fully developed as to warrant the introduction of Canon Law." [281] To Corrigan's mind, the presence of a delegate "could in no manner *add to the supreme power which our Bishops already possess,* but . . . it might materially *add to the power of the Clergy.*" [282] He insisted, however, that a delegate would have to possess a perfect knowledge of the language of the United States. Another observation was that the priests gathered up the funds that brought consolation to the heart of the Holy Father and yet had hardly any channel of communication open between themselves and the Propaganda. In a practical way he suggested that some of the graduates of the American College in Rome be retained after their ordination "as assistant-clerks" in the Propaganda in order to facilitate communication with the American clergy; then "the pious lady convert at Rome" would not be needed "to do all the talking for us." [283] It appeared desirable to him that one of the cardinals of the Propaganda, such as Lucido Parocchi, come to the United States in an unofficial capacity for an extensive visit.

Father Corrigan forestalled an objection that could be based on his own advocacy of the principle of representation, saying:

> In this country, where the interests of Priests and people have been so identical, the people are willing to leave their choice to the judgment of the Priests. In giving the Priests the power asked, you give the people all they desire in the United States.[284]

He thought that the only priests who would not favor the change were some who had recently come from other lands. He denied that the proposed system would excite inordinate ambition among the priests; on the contrary, he reproached the bishops for arousing the ambition of certain priests by obtaining for them from Rome "titles and distinctions hitherto unknown, and certainly without apparent usefulness to the Church in this country." He feared that such honors would "injure the old Apostolic and democratic spirit of the American Priesthood" by introducing castes and a sense of inferiority. Hence, he expressed the hope that the "shrewd and *far-seeing fathers of the coming* Council" would give those responsible for this noxious novelty "*a polite hint not to ask for any more* Monsignori, at least for a very long time to come." [285]

Patrick Corrigan proceeded to echo many of the sentiments of William Mahoney — that the law should be sharply defined for bishops as well as for priests and that the bishop should "govern as a tender father and not as a magistrate who ever holds the rod *in terrorem*." [286] He also added some complaints of his own — that bishops could remove a parish from a rector by dividing it or erecting a national parish within its limits or letting a religious order build a church there, that begging sisters annoyed businessmen, and that mendicant orders, building extravagant edifices, deprived the parishes of money needed for schools, "rudely cropping whatever is green."[287]

In the last chapter Corrigan predicted that the forthcoming plenary council would be a great blessing if this question should be "fairly met and solved," for in his opinion it underlay all the other questions pressing for immediate consideration. He had confidence in the leadership of James Gibbons, "an apostolic Bishop," who was to preside over the council, because he believed Gibbons to be "heart and soul in sympathy with the Priests." [288] He deprecated bringing in as bishop a priest from another diocese, because such a man would not understand the local problems. Mixing up topics with his usual lack of logical order, Corrigan then asserted that the American bishops have "a supreme and dictatorial power hardly ever wielded by any other body of Bishops in any other time or nation from the foundation of Christianity," and he warned that no people "have a more supreme contempt for the arbitrary exercise of absolute power than the . . . American people." [289] He continued:

> The temper of the Clergy and the educated classes of the laity of the United States should be heeded, for it is one of righteous impatience with the many reproaches to which the inexperience and want of ability on the part of some of their otherwise pious and amiable guides oblige them to submit.[290]

Verbosely he appealed to the best class of priests to exert themselves lest a less representational form be adopted by the council. Passionately he asked, "Must the relics of civil tyranny that deprived the Clergy of a vote in the election of Bishops in other times and other lands be maintained and perpetuated in the United States?" [291] Corrigan felt sure that the priests would choose men of the same caliber as John Carroll, who was elected by his fellow priests. He concluded this tract with the same diffuse paragraphs as the first one.

This time Father Corrigan was not molested by his bishop for having published an offensive pamphlet. Archbishop Corrigan commented to Bishop McQuaid:

> You will notice that he shelters himself under the mantle of a Roman Cardinal (Parocchi), because he said nothing in his first essay against faith or morals. He certainly sins against good order and discipline in the second and respect for episcopal authority; and I believe that his Ordinary could very well forbid the publication on the strength of general principles as well as by reason of the special authority given by the Holy See in the letter published in the Council of Baltimore, p. 333 & 334 (last paragraph).[292]

Bishop Wigger had written to Archbishop Corrigan that he was "thinking seriously of writing to the Holy Father, direct, on the subject; and also resolving in his mind whether and how far he ought to punish the offender." The archbishop had advised him differently:

> It would be as well to *ignore* the work and its author here, though he [Wigger] might write to the H. See if he deemed it advisable. Rome will not so easily understand *our* circumstances, and Card. Parocchi is already on the author's side; and the sympathies of many others are no doubt also with him.[293]

Encouraged by Bishop Wigger's unwonted permissiveness, Father Corrigan published yet another pamphlet in October, 1884. Although the title was different ("The Bishop and the Priest"),[294] the contents were the same as in the second pamphlet with the addition of an "appendix" at the beginning. Here he reprinted a philippic that he had written to the editor of the *New York Tablet* in reply to the criticisms of Denis McCartie, chancellor of the Diocese of Newark and secretary to Bishop Wigger, to defend himself against the "absurd and dishonest charges" of "this queer Father."[295] He accused "this eccentric theologian" of being opposed to the proposed change because his "chances of adoption or promotion in this country would be much diminished by the establishment of ecclesiastical law, . . . and his almost total ignorance of this country makes him believe that the clergy are neither anxious nor even qualified to exercise such a power."[296] Corrigan demanded that the "wind-bag" retract his slanderous public charges of false doctrine and insubordination to the bishop. To refute these charges Corrigan boasted that the pamphlet "Episcopal Nominations" had been translated into Italian and had not been suppressed by the Roman authorities. He also said that Cardinal Jacobini, Secretary of the Propaganda,[297] had given permission to circulate the pamphlet, in English or in Italian, even in Rome. The author was content with this negative approval.

Then in a preface to the present brochure Corrigan gave way to vainglory, exclaiming: "Nothing published in the United States has ever attracted so much attention among Catholics, or has ever created such a complete revolution, in so short a time, in favor of any question of church government, as this same pamphlet."[298] He also mentioned the recent action of the priests of the Diocese of Davenport, who of their own volition assembled and voted for their bishop with the subsequent sanction of the bishops of the province and of Rome. Taking some credit for this achievement, he trumpeted: "The election of Bishop Cosgrove is a great historical event in the church of the United States." It was "the deathknell of the old regime and the bright beginning of the new dispensation." [299] He was deluded into thinking that the movement had progressed so far that "the great work" could be regarded as already completed and hardly anything remained to be done. It was his recommendation that an organization of priests designed to influence the forthcoming council or to appeal to the Propaganda should not be brought into existence unless the council failed to act, for the Propaganda had already decided that a certain percentage of the priests should have a vote in the election of the bishops, and the council, if not embarrassed by such an organization, might anticipate the wishes of the priests by increasing the percentage. Still the threat of an eventual organization would have "*its due weight* at Baltimore." Apparently unconscious of his stark want of humility, he said that his own connection with the movement was, perhaps, providential.

Being suspicious of Father Corrigan's claim of Roman approbation of his first pamphlet, Bishop Wigger sent an inquiry to the prefect of the Propaganda, Giovanni Simeoni. The cardinal replied that Archbishop Jacobini had neither read nor approved the pamphlet.[300] It seems that Corrigan had been misinformed by his Roman agent, Monsignor Paolo Mori. In any case, lacking any other Roman skirts behind which he could hide, Corrigan on March 10, 1885, was peremptorily suspended by Bishop Wigger for three weeks on the grounds that he had notoriously disregarded and defied his episcopal authority by republishing substantially a pamphlet which the bishop had suppressed for many reasons and to republish which, in whole or in part, he had refused permission. The suspension of the popular pastor caused a sensation in the press; the *Mercury* commented: "No event in the history of the Catholic Church in the United States for a long time will create as much excitement or cause such warm discussion as the peremptory suspension of the Rev. Father Corrigan." [301] Corrigan wrote to the editor of the *Herald* that he was entitled to a formal hearing before an official tribunal and avowed that he would appeal to Rome. Although Wigger disliked the notoriety, he too used the secular newspapers to vindicate his action; he translated and published in the *New York Sun* Simeoni's letter denying that Jacobini had given the approbation claimed by Corrigan and suggesting that Wigger could punish the priest "in the manner, and according to the measure, that zeal and charity and prudence will suggest." Trying to justify the manner of imposing the suspension, to which Corrigan had taken exception, the bishop asserted that the case was notorious and that no formal hearing was required.[302] As far as is known, Corrigan never carried out his threat of taking the case to Rome, but he waited over a year to inform Wigger that he was willing to give up all thought of an appeal. The bishop then apprised Cardinal Simeoni of the quiet end of the affair and even palliated Corrigan's fault by adding that the priest had been misled by a false report of official approval of the first pamphlet sent by his agent in Rome.[303]

Some of Mahoney's and Corrigan's demands were voiced much more dispassionately and judiciously by the eminent American Catholic historian, John Gilmary Shea, in an article on "The Coming Plenary Council of Baltimore." [304] Having pointed out that there were no canonically erected parishes in the country, Shea stated:

> The time is coming, as all feel, when regular parishes must be instituted, with parish priests unremovable except for cause and after trial. Yet in this country, where building of churches and schools, as well as their maintenance and the reduction of debts, devolves in a great measure on the pastor, the bishop must have power to remove a priest who is not able to manage affairs for the good of the parish. A priest may have learning and piety and be of unimpeached morality, and still be one who will bring the church to ruin.[305]

Shea mentioned a few cases in which priests, deeming themselves aggrieved by their bishops, had sought redress in the civil courts, often at great expense, and "judges with more bias against the church than sound legal principle" had given "the wildest decisions." He declared that the Propaganda's instruction of 1878, requiring the appointment of *judices causarum*, had in practice "proved inadequate." He continued with clearer insight than those who advocated the indiscriminate introduction of canon law into the United States:

> Whenever cases have arisen, there seems a want of a clear code, defining rights, powers, duties, and obligations, with the distinctness of the Code Napoleon; with classification of the clergy in grades; regulations as to the appointment to each; a distinct statement of offenses, and the punishment for each on conviction by a recognized tribunal, in suspension, loss of grade for a longer or shorter period, providing for appointment to inferior positions after a specified period spent in some religious house. If it were possible to lay down all this clearly and distinctly, much of the confusion, delay, and uncertainty which now environ every case that comes before the courts would disappear. At present nothing

can be more confused or confusing than the opinions of those summoned as canonists to apply the canons of the Church, as understood in other times and countries, to the affairs of the Church in this country at the present time; canons based on a condition of affairs where churches were already built and endowed, the clergy paid by tithes, and the duties clear and limited, but which can apply here in many cases only by analogy.[306]

Thus the expectations of laymen as well as of priests were focused on the forthcoming plenary council.

Part V: The Climax — The Third Plenary Council

When Father Corrigan published his first pamphlet, he did not know that the Holy See had already decided to convoke the American bishops in another plenary council. Cardinal McCloskey had been consulted by the Propaganda on this subject at the beginning of 1882 and had been asked to ascertain the opinions of the bishops of his province. In relating the news to Bishop McQuaid, McCloskey's coadjutor wrote:

> Card. Simeoni's letter recites that some Bishops have expressed the wish that a Council be convened as soon as possible, in order to regulate Church matters better, — especially, the relations of Bishops and Priests, and adapting the training of Clerics to the wants of the present time.[307]

McCloskey was of the opinion that these purposes could be attained more readily and efficaciously in provincial councils, and McQuaid expressed a similar opinion in reply. Eventually, nevertheless, the Holy See became convinced of the immediate need for a plenary council. Late in May, 1883, therefore, the prefect of the Propaganda invited most of the metropolitans of the United States to attend preliminary conferences with the cardinals of the Sacred Congregation in Rome the following November. Gibbons' successor in the See of Richmond, John J. Keane, who had spoken with Leo XIII and officials of the Propaganda while he was in Rome that summer, wrote to the Archbishop of Baltimore:

> After my conversations with all these, it is perfectly clear to my mind that the summons had been issued in a spirit of the most entire friendliness towards the American Hierarchy, and through the desire to have all their relations with their priests & with the Holy See placed on the footing that will be the most advantageous

& agreeable to our Hierarchy. I am told on all hands that the
Holy See is *pestered* with appeals of all sorts from priests of our
country; — that the authorities here, while bound on the one hand
to entertain any appeals that are not evidently without foundation,
yet always, on the other hand, take their stand on the side of the
authority of the Bishops, and adhere to that unless forced to
side with the priest by the force of evidence adduced. But they
complain that while the priests are active in offering evidence,
the Bishops too often fail to offer anything that can stand as real
evidence, and thus the authorities are sometimes forced, to their
great regret, to decide ag'st the Bps.[308]

It was evident, therefore, that some better regulation was needed.

In August Archbishop Corrigan, who was to attend the conference
in place of the ailing Cardinal McCloskey, informed McQuaid that
according to the Bishop of Fort Wayne, Joseph G. Dwenger, "It is
commonly supposed that the *Instructio* [of 1878] will go by the
board." The archbishop asked, however, "What can we propose to
take its place?"[309] The answer to his question had already been
prepared in Rome.

In anticipation of the conference at Rome and of the council at
Baltimore, the Propaganda drew up an Instruction on cases of clerics
intended to meet the needs of the times, ensure the regular administration of justice, protect the authority of the bishops, and prevent complaints from those accused. It supplanted the Instruction of 1878, and
thus the commissions of investigation were abolished. Since episcopal
curias or courts were to be required in all dioceses, they were employed in the new form of trial, which was to be conducted in summary
fashion without the full apparatus of a formal court. Functions were
assigned to the vicar-general, the chancellor, and the *procurator fiscalis*
(prosecuting attorney).[310]

These new rules were discussed by the cardinals and other officials
of the Propaganda with the American archbishops and bishops who
went to Rome in the autumn of 1883 to prepare decrees for the forthcoming council. In the agenda it was proposed that the instruction of
1878 be observed only in those articles which could be reconciled with
subsequent legislation.[311] From this frank discussion there resulted
certain modifications and clarifications. When the Archbishop of
Chicago, Patrick A. Feehan, asked whether an archbishop would be
obliged to accept an appeal before the bishop had rendered judgment,
the cardinals replied that an archbishop was not allowed to accept an

appeal in such circumstances, whether it be on the merits of the issue or on incidental questions. In response to another question the cardinals said that an archbishop on receiving an appeal was not obliged to follow the whole process as had been done in the first instance; he was allowed to use the record of the suffragan court and to render judgment on the basis of its contents unless something appeared to be irregular or omitted or insufficiently investigated therein.[312] The cardinals also declared that although there was no further reason for the commission set up in accordance with the Instruction of 1878, in those dioceses in which, by virtue of a dispensation of the Holy See, episcopal curias had not yet been established, the old Instruction was still to be observed for the time being. Answering Archbishop Feehan's question about the time at which the new Instruction would become operative, the cardinals stated that it was immediately obligatory inasmuch as it was imposed by the Holy See independently of the future holding of the council.[313] Finally, it was asked which would be the court of appeals in the case in which judgment was rendered in the first instance in an archiespiscopal court, and it was decided that the appeal should be taken to the nearest archiepiscopal court; the forthcoming council was to determine which archiepiscopal courts were to be considered nearest to each other.[314]

The most significant modifications of the new Instruction were requested by Archbishop Corrigan in regard to the advocates of those subject to inquiry. He asked first that instead of allowing laymen to serve as defense counsels, as the Propaganda had done, only priests be admitted, for he feared the danger of scandal if lay attorneys were permitted to act in the criminal cases of clerics and that artful, cunning, crafty, and evil advocates would be chosen who would strive by every stratagem to upset the bishop's judgment. Secondly, he asked that no defense counsels, either ecclesiastics or laymen, be permitted to appear in person before the episcopal tribunal for the purpose of entering an oral defense, for he feared that gradually there would grow up in America an odious brood of ecclesiastical lawyers to whose advantage it would be to multiply legal cases and to drag them out indefinitely. Corrigan proposed, therefore, either that the accused be able to defend himself or that his defense be presented only in writing or that in each diocese the bishop appoint three or four qualified ecclesiastics among whom the accused could choose his counsel. The cardinals replied that the right of defense had already been partially restricted in the Instruction by the provision that the defense counsel chosen by the accused must be approved by the bishop. They agreed, however, that the defense should be presented only in writing.[315] Corrigan, nevertheless, was still not content

Among the other topics discussed at the preparatory conferences in Rome were the erection of cathedral chapters of canons, the appointment of irremovable pastors, and the manner of proposing candidates for the episcopacy. As far as the erection of chapters was concerned, the Propaganda proposed that the plan just approved for Scotland should be adopted, according to which each chapter was to consist of at least six canons with a provost or dean. Where it was impossible to establish a chapter immediately, four or six consultors were to be named, one-half of whom were to be chosen by the bishop independently and the other half also by the bishop but only after they had been proposed by the clergy; the consultors would not have the right, as the chapter would, of proposing either a vicar-capitular or candidates for the see in case of a vacancy. The bishop would have to convoke the chapter or the consultors as often as he might need their consent or counsel, but at least four times a year, to consider the matters that he would refer to them.[316]

At the very first meeting Archbishop Gibbons in the name of all his colleagues said that it was not expedient to establish chapters, but that their place could adequately be supplied by a body of diocesan consultors. The cardinals of the Propaganda, on the contrary, insisted that it was desirable to appoint canons and to institute chapters; they observed that in the present condition of the American Church it would be about the same thing to choose canons as to name consultors, and that the only difference was that the canons would enjoy permanent tenure while the consultors would be removable at the wish of the bishop. The cardinals also presented a list of cases in which the bishops would be bound by law to seek the advice only or the consent of the chapter or of the consultors. Since the American prelates requested more time to examine this question,[317] the discussion was continued at the second meeting. Now Gibbons presented and read a paper containing the reasons impelling him and his colleagues to regard the establishment of chapters as not expedient, namely:

> (1) chapters are not in accord with the character of the American people; (2) qualified priests are not readily available because the priests, scattered in districts far removed [from the cathedral], cannot be brought together without serious inconvenience and great expense; (3) it is to be feared that once priests are raised to the rank of canons they will become insolent in their attitude toward the bishop and will seek to demand unwarranted priv-

ileges; (4) there is the risk of controversies between the bishops and the canons, as experience shows to be the case where chapters exist.[318]

The Coadjutor Archbishop of St. Louis, Patrick J. Ryan, added that if those dangers were not present at the moment, they could easily arise in the future. The cardinals tried to refute the arguments thus advanced; they noted in particular that for the present chapters would be established only in those dioceses in which they were feasible, and, therefore, they dismissed the objection drawn from the lack of priests. They showed, moreover, that the chapters to be established would not be moral bodies independent of the bishops but only their senate and that the danger of unwarranted interference in the affairs of the diocese would be precluded by the fact that the canons would need to be convoked by the bishop and that they could deliberate only on those matters that were set before them by the bishop. It was pointed out that such chapters existed in England and Holland and that no harm, but rather great good, had resulted from them. The conclusion was reached that in the forthcoming council the question of the institution of chapters should not be excluded from its consideration and that in any event the establishment of diocesan consultors should be imposed on all.

Once the cardinals had consented to this compromise, the American prelates were intent only on restricting the rights of the consultors as much as possible and on clarifying certain details. The Bishop of Little Rock, Edward Fitzgerald, stated that it would be impossible for him to have more than two consultors and that this was true of all the dioceses in the Province of New Orleans, which he represented. The cardinals replied that the number of consultors could vary from diocese to diocese but that there should be six if possible; otherwise four or at least two would be sufficient for the time being. When the Archbishop of Oregon City, Charles J. Seghers, asked by whom the consultors should be appointed, the officials of the Propaganda replied that, as in Scotland, one-half of them should be chosen by the bishop himself while the other half should be appointed also by the bishop but from the candidates proposed by the clergy. The Archbishop of Boston, John J. Williams, then inquired what should be done in case the bishop might think that the candidates proposed by the clergy could not or should not be admitted. In response the method of election on the part of the clergy was determined thus: The clergy were to submit to the bishop a list of those priests whom they deemed suitable or capable of discharging the function of consultor without naming any exclusively; then the bishop would choose from that list those whom he preferred. This method was approved by all.

As far as the rights of the consultors were concerned, at the next meeting Gibbons on behalf of his colleagues read a paper regarding the cases in which bishops were to be required to seek the consent or the advice of the consultors. Their position was summarized in the official minutes as follows:

> (1) In summoning a diocesan synod and publishing its acts, they need only the advice of the consultors. (2) For the acquisition and the alienation of church property all the bishops with one exception were of the opinion that the consent of the latter was needed on condition that when this consent is given the bishops should be entirely free in regard to details and to the method in which the transaction as a whole should be concluded. (3) For the division of missions and parishes all the bishops agreed that it was necessary to seek only the advice, not the consent, of the consultors and of the interested rector of the church, and this for the following reasons: (a) the consultors would be pastors themselves and therefore would be easily persuaded by other pastors to refuse their consent to the division; (b) as pastors the consultors would be promoting their own interests in opposing divisions; (c) since pastors are to have a voice in the proposing of candidates for vacant episcopal sees, consultors would be careful not to offend them since the latter would be able to vote for or against them; (d) since in order to establish a new parish it is often necessary to detach portions from several existing parishes, innumerable difficulties would ensue if it were necessary to seek the consent of all the interested pastors; (e) because of continuing immigration the establishing of new missions has become almost a daily occurrence and, as a consequence, the bishops need the utmost liberty in establishing parishes in order that they may provide for the welfare of the sheep entrusted to them.[319]

It was later decided that the details (*minutiae*) to which Gibbons referred would be understood as items not exceeding a value of three thousand dollars. All the prelates admitted that the consent of the consultors would be required for the appointment of a new consultor or of extra-synodal examiners and for the imposition of a new tax for the bishop but that their advice would suffice for the entrusting of a parish to a religious institute, especially since for this the permission of the Holy See was required anyway. In spite of this agreement, in the council itself some of the fathers were to insist that the consent of the consultors should not be required in any case.

With respect to the irremovability of pastors, the agitation of the American priests had obviously produced some effect on the Propaganda. The cardinals had proposed that parishes containing at least 1,500 Catholics and having a church, rectory, and school should be declared "irremovable" within a period to be determined by the forthcoming council. Only priests who had worthily exercised the ministry in the diocese for five years and had been passed in a general *concursus* could be appointed rectors of such parishes; where the *concursus* could not be held, a longer time of creditable ministry, for example, ten years, was to be required of candidates for these parishes.[320]

Recognizing the need for compromise also on this question, Gibbons on behalf of his colleagues agreed to the establishment of parishes of irremovable tenure but only under three conditions: "(1) that the decision regarding the fitness of appointees be left to the bishop; (2) that the appointee undergo a *concursus* or competitive examination; (3) that only those be eligible who for ten years had successfully exercised the ministry in some church of the diocese." [321] These conditions were acceptable to the Propaganda. At the next meeting, nevertheless, Archbishop Seghers reopened the question, denying the existence of any serious reason for the establishment of parishes of irremovable tenure. The cardinals replied to his arguments by offering the general reason acknowledged by law as well as particular reasons, especially the need to prevent the complaints of the priests who were demanding that some provision be made for the stability of their condition. Seghers persisted, saying that in that case only a few parishes of irremovable tenure should be established because, as a result of the mobility of the population in America, it could easily happen that in a given place the majority of the people might be of one nationality today and of another tomorrow, and consequently it would be necessary to change the pastors. The officials of the Sacred Congregation replied that this consideration was true of some parts of the United States but not of the whole country and that in any event there were means of providing for such cases, namely, either through the appointment of a coadjutor pastor or through the transfer of the pastor to another parish; anyway, since such a case could not be ordinary, it could not hinder the general law. Tenaciously holding his ground, Seghers then asserted that he had many younger priests to whom it did not seem proper to entrust parishes of irremovable tenure. This objection the representatives of the Propaganda answered by pointing out the attached condition by which only those priests who had had the experience of ten years in the parochial ministry could be appointed irremovable pastors. When he went on to ask whether such pastors should have ordinary or delegated power, he was told that they must have ordinary authority as true pastors have.

Since the American prelates were eager to limit this concession to their priests as much as possible, they kept returning to the subject. At the third meeting they declared it to be their understanding that in demanding the establishment of parishes of irremovable tenure, the Sacred Congregation intended to grant to the rectors of churches only the quality of irremovability and not all the privileges and rights of genuine pastors and that it was only in this sense that they had given their consent to the proposal. Archbishop Ryan suggested that it would be preferable to appoint only irremovable rectors of missions, as in England, instead of attaching the irremovability to the parish. Seconding this proposal, Archbishop Feehan remarked that this method would guarantee the priests' security of tenure according to the intention of the Sacred Congregation without placing an obstacle in the way of the extremely useful division of missions. The cardinals acquiesced in the demand of the Coadjutor of St. Louis and of the Archbishop of Chicago to the extent that the right then possessed by the bishops relating to the division of missions should remain intact although there would be some parishes whose rectors would be irremovable; they added, however:

> (1) once a mission is established as of irremovable tenure, it always continues to enjoy that status even though some part of it may be taken away; (2) an irremovable rector has ordinary jurisdiction as if he were a true pastor; (3) neither new parishes formed through division nor their rectors are irremovable unless they are established as such by the bishop; (4) parishes established through a division can be independent of the mother parish and it is desirable that they be so established; (5) missions properly so called are not to be included among the missions of irremovable tenure . . .[322]

Not resigned to his defeat, Archbishop Seghers raised the question of the rights and privileges of irremovable rectors once again at the fifth session. The cardinals tried to maintain their position that such rectors should be regarded as true pastors in the canonical sense, but in the face of the firm opposition of several American prelates they yielded by agreeing that the reasons against this proposal, if presented in writing, would be examined in a general congregation of the Propaganda. At the next meeting, however, it was announced that although the question would not be considered in a general congregation, it should be answered as follows: "For the present, irremovable rectors are to be appointed as in England," [323] that is, they would enjoy only the character of irremovability without the rights and privileges of true pastors. Through their persistence, then, the bishops won a partial victory in the end.

The last question to be discussed in Rome was the manner of nominating candidates for episcopal sees. The Propaganda had proposed that in case of a vacancy the canons, where they existed, and the irremovable rectors of the diocese should be assembled under the presidency of the administrator of the diocese and should submit to the bishops of the province the names of three men whom they judged most worthy, adding pertinent information about each one. Before voting, they should swear that they were not swayed by any favor. This vote would be only consultative. The chairman should send the procès verbal of this meeting to the Sacred Congregation and to the archbishop (or to the senior bishop if the metropolitan see was to be filled), who would communicate it to all the suffragans. Then the bishops of the province would meet and discuss these three candidates and would draw up a terna for presentation to the Holy See.[324]

At the first meeting held in Rome Archbishop Gibbons, speaking for all the Americans present, said that the proposed plan was acceptable but that the following addition should be made: "either the archbishop or, if he is unable, a suffragan bishop delegated by him should preside over the meeting of the clergy: in case an archbishop was to be proposed, the senior suffragan bishop should preside, or, if he is unable, another bishop delegated by him." [325] This proposal was accepted without any opposition. In the next session some further details were adjusted. Archbishop Corrigan asked whether regulars who were rectors should be allowed to cast a vote; the reply was that such regulars were not irremovable pastors even though their church was perpetually given over to their religious order. Then Archbishop Williams inquired whether the bishops should discuss only the names proposed by the clergy or also others of their own choosing; the reply was that they should discuss both, because the vote of the clergy was only consultative; the bishops, however, were obliged to set forth to the Sacred Congregation their reasons for rejecting the names proposed by the clergy. On these terms the Roman phase of the preparation for the Third Plenary Council was brought to a close.

After the discussions with the officials of the Propaganda were concluded, Gibbons, who had been appointed apostolic delegate for the council, sent to all the American bishops a revised statement of the decrees proposed for their deliberation. In this document the modifications and clarifications that had been agreed to were incorporated. For example, the method by which the clergy were to nominate the consultors was specified thus: each priest who was engaged in the sacred ministry within the diocese was to submit to the bishop a list of those whom he deemed fit for that office without designating any exclusively; from these nominees the bishop was to choose those whom he judged most suitable. (This method hardly restricted the bishop's freedom of choice, for unless the priests of a diocese were perfectly unanimous, at least one of them could be expected to nominate the persons whom the bishop favored, and then the bishop could proceed to appoint them in spite of the preference of the majority of his clergy.) The consent of the consultors, however, would be necessary in the choice of a new consultor. In appointing an irremovable rector, the bishop was also free to choose the one whom he considered the most worthy among the priests who had satisfied the conditions of passing the *concursus* and spending ten years in the diocese. At least one-tenth of the parishes were to have irremovable pastors. In nominating candidates for a bishopric, moreover, the metropolitan and/or suffragans could add names to those proposed by the clergy or substitute others, but if they believed that the names proposed by the clergy should not be accepted, they would have to state their reasons to the Propaganda. Finally, the council was to adopt the procedure for criminal cases laid down in the Congregation's recent instruction.[326]

Neither the participants in the conferences nor the bishops who had not been invited were entirely satisfied with the fruits of that Roman autumn. After the archbishops had returned home, Ryan wrote to Gibbons, "We shall have something to do to defend our 'schemata' in the Council, but I do not see that we could have done better, especially when the result shall be compared with what the Cardinals submitted to us for adoption. The new 'Instructio' will not, I fear, satisfy without some changes." [327] Archbishop Corrigan was one who was determined to modify the procedure prescribed in the Instruction. He wrote to McQuaid that in his opinion "the mode of trying clerical cases" was "the only paper to which exception" could justly be taken. He went on to say:

> It seems to me that the important point *now* is to represent to the Holy See all the objections against the proposed method of clerical trials. . . . These difficulties should be stated clearly

and strongly before the Council meets and permission obtained to revise the *Instructio*, either by individual or concerted Episcopal action.[328]

He also reminded Gibbons of the "matter of the verbal pleading of lawyers," [329] and when Gibbons sent out the original version of the text, Corrigan enumerated to him the precise changes which it had been agreed at Rome to make in the Instruction in order "to exclude oral pleadings of lawyers." [330] Gibbons promptly took heed of the corrections, and the Coadjutor of New York then replied: "I am delighted that the amendments have duly been inserted in the Instructio regarding trials. This change will give great satisfaction [to the bishops!]." [331] In the summer Corrigan informed his friend in Rochester that Gibbons had inserted into the *schemata* Chapter XV (*De Judiciis Clericorum*) of the Provincial Council of New York which had been held the previous year but had not yet been approved by the Holy See. Gibbons had told him that several prelates had expressed "a desire for specific legislation on this subject." [332]

One of the bishops to whom Gibbons was referring, perhaps, was Gilmour of Cleveland. He called the new Instruction "cumbersome & vexatious" and considered the old one, "somewhat improved," to be better. He also commented on another point:

> The question of rectors needs to be somewhat modified – & percision, as to the character of the rectories to be created & the causes for removal, be clearly defined. I proposed at our Council the *ten per cent* phase, but for the next twenty years forbade its extension, so that its workings be felt & considered, while it was manageable. With the above or something similar I think it excellent.[333]

Another bishop whom Gibbons may have had in mind was John J. Kain of Wheeling, who rejoiced over "Archbishop Elder's petition to the Holy See against allowing laymen to enter *our* ecclesiastical courts, & his suggestion to dispense with the concursus in appointment of first *Rectores inamovibiles*." [334]

The apostolic delegate assigned each of the *Capita proposita* to one of the ecclesiastical provinces of the United States for comment and development. Chapter II, on chapters of canons and parishes, was given over to the Province of Boston. After discussing it with his suffragans, the metropolitan, John J. Williams, replied to Gibbons that in their opinion "the number of the Consultors should depend on the number of the clergy, or of the parishes, in each diocese." They also suggested that the advice of the consultors be asked in the appointment of permanent rectors and that one of the conditions for that office be "that he should have been three years in charge of a church, and have proved himself, in his administrative and financial capacity." The comprovincials of New England, moreover, remarked that they had not yet received from the Propaganda "the promised form for the examination or *concursus* of the candidates," which they called "a most important item of this question," and they expressed the fear that the proposed right of appeal from the bishop's judgment in the appointment of rectors might "in time give much trouble" and "place the Bishop in a very unpleasant position." [335]

The Province of Santa Fe, to which Gibbons had assigned Chapter III, on the mode of proposing to the Holy See candidates for vacant dioceses, had no criticisms to make.[336] The Province of Cincinnati, on the other hand, commented on several chapters, and the metropolitan in separate letters to Gibbons added his glosses in English to the Latin report of the meeting. The bishops "agreed that the consent of the Consultors should not be required for the acquisition of property, but only for its alienation," and they thought that it would be "enough to require *consent* for contracting debts of more than three thousand dollars in any one transaction." Archbishop Elder commented:

> Indeed, as far as my observation has extended, the abuses would have been hindered, if only the older priests had possessed an official *right to know* what the Bishop was doing, because they could have drawn the attention of the Metropolitan or other authority: so that in the whole matter I prefer *consilium* to *consensus*.

The bishops of this province also wished to limit the number of irremovable pastors to the proposed ratio of one to ten for twenty years. "The object was to hinder one Bishop from burdening the diocese with Rectors, to the embarrassment of his successors." They desired, furthermore, to add to the requirements of the parish which was to have an irremovable pastor that it be equipped with a school for each sex and a house for the teachers and that its ordinary income be sufficient to pay the annual interest on any debt that it might have and a part of the principal. Elder explained, "This will stimulate priests to bring their churches to this condition." Finally, these bishops decided to beg the pope not to allow laymen to defend priests in episcopal courts; they drew up a petition to this effect and sent it to the apostolic delegate so that it could be forwarded to all the ordinaries of the country and signed by them also. In this letter they expressed their fear that because of the peculiar circumstances of the United States lay pleaders, nominally Catholic, would show themselves ready to defend the worst cases for the sake of profit, and if they were excluded by the ordinary's decision from defending the accused cleric, they would stir up hatred, murmuring, and prejudice. Elder asked Gibbons' opinion of this petition, adding:

> In this country there is a class of petty lawyers, who would gladly devote themselves to such cases, on purpose to give trouble, and make for themselves a cheap reputation. With the technicalities of the process we are not yet familiar, so that it would be easy for petty lawyers to make annoyances. If rejected by the Bishop, he and the unworthy priest would make capital out of that.[337]

Apparently Elder did not think it necessary to await the outcome of a trial before calling an accused priest unworthy, nor did he envision the possibility of an innocent priest ever being wrongly suspected.

The province to which Chapter VI, on the procedure for criminal and disciplinary cases of clerics, was referred, namely, that of San Francisco, did not make any such objection to the Propaganda's instruction. It uttered the caution, however, that the creation of irremovable pastors could be harmful to ecclesiastical discipline unless not only the causes for removal which were defined in law but also other causes peculiar to American circumstances were enumerated; these Western prelates proposed, therefore, that the section "De judiciis clericorum" of the recently held Provincial Council of New York be adopted by the plenary council.[338]

The bishops of the Province of Milwaukee shared this belief in the absolute necessity of increasing the number of canonical causes for which an irremovable rector could and should be removed, and they mentioned specifically drunkenness as the first among them, warning: "Let that excessive mildness of the law be taken away by which a rector, although he has given great and public scandal, cannot be removed as long as he promises to amend his life." They predicted that the institution of irremovable rectors would be more injurious than useful if such priests could not be touched except for reasons then specified in ecclesiastical law.[339]

Finally, the bishops of the Province of Chicago recommended briefly that in cases of appeal to the metropolitan, "his court be composed of Bishops of the Province exclusively," and that the number of irremovable priests be neither more nor less than ten per cent "until a future Council." [340]

With the aid of these suggestions decrees were drafted by the theologians whom Gibbons had invited to go to Baltimore in the late summer of 1884. The resulting schema was then printed and was used as the basis of discussion in the council.[341] The debates and votes in the private congregations were carefully recorded in the *acta*, which were subsequently published in a private edition along with the *decreta*. [342]

In regard to diocesan consultors, the bishops discussed the number of names that the clergy was to propose. Upon the motion of Archbishop Williams they at last agreed unanimously that as a general rule, since the number of consultors would vary from diocese to diocese, the clergy should propose three names for each consultor who was to be chosen by the bishop. Since the draft retained the requirement of the consultors' consent for the acquisition and disposal of ecclesiastical property and for the taking out of mortgages as well as for the other actions mentioned above, Archbishop Heiss, echoing the written suggestion of Archbishop Elder, moved that wherever the word "consent" was used in this paragraph it should be replaced by the word "advice." The Bishop of Charleston, Henry P. Northrup, on the other hand, thought that the text should not be altered, for by the consultors' consent the bishop's mind was freed from worry, or, in other words, his responsibility was lessened. Bishop Dwenger warned his colleagues that the Propaganda insisted on the consultors' consent for the specified matters, and he assured his colleagues that the consultors would never refuse their consent if what was proposed was just and reasonable. The Vicar Apostolic of Dakota, Martin Marty, O.S.B., however, observed that a bishop ought not to be less free than an abbot of a monastery, who asks counsel and not consent. The Vicar Apostolic of Nebraska, James O'Connor, maintained that the matter was no longer an open question; Rome wished to have the council introduce into the United States, at least approximately, that provision of the law which prohibited a bishop from alienating church property without the consent of the chapter, and the consultors were to take the place of the chapter. Archbishops Seghers and Feehan, nevertheless, asserted that the Sacred Congregation had left the matter to the judgment of the prelates assembled in the council. The motion of the Archbishop of Milwaukee was then carried by sixty-five votes cast in its favor. Next the Bishop of Providence, Thomas F. Hendricken, moved that the opinion of the consultors should be given in writing, and Archbishop Kenrick, seconded by Bishop McQuaid, moved that the consultors should give their advice as a body (not individually). These motions were also passed. The amount of money which the bishop could spend independently of the consultors was reduced to five hundred dollars, since he would only have to consult them anyway. The committee which reported on this chapter recommended that instead of keeping the provision which made the consultors permanent after they were once named, the paragraph be modified to say, "Let the consultors be chosen for a three-year term." This proposal was adopted by a vote of sixty to nine.[343]

In the final version of the decrees the fathers stated in the first paragraph of the chapter on diocesan consultors, perhaps as a concession to the Propaganda and to the clergy, that it was greatly to be desired that the canons regarding cathedral chapters could be carried into execution forthwith. They added, however, that the circumstances of the dioceses did not permit the erection of chapters at that time. Hence, it seemed good to them to institute diocesan consultors until other provision be made.[344] In this way the fathers acknowledged that the consultors were to be regarded only as temporary substitutes for canons.

The chapter on irremovable rectors occupied much of the conciliar fathers' time. The qualifications of a parish to which this privilege would be attached were considered in detail. The Bishop of Savannah, William H. Gross, said that the church must be entirely free of debt. The Bishop of Vincennes, Francis S. Chatard, replied more realistically that if this condition were imposed, irremovable rectors could be instituted in very few places, and even if a rector accepted a church free of debt, he might be forced to contract a debt later on. Bishop Dwenger agreed that if complete freedom from debt were demanded, there would be no place for an irremovable rector in the diocese. Thereupon the Bishop of Peoria, John Lancaster Spalding, declared that the fathers should decide whether or not irremovable rectors ought to be instituted at all before they discussed such accidental questions.[345] By a vote of forty-seven to fourteen it was decided, therefore, that the fathers should first deliberate on the substantive issue.

Many of the bishops expressed a basic opposition to the proposed decree. The Archbishop of San Francisco, Joseph S. Alemany, stated that the time had not yet come for the creation of irremovable rectors, at least on the Pacific Coast, and the bishop of Portland, James A. Healy, expressed his agreement for Maine. Archbishop Kenrick feared that many and grave inconveniences for bishops and dioceses would arise as a result, and the Bishop of Dubuque, John Hennessy, asserted that more than a tenth of the clergy were already virtually irremovable; hence, he questioned the need of a new law that would create difficulties. The Bishop of St. Paul, John Ireland, remarked that there were often reasons to remove a rector which could not be proved canonically, that rectors were, in fact, irremovable, and that it would be better to decree that a priest could not be removed without first obtaining the counsel of the consultors. He was convinced that there would be a perpetual foment of envy and discord if one in ten were declared irremovable. Bishop Spalding asserted that the advice of the Holy See should not be urged, since the bishops were convoked to decide this matter according to their own judgment. Instead of remedying litigation and discord, the law would increase them from day to day. Bishop Dwenger rejoined that the Sacred Congregation wished this decree, and the Second Plenary Council had also desired it, and that litigation and discord were less to be feared in the future, since the reasons for removal would be so clearly set forth. Bishop Gross expressed his agreement and added that the honor and esteem entertained by priests for bishops would be much decreased if this part of the schema were rejected, for all knew that it had been drawn up on the model of the Roman schema which was approved by the cardinals of the Propaganda. He feared that if priests were disappointed in their expectations they would tire out the Holy See with petitions and complaints, and in the end a law would be imposed on the bishops against their will.

As the debate continued, Bishop McQuaid said that when he had been in Rome he had advised the creation of irremovable rectors instead of chapters. Archbishop Williams observed that rectors in some places were trustees or wardens of churches by virtue of civil law and so even if they were removed they could remain in possession against the will of the bishop while their appeal was pending. Bishop Spalding, however, insisted that all zeal and devotion to the good of the faithful would die out in the rectors once they became irremovable. Bishop O'Connor admonished his colleagues that they would have to yield to some extent to the will of the Holy See and to the almost unanimous wish not only of factions but also of pious priests. He maintained that there was no force to the objections made till then; that the provisions contained in the schema were quite sufficient to uphold sacred discipline; and that, in case of need, new reasons for removal could be established by provincial councils. Then the fathers heeded the advice of Bishop Healy to defer further deliberation on this matter for a few days.[346]

When the council returned to this question at the end of that week, Archbishop Alemany moved that the whole matter of irremovable pastors be left to provincial councils to settle, but he was supported by only two votes. Bishop Healy said that the paragraph should be retained because the irremovability of some priests would make it clear that the rest were removable; he moved, however, that the clause allowing parishes with debts (but also with adequate income) to receive irremovable pastors be eliminated. A majority of fifty-two fathers voted for this deletion, thus requiring that the parish be entirely free of debt. When Archbishop Kenrick moved, and Bishop Spalding seconded his motion, that all the rectors of churches who had laudably exercised the sacred ministry for ten years be reckoned among the irremovable rectors, only fourteen fathers voted in favor and fifty-one voted against.

Archbishop Gibbons, having been asked by Bishop Ireland to disclose his view on this question, spoke "with very grave words as on a subject of the greatest importance." He recalled to the bishops the explicit and often repeated statements of the cardinals of the Propaganda by which it was clear that they were unshakably attached to the principle of irremovable rectors. He feared that if the American bishops did not institute them voluntarily, they would be forced to do so against their will and to the discredit of the episcopacy. He warned that neither their decrees nor their prayers would budge the cardinals from this intention. In his opinion, however, it would be easier in the future to remove irremovable pastors, if they should render themselves unworthy, than those who were then considered movable. Gibbons believed, furthermore, that the council had to satisfy to some extent the desires of the clergy, for this privilege was insistently requested by very many learned and pious priests. To him, moreover, it hardly seemed fair to suspect in advance the prudence and loyalty in the administration of parishes of those who were as highly qualified as irremovable rectors would have to be according to the draft. In fact, he remarked, more qualities were demanded for the office of irremovable rector, to whom the care of only one mission would be entrusted, than were commonly required of a bishop, to whom the government of a whole diocese would be committed. The apostolic delegate concluded his discourse by referring to the causes for removal which would make it difficult for any harm to arise from the new legislation.

Several other speakers then added arguments to those offered by

Gibbons. The Bishop of Burlington, Louis de Goesbriand, spoke in favor of passing the decree because it was desired by the Propaganda, which understood very well the condition of the American churches. Bishop Hendricken said that twenty years previously he had been ordered to consult the clergy about the privilege of irremovability and that though they received the news with joy they were prevented by fear from expressing their opinions. Archbishop Heiss reminded the fathers that the prelates in the meeting at Rome in the preceding year had unanimously agreed on the institution of irremovable rectors, and he said that if the council were now to reject it, the bishops would be judged at Rome as having acted against the obedience and reverence due to the Holy See. Bishops Dwenger and O'Connor praised the proposed decree also because it would stimulate the younger priests to study more diligently in view of the *concursus*.

All these arguments, however, failed to convince Bishop Spalding. He attacked the proposal because if it once became law it would never be abrogated. He thought that the existing discipline was closer to that of the early Church and to that which existed in all the countries where the Catholic religion was making progress. In his opinion, the Propaganda wanted to concede this privilege because it thought that the clergy desired it; he retorted:

> That is false; it is not the good and pious priests who desire it but only the factious and scurrilous who charge the bishops with tyranny. The status of our Church is not well known to the Sacred Congregation as is evident from the instruction recently issued and then recalled. Vain is the hope conceived by some that rectors appointed by the bishop will always stand by him if troubles arise. Perhaps they will be against him. What if a new bishop comes, an unwelcome person? They will be unanimous against him as if they had conspired. From this new legislation we can expect nothing but everlasting dissensions, quarrels, and disputes. The fervor of zeal will come to an end in our priests, as has happened in Italy, once they know that they can be removed only by a judge. It would be better to defer this whole matter to the next plenary council.

To relieve his conscience of responsibility for the evils and scandals that he foresaw, Bishop Ireland also argued against the proposal of irremovable pastors, saying among other things:

> A rector can live in a very holy manner and still be a great hindrance to his church. Catholics, especially the Irish, are gen-

erally unwilling to be witnesses against a priest, however unworthy he may be. The Sacred Congregation does not know this; it gives credence too easily to factious priests who slander their bishops.

Obtaining the floor, Archbishop Seghers complained that the bishops were being pressed from both sides on this matter — by the authority of the Propaganda on the one hand and by the desires of the lower clergy on the other. He feared that an irremovable rector would become a genuine pastor with a right to the collections at Mass and a right to name his assistants and that the Holy See might eliminate the conditions attached by the council. Archbishop Ryan promptly scotched this notion, saying that it was clearly understood at Rome that the new rectors would have the same standing as those in England. He also denied what Spalding had asserted about the conformity of the present discipline with that of the ancient Church. Archbishop Williams corroborated Ryan's statement about the English model for the new rectors and acknowledged the usefulness and desirability of the proposed law, although he also recognized the danger of giving the civil courts an opportunity to interfere, for even though a rector who was a trustee or warden might be removed by the bishop for sufficiently grave reasons, he would still remain a trustee before the civil law. To dispel all doubt, Marty and Williams proposed that explicit references to England and to the explanation given during the discussions in Rome be added to the text in a footnote. After this motion was passed, the amended paragraph was finally approved.

Bishop Dwenger attempted to prevent any bishop from making more than one-tenth of the rectors irremovable, but the word for "at least," which he wished to expunge, was retained by a vote of thirty-seven to thirty. Spalding, nevertheless, persuaded his colleagues to prohibit any increase of the established ratio for twenty years from the promulgation of the decrees. With a few other minor amendments this paragraph too was at last approved.[347] In the afternoon, however, at the urging of Bishop Dwenger, the original wording was restored to the extent of permitting a bishop to exceed the ratio upon consultation. Dwenger supported Seghers in the latter's desire to enable a bishop to number among the irremovable rectors a priest who had spent less than ten years in the sacred ministry lest the bishop's freedom be restricted, but this motion failed by a vote of thirty-six to thirty-four. Another motion that was rejected, but by a larger margin (forty-four to sixteen), was made by the Bishop of Columbus, John A. Watterman, with Spalding's support, namely, that a priest who was to be named a rector should have previously shown himself to be zealous especially with regard to the commanded collections. Spalding was also unsuccessful in his effort to have the right of appeal taken away from a priest who would have satisfied all the requirements but would not have been appointed by the bishop.

Then the council took up the proposed causes for the removal of an irremovable rector. The draft revealed how grudgingly the bishops were allowing the privilege when it said that they feared that it would tend "to the detriment of religion and the weakening of ecclesiastical discipline, as well as to the disgrace of the Church," unless to the causes established by law there were added others adapted to the circumstances of the United States.[348] The first of these was grave incapacity of governing either spiritually or temporally the mission entrusted to the rector. Upon the recommendation of the theologians the fathers added by a vote of thirty-seven to thirty-four the clause, "If, however, the incapacity does not result from his own fault, the mission should be burdened with the becoming support of the removed rector insofar as the revenues of the church permit." The second cause was obstinate disobedience to the rules laid down by the ordinary for the administration of the temporal affairs of his mission. Almost all the fathers agreed to add the phrase suggested by Bishop Healy, "or for the support of the obligations of the diocese." Thirdly, an irremovable pastor could be removed for "open refusal or supine negligence in building Catholic schools after the ordinary, upon mature consideration and in view of the condition of the mission, has declared that those schools can and should be built." The other causes for removal were rash assumption of a loan for the parish and inexcusable negligence in paying its debts, collusion with the lay trustees in giving a note on the parish for money rightly or wrongly due to the rector without the consent of the ordinary, voluntary and deliberate falsehood in the annual report on the spiritual and temporal state of the parish in a matter of greater importance, drunkenness on the part of a rector who would thereby cause serious scandal to the faithful and harm to religion, and a well founded suspicion of incontinence which would seriously prejudice his ministry. With little discussion or modification all these provisions were accepted by the council.[349]

Then the conciliar fathers turned to the proposed mode of nominating candidates for vacant sees. Archbishop Kenrick, who had been represented at the Roman meetings by his coadjutor, suggested, apparently with the Irish system in mind, that on the thirtieth day after the funeral of a bishop all the rectors of churches, religious included, who had exercised the sacred ministry for ten years should assemble and submit three names to the bishops of the province; then the latter should convene under the metropolitan to consider these names and should nominate one of them to the Holy See; the same procedure would be followed when a coadjutor with the right of succession was to be appointed. Archbishop Elder praised this proposal because it would avoid delay in the appointment of a new bishop and would allow a greater number to give their vote and opinion, but he did not approve of sending only one name to Rome. Archbishop Ryan agreed with his colleague from Cincinnati, saying that all rectors having ten years' experience should be allowed to express their opinions; otherwise the number of electors would be improperly small. Bishop McQuaid shared these views and recommended that the chancellor, deans, rector of the cathedral, and superiors of seminaries be granted a voice, and others observed that the greater the number of persons who had recommended a candidate, the more welcome and acceptable he would be as bishop. Dwenger and Goesbriand, on the contrary, spoke for the schema. Spalding expressed his disagreement both with the schema and with Kenrick's proposal, as he cautioned his colleagues: "We are entering upon a rough road and may never be able to go back. If priests are given the right of electing [their bishop], the people will also covet it." He thought that irremovable rectors and all others except the consultors should be denied this privilege. His position was reinforced by the Bishop of Louisville, William G. McCloskey, and Archbishop Corrigan. Archbishop Gibbons, however, believed that the Propaganda would not readily retreat from its instruction; he thought it would be helpful, nevertheless, if the priests submitted the names to the bishops on the very day of the funeral so that the latter might have time to consider the merits of the candidates before the thirtieth day; as he reminded his colleagues, the Propaganda complained that names were often sent to Rome without adequate information about the candidates' qualifications.

In the voting, both parts of Kenrick's proposal were rejected; only two fathers were in favor of sending a single name to Rome. Spalding's attempt to restrict the election to the consultors, being supported by only twenty-three votes, was also defeated. McQuaid's motion likewise was voted down by a small margin. In a similar way the council refused to admit Alemany's amendment which would have required the clergy to name six candidates (instead of three) in order to leave the bishops of the province more freedom of choice. Finally, the section as a whole was adopted.[350]

The last important item discussed in the council was the procedure to be followed in disciplinary and criminal cases involving clerics. Archbishop Kenrick reminded his colleagues of the decree of his provincial council of 1855, which had been subsequently recommended by the Propaganda and approved by the Second Plenary Council and had never been explicitly abrogated. He presented several reasons for retaining this legislation, namely, that it made no distinction between rectors and other priests; that it revealed the identity of the accusers; and that it did not adhere so closely to legal forms. He said that he himself had followed this procedure in the past and would continue to do so until it should be explicitly abrogated. When Bishop O'Connor asked him whether he offered the St. Louis procedure as a substitute for the one in the schema or as an alternative which the bishops could freely choose, Kenrick replied that he offered no substitute, for that would be irreverent to the Holy See, but he submitted an easier method for the consideration of the prelates, and if they judged it proper, they might propose it respectfully to the Holy See for approbation.

Bishop Spalding, who thought that the question had been examined by the archbishops in Rome, requested information as to what had been agreed upon by them. Ryan replied that the matter had not been examined by the archbishops, because they knew that the form of ecclesiastical trials had been enjoined by the Holy See. He himself preferred the form prescribed by the First Provincial Council of St. Louis and regretted that it had rarely or never been employed in the dioceses. Hence arose so many appeals, the remedy for which the Propaganda was seeking in this new form of trial, and the schema, therefore, could not be changed except by humble petition to the pope himself. Bishop McQuaid then said that it was the right and duty of the council to point out the difficulties entailed in the new method under which it would rarely happen that the guilty would be punished. The Bishop of Springfield, Patrick T. O'Reilly, was of the same opinion, stating that two years before at Rome he had heard men of authority and distinguished position express their wonderment at the fact that the American bishops had accepted the instruction of 1878 with hardly any protest. Bishop Keane also testified that he had heard at Rome that the Propaganda wanted to impose nothing but what the bishops were both willing and able to do, but that the Holy See absolutely required accurate information on the whole judicial process; the testimony had to be judicially unimpeachable, with papers, documents, and other reliable material and not simply affirmations or opinions. The Bishop of Richmond also preferred the St. Louis procedure, which he was sure the Holy See would not refuse if the bishops properly requested it. McCloskey thought that such a petition should be signed by all. The Vicar Apostolic of Nebraska agreed that the bishops should request permission to use either form; he himself preferred the St. Louis procedure, because he could hardly send a commission to investigate in a place 1,800 miles from his see city, as actually happened. But Dwenger, acting again as a spokesman for Rome, denied that there was any danger of delay or scandal in the new form, and he doubted that the Holy See would grant the proposed petition, for Leo XIII had devised this procedure for his clergy when he was Archbishop of Perugia, and the clergy of France had adopted it.

Once again, however, Bishop Spalding led the opposition, criticizing the new procedure:

> It is full of details, and if they are omitted the sentence may be annulled at Rome. The bishops desire a fair form of trials, without any noise, not like those of the Protestant clergymen who have consequently suffered notable damage to their reputation among their citizens, for the newspapers spread these things throughout the whole country every day. As a result, the life of bishops will be made miserable with constant suits, appeals, trials to be repeated, etc.

Spalding declared that he would rather resign the episcopacy than prosecute a cleric at Rome.

Bishop Chatard thought that the new form, although perhaps inconvenient, would be very useful, and that there would be fewer appeals if the trials were conducted in a properly judicial manner. He pointed out that the St. Louis procedure, in spite of the approval of the Second Plenary Council and of the Propaganda, was not followed by the bishops, and for this reason the metropolitans were unwilling to accept appeals. Kenrick denied that there were ecclesiastical trials properly so called in the United States, for in these trials the accusers must be brought face to face with the accused, witnesses must be cited, and perjurers punished, but none of these things were possible because of the civil law. He agreed that metropolitans had been unwilling to accept appeals because the judgments of the lower courts were not legal.

Archbishop Ryan was certain that the Propaganda would not revoke its instruction before the bishops ascertained through experience the effectiveness of the new procedure. He proposed, nevertheless, that the Holy See be asked to permit a bishop to use the St. Louis form in those cases in which he could not follow the new procedure without grave inconvenience. This motion was passed with fifty-two affirmative votes.

Archbishop Williams proposed that the Holy See be further asked not to admit any appeal unless the case had already been appealed to the metropolitan. Although the Bishop of Scranton, William O'Hara, feared that Rome would thus be renouncing its right, Williams explained that it was not a petition to take this right away from the Holy See but rather to have the Holy See forgo the use of it for a while for the greater good of the Church; he believed that Rome would grant this with equanimity, as it had done in the case of English clerics. The same opinion was expressed by Archbishop Corrigan, who recommended that the Holy See be asked to require that a case always be tried twice in this country, so that a subject of a metropolitan would have to appeal to the nearest metropolitan before he could carry his case to Rome. With this amendment the council adopted Williams' motion almost unanimously.[351] Later the apostolic delegate appointed a committee consisting of Archbishops Kenrick, Williams, and Corrigan and Bishops Keane, McQuaid, O'Connor, and Michael J. O'Farrell of Trenton to draw up a petition to the Pope for the retention of the old form of trials in dioceses in which the new procedure could not be used without serious hardship,[352] and when it was read at a subsequent private congregation it was approved by nearly all.[353]

In the last private congregation Gibbons observed that the fathers still had to designate the metropolitans to whom a defendent could appeal against his own metropolitan before having recourse to Rome. Although Chatard wished to leave this task to the Holy See, Corrigan insisted that it be done by the plenary council. In Gibbons' opinion, Rome could not object if the appeal were made to the senior bishop of the province instead of another metropolitan. Bishop Hennessy proposed that a supreme court of appeals consisting of bishops as judges be constituted in order that cases could be tried also in the third instance in this country and the Propaganda would not be bothered with so many frivolous appeals. The apostolic delegate, however, doubted that the Holy See would approve such a court. Dwenger then asked that the archbishops decide whether a defendant who was condemned in the metropolitan court could appeal either to the nearest metropolitan or to the senior bishop of the province, as he might choose, and that this favor be requested of the Holy See. A majority of ten archbishops carried the motion. Ever eager to preserve episcopal authority, Bishop Spalding proposed that in case of an appeal from a suffragan to the metropolitan, the latter should employ bishops and not priests in the metropolitan court, for it seemed to be improper for a bishop to be judged by priests. Gibbons quashed the suggestion by replying that in many provinces this would be impossible. Thus the month of deliberations was ended.[354]

After the council it was feared that the Holy See might not approve the decrees as modified by the bishops. Hence, Archbishop Gibbons appointed two bishops, Dwenger and John Moore of St. Augustine, to take the decrees to Rome and to try to have them approved without change.[355] McQuaid thought that such representation would not be strong enough; he wrote to Gibbons:

> . . . Again the Statutes for immoveable rectors can not be safely disturbed, if we are to exist as bishops. This rebellious & insolent element must be met with something else than honey or sweet words. Now, with the prejudice of Franzelin & others, are the men, who have gone, equal to cope? I gravely doubt. . .[356]

In fact, the two envoys encountered great difficulties in persuading the cardinals of the Propaganda to permit the substitution of "counsel" for "consent" of the consultors in the decree concerning the purchase and sale of church property. Hence, Gibbons in concert with several other archbishops later appointed a third representative, Bishop Gilmour. After a long struggle the three bishops accomplished their mission successfully.

The Propaganda with the approval of Leo XIII issued an indult exempting the American bishops for ten years from the solemnities required by canon law for contracting major financial obligations on the Church; they were enjoined merely to seek the counsel of their consultors on the need or usefulness of the proposed transaction.[357] As far as the petition for the continued use of the St. Louis form of trials was concerned, Rome insisted on the erection of episcopal courts within three years after the promulgation of the council's decrees unless a further dispensation was obtained from the Propaganda; meanwhile in such places the instruction of 1878, as subsequently interpreted, was to be observed. In the final decree more safeguards were provided for the accused in the acceptance of testimony; the accused could learn the names of the witnesses (but only after they had made their own depositions) and then take exception to particular ones, but he still could not cross-examine them; he could also produce witnesses on his own behalf, but only the judges could examine them.[358] Thus the procedure in such trials continued to differ greatly from that of the Anglo-American legal tradition. The decrees were finally published in 1886.

The pastoral letter of the Third Plenary Council, on the other hand, was published immediately. In it the bishops appeared to be eager to reassure their priests of their concern, respect, and affection. Perhaps they also wished to allay any unrest that might cause the clergy to apply pressure to the Propaganda during the revision of the conciliar decrees. They addressed the faithful in these words:

> No small portion of our attention has been bestowed on the framing of such legislation as will best secure the rights and interests of your pastors, and of all ranks of the clergy in this country. It is but natural, beloved brethren, that the first and dearest object of our solicitude should be our venerable clergy. . . .
>
> The rights of the clergy have reference chiefly to their exercising the sacred ministry in their missions, to the fixity of their tenure of office and to the inviolableness of their pastoral authority within proper limits. It is the spirit of the Church that the various grades of authority in her organization should in no wise be in rivalry or conflict, but orderly and harmonious. This she has secured by her wise laws, based upon the experience of centuries, and representing the perfection of Church organization. It is obvious that in countries like our own, where from rudimentary beginnings our organization is only gradually advancing towards perfection, the full application of these laws is impracticable; but in proportion as they become practicable, it is our desire, not less than that of the Holy See, that they should go into effect. For we have the fullest confidence in the wisdom with which the Church devised these laws, and we heartily rejoice at every approach towards perfect organization in the portion of the vineyard over which we have jurisdiction. This has been to some degree accomplished by regulations enacted during recent years, and still more by the decrees of the present Council.[359]

These words appear to have been calculated to disarm the critics of the bishops by agreeing in principle but making important reservations in practice.

One question relating to priests was left unanswered even when the decrees of the Third Plenary Council were approved in Rome. It was not determined in which cases bishops would be held to the formality of a legal trial when they might wish to deprive movable rectors of missions of their office or to transfer them to another post. Hence, the cardinals of the Propaganda, meeting on March 28, 1887, decreed:

> In cases of carrying out a removal or total deprivation of the office of rector, as a punishment for a crime or disciplinary misdeed, a canonical trial must be conducted according to the Instruction *Cum magnopere* and the decrees of the Third Plenary Council. If, on the other hand, it is a question of transferring a rector from one mission to another or to another office, even a lower one, the ordinaries are not bound to conduct a canonical trial; it is necessary, however, that this be done for grave reasons and with consideration of his merits. . . If in the case of a transfer an appeal is made to the Sacred Congregation, it will be remanded to the metropolitan, or if it concerns the metropolitan, to the closest metropolitan.[360]

When Gibbons at the request of the prefect of the Propaganda communicated this decision to the other American bishops, they received it with great satisfaction.

Part VI: Fulfilment and Loss

Before long, nevertheless, it became evident that the decrees of the Third Plenary Council were failing to effect the desired harmony between bishops and their priests. Cases such as the suspension and excommunication of Dr. Edward McGlynn, pastor of St. Stephen's Church in New York, beginning in 1886, were widely publicized in the secular press.[361] McGlynn's "counselor, defender, and abettor," as Archbishop Corrigan called him, was Dr. Burtsell, who also had served as the advocate of several other priests, among whom was one in Rochester, James M. Early, engaged in a dispute with Bishop McQuaid.[362] Burtsell was also a friend of Patrick Corrigan.[363] In 1887 the canon lawyer published a series of articles in the *New York Tablet* and then republished it without change as a booklet of 106 pages under the title, *The Canonical Status of Priests in the United States*. Much of his treatment was narrative, descriptive, or expository; it was generally not argumentative, but it was throughout definitely tendentious and in places sharply critical of the American bishops while reverential toward the Propaganda. As a trained canonist, Burtsell avoided the strained and indefensible interpretations given by William Mahoney, but in the latter's spirit he seemed to point out every conceivable situation in which a priest could appeal to higher authority against his bishop; he frequently asserted, however, that such recourse did not imply any lack of respect.

At the outset Burtsell refuted the false idea that canon law was not in force in the United States because of the missionary status of the country and that therefore everything was left to the will of the superior or the bishop.[364] He found the first generic relation of a priest to his diocese to be that just as a priest is not free to leave it without the bishop's permission, so the bishop is not free to cut him off from it. The author argued that even removable vicars could not be removed at the mere whim or caprice of the bishop,[365] and that removals without reasonable and just cause could be appealed and annulled, especially if the transfer was so made as to imply any blame or fault in the one removed. "Hence a fair similarity, as far as possible an equality of positions must be clear in the transfer." [366] Discoursing on the title of the mission for ordination, Burtsell stated: "As long as the bishops use this extraordinary title they must be prepared for the exercise of the Sacred Congregation's ordinary right to inquire directly into the case of each priest whose title or right to maintenance derived therefrom is in any way touched." [367] His object was to increase the stability and security of all secular priests in their positions.

Burtsell also upheld the right of the clergy to remonstrate to the bishop against harmful diocesan legislation and, if necessary, "to have recourse to the Supreme Authority" to seek the amendment of such statutes; he likewise defended such appellants against any charge of disrespect and said that the intermediate authority obstructing such an appeal would thereby show that the regulation or decision being questioned was "the offspring of personal views." [368] In treating of the establishment of new parishes, he maintained that "the rectors of parishes from which portions are to be taken . . . are entitled to have their objections carefully weighed before the dismemberment of any part of their parish is made." [396] If their reasons are overruled and they deem themselves aggrieved, they may appeal to higher authority. With respect to the number of irremovable rectors, he emphasized the contrast between the Propaganda, which wished to enlarge the proportion, and the bishops, who discountenanced "as great a multiplication of these privileged rectors as the Propaganda instructions seemed to encourage." [370]

By way of preface to a sketch of the various procedures designed for successive use in this country, Burtsell enunciated the principles that no one should ever be condemned unheard and that every accused person has a right to the aid of counsel and to freedom in choosing his counsel. As for the procedure laid down for the Province of St. Louis in 1855 and extended to the whole country in 1866, he said: "I am not aware of any cases that were ever settled in accord with this decree." [371] Hinting at his own experience, he remarked that "the rejection of anyone as counsel without a very serious reason is very strong evidence that passion, dislike and prejudice, not zeal for souls or God's glory, are at the bottom of the charges made." [372] Another blow was struck against the bishops in the following words: ". . . in this country the limitations which the canon law places upon the power of bishops has never been realized by them and nowhere else has there ever been such dependence upon the bishops' will as in this country." [373] Burtsell enumerated some "special reasons why in this country for the welfare of the Church strict adherence to the substantial forms of the prescribed trial [for priests] will always be found to be of the gravest importance," especially the fact that the "natural temperament of the people is opposed to any appearance of arbitrary treatment." [374] With deep personal feeling he lamented that the lawyer for the accused had been "lowered from his high estate to be reputed among a low and hateful brood, subject to the suspicion of being intent only upon evil." [375] He criticized the method of ecclesiastical procedure founded on Roman law which put so much responsibility on the judges and left so small a role to the advocate. He was in favor of having the vicar-general (provided he was trained in jurisprudence) rather than the bishop serve as judge, as was the practice in Italy. Again and again he repeated that a sentence or penalty imposed without due process did not bind the accused in conscience. Describing the American bishops, he wrote: "When men have for a long period had almost unrestricted sway, it is not surprising that its curtailment in accord even with the common law of the Universal Church should make upon them the impression of being an innovation much to be regretted." [376]

With respect to diocesan consultors, Burtsell stated that it was the unanimous wish of the committee of the Third Plenary Council charged with this section of the decrees that the clergy should be assembled to designate three names for each position to be filled and the bishop should choose one of these three; instead it had become the practice in some dioceses that each priest individually sent in three names for each vacant position, so that a great number would be nominated and the bishop would then have an almost unlimited choice; this increase in the number of candidates decreased the representation of the clergy which was the purpose of allowing such nominations.[377] In his opinion, furthermore, the fact that the consultors were appointed only for three-year terms, instead of for life as the Propaganda originally intended, constituted a deterrent to their freedom in designating candidates for a vacant see, because those who had been opposed to the man eventually named bishop might not be reappointed by him at the expiration of their terms.[378] Burtsell does not seem to have adverted to the possibility of a secret ballot, which was expressly permitted by the Third Plenary Council.[379]

It is obvious that in spite of the canonical and historical erudition with which it was composed, this presentation was strongly biased. A pink slip, moreover, was inserted in the pamphlet, suggesting that the reader send one dollar to a given address and promising that Burtsell would use the money "to aid priests, who are deprived of the exercise of the ministry to regain it in accordance with the laws of the Church." [380]

In December Archbishop Corrigan forbade Burtsell to circulate the booklet any farther and ordered him to withdraw it from sale until the regulations of the synod and councils were complied with.[381] The author replied that it had not crossed his mind "that the alleged regulations were applicable to the printing in pamphlet form of a series of articles that had been published with the writer's name in a Catholic paper of this city" and "that all the copies of the pamphlet intended for distribution" had been sent out already. He explained to his archbishop: "The circulation was restricted to priests outside the diocese of New York. It was not for sale nor in the hands of any publisher." [382]

Since Corrigan could not stop the circulation of Burtsell's pamphlet, he endeavored to have it severely criticized in the press.[383] Soon the *Freeman's Journal* devoted a brief editorial to it, saying:

> . . . as it had been sent to the press for review, as it is likely to be read by laymen, we take the liberty of saying that it shows a spirit of bitterness, of insubordination, of disloyalty to authority, which must fill any well-instructed Catholic layman with regret. . . . we say, representing as we do the best lay Catholic element in this community, that if there are many priests who can publicly sneer at authority and defend themselves for so doing by sophistries, God help their flocks.[384]

This newspaper also published a long review of the booklet by "A

Reader of Canon Law." The anonymous critic lamented Burtsell's "tendency to plead against authority" and said that he spoke "of episcopal authority with a constant undercurrent of distrust and opposition" and presented the bishops "in general as arbitrary taskmasters," who, " 'when peevish from indigestion or sleeplessness, or from other causes,' enact statutes . . . the principal purpose of which is 'to trip up or hold fast some innocent lamb that is gambolling too friskily near by.' " The reviewer criticized the author for giving the "impression that assistants in this country, or temporary vicars, have a right similar to that of movable rectors, not to be transferred against their will, unless to a mission which they consider equally good and desirable," and exposed the lack of foundation for such a thesis. Accusing Burtsell of frequently misleading the reader by the *suppressio veri*, the reviewer offered as an example of this fault the treatment of the transfer of movable rectors, where the author suggested "that the decision of 1887 settled a disputed question against the authority of the Bishops; whereas, if it settled anything, it rather increased the episcopal authority in regard to removals of rectors." In conclusion the "Reader of Canon Law" declared it "a pity to see so much study and learning used, not to promote reverence, obedience, peace, and discipline, but to foster a spirit of dangerous independence and of clerical distrust toward the bishops." [385]

Burtsell was convinced that the "Reader of Canon Law" was Archbishop Corrigan himself.[386] In any case, he prepared an answer, which appeared in the *New York Tablet* on February 4, 1888, with an introduction by the editor, who said that Burtsell had left his opponent without his mask or a leg to stand on.[387] Keeping his mask, nevertheless, the "Reader of Canon Law" re-entered the lists a fortnight later with a three-column rejoinder in the *Freeman's Journal*. He praised Burtsell for having disclaimed "any intention of knowingly seeking to weaken the lawful authority of Bishops" but he reiterated his charges "that the 'Canonical Status' contains misleading *ex parte* statements; that its doctrines suppose an un-Catholic spirit of distrust to the Bishops; and that its effects upon the priests would, if followed by them, be most demoralizing and injurious." After quoting passages from the pamphlet to substantiate his original accusations, the "Reader" proceeded to prove "from some actions of the writer," the "Reader's" assertion "in regard to the general tone of the book as intended to foster a disposition of discontent and resistance to authority." First he asked:

Now why, in the name of respect to episcopal authority, that little slip glued in the pamphlet, asking from the reader a contribution of one dollar, to be used for the reinstatement of suspended priests? Would one, unacquainted with the real state of things, not infer from that request that there are numberless priests, innocent of all crime, illegally deprived of their priestly status by the Bishops, about whose government there are so many complaints in the dissertation? Yes, it may have happened that the guiltless were condemned. But how many? It is sufficient to glance at the history of those who, in our knowledge, incurred the penalty of suspension, to see that nearly all, if not all of them, had richly deserved their fate. It was not undue severity of the Bishops, but their excessive patience and leniency, that often called for comment. Some of the punished clerics went into appeal with success, it is true; but how many of these were thereby reinstated in the public esteem? Was it not on the strength of a writ of error that they conquered, rather than on the intrinsic merits of their case? The martyrs of episcopal injustice have still their niches empty in the palace of clerical vindication. The truly innocent ones, when unduly struck, have generally found it easier to demonstrate their guiltlessness before their own Bishops than by collecting dollars to be reinstated on this novel plan.

The "Reader" went on to assail Burtsell in a personal way. He reproached him for having attended and applauded the lecture of a "rebellious priest," presumably McGlynn, who had "delivered himself of a virulent attack on ecclesiastical authority." He stated, moreover, that Burtsell had invited an excommunicate, undoubtedly McGlynn again, to the celebration of the twenty-fifth anniversary of his ordination. If Burtsell really wished to respect the lawful authority of the bishops, why, the "Reader" asked, did he write and act in this way? He answered his rhetorical question thus:

Is it not because the author and his friends have the habit of making to themselves an ideal Church, an abstraction of their brain, consisting of Pope and Cardinals and Bishops, not as we have them before us, of flesh and blood, living and acting as Leo XIII, as Cardinal Simeoni, as Archbishop Corrigan, but as Pope and Cardinals and Bishops exist without a concrete entity in the Decretals and the books on Canon Law? These abtractions can — but do not in fact — command, rebuke, or punish; and hence it is easy to profess allegiance and submission to their authority and decrees. Good Catholics do this, but they moreover heed the commands and punishments of such living masters as Leo XIII. . .

The "Reader of Canon Law" concluded his reply by describing the effects that Burtsell's pamphlet would have on a priest carrying out its counsels. He would be "constantly poring over the Corpus Juris and some canonical treatise, to find out how he may enforce his rights and have them respected." With such a self-centered man the "Reader" contrasted the priest "who is more anxious about his priesthood than his manhood, but who is none the less a man, because in him the interior quality has been absorbed in the higher dignity." Such a priest, he said, "knows he has his rights, but he is not always intent on parading them, and as a rule has them in consequence much more respected." He continued:

> Should he, innocent or guilty — for both have happened and will happen again — be accused before his Bishop of some transgression that may call for a punishment or a removal, he certainly defends himself, as the ecclesiastical and natural laws both either allow or sometimes command; but he looks more to the good of souls and to the glory of God than to his own vindication. He is even willing to bear punishments, especially if deserved, although not inflicted according to all the forms of law, suffering even wrong, not to give scandal by protracted litigation, or by the raking up of forgotten or unknown miseries, or by captious appeals. And does he not in the end rise out of his troubles more successful, even before men, than the denying, excepting, appealing litigant? [388]

With this trenchant blow the *Freeman's Journal* let the pamphlet sink into oblivion.

Burtsell noted in his diary that this reply "gives abuse, shows venom, and manifests more and more Abp. Corrigan to be the writer." [389] Hence, he published another rebuttal in the *New York Tablet*.[390] Meanwhile he continued his activity on behalf of the excommunicated McGlynn and appealed to Rome against the metropolitan in the case of Louis A. Lambert, another priest of the Diocese of Rochester disciplined by Bishop McQuaid.[391] Archbishop Corrigan chastised Burtsell by transferring him, allegedly for "administrative reasons," in December, 1889, from his affluent parish in New York to the rural mission of St. Mary in Roundout. Burtsell appealed to the

Propaganda but received an adverse decision the following July, and in November he took up his pastoral duties in the small town.[392]

Bishop McQuaid had predicted long before that Burtsell would lose favor with the Holy See because of his pamphlet. He had written to Corrigan:

> Burtsell's pamphlet may well startle them in Rome, but the mischief came from Rome. When Rome encouraged every malcontent, no matter how unworthy, is it any wonder that Bishops were snubbed and defied? Rome regarded us as despots, ignorant of Canon Law, whimsical, etc., etc., while all virtues were found in the oppressed clergy.[393]

Now McQuaid surmised that Rome had ordered Burtsell to obey his archbishop without a formal investigation, but he waxed indignant at the Holy See's involvement in the affair:

> . . . Sending this simple case of insubordination and revolt, on the part of such a priest as Burtsell, to a General Congregation is practically making government impossible in America. A Bishop will cease to be able to govern when his acts may be upset by Rome on the grounds of expediency or through fear of a recalcitrant priest.[394]

Although Burtsell reluctantly accepted his new assignment, his loyal supporters in his old parish continued for several years to agitate for his reinstatement.

In addition to controversies between individual bishops and priests, troubles involving large groups also plagued the Church in the United States in these years. In Milwaukee after Archbishop Heiss died on March 26, 1890, the English-speaking priests of the archdiocese wrote to all the archbishops individually, begging them to use their influence to have an English-speaking ordinary appointed. Although the archbishops, sharing their sentiments, spurned the terna of the consultors and of the suffragan bishops, who had proposed three bishops of German extraction, the Holy See passed over the nominations of the archbishops and appointed to the see Frederick X. Katzer, who had been put in first place on the original terna. Then in Cleveland after Bishop Gilmour died on April 13, 1891, the consultors, a majority of whom were German-Americans, included no Irish-American among their three candidates, but the suffragan bishops recommended Thomas Byrne as most worthy. The newspapers devoted much space to this conflict and stirred up the national feelings dividing the priests and people of the diocese and the bishops of the country. In the end Ignatius F. Horstmann, who had been second on the terna of the suffragans, was named.[395]

A few months later, the Prefect of the Propaganda, Miecislaus Cardinal Ledochowski, sent a letter to the bishops of the United States on the subject of the selection of bishops. He directed their vigilant attention to a growing practice which needed to be corrected. He reminded them of the letter that the Secretary of State, Cardinal Rampolla, had written to Cardinal Gibbons the previous summer to scotch the rumors about a change in the character of the American hierarchy, by which bishops would be placed in charge of the Catholic immigrants on the basis of their nationality; Rampolla, on the contrary, had insisted that the existing system would be preserved without alteration. Ledochowski said that contrary customs which were growing up would not be tolerated. He referred to the agitation that had been stirred up on the occasion of some vacancies in episcopal sees, among the clergy and the people, and stated that these dissensions were gradually becoming more serious and frequent. The clergy and people became excited over the presentation of candidates for the episcopate; the struggles were publicized in the public newspapers; meetings were held publicly and privately in which each faction extolled its own candidates and denigrated the others. What especially fostered these disputes, he said, was the vehement desire of each faction to have a bishop of its own nationality, as if the choice of a bishop were intended to serve their own interests rather than the good of the Church. The Holy See, nevertheless, was concerned only with the latter, particularly in the United States, where various European nationalities were coming together to form one country. Consequently, the prefect admonished the bishops to eliminate all contrary attempts, and he asked them to warn the clergy and people in each diocese about the regrettable result of these controversies and to inform them that such efforts were useless, because the Holy See, as the champion of order and peace, could not be swayed by anything done contrary to ecclesiastical law.[396]

Since the existing ecclesiastical law, however, did not seem capable of maintaining good order and since other problems, especially those arising from disagreements over the spiritual care of immigrants and the education of Catholic children, defied solution, Pope Leo XIII and his advisors thought of sending a permanent apostolic delegate to the United States. This prospect displeased and alarmed the American bishops. An example of their attitude was the reply that Cardinal Gibbons gave to Archbishop Elder of Cincinnati, who had asked him how priests could be prevented from appealing from the metropolitan's court to Rome as a pastor in the Diocese of Cleveland had just done. Gibbons wrote back:

> The numerous complaints, sent to Rome by priests who have real or fancied wrongs, are much to be deplored. I think that their number would be diminished, if the influence of Metropolitans were invoked and exercised in the early stages of the difficulties in effecting a settlement.
>
> I fear much that the Holy See may use these appeals as a pretext for sending us a permanent legate or delegate, who would soon become the center of intrigues, and that the dignity and authority of the ordinaries would be seriously impaired.[397]

The fear of losing control over their priests was one of the main motives for the American bishops' opposition to the creation of a permanent delegation.

Although Leo XIII was aware of these sentiments, he finally decided to send a delegate to the United States.[398] He took advantage of an opportunity afforded by the federal government, which invited the Holy See to lend some fifteenth-century maps and charts for exhibition at the World's Columbian Exposition in Chicago and to entrust them to the care of a personal representative. For this mission he chose Archbishop Francesco Satolli, who had previously represented him at the centennial of the American hierarchy and the opening of the Catholic University of America in November, 1889. While the papal ablegate (as he was at first called) was residing at the university in December, 1892, he received from Cardinal Ledochowski certain faculties which had been approved by the Pope on October 30; by virtue of these he was empowered to settle definitively all religious questions between bishops and priests in the United States. His host, Bishop Keane, rector of the university, hastened to prepare Cardinal Gibbons for the visit that Satolli was about to pay him:

> Permit me to ask the attention of your Eminence to the fact that they are *not* the *powers of a legate,* but only of a *representative of the Propaganda* for cases between priests and bishops; — not the powers, therefore, that would give final authority to his action with the Archbishop, — not the credentials of his position as *representative of the Pope.*

Keane was anxious to guard the cardinal against any possible misunderstanding, because some of the professors at the university had interpreted the powers in the broader sense. The rector asked Gibbons to impress on the ablegate that he should receive cases as the Holy See did, that is, after they had passed through the court of the metropolitan, and he added, "Were he a *court of first instance,* it is easy to imagine how much confusion & disorder would be occasioned." [399]

The secular newspapers immediately reported the grant of faculties to Satolli, and the religious newspapers commented on it. The *Freeman's Journal* prophesied that the ministration of the powers with which the Pope had invested him could not fail "but to result in good to the Church on this continent." The editorial continued:

> The reference of disputed cases to him will be as but the first step towards a more perfect definition of the limits of authority in ecclesiastical affairs, and from his labors, viewing the man as one of the ablest and most conscientious doctors of our time, we can look with confidence to the law-abiding American people getting a better idea of the true constitution of the Church than it has ever been able to arrive at from the necessarily imperfect organization incident to its incipient growth in a new country.[400]

These special faculties attracted to Satolli, like flies to honey, many priests who were at odds with their bishops. On December 23 Satolli absolved the most notorious of them, Edward McGlynn, of his censures after having obtained from him a statement of his teachings and having had it examined by four professors at the Catholic University of America. This bold action made the ablegate to a still greater extent a *persona non grata* to many American bishops.[401]

In January, 1893, nevertheless, Pope Leo established the apostolic delegation and appointed Satolli the first delegate. The announcement was greeted with shouts of joy by priests who expected to use this new ally in their war against their bishops. Patrick Corrigan, who had just been formally reconciled with Bishop Wigger after having been cited to appear before the ecclesiastical court in Newark for publishing statements which the bishop claimed were false in regard to the recent German Catholic Congress and the *Priesterverein* and had been defended by Burtsell during the trial, was elated by the Pope's action. He declared in the *Freeman's Journal*:

> . . . The Bishops were naturally disinclined to have a delegate appointed because they had been in the habit of exercising almost absolute power themselves, and no man desires to relinquish power. Ecclesiastics are no exception to the rule. The Pope put on the needed pressure.

The permanent appointment of Archbishop Satolli means a curtailment of the extraordinary power hitherto exercised by the American episcopacy. It means more liberty and more protection for the priests, because they now have the authority at their own doors to decide their difficulties with the Bishops . . . . I advocated it [the appointment of a delegate] in the pamphlet I issued in 1883, which was condemned by episcopal authority. I advocated the coming of some of the great men from Rome to learn and understand the Church in this country and legislate for its wants. The Pope has sent Archbishop Satolli to this country with that object in view.[402]

In the spring Father Corrigan entertained Satolli at an elaborate banquet held in his parish in Hoboken and attended by the Governor of New Jersey, several mayors, Protestant ministers, and nearly 200 priests.[403] Bishop Wigger not only declined the invitation but also pointed out that most of the priests from other dioceses who planned to be present had had difficulties with their bishops and the thirty from his diocese, out of a total of 183, constituted what some called the "Corrigan Coterie." [404]

In September, Edward McGlynn, who had gone to Rome in May and had had an audience with the Pope, published an article, "The Vatican and the United States," in *The Forum*.[405] To provide a background for the establishment of the Apostolic Delegation, he disparaged the past government of the American bishops. He asserted that the system of choosing bishops without the slightest reference to the wishes of the clergy or the people still perdured, and in proof he cited the recent appointment of Archbishop Corrigan's secretary, Charles E. McDonnell, as Bishop of Brooklyn. He warned:

Such a system can hardly fail to be a serious detriment to the spiritual character of the man who is thus invested with almost despotic powers and of those who must pay court to him to acquire his favor or to avoid his frowns or his active persecution.

Under this system the bishops of the United States . . . have practically a free hand to govern despotically both clergy and people and to lay upon them what burdens they pleased and to refuse them justice and even a hearing. Until very recently the government of the bishops in the United States was practically arbitrary, without other remedy than an appeal or recourse to Rome. To the clergy and laity who felt aggrieved it was in most cases physically impossible to make such appeals effectual.[406]

He castigated the bishops for not allowing an accused priest the benefit of counsel in his trial until they were compelled by Rome, and then for rejecting the counsel chosen by the defendant and even for trying to coerce the defendant into accepting as counsel a clergyman of their own choice, and finally, for contemptuously overruling the decisions and recommendations of their own judges. To redress these wrongs and to lift these burdens, he said, the Pope had established the delegation and had appointed Satolli, "a man of great ecclesiastical learning, possessed of an open, perspicacious and logical mind," who had "absolute single-mindedness in the perception of righteousness and absolute fearlessness in doing, and compelling the doing, of justice." [407] He accused some of the bishops of having entered into a conspiracy to drive Satolli out of the country by intrigue and misrepresentation, though, of course, he did not name them.

Pope Leo XIII was concerned about the relations between the apostolic delegate and the American bishops. Hence, in his encyclical letter addressed to the Church in the United States, *Longinqua oceani*, on January 6, 1895, he said: "But how unjust and baseless would be the suspicion, should it anywhere exist, that the powers conferred on the legate [that is, the apostolic delegate] are an obstacle to the authority of the bishops." Having dilated on their rights, the Pope concluded:

> Therefore, since it is the office and function of an apostolic delegate, with whatsoever powers he may be vested, to execute the mandates and interpret the will of the Pontiff who sends him, thus, so far from his being of any detriment to the ordinary power of the bishops, he will rather bring an accession of stability and strength. His authority will possess no slight weight for preserving in the multitude a submissive spirit; in the clergy discipline and due reverence for the bishops, and in the bishops mutual charity and an intimate union of souls.[408]

A more placid analysis than McGlynn's of "the fruits expected by the Holy Father from the delegation" was offered by Thomas Bouquillon, professor of moral theology in the Catholic University of America, who was well disposed toward Satolli personally because of the latter's position in the controversy over Catholic schools.[409] One of these benefits, he wrote, would be "the strengthening of episcopal authority by virtue of the enlightened support which each bishop will receive in the discharge of his delicate duties."[410] Another would be "the security of the sacerdotal body by the development of a spirit of justice and equity on the one hand, of respect and noble obedience on the other." [411] In conclusion Bouquillon attributed three qualities to the present delegate — theological and canonical science, understanding and love of the institutions and people of the United States, and sacerdotal piety.

After Satolli was elevated to the cardinalate and recalled to the Roman Curia in 1896, McGlynn was asked to contribute another article to *The Forum*.[412] Here he recalled that until recent years the Catholic Church in the United States had been governed by "a benevolent paternal despotism," in which the bishops ignored the spirit and often disregarded the letter of laws imposed by Rome. Even the new procedure for naming candidates for the episcopacy he declared to be an ineffectual remedy, since the smallness of the number of the priests participating and the fact that they were appointees of the bishop meant that they were not fairly representative of the body of the clergy. The list presented by these priests, furthermore, was revised by the bishops, who drew up a secret list of their own. In the final appointment, he asserted, "quite frequently the choice of the privileged clergyman" had been overruled. McGlynn suggested that the best solution would have been "to broaden the electorate, as in Ireland, so as to include all the rectors of churches." Failing that, the next best thing was "that the Holy Father should have, outside the bishops of the province and the limited number of privileged priests, some other regular source of accurate and unprejudiced information." [413] Hence, Leo XIII wisely and courageously established the apostolic delegation. McGlynn had high praises for the first delegate:

> . . . from the very beginning of his administration and in the nearly four years of its duration, Monsignor Satolli has done, in numerous instances and in many directions, more than enough to justify the Pope's judgment and expectation that the Delegation would do much to remedy the evils and to supply the wants . . . Time and again he has lifted oppressive burdens from clergy and people, righted wrongs, compelled the tempering of justice with mercy, made judicial hearings accessible and easy; and, by the happy interposition of his authority and by his tact and good offices, he has been able to bring about reconciliations and compromises extrajudicially.
>
> The mere presence in the country of such a man, invested with such authority, has prevented much matter for discord and litigation. It has made cautious some prelates who, in their inexperience, or excessive estimate of their own authority, would

otherwise have been more ready to lay undue burdens upon clergy or people, and to stretch their authority beyond its due limits. He has restored priests who had been condemned by their bishops; in some cases because he found that they were innocent, and in others because he found that they had already been too severely punished.[414]

Actually, by the time of his departure from the United States Satolli had begun to detach himself from the liberal group that was overwhelming him with fulsome flattery.

Further strictures on the functioning of the diocesan consultors were expressed in the spirit of Burtsell by a canon lawyer of the Diocese of Detroit, Peter A. Baart, in his *Legal Formulary*. Calling the proposition of candidates by the clergy nugatory when the vote was taken by letters sent by the individual priests to the bishop's office, he stated: "While it might have been intended that a vote should be taken in synod and that the bishop should recognize the wish of the clergy by selecting those three for consultors for whom most priests had voted, still practice has developed something very different." Baart also thought that the short term of the consultors had proved detrimental; he regarded as a defect of the law bearing on the practical efficiency of the consultors the fact that if they were "outspoken in meeting or opposed to some imprudent or illegal act of the bishop," they could be dropped at the expiration of their terms; thereby "one of the chief objects intended by establishing" them was defeated. He pointed out the incongruity in the existence of chapters in England and other countries and their absence in the United States, where the Church was in much better condition. His final judgment was: ". . . the experience of the fourteen years elapsed since the council has shown that in most dioceses the establishment of consultors has by no means satisfied the want of cathedral chapters." [415] There can be no doubt that insofar as the peculiar arrangement which the Holy See had allowed to the American bishops fell short of the ideal embodied in the law of the universal Church, it failed to content a majority of the priests.

The delicate system of episcopal nominations seemed to be threatened on the one side by the excesses of nationalist sentiments and rivalries and on the other by the attacks of critics such as McGlynn. To bolster the existing structure the mercurial French professor of canon law in the Catholic University of America, George Peries, composed an article on "Episcopal Elections." [416] It consisted mainly of an historical survey of the practice, concentrated on the early centuries of Christianity and the Middle Ages. Peries said that the American system "safeguards, as much as possible, the most ancient practices of the Church, taking into account abuses which the experience of centuries has shown to exist." In his opinion the consultors and irremovable rectors represented "the most healthy element of the clergy" and also in a certain measure were "the spokesmen of the Christian people whose aspirations, needs, and desires" they knew. The bishops of the province, secondly, were, "in a sense, the successors of the first electoral colleges." The professor idealized their function thus: ". . . they listen to the voice of the multitude, they gather various testimonies, they ask the advice of the clergy belonging to the vacant see, and, under the eye of God, they ask Him who will be the most worthy to enter their 'corps d'honneur.' Generally, they have not to go outside the list presented them." [417] He defended the preponderant influence of the bishops in the process because of their experience of church government and of the people's needs: "More detached from the spirit of companionship, more penetrated with the heavy responsibility for souls, they are better able to reject human considerations, to regard only religious interests." He also extolled the role played by the Propaganda, which, "away from local excitement and national prejudice," made the final choice "as a rule from among the names presented." Summing up, Peries stated:

> This seems to us the most perfect organism the Church has yet set to work to effect useful and wise elections. Every element interested is represented, and in proportion to its worth and importance . . . .
> We ask any unprejudiced man, is there aught more grand, more wise, more regardful of all interests than this manner of selecting the pastors of the faithful? Surely the Roman Church has not degenerated from the primitive Church . . . . Full of reverence for sacred antiquity, yet attentive to the needs of the present, she applies herself by an intelligent adaptation to preserving in their purity and developing in all their fruitfulness the institutions of the Saviour.[418]

Most of the gains made by the American clergy in the latter part of the nineteenth century were lost early in the twentieth, and in spite of the efforts of such writers as Peries, the system of episcopal nominations was the first to be taken away. The priests' right to participate through certain representatives in the designation of candidates for vacant sees was imperiled by the frequent violations of secrecy.

In 1910 the Sacred Consistorial Congregation issued a decree to remedy this abuse. It said that when the names of candidates, as often happened, were made known, they were exposed to public discussion, which was sometimes fair but more often unjust and wrong. Thus the reputation of the candidates was sometimes injured and could not easily or fully be repaired, and the Holy See's calm judgment and proper freedom of choice was impeded. As a result, many excellent men shrank from being nominated not only from a reasonable fear of the episcopal office but also from a dread of public vituperation. For this reason, a number of bishops and other distinguished men had asked the Holy See to take appropriate precautions. Accordingly, the cardinals of the Congregation ordered that, when the diocesan consultors and irremovable pastors should meet to draw up their terna, at the beginning of the session they should all take an oath before the presiding prelate to keep secret the names that would be discussed and those that would be selected by voting. If any consultor should violate his oath, he was immediately to be removed from office and could be liable to other penalties as well; if the offender was a pastor, he was to be forever deprived of the right to vote. The bishops and the officials of the Apostolic Delegation were also obliged *sub gravi* to observe secrecy, as well as those from whom the delegate might request information about the candidates.[419]

Even with these safeguards the system was not found to be satisfactory and, consequently, was radically altered in 1916. In that year the Consistorial Congregation issued another decree saying that although the method of the terna had been improved, it did not seem to meet the present needs of the Church in the United States. It was subject to long delays so that vacancies were unduly protracted — to the annoyance of the faithful and the loss of ecclesiastical discipline. It seemed inadvisable, moreover, that a matter of such importance should be handled hastily, only when the urgent necessity arose, for vacancies were bound to occur eventually and therefore the names of the candidates whom the bishops deemed worthy and suitable could be presented to the Holy See in advance. To overcome these drawbacks and to ensure greater tranquility in this business, the Consistorial Congregation proposed a system which had already been introduced in other places. First it asked the individual bishops of the United States for their views, and the great majority of them approved of the proposal although some suggested changes which the Pope allowed on the advice of the Congregation. Then Benedict XV sanctioned the new law, and the Congregation promulgated it.

According to this decree, every other year the bishops were to send to the metropolitan the names of one or two priests who could also be outside their diocese or province. But before deciding on these names, the archbishops and bishops were to ask their diocesan consultors and irremovable pastors to recommend some priest as worthy of becoming bishop of some (not of a particular) diocese. The consultors and pastors, however, were not to be convoked in a meeting but rather were to be asked separately and individually under the grave obligation of secrecy, and the bishop was not to reveal their advice to anyone except perhaps to his fellow bishops in a later meeting. The bishop could also consult prudent men, even among the regular clergy, in regard to both the qualities of a candidate and the recommendation of new candidates. The bishops could follow the advice received in these ways, but they were not obliged to do so, for they were "to render an accounting to God alone in this respect." [420] Obviously, the role of the clergy in this process was greatly diminished. This method remained in force after the Code of Canon Law went into effect in 1918.[421]

The Code of Canon Law also destroyed the representational character of the diocesan consultors. A canonist has compared the old and the new legislation in these terms:

> As to the method of choosing the body of Consultors the [Third Plenary] Council in number 19 legislated that the Bishop choose the Consultors but in this manner that half the number be taken from names proposed by the clergy and the other half, as it implies, freely. The Code in canon 424 decrees that the Bishop chooses the Consultors with due regard to canon 426 which in turn provides that every three years the Consultors be reappointed or new ones substituted and that should a vacancy occur during the three year term, the Bishop with the advice of the remaining Consultors fill it. The Code clearly shows, especially in requiring merely the advice of the Consultors and that only when supplying a vacancy in their body, that it wants the Bishop to be free in the choice of his advisors. In so far, then, as the Council by giving the right of proposal to the clergy curtails the liberty granted to the Bishop by the common law, it is opposed to the latter and, therefore, abrogated. Inasmuch, however, as the Code does not specify the manner of making the selection the Bishop is still free to borrow what he wishes from the conciliar method.[422]

Finally, the Code altered the categories of affairs for which the bishop would be bound to obtain even the counsel of his consultors.[423]

The Code, on the other hand, preserved the institution of "irremovable parishes." It decreed that pastors in general should be permanent, that "irremovable parishes" could not be made "removable" without the permission of the Holy See, that "removable parishes," on the contrary, could be declared "irremovable" by the bishop upon the advice of the consultors, and that new parishes should be "irremovable" although it allowed the bishop at his own prudent judgment, in view of the special circumstances of persons and places, and after hearing the consultors, to decide that "removability" was more appropriate for a new parish.[424] It could be foreseen, nevertheless, that the ten-to-one ratio of irremovable pastors decreed by the Third Plenary Council would thereafter decrease rather than increase.

As far as the removal of irremovable pastors is concerned, the Consistorial Congregation in 1910 provided a new and easier process called "economic" or disciplinary, which was to be carried out in an administrative way without judicial formality. This could be employed only when the object was the good of the faithful and not the punishment of the pastor.[425] Since the former motive rather than the latter could colorably be asserted in most cases, the security of tenure that irremovable pastors previously enjoyed was greatly diminished. A doubt was then raised whether removable pastors could be removed or transferred only according to the procedure prescribed in this decree of 1910 (*Maxima cura*). In 1915 the Consistorial Congregation replied negatively; in other words, they could still be removed *ad nutum Episcopi*, but the bishops were reminded of the still valid warning of the Second Plenary Council that they should not make use of this right except for serious reasons and with due regard for the merits of the priest concerned.[426] The decree of 1910, therefore, did not give greater stability to movable pastors but rather left their condition untouched; they remained the vicars of the ordinary.[427]

This legislation, however, was modified by the Code. With a few exceptions, as a student of the question has written, "the Code practically abolished removability *ad nutum* as had been decreed in the 'Maxima cura.' " No pastor could be removed thereafter except by due process, even when there was no question of crime or punishment. In regard to removal as a penalty, there was a slight difference between irremovable and removable pastors in that the procedure was somewhat easier and shorter for the latter than for the former. In regard to transfer, the irremovable pastor was not to be moved without special permission of the Holy See if he was unwilling to accept another parish, but the movable pastor could be transferred even if he was unwilling.[428] After 1918, therefore, the bishop was never to act at will (*ad nutum*) in dealing with his priests, but he was at liberty in most cases to act as he saw fit.

From the promulgation of the Code of Canon Law to the convocation of the Second Vatican Council there seems to have been very little public discussion of the relations between bishops and priests in the United States. In this respect American Catholics were hardly different from their co-religionists in other countries. The clergy were taught to regard the Code as the nearly perfect and almost immutable legislation for the Western Church. It could not be altered even by the bishops, who held no more provincial or plenary councils and few diocesan synods during this period. The National Catholic Welfare Conference which they organized possessed no legislative power. The monarchical character of the papal government of the universal Church was imitated by the bishops within their respective domains. The administrative manner of dealing with most of the ecclesiastical matters except certain kinds of marriage cases spread from Rome to the lower levels of jurisdiction. The climate was not propitious, therefore, for raising provocative questions or for arousing disgruntled clergymen.

Conclusion

It would be bootless to try to determine whether on the whole the bishops or the priests were more blameworthy for the discord that so often marred their mutual relations in the nineteenth century. It is possible, however, to characterize their attitudes toward each other in the light of the foregoing study.

As far as the bishops are concerned, it is clear that some of them frequently, even habitually, treated their priests in an arbitrary manner and — what was worse — that the legal system permitted such treatment. To account for their attitude, several factors should be kept in mind. First, the bishops, as a result of their education and observation, held an exaggerated idea of their own importance in the Church. They viewed their responsibility in so exclusive a way that they insisted on bearing their burden alone, as if they could not share it with their priests. Hence, they tended to be jealous of their authority, unwilling to listen to advice, and paternalistic rather than fatherly. Secondly, though few of them were so contemptuous of the priests as McQuaid and John Lancaster Spalding were, most of them were needlessly distrustful of the clergy. Thirdly, through an excess of what they regarded as prudence, they were secretive about the affairs of the diocese which directly concerned their priests and people, and thus even when their decisions were wise and just they were often not recognized as such because the reasons for them were unknown. Fourthly, the bishops were suspicious and resentful of Roman interference which they tried to explain away as if it were necessarily based on imperfect knowledge or incorrect understanding of the local situation. Each one wanted to be let alone to handle the business of his own diocese as he deemed best. Fifthly, when they were confronted with requests or proposals, they often failed to distinguish between the distasteful husk of intemperate language and the wholesome kernel of useful reform. They tried to deny that any general problems existed through faults in the system and attributed concrete cases of trouble merely to the wickedness or perverseness of the priests involved. Instead of creatively devising solutions, they spent their energy in striving to avert changes imposed by the Holy See. In public they assumed a defensive position and neglected to present their side in any forceful or convincing way. They found it difficult to act in concert because they held no regular meetings of the whole episcopate until the 1920's and in the latter part of the nineteenth century were divided among themselves over other issues. To an observer of a later age they seem to have harped more loudly than was warranted on the one string of the peculiarities of the American scene in order to ward off the application of the general laws of the Church. They had a valid argument, to be sure, in their need for a certain flexibility of administration, unhampered by rigid laws, amid the rapidly changing conditions of the Church in the United States, but they never set it forth clearly to their priests.

The priests, on the other hand, were not merely the oppressed subjects or innocent victims that some of them pretended to be. The good ones had the misfortune of being represented by unworthy spokesmen of their own order. Aside from the layman McMaster and the canonist Smith, the most prominent polemicists for the clergy had their own axes to grind and could not be regarded as unselfish, disinterested champions of their less articulate brethren. O'Callaghan was unscrupulous; Mahoney was incorrigible; Corrigan was bellicose; and Burtsell was bitter. They all tended to be censorious and even captious. Secondly, the priests professed unbounded confidence in the wisdom and justice of the Holy See and tried to pit Rome against their bishops. Thirdly, preoccupied with concern for their rights rather than with the service of their people, they seemed to demand changes for the exclusive benefit of their class. Too often they sounded as if they merely longed to acquire some of the bishops' power for themselves and not to win broader opportunities for the exercise of the pastoral ministry. Fourthly, they failed to organize themselves in any national movement. Fifthly, a certain amount of their discontent was due to a conflict of nationalities, especially when Irish priests rebelled against German bishops. Finally, many of the pastors were as tyrannical to their assistants (if they had any) and parishioners as they claimed the bishops were to them.

The bishops and priests, moreover, held certain common assumptions. They both professed respect for law, but the former were content with the law that they had inherited, and the latter were eager for the law that they had never experienced. Secondly, they both invoked the American spirit but interpreted it to prove contrary contentions, for example, regarding the harmony of cathedral chapters with the spirit of a democratic country. Thirdly, they both regarded the laity as mostly passive members of the Church. Fourthly, they both discussed their differences in terms of ecclesiastical discipline and not of sacred theology. Lastly, they were both prone to impute the follies or excesses of a few to the whole order to which the few belonged.

One might ask to what extent the movement for priests' rights was indigenous to the United States and to what extent it was imported from Europe. It seems to have been inspired and nourished mainly by the American milieu though it was partially justified by appeals to foreign examples. Yet the "Americanizing" bishops such as John Ireland, John Keane, and James Gibbons did not support the movement any more than their conservative colleagues did. Perhaps the priests, being closer to the people, were more influenced by the typically American values than the bishops were.

Certainly there was great need for law to regulate the relations between bishops and priests. This law might have been originated abroad, but it had to be adapted to American circumstances. It had to be consistent with the essential principles of universal church order and sanctioned by the Holy See. Perhaps it was not understood that in order to be efficacious in maintaining and fostering serene and fruitful relations between bishops and priests, law had to be recognized as necessary and appropriate by both sides and that to this end both sides ought to have been consulted in its formulation.

It might be concluded from the narration of so much strife that the chief characteristic of the relations between bishops and priests in the nineteenth century was mutual distrust and even hostility. Yet it should not be overlooked that if there had not been, to a much greater extent, generous co-operation from both sides, the churches would not have been built, the educational and charitable institutions founded and developed, the immigrants assimilated, or the vocations fostered — in short, the enormous and rapid expansion of the Church during the same period could not have been realized, nor would the Church be what it is today.

KEY TO THE ABBREVIATIONS:

AAB — Archives of the Archdiocese of Baltimore
ACQR — American Catholic Quarterly Review
ADP — Archives of the Diocese of Pittsburgh
APF — Archives of the Sacred Congregation de Propaganda Fide (Rome)
CHR — Catholic Historical Review
CL — Acta et Decreta Sacrorum Conciliorum Recentiorum. Collectio Lacensis, Volume III (Freiburg im Breisgau, 1875)
FJ — New York Freeman's Journal and Catholic Register
MCUND — Manuscript Collections of the University of Notre Dame
RACHS — Records of the American Catholic Historical Society of Philadelphia

1. Charles Florence McCarthy, "The Historical Development of Episcopal Nominations in the Catholic Church of the United States (1784–1884)," *RACHS*, XXXVIII (December, 1927), pp. 297–354.

2. Peter Guilday, *The Life and Times of John Carroll, Archbishop of Baltimore (1735–1815)* (Westminster, Md., 1954; reprinted from 1922), p. 348; for the original Latin see p. 350, fn. 4. At the second General Chapter of the Clergy, held at Whitemarsh in November, 1786, it had been resolved: "That the representatives of the clergy of the United States are the only proper persons to chuse [*sic*]" the bishop (*ibid.*, p. 326). Among the motives for this resolution was an eagerness to ensure the appointment of one of their own number of ex-Jesuits, lest the Holy See name someone who might not share their longing for the restoration of the Society of Jesus in the United States.

3. *Ibid.*, pp. 351–352.

4. On the election of John Carroll see also Annabelle M. Melville, *John Carroll of Baltimore, Founder of the American Hierarchy* (New York, 1955), pp. 104–109.

5. Guilday, *op. cit.*, pp. 354–355.

6. Rome, November 6, 1789; Latin text in Donald C. Shearer, O.F.M.Cap., ed., *Pontificia Americana. A Documentary History of the Catholic Church in the United States, 1784–1884* (The Catholic University of America Studies in American Church History, Vol. XV [Washington, D.C., 1933]), pp. 81–84; English translation in John Tracy Ellis, ed., *Documents of American Catholic History* (Milwaukee, 1956), No. 53, pp. 167–171.

7. Guilday, *op. cit.*, pp. 443–445, 568–570.

8. Carroll to Antonelli, Baltimore, June 17, 1793, AAB, Carroll Papers, autograph draft.

9. Antonelli to Carroll, Rome, January 4, 1794, quoted in a "Nota di Archivio" composed for a much later case, APF, Acta, Vol. 222 (1858), fol. 30v–31r; the "Nota" is also to be found in Scritture riferite nelle congregazioni generali, Vol. 983 (1858), fol. 180r–186v.

10. Guilday, *op. cit.*, pp. 581–586.

11. See Finbar Kenneally, O.F.M. (comp.), *United States Documents in the Propaganda Fide Archives*, First Series, Vols. I and II (Publications of the Academy of American Franciscan History [Washington, D.C., 1966, 1968]), *passim.*

12. "Nota di Archivio," APF, Acta, Vol. 222 (1858), fol. 31v–32r.

13. Poynter to Maréchal, July 30, 1821, in Peter Guilday, *The Life and Times of John England, First Bishop of Charleston (1786–1842)* (New York, 1927), II, p. 78 and fn. 14. (Hereafter cited as *England.*) Cardinal Francesco Luigi Fontana was prefect of the Sacred Congregation de Propaganda Fide from 1818 to 1822.

14. Ronin John Murtha, O.S.B., "The Life of the Most Reverend Ambrose Maréchal, Third Archbishop of Baltimore, 1768–1828" (Unpublished Ph.D. dissertation, The Catholic University of America, Washington, D.C., 1965), p. 223 and fn. 27.

15. Hugh J. Nolan, *The Most Reverend Francis Patrick Kenrick, Third Bishop of Philadelphia, 1830–1851* (The Catholic University of America Studies in American Church History, Vol. XXXVII [Washington, D.C., 1948]), pp. 70–71. The memorial was dated May 12, 1827.

16. Guilday, *England*, II, pp. 100–102. The letter was received in April, 1827.

17. *Ibid.*, pp. 105–108.

18. Thomas F. Casey, *The Sacred Congregation de Propaganda Fide and the Revision of the First Provincial Council of Baltimore (1829–1830)* (Analecta Gregoriana, Vol. 88 [Rome, 1957]), p. 55.

19. *Ibid.*, p. 64.

20. *Ibid.*, pp. 57–58.

21. *Ibid.*, p. 62.

22. *Concilia Provincialia, Baltimori habita ab anno 1829 usque ad annum 1849* (2d ed.; Baltimore, 1851), pp. 64–65.

23. Casey, *op. cit.*, pp. 59–60 (Latin text).

24. Guilday, *England*, II, p. 132.

25. "Papers Relating to the Church in America from the Portfolios of the Irish College at Rome," *RACHS*, VIII (1897), pp. 460–461.

26. *Decreta Synodi Mobiliensis Primae die 19a Januarii 1835 congregatae* (Notre Dame, Ind., 1890), p. 3, No. XI. See also Oscar Hugh Lipscomb, "The Administration of Michael Portier, Vicar Apostolic of Alabama and the Floridas, 1825–1829, and First Bishop of Mobile, 1829–1859" (Unpublished Ph.D. dissertation, The Catholic University of America, Washington, D.C., 1963, c. 1965), p. 168.

27. Decree *Cum ad gravissimum*, October 17, 1829, in *Collectanea S. Congregationis de Propaganda Fide* (Rome, 1907), I, pp. 470–472, No. 808.

28. John H. Whyte, "The Appointment of Catholic Bishops in Nineteenth-Century Ireland," *CHR*, XLVIII (April, 1962), 12–32 at 17.

29. Wilfrid Ward, *The Life and Times of Cardinal Wiseman* (London, 1900), II, pp. 55–60, 65.

30. See the apostolic brief of November 19, 1850, and the decree of the Propaganda of April 21, 1852, *CL*, Vol. III, coll. 955–960; also the "Statuta Capitularia in Synodo prima provinciali West. approbata," *ibid.*, coll. 946–951.

31. Cuthbert Butler, *The Life & Times of Bishop Ullathorne, 1806–1889* (London, 1926), I, pp. 198–199.

32. See the "Decreta Concilii Provincialis Westmonasteriensis I," *CL*, Vol. III, coll. 922–926.

33. See the "Modus procedendi in consilio capiendo a Concilio investigationis priusquam finaliter dejiciatur rector missionarius," August 4, 1853, *ibid.*, coll. 960–961.

34. *Concilium plenarium totius Americae Septentrionalis Foederatae, Baltimori habitum anno 1852* (Baltimore, 1853), Decree VI, p. 45.

35. *Ibid.*, pp. 29 and 30.

36. John P. Marschall, C.S.V., "Francis Patrick Kenrick, 1851–1863: The Balti-

more Years" (Unpublished Ph.D. dissertation, The Catholic University of America, Washington, D.C., 1965), pp. 105–106 and fn. 64.

37. Francis Patrick Kenrick to Peter Richard Kenrick, n.p., July 4, 1853, in *The Kenrick-Frenaye Correspondence, 1830–1862*, translated, arranged, and annotated by Francis E. Tourscher (Philadelphia, 1920), No. CCXVII, p. 371. The Kenrick brothers corresponded with each other in Latin.

38. James Bradly to Heyden, Newry, Pa., November 5, 1853, ADP, Letter Collection, No. 680. Bradly (or Bradley) emigrated from Ireland in 1825, was ordained five years later, and in 1832 went to Newry, where he remained as pastor over fifty years. See Ambrose A. Lambing, *A History of the Catholic Church in the Dioceses of Pittsburgh and Allegheny* (New York, 1880), pp. 265–267, and *Brief Biographical Sketches of the Deceased Bishops and Priests Who Labored in the Diocese of Pittsburgh*, Vol. I (Pittsburgh, 1914), pp. 99–102.

39. James F. Connelly, *The Visit of Archbishop Gaetano Bedini to the United States of America* (June, 1853 — February, 1854) (Analecta Gregoriana, Vol. 109 [Rome, 1960]), p. 218.

40. *Ibid.*, pp. 221–222.

41. "Decreta Concilii Baltimorensis Provincialis VIII," No. VI, *CL*, Vol. III, coll. 161–162.

42. "Acta Concilii Baltimorensis Provincialis VIII. mense Majo anno 1855 habiti," third private congregation, May 9, 1955, No. 1 of the *Sommario* of the *Ponenza* of Cardinal Alessandro Barnabò, prefect, for the general congregation of September 1, 1856, APF, Acta, Vol. 220 (1856), fol. 431v–432r.

43. "Voto del Rmo P. M. Gavino Secchi-Murro, Consultore della S. C. di Propaganda Fide," *ibid.*, fol. 402v.

44. "Dubbj" and "Responsa," No. 24, September 9, 1856, *ibid.*, fol. 389r–v, 391v.

45. "Decreta Concilii Provinciae Sancti Ludovici, No. VI, *CL*, Vol. III, col. 308.

46. APF, Acta, Vol. 220 (1856), fol. 456v.

47. "Osservazioni sulli Decreti del primo Sinodo Provinciale di St. Louis," in "Voto del Rmo P. M. Gavino Secchi-Murro," January 5, 1856, *ibid.*, fol. 418v–419v.

48. *Ponenza* of Barnabò, *Ristretto*, par. XXX, *ibid.*, fol. 385v.

49. "Dubbj" and "Responsa," No. 42, September 9, 1856, *ibid.*, fol. 390r, 392r.

50. Barnabò to P. R. Kenrick, Rome, February 17, 1857, *CL*, Vol. III, coll. 310–311. In fact, this decree was appended to the decrees of the Eighth Provincial Council of Baltimore held in the same year (*ibid.*, col. 168).

51. Unsigned, unaddressed memoir in Italian, n.p., n.d., APF, Scritture riferite nelle congregazioni generali, Vol. 982 (1857), fol. 214r, 215r.

52. Edward J. O'Brien, pastor of St. Mary's Church, New Haven; Thomas Quinn, pastor of St. Joseph's Church, Meriden; and M. A. Wallace, pastor of Wallingford, to Bedini, Meriden, Conn., November 8, 1856, *ibid.*, fol. 206r–v. For the vacant see they recommended Jeremiah Cummings, D.D., an alumnus of the Propaganda and pastor of St. Stephen's Church, New York; he was never appointed a bishop.

53. Bedini to O'Brien, Rome, December 26, 1856, APF, Lettere, Vol. 347 (1856), fol. 670v.

54. Mazzuchelli to Bedini, Benton, Wis., March 5, 1857, APF, Scritture riferite nei congressi, America Centrale, Vol. 17 (1855–1857), fol. 841r–v.

55. Bedini to Mazzuchelli, Rome, April 7, 1857, APF, Lettere, Vol. 348 (1857), fol. 224v.

56. O'Connor to the Propaganda, Pittsburgh, July 6, 1858, APF, Scritture riferite nelle congregazioni generali, Vol. 983 (1858), fol. 730r–733r.

57. Heyden had served as a priest in Pennsylvania since he was ordained in 1821; in 1829 he had been nominated by Henry Conwell, Bishop of Philadelphia, as his coadjutor, and in 1837 by the Third Provincial Council of Baltimore for the See of Natchez; he had been theologian for Francis Patrick Kenrick in the Council of 1843 and for O'Connor in the Council of 1846.

58. Hughes to Heyden, New York, August 31, 1858, ADP, Letter Collection, No. 776. Heyden followed Hughes' advice, writing to Archbishop Bedini from Bedford, Pennsylvania, on September 6, 1858, APF, Scritture riferite nei congressi, America Centrale, Vol. 18 (1858), fol. 354r–355r.

59. F. P. Kenrick to O'Connor, Baltimore, June 10, 1859, Archives of the Archdiocese of Omaha, O'Connor Papers.

60. O'Connor to Heyden, Pittsburgh, April 25, 1860, ADP, Letter Collection, No. 834.

61. Mullen to Heyden, Allegheny, April 27, 1860, *ibid.*, No. 835.

62. F. P. Kenrick to James O'Connor, Baltimore, June 18, 1860, Archives of the Archdiocese of Omaha.

63. M. O'Connor to F. P. Kenrick, Loretto, Pa., June 20, 1860, AAB, 30-Y-41.

64. F. P. Kenrick to M. O'Connor, Baltimore, July 11, 1860, Archives of the Archdiocese of Omaha, O'Connor Papers. See also *Kenrick-Frenaye Correspondence*, pp. 445–446.

65. Leitner to Bedini, St. Peter's Church, Columbia, Lancaster Co., Pa., February 1, 1859, APF, Scritture riferite nei congressi, America Centrale, Vol. 18 (1858), fol. 766r–767v.

66. Barnabò to the Archbishops of the United States, Rome, May 29, 1859, APF, Lettere, Vol. 350 (1859), fol. 345r–v.

67. F. P. Kenrick to Barnabò, Baltimore, May 18, 1860, No. 1 of the *Sommario*, APF, Acta, Vol. 225 (1861), fol. 28r. Kenrick here refers to his earlier reply of June 17, 1859.

68. *Ponenza* of Barnabò for the general congregation of January 26, 1858, Art. III, parr. 9–10, APF, Acta, Vol. 222 (1858), fol. 23r–v, and Kenrick's letter in the *Sommario*, No. 2, fol. 28v.

69. "Nota di Archivio," *ibid.*, fol. 30v, 32v–33r, 34v.

70. "Dubbj" and "Responsa," Nos. 5, 6, and 7, *ibid.*, fol. 24r, 25r.

71. Francis Patrick Kenrick, *Theologia Moralis* (2d ed.; Mechlin, 1860–1861), II, 375, parr. 84 and 85.

72. "The Church not a Despotism," *Brownson's Quarterly Review*, 3d series, III (April, 1862), 137–172 at 163–164; reprinted in *The Works of Orestes A. Brownson*, ed. Henry F. Brownson (Detroit, 1882–1907), XX, 215–248 at 240.

73. David Spalding, C.F.X., "Martin John Spalding, Legislator," *RACHS*, LXXV (September, 1964), 131–160 at 142 ff.

74. P. R. Kenrick to Spalding, St. Louis, November 6, 1865, AAB, 34–M–17.

75. Same to same, St. Louis, April 8, 1866, AAB, 34-N-24.

76. Same to same, St. Louis, May 16, 1866, AAB, 34-N-26.

77. Spalding to P. R. Kenrick, Baltimore, May 22, 1866, AAB, Letterbook I, p. 237. Cf. John Lancaster Spalding, *The Life of the Most Reverend M. J. Spalding* (New York, 1873), p. 312.

78. P. R. Kenrick to Spalding, St. Louis, May 29, 1866, AAB, 34-N-28.

79. Spalding to P. R. Kenrick, Baltimore, June 11, 1866, AAB, Letterbook I, p. 241.

80. Same to same, Baltimore, July 16, 1866, *ibid.*, p. 250.

81. Draft of Decrees for the Second Plenary Council of Baltimore, 1866, Titulus II: "De Hierarchia et Regimine Ecclesiae," Caput V: "De Capitulis Cathedralibus Constituendis," par. 71, p. 30.

82. *Ibid.*, parr. 73–76, pp. 31–32.

83. *Ibid.*, parr. 102–110, pp. 43–47.

84. *Ibid.*, parr. 130–135, pp. 50–51.

85. "Animadversiones Theologorum Tertiae Congregationis circa Titulum III," AAB, 39A-D-3, p. 15. The names of the members of this committee are given *ibid.*, 39A-D-7, p. 2. Cf. the *Ponenza* of Cardinal Teodolfo Mertel on the Acts and Decrees of the Second Plenary Council of Baltimore, "Sommario," No. X: "Ristretto delle

Relazioni delle sette Congregazioni dei Teologi sopra tutti i Titoli del libello presentato ai Padri," APF, Acta, Vol. 232 (1867), fol. 397r.

86. Fifth private congregation, October 12, 1866, in *Concilii Plenarii Baltimorensis II., in Ecclesia Metropolitana Baltimorensi, a Die VII. ad Diem XXI. Octobris, A.D. MDCCCLXVI., habiti, et a Sede Apostolica recogniti, Acta et Decreta. Praeside Illustrissimo ac Reverendissimo Martino Joanne Spalding, Archiepiscopo Baltimorensi, et Delegato Apostolico* (Baltimore, 1868), pp. lxvii–lxviii.

87. Spalding to Cardinal Prefect, Baltimore, March 8, 1867, in the *Ponenza,* "Sommario," No. IX: "Commenti privati del Delegato Apostolico sopra alcuni Decreti e circa alcuni cangiamenti proposti dai PP.," *ibid.,* fol. 395r.

88. *Ponenza,* "Dubbj," No. 7, and "Responsa," No. 7, *ibid.,* fols. 373r and 377v.

89. Sixth private congregation, October 13, 1866, in *Concilii Plenarii Baltimorensis II.,* p. lxxi.

90. *Ponenza,* "Ristretto," par. 27, APF, Acta, Vol. 232 (1867), fol. 350v.

91. *Ponenza,* "Dubbj," No. 9, and "Responsa," No. 9, *ibid.,* fols. 373r and 377v.

92. *Concilii Plenarii Baltimorensis II., in Ecclesia Metropolitana Baltimorensi, a die VII., ad diem XXI. Octobris, A.D. MDCCCLXVI., habiti, et a Sede Apostolica recogniti, Decreta* (Baltimore, 1868), Titulus III: "De Personis Ecclesiasticis," Caput IV: "De Sacerdotibus curam animarum habentibus," Nos. 108 and 109, pp. 75–76; Titulus II: "De Hierarchia et Regimine Ecclesiae," Caput V: "De Consultoribus, Vicario Generali, Archidiacono, caeterisque Episcopi Officialibus," No. 71, p. 54, and No. 77, pp. 57–58.

93. "The Second Plenary Council of Baltimore," *Catholic World,* VII (August, 1868), 618–625 at 620 and 625.

94. "Our Roman Catholic Brethren," *Atlantic Monthly,* XXI (April, 1868), 432–451 at 447. Parton wrongly supposed that an archbishop or bishop was "practically elected by the very men whom he is afterwards to govern." He thought that "the higher clergy of the province" drew up the terna and that the "office is almost invariably assigned to the person whom his brethren thus indicate as their choice" (*ibid.*).

95. *FJ,* January 1, 1870, p. 4.

96. Henry F. Brownson, *Orestes A. Brownson's Middle Life: From 1845 to 1855* (Detroit, 1899), p. 446.

97. *FJ,* October 3, 1868, p. 5.

98. On this lamentable episode see the paper, "Dynamics of Ecclesiastical Authority: The Crisis of the Chicago Succession, 1865–1881," read by James P. Gaffey at a joint session of the American Catholic Historical Association and the American Society of Church History in New York on December 29, 1968.

99. *FJ,* October 3, 1868, p. 4.

100. *FJ,* October 10, 1868, p. 4.

101. *FJ,* October 17, 1868, p. 5: "Parishes versus Pariahs," and p. 4: "About the Completion of Catholic Order in These States."

102. *FJ,* October 31, 1868, p. 1: "The Pittsburgh Catholic on the Sacerdotal Question, Once More," and p. 4: "The Pittsburgh Catholic on the Rights and Remedies of Priests."

103. *FJ,* November 21, 1868, p. 4: "The 'Freeman's Journal' and 'Placidus.'"

104. Wheeler to McMaster, St. Louis, October 19, 1868, MCUND, McMaster Papers, 1866–1870, 2, I-1-M. (The location is the same for subsequent references to the McMaster Papers.) Wheeler was to be the theologian of Patrick A. Feehan, Bishop of Nashville, at the First Vatican Council. See John Rothensteiner, *History of the Archdiocese of St. Louis* (St. Louis, 1928), II, p. 102.

105. Mahoney to McMaster, Paquette, Manitowoc, Wis., November 7, 1868, MCUND, McMaster Papers.

106. *FJ,* November 7, 1868, p. 1: "The Status of the Catholic Priesthood," and "The Value of Ecclesiastical Law" (dated October 24, 1868).

107. O'Callaghan was born in 1831 in Kanturk, County Cork, emigrated to the United States in 1847, enrolled at the University of Notre Dame in 1849, entered St. Mary's Seminary, Cleveland, in 1855, was ordained in 1859, and was appointed pastor in Youngstown in 1861.

108. Having earlier been accused of national prejudice for trying to Americanize the European immigrants too rapidly, the French-born bishop at this time was being attacked by a group of Irish priests for admitting too many French and German students to the diocesan seminary. See George F. Houck, *A History of Catholicity in Northern Ohio and in the Diocese of Cleveland* (Cleveland, 1903), I, pp. 89–91, and the unpublished biography of Bishop Rappe by William A. Jurgens.

109. O'Callaghan to McMaster, Youngstown, November 27, 1868, MCUND, McMaster Papers.

110. *FJ*, December 12, 1868, p. 1.

111. *FJ*, December 26, 1868, p. 4. Very few of these letters are preserved in the MCUND, McMaster Papers. One of them, intended for the recipient's information only, was sent by E. Audran to help, "if necessary, to enlighten you a little more on the arbitrary doings of some of our good bishops and on the à propos of your late articles on this subject." Audran stated that Bishop James de Saint-Palais "in a fit of unjust jealousy" had removed him as pastor of the cathedral of Vincennes, where he had spent more than twenty-two years of hard and faithful labor. Audran to McMaster, Jeffersonville, Clark Co., Ind., December 17, 1868.

112. *FJ*, February 6, 1869, p. 1.

113. *Ibid.*, p. 4.

114. *FJ*, February 27, 1869, p. 1.

115. *Ibid.*, p. 4.

116. On the O'Flaherty case see Frederick J. Zwierlein, *The Life and Letters of Bishop McQuaid* (3 vols.; Rochester, N.Y., 1925–1927), II, pp. 11–41.

117. Spalding to McCloskey, Baltimore, March 1, 1869, AAB, Letterbook I, p. 437. On Edward McGlynn *vide infra*. Writing to Bishop James Gibbons, Vicar Apostolic of North Carolina, a few days later, Spalding instructed him to include in the pastoral letter of the Tenth Provincial Council of Baltimore, which was to be held in the latter part of April, a section on the duties of the clergy with references to the "late scandalous disturbances" (Baltimore, March 4, 1869, AAB, 71-U-1). Apparently he had second thoughts on this matter, for shortly before the council he asked Archbishop Purcell whether the pastoral should allude to the "late troubles" or would do better to be silent on the subject (Baltimore, April 15, 1869, MCUND, Purcell Papers). In the end no allusion to the troubles was made in the pastoral, but the clergy were exhorted to study carefully the decrees of the Second Plenary Council so that the "harmonious relations hitherto always existing between us, may be thereby still further strengthened and perpetuated" (*Catholic Mirror*, May 15, 1869).

118. McCloskey to Spalding, New York, March 3, 1869, AAB, 36A-N-11. "The late Archbp." was John Hughes, who died in 1864.

119. *FJ*, March 16, 1869, p. 4: "A Scandalous Hubbub."

120. *Ibid.*, "Art Thou He That Troubles Israel?" The Boston *Pilot*, March 6, said, "We fully endorse this sentiment from the *Telegraph*." The *New York Tablet*, March 6, said, "The *Telegraph* on this . . . exactly expresses our opinions."

121. *FJ*, March 13, 1869, p. 4; "What Is Canon Law?"

122. *FJ*, March 20, 1869, p. 4: "Questions and Answers."

123. *Ibid.*, p. 1.

124. *FJ*, April 24, 1869, p. 1.

125. A fortnight previously McMaster had chided the priests for their "singular lack of concentrated action." He urged them either as individuals or as "bodies of clergymen of given dioceses" to have recourse to the Propaganda promptly while there was still time before the ecumenical council: *FJ*, April 10, 1869, p. 4.

126. *FJ*, April 24, 1869, p. 1. On the following day the Tenth Provincial Council of Baltimore convened. Three of its eight decrees dealt with the clergy; it ordered that consultors and judges be appointed in every diocese of the province, that priests have a share in the formulation of recommendations of prospective bishops, and that suspended priests not be left entirely without support; the decree concerning the role of priests in the naming of candidates for the episcopacy was subsequently modified by the Propaganda. See the *Ponenza* for the general congregation of January 26, 1870, APF, Acta, Vol. 236 (1870), fol. 13r ff.; and *Concilii Provincialis Baltimorensis X in Metropolitana Baltimorensi Ecclesia, Dominica quarta post Pascha, quae festo S. Marci Evangelistae incidit, A.R.S. 1869, Inchoati, et Insequenti Dominica Absoluti, Acta et Decreta* (Baltimore, 1870), pp. 60–62.

127. *FJ*, May 1, 1869, p. 4.

128. *FJ*, May 8, 1869, p. 1: "Dioceses and Parishes versus Districts and Missions." Wiseman had died in 1865.

129. *Ibid.*, p. 4: "Cardinal Wiseman on Canon Law." This issue also carried a story, borrowed from the *Chicago Tribune* of April 13, on the "Insanity of Bishop Duggan," in which his "mental derangement" was described as related by his physician. The bishop had to be taken to an asylum in St. Louis, where he was confined for the rest of his life. McMaster never admitted that Duggan's treatment of the three priests, due to his illness, was not a valid example of episcopal arbitrariness.

130. *FJ*, May 15, 1869, p. 4. A priest wrote to the editor that "Jus" had "received all but universal approval from the priests every where," but he added the admonition: "It is nearly time that he should propose some practical way for the drawing up, approval and signing of the petition. It is the most difficult part of the work though he may not think so." The writer admitted that he himself could not suggest "a good practical plan" because of the many difficulties. O'Farrell to McMaster, St. Joseph's, May 14, 1869, MCUND, McMaster Papers.

131. *FJ*, July 17, 1869, p. 4. This letter relieved the anxiety of a priest who then wrote to the editor: "*Ius* having been so long silent, I feared he was hanged. I am happy to discover from your last issue that he is living. God bless him." The writer offered ten dollars and asked that "Jus" go to Rome, adding, "I trust all to *Ius*. . . Lay our case before the coming Council in such a manner that Episcopal tyranny shall rule no longer." Thomas Murray to McMaster, Stillwater, Minn., July 19, 1869, MCUND, McMaster Papers.

132. *FJ*, July 31, 1869, p. 1.

133. James M. Doyle to McMaster, Janesville, Rock Co., Wis., August 13, 1869, MCUND, McMaster Papers. Doyle also suggested that, as had been done with immediate success in England some years before, a printed card be sent to each priest to be signed and returned to the agent who would present them at Rome with a petition to the Pope. He remarked, "We could then see the men who are sincere in this great and all important movment."

134. *FJ*, August 28, 1869, p. 1.

135. The two predecessors of Bishop Duggan who left the Diocese of Chicago after brief and unhappy episcopates were James Oliver Van de Velde, S.J., who at his own request was transferred to the See of Natchez in 1853, and Anthony O'Regan, who resigned at the age of forty-nine in 1858. See Gilbert J. Garraghan, S.J., *The Catholic Church in Chicago, 1673–1871* (Chicago, 1921; reprinted Ann Arbor, Mich., 1968), pp. 161–163 and 178–179.

136. *FJ*, August 7, 1869, p. 4.

137. *FJ*, August 14, 1869, p. 4.

138. *FJ*, September 4, 1869, p. 4. In providing this convenient summary, "the sum and substance of all that the *Freeman's Journal*, and its distinguished correspondent '*Jus*' has ever proposed," McMaster may have been suggesting to the priests a possible formulation of their petitions to the Pope.

139. *FJ*, November 6, 1869, p. 4.

140. In a letter undated but probably written shortly before his departure for Rome, O'Callaghan informed McMaster about the campaign against himself in his parish in Youngstown, which he thought had been instigated by Bishop Rappe out of vengeance. He continued: "I understand the Bishop *suspects* me of being '*Ius*' but lately I think they (he and his friends) are on the wrong scent. Opinion is settling down upon ex-bishop O'Connor as the writer. I say: *good*; this will bring extrinsic motives to make converts to our scheme. I have even written to a friend or two expressing my opinion that from certain expressions in Ius's letters it would appear that he is the writer. One of our vicars general appears convinced that it is the ex-bishop. If the whole truth were known, not all the waters of the Jordan could cleanse me from my great guilt and Bishop Rappe would sing the Canticle of Moses over my being swamped." O'Callaghan to McMaster (n.p., n.d.), MCUND, McMaster Papers. Michael O'Connor had resigned the See of Pittsburgh in 1860 and at this time was a Jesuit. He was supposed to be a friend of O'Callaghan whom he visited.

141. *FJ*, November 20, 1869, p. 1.

142. *Ibid.*

143. Only one letter from priests dated within this interval is preserved in the McMaster Papers, and it contains no reason for abandoning the petition: James Drummond and Patrick Canavan, Priests of the Diocese of Portland, to McMaster, Dover, N.H., November 19, 1869.

144. *FJ*, November 27, 1869, p. 4.

145. In the McMaster Papers fewer than two dozen letters covering contributions have been preserved. Some were written by individuals, and others in the name of groups of priests. The great majority of the writers had Irish names. Several lived in Pennsylvania and New York; others in New England, the Middle West, and California. Many of them expressed their thanks to McMaster and "Jus" for their efforts on behalf of the clergy. Some of them offered to contribute again, should more money be needed, or to sign a petition, should that course be considered advisable. One said: "Jus is a noble man, a champion of our rights, speaking & writing for us and strenuously advocating our cause &c. when we ourselves dare not do so, because we are not men of the right stamp, but like tenants at will before unjust and oppressive grinding landlords." (James S. O'Sullivan to McMaster, Hudson, N.Y., December 1, 1869, MCUND, McMaster Papers.) Another remarked: "The present state of things is calculated, in many instances, either to drive the good men out of the ministry or to induce them to become hypocrites." (Thomas F. Mangan to McMaster, Mattoon, Ill. [Diocese of Alton], December 1, 1869, *ibid.*) A third commented: "We need such a representation for, at present, we have *no right to breathe* unless thru the nostrils of our Bishops." (P. McNulty to McMaster, Baldwinsville, N.Y., December 7, 1869, *ibid.*) Since it is impossible to ascertain what percentage of the total response the preserved letters constitute, it would be useless to try to tabulate and analyze the reaction of the priests geographically.

146. *FJ*, December 4, 1869, p. 4.

147. *Ibid.*, p. 1.

148. *Ibid.*, p. 4. McMaster was so convinced that O'Callaghan was "a true Catholic Priest," that he added: "All this we state, with the full knowledge that, in a future not probably distant, it will be known who is the writer of the articles that have been signed 'Jus.' If we now say of him what is not true, it will redound greatly to our personal discredit. This is what those that know us are aware we would not, knowingly, subject ourselves to."

149. *FJ*, December 18, 1869, p. 4. No letter from a vicar-general fitting McMaster's description has been found for this period. Later, however, the vicar-general of Walla Walla, J. Bt. Brouillet, wrote him: "I heartily subscribe to the various points of disciplinary changes petitioned for by the American priesthood, as analysed in your Editorial of the 1st inst." Brouillet to McMaster, Walla Walla, Wash., January 22, 1870, MCUND, McMaster Papers.

150. *FJ*, January 1, 1870, p. 4. When the Bishop of Louisville, Benedict Joseph Flaget, was seeking a coadjutor in 1847, he nominated John MacElroy, S.J., in first place and Martin J. Spalding only in second; the clergy of the diocese then let the Propaganda know that they preferred a native of Kentucky. See Robert F. Trisco, *The Holy See and the Nascent Church in the Middle Western United States, 1826–1850* (Analecta Gregoriana, Vol. 125 [Rome, 1962]), pp. 92–93, 143–145.

151. McQuaid to James M. Early, Rome, December 16, 1869, in Henry J. Browne (ed.), "The Letters of Bishop McQuaid from the Vatical Council," *CHR*, XLI (January, 1956), pp. 414–415.

152. *FJ*, January 22, 1870, pp. 1 and 4. The editorial was entitled, "Opposition to a More Fixed Status for the Clergy of the Second Order." The covering letter from Stephan, dated December 30, 1869, contains the postscript: "It should go in unabridged." MCUND, McMaster Papers.

153. *FJ*, February 5, 1870, p. 1. In this issue McMaster wrote: "We have had, in the last eighteen months, some two or three, only, wheeping [*sic*] communications, from ecclesiastics without experience, age, information, or authority to speak, who wanted to have their little say *against* the establishment of a regular ecclesiastical *law* in this country. Their communications have been put with *scores* of communications from the side *in favor* of *canonical law*, that, also we have not thought it proper to publish. Many of the latter may have felt *hurt*, at our putting their communications, so brilliantly and ably written, aside. A cause that *we* have the responsibility for, we must be permitted to manage in our own way."

154. *FJ*, February 12, 1870, p. 4.

155. Browne to McMaster, Rome, February 3, 1870, MCUND, McMaster Papers.

156. McQuaid to Corrigan, Rome, February 6, 1870, in Zwierlein, *op. cit.*, II, p. 37.

157. O'Callaghan to McMaster, Rome, February 26, 1870, MCUND, McMaster Papers. O'Callaghan asked McMaster to read the last part of the "Jus" letter carefully before publishing it lest his remarks about the necessity and the manner of preparing the petition not agree with what the editor might already have said in the issues that had not yet reached Rome. He feared that any contradiction of this kind might indicate that he did not see the *Freeman's Journal* for some weeks after its appearance and might excite some suspicion of his being in Rome.

158. O'Callaghan to McMaster, Rome, March 16, 1870, MCUND, McMaster Papers. O'Callaghan gloated over the impatience of the American bishops chafing at their detention in Rome: "They may learn to appreciate the sentiments of subjects whose conscientious circumventions [?] are overruled by superior authority. They may also learn a fortiori how goading arbitrary rule is to subjects having ordinarily no redress. But it may happen that their being snubbed in Rome may make them more arbitrary in America and like the Evil One seeing that their time of arbitrary rule is short they may perhaps exercise their power with greater excesses. However I think they will not." O'Callaghan seems to have been the one who was obsessed with the notion of arbitrary rule.

159. *FJ*, March 26, 1870, p. 1.

160. A number of letters from priests, dated in the latter part of March and in April, are preserved in the MCUND, McMaster Papers. More letters were sent from Iowa than from any other state except Wisconsin, where one priest presumed to send a list of thirty-seven names, his own included, of English-speaking priests of the Diocese of Milwaukee even though he had not spoken with some of them since the previous summer. James M. Doyle to McMaster, Janesville, Wis., April 7, 1870, *ibid.*

161. "Sacerdos" to McMaster, March 16, 1870, MCUND, McMaster Papers. Baltes was consecrated on January 23.

162. A. J. Verbeck to McMaster, Appleton, Wis., April 5, 1870, MCUND, Mc-

Master Papers. The writer added: "Perhaps scores of true missionary priests would send their names to petition for having the laws of the Church proclaimed here, if they had been able to carefully examine the question, or, if they were not afraid of what might follow. As it is, they remain silent, inactive, and may be counted as so many votes against the establishment of law instead of arbitrary rule. Is there no remedy against this awkward position? If there is, let the Freeman speak out."

163. See Sister Mary Augustine Kwitchen, O.S.F., *James Alphonsus McMaster. A Study in American Thought* (Washington, D.C., 1949), p. 195.

164. James S. O'Sullivan to McMaster, Hudson, N.Y., May 27, 1870, MCUND, McMaster Papers. O'Sullivan had previously written to McMaster on December 1, 1869 (*vide supra*, fn. 145), thanking him for his "great efforts & exertions on behalf of the priesthood of this country," praising "Jus" as "a noble man, a champion of our rights," and contributing ten dollars to the fund for the representative in Rome.

165. *FJ*, June 18, 1870, p. 5: "The Rule of Catholic Law."

166. *FJ*, August 6, 1870, p. 4: "The Council." Unfortunately, the "private communications" from bishops which McMaster mentioned have not been preserved.

167. *FJ*, September 10, 1870, p. 4.

168. McQuaid to Early, Rome, April 25, 1870, in Browne, *op. cit.*, p. 425.

169. Luers to Spalding, Fort Wayne, March 30, 1870, AAB, 34-S-11.

170. Luers to Barnabò, Fort Wayne, June 9, 1870, APF, Scritture riferite nei congressi, America Centrale, Vol. 23 (1870–1871), fol. 369r-370v. As a sample of the way in which priests were sometimes dismissed, Luers quoted in Latin the following note, which John O'Donnell, administrator of the Diocese of Portland, wrote to a priest named Patrick McGreary: "Since you have expressed to us your interest in leaving the Diocese of Portland, acceding to your wishes, we grant you permission to subject yourself to any bishop enjoying communion with the Holy See. We dismiss you in the Lord." Luers sketched the circumstances of this case and commented that such notes were likely only to embarrass other bishops.

171. Evrard to Barnabò, Rome, June 29, 1870, *ibid.*, fol. 397r-v.

172. O'Callaghan had written to McMaster in March, ". . . if questions at issue now against my Bishop are decided against him I will press my cause with strong hopes of success" (Rome, March 16, 1870, MCUND, McMaster Papers). After he returned home, O'Callaghan was suspended again, this time by the administrator of the diocese for making under subpoena of the Court of Common Pleas in Cleveland a deposition, which later appeared in a newspaper, on the manner in which dioceses held property in the United States. He was given a hearing before the metropolitan court of Cincinnati and was found guilty; accordingly, he was forced to publish a retraction (dated February 22, 1872) of "statements relative to Church authority, and the powers and duties of bishops and administrators" which had been submitted to the ecclesiastical tribunal according to the direction of the Holy See. See Houck, *op. cit.*, I, 99–100.

173. *FJ*, August 24, 1896, p. 1. O'Callaghan died in 1901.

174. "Nonnulla quaesita circa disciplinam ecclesiasticam quae episcopis . . . Romae praesentibus proponuntur," Nos. 13 and 14, June 6, 1867, in Giovanni Domenico Mansi (ed.), *Sacrorum Conciliorum nova et amplissima collectio*, XLIX (Arnhem and Leipzig, 1923), col. 244. On the canonical concept involved, see Edwin J. Murphy, C.PP.S., *Suspension "ex informata conscientia"* (The Catholic University of America Canon Law Studies, No. 76 [Washington, D.C., 1932]), pp. 10–35.

175. "Summarium responsorum ab episcopis datorum de gravioribus disciplinae ecclesiasticae capitibus in concilio tractandis," Questione XIII, par. 328, mansi, col. 392, and Questione XIV, par. 348, col. 403.

176. "Memoranda pro Concilio Oecumenico," AAB, 39-M-6, pp. 5–6. The covering letter, Spalding to Barnabò, Baltimore, August 15, 1869, APF, Scritture riferite nei congressi, America Centrale, Vol. XXII (1869), fol. 1115r.

177. *Collectanea S. Congregationis de Propaganda Fide, seu Decreta, Instruc-*

tiones, Rescripta pro Apostolicis Missionibus (2 vols.; Rome, 1907), No. 1394 (February 4, 1873), II, p. 70. Cf. Kenneth R. O'Brien, *The Nature of Support of Diocesan Priests in the United States of America. A Historical Synopsis and a Commentary* (The Catholic University of America Canon Law Studies, No. 286 [Washington, D.C., 1949]), pp. 16–17, 66, and 77–78.

178. *Notes on the Second Plenary Council of Baltimore* (New York, 1874).

179. *Ibid.*, p. 66.

180. *Ibid.*, p. 96.

181. *Ibid.*, p. 99.

182. *Ibid.*, p. 101.

183. *Ibid.*, p. 110 n.

184. *Ibid.*, p. 370.

185. *Ibid.*, p. 377.

186. *Ibid.*, p. 401.

187. *Ibid.*, p. 405.

188. *Ibid.*, p. 406.

189. *ACQR*, III (October, 1878), pp. 709–721. Strictly speaking, this was a review of two canonical books.

190. *Ibid.*, p. 718. In 1884 Smith at the invitation of Archbishop Gibbons helped to prepare the decrees for the Third Plenary Council of Baltimore and then served as the theologian of his bishop, Winand Wigger.

191. Unsigned and undated report (Italian), APF, Scritture riferite nei Congressi, America Centrale, Vol. XXXVI (1882), fol. 198.

192. *Ibid.*, fols. 209–210.

193. *Ibid.*, fols. 211–212.

194. *Ibid.*, fols. 212–215.

195. *Ibid.*, fols. 215–217.

196. Diary of Richard L. Burtsell, May 14, 1878, p. 199. Conroy stayed at Burtsell's house for two days; together they called on McGlynn. Burtsell wrote: "The De[legate] will recommend to Rome the custom introduced to Baltimore by Abp. Kenrick that the pastors of the diocese have a right of 'recommending' for the episcopacy: that the bishops have assigned rules to guide them in suspending" (p. 200).

197. "Instructio S. Congr. de Propaganda Fide de modo servando ab episcopis Foederatorum Septemtrionalis Americae Statuum in cognoscendis et definiendis causis criminalibus et disciplinaribus clericorum (*Quamvis*)," June 20, 1878, in *Acta Sanctae Sedis*, XII (1879), pp. 88–92; reprinted in *Acta et Decreta Concilii Plenarii Baltimorensis Tertii A.D. MDCCCLXXXIV* (Baltimore, 1886), pp. 292–296. An English translation as well as the Latin text in parallel columns is given in *The Pastor*, I (April, 1883), 171–178.

198. Corrigan to McQuaid, September 20, 1878, in Frederick J. Zwierlein, *Letters of Archbishop Corrigan to Bishop McQuaid and Allied Documents* (Rochester, N.Y., 1946), p. 22.

199. Corrigan to Gibbons, January 4, 1879, in Zwierlein, *McQuaid*, II, p. 181.

200. Same to same, February 1, 1879, *ibid.*

201. Corrigan to Gilmour, March 10, 1879, *ibid.*, p. 183.

202. Reprinted in *Acta et Decreta Concilii Plenarii Baltimorensis Tertii*, pp. 296–297.

203. McQuaid to Corrigan, Paris, March 29, 1879, in Zwierlein, *McQuaid*, II, p. 184.

204. Corrigan to Gilmour, April 7, 1879, *ibid.*

205. Zwierlein, *Letters*, p. 25.

206. Corrigan to McQuaid, June 11, 1879, *ibid.*, pp. 26–27. Giovanni Battista Agnozzi was secretary of the Propaganda.

207. McQuaid to Corrigan, December 2, 1879, in Zwierlein, *McQuaid*, II, p. 191.

208. McQuaid to Gilmour, October 25, 1880, *ibid.*, pp. 191–192.

209. Same to same, April 12, 1885, *ibid.*, p. 181.

210. Gibbons to Elder, Baltimore, February 1, 1882, in John Tracy Ellis, *The Life of James Cardinal Gibbons, Archbishop of Baltimore, 1834–1921* (2 vols.; Milwaukee, 1952), I, p. 200.

211. M. J. Spalding to John B. Purcell, Archbishop of Cincinnati, Baltimore, February 28, 1865, MCUND, Purcell Papers, II-5-c: "If a certain Rev. Wm. Mahoney, late of Balt^e, should call on you, do not trust him: he is wholly unreliable & unprincipled, I fear. Having found him deprived of all faculties, I could not conscientiously restore him, after consultation with a special court of ecclesiastics convened for the purpose." For a sketch of the unstable career of this priest, who was born in Carlyle, Pennsylvania, in 1838, was a curate at St. John's Cathedral in Milwaukee when he published his book, and died in Denver, Colorado, in 1890, see Benjamin J. Blied, "Our Cathedral Curate Wrote a Book," *Salesianum*, XLII (October, 1947), pp. 158–163.

212. *Jura Sacerdotum Vindicata* (New York, 1883). The publisher was James Sheehy. The book bore no imprimatur, for the writer denied that he needed one; he attempted to prove this contention, but he submitted his work to the judgment of the Holy See (pp. 21–23 and 27).

213. *Ibid.*, p. 7.

214. *Ibid.*, p. 13.

215. *Ibid.*, p. 14.

216. *Ibid.*, p. 32.

217. *Ibid.*, p. 35.

218. *Ibid.*, p. 39.

219. *Ibid.*, pp. 42–43.

220. *Ibid.*, p. 44.

221. *Ibid.*, p. 46. Cf. p. 62 ("The statute [of the Second Plenary Council] which ordains ecclesiastical trials (N. 77) has been a dead letter from the day it was promulgated to this day. The realization of its salutary ends never took place.") and p. 347 ("I doubt very much if there has been one case tried in the United States according to the spirit and letter of the 'Instructio' since its promulgation.").

222. *Ibid.*, p. 47.

223. *Ibid.*, p. 51.

224. *Ibid.*, p. 55.

225. *Ibid.*, p. 56.

226. *Ibid.*, p. 59.

227. *Ibid.*, p. 62.

228. *Ibid.*, p. 100.

229. Ibid., p. 154. He ignored the fact that the decrees of the Second Plenary Council had been expressly approved by the Propaganda acting in the name of the pope. The bishops of the Fourth Provincial Council of New York in September of that same year were to renew explicitly Decree 77 of the Second Plenary Council: *Acta et Decreta Concilii Provincialis Neo-Eboracensis IV., in Ecclesia Metropolitana S. Patritii, Neo-Eboraci, a die XXIII. ad XXX. Septembris, A.D. MDCCCLXXXIII., praeside Eminentissimo ac Reverendissimo Joanne McCloskey, . . . habiti, et a Sede Apostolica recogniti* (New York, 1886), Caput V: "De Statu Clericorum," Art. V, p. 23. On the bishop's obligation to support a delinquent cleric under the present Code of Canon Law, see Philip M. Hannan, *The Canonical Concept of "congrua sustentatio" for the Secular Clergy* (The Catholic University of America Canon Law Studies, No. 302 [Washington, D.C., 1950]), pp. 185–199.

230. *Jura Sacerdotum Vindicata*, pp. 192 ff. He apparently supposed that most priests would consider an ecclesiastical prison preferable to uncanonical dismissal.

231. *Ibid.*, p. 314.

232. *Ibid.*, p. 320.

233. *Ibid.*, pp. 329–330.
234. *Ibid.*, p. 334.
235. *Ibid.*, p. 338. Mahoney thought that a few months only spent in a monastery would be almost useless: "A year, in my humble judgment, should be the least penance as a rule inflicted for ordinary faults. Frequently a longer probation would be advisable and oftentimes necessary" (p. 360).
236. *Ibid.*, pp. 344–345.
237. *Ibid.*, pp. 354–355.
238. Mahoney to Gibbons, Milwaukee, February 27, 1883, AAB, 77-C-12.
239. Corrigan to Gibbons, New York, March 13, 1883 (*Private*), AAB, 77-D-8.
240. Gibbons to Corrigan, Baltimore, March 15, 1883 (*Private*), in Ellis, *Gibbons*, I, p. 201.
241. Corrigan to Gibbons, New York, March 19, 1883, AAB, 77-E-2. Michael Heiss was Archbishop of Milwaukee.
242. Same to same, New York, March 21, 1883, AAB, 77-E-4.
243. *FJ*, April 7, 1883: "The Priesthood Vindicated in Its Honor, as in Its Rights."
244. Mahoney to McMaster, Milwaukee, April 7, 1883 ("Confidential"), MCUND, McMaster Papers.
245. Since Mahoney asked McMaster to return the letter to his publisher, Sheehy, if he should decline to publish it, it is not to be found among the editor's papers.
246. Corrigan to McMaster, undated but later marked "1883," MCUND, McMaster Papers: "I will let you know in a few days whether it be worth while to answer Rev. Mr. Mahony's [*sic*] wild talk."
247. Mahoney to Gibbons, Milwaukee, April 27, 1883, AAB, 77-F-14.
248. Same to same, Milwaukee, May 7, 1883, AAB, 77-G-3.1.
249. Gibbons to Corrigan, Baltimore, May 23, 1883, in Ellis, *op. cit.*, I, p. 201.
250. Corrigan to Gibbons, New York, May 24, 1883, AAB, 77-G-14.
251. *Jura Sacerdotum Vindicata*, p. 25.
252. (New York, 1885). This edition was also published by James Sheehy.
253. "Episcopal Nominations" (New York, 1883). The pamphlet, containing forty-five pages, was published by Sullivan & Schaefer in June. The writer said that he had been born in Ireland, had come to the United States as a boy, had been ordained in 1860 for the Diocese of Newark, had been successively pastor of four large congregations, and had been active in building Catholic schools (p. 3).
254. *Ibid.* Patrick Corrigan was not the only, and perhaps not the first, priest of the Diocese of Newark to hold this view. After Bishop Corrigan was promoted to be coadjutor archbishop of New York in 1880, some of the clergy displayed a certain initiative. One of them, William McNulty, wrote to his friend Bishop McQuaid that the method of naming bishops ought to be changed. Like many before him, he believed that the diocesan clergy knew the merits of their fellow priests better than did the bishops of the province who had the responsibility of recommending candidates to Rome. Accordingly, he suggested a concrete system: "Let the Priests of a diocese in need of a bishop assemble and elect as many of their number to represent them as there are bishops in the province of which a bishop is to be elected — let this body of bishops and priests meet and do what now is done by bishops alone. This would be approximating to what the Church has laid down in her laws" (McNulty to McQuaid, Paterson, October 22, 1880). When McQuaid heard reports of clerical meetings in which the candidacy of certain priests for the vacant see was advanced, he commented disdainfully to Archbishop Corrigan: "They would do well to keep quiet, mind their own business, leave the nomination where it belonged, and all would come out right" (McQuaid to Corrigan, Rochester, February 11, 1881). In the end Winand Wigger, whom McNulty had recommended to McQuaid, was appointed Bishop of Newark. See Carl Derivaux Hinrichsen, "The History of the

Diocese of Newark, 1873–1901" (Unpublished Ph.D. dissertation, The Catholic University of America, Washington, D.C., 1962), pp. 153–154.

255. "Episcopal Nominations," p. 4.

256. *Ibid.*, p. 5.

257. *Ibid.*, p. 33.

258. *Ibid.*, p. 35.

259. *Ibid.*, p. 38.

260. *Ibid.*, p. 39.

261. *Ibid.*, p. 42.

262. Wigger to Sullivan and Schaefer, South Orange, June 30, 1883, cited by Hinrichsen, *op. cit.*, p. 202.

263. *Ave Maria*, XIX (July 14, 1883), p. 557.

264. Wigger to Hudson, South Orange, July 18, 1883, cited by Hinrichsen, *loc. cit.* Perhaps Wigger, the son of German immigrants and the president of the newly organized American branch of the St. Raphaelsverein, also resented Patrick Corrigan's disrespectful remarks about German bishops ("Episcopal Nominations," p. 36).

265. M. Corrigan to McQuaid, July 23, 1883, in Zwierlein, *Letters*, pp. 60–61.

266. Same to same, August 23, 1883, *ibid.*, p. 62.

267. *Acta et Decreta Concilii Provincialis Neo-Eboracensis IV.*, Caput XIV: "De quibusdam capitibus disciplinae," Art. VII, pp. 72–73.

268. "What the Catholic Church in the United States Needs Most" (New York, 1884). This pamphlet, containing seventy-seven pages, was published by the American News Company.

269. *Ibid.*, p. 5.

270. *Ibid.* He later commented: "Any Bishop may invoke this law [requiring the imprimatur] at his pleasure, but it is seldom done, except in the case of works that treat of faith and morals. The rigid laws regarding printing of books have been modified very much by custom even in Catholic countries" (p. 10).

271. *Ibid.*, p. 6. Bishop Wigger was consecrated on October 18, 1881.

272. *Ibid.*, p. 16.

273. *Ibid.*, p. 17.

274. *Ibid.*, p. 18.

275. *Ibid.*, p. 19.

276. *Ibid.*, p. 23.

277. *Ibid.*, p. 30.

278. *Ibid.*, p. 32.

279. *Ibid.*, p. 36.

280. *Ibid.*, p. 42.

281. *Ibid.*, p. 45.

282. *Ibid.*, p. 46.

283. *Ibid.*, pp. 49–50.

284. *Ibid.*, p. 51.

285. *Ibid.*, pp. 54–55. About the same time Archbishop Corrigan wrote to Archbishop Gibbons that he could think of only nine domestic prelates then living in the United States (see Ellis, *op. cit.*, I, p. 228).

286. "What the Catholic Church," p. 57.

287. *Ibid.*, p. 59.

288. *Ibid.*, p. 68.

289. *Ibid.*, p. 71.

290. *Ibid.*, p. 72.

291. *Ibid.*, p. 74.

292. M. Corrigan to McQuaid, May 29, 1884, in Zwierlein, *Letters*, p. 66.

293. *Ibid.*, p. 67.

294. "The Bishop and the Priest" (New York, 1884). This was also published by the American News Company.

295. It is impossible to find out exactly what criticisms McCartie made, for no issues of the *New York Tablet* from 1884 are known to be extant. See Eugene P. Willging and Herta Hatzfeld, *Catholic Serials of the Nineteenth Century in the United States. A Descriptive Bibliography and Union List*, 2d series, Part 14, Vol. I: *New York City* (Washington, D.C., 1967), p. 124.

296. "The Bishop and the Priest," p. vi.

297. Corrigan meant Archbishop Domenico Jacobini, not his brother Lodovico, the cardinal. He corrected the error in the preface to the present pamphlet.

298. "The Bishop and the Priest," p. 1.

299. *Ibid.*, p. 2. Henry Cosgrove had served as a priest in Davenport from the time of his ordination in 1857. The first Bishop of Davenport, John McMullen, had appointed him vicar-general, and when the bishop died on July 4, 1883, Father Cosgrove became administrator of the diocese. After the bishops of the province met to choose candidates for the vacant see, the rumor was spread that Cosgrove had not been recommended to Rome. Thereupon some of the priests sent a cablegram to the Propaganda, asking that no action be taken in this matter until the priests of the diocese could be heard from. The priests then assembled and signed a petition for the appointment of Father Cosgrove, which was dispatched to the Propaganda. The Sacred Congregation asked the bishops of the province to discuss the question again, and in the end, with the consent of Leo XIII, it named Cosgrove the second Bishop of Davenport. See George Giglinger, "Rt. Rev. Henry Cosgrove, D.D., Bishop of Davenport, Iowa. A Biographical Sketch," *Acta et Dicta*, II (July, 1910), 211–218 at 214.

300. Simeoni to Wigger, Rome, January 14, 1885, cited by Hinrichsen, *op. cit.*, p. 203.

301. *Mercury*, March 15, 1885, cited *ibid.*, p. 204.

302. See *ibid.*, p. 205. Referring to Patrick Corrigan's threat of appealing to Rome, Wigger wrote to McQuaid: "My impression is that the 'Instructio' of 1878 has turned the heads of many American priests, especially Rectors. . . . At present too many of them seem to think that the *rights* are all on the side of the clergy, and the *duties* only devolve on the Episcopacy." (Wigger to McQuaid, South Orange, March 26, 1885, in Hinrichsen, *op. cit.*, p. 205, fn. 52)

303. Wigger to Simeoni, South Orange, September 1 (?), 1886, cited *ibid.*, p. 206. In 1892 Patrick Corrigan became involved in another widely published controversy with Bishop Wigger — this time over the proposals of Peter Paul Cahensly and the German-American Priests' Union regarding the spiritual care of immigrants; Richard L. Burtsell was his defender, and Sebastian B. Smith was the prosecutor in the ecclesiastical court; an agreement was reached before the trial could be completed (see *ibid.*, pp. 226–239). At the time of his death in 1894 he was engaged in still another dispute with Wigger; he was a partisan of Archbishop Ireland on the school question and closed his parish school (see *ibid.*, pp. 274–287).

304. *ACQR*, IX (April, 1884), pp. 340–357.

305. *Ibid.*, p. 352.

306. *Ibid.*, p. 353.

307. Corrigan to McQuaid, January 31, 1882, in Zwierlein, *Letters*, p. 44.

308. Keane to Gibbons, Rome, June 25, 1883, AAB, 77-H-8.

309. Corrigan to McQuaid, August 23, 1883, in Zwierlein, *Letters*, pp. 61–62.

310. "Instructio S. C. de Prop. Fide, 1883. De modo servando in cognoscendis et definiendis causis criminalibus et disciplinaribus clericorum in foederatis Statibus Americae Septentrionalis (*Cum magnopere*)," in *Collectanea S. Congregationis de Propaganda Fide* (Rome, 1907), II, pp. 169–172, No. 1586.

311. "Capita praecipua quae Emi Cardinales S. C. de Propaganda Fide cen-

suerunt a Rmis Archiepiscopis et Episcopis Foederatorum Statuum A. S. Romae congregatis praeparanda esse pro futuro Concilio," (1883), Caput VI, p. 5.

312. "Minutes of the Roman Meeting Preparatory to the Third Plenary Council of Baltimore," Fourth session, November 20, 1883, *The Jurist*, XI (April, 1951), 309. This translation has been corrected, where necessary, through a comparison with the Latin text, "Relatio collationum quas Romae coram S. C. de P. F. Praefecto habuerunt Archiepiscopi pluresque Episcopi Statuum Foederatorum Americae, 1883."

313. Fifth session, November 22, 1883, *ibid.*, p. 310.

314. Ninth session, December 4, 1883, *ibid.*, (October, 1951), p. 542.

315. Tenth session, December 10, 1883, *ibid.*, p. 546.

316. "Capita praecipua," Caput II, pp. 1–2. The action regarding Scotland was taken on June 18, 1883.

317. First session, November 13, 1883, "Minutes of the Roman Meeting," XI (January, 1951), pp. 124–125.

318. Second session, November 15, 1883, *ibid.*, p. 129.

319. Third session, November 17, 1883, *ibid.*, (April, 1951), pp. 302–303.

320. "Capita praecipua," Caput II, p. 2.

321. First session, November 13, 1883, "Minutes of the Roman Meeting," XI (January, 1951), pp. 124–125.

322. Third session, November 17, 1883, *ibid.*, (April, 1951), p. 304.

323. Fifth session, November 22, 1883, *ibid.*, p. 310.

324. "Capita praecipua," Caput III, p. 2.

325. First session, November 13, 1883, "Minutes of the Roman Meeting," XI (January, 1951), p. 126.

326. "Capita proposita et examinata in collationibus, quas coram nonnullis Emis Cardinalibus Sacrae Congregationis de Propaganda Fide ad praeparandum futurum Concilium plenarium habuerunt Rmi Archiepiscopi et Episcopi foederatorum statuum Americae Septemtrionalis Romae congregati," Capita II, III, VI, pp. 3–5, 7.

327. Ryan to Gibbons, St. Louis, March 14, 1884, AAB, 77-O-9.

328. Corrigan to McQuaid, February 14, 1884, in Zwierlein, *Letters*, p. 65.

329. Corrigan to Gibbons, New York, March 18, 1884, AAB, 77-P-2.

330. Same to same, New York, April 1, 1884, AAB, 77-S-2: "Such were the changes agreed to at the time as I am able to state positively because then and there, at Card. Franzelin's dictation, the words cited above were ordered to be inserted into the Instructio, and I then marked them with ink on the copy now before me. The alteration has probably been accidentally overlooked and omitted." Johannes Baptist Franzelin, the distinguished Austrian Jesuit theologian, had been a cardinal since 1876 and a member of the Congregation de Propaganda Fide.

331. Same to same, New York, April 5, 1884, AAB, 77-T-5.

332. Corrigan to McQuaid, July 15, 1884, in Zwierlein, *Letters*, p. 68. The Fourth Provincial Council of New York, meeting in September, 1883, enumerated several reasons which would be sufficient for the transfer of rectors from one mission to another (even to one of lower esteem) or even for their complete removal from office if the gravity of the case demanded such action. This chapter (XV) had been prepared by the congregation *De personis ecclesiasticis* under the chairmanship of Bishop McQuaid. *Acta et Decreta Concilii Provincialis Neo-Eboracensis IV.*, pp. 74–75. These provisions, however, were not adopted by the Third Plenary Council of Baltimore.

333. Gilmour to Gibbons, Cleveland, March 28, 1884, AAB, 77-Q-10. Later he wrote: "The Rectors, incardinations, & trials need careful handling, as also the management of our temporalities. The dismissing of priests & receiving of same, as also seminarians, is so loose that both are a scandal & grave disorder." Same to same, Cleveland, April 6, 1884, AAB, 77-T-6.

334. Kain to Gibbons, Wheeling, August 11, 1884, AAB, 78-J-11.

335. Williams to Gibbons, Boston, July 14, 1884, in *Relationes eorum quae disceptata fuerunt ab Illmis ac Revmis Metropolitis cum suis suffraganeis in suis singulis Provinciis super schema futuri concilii praesertim vero super capita cuique commissa* (Baltimore, 1884), p. 5.

336. "Relatio Provinciae Sanctae Fidei," J. B. Lamy *et al.* to Gibbons, Santa Fe, July 9, 1884, *ibid.*, pp. 6–8.

337. "Relatio Provinciae Cincinnatensis," Elder to Gibbons, Cincinnati, June 6 (Latin and English) and 17, 1884, *ibid.*, pp. 9–13.

338. "Relatio Provinciae Sancti Francisci," *ibid.*, p. 15.

339. "Relatio Provinciae Milwauchiensis," *ibid.*, p. 21.

340. "Relatio Provinciae Chicagiensis," Feehan to Gibbons, Chicago, June 11, 1884, *ibid.*, p. 37.

341. *Schema Decretorum Concilii Plenarii Baltimorensis Tertii* (n.p., n.d.).

342. *Acta et Decreta Concilii Plenarii Baltimorensis Tertii in Ecclesia Metropolitana Baltimorensi habiti a die IX. Novembris usque ad diem VII. Decembris A.D. MDCCCLXXXIV., praeside Illmo. ac Revmo. Jacobo Gibbons, Archiepiscopo Balt., et Delegato Apostolico* (n.p., n.d.). This private edition of the *Acta et Decreta* is the only extant record of the debates in the council and of the views expressed by the several bishops. A selection from these minutes has been translated in paraphrase by Zwierlein, *McQuaid*, II, pp. 312–317.

343. Fourth private congregation, November 14, 1884, *Acta et Decreta*, pp. xxxiii–xxxiv. The council returned to the question of the consultors' role in the alienation of church property in the next private congregation, November 15, deciding that in an emergency the opinion of only two consultors would suffice (*ibid.*, p. xxxvi).

344. *Acta et Decreta* (public edition, as in fn. 197), p. 14: Titulus II: "De Personis Ecclesiasticis," Caput II: "De Consultoribus Dioecesanis," par. 17.

345. On Spalding's role in the Third Plenary Council see David Francis Sweeney, O.F.M., *The Life of John Lancaster Spalding, First Bishop of Peoria, 1840–1916* (New York, 1965), pp. 159–166. Spalding's opposition to the theory and practice of democracy within the Church is here explained.

346. Eighth private congregation, November 19, 1884, *Acta et Decreta*, pp. xli–xlii.

347. Eleventh private congregation, November 22, 1884, *ibid.*, pp. xlvi–xlix. In the thirteenth private congregation, November 24, the council adopted Spalding's motion prohibiting rectors of cathedrals from ever being made irremovable, *ibid.*, p. li.

348. *Schema Decretorum*, par. 43, pp. 11–12.

349. Twelfth private congregation, November 22, 1884, *Acta et Decreta*, pp. xlix–l. In the twenty-seventh private congregation, December 4, the council, at the suggestion of Bishop Dwenger, added that a rector, instead of being definitively removed, could also sometimes be transferred to another mission (*ibid.*, p. xci).

350. Thirteenth private congregation, November 24, 1884, *ibid.*, pp. lii–liii.

351. Twenty-sixth private congregation, December 4, 1884, *ibid.*, pp. lxxxiii–xc.

352. Twenty-seventh private congregation, same day, *ibid.*, p. xci.

353. Thirty-first private congregation, December 6, 1884, *ibid.*, p. xcviii.

354. *Ibid.*, p. c.

355. This episode has been narrated by Zwierlein, *McQuaid*, II, pp. 345–356, and by Ellis, *op. cit.*, I, pp. 252–262.

356. McQuaid to Gibbons, March 21, 1885, in Zwierlein, *McQuaid*, II, p. 346.

357. "Decretum de alienatione bonorum ecclesiasticorum," Rome, September 25, 1885, in *Acta et Decreta* (public edition, as in fn. 197), p. ciii.

358. *Ibid.*, pp. 171–174; Titulus X: "De Judiciis Ecclesiasticis," Caput II: "De Officialibus Curiae Episcopalis," sect. 1: "In Causis Disciplinaribus Clericorum."

359. Peter Guilday (ed.), *The National Pastorals of the American Hierarchy*

(1792–1919) (Westiminster, Md., 1954; reprinted from 1923), pp. 240–241. The principal author of the pastoral of 1884 was Bishop Keane, if his biographer is correct, although the names of Archbishop Corrigan and Bishop O'Farrell preceded Keane's on the list of the committee appointed for this purpose. See Patrick H. Ahern, *The Life of John J. Keane, Educator and Archbishop, 1839–1918* (Milwaukee, 1954), pp. 58-59.

360. Simeoni to Gibbons, Rome, May 20, 1887, AAB, 82-R-1.

361. On the McGlynn case see Zwierlein, *McQuaid*, III, pp. 1–83, and *Letters*, pp. 90–126; Ellis, *op. cit.*, I, pp. 547–594; and the unscholarly and uncritical work by Stephen Bell, *Rebel, Priest and Prophet. A Biography of Dr. Edward McGlynn* (New York, 1937), pp. 30–234. Archbishop Corrigan's words about Burtsell are on p. 128.

362. See Zwierlein, *McQuaid*, II, pp. 372–375. In 1888 Burtsell was to defend another priest, Louis A. Lambert, against McQuaid, *ibid.*, III, pp. 103–126.

363. On February 10, 1887, Burtsell recorded in his diary: "Fr. Corrigan called to ask me about getting up a grand collection by priests to the Holy Father for his sacerdotal jubilee, petitioning at the same time to have the rectors' position restored to them as before the 3rd Plenary Council of Baltimore. All the bishops were placing in their synodal decrees that all rectors *non inamovable* were amovable ad nutum. I said that their status was the same as before: no rector *amovable ad nutum* could be removed for crime without a trial, though for poor financial administration he could be, as before. I was willing to sign a petition that all rectors of parishes of any account should be declared inamovable; but I would not take part in any special collection at the same time, for I would not try to purchase with money what I thought to be for the welfare of the Church. He said that money was the only way to reach Italian Ecclesiastics. He spoke of Dr. McGlynn as a rebel. . . . I told him that Dr. McGlynn had never said anything as bad against Rome, as he had just now, when he said that 'Money was the only way to reach Italian Ecclesiastics'; and he was speaking of a practical bribe to the pope to give us spiritual rights" (pp. 185–186).

364. *The Canonical Status*, p. 5.

365. *Ibid.*, pp. 13–14.

366. *Ibid.*, p. 16.

367. *Ibid.*, p. 21.

368. *Ibid.*, p. 29.

369. *Ibid.*, p. 39.

370. *Ibid.*, p. 42.

371. *Ibid.*, p. 52.

372. *Ibid.*, p. 56.

373. *Ibid.*, p. 58.

374. *Ibid.*, p. 62.

375. *Ibid.*, p. 66.

376. *Ibid.*, p. 78.

377. *Ibid.*, pp. 85–86.

378. *Ibid.*, pp. 96–97.

379. *Acta et Decreta* (public edition, as in fn. 197), p. 16, par. 21.

380. Zwierlein, *Letters*, p. 118.

381. Burtsell's Diary, December 15, 1887, p. 307.

382. *Ibid.*, December 16, 1887. Cf. Corrigan to McQuaid, January 12, 1888, in Zwierlein, *Letters*, p. 117.

383. Corrigan wrote confidentially to the editor of the *Pastor*, William Wiseman, informing him that if he intended to review the pamphlet "he should know that it was published in contradiction to the laws of the Church, without revision by the Eccl. Authority of the diocese. Dr. Wiseman wrote back that he did not intend to review it, as it was a reprint of articles in the N.Y. Tablet, therefore stale: . . .

but that he did not agree with the Abp. in the application of the rules of the Index, which were obsolete." Burtsell's Diary, January 13, 1888, p. 5.

384. *FJ*, January 28, 1888, p. 4. McMaster had died on December 29, 1886.

385. "The Latest Addition to Canonical Jurisprudence in the United States," *ibid.*

386. Burtsell's Diary, January 31, 1888, p. 11.

387. *Ibid.*, February 4, 1888, p. 14. For the reason given above (fn. 295) this reply cannot be found.

388. *FJ*, February 18, 1888, p. 1.

389. Burtsell's Diary, February 18, 1888, p. 18.

390. *Ibid.*, March 23, 1888, p. 32: "He [the editor, Kerwin] considered my last letter in the Tablet wonderfully clever, and was surprised that I was allowed to keep on my (sacerdotal) head. I said simply that I kept within the law."

391. On the Lambert case, see Zwierlein, *McQuaid*, III, pp. 84–149.

392. See Burtsell's Diary, December 6, 16, 21, 23, and 27, 1889, pp. 254, 258 260, 261–262; and July 7, 8, 14, and 17, 1890, pp. 345–346, 351, 352.

393. McQuaid to Corrigan, March 2, 1888, in Zwierlein, *McQuaid*, II, p. 374, and III, p. 59.

394. Same to same, May 6, 1890, in Zwierlein, *Letters*, p. 132.

395. Colman J. Barry, O.S.B., *The Catholic Church and German Americans* (Milwaukee, 1953), pp. 128–129 and 154, fn. 30.

396. Ledochowski to the Ordinaries of the United States, Rome, May 15, 1892, in *Acta Sanctae Sedis*, XXIV (1891–1892), pp. 684–686, and *American Ecclesiastical Review*, VII (July, 1892), pp. 63–64.

397. Gibbons to Elder, Baltimore, March 21, 1889, in Zwierlein, *McQuaid*, III, pp. 156–157; cf. Ellis, *op. cit.*, I, p. 617.

398. On the establishment of the Apostolic Delegation in the United States, see the article *s.v.*, *New Catholic Encyclopedia*, I, pp. 690–693.

399. Keane to Gibbons, Washington, December 4, 1892, AAB, 90-T-4.

400. *FJ*, December 3, 1892.

401. Satolli also compelled McQuaid to absolve Thomas O'Flaherty of the suspension that he had imposed on him in 1869. See Zwierlein, *McQuaid*, II, pp. 39–40.

402. *FJ*, January 21, 1893.

403. *FJ*, May 20, 1893. In November Corrigan unveiled a bust of Satolli commorating the visit.

404. Hinrichsen, *op. cit.*, p. 244.

405. *The Forum*, XVI (September, 1893), pp. 11–21.

406. *Ibid.*, p. 14.

407. *Ibid.*, p. 17.

408. Ellis (ed.), *Documents*, No. 140, p. 521.

409. "The Apostolic Delegation," *ACQR*, XX (January, 1895), pp. 112–130. On Bouquillon, see Daniel F. Reilly, O.P., *The School Controversy, 1891–1893* (Washington, D.C., 1943), pp. 88 ff.

410. "The Apostolic Delegation," p. 128.

411. *Ibid.*, p. 129.

412. "The Results of Cardinal Satolli's Mission," *The Forum*, XXII (February, 1897), pp. 695–705.

413. *Ibid.*, p. 696.

414. *Ibid.*, p. 700.

415. *Legal Formulary, or, A Collection of Forms to be used in the Exercise of Voluntary and Contentious Jurisdiction, to which is added an Epitome of the Laws, Decisions and Instructions pertaining thereto* (New York, 1898), pp. 43–44.

416. *ACQR*, XXI (January, 1896), pp. 81–105. On Peries, see Patrick Henry Ahern, *The Catholic University of America, 1887–1896. The Rectorship of John J. Keane* (Washington, D.C., 1948), pp. 54 and 152–156.

417. "Episcopal Elections," p. 103.

418. *Ibid.*, pp. 104–105.

419. S. Congregatio Consistorialis, "Decretum de secreto servando in designandis ad Sedes Episcopales in Foederatis Statibus Americae Septentrionalis," Rome, March 30, 1910, *Acta Apostolicae Sedis*, II (1910), pp. 286–287; also *Ecclesiastical Review*, XLII (June, 1910), pp. 718–719. The Consistorial Congregation now had competence in this matter, because the American Church had been removed from the jurisdiction of the Propaganda in 1908.

420. S. Congregatio Consistorialis, "Decretum circa proponendos ad episcopale ministerium in Foederatis Americae Septentrionalis Statibus," Rome, July 25, 1916, *Acta Apostolicae Sedis*, VIII (1916), pp. 400–404; also *Ecclesiastical Review*, LVI (January, 1917), pp. 58–63.

421. John Daniel Mary Barrett, *A Comparative Study of the Councils of Baltimore and the Code of Canon Law* (The Catholic University of America Canon Law Studies, No. 83 [Washington, D.C., 1932]), pp. 58–59.

422. Ibid., pp. 74–75. Cf. Peter J. Klekotka, *Diocesan Consultors* (The Catholic University of America Canon Law Studies, No. 8 [Washington, D.C., 1920]), pp. 52–53.

423. Barrett, *op. cit.*, pp. 78–83; Klekotka, *op. cit.*, pp. 112–169.

424. Canon 454, parr. 1 and 3.

425. S. Congregatio Consistorialis, "De amotione administrativa ab officio et beneficio curato Decretum (*Maxima cura*)," Rome, August 20, 1910, *Acta Apostolicae Sedis*, II (1910), pp. 636–648. When a doubt was raised whether this decree applied to the dioceses of the United States, the Congregation replied affirmatively on March 13, 1911 (*ibid.*, III [1911], p. 133). Cf. Maurice Connor, *The Administrative Removal of Pastors* (The Catholic University of America Canon Law Studies, No. 104 [Washington, D.C., 1937]), pp. 37–46; and William Anthony Galvin, *The Administrative Transfer of Pastors* (The Catholic University of America Canon Law Studies, No. 232 [Washington, D.C., 1946]), pp. 60–65.

426. The decision was made by the cardinals on June 28, 1915, and was approved by the Pope on the following day. *Acta Apostolicae Sedis*, VII (1915), pp. 378–382. Thus *Maxima cura* was declared not to apply to removable pastors. See Galvin, *op. cit.*, p. 31.

427. John Joseph Coady, *The Appointment of Pastors* (The Catholic University of America Canon Law Studies, No. 52 [Washington, D.C., 1929]), pp. 88–89.

428. *Ibid.*, pp. 90–93; on the transfer of pastors, see also pp. 110–112. Cf. Galvin, *op. cit.*, pp. 93–97.

MICHAEL V. GANNON

BEFORE AND AFTER MODERNISM: THE INTELLECTUAL ISOLATION OF THE AMERICAN PRIEST

INTRODUCTION

The Fathers of the Second Vatican Council, in their Decree on Priestly Formation, promulgated in 1965, directed that candidates for the priesthood in theological seminaries be made knowledgeable in the major fields of contemporary secular thought, philosophical and scientific. They should be conversant, the Fathers said:

> . . . with contemporary philosophical investigations, especially those exercising special influence in their own country, and with recent scientific progress. In this way, thanks to a correct under-standing of the character of modern times, students will be properly prepared in dialogue with the men of their own day.[1]

Together with similar expressions contained in the encyclical letter *Ecclesiam Suam* issued by Pope Paul VI the previous year,[2] this decree placed the Catholic Church officially and squarely on the side of those who in this country, since 1955 at least, had been arguing for higher intellectual standards for American priests in training, and for closer, friendlier contacts between the clergy and the United States intellectual community at large.

The Council directive may not have been especially innovative or original; indeed, it said no more and not quite as much as was said on repeated occasions by Archbishop John Ireland of St. Paul and Bishop John Lancaster Spalding of Peoria during the last two decades of the nineteenth century.[3] As official doctrine, however, it did con-stitute a major step in a new direction, as is plain if one remembers that barely four years earlier the Apostolic Delegate to the United States, speaking at Marquette University, excoriated efforts being made at that time:

> . . . to build a bridge between modern secular thought and Catholic thought, even to the point of digressing from positions

293

traditionally accepted in the past, in the expectation of being
acknowledged and accepted in the intellectual circles of today. . . .
Even if our bishops and priests cannot all be scholars . . . with
the long years of their seminary training, with the large
amount of reading most of them do, they are equipped to understand and evaluate anything that the intellectuals can say and
write about religion.[4]

Those words might jar the post-conciliar ear, as indeed they jarred
certain pre-conciliar ears, but, even if touched with a certain *Romanità*,
they give a fair estimate of the attitude toward secular and Protestant
scholarship that prevailed generally among the American clergy
throughout most of our history since the inauguration of the Church
in the United States under Bishop John Carroll in 1790.

The purpose of this essay, then, is not to enumerate the instances
of inter-relationship and influence between the clergy and the American
intellectual community. The finding of this researcher is that, with the
exception of the period 1890–1908 and the very recent years, there
have been precious few such instances.[5] Rather, what is attempted
here is a presentation of the major historical reasons for the estrangement, if not hostility, that generally existed between the two. In
that attempt one cannot pass over the much-agitated question why
American Catholics generally, both clergy and lay, showed such
lamentable lack of scholarly accomplishment in categories that would
be likely to win secular recognition, since the question of the educated
clergy cannot be divorced entirely from certain considerations of
Catholic intellectualism at large.[6] All the commentators seem agreed
that if any class of Catholics was likely to make its mark on the
American intellectual scene, it was the clergy.

Not only did the nineteenth and early twentieth century priest charis-
matically represent intellectual leadership to his immigrant charges,
who brought that adulation of priestly learning with them from the
home country, but in point of fact his long seminary training, with its
abundant leisure and its opportunities for study and reflection, gave
him, if it gave to any American Catholic, an acquaintanceship with
books, a taste for culture, and a chance to become a man of scholarly
distinction.[7] The celibate seclusion of his subsequent priestly life, one
would feel, provided the necessary atmosphere for bringing those
pursuits to a point of fruition. In the religious orders, where education was often the principal priestly work, and well-supplied libraries
were just down the hall, intellectual and cultural achievements would
seem to have been particularly promising. A sociologist tells us that

Catholic priests "have long been the best educated clergymen in the United States." [8] And as recently as 1956, the President of Hunter College said that "in any comparison between Catholic-trained laymen as a group and the genus 'scholarly priest' as a group, a larger proportion of the men-in-orders will attain to true intellectual distinction." [9] Those groups have now come abreast of each other, if one accepts the findings of Andrew Greeley, [10] or have been reversed, if one accepts the views of Daniel Callahan. [11]

There is no denying that certain of the American clergy have achieved intellectual distinction. For that fact to be borne home, one need only recall such names out of the present century as Francis E. Gigot, John B. Hogan, William J. Kerby, Edward A. Pace, John M. Cooper, Peter Guilday, John A. Ryan, Thomas Verner Moore, John LaFarge, Gustave Weigel, and John Courtney Murray. Certain of those named, notably John Courtney Murray, had influences outside the Catholic communion and may be said to have made some impact on the national intellectual scene. For the most part, however, whatever intellectual lamps the clergy lit in this century cast their light in magnificient isolation. And it must be said that the majority of the clergy did not even have oil for the lamps. Why? Was it because they did not, as it turned out, have sufficient leisure and opportunity for research? Perhaps, but that does not seem to be the major reason. Neither does it appear that certain of the other reasons, advanced in the 1950's to explain the Church's intellectual lag, apply specifically to the failure of the clergy to make a significant intellectual contribution. We can summarize those reasons: (1) the pastoral emergency occasioned by the vast influx of Catholic immigrants up to 1929; (2) the preoccupation with building churches, schools, and charitable institutions, a preoccupation which became known as the "brick-and-mortar" excuse; (3) the long-nurtured anti-Catholic bias of many Americans; (4) the failure of bishops and religious superiors to give effective leadership and, especially, encouragement to intellectual endeavors; (5) the deliberate aloofness of many clergy from humanists; and (6) the subordination of everything human to the development of the supernatural life. [12]

Each of these reasons has its justification in particular instances and contexts. Beneath them all, perhaps, like a bedrock, lies another reason, more deep-seated and encompassing than those just rehearsed — a reason of which the other reasons are in part manifestations. Perhaps the reason for the failure of the educated clergy to establish itself in the eyes of the American intellectual community lay within Catholic intellectualism itself. [13] Intellectuals there were among the clergy, but perhaps the intellectualism in which they were formed and which they themselves evidenced, was such as to restrict rather than to expand the mind, to seek simple preservation and elaboration of antique truths rather than their creative development; to promote a defensive style of apologetics rather than open historical criticism; to build fences instead of bridges. It was an intellectualism fairly bristling with non-intellectualism, and its name was *scholasticism* — not that neo-scholasticism which was fostered in the Thomistic revival of Pope Leo XIII, nor that academic scholasticism which even today commands the respect of Protestant and secular scholars in the Medieval Academy of America and elsewhere, but that artificial, gerrymandered scholasticism composed of syllogisms piled Ossa on Pelion, frozen into textbook form, and memorized by unnumbered seminarians. It was the scholasticism of the counter-modernism repression, and it swept onto the American scene at just that point in time, the opening decade of the present century, when it appeared that the clergy were at last moving out of the darkness of a self-imposed isolation from modern currents of thought and were holding aloft the first promising lights of independent learning.

BEFORE MODERNISM

A. The American Priest

In the past, most historians of American cultural and intellectual life accepted an interpretation of American civilization that stressed the continuity of American values, modes of thought, and institutions with those of Europe.[14] As late as 1946 philosopher-historian Herbert W. Schneider maintained, "We still live intellectually on the fringe of European culture." [15] More recently, there has been a search for qualities that are "unique" to American life, that owe no special allegiance to Anglo-Saxon traditions, and that explain presumably better than non-indigenous qualities the peculiar process called "the American experience." [16] If one were to combine all the unique qualities attributed to Americans, he would have a people who, throughout the greater part of the nineteenth century, exhibited "restless energy," "activism," "voluntarism," "power of practical observation," "love of risk and adventure," "inventiveness," "irrepressible optimism," and a "hunger for the novel"; a people who dealt constantly with what John Dewey called "the unprecedented, the hazardous, the unpredictable"; who, because they lived amid perpetually shifting conditions, were suspicious of attempts to find unchanging principles in nature or fixed goals for man; who, because they lived in an open democratic society, resisted the effort to make wisdom into a professional speciality; who, because they lived in a practical and successful society, inclined to feel that the ultimate problems solve themselves — or dissolve themselves — when men concentrate on the penultimate ones; who, as Alexis de Tocqueville was the first to observe, accept tradition only as information, tend to results without being bound to means, and aim at the substance through the form; who solved the tensions existing between their thought and their action by devising fluid, non-conceptual systems of philosophy, which came eventually to be called "pragmatic," "process," or "behavioristic." [17] The list could be continued. What emerges in the end is the picture of a people who were basically inhospitable to men of thought, or "intellectuals." [18] More important for our present purposes is the emerging picture of a people equally inhospitable to the Roman Catholic priest.

The priest and the intellectual occupied similarly precarious positions at the onset and throughout much of the nineteenth century. It was an age when the nation's people were building a business society, forging new political and social institutions, throwing canals, trunk-line railways, and themselves across the Alleghenies into the forested West. The intellectual was ridiculed because he was unworldly, unmasculine, and impractical. The priest received opprobrium primarily for reasons very different: 1) as an immigrant (from France, Ireland, or Germany in the main) he was not a charter member of the native Anglo-American society; 2) he and his immigrant charges seemed to threaten the economic stability of cities and states into which they poured at phenomenal rates; [19] 3) his presence on American soil was an affront to Protestant Christianity with which the nation was identified by most "nativists," who launched an *odium theologicum* against him and his religion.[20]

But there were other grounds, too, specifically cultural and intellectual, on which the priest was mistrusted by many Americans. Like the intellectual, he had nothing to contribute, seemingly, to the ongoing conquest of wilderness. Like the intellectual, he dwelt in the aery reaches of speculative reason far removed from the practical concerns of men. Quite unlike the intellectual, however, he confronted the emerging nation with principles, points of view, and practices that ran directly counter to the popular experience: he represented institutional immutability in a land committed to change; unbending theological doctrine to a people accustomed (ever since the Halfway Covenant) to doctrinal compromise and adjustment; a complex and relatively inflexible intellectual system to men whose minds refused to be clamped in place; a negative approach to mammonism, divorce, sexuality, and other moral problems which most Americans seemed content on leaving to heaven or to the courts; and a curious devotional apparatus, including such practices as Forty Hours and Perpetual Adoration, which, the American Protestant ethic held, took men's time and energy away from their God-appointed industry, enterprise, and manifest destiny.[21] By all these criteria the priest seemed reactionary and out of step. True, the typical immigrant cleric became at once an American citizen, proclaimed a firm allegiance to the Constitution, and evinced a strong loyalty to the nation's basic institutions. But these free political commitments he held in tension with his religious ethos, which was not, as most of his fellow citizens saw it, "American." De Tocqueville wrote: "The Catholic priests in America have divided the intellectual world into two parts: in the one they place the doctrines of revealed religion, which they assent to without discussion; in the other they leave those political truths which they believe the Deity has left open to free inquiry." [22]

In his alienation from the mainstream, then, the priest was like the secular or Protestant intellectual. In the resolution of his alienation he was not like the latter at all. The secular intellectual went on eventually to find philosophical constructs in Darwinism, pragmatism, and related movements which served both to explain the American experience and to provide him an acceptable, if not yet respectable, place within that experience. The Protestant intellectual, for his part, concluded in time that churchmen had neither an intellectual vocation nor an intellectual responsibility, hence simply appropriated and baptized the findings of supposedly objective scholarship in biology, anthropology, physics, history, and sociology, and at the same time redefined religion in what he believed to be more acceptably American terms as "social concern," "sincerity," "sentiment," and "openness of mind." [23] Thus were born in the latter half of the nineteenth century: on the one hand, a secular, science-oriented, and pragmatic intellectual community, preaching humanistic alternatives to religion; and, on the other hand, a Protestant intellectual community "with no independent intellectual content" preaching adjustment to science and to the reigning secular social ideals.[24] Neither of these two solutions was possible for the priest. Indeed, it was against the concept of secular society and against the flexibility of Protestant doctrine that his church leadership most vigorously declaimed. Paul Tillich could write as late as 1938, "Since the Counter-Reformation, Catholicism has been fighting a defensive war equally against Protestantism on the one hand and autonomous civilization on the other." [25] It was not to be expected that the American priest would find intellectual peace on the American scene so easily or so soon.

Who was this priest? Originally, he was, in the main, Anglo-American and a former member of the English province of the suppressed Society of Jesus. About twenty-five in number, this select body of the clergy was the total force of clergy available to Father John Carroll upon the latter's appointment as Superior of the American missions in 1784.[26] The faithful to whom these priests ministered tended to be well-established Anglo-American families centered principally in Maryland. Very quickly, however, this clergy, to whom not only the English language but also English traditions in literature and politics were native, yielded prominence to French and Irish immigrant clergy. Father François Nagot led the first group of French émigré priests to this country in the summer of 1791. Refugees from a France where the Civil Constitution of the Clergy, promulgated the year before, to all practical purposes severed the French Church from the See of Rome, this first group of four priests and five seminarians, all members of the Society of Saint Sulpice, founded the mother seminary of the American Church, St. Mary's, in Baltimore.[27] Not only their seminary but also the Sulpician faculty, a considerable number of whom went out to the frontier as missionaries during the next quarter century, had an important and salutary influence on the state of the Church during the early national period.

It was the Irish, however, who eventually would predominate, in numbers, in manner, and in influence. Irish priests — Augustinians, Capuchins, Dominicans, and seculars — filtered into the seaboard towns during the late 1780's and already by 1792 had changed the composition of the American clergy in their favor. Indicative of the strongly ethnic mentality introduced by the Irish was the request made to Rome in that year by the now Bishop Carroll to abandon the Missal and Breviary supplements for England, since, as he wrote, ". . . The Irish clergy in the United States refused to celebrate the English saints." [28] From St. Patrick's College, Maynooth, All Hallows College, Dublin, and from the lesser known colleges of Carlow, Thurles, and Kilkenny, the Irish clergy poured into the port towns of the east coast. With them and ahead of them came thousands of their fellow countrymen: a total of 1,683,791 from the time of Carroll's death in 1815 until the close of the Civil War in 1865. Before the next century they could be found everywhere in the young nation:

in industrial centers of New England and the Middle Atlantic states, in mill towns and coal mining regions, in railheads of the middle continent, and in mining frontiers of the West. The result for American Catholicism has been summed up by Will Herberg: "Irish Catholic and American became almost identical in the Irish-American mind, and the Americanism of the Irish Catholic developed into something much more than merely the sense of national 'belonging.' To a greater or lesser degree all American Catholicism has tended to take on this peculiar nationalistic coloration." [29] This is not to say that Irish clerical dominance went unchallenged. The German states provided the second largest immigration of Catholics, clergy and lay, some 606,791 in the period 1815–1865, and another 680,000 between 1865 and 1900, while Irish immigration in the latter period amounted to only 520,000. For the most part German Catholics settled in the triangle from Cincinnati to St. Louis to Milwaukee, but there were also concentrations in Buffalo and western Pennsylvania, in Cleveland and along the upper Mississippi. The last two decades of the century would see frequent occasions when German priests expressed bitter resentment at the Irish ascendancy, especially at the Irish monopoly of bishoprics; however, thanks to the pacific influence of prelates such as James Gibbons, Cardinal Archbishop of Baltimore, of Irish extraction, the two great ethnic clergy groups settled their differences and proved, as Gibbons predicted, that "the ties formed by grace and faith are stronger than flesh and blood." [30]

The pioneer Anglo-American clergy, though few in number, became the cultural nucleus of Maryland-Kentucky Catholicism, and some American clergy of English ancestry attained positions of leadership, e.g., Bishops Martin J. Spalding (1810–1872), John Lancaster Spalding (1840–1916), and William Henry Elder (1819–1904); and the convert Bishops Josue Young (1808–1866), Alfred Curtis (1831–1908), Thomas Becker (1832–1899), and Frederick Wood (1813–1883). A considerable number of the French Sulpician clergy, disappointed at the scarce supply of students for their Baltimore seminary — only one native, William Matthews, was ordained from the seminary during its first ten years — volunteered to serve on the American missions, where together with other émigré priests they accommodated themselves astonishingly well to frontier society. Between 1792 and 1815, when their numbers dwindled, they were the leading presence of the Church in Kentucky and the Illinois Country, as Sulpician-trained priests were in parts of New England.[31]

Of the four major national groups, Irish, German, Anglo-American, and French, the French émigré priests may be said to have been the outstanding men, intellectually. The Anglo-Americans were polished gentlemen, of cultured background, and no one can gainsay a tradition which gave the American Church its two Spaldings. They were few in number, however, and lacked the strong intellectual formation of the French, most of whom had received excellent training at French classical colleges in Latin and Greek, grammar, *belles lettres*, rhetoric, philosophy, mathematics, and the natural sciences. The instruction they in turn gave at St. Mary's College, founded by the Sulpicians at Baltimore in 1799, was of such high quality that practically all the prominent families of Baltimore, together with families of substance in other cities of the country, had sons in attendance. The historian of the émigrés tells us that "the seminary professors and the other émigré priests who came to the United States were welcome in the best circles of society," where presumably their education and refinement won respect not only for themselves but for their Church.[32] Certainly the missionaries among them were the most learned clergy on the frontier. Bishop Simon Bruté de Remur (1779–1839) amazed Vincennes, Indiana, with his library of 5,000 volumes.[33] Father Stephen Theodore Badin (1768–1853) in Kentucky thought that he had probably the best French library in the state at the turn of the nineteenth century.[34] Badin donated the land on which Father Edward F. Sorin (1814–1893) and the Fathers of the Holy Cross founded the University of Notre Dame in 1842.[35] Most of the émigrés were engaged in the founding of Catholic schools, such as Gabriel Richard, S. S. (1767–1832) who built primary and high schools in Detroit, established Indian schools at numerous sites in the Territory of Michigan (for which he served in Congress as delegate from 1823 to 1826), and became vice-president of the University of Michigan when that institution was founded in 1817.[36] Similar academic interests occupied Bishops Benedict Joseph Flaget, S.S. (1763–1850) in Indiana, and John Baptist David, S.S. (1761–1841) in Kentucky; secular Bishop Jean Cheverus (1768–1836) and Father François Matignon (1753–1818), Boston's first bishop and most respected pioneer priest, respectively.[37] Although they held basically conservative political opinions, and some few were outspoken in their preference for the Bourbons, most French frontier clergy accepted and grew to like American institutions, and with their "sturdy, hard working, abstemious, obliging, neighborly" manners endeared themselves to the Americans, even among the Yankees and Puritans.[38]

Not everything favored the intellectual contribution of the French priest, however. The Sulpician piety that permeated the clergy leaned strongly on the rigorism of Jean Joseph Surin, S. J. (1600–1665), placed great stress on humility and obedience, which meant in practice a near military subjection of priest to bishop, and cautioned darkly against the "vanity" of learning. Said Sulpician founder Jean-Jacques Olier, in 1659: "The more learned you become, the drier will be your devotion. To be learned without being puffed up is a miracle: *"Scientia inflat.*' " [39] In the American environment learning beyond the *scientia competens* required for professional ministry seemed to some not only vain but useless, as Archbishop Ambrose Maréchal, S.S. (1768–1828) of Baltimore suggested in 1826 to Father Samuel Eccleston, an American convert priest then at the Sulpician solitude in Issy, France. Noting that most newly ordained priests in this country read and preached the gospels so abominably that they caused Protestants to laugh and Catholics to be ashamed, Maréchal urged Eccleston to learn a "grave and just way of speaking," for thus he would "render to the Church of America an infinitely more important service than if he taught them the learned works of our most celebrated Theologians. . . ." [40] The statement may fairly stand as a symbol of the manner in which practical exigencies of the American situation gradually overcame among the French the advantages of intellectual attainment, and, together with Sulpician piety, dictated for a century and a half to come the less bookish purposes for which Sulpician seminaries in this country would stamp native-born *ordinandi.*

When Archbishop Gaetano Bedini, newly appointed Nuncio to Brazil, visited the United States in 1853, he found that on the whole the German priest gave evidence of better training than that claimed by the Irishman — "if he is not better, at least he does not suffer by the comparison." [41] Bedini had occasion to meet German religious, such as Jesuits, Redemptorists, and Precious Blood Fathers, as well as secular clergy, and he passed few criticisms of them apart from what he saw as their excessive nationalism and pride of language. It was these two very factors, however, which made it difficult for the German priest to speak effectively to the American mind in the nineteenth century, despite what commentators such as Richard Hofstadter have described as the "impressive German scholarship" of the period.[42] The German priest believed that the United States was a country but not yet a nation; like Europe, the continent was spacious enough to accommodate many different languages and national customs. For that reason the German priest felt himself under no necessity to "Americanize" himself. Proud of his language and traditions, and conscious of the strong bond that existed in his people's minds between the Catholic faith and the German culture, the priest sought to imitate within his parish all the features that he remembered from parish life in the Rhineland or Bavaria. Understandably, language played an important role in this determination to keep German Catholic communities insulated from the majority Irish Church. "Language saves the Faith" was the slogan of many, including the first German bishop in the United States, John Martin Henni (1805–1881) of Milwaukee, Bishop John Nepomucene Neumann (1811–1860) of Philadelphia, and missionary Father Francis X. Weninger, S.J. (1805–1888).

In time, other voices were heard among the German clergy warning that, in the long run, it would prove impossible to sustain German language, customs, and patriotism on American soil. "How laughable it is to think otherwise," said Redemptorist missionary Joseph Prost.[43] In 1887 Father John Gmeiner, editor of the German weekly *Der Seebote* and professor at St. Francis Seminary in Milwaukee, the nation's first German language seminary (founded 1845), urged German Catholics to conform themselves to their surroundings as far as prudence and conscience allowed.[44] It is striking that by this date even the priest who gave the most characteristically German response to Gmeiner, Father Anton H. Wolburg, pastor of St. Augustine's Church in Cincinnati, expressed doubt that the immigrants who labored to perpetuate German nationalism would succeed. "They will Americanize in spite of themselves," he lamented. "The American nationality will finally prevail. . . . Foreign nationalities will be absorbed by it and flow in the current of American life."[45] His prognosis proved correct, but too late for German priest-scholars to make a significant entrance into the "American experience" before the close of the century. The best minds among them were engaged in a defensive struggle and the atmosphere in the German triangle was hospitable neither to Americanism nor to the free play of intellect. At stake was not only their faith but their sacred honor.

As late as the *fin de siècle* the German clergy were still objecting mightily to the "Americanizers," "liberals," and "minimists," as they called such leading Irish-American figures of the time as Cardinal Gibbons and Archbishop Ireland; Bishop Denis J. O'Connell (1849–1927), Rector of the North American College in Rome; and Bishop John J. Keane, Rector of The Catholic University of America, which had been founded at Washington, D. C. in 1889. The new university itself became the scene of several critical struggles over the nationalism issue, and Monsignor Joseph Schroeder (1849–1903), professor of dogmatic theology from Cologne (along with Joseph Pohle, the first German members of the faculty), became during his tenure at Washington (1889–1898) the intellectual leader of the German Catholic societies in the United States. When Schroeder was forced out of the university in the spring of 1898 (by a ten-four vote of the trustees the previous October), German priest-supporters were acutely embittered and many took special satisfaction at the discomfiture caused Irish-Americans by the papal condemnation in 1899 of the alleged heresy of "Americanism." [46] It takes no effort of the historical imagination to understand that these years of enmity, suspicion, and *parti-pris* had no beneficial effect on the development of Catholic intellectual life.

The largest clergy group, though by no means the best educated, was the Irish. When New York was erected a diocese in 1808, Father Richard Luke Concannen, O.P. (1747–1810) of County Roscommon, trained at the Irish Dominican College of San Clemente in Rome, was appointed first ordinary of the see. Concannen died en route, but his place was taken by another Irishman from San Clemente, John Connolly, O.P. (1751–1825), of County Meath. Within the short space of twelve years' time, Irish prelates also occupied the sees of Philadelphia, Richmond and Charleston. Thus early notice was given of the extent to which Irish clergy would assume responsibility for the Church in English-speaking America. As the first half-century progressed, the Irish priests whom the bishops governed far outnumbered their Anglo-American and German counterparts, but it was clear that many were not quite as cultured, nor for that fact as governable.[47] Some, it appeared, had left Ireland for New York harbor with rather more encouragement than permission of their Irish bishops or superiors. Archbishop Maréchal of Baltimore, in a letter to the Holy See dated September 18, 1819, stated that out of the ten Irish priests who came to his diocese, eight had turned out badly. He went on to say that most of the scandals of the day could be attributed to Irish priests in Philadelphia, Norfolk, Richmond, and Charleston.[48]

Maréchal's testimony may not have been altogether disinterested, since there was obvious dismay at this time on the part of the French clergy both over the cultural rudeness of the Irish soggarth and over the continuing necessity of turning over the Church to such hands as his. Also, it was clear to observers such as Archbishop Bedini that, if the Church was not to falter in this new land, perhaps less disciplined hands than those of the French ought to guide it. "If someone were to complain about them," Bedini said of the French, "it would be about their excessive discipline and restraint, which completely oppose the free American spirit." [49] Again, it should be noted that there were in the early years a number of outstanding Irish clergy below the dignity of bishop. Fathers John Power (1792–1849) in New York and Francis Patrick Kenrick (1796–1863) in Bardstown, Kentucky, are good examples. As pastor of St. Peter's Church, vicar-general and administrator of the diocese, exponent of Catholic doctrine, author, translator, and linguist (Latin, Greek, French, Spanish, Italian, Gaelic), Power was one of the most cultured men in New York and one who hardly matched Maréchal's image of the rowdy Irish priest. Kenrick, later ordinary of Philadelphia (1842–1851) and Archbishop of Baltimore (1851–1863), taught theology, history, Greek, and liturgy on the Kentucky frontier, published there a distinguished treatise on the Eucharist (*Letters of Omega and Omicron on Transubstantiation*, Louisville, 1828), and went on to become the foremost theological scholar in the American Church.[50] Many Irish clergy sent to America who exhibited brilliance of mind and refinement of manner were promoted to the episcopate. An early example was the celebrated John England (1786–1842) of Charleston, who was already a bishop when he arrived in this country from Cork in 1820. A writer and orator of marked ability, Bishop England expended much of his energy in explaining the harmony of Catholic teachings with republican institutions. This he did in public squares, in courthouses, in churches of other faiths, in the pages of the weekly *United States Catholic Miscellany* which he founded at Charleston in 1822, and even from the rostrum of the House of Representatives in Washington. Archbishop John Hughes (1797–1864) was undoubtedly the outstanding Catholic clerical mind in New York during his episcopacy (1842–1864), as probably Bishop Michael O'Conner, S.J. (1810–1872) was the most erudite between the Delaware River and Lake Erie.

Learning and acumen were not limited to those men raised to the episcopate, however. Taking all the nationalities together one finds among the lower clergy, too, occasional personalities whose cultivated intellects lent distinction to the Church in the nineteenth century. One may mention in this connection: the New York pastor Jeremiah W. Cummings (1814–1866), first American graduate of the Urban College of the Propaganda in Rome, counselor of Orestes Brownson, contributor to *Brownson's Review*, and acerbic critic of seminary training in the United States; James A. Corcoran (1820–1889), that "rare genius" as the New York *Freeman's Journal* called him,[51] who taught theology in Charleston and Philadelphia, served as a *peritus* in two provincial and two plenary councils, represented the American bishops on the preparatory commission for Vatican Council I, and founded in 1876 the *American Catholic Quarterly Review*; the converts Isaac Hecker (of whom more will be said), Augustine L. Hewit, Francis Baker, George Deshon, and Clarence Walworth, all of whom became Redemptorists and later (except Walworth) Paulists; the convert-priests Dwight Lyman, William Everett, Thomas S. Preston, and Donald McLeod; such noted secular priests of New York as pastor and social reformer Thomas Farrell (1823–1880), canonist and civic leader Richard Burtsell (1840–1912), historian and controversialist Henry A. Brann (1837–1921), and Edward McGlynn (1837–1900), who, though remembered primarily for his espousal of Henry George's single tax theory and for his brief excommunication on disciplinary grounds, was already by the 1870's proposing social reform themes later made popular in Protestantism by Washington Gladden and Walter Rauschenbusch;[52] John Gmeiner and Anton H. Wolburg, both previously mentioned, theologian Peter Abbelen (1843–1917), and Joseph Jessing (1836–1919) who founded the Pontifical College Josephinum in 1894; and finally, Félix Francisco José María de la ConcepcíonVarela y Morales (1788–1853), Cuban exile, who as pastor of the Church of the Transfiguration in New York and vicar-general of the diocese from 1837 to 1853, contributed from the store of Latin culture a mind rich in philosophy, law, and natural science.[53] These are not, of course, the only outstanding minds below the rank of bishop which could be produced from the roll of the American clergy during the nineteenth century, and indeed we shall see others in the section which follows, but at this point in the narrative they can stand for the rest.

It remains to be said that wherever the immigrant priest exercised his pastoral ministry, whether in the slum sections of the large cities, in shanties along the railroad tracks, in the farming regions of the Middle West, or in the mines of Pennsylvania or California, he was the charismatic, central figure in his Catholic community. Irrespective of how his intellectual life might be judged by secular and Protestant critics of his own time, or by Catholic historians of the present time, the priest of the immigrants was to his own people nothing short of an intellectual giant, skilled in theology but, because of his educational advantages, competent also to give advice on politics, law, education, mechanics, pharmacy, banking, and social reform. The immigrants' view of him as intellectual leader and representative of learning in general was part of the European heritage which they transplanted in the United States; it was likewise born of many fruitful experiences in this country where the American priest rather remarkably lived up to the expectations his people had of him. As a result, the priest belonged to a "class," enjoyed a position or community status, a kind of *métier*-substitute. De Tocqueville saw this as early as 1832: "The priest alone rises above the rank of his flock, and all below him are equal." [54] It was still true in the heady days of Archbishop Ireland (1838–1918) who declared in 1889: "Priests are officers, laymen are soldiers." [55] The presumption of universal competence was noted by Bedini among the Irish immigrants, who, as he wrote, "see in their priests not a simple minister of religion; but their father, their magistrate, their judge, their king, their 'papa,' their idol." [56] And, somewhat the same presumption could be found as late as a generation ago when, as Monsignor William J. Kerby reported, a priest-friend of his in the West contended that on *all* matters of importance he was the "best-posted and ablest man in his county." [57]

The demanding toil of recreating the Church of Ireland and Europe in a new land caused in time the adoption of a particular scale of values on which intellectual pursuits ranked lowest and pastoral-administrative-building achievements ranked highest. "The most outstanding priest," Bedini wrote, "is the one that has built the most churches and begun the most institutions." [58] In this hierarchy of merit, it must be repeated, the priest was not unlike the average American of his time. Richard Hofstadter reminds us:

> During the nineteenth century, when business criteria dominated American culture almost without challenge, and when most business and professional men attained eminence without much formal education, academic schooling was often said to be useless. It was assumed that schooling existed not to cultivate certain distinctive qualities of mind but to make personal advancement possible. [59]

Where the priest did differ was in his intellectual isolation from such "distinctive qualities of mind" as *were* being cultivated by way of thoughtful response to the ongoing American adventure — a response that was characteristically pragmatic, nondoctrinal, this-worldly, and open to correction. This kind of response, by and large, the priest was unable to give. His purposes were nonfunctional, strictly doctrinal, supernatural, and philosophically certain. True, he participated as everyone did in the great labor of clearing the forests and building the cities, and to that extent he was caught up in the external nimbus of the American experience. Intellectually, however, he was a man set apart. Even when the learned French clergy accommodated themselves to American frontier conditions, they did precisely that — they *accommodated*. They did not directly enter the cultural mainstream of the Americans, neither did they mediate significantly between the Catholic mind and the secular or Protestant mind. The French clergy, like the Irish and German who followed them, lived off the borrowed capital of other lands; furthermore they were committed to continue doing so since their philosophical and theological commitments were intimately dependent on European culture. The Germans were still further indisposed to embrace the American ethos by their extreme nationalism. And the Irish, with their general lack of interest in American cultural traditions, were isolated by choice. Archbishop Ireland wrote in 1894:

> No one need remind me that immigration has brought us inestimable blessings . . . [but] Priests foreign in disposition and work were not fitted to make favorable impressions upon the non-Catholic American population, and the American-born children of Catholic immigrants were likely to escape their action. . . . Even priests of American ancestry ministering to immigrants not infrequently fell into the lines of those around them, and did but little to make the Church in America throb with American life.[60]

For all these reasons, together with the prevailing anti-Catholic bias of many Americans, it is not surprising that most of the intellectual labor of the nineteenth century priest was defensive in nature. In the parochial school his instruction was directly calculated to preserve religious and/or ethnic loyalties against the threats posed by prejudice and Protestant proselytizing. In social philosophy he tended to form a closed Catholic circle amid the alien corn, thus giving rise to what since has been called the Catholic "ghetto" or "siege" mentality. And when he wrote or spoke for public consumption it was nearly always for apologetical reasons. As Orestes Brownson noted, ". . . Our Catholic authors, very naturally and very properly, have confined themselves, when addressing those without, either to the defense of Catholicity against the objections of Protestants, or to the refutation of the errors of non-Catholics." [61]

B. The Clerical Mind at Work

Anti-Catholicism, it has been said, was the pornography of the Puritan.[62] The evangelical American Protestant looked upon the hordes of Catholic immigrants with both fear and fury: fear because he saw in them a threat to his livelihood, his free institutions, and his prevailing social peace; fury because he saw the noble Protestant nation-state swarming with ignorant, superstitious, priest-ridden papists who infected the evangelical body with all the diseases of European Catholicism. And so he vented his spleen in an outpouring of books, pamphlets, magazines, lectures, and sermons that ranged from intense theological rebuttals on "Romanism" down to scurrilous fantasies about libertine priests, licentious convents, gluttonous bishops, and popes who stood ready (with their vast navies) to seize the American continent once Protestants relaxed their vigilance. The hysteria reached its heights in the nativist movements of the 1840's and 1850's and in the American Protective Association of the 1890's. The story has been told many times, and to rehearse it here would take us too far afield.[63] It needs mentioning, however, if we are to understand how the literary abilities of American priests first became absorbed almost exclusively in the task of apologetics.

The ranking Catholic priest-author of the 1840's, for example, was undoubtedly Father Martin John Spalding (1810–1872) of the Diocese of Louisville, later Archbishop of Baltimore (1864–1872). Of Anglo-American descent, Spalding devoted his three major writings, (1) *D'Aubignés "History of the Great Reformation in Germany and Switzerland," Reviewed,*[64] (2) *General Evidences of Catholicity,*[65] and (3) *Miscellanea,*[66] to the task of demonstrating not only the divine origin of his Church but also, from history and reason, the harmony of that Church with the major stated ideals of American Protestant faith and culture. The latter was the more pressing purpose, for Protestant writers were finding that theological arguments against Catholicism proved less effective than did social, political, and cultural arguments. Spalding's native upbringing enabled him to speak to these arguments in direct, matter-of-fact language weighted with a kind of reasoning that was most likely to win a favorable hearing from his countrymen.[67] In this respect he seems to have enjoyed more success than the Irish-born, Roman-trained, and more erudite Francis Patrick Kenrick, who, referring to his own major apologetical effort, *Vindication of the Catholic Church* (1855), conceded, "Controversial writing seldom convinces the adverse party. Prayer is more effectual."[68] When Kenrick published *The Book of Job and the Prophets* (1859), Brownson took the occasion of a review to suggest: "Most of our English Catholic literature has, at least to one not brought up a Catholic, something of a foreign air. . . . Most of our Catholic writers, educated abroad and in a foreign tongue . . . rarely write it [English] as their mother tongue. Their thoughts flow in Latin or French channels." [69] Other Irish apologists seem to have had equal difficulty, though not always for reasons of rhetoric, in addressing the American mind. A recent commentator contends that Bishop John Hughes of New York, through his inability to see the actual valid aspirations of Protestant New Yorkers, as well as through his occasional arrogance of expression, helped to incite the very bigotry or prejudice that he opposed in his diocese, and to bring into existence the now much-lamented "ghetto-mentality." [70] Of a similar sort was the Irish, American-born French-trained Bishop John Bernard Fitzpatrick (1812–1866) of Boston, whom Isaac Hecker described as one who ". . . was indeed a first-class mind both in natural gifts and acquired cultivation, but his habitual bearing was that of suspicion of error. . . . He was a type of mind common then and not uncommon now — the embodiment of a purpose to refute error, and to refute it by condemnation direct, authoritative, even if argumentative." [71] Fitzpatrick it was who persuaded Brownson to read the *Summa Theologica* of Thomas Aquinas and to refashion his apologetics in scholastic terminology, with the result that Brownson lost much of his free and persuasive touch with the American audience.

Until 1855 clerical apologetical literature aimed exclusively at diminishing prejudice and correcting misrepresentations. It contended that the Church deserved equal social status with other religious denominations, and sought to prove the external affinity of Catholicism to American institutions. In February, 1855, the convert Redemptorist Father Isaac Hecker published a small volume, *Questions of the Soul*, which inaugurated a modest shift in apologetical strategy from defense to offense.[72] Hecker was in an admirable position to approach the Protestant and secular minds in terms that they could appreciate. Born into a family that offered little in the way of religious training, Hecker found his way, with Brownson's help, to Brook Farm, a social experiment at West Roxbury, Massachusetts. There he discussed the great questions of life with Ralph Waldo Emerson, Henry Thoreau, Bronson Alcot, and other luminaries of the infant New England intellectual community. Dissatisfied with their answers, and again guided by Brownson, he entered the Catholic Church in 1844 and was ordained a priest of the Redemptorist order in England two years later. It would be difficult to imagine a better background for one who sought to mediate between the rich content of European Catholic intellectualism and the American mentality, as Hecker sought to do on the printed page and from the pulpit during the course of a long sacerdotal career as Redemptorist, and later, as a member of the Society of Missionary Priests of St. Paul the Apostle (Paulists), which he founded at New York in 1858.[73]

Questions of the Soul was the first published evidence of Hecker's ability to say the right things. He did not begin by arguing a logical defense of Catholicism from reasons drawn out of Scripture or history, but began, as most Americans seemed to begin when they examined great personal questions, by delineating the positive instincts and aspirations of man's nature. From that point he went on to ask, can Protestantism or representative philosophers, foreign or American, satisfy those legitimate instincts and aspirations? His negative answer led him then to suggest that Catholicism alone responded adequately to the cravings of the human heart. The method would be commonplace later in the century, in the days of Gibbons and Ireland, but at the time Hecker presented it, at the height of the Know-Nothing movement, it was startlingly new. The New York *Observer* noted its appearance as "a cunning artifice of Popery to catch the unwary," but in point of fact it was an artifice of native American genius.[74] Two years later, at Rome, Hecker expressed his conviction that, ". . . The longing after a more spiritual life is one of the principal characteristics of the American people. . . . Far from being a nation absorbed in commerce and in accumulating material wealth, there is no people who are so easily kindled to a religious enthusiasm." [75] Hecker may have been somewhat naïve in his appreciation of the Americans, but without a doubt his positive attitude was more likely to win a hearing for his faith than would be a censorious one. To him it was not necessary to graft Catholic thought onto the American main stem, for the two, in his view, were meant in God's providence to grow as one from seed-bed. Soon, he predicted, Catholic principles and American institutions would come together in intimate life and growth as they were meant to do from the beginning. It was an audacious proposition, and Hecker had his detractors among conservative Catholics as well as Protestants, but his vision and his labors helped build the first real bridge from "Romanism" to the American culture.[76] On the occasion of his death in 1888, the great English Cardinal John Henry Newman said: "I have ever felt there was a sort of unity in our lives, that we had both begun a work of the same kind, he in America and I in England." [77]

The Civil War (1861–1865) was probably a watershed in the maturation of the American Church, for with the onset of sectional warfare, bishops and priests for the first time entered national politics on an issue not directly affecting Catholicism as such. A presentation of the reasons why they had not done so before has already been attempted by the present writer.[78] Only after the guns began to roar, when it appeared that they could no longer stand apart from the civil agony and still claim the full loyalty of their subjects, did the clergy commit their pulpits to the fire of politics and war. As everyone else, bishops and priests lined up along geographical lines. It was a strange moment for the Church that had "left to worldlings the cares and anxieties of political partisanship." [79] But by the time peace settled over the charred ruins and the flag of the Confederacy was furled forever, it was clear that the American Church, like the nation, had changed. In October, 1866, the bishops of North and South assembled at Baltimore for a Second Plenary Council, as though nothing had happened, but something *had* happened, and because of it the Catholic clergy were of necessity more closely bound up with the nation, with her problems, social and economic, with her commonweal in general, with her destiny.

One indication of the modest degree to which churchmen drew close to the American experience during those years came in the surprisingly pragmatic, or one may even say ecumenical, approach taken toward Protestant society by American bishops attending the First Council of the Vatican at Rome in 1869–1870. The historian of American participation in that council tells us that the majority of bishops from this country opposed the definition of papal infallibility as "inopportune," on the very pragmatic grounds that it would worsen relations between Catholics and the dominant Protestant majority of their homeland. "Not all the Americans moved from this pragmatic position into a theoretical opposition. In the final analysis, only a handful did so. The basic American objection to the definition was a practical one." [80] Not the least surprised by that objection was the Catholic press at home. At the first, when news that infallibility might be defined reached American shores, in January, 1870, Catholic papers came out strongly in the dogma's favor. Later, after it became apparent that certain of the American bishops opposed the definition, papers under the jurisdiction of those prelates had to turn about sharply and begin writing about "inopportuneness," an idea that seems not to have troubled them before. It was a curious episode, but a significant one as well, because it showed the extent to which the bishops, including many of Irish extraction, were in advance of their priests and people at home. It suggests that the early development of a conciliatory Catholic approach to the American environment took place from the top down —

that the hierarchy, customarily thought of in America at the time as an eminently conservative group, in fact took the lead in seeking a mitigation of the tensions existing between Catholicism and American life.[81] Equally surprising to many were the unconventional, humorous, but thoroughly practical interventions of the French-born erstwhile Sulpician, Augustin Verot (1805–1876), Bishop of St. Augustine. Confounding the predictions of John England that a French priest "never can become American,"[82] Verot delivered some of the most characteristically American words at the council, and it is not too much to say that his allocution of May 28, 1870, would have delighted American ecumenists at Vatican II:

> I confess frankly that this council gave me high hopes of obtaining some reconciliation for the Protestants — high hopes, to be sure, if the exposition of doctrine made by this council were made plain, mild, and soothing — as far as the truth will bear — concerning those points which are subjects of controversy between Catholics and Protestants. . . . It seems to me that if the exposition on those points is softened and moderated by the council, then at least the door will be open. . . .[83]

Verot was not alone in his irenics. Many of the other Americans at Vatican I shared his conviction that more could be accomplished for Catholicism by the free exchange of convictions than had been accomplished to that date by hostile aloofness, by dogmatic pronouncements, or by the imputation of unworthy motives to the Protestant and secular majority. Their words and actions at Rome indicated to the highest assembly of the Church that they had decided to choose conciliation over stubborn resistance as the proper response to the new species of problems facing Catholicism in the United States.

One of the species of problems unforeseen by the bishops at that time, however, was the evolution of species. One year after the abrupt closing of Vatican I, Charles Darwin published *The Descent of Man* (1871), in which he made explicit what was only suggested in his 1859 work, *The Origin of Species* — the animal origins of man himself. For the first time, or at least since the Enlightenment, American Catholics were confronted by a major challenge to their religion that came not from Protestantism but from natural science. During the course of the next thirty years Darwinism, which began as a theory of "natural selection," "transmutation," and "survival of the fittest" to explain the development of the plant and animal kingdoms, was extrapolated by American and European thinkers, principally the latter, to explain the development as well of the inanimate earth and solar system, even of the cultures, societies, religions, and institutions of man. A new "religion of humanity" was born.[84] The same thirty years provides a typical case of the American Catholic clerical mind at work when placed in contact with secular sciences, as priests and bishops alike vacillated between granting the probability of evolution without fully accepting it and rejecting it without fully condemning it.[85]

For this reason probably more than any other the voluminous clerical literature on evolution in this period had, with but few exceptions, no apparent influence on Protestant and secular thought. It was a time when American society was polarizing intellectually to form a fundamentalist Protestant position on the one hand and a liberal Protestant secular position on the other. Catholic clerical leadership, which had only recently begun to sense that the American experience up to that moment had been basically non-ideological and middle-of-the-road, tried to steer a middle course in the controversy over evolution, with the result that it spoke effectively to neither side. By an unhappy irony, at the very time when clerics determined to try conciliation in place of stubborn resistance as the proper American strategy, conciliation was beside the point. It was not until 1896 that this species of intellectual isolation was discovered and exhibited, by Father John A. Zahm, C.S.C., professor in the University of Notre Dame and outstanding American priest-scientist of the nineteenth century. Wrote Zahm:

> Between the two theories, that of [immediate and total] creation and that of Evolution, the lines are drawn tautly, and one or the other theory must be accepted by all who make any pretensions intelligently to discuss the subject. No compromise, no *via media*, is possible. We must needs be either creationists or evolutionists. We cannot be both.[86]

Father Hecker and Brownson had a falling out very early on this matter. Brownson greeted *Origin of Species* and Sir Charles Lyell's *Antiquity of Man* (1863) as signs of "the deterioration of science," and stated that "St. Thomas had more science" than any of the Darwinists.[87] Hecker's periodical the *Catholic World* (founded by him in 1865) vacillated, taking a generally tolerant view of the theory in 1865–1867, turning to hostility in 1868–1872, reverting to a favorable opinion early in 1873, and then turning hostile once more in August, 1873, when it argued that, owing to the influences of such men as Herbert Spencer, Thomas Huxley, John Fiske, John Tyndall, Louis Buchner, Edward L. Youmans, and others, Darwinism was drawing many Americans away from Christian principles and toward those of materialism.[88] Most other clerics, meanwhile, looked for some authority who could represent an acceptable halfway house between the two. They found him in the English convert-biologist, St. George Mivart (1827–1900), whose book, *On the Origin of Species* (1871), put forward a theory that many thought compatible with both science and religion. Mivart accepted evolution, but not Darwinism (particularly not natural selection). He accepted the evolution of lower animal life, but not that of man. Persuasively argued, the solution was seized on by many priests who seemed as much comforted by it as convinced. Archbishop Ireland failed in an attempt in 1889 to have Mivart appointed to the chair of natural science in the infant Catholic University of America at Washington, but for American Catholics the biologist continued as the major alternative to Darwin until his death in 1900.[89]

Heavy criticism of evolution in any form continued to be heard from time to time. Father Edward Garesché, S.J., St. Louis University, arguing *ad hominem,* saw the evolutionists as men who worshipped matter and looked with ill-concealed scorn on supernaturalism and Catholic doctrine. When Professor John W. Draper of New York University published his famous pro-Darwin *History of Conflict Between Science and Religion* (1874), Garesché called it the "most trashy" book he had ever read.[90] Father Camillus Mazella, another Jesuit and professor of dogmatic theology in Woodstock College, Maryland, published a treatise, *De Deo Creante,* in 1877, in which various theories of evolution then current came in for rough handling.[91] Father Corcoran's *American Catholic Quarterly Review,* which began appearing in 1876, also took a strongly conservative position. Most priest writers struck a conciliatory note, however, and sought to develop a theistic understanding of evolution that protected the essential doctrines of Christianity. This was the case, particularly, in the 1880's when it became obvious that nearly all American scientists had gone over to the leading principles of evolution, and practically every Protestant theologian of reputation had embraced the theory.[92]

The increased openness of clerics to new currents of scientific thought was probably encouraged also by the intellectual interests of Pope Leo XIII, who had acceded to the papacy in 1878. Leo's encyclical letter *Aeterni Patris* (August 4, 1879) commanded the study of scholastic philosophy in Catholic seminaries and universities, but also urged greater familiarity by clerics and lay students with the findings of modern science. At the Third Plenary Council of Baltimore in 1884, the American bishops urged, "that the priest should have a wide acquaintance with every department of learning that has a bearing on religious truth." [93] For all these reasons and perhaps for others, where once the cleric sought to associate evolution with atheism he now sought to show that there was no necessary connection between the two. Father Hecker's successor as Superior General of the Paulists, Augustine F. Hewit, took a moderate stand on the question in the 1880's. Father John Gmeiner, at the time a professor in Archbishop Ireland's Theological Seminary of St. Thomas in St. Paul, wrote the first American Catholic book on the subject, *Modern Scientific Views and Christian Doctrines Compared* (1884), in which he not only presented a theistic interpretation of Darwin's theory but proposed evolution as a potential source of support for Christianity. God's providence and design, he said, were all the more wonderful for having been executed gradually. In his own way he was repeating, as were many Catholic clerics, an assertion by Henry Ward Beecher, pastor of Plymouth Church in Brooklyn, that, "design by wholesale is grander than design by retail" — a perfect expression for a business society.[94] Other priests, too, showed warm support for the theory, including the Paulist mathematician and astronomer George M. Searle (1839–1918), who, though he hesitated on the specific hypothesis of human evolution, accepted the general theory explaining lower forms as proven fact.

It was Cardinal Gibbons who gave the most representative evaluation of the whole controversy during the 1880's. Writing in the *American Catholic Quarterly Review,* Gibbons set out to put everyone's mind at ease on the question whether there could be any real conflict between revealed truth and scientific truth. There could not be, he assured his reader; and, furthermore, if Huxley and Draper were agnostics it was because they had been so prior to their scientific investigations. They were men blinded to the controlling supernatural mind whose workings were revealed in the natural sciences. "Small draughts of philosophy lead to atheism," he quoted from Francis Bacon, "but larger ones bring back to God." [95]

Lines appeared to harden in the last decade of the century. Those priests who thought at all about the problems posed to theology by evolution tended to form two sharply dissident factions. A conservative reaction was forming to the liberal-progressive direction being taken by many of the clergy, particularly those whose efforts to accommodate Catholicism to the American scene would earn them the epithet, "Americanists," and lead, unwittingly, to the repressive letter of Leo XIII, *Testem benevolentiae*, in 1899.[96] The intramural Catholic controversy over evolution during the 1890's did not, however, interest most thinking Americans. To secular and Protestant evolutionists the Catholic arguments, whether for or against the theory, seemed antiquated, parochial, and outside the current of important academic discourse. Perhaps more striking was the fact that Catholic objectors to the theory did not feel any affinity to Protestant fundamentalist objectors; on the contrary, priests were quick to disavow Protestant support and to point out that materialism was Protestantism's legitimate child, now turning against the parent. Again the isolated intellect prevailed.

As for Father Zahm, probably the ablest American Catholic scientist of the day, he had the unfortunate experience of following his own advice. After wavering for several years between creationism and evolution, in 1896 Zahm finally came down hard on the side of evolution, including that of the human body. On the lecture platform, at the Catholic Winter School in New Orleans, and the Madison (Wisconsin) Summer School, and in a much-noted book, *Evolution and Dogma* (1896), Zahm declared that a theistic understanding of man's evolution was justified theologically and philosophically, as well as scientifically. The book contained little that was new, but the vigorous, even provocative, style with which its ideas were put forward gave rise to a storm of controversy. The excitement was not helped by Zahm's incautious behavior and his curious penchant for sensation; it is said that Zahm himself edited a story which appeared in the New York *Herald* under the title, "Is Zahm a Heretic?" [97] Clerics who censured him included Bishop Sebastian G. Messmer of Green Bay, Monsignor Joseph de Concilio, who was reputed to have been the author of the Baltimore Catechism (1885), and Jesuit theologian Joseph Selinger. His chief clerical defenders were Louis A. Lambert, Dr. Edward A. Pacc (1861–1938), professor of philosophy in the Catholic University of America, and reviewers in every major American Catholic periodical. Zahm was promoted in 1896 to Procurator of the Congregation of Holy Cross at Rome and afterwards to Provincial of the American Province in 1898. During that same period, however, anti-"Americanism" forces were gathering strength at Rome and Zahm was taken in some Vatican quarters as a vulnerable symbol of the much suspected liberal Catholic movement in the United States. On September 10, 1898, the Sacred Congregation of the Index promulgated a prohibition against *Evolution and Dogma*. Monsignor Denis J. O'Connell, vicar of Santa Maria in Trastevere, Gibbons' titular church, wrote to Zahm, "Naturally one must consider the maneuver as a recognition of the part you played in Americanism." [98] Another friend at Rome, Cardinal Serafino Vannutelli, intervened to prevent publication of the decree, but the secretary of the Sacred Congregation of the Index demanded withdrawal of the book in all languages. A letter from Zahm to his Italian publisher asking that this be done became public and gave much satisfaction to his conservative critics.[99] Under the displeasure of the Holy See, Zahm's defenders fell silent. Zahm himself, censured at Rome and rejected as Provincial Superior by his own congregation, went off on world travels with Theodore Roosevelt and turned to writing travel books. The gulf between American Catholic thought and American scientific thought was fixed.

Much has been written in recent years about the alleged low state of higher education in American Catholic seminaries, colleges, and universities, as well as about what has been claimed to be the dearth of intellectuals among both clergy and laity in the American Church.[100] Particular criticism has been raised against deficiencies manifested in the present century, but the nineteenth century Church has not escaped blame either. It is not the purpose of this essay to rehearse that criticism, nor to evaluate it, except to point out that Catholic higher education in the last century was not alone in its inadequacies as judged by present standards. In 1869 the National Teachers' Association meeting in Trenton, New Jersey, declared: "We have, as yet, no near approach to a real university in America." [101] Seven years later the Catholic convert Bishop Thomas A. Becker (1832–1899) of Wilmington, himself a former student in the University of Virginia, pronounced the same judgment: "There is not *to-day*, in the entire country, a single institution, Catholic, Protestant (of any shade) or non-descriptive, entitled to the name of *university* in the European sense of the word." [102] The justice of these criticisms may be appreciated if one remembers that it was not until after the introduction of the German historical seminar system at the University of Michigan in 1871, and the organization of the first American graduate school at the Johns Hopkins University in 1876, that American secular and Protestant universities began to develop faculties, programs, and standards comparable to those found in German universities, by universal acknowledgement the finest in existence at that time.

Given the generally prevailing condition of American higher education in general, the anti-intellectual atmosphere of most American business society, and the special socio-economic handicaps facing American Catholics in the same period, it is not strange to find an even lower standard of higher education prevailing in Catholic institutions.[103] The quality of those institutions — there were some sixty colleges and seven so-called universities as the Church entered the last quarter century — was further handicapped by an overconfident academic presumption of already possessing the necessary truths of life, together with a conception of the university — a conception akin to that of John Henry Newman — as being a center for the diffusion of knowledge, not for research of new knowledge.[104] The professional education of the clergy was also of mediocre quality in this period, particularly of those clergy who matriculated at Sulpician and Vincentian institutions. Irish priests who studied at Maynooth or at All Hallows College, Dublin, may have fared slightly better, and this certainly can be said for German-born priests who completed their studies in Catholic faculties of the German state universities before emigrating to the United States. Some few Americans received their training in the Urban College of the Propaganda in Rome, after 1857 in the American College of the University of Louvain, and after 1859 at the North American College in Rome. In none of these institutions, however, with the exception of Louvain, was the young cleric who studied abroad put in touch with authentic university traditions and standards as they were taking shape in the latter half of the century.[105]

What is more important for the purposes of the present essay is the fact that neither the seminaries at home nor those abroad gave the candidate for priesthood any deep understanding of, much less any affinity to, the newly developing forms of natural and historical science. On the contrary, much seminary training of the time seemed directly calculated to insulate the cleric's mind from contamination by bacilli then circulating in the academic world. Even Thomism, or scholastic philosophy, which had been prompted by Leo XIII's encyclical *Aeterni Patris*, was seized on by some American Catholic figures as a protective instrument, indeed one whose claims to intellectual excellence far surpassed those of secular science. Cardinal William O'Connell (1859–1944) of Boston, remembering his days as a student in Rome (1881–1884), let it be known that, "The somewhat flamboyant mentality of the scientists of that time had little reverence for the exact intellectual processes of the Thomistic system." "Scholasticism . . . ," he complained, "the world of physical science was striving to bury beneath the disorderly mass of mere speculation. . . ." But no matter: ". . . Thomism very quickly regained a triumphant ascendancy over the whole world." [106] Such naïvete was not uncommon among churchmen on both sides of the Atlantic during the last decades of the century.

It caused many to bask not only in the presumed superiority of the scholastic system, but also in the equally presumptive scholarship of the typical American priest. The value of secular education was not even averted to. When a prospective Jesuit, Walter Drum, presented himself to a Jesuit provincial and suggested that he might first take a Ph.D. in English literature at Harvard, he was told: "Either you are going to be a Jesuit or not. If you are going to be a Jesuit, enter the Society now, and don't waste two years at Harvard. If you are not going to be a Jesuit, take up your life career at once, and don't waste two   years   at   Harvard." [107]   Either   way   a   Harvard   Ph.D.   was useless.

Certainly there was some intellectual arrogance at work among the clergy who spoke this way. There were cocksure clergy who tended to pontificate and to arrogate to themselves knowledge and authority not actually possessed. There were others who were simply smug, who manifested a quiet but immense satisfaction in the ownership of final answers to all the questions that really mattered. The mentality of the latter group might well have been represented in the opinions expressed by Monsignor M. O'Riordan, rector of the Irish College at Rome, writing in the pages of the New York *Freeman's Journal.* O'Riordan admitted that he knew little about science and the findings of contemporary researchers, since his time was more profitably spent in other studies, namely, metaphysics. Scholastic philosophy having given him one conception of the origin and nature of life, he resented the pretensions of physical science, an inferior discipline, to give him another one. Thus, as he stated proudly, he made no effort to understand the claims of contemporary academicians and instead rendered himself impervious to all the evidence in their favor.[108]

More realistic than the average clergy about the quality of the average American priest's mind were Father James F. Loughlin, erstwhile professor in St. Charles Seminary, Philadelphia; Bishop Becker; and Bishop Spalding. Writing in 1890, Loughlin argued that those who descanted glibly on the "intellectual status of our clergy" seemed to overlook the fact that clerical scholarship, such as existed, lay in areas "for which there happens *hic et nunc* to be a lamentably scant demand in the public market." He went on: "Our clergy may, indeed, and ought to 'shine before men' by their good works, by their zeal and energy; but their education has not been conducted along the lines best calculated to enable them to shine with brilliancy in point of scholarship in the midst of a population but slightly tinctured with classical lore, and unspeakably averse to metaphysical and theological investigations." [109] Becker had pointed to the same deficiencies a decade earlier, when he described "the utter superficiality" of many of the younger members of the clergy. "The age demands that we should keep pace with whatever is good in progress," he wrote, but

> . . . we suffer, as we do now frequently, because some ignorant men, to whom no institution ever accorded a diploma, make a false pretense of learning to the detriment of the good name and fair character of the sacerdotal office. [110]

No one, however, better expounded the need for higher education of the clergy than did John Lancaster Spalding. The Louvain-trained Bishop of Peoria spoke on the subject at the silver jubilee of St. Francis Seminary in Milwaukee on June 30, 1881, and reminded his hearers that, truth be told, seminaries such as St. Francis were "elementary schools of theology" whose purpose was to impart basic professional skills for the ministry and not necessarily to inculcate in young clerics the "best intellectual culture." Even the American colleges at Louvain and Rome must be seen as serving the first purpose; only the Jesuit seminary at Woodstock, Maryland, served the second, but "the secular priests of this country are not and cannot be brought under its influence." This being the case, what was needed, Spalding said, was a "High School" of philosophy and theology, on the order of the Dunboyne Establishment at Maynooth and the theological faculty of Louvain: "I am not speaking of a university, but of something far simpler, less expensive, and in my opinion, better fitted to supply the most pressing want of American Catholics. The institution of which I am thinking might be called a High School of Philosophy and Theology." [111]

Such a high school never materialized, but three years later, at the Third Plenary Council of Baltimore, Spalding *was* speaking of a university. His sermon during the Council on "University Education Considered in its Bearing on the Higher Education of Priests," delivered on November 16, 1885, repeated the criticisms he had made earlier of the typical American seminary:

> Its text books are written often in a barbarous style, the subjects are discussed in a dry and mechanical way and the professor wholly intent upon giving instruction, is frequently indifferent as to the manner in which it is imparted, or else not possessing himself a really cultivated intellect, he holds in slight esteem ex-

pansion and refinement of mind, looking upon it as at best a mere ornament.

Only a university, he had now decided, could provide the clergy with opportunities to pass beyond the requisite skills for the ordinary exercise of the ministry and to develop true intellectual culture. In an age when persecution of the Church was losing its harshness, when abuses had disappeared and heresy had, as Spalding thought, run its course, the challenge facing the Church in the modern world was "almost wholly intellectual," and it was not possible for her ministers to have too great power of intellect. ". . . When numbers of priests will be able to bring this cultivation of intellect to the treatment of religious subjects, then will Catholic theology again come forth from its isolation in the modern world." [112]

Spalding's university was subsequently founded in 1889, at Washington, D.C., under the title The Catholic University of America. Canonically erected with pontifical status, it was the only Catholic institution in the United States that professed to offer graduate studies exclusively. Bishop John J. Keane of Richmond was chosen as first rector (Spalding having declined the post). Of the ten faculty, one was a layman, Charles W. Stoddard, lecturer in English; two were Sulpicians, John B. Hogan, librarian, and Alexis Orban, spiritual director; two were American Paulists, Augustine F. Hewit, lecturer in church history, and George M. Searle, lecturer in science; and five were recruited from Europe: Henri Hyvernat, professor of Scripture; Joseph Schroeder, dogmatic theology; Thomas J. Bouquillon, moral theology; Joseph Pohle, philosophy; and Joseph Graf, music. For six years, from the date of its opening on November 13, 1889, the university served as a graduate school of theology for the clergy only. In October, 1895, its School of Philosophy and School of Social Sciences were opened to all qualified male applicants.

The benefits accruing to the clergy in the opening decades of the institution's history apparently were minimal, for at least three reasons: 1) Contrary to Spalding's expectations, only a handful of the clergy proved to be either prepared for or interested in graudate instruction. The clerical enrollment never rose much above the forty-six students counted in the first year. This fact together with the threat of financial bankruptcy in 1904 made it necessary to open the university to undergraduate lay students in 1905. 2) The university met with persistent opposition by Bishop Bernard J. McQuaid of Rochester, on the grounds that diocesan seminaries should have been erected first, and later because he disagreed with the choice of Washington as the site of the institution; [113] as well as opposition by the conservative Archbishop Michael A. Corrigan of New York, by many American Jesuits, and by most of the German bishops and priests of the country, who saw the university as a seedbed of Americanism and other forms of censurable liberalism. 3) The university and its faculty were very early caught up in the stormy controversies that swept the American Church in the 1890's. Professor Schroeder became the chief voice of German nationalism in the German-Irish contest already described; Professor Bouquillon supported Archbishop Ireland (and opposed his colleague Schroeder) on the advisability of seeking reconciliation of parochial and public education; [114] church historian Thomas O'Gorman, member of the faculty from 1890 to 1895, and the brilliant young professor of psychology and philosophy, Edward A. Pace, who joined the faculty in 1891, supported nascent Catholic movements, eventually labeled "Americanist," which sought to build intellectual bridges between Catholic thought and American culture; [115] Keane himself was dismissed as rector in 1896 for his part on the liberal, or progressive, side in the German-Irish, school, and "Americanism" questions. [116] Beset by these difficulties and divisions, it was unlikely that the new institution would be in a position to improve substantially the academic competence of the average American priest of talent, or to give him what Spalding prized so much, a *hauteur intellectuelle*. Indeed, as late as half-way into the next century the Catholic University of America would be not much more than an official training school for clerics, but that would be for different reasons than those which were at work in the 1890's.

The seminaries, meanwhile, were on the whole producing no better a product intellectually at the close of the 1890's than they were at their start, when Father Loughlin, one recalls, found the young clergy generally out of touch with the currents of contemporary American thought. Without examining in detail the condition of seminary studies at this time — for that is the purpose of Monsignor Ellis' companion essay in this volume — it is enough to say that the most penetrating critic of the *fin de siècle* seminary found that the institution's typical product was "an intellectually crude soul," and, what is more pertinent to the inquiry made in this present essay, that "in the presence of the questions of the day he is dumb." How did that intellectual isolation come about? The critic, Father John Talbot Smith of the Archdiocese of New York, explained:

> The habits of intellectual life in the seminary have dwarfed him [the young priest]. The curriculum rarely recognizes any-

thing but theology and philosophy, and these often isolated from present conditions and without practical application. The serious political life of the times is shut out deliberately from most seminaries with the exclusion of the journals and reviews; the great literary movements, the leaders of current literary thought are also shut out as unnecessary matters; scientific discussion has small place, and appreciation of scientific progress is impossible, because the whole round of the sciences is mostly ignored. History is taught in random, unscientific fashion, to judge the method by the results. . . . [The young priest] knows nothing of Emerson but that he may have been a pantheist, and is unable to appreciate the circumstances that bred any school of popular essayists, novelists, journalists. Such a man is no leader in the modern parish. . . . The priest must either lead or die. He cannot follow. He must be abreast of his day and ahead of it.[117]

Archbishop Ireland had been preaching the same theme all through the 1890's: "This is an intellectual age," he had said at the dawn of the decade. "It worships intellect." Priests, indeed all Catholics, should be in the foreground of intellectual movements of all kinds. "The age will not take kindly to religious knowledge separated from secular knowledge." [118] In 1893 Archbishop Ireland was warning that too many leaders of thought in the Church had made the mistake of being slow to understand the new age in which they ministered, and too slow to extend to it the conciliatory hand of friendship. The churchman's work was to "bridge the chasm separating the Church from the age." Ireland exulted: "I preach the new, the most glorious crusade. Church and age! Unite them in the name of humanity, in the name of God." [119]

Although not nearly so grandiloquently, Ireland was joined in this "crusade" by at least three other prelates of the time: his longstanding friend, Cardinal Gibbons, and Bishops Keane and Spalding. All were friendly to the American civil order. All were in tune with the Progressive Era concerns of political, social, and economic reform. All were engaged in efforts to accommodate the immigrant Church to American culture, and thus championed open, considerate, and pragmatic approaches to other faiths and culture-groups — approaches that would be elaborated by French theologians into the imaginary heresy of "Americanism." Ireland was perhaps immoderately American: his enthusiastic manner, combined with a mind never given to qualification, sometimes outraged conservative clerics. Gibbons, on the other hand, with his diplomatic habits and stately bearing, smoothed the rough edges of progressive Catholicism, dealt intimately and cordially with political leaders of the nation, and caused the Church he represented to be respected and admired by many Americans outside his communion. Gibbons vigorously supported movements to improve the intellectual tone of the clergy, and in a volume published in 1896, *The Ambassador of Christ,* argued that "there is no spectacle more deplorable and humiliating to the Church, than that of an ignorant and torpid clergy." Although piety was indispensable in a priest, it "can never be," he warned, "an adequate substitute for learning." [120] Nearly half the 400 pages in his book were devoted to the standards of learning that priests ought to maintain in a modern society.

Keane, with his fine mind and oratorical skills, took Catholic thought into forums where it had not appeared before, lecturing at Harvard University (1890), the University of Michigan (1891), Yale University (1891), Brooklyn Institute of Arts and Sciences (1892), and Brown University (1895). Keane associated freely with non-Catholic religious leaders and in 1893, with the consent of the archbishops, he took the lead in organizing Catholic participation in the Parliament of Religions at that year's World Columbian Exposition in Chicago. For the first time, American Catholic speakers shared equally a public platform with Protestants, schismatics, Buddhists, Parsees, and representatives of other world religions and sects. Keane spoke at the parliament himself, as did Gibbons and Ireland. Papers explaining Catholic doctrine were given by a team of articulate priests which included Augustine Hewit, C.S.P., Walter Elliott, C.S.P., Thomas O'Gorman, John Gmeiner, and John R. Slattery, among others.[121] Keane contended, in an ecumenical spirit worthy of a later time that, "It is only by a friendly and brotherly comparison of convictions that reasonable men can ever come to an agreement about the all-important truths which are the foundation of religion. . . ." [122] But the Catholic part in the Parliament met with severe criticism, even shock, in some Catholic quarters. Fr. David S. Phelan's *The Western Watchman* of St. Louis, always watchful for signs of theological liberalism, said of the Catholic participators: "They were indiscriminately *levelled* with publicans and heathens in that heterogeneous gathering making up a discordant babel of creeds." [123] And despite a favorable account of the proceedings sent to Rome by Gibbons, Pope Leo XIII shared the conservatives' concern. In a letter to the Apostolic Delegate Francesco Satolli, dated September 18, 1895, Leo condemned any further participation by Catholics in gatherings similar to the one held in Chicago.[124] The premature ecumenism of the progressive clergy, born out of the American experience, expired before it could be taken from the incubator, and its like would not be seen again for half a century.

Like Gibbons, Ireland, and Keane, Bishop Spalding participated in many of the public economic and social reforms advocated in the Progressive Era. He possessed probably the finest mind in the American clergy, and seems to have been recognized generally for that distinction. Some historians single him out as the best example in the period of a thoroughly American Roman Catholic intellect.[125] It needs to be said, however, that Spalding and his like-minded confrères were not typical of the episcopacy at large. On the contrary, in any estimate of the intellectual attainments or interests of the other eighty-three archbishops and bishops of the country during the most exciting decade in American Catholic history prior to the 1960's, one would have to conclude that no more than twenty were deserving of special notice, and none, with the exception of the conservatives McQuaid of Rochester and Corrigan of New York, ever approached the distinction of Spalding and his friends.

Still, it was the bishops, and not the younger clergy, who formed the cutting edge of the American Church. Just as at Vatican I the bishops led the way in seeking to adjust Catholic thought and practice to the exigencies of the American situation, so now it was the older clergy, specifically four or five bishops, who attempted to propel the priesthood into the twentieth century. For their pains they were condemned as "Americanists" and Leo XIII communicated to them and to their supporters his "suspicion that there are some among you who conceive of and desire a church in America different from that which is in the rest of the world." [126] The principals concerned denied that they had any such conception or desire, and pledged their unswerving loyalty to the Holy See.[127] Still, the sword had been dropped, and its action left the Church in the United States not sundered, but gravely bruised. Like the lame and the halt, a cautious priesthood hobbled over the threshold of the new century. As the historian of the "Americanism" episode recounts: "The story of the Catholic Church in the United States during the next two decades is the story of the rejected Americanists hoping for changes that did not come and their opponents trying to solve the problem of getting Catholicism accepted in American circumstances without adopting the policies they had condemned in their opponents." [128] Why the changes did not come is a story in itself, and is best entitled: "Modernism."

MODERNISM

There was a modest flowering of American Catholic clerical culture in the first seven years of the twentieth century. Despite the pall cast by the condemnation of Americanism, the American priest during this period displayed a surprising intellectual activity. He may have been daunted politically, socially, and ecumenically by the condemnation, but intellectually he ranged farther and more freely than he ever had before, seeking to know whatever was true in the relationships between religion and the new physical and historical sciences. Why this was the case it is difficult to explain. The encouragements to learning given by the Church's most prominent personalities from the Third Plenary Council through the 1890's, the presence and influence of a national Catholic University, the increased frankness and openness of the Catholic press, and the growing number and quality of clerical publications certainly were contributing factors. In addition, the excitements of the previous decade had caused clerical minds to question, to search, and to experiment, all processes which, once started, were hard to brake. Beyond these reasons it is not safe to go: the plain, startling fact is that the American Church seemed suddenly ready to enter an intellectual renaissance, a "golden age," as inexplicable, at bottom, as all such ages in human history. Paradoxically, at the same moment, officials of the new pontiff, Pope Pius X (1903–1914), were moving along non-parallel lines, anxiously alert for any signs of theological compromise. The disjunction of movements did not bode well.

The American Catholic Quarterly Review was probably the foremost exemplar of clerical intellectualism at the onset of the century. Its pages, published by Archbishop Patrick John Ryan, carried accounts of the latest scientific discoveries, articles on the most recent advances in scriptural exegesis, historical science, and evolution studies. In general, the *Quarterly* demonstrated an open approach to the major scholarly questions of the day and provided a forum for gifted clerics such as James A. Burns, C.S.C., Thomas Shahan, Walter Elliott, C.S.P., William J. Kerby, and Charles P. Neill. The *Catholic University Bulletin*, damaged somewhat in the Americanism controversy, showed new vigor and a high intellectual quality. The *American Ecclesiastical Review*, owned and edited by Father Herman J. Heuser, professor of scripture at St. Charles Seminary in Philadelphia, carried both signed and unsigned articles on recent scriptural studies and the European-bred "higher criticism." Articles by and about the soon-to-be-condemned Alfred Loisy and George Tyrrell, S.J. appeared in its pages, as did lively discussions on the new apologetics of Maurice Blondel, historical criticism, and the advantages and the disadvantages of Scholastic methodology.[129] Tyrrell's writings were also carried in the *Dolphin*, a monthly periodical published briefly in conjunction with the *AER*, first (1901) as a book review and literary supplement, and afterwards (1902–1905) as "An Ecclesiastical review for educated Catholics."

The *Homiletic and Pastoral Review* began to appear in October, 1900, under the title, *The Homiletic Monthly and Catechist*, but it limited itself during the first decade to sermon topics and outlines for pulpit use. The American priest had access to Catholic literary culture in publications such as the *Catholic World* and *Ave Maria*, and to American Jesuit writings in the *Sacred Heart Messenger*. Father John O'Brien of East Cambridge, Massachusetts, edited the *Sacred Heart Review*, which had an attractive variety of departments and foreign correspondents. Interested priests could also read, and many did, foreign theological periodicals such as the *Nouvelle Revue théologique* from Belgium; *L'Ami du Clergé* from France; *La Scuola Cattolica, Civiltà Cattolica,* and *Divus Thomas* from Italy; the *Irish Ecclesiastical Record* from Ireland; and *Theologische Quartalschrift* from Germany and *Theologisch-Praktische Monatsschrift* from Austria. Until the middle of the decade, however, there would be no American scholarly product of merit comparable to the periodical and book literature of the European Church. Then, in 1905, two events occurred which revealed how deeply the American priesthood was penetrating, and was being penetrated by the currents and standards of modern scholarship. In that year Sulpician priests of the faculty of St. Joseph's Seminary, Dunwoodie-Yonkers, New York, founded the *New York Review*, the first scientific Catholic theological journal in this country. And a joint clerical-lay board of editors began commissioning articles for the *Catholic Encyclopedia*, a scholarly compendium which, when published (1907–1914), would stand for half a century as the most significant Catholic reference work in the English language.[130] Of the *New York Review* more will be said later.

The major centers of Catholic intellectual life were the Catholic University of America, where men like the Louvain-trained sociologist, Father William J. Kerby (1870–1936), were breaking new ground in the social sciences, and three of the country's seminaries: St. Joseph's in Dunwoodie-Yonkers, St. Charles in Philadelphia, and St. Bernard's in Rochester. For the first year of the decade St. John's Seminary in Brighton, Massachusetts, boasted one of the finest individual minds of the American Church in its rector, John B. Hogan, S.S. (1829–1901). And for the whole of the decade St. Paul Seminary in St. Paul, Minnesota, possessed the pioneer social philosopher John A. Ryan (1869–1945), whose work, *A Living Wage: Its Ethical and Economic Aspects*, published in 1906, won national attention.[131] None of the seminaries had graduate faculties, at a time when graduate schools were beginning to direct the course of American thought. Their principal function continued to be to produce a parochial clergy, but in this they seemed to be producing on the whole a more knowledgeable cleric than they had in the past, and Archbishop Ireland told the Baltimore *Sun* in 1903, "I believe that in the very near future the Catholic clergy of the United States will be as thoroughly educated and as thoroughly well adapted to meet the conditions and requirements of the day as any clergy of the day, even that of Rome." [132] Ireland was certainly too optimistic, however. Seminary faculties were overworked, many instructors having to serve in parochial capacities on weekends, with the result that there was little time given for reflection, much less for writing. The major writing continued to be done in Europe. This observation applies to the religious as well as to the secular clergy. The Jesuits, with their graduate theology faculty at Woodstock, and numerous colleges and universities, were best prepared of all the orders to influence the American intellectual scene, and they may have done so in a very modest measure. The Paulists continued to work among Protestants and non-Christians. However, the remaining communities — Franciscans, Dominicans, Redemptorists, Augustinians, Vincentians, Holy Cross Fathers, Marists, *et al* – appear to have had no impact on currents of thought outside their faith, even outside their respective communities.

The Paulists entered university life during this period as chaplains to Catholic students attending secular institutions. Thomas Verner Moore, C.S.P. went to the University of California at Berkeley in 1906, to take direction of the Newman Club founded there seven years before under a curate of the local parish, Father John J. Cantwell. The thirty-year-old Moore had impressive scholarly credentials, including a doctorate in psychology from the Catholic University of America and post-doctoral training in Leipzig under Wilhelm Wundt. He was ill-suited to chaplaincy work, however, and recurring conflicts with San Francisco Archbishop Patrick W. Riordan led to his dismissal in 1909. Riordan strongly supported the university apostolate but thought that Moore was too young, saying ". . . it cannot be handed over to boys." "The chaplain," Riordan said, "is brought into contact day by day with Professors of the University, and he must be looked up to by them." [133] To replace Moore, the Archbishop of San Francisco succeeded in persuading the Paulists to assign George M. Searle, the seventy-year-old former superior general, an esteemed astronomer, who earlier in life had taught at the United States Naval Academy and at the Catholic University of America. Meanwhile, interest in the university ministry grew in other parts of the country: at the University of Pennsylvania in Philadelphia where the first Newman Club in the country had been founded in 1893; at the University of Wisconsin in Madison where Archbishop Messmer of Milwaukee appointed Henry C. Hengell as chaplain in 1906; and in Rochester, New York, where in the same year, 1906, Bishop McQuaid proposed to the archbishops of the country his "Cornell Plan" for attaching a Catholic college, similar to the university colleges at Oxford, to Cornell University in Ithaca.[134] The "Cornell Plan" would never materialize, owing both to more immediate building needs at St. Bernard's Seminary and to McQuaid's failing health — he died in 1909 — but Riordan, a supporter of the Plan, predicted the future only too clearly when he wrote to McQuaid: "No matter what we do or say, these secular universities are going to be frequented by a large number of Catholics, both boys and girls, and unless we provide for their religious necessities such as is done in Oxford and Cambridge these students will drift away from us." [135]

Of all the geographical districts in the American Church, New York City and vicinity had the greatest concentration of Catholics in the opening years of the new century, with about 825,000 in the Archdiocese of New York, 500,000 in the Diocese of Brooklyn, and another 272,000 across the river in the Diocese of Newark. Socially, economically, and politically, New York also had at this time the most influential clergy of any major Catholic center, numbering among its pastors such men as McGlynn and Burtsell, Joseph H. McMahon, Joseph Mooney, James Flood, John Edwards, James H. McGean, Patrick McSweeney, James Nilan, Frederick Wayrick, Anthony Kessler, and Anthony Lammel.[136] Intellectually, the most distinguished body of priests in New York, possibly in any diocese, formed the faculty of St. Joseph's Seminary at Dunwoodie-Yonkers. Although the seminary was officially under the direction of the Sulpician Fathers, no less than eight of its fourteen-member professorial staff were secular priests at the time James F. Driscoll, S.S., D.D., professor of Semitic Languages, became rector in 1902. Several of the faculty who served during the decade were distinguished for their scholarly achievements. Francis E. Gigot, S.S. (1859–1920), was undoubtedly the most advanced Catholic scripture scholar in the American Church, and its most knowledgeable authority on European Catholic studies in higher criticism. Scholars of various faiths acknowledged the scholarship demonstrated in his many articles and in two widely used manuals, *General Introduction to the*

Study of the Holy Scriptures (1900) and *Special Introduction to the Study of the Old Testament,* two volumes (1903–1906). A fair insight into his mind can be gathered from these remarks in a 1900 article on "The Study of Sacred Scripture in Theological Seminaries":

> . . . The time is gone when the questions involved in the higher criticism might be simply identified with rationalistic attacks upon the revealed word. Again, one can no longer afford to be ignorant of topics which, perhaps more than any others at present, engross the attention of the intellectual and religious world. . . .[137]

Joseph Bruneau, S.S., S.T.L. (1866–1933), professor of dogmatic theology at Dunwoodie, enjoyed a wide reputation as an expert on apologetic writing, particularly that emerging from the Blondel school in France. Dr. Gabriel Oussani (1875–1934), Baghdad-born secular priest, came to Dunwoodie in 1904 as professor of Oriental history and Biblical archeology. He had studied classical Arabic, Syriac, Turkish and French at the Patriarchal Seminary in Mosul (ancient Niniveh), Mesopotamia, received ordination from the Urban College of the Propaganda at Rome in 1900, and arrived in the United States in the following year to become a fellow in Semitic languages at the Johns Hopkins University. From the time of his inaugural lecture at Dunwoodie and for the next thirty years, New York could claim one of the most distinguished Orientalists in the country.[138] Less distinguished, perhaps, but better known to American Catholics for his later service as a chaplain with the Rainbow Division in World War I, was Francis P. Duffy (1871–1932), professor of philosophy and a priest of the archdiocese. Duffy, whose statue stands in Times Square, was a man of wide scholarly interests — theology, history, science, literature, as well as philosophy — and he enjoyed both professional and friendly relations with the English Jesuit Tyrrell. Of him the Sulpician vicar-general in the United States, Edward R. Dyer, S.S., said in 1905: "Father Duffy is one of the most efficient men I have ever seen at work in a seminary, — he is near enough to the ideal Professor and Director to say that he is It." [139]

It was Duffy and another diocesan priest on the faculty, John F. Brady, professor of philosophy, who conceived the *New York Review,* to which allusion has already been made. Its origins are described in a letter from Driscoll to Dyer, dated January 11, 1905:

> Not long ago a scheme was proposed to me which, without my knowledge, had for some time previous been maturing in the minds of a few of the professors, notably Fathers Duffy and

Brady. It referred to the founding of a review, the headquarters of which would be in the seminary, and the editorship in the hands of the Faculty, myself and Father Duffy assuming the chief responsibility. The object of the publication (which would be brought out every two months) would be to discuss in a scholarly way, yet in a manner intelligible to ordinarily cultured persons, lay or cleric, the various questions with which the modern Christian apologist has to deal — mainly those pertaining to Scripture and Philosophy. . . . We decided to lay it before the Archbishop [John M. Farley (1842–1918), Ordinary of New York since 1902], for which purpose Father Duffy and myself went to see him. . . . It was just what he wanted. He expressed his deep, long-standing regrets at the backwardness of Catholic writers in matters of modern scientific interest, and gave as his opinion that it was due in great measure to the exaggerated restrictive policy of the ecclesiastical authorities, who through their unreasonably stringent methods of censorship (Index, etc.) only succeed in stifling all initiative on the part of the ablest and best-disposed Catholic scholars.

Driscoll went on to name the scholars whom he and Duffy were soliciting as writers, and he assured Dyer that he would not have to accept responsibility for the review: "All we desire and expect is to be let alone." [140] Dyer was only too willing to decline responsibility; indeed, he wrote to Farley asking if the archbishop would write a letter stating that *he* was assuming responsibility as Farley subsequently did, in March of the same year.[141] At the same time, Dyer was irked that he had not been asked permission to begin the review. "Is it the right thing," he asked Driscoll, "that a man who has a duty and consequent right to speak, to give a decision, be set over in a corner to look on at the performance, and told to approve if he feels like it, but that he is not expected to manifest any disapproval should such be his judgment, for if he does, what is he going to do about it?" [142]

For their part, the Sulpician members of the Dunwoodie faculty were also irritated, but for other reasons, mainly the repressive Sulpician censorship under which they labored. Gigot, for one, had been trying since 1902 without success to obtain a *nihil obstat* for the second volume of his Old Testament textbook. By January, 1906, he was sufficiently frustrated to tell Dyer that he had reached the limit with St. Sulpice, "that he had had enough of its killing repression; that it was impossible under such a system, to accomplish any real work. . . ." [143] With the exception of Bruneau, the other Sulpicians shared Gigot's misgivings about the future of authentic scholarship under Sulpician auspices, and on January 9, 1906, they addressed a joint letter to Dyer announcing: ". . . We have decided to sever our connection with the Company of St. Sulpice, and have accepted the offer of the Most Rev. Archbishop and his council to continue the seminary work as priests incorporated into the Archdiocese of New York." [144] As might be expected, this news, together with another report that Farley was taking over the seminary, came as a hard blow to Dyer, who worked quickly in an attempt to repair the breach. But it was too late, and Dyer had to content himself with expressions of pique, which he published and distributed widely.[145] The Sulpician superior attempted to cast blame for the defections, not on his own failure to improve the censorship problem (which is where the defectors cast it), but on the arrogance of the Dunwoodie faculty in founding the *Review* without the Sulpician superiors being consulted beforehand. Driscoll said vaguely that their leaving was "not the outcome of any controversy concerning their orthodoxy or that of the *Review*, but was due to a concurrence of circumstances quite foreign to that matter." [146] At Dunwoodie the transition of five faculty from Sulpician to diocesan status took place almost without notice, except that the one Sulpician loyalist, Bruneau, repaired to Baltimore where he became professor of dogmatic theology at St. Mary's Seminary, and his courses at Dunwoodie were taken over by Brady.[147]

In the meantime, the *New York Review* was underway, the first number having appeared in June-July, 1905. Driscoll was editor, Duffy, associate editor, and Brady, managing editor. The "Announcement" introducing the *Review* repeated the purposes described in Driscoll's letter to Dyer, and further stated that the reviews of material bearing on theology, scripture, philosophy and the cognate sciences would "draw attention to the needs of the present intellectual situation in matters of religious belief." In this and in the numbers which followed during the *Review's* brief lifetime the list of contributors included such names as: George Tyrrell, Wilfrid Ward, Vincent McNabb, Ernesto Buonaiuti, Henri Bremond, and Pierre Batiffol from abroad; Gigot, Duffy, Oussani, William L. Sullivan, C.S.P., John A. Ryan, and Pace from the United States. So advanced and open was the publication that Driscoll had to defend its editors against the suggestion, made in the editorial pages of the Boston *Transcript*, that the *Review* represented a "new liberal Catholicism." [148] Driscoll asserted:

> . . . It is hardly necessary to say that there is not the least intention on the part of the founders and promoters of the *Review*

to inaugurate a movement that could in any sense be termed a 'new Catholicism.' To entertain such an idea would be absurd — there could be no surer means of defeating the real purpose we had in view. This purpose . . . is not to abandon the old in favor of the new, but rather to interpret with becoming care and reverence the old truths in the light of the new science. The task, as it appears to us, is not one involving doctrinal change, but restatement and readjustment — in other words, the preservation and not the rupture of continuity.[149]

Driscoll had implemented these purposes in other ways besides the *Review* since becoming rector of St. Joseph's in 1902. A former student at the Catholic Institute of Paris, where he was, according to a close friend, "a much-beloved pupil of Loisy," [150] Driscoll had long been convinced that the work of a seminary was to produce priests who were not only pious, but cultivated in the things of the mind. The effective ministry of priests in the modern world, he thought, depended on their being made aware of what was happening on the American and world scenes, intellectually, culturally, and socially. To this end he did away with the usual round of seminary lectures on "The Novel," "Medieval Guilds," "Literature of the Grail," and such topics, and in their place substituted guest lectures by Protestant as well as Catholic authorities, on such more pertinent topics as "The Catholic Church and Twentieth Century Thought," "Theological Needs," and "Socialism." To Dunwoodie came Dr. Charles A. Briggs (1841–1913), president of Union Theological Seminary, and professors from the faculty of Columbia University, as well as knowledgeable Catholics such as philosopher Father James J. Fox (18?–1923), of the Catholic University of America; the biographer of Hecker, Father Walter Elliott, C.S.P. (1842–1928); Father Edward J. Hanna (1860–1944), professor of dogmatic theology at St. Bernard's Seminary, Rochester, New York; and Father Giovanni Genocchi, M.S.C. (1860–1926), an Italian, consultor of the Pontifical Biblical Commission, whose progressive views would cause him some trouble in Rome after 1907.

Nor did Father Driscoll content himself with bringing outside authorities to the seminary: he encouraged his students to pursue courses in their spare time at New York University, and with President Nicholas Murray Butler and the Trustees of Columbia University he negotiated an arrangement whereby Dunwoodie students were accepted as graduate students in that institution and permitted to attend lectures, at no tuition cost.[151] In sum, Driscoll's was a bold program, of which the

Review was but the chief external result and evidence. New York appeared to be leading the American priesthood into a new day. More than any diocese, religious order, or seminary elsewhere in the country, New York was opening its eyes and ears to the proclamation of truth in the natural, historical, and social sciences. More than any other it was promoting the study of theology and scripture in depth, in consort with the best minds in Europe, and in conjunction with the full range of human wisdom. More than any other it was preparing American Catholicism for what a later epoch would call *aggiornamento*. And for all these reasons, New York, more than any diocese, order, or seminary elsewhere, stood in an acutely vulnerable position as storm clouds boiled on the Atlantic horizon.

The lightening struck finally in 1907. On July 3 of that year, the Holy Office issued a syllabus, *Lamentabili sane exitu*, listing sixty-five heretical propositions taken mostly from the writings of Loisy.[152] And on September 8, Pius X issued an encyclical, *Pascendi Dominici gregis*, condemning the errors of what the pontiff called "modernism." What were these errors? An exhaustive answer would take us too far from the focus of this essay. Suffice it to say they included most attempts then being made by European Catholics, priests and laity, to incorporate the most recent non-scholastic research and scholarship into the development of theology and scripture studies. Implied in the encyclical's description of "modernism" were such diverse tools or directions of thought as historical criticism, literary exegesis separate from dogma, naturalistic evolutionary philosophy, the immanentist or experiential theologies of Friedrich Schleiermacher and Albrecht Ritschl, the pragmatism of William James, the intuitionism of Henri Bergson, Neo-Hegelianism, and Neo-Kantianism. Nor does that complete the list of the categories that Pius X had in mind. The encyclical cautioned, *in globo*, against all systems of thought by whatever name which expounded an evolutionary theory of religion, or suggested that the Church had reshaped external truths in every period of history according to its understanding, or otherwise threatened the validity and the stability of dogma.

But just as modernism itself was too varied to admit of precise definition, its proponents too were never so like-minded that they formed one school; and even within the single modernist breast there beat the heart of many different interests. As the encyclical observed, the typical modernist was a manifold personality: he was a philosopher, a believer, a theologian, an historian, a critic, an apologist, and a reformer. His heresy was, not that he had many interests or had learned many things, but that he had used his knowledge "to subvert the very kingdom of Christ," principally by his suggestion that the essence of Christianity lay not in intellectual propositions nor in creeds, but in the very processes of life. Pius X obviously had in mind such men as Loisy and Tyrrell. Of them and others like them the pontiff said:

> . . . None is more skilled, none more astute than they, in the employment of a thousand noxious devices; for they play the double part of rationalist and Catholic, and this so craftily that they easily lead the unwary into error; and as audacity is their chief characteristic, there is no conclusion of any kind from which they shrink or which they do not thrust forward with pertinacity and assurance. To this must be added the fact, which indeed is well calculated to deceive souls, that they lead a life of the greatest activity, of assiduous and ardent application to every branch of learning, and that they possess, as a rule, a reputation for irreproachable morality.[153]

If the modernists had any fundamental faults, it was unregulated curiosity and excessive pride. On the first point Pius X quoted Gregory XVI from the latter's encyclical, *Singulari nos*, of 1834:

> A lamentable spectacle is that presented by the aberration of human reason when it yields to the spirit of novelty, when against the warning of the Apostle it seeks to know beyond what it is meant to know, and, when, relying too much on itself, it thinks it can find the truth outside the Catholic Church, wherein truth is found without the slightest shadow of error.[154]

As for pride, "It is pride which puffs them up with that vainglory which allows them to regard themselves as the sole possessors of knowledge." Not only that, "It is pride which arouses in them the spirit of disobedience, and causes them to demand a compromise between authority and liberty." For these reasons, Pius X advised the bishops in every diocese, ". . . It will be your first duty to resist such victims of pride, to employ them only in the lowest and obscurest offices." [155] This first duty was then followed by other commands equally restraining: e.g., committees of vigilance were to be set up in each diocese for the purpose of detecting the presence of heresy; professors sympathetic to modernist views in seminaries or in Catholic universities were to be discharged "without compunction"; books, periodicals, and newspapers dealing with religious matters were to be subjected to the closest scrutiny and, where necessary, censorship; all future congresses of priests were prohibited, except on rare and prudently guarded occasions; and priests were forbidden to pursue studies in secular universities if the same courses were available in Catholic institutions. In his *motu proprio, Praestantia Scripturae,* dated November, 1907, Pius X declared as binding all doctrinal decisions, both past and future, of the Pontifical Biblical Commission, thus placing tight reins on Catholic scriptural interpretation. Three years later, in another *motu proprio, Sacrorum antistitum,* dated September 1, 1910, the pope further restrained clerics from the dangers of modernism by the celebrated Oath Against Modernism, required of all candidates before ordination to the subdiaconate, and of priests before assuming certain offices, especially the episcopacy. And corollary documents, issued through 1913, prescribed strictures on seminaries and their courses of study, making the scholastic method mandatory, establishing Thomism as the sole system of thought in Catholic institutions, and, in general, discouraging all disinterested intellectual activity among clerics preparing for ordination.[156]

The impact of *Pascendi* on the Church in the United States was not immediately discernible, for at least three reasons: 1) The matters treated by the 1907 encyclical were not subjects of popular interest in the American Church. They were of interest solely or primarily to those comparatively few bishops and priests who had access to official Roman periodicals or who read regularly one or more technical theological journals from Europe. Knowledge of the encyclical's contents did not become generally known in this country until 1908, when the *Ecclesiastical Review* devoted three articles to the subject and four books were published explaining both modernism and the pope's condemnation of it.[157] Even then, popular interest did not run high. 2) There was no great passion among American church leaders in support of the root principles of modernism as there had been certain enthusiastic, though unavowed, episcopal supporters of the root tendencies condemned as Americanism. Indeed, there was probably no real connection between the Americanist and modernist movements either by way of cause or practical preface.[158] The former was an alleged attempt by some churchmen in the United States to accommodate Catholic teachings and practices to the American lifestyle, and as a movement it was largely devoid of theological content. What little there was of theological activity in the American Church was conducted apart from the national culture. For that matter, most theology taught in the schools was still imported in packaged form from Europe, and thus was hardly susceptible to Americanist influences.

Modernism, on the other hand, was a specifically theological phenomenon, with origins in European endeavors to adapt dogma, not to
social or political life-styles, but to what was considered sound in
modern thought. Where Americanism with its pragmatic and earthy
themes very plainly touched the exposed nerves of the Church in this
country, it was not to be expected that modernism, with its purely
intellectual concerns, would touch American Catholics with the same
intimacy. The Church in the United States was a different community
from that in Europe. 3) The number of actual American modernists
was small, so small as to be insignificant. The unidentified author of
"Modernism in the American Church," in the *Ecclesiastical Review*
for January 1908, wrote: "It is our frank opinion that the evils of
which the Pontiff chiefly complains exist to a very large and dangerous
extent in the United States." [159] However, no other writer seems to
have had that opinion, including Anthony Viéban, S.S., of the St.
Mary's Seminary, Baltimore, who in the same publication four months
later expressly directed himself to the question, "Who are the Modernists of the Encyclical?" and gave no indication that any Americans
held the condemned doctrines.[160] A Redemptorist, Charles Warren
Currier similarly surveyed the modernism problem in the November and December, 1908, issues of the *Ecclesiastical Review* without
citing any American names.[161] Still, there were certainly some identifiable modernists, the best-known of whom was William L. Sullivan
(1872–1935).

A graduate of St. John's Seminary in Brighton and the Catholic
University of America, Sullivan had been ordained a priest in 1899.
He joined the Paulists, and in 1902–06 taught at St. Thomas College
(the Paulist house of studies) in Washington; in 1906–08 he worked
at the Paulist Center in Chicago, and in 1908–09 took charge of the
newly opened Catholic chapel and lecture hall at the University of
Texas in Austin. He was a prolific writer on religious subjects and an
enthusiastic backer of the *New York Review*, to which he contributed.
On May 1, 1909, a convinced modernist, Sullivan resigned his pastorate in Austin and five days later formally announced his withdrawal
from the Paulist community and the Catholic Church. He spent most of
the remainder of his life as a Unitarian minister in New York,
Missouri, and Pennsylvania, dying at Germantown, Pennsylvania, in
1935.[162]

John R. Slattery (1851–1926) was another priest of pronounced
modernist convictions. Ordained in the Mill Hill community in 1877,
Slattery served as Provincial of the American Province of the Mill

Hill Fathers (1878–1883), and later as first Superior of the St. Joseph's Society for Colored Missions (Josephite Fathers), from 1892 to 1903. He read widely, in Protestant and secular fields as much as Catholic, studied abroad under Loisy in Paris and Adolph von Harnack in Berlin, and wrote articles for the New York-based Protestant weekly, *The Independent.* Slattery resigned his priesthood in 1904 and publicly renounced it two years later in an article, "How My Priesthood Dropped From Me," published in *The Independent.*[163] There is no doubt that Slattery was a "modernist," and to him we owe one of the most informative articles on the subject, "The Workings of Modernism," which he wrote in 1909 for publication in the *American Journal of Theology.*[164]

A third identifiable modernist was Thomas J. Mulvey, ordained at the Urban College of the Propaganda at Rome in 1899, who served as assistant pastor in two Brooklyn parishes, St. Francis of Assisi (1899–1904) and St. Edward's (1904–1908), before resigning his priesthood on July 17, 1908. In an interview published in the next day's New York *Sun* Mulvey explained that he had long considered the condemnation of modernism by Pius X and had reached the conclusion that in conscience he could not accept it.[165] One day later, the New York *Times* carried a statement on the Mulvey departure by Cardinal Gibbons, in which the prelate expressed the opinion, probably correct: "This is the first defection from the Church on the grounds of modernism since the Pope's encyclical letter defining and condemning that heresy."[166]

There were, then, at least three American clerics to whom the appellation "modernist" could be applied with justification. That there were not more is owed to the first two of the three reasons offered above. The English historian, Alec R. Vidler, wrote in 1934: "American Catholics do not seem to have been much troubled by doctrinal difficulties; absorption in 'practical Christianity' was their besetting weakness."[167] George Tyrrell had earlier said much the same thing to Sullivan, complaining:

> I cannot understand America. . . . Modernism has produced there hardly an echo. The Church in America is asleep; and I can conceive nothing that will awaken it, but the production of some book native to the soil.[168]

Even more critical was Sullivan himself. Although the period 1900–1907 had been a time of modest intellectual increase among American seminarians and priests, when many were beginning to move off the foothills of defensive apologetics and to test their energies on the higher slopes, it is still true that a great distance separated them from the mountaintops, and, allowing for the bitterness, there is more than a grain of truth in Sullivan's reason why there were so few American priests susceptible to modernist influence:

> Modernism, while not wholly, is predominately an intellectual movement . . . [and] the men sent to the seminaries by Catholic colleges are in a condition of almost scandalous unfitness for prosecuting the higher studies of an ecclesiastical course. . . . Not only were these candidates deficient in positive erudition, but . . . they were mentally untrained, unable to grasp a problem, incapable of thinking for themselves and formulating an independent personal conclusion on a matter of scholarship.[169]

The above three reasons suggest why there was little initial excitement in the American Church as a consequence of *Pascendi,* to which the bishops made the normal, expected responses. Many hastened to express their obedient acceptance of the document in letters to Pius X, disclaiming at the same time any modernist persons or tendencies in their respective dioceses. Others addressed pastoral letters to their people or, as in New York and Philadelphia, gave public discourses on the subject.[170] Predictably, the Board of Trustees of the Catholic University of America, meeting at Washington on November 13, 1907, agreed that modernism was a serious danger to the Church, established a committee of revision to survey modernist books in the library of the University, and instructed Cardinal Gibbons, Chancellor of the University and President of the Board of Trustees, to write a letter to Pius X declaring the complete submission of the University and its trustees to the encyclical.[171] At Saint Charles Borromeo Seminary in Overbrook, Pennsylvania, Father Herman J. Heuser, editor of the *Ecclesiastical Review,* gave assurance of his orthodoxy in a proclamation to the faculty assembled in the seminary chapel.[172] Similar scenes, though less dramatic, were repeated elsewhere.

There was never any question that the American Church would comply with the Roman directives. The encyclical was accepted quietly, obediently, and, for the reasons advanced above, with no marked trauma. For all that one could see, nothing special had happened. Seminaries continued classes as before, bishops and priests continued on their accustomed rounds, and the poor had the gospel preached to them. The face that the Church presented to the nation at large remained the same. Still, something, indeed, occurred, something unperceived at the moment, something whose long-range impact on American Catholic thinking would be hard to exaggerate. The Church

of the United States was overcome by a *grande peur*. As 1908 proceeded on its course a gradually enveloping dread of heresy settled
over episcopal residences, chanceries, seminaries, and Catholic institutions of higher learning. Security, safety, conservatism became national
imperatives. Free intellectual inquiry in ecclesiastical circles came to a
virtual standstill. The nascent intellectual movement went underground
or died. Contacts with Protestant and secular thinkers were broken
off. It was as though someone had pulled a switch and the lights had
failed all across the American Catholic landscape.

The chief example of this blackout, as might be expected, occurred in
the Archdiocese of New York. And the first object to fall under darkness,
as might likewise be expected, was the *New York Review*. In middle
January, 1908, Archbishop Farley received a communication from the
Apostolic Delegate to the United States, Archbishop Diomede Falconio,
which expressed dismay that the most recent number of the *New York
Review* carried an advertisement for the books of George Tyrrell.[173]
The delegate declared the advertisement to be a violation, both in letter
and in spirit, of the encyclical *Pascendi*, which — he found it worth
an exclamation mark — was reproduced "in the same number of the
New York Review!" He continued:

> Knowing well how much you have at heart the execution of
> our Holy Father's dispositions, I take also the liberty of sug-
> gesting that for the future Your Grace should see that writers
> who have a tendency for the condemned doctrines of modernism
> should not write for the Review, or, at least, that they should
> first submit their communications to your approval.
>
> *In confidence* I tell you that it has made no favorable im-
> pression in Rome to see in the Review articles contributed, not
> only by Rev. Fr. Tyrrell, but also by Ernesto Buonaiuti, Nicola
> Turchi of Rome, and by the Abbés [Ernest] Dimnet and [Albert]
> Houtin of France.[174]

Farley replied at once. Quite out of character with his other actions
in the modernism crisis, the episcopal patron of the *Review* exhibited
in this instance a rare courage. Both his facts and his language must
have taken the delegate by surprise. He began by naming points on
which Falconio's informant was in error:

> On making diligent search through the Review and on inquiry
> from the editors, I find that neither the Abbé Dimnet nor Abbé
> Houtin ever wrote a line for the Review, nor were they ever in-

vited to do so, nor did their names ever appear on the list of its contributors. There are only two references in the whole Review to Abbé Houtin and these references condemn him.

Farley then cited the two passages in which Houtin came in for a scolding, and he concluded:

> Certainly Your Excellency will admit that it must be the very spirit of malevolence which prompted the party who complained to you, to say that the Review in any way favored either Houtin or Dimnet, and I feel that you will not fail to so inform this person whoever he may be.

The Archbishop of New York's implication would appear to be that Falconio should have read through the numbers of the *Review* himself. In the paragraphs which followed, Farley admitted that Tyrrell, Turchi, and Buonaiuti had, indeed, published articles in the *Review*. Of Tyrrell's two articles the archbishop said that they were "both written while he was yet a Jesuit and supposed to be in good standing." As for Turchi, who contributed one article, Farley said, with what might have been a delicate touch of sarcasm:

> Neither this article nor anything we knew of the writer would lead us to suspect that he was in any way identified with the Modernist movement, especially as he is employed as a professor in the College of the Propaganda, Rome.

Buonaiuti had contributed two articles, but, as Farley observed, "He was editor of a Review in Rome and it was naturally supposed that he was all right." The Archbishop then turned to the question of the advertisement for Tyrrell's books. This appeared, he explained, through the inadvertence of Father Brady, the managing editor, whose father lay near death at the time the proofs of the advertisement came to the editor for approval. From want of sleep, Brady was worn out, "and not expecting anything wrong did not examine [the advertisement] and sent it to the printer. No one regrets this blunder more than he does; it has filled him with mortification." [175] Farley enclosed a letter for the delegate from Brady, who, curiously, gave a slightly different explanation, stating that he never even saw the proofs, and in the normal course of preparing the *Review* would not have done so. Advertising proofs, he wrote the delegate, "are not sent to me for correction but to the advertising parties, and so the contents of the page did not come under my notice until the issue of the Rev[iew] was printed." [176]

This, in any event, appears to be the last time that Archbishop Farley stood by the *Review* and its editors. The next two numbers would be the last. Without having received any formal condemnation from the ordinary or from Rome, the *Review* simply ceased publication. Dated Volume III, No. 6 (May-June, 1908), the final offering contained an announcement from the editors on the front inside cover informing subscribers that "the number of Catholics interested in questions which are of importance to the thinkers of the present generation — and which will be vital to all classes in the next" had proved to be disappointingly small, hence, lacking sufficient financial support, the *Review* would have to discontinue publication. It is doubtful, however, that financial reasons alone explain the whole story of the *Review*'s demise, although it must have been true, with the modernism scare spreading through the ranks of the clergy, that the audience for original scholarship was drying up; with vigilance committees established in most dioceses, it is not likely that most priests would want to be discovered with the *New York Review* on their lamp tables. Other causes of its demise can be cited. For example, in all likelihood Archbishop Farley developed a case of acute prudence. Falconio had sounded the tocsin. So had Farley's own Roman informants, as we shall see. The Archbishop of New York could not afford to be connected with heresy or heretics, however remotely. And probably, in his capacity as censor, he did not believe himself capable of deciding what was orthodox and what was not: after all, as his letter to Falconio complained, the orthodox thinker of yesterday was the heretic of today, even when he was a professor at Rome! In support of this view, the American modernist William Sullivan wrote in 1944 that "Cardinal Farley told Dr. Driscoll that intimations from a certain quarter counseled its [the *Review*'s] suspension." [177] Houtin, for his part, held the opinion that articles in the *Review* by Edward J. Hanna, Joseph McSorley, C.S.P., and Cornelius Clifford "motivated its suppression." [178] Whatever the exact reasons, the *Review* passed into the oblivion prepared for it by *Pascendi*, and its like would not be seen again until the appearance of the Jesuit-edited *Theological Studies* in 1940.

Archbishop Farley had his own informants in Rome, and one of them, Monsignor Thomas F. Kennedy, Rector of the North American College since 1901, wrote in December, 1907, three days before his consecration as bishop, that he had not only heard "very harsh criticisms" of the *Review*, but that he was concerned as well about the *Catholic Encyclopedia,* the first volume of which had appeared in 1907 under Farley's sponsorship. "In confidence and as a friend," he said:

I beg you to keep a close watch on all the articles published therein. It bears your imprimatur or at least you are held responsible for it. So it would be terrible if any sentence had to be struck out. That thought came to me when the Card[inal]. Prefect of Prop[aganda]. sent over here for a copy to examine the article on Absolution written by Dr. Hanna. I told the messenger (Msgr. Conte) that the only copy I know of in Rome was that I presented to the Pope. He said he would send to the Secretary of State for that. So you see they mean business.[179]

Learned reviews and encyclopedia articles were not the only ground on which the Archbishop of New York felt tremors. A fault ran through the city of Rome itself, as Farley learned from an unnamed correspondent, who advised that four of Farley's priests, who had been sent to Rome for graduate studies to prepare them to teach in the seminary, were consorting with known "modernists," specifically Giovanni Genocchi and Antonio Fogazzaro.[180] The four clerics were John J. Mitty, future Archbishop of San Francisco (1935–1961), Francis X. Albert, Edwin Ryan, and Daniel W. Sheeran. To them Farley wrote in January, 1908, expressing his uneasiness at the reports received, and urging the priests to exercise extreme caution in their personal contacts. Before the priests could reply, Farley received an explanation of the Genocchi contact, probably from some acquaintance of the priests at the seminary. He would use it in reply to Archbishop Falconio, who, in his letter of charges against the *Review* written on January 15, concluded with this allusion to the New York priests in Rome:

> Even some fear is entertained in regard to the students of your diocese who frequent the Universita Gregoriana in Roma and who board at the Convent of the F[athe]rs Pallottini, Via S. Silvestro, on account of their familiarity with some one of the above mentioned modernists.[181]

In his reply Archbishop Farley told the delegate that, on inquiry, he had learned that when the priests first arrived in Rome they knew no Italian, and, wishing to receive the Sacrament of Penance, confessed to Father Genocchi, whom they knew from his visit to Dunwoodie the year before as one who spoke English. But having heard of their contact with Genocchi, and that he was suspect in some quarters, Farley had written his priests "warning them to have no association with any person suspected of the new errors." There may have been a trace of acid in his final remark that he had sent them to Rome in preference to Innsbruck, Freiburg, or Jerusalem so that they would be "farther removed" from doctrinal heterodoxy: "Surely, I said, they will be safe in some religious house in the Centre of Christianity." [182]

Farley's assumption appears to have been that Genocchi was the "some one of the above mentioned modernists" in Falconio's letter, even though Genocchi was not mentioned by the latter. Curiously, when Mitty replied to Farley in the name of all four priests he seems to have assumed that Fogazzaro was the leper. Mitty wrote:

> As to the reports you have heard concerning us, I would say: Some days after our arrival in Rome, we paid a visit to Father Genocchi, the head of the Novitiate of the Missionaries of the Sacred Heart. Just before we left Signor Fogazzaro entered and we were introduced to him. We conversed with him for about two or three minutes on different topics (what part of America we came from, the time of our arrival in Rome, and the length of our stay here) and then we took our departure. The meeting was unexpected and accidental. From that moment to this we have never seen Signor Fogazzaro, nor held any communication of any kind with him and I doubt very much if we should even be able to recognize him again. The statement of having met him at dinner is entirely untrue.[183]

In April, the other three New York priests wrote to Farley disclaiming any guilt by association with known modernists. Albert reasserted "our faithful and devoted stand towards the authoritative teaching of the Church and . . . our distant attitude toward everything and everybody tainted with Modernism as condemned in the recent Encyclical." [184] Ryan allowed that Farley's letter of caution "cast something of a cloud over our life here," and expressed disappointment that "there are persons in Rome — perhaps even at San Silvestro — given to purveying news of much the same character and value as that which reached you." [185] Sheeran, the last to write, promised "a more rigid avoidance of all suspicious circumstances" and thanked the archbishop for his "kindly note of warning." [186] The correspondence reveals the tension of the four young clerics as they sought to pursue studies in the midst of a witch hunt. The experience was hardly calculated to open their minds to the world of disinterested scholarship. And their travail was not soon ended. In August of the same year, with Farley's permission, Mitty, Ryan, and Sheeran moved to Munich. Albert visited them for a time in the fall, before resuming his courses at Rome, and communicated to them yet another warning from Farley, "to take every precaution against any suspicions of Modernistic tendencies." Albert reported his confrères as being "greatly surprised" to receive this second warning, but it was well-conceived.[187] Roman eyes saw as far as Munich, as Farley would learn from his gossipy friend, the Rector of the North American College, who wrote:

> Cardinal Merry del Val told me to write you in confidence to keep a close watch on your students at Munich i.e. those young priests who were here at S. Silvestro last year. He says Munich is no place for young priests at this time. . . . (Now I know that those young priests go around with turn down collars and red and white neckties. One attends the lectures in a travelling cap. That is causing comment and has been reported at the Vatican.)[188]

Bishop Kennedy was not done with his tale-bearing. Informing the Ordinary of New York about the sartorial indiscretions of his priests at Munich could perhaps be considered as well-intentioned and friendly counsel. But how account for his telling the same things to the delegate in Washington, Archbishop Falconio? No doubt this is what Farley wondered when, in January, 1909, he received a précis of a conversation between Falconio and Kennedy, who was visiting in Washington. The report came from William Hughes, a priest of the Archdiocese of New York, and former professor of church history at Dunwoodie (1904–1908), who had recently been appointed secretary to the Apostolic Delegation. Hughes' communication provides perhaps the best example in the period of the degree to which the inquisitorial spirit and intramural abuse infiltrated the calm of American Catholicity. Hughes began by saying that Kennedy had arrived at the Delegation on the morning of the day he wrote, January 4, and entered at once into a discussion with Falconio on the subject of the former Sulpicians on the faculty at Dunwoodie. The conversation then turned to Farley's priests at Munich, about whom Kennedy had worse things to tell Falconio than he had told Farley. Hughes wrote:

> First of all the Bishop [Kennedy] told me, and the Delegate just reiterated it from his own inner consciousness, that the young priests together with the Dunwoodie professors (the ex Sulps.) had done the Archdiocese much harm. Despite the fact that Bp Kennedy warned the young men, they were repeatedly seen on the streets with the suspected men and while in Munich the doffing of the Roman collar was merely by-play. The real offense was

attendance at the lectures of the suspected and — in one case at least — the condemned professors.

Hughes concluded with even darker news:

> The last point is this. The Delegate says that it is positively sure that there is a group of eight Modernists in the Diocese. He does not know their names for he refused to accept the information. He has no doubt of the accuracy of his information, and from what I gather, the Holy See knows of the existence of the coterie.[189]

No such coterie was ever assembled for condemnation, but with communications of this sort coming into Farley's hands, it is no marvel that the Archbishop of New York should have put the clamps on his seminary professors, his student priests, and his clergy at large. In fact he had begun these actions in the preceding June with the demise of the *New York Review*. In the following month, while in Rome, he sent a cablegram directing his vicar-general to remove the progressive rector of the seminary, Father Driscoll, and to assign in his place John P. Chidwick, New York police force chaplain. Driscoll was appointed to Chidwick's parish, St. Ambrose in Manhattan, and little was heard from him again.[190] Chidwick implemented the new dispensation by severing all connections with Columbia University and for the first time making Latin mandatory for all classes.[191] The repression was on. Brady left Dunwoodie in 1910 to become vice president of the College of Mount Saint Vincent at St. Vincent on-the-Hudson. Francis Duffy survived at the seminary until 1912 when, at his request, he was named pastor of a newly established parish in the Bronx which he named Our Savior. In point of fact, his scholarly work had come to an end in 1908. Another professor whose scholarly writing ceased in that year was the Chaldean, Gabriel Ousanni. For the next quarter century, Ousanni obediently taught from acquired knowledge rather than from original research. Such is the recollection of those who knew him. Once when a seminarian asked him if a certain French writer had been suspected of modernism, Ousanni replied that everybody who was not dead at that time was suspected of modernism.[192] No doubt there were other intellectual casualties at Dunwoodie and in the New York clergy resulting from the bomb dropped by Farley, but the scholarship that might have been is not such as can be recorded in chronicles or archives. What E.E.Y. Hales said about the post-modernism Church in general could be said about New York's priest-intellectuals in particular:

We shall never know how many valuable shoots, which might have brought forth good fruit, were killed, alongside the dangerous errors, when the bomb dropped, nor how many men were prevented, thereafter, from ever thinking at all because some had fallen into error in their thinking. The price that has to be paid when such high explosive is used can be tremendous; a kind of intellectual sterilization may be included when thinking becomes so dangerous.[193]

Nor was New York the only example of the new philistinism, although it was no doubt the best. Rochester, New York, and Washington, D.C. also had their moments. At Rochester, forty-seven-year-old Edward J. Hanna, professor of dogmatic theology in St. Bernard's Seminary, learned during the summer of 1907 that his name had been submitted to Rome as a candidate for coadjutor to Archbishop Riordan of San Francisco. The professor was *dignissimus* on the *terna*, an honor that owed much to the support of his ordinary and Riordan's good friend, Bishop McQuaid. Unfortunately, Hanna had written. During 1905 and 1906 he had published an essay, "The Human Knowledge of Christ," in three short installments in the *New York Review*;[194] in 1906 he had published a short survey, "Some Recent Books on Catholic Theology," in the Protestant periodical, the *American Journal of Theology*;[195] and he had contributed the article on "Absolution" to the first volume of the *Catholic Encyclopedia*, which appeared in 1907.[196] Unfortunately, too, Hanna had, unknown to him, a delator among his colleagues on the Rochester faculty who would turn the first of these writings against him.

The delator was Andrew E. Breen, for twenty-five years professor of Sacred Scripture, whom McQuaid would describe later as being "possessed with insane jealousy of Hanna."[197] When he learned of Hanna's candidacy, Breen wrote a friend at Rome, who would be certain to pass the letter upward to the proper authorities, attacking the articles on the human knowledge of Christ for being based on the writings of "rationalists"; the series should rather have been entitled, he charged, "The Ignorance of Christ." Breen's letter also attacked Hanna personally, alleging that he was a "man who covets his own advancement, and who lacks firmness of character, a courtier, shifting where the wind blows."[198] At the same time, from another and unknown source, Roman authorities received accusations that Hanna's encyclopedia article, "Absolution," violated proposition forty-six of the 1907 papal decree *Lamentabili*, specifically, that sentence of the article which read: "But it is one thing to assert the power of absolution was granted to the Church, and another to say that a full realization of the grant was in the consciousness of the Church from the beginning." [199] Riordan went to Rome on Hanna's behalf, and Hanna himself attempted to vindicate his orthodoxy with a fourth article on "The Human Knowledge of Christ," followed by another entitled "The Power of the Keys (I)" which clarified the encyclopedia article on absolution, both of which appeared in the same number of the *New York Review*.[200] But it was to no avail. Discovery of the *Journal of Theology* article, and a criticism of it as tending toward modernism by the Servite theologian Lépicier, voided the value of his contributions to the *Review*, and Hanna was passed over in favor of Denis O'Connell, Rector of the Catholic University of America. O'Connell was appointed auxiliary to Riordan on December 24, 1908. Four years later he was translated to the See of Richmond, whereupon Riordan asked again for Hanna. This time Hanna made it. He had passed through the valley of the shadow of modernism.[201]

At Washington, well before *Lamentabili* and *Pascendi*, suspicion had fallen on Father Charles P. Grannan, head of the Department of Sacred Scripture in the Catholic University of America. In April, 1907, Grannan was accused by some in the University community of teaching opinions contrary to decisions of the Biblical Commission. The trustees adopted a resolution asking his resignation, but the rector, Denis O'Connell, refused to support the action, and the resolution was rescinded by majority vote of the trustees on April 10.[202] The incident was an unfavorable omen for Grannan's associate professor of Scripture, Dutch-born Henry A. Poels, who at the same time was wrestling with the problem of the Mosaic authorship of the Pentateuch. That Moses was the author of the first five books had been ordained as normative teaching in a four-part decree dated June 27, 1906, of the Biblical Commission, to which Poels was a consultor, and in the summer of 1907, to set his mind at ease, the exegete went to Rome to see Pius X. Receiving what he thought was sanction from the pope to continue teaching despite his doubts, and encouraged by Genocchi and Lawrence Janssens, O.S.B., secretary of the Biblical Commission, to do the same, Poels returned to his Washington classroom. Thereupon followed over the course of the next three years a muddled series of misunderstandings, mistaken identities, lapses of memory, accusations, and exonerations, involving such high personages as Pius X, Merry del Val, and Gibbons — events of a nature too complex to be rehearsed here.[203] It is enough to say that the whole murky story reflected the fears, the anxieties, and the inquisitorial atavism of the counter-modernism period and Poels, though no doubt innocent of most aspersions made against him, and undeniably loyal to the Holy See, was finally forced into resignation at the end of the 1909–1910 term. He returned to his native Holland, after shaking the dust off his feet in a pamphlet entitled, *A Vindication of My Honor.*[204]

There was little doubt by 1910 that a decisive pall had fallen over intellectual activity in the teaching and, *a fortiori*, the pastoral priesthood of the United States. No cleric wanted to be counted part of a subversive conspiracy against *Mater Ecclesia*, and none wanted, by his writing or instruction, to lead others into temptation. Original research became original sin. The study of theology became the study of approved manuals, usually bad translations from the German. Critical studies in scripture yielded preeminence to *parti pris* history of the Church and to moral theology. The seminary faculties devoted themselves exclusively to the training of assistant pastors. The ordinary clergyman and layman lapsed into silence on matters bearing on doctrine. Bishops were selected for their orthodoxy, and almost all for the next two decades came out of Roman seminaries. The *Catholic Encyclopedia* continued to appear, but its editors paid a visit to Rome to assure Vatican authorities of the publication's orthodoxy.[205] The *Ecclesiastical Review* became strictly pastoral in character; the *Catholic University Bulletin* shed the high intellectual quality that it had exhibited for several years and became a small information bulletin; and the *Catholic World* went into the literary field. The American clerical mind turned in on itself, became romanticist, read Gilbert Keith Chesterton's new book, *Orthodoxy* (1908), with self-congratulatory fervor, and agreed with the great "G. K." that, "If there is one class of men whom history has proved especially and supremely capable of going quite wrong in all directions, it is the class of highly intellectual men." [206] In these circumstances, it goes without saying that in the years following 1907 there was exceedingly little communication between the Catholic priest and the American intellectual community. The critical mind lay at ruinous discount.

AFTER MODERNISM

The *Ecclesiastical Review*, which was the most representative journal of the clergy during the first quarter century after *Pascendi* and the only continuous source of clerical thought we have from 1900 to the present, waited twenty-two years before it carried an article urging priests once again to build bridges to the American intellectual community. "There is need for modern scholarship," said its author, the young Father John A. O'Brien of the Catholic chaplaincy at the University of Illinois. "There is need of familiarity not merely with the thought of the thirteenth century, but with the thought of the modern world." He mentioned the new advances in physics, astronomy, anthropology, comparative anatomy, paleontology, archaeology, psychology, biblical criticism, and historical sociology. "By identifying the new learning with heresy," said O'Brien, quoting Erasmus, "you make orthodoxy synonymous with ignorance." [207] But even at that date, 1930, no one was listening. At that time the thirteenth century was everywhere the model of orthodoxy, and worshipful Thomism was the normative science. That the scholastic method was the sole approved mode of thinking for clerics, *Pascendi* had left no doubt. One of the 1908 volumes explaining the condemnation of modernism to the American public had arranged the encyclical's passages in question and answer form: In discussing the intellectual causes of Modernism the encyclical was quoted as citing in the first place, "ignorance." The interlocutor exclaimed at that point: "Ignorance! — in the Modernists who think themselves so learned! — can that really be true?" To which the encyclical replied: "Yes, these very Modernists . . . who speak so loftily of modern philosophy, and show such contempt for scholasticism, have embraced the one with all its false glamor precisely because their ignorance of the other had left them without the means of being able to recognize confusion of thought and to refute sophistry." Two pages later the encyclical was quoted to this effect: ". . . There is no surer sign that a man is tending to Modernism than when he begins to show his dislike for the scholastic method." [208]

No wonder the seminaries ignored John A. O'Brien and stuck to their mandate as *laudatores temporis acti*. It was unsafe to do otherwise. In philosophy, scholasticism, mostly of the manual variety, was pursued with undivided vigilance. The manuals hesitated before no problem, and they rendered universal everything they touched. "Catholic philosophy alone has the whole truth," wrote one seminary professor in the *American Ecclesiastical Review*. "Every other system has some truth, exaggerated or perverted." And he allowed himself this exuberance in closing: "Until the heavens be no more, the Scholastic philosophy will endure." [209] All across the country seminarians were indoctrinated in the science of matter and form, substance and accident, essence and existence. They were asked to memorize, in Latin, answers to questions and problems that had not been posed for hundreds of years. A combative atmosphere prevailed. Adversaries were seldom considered in their context; instead straw men were set up for swift knocking down. Students developed the weakest of all attitudes toward adversaries, that of contempt.[210] Thus the young priest went "out into the world" with an unarticulated protective tariff against threatening ideas and a sufficient number of absolute first principles to allow him to bask in certainty all his days. Indeed, as Albert Power, S.J., pointed out in a 1929 book:

> Once you know the facts of any particular subject, you can think about that subject only in one way — you cannot hold any view you like about it, e.g., if I ask you whether it is night or day, you cannot have two opinions on the subject — your freedom to think as you please is limited by the fact that you know which it is. . . . The truth has put a stop to the swaying of the mind.[211]

The presumed certainties of scholastic philosophy overflowed naturally into the field of church history where, true to the maxim, what was not permissible could not have happened — *nicht sein kann, was nicht sein darf* — a retouched picture of the Church was often presented as a means of showing future priests that the Church had overcome all intellectual attacks, that the thirteenth truly was the "greatest of centuries," [212] and that Catholicism would "still exist in undiminished vigour when some traveller from New Zealand shall, in the midst of a vast solitude, take his stand on a broken arch of London Bridge to sketch the ruins of St. Paul's." [213] Having all the answers, as unfortunately the seminaries seemed to claim, made not only unattractive but also unnecessary anything like intellectual inquiry. Thus, students were rarely, if ever, required to do research or collateral reading. One consequence of that dogmatic slumber was described by a young priest in the pages of the *Homiletic and Pastoral Review* in 1923. Writing under the name "Victim" and addressing himself to the question, "Are Our Priests Intellectual?" he gave the following reasons from his seminary experience to support a negative answer:

> Study time was consumed in reading papers, magazines, and the modern novel. Conversations were about sports, theaters, parties, the latest 'dope' and scandals of the diocese, defects and faults of professors, fellow students, seminary rules, and generally the meals. The individual who talked about class matter at any time was branded contemptuously as a 'highbrow' or an 'intellectual.' The very term 'intellectual' was a term of opprobrium.[214]

In such descriptions one sees all too clearly the bleak effects of a pedagogy that fixed the mind in mindless certainties. It was not Thomism, as such, which created the intellectual desert which was the

American seminary system, but the manner in which Thomism was masticated, pre-digested, and force-fed. When Thomas à Kempis, read in chapel, declared, "I would rather feel compunction than know its definition," most seminarians knew exactly what he meant. Passing to theology, one hardly felt the passage. As one theologian said recently, "The theology of this period was actually taught more as a 'stepped-up' philosophy course than as a true science of faith." [215] The only real difference: selected scripture quotes were added. Nor surprisingly, the saying originated, "If you make it through philosophy, you can more or less sleep through theology." Here everything was arranged on a philosophical base, perennially fixed theses were provided for the benefit of rote memory, and the Bible was available as a source-book for rational-historical "proofs." One came out of the course equipped with a consoling number of immutable certainties of faith, not to mention a strong orientation toward apologetics, which was needed, it goes without saying, to show that the intellectual world outside the Catholic system was one of bewildering confusion.

As for further studies in theology, Father Charles Bruehl told the reader of the *Homiletic and Pastoral Review* that he need not worry much about theology, which is, he said, "fairly standardized." "All that is required of him," he added, "is to review what he has learned, here and there to expand it and to gain a deeper insight into its meaning." [216] The whole process was a veritable "cult of pure reason," and, indeed, in its often arid rationalism it resembled, of all things, the Puritan theology of early New England, in accordance with which the first body of College Laws at Harvard required the student to be able not merely to read the scriptures, but "to Resolve them Logically." Perry Miller stated that for the Puritan minister "interpretation of scripture was an abstruse art, to be learned with diligence, to be employed with caution, and to be regulated by the immutable laws of right reason and infallible logic." [217] Or, of course, one could go back to medieval Christianity for parallels, which is exactly what Winfred Ernest Garrison did in 1928 for his book, *Catholicism and the American Mind*: "Catholicism today," he said, "is less modern and more medieval in both doctrine and discipline than it was a generation ago. . . . The liberalizing movements within the church which were active thirty years ago have been either crushed out or driven under cover." [218]

What of the priests out in the field? Why could not an intellectually oriented priest come out of a parish into academic centers of national influence as Reinhold Niebuhr came out of a busy industrial parish in Detroit where he had served for thirteen years? [219] Was it for lack of study time? A priest correspondent in the *Homiletic and Pastoral Review* in 1923 argued no, saying: "Let it not be said that the busy parochial life of this country is responsible. For any priest who has had wide experience knows that many of those who are most intellectual are most active in practical affairs. . . . Neither let it be alleged that our clergy have no time, for they find plenty of spare time and opportunity to do the things they like." [220] Another priest correspondent in the same year agreed with this argument and explicitly rejected by name the "brick and mortar" excuse. "Pressure of parochial work" and "lack of time," he added, "may be excuses for not being able to *satisfy* intellectual tastes, but surely not for the *lack* of them." [221]

This is not to say, however, that there were not many priests who regarded their position *vis-à-vis* the general intellectual in the best possible light. One enthusiastic cleric, again in 1923, told the readers of the *Homiletic and Pastoral Review* that priests formed intellectually a *gens electa*. "I dare say" — he did in fact dare to say — "any of us could put out a weekly magazine at two dollars a year that would make the *Atlantic Monthly* . . . look like a kindergarten primer, provided, of course, that we had a Rockefeller Foundation at our back." [222] Such conceit showed especially in matters scientific. Here, of course, it was impossible for the priest to hold himself apart from influences that came from the general intellectual community. Science was too obviously successful to be ignored; its accomplishments were incontrovertible. And although clerics were quick to attack the occasional scientist who wandered out of his field to discuss a problem in religion, by and large the clergy showed considerable deference to the company of physical scientists. That deference usually took the form of counting up the number of prominent scientists who were Catholics — in name at least. Most of the Catholic scientists the priest knew nothing about — men like Linacre, Vesalius, Galvani, Mendel, Müller — but when a popularly known figure like Nobel Prize winner Alexis Carrel turned out to be a Catholic, the priest fairly danced around the pamphlet rack.

There is a fascinating clerical literature on the history of Catholic contributions to science. Most of it is glib, superficial, puerile, and beside the point. [223] When the history of Catholic clerical thought in this period is researched in detail, it will be interesting to see (if such information is available) what percentage of priests was sufficiently in touch with contemporary currents in scientific thought to know that the Newtonian conception of the cosmos had been overthrown in this century, and that in the names of quantum mechanics and relativity theory, entirely new conceptions of social and cultural life were being forged; what percentage knew that the relativism already implicit in evolutionary and pragmatic thought was being applied to the fields of history, law, anthropology, psychology, and political science; what percentage knew the names Max Planck, Carl Becker, Ruth Benedict, and Jerome Frank? In other words, what percentage was aware that a new world was being born — a world of anti-metaphysical sociology, positivistic psychology, non-religious depth psychiatry, cybernetics, and atomic technology — a world in which the cleric who was out of step with the surrounding intellectual milieu might one day find his position markedly precarious?

New York, which provides such good examples of other moments in this history of clerical thought, is equally instructive on the "myth" of intellectual attainment nurtured by some American priests. Interviews conducted during 1969 with fifty New York priests ordained from St. Joseph's Seminary, Dunwoodie, in the years 1915 to 1929 reveal that the typical Dunwoodie product of that period felt secure in the assumption that he had passed through a superior regimen of intellectual formation.[224] This, despite the fact that the course work required little or no reading outside the textbooks and some notes; no papers to do; a library open to students only two hours on Sunday and Wednesday mornings; and an institutionalized four hours and forty minutes of study in the horarium. It was not modernism alone which caused this reality behind the myth. Archbishop (Cardinal in 1924) Patrick J. Hayes of New York (1919-1938) had little interest in the seminary, even less in its academic side. As a result, the seminary budget during his administration was always small, with never any more than $500.00 allotted each year to the library for the purchasing, processing, and maintenance of books. The cardinal's man in the seminary was the procurator.

Hayes appointed to the rectorship a priest who had no academic experience, had been in parishes all his priesthood, and was already an old man at the time of his appointment. The cardinal looked on priests as "soldiers of Christ," hence he conceived the seminary as a kind of West Point.[225] A priest who served as vice-president at Dunwoodie in the 1920's recalled: "The old seminary notion was on a militaristic basis. It was a West Point, an Annapolis. . . . The spiritual was dominant, and authority, discipline, order and so forth." [226] Ignatian spirituality also had a military cast and this would appear in the retreats given seminarians and priests by Jesuits of the New York Province. The seminary was, then, not so much a place of intellectual training as it was a place of character training.[227] And not surprisingly, the attributes of a priest frequently stressed in eulogies or testimonials were courage, heroism, patriotism, discipline, obedience, and loyalty to the "corps." What was also esteemed in the New York seminarian and priest was the quality of the "cultured gentleman." The model New York priest was refined, careful in speech, literate in tastes, and courteous in manner. He was a paragon of what the seminary curriculum called *urbanitas*. When the Dunwoodie seminarians came to ordinations they wore top hats and coats *usque ad genua*. Hence, the popular name, "Dunwoodie Dudes." One more characteristic of the New York priest that was admired and promoted by his superiors was manly activism. The ideal priest demonstrated masculine, athletic, ambitious qualities. He was not the inoffensive, effeminate silver-haired smiler portrayed as the typical Protestant minister in motion pictures. Rather, as Martin E. Marty wrote in 1958, citing two movie portrayals of New York priests, "Roman Catholic priests, from *Going My Way* to *On the Waterfront,* are real persons with authentic individuality. The Protestants may be 'God's kind of guys' but the Catholics are men's kind of guys." [228]

It was not to be expected against this background that the typical New York priest of the 1920's and 1930's was much of a reader. When he did read seriously it was such works as Henry Edward Cardinal Mannings' *The Eternal Priesthood*; [229] James Cardinal Gibbons' *The Ambassador of Christ*; [230] James Keatinge's *The Priest, His Character and His Work*; [231] Jacques Millet's *Jesus Living in the Priest*; [232] the Canon Patrick Augustine Sheehan novels, particularly *My New Curate*; [233] and the works of Basil William Maturin, for example, *Laws of the Spiritual Life* [234] and *Some Principles and Practices of the Spiritual Life*.[235] What is important to notice is that none of the books was published after 1907. No one, apparently, was writing anything "worthwhile" after that date. Equally important, aside from the fiction, the priest's serious reading rarely extended beyond specifically Catholic interests. About the only published means he provided himself for keeping up to date with the world around him were the daily newspapers, popular magazines, the diocesan paper, the *American Ecclesiastical Review*, the *Homiletic and Pastoral Review*, and the Jesuit-edited journal of opinion, *America*. Arthur Barry O'Neill, C.S.C., wrote in 1922:

> It is doubtless a bit extravagant to assert that the reading of a goodly number of American priests, apart from the breviary, is restricted to newspapers, popular magazines, and 'best-sellers;'

but it is well within the truth to say that far too much clerical time is wasted on these ephemeral productions. Nor is waste of time the only evil of such action. Such desultory, unmethodical reading is a positive obstacle to the acquisition of really valuable knowledge.[236]

And yet one may ask if the serious religious reading that the average priest *did* do at this time was not itself prejudicial to "the acquisition of really valuable knowledge." Although most of the books cited above as typical reading of the New York priest exhorted him to keep up his studies in the years following ordination — Gibbons, for example, wrote that the priest could no more lay aside books and learning after graduation than could the lawyer or judge: "The foundation was laid; the superstructure is the work of his whole life." [237] — still the general tone of the books he read was such as to corroborate his assurance that "The ordinary priest is the best all-round educated man in his community," [238] to confirm him in his possession of "certitude," and *volte face* to make serious investigative reading the more dangerous use of time. Maturin, for example, told him:

> . . . The air is full of controversy and questionings. . . . Under such circumstances the position of the Catholic is a very difficult one. For amidst all the Babel of opinion around him he has a certainty that he has the truth, of a different character and in a far intenser degree than that of a member of any other body of Christians. He knows in fact that the Catholic Church is the pillar and ground of truth, and in so far as other bodies differ from Her in matters of faith he knows that they are wrong.[239]

Not only in New York, but elsewhere in the country as well, priests of the post-modernism decades had, by dint of training, reading, and acculturated isolation from Protestant and secular thought, a low tolerance for the provisional, the tentative, the experimental. The same low tolerance could be found in the place where it should least be expected: in the Catholic university. There the priest who learned as well as the priest who instructed was concerned almost exclusively with the transmission of already accumulated knowledge. As late as 1953 Professor Julian Pleasants of the University of Notre Dame could observe that the typical Catholic looked on original research as "a sort of hobby for the human race, [having] nothing to do with the real business of existence." [240] Original research was made by and large unnecessary by the fact that perennial wisdom was already available, even in published volumes, and to answer the questions posed by life's changing situations one had only to drink deeply from the Pierian spring. The *Summa Theologica* of Thomas Aquinas was the matchless aqueduct through which the waters of wisdom flowed and, as the Talmudic rabbis did with the Torah, one had only to "turn it and turn it again" to find the answers to life's perplexing problems.

There are at least three general reasons why the priest-academician eschewed original research, which formed the principal occupation of his counterpart in secular universities. The first and most obvious reason was the pall cast over such activity by the condemnation of modernism. The second was the near universal deference paid to Cardinal Newman's *The Idea of a University* as the exemplar and charter of higher learning. Newman had described the university as ". . . a place of *teaching* universal *knowledge*. This implies that its object is, on the one hand, intellectual, not moral; and, on the other, that it is the diffusion and extension of knowledge rather than the advancement. If its object were scientific and philosophical discovery, I do not see why a University should have students. . . ." [241] The third reason was the widely held conviction that original research, such as that conducted in the typical American graduate school, threatened the secure foundations of the Catholic mind and added nothing to that mind except the empty exhilaration of discovery. The typical graduate school, explained George Bull, S.J., in 1938, saw its purpose as "to add to the sum of human knowledge." But why go to all that bother, asked Father Bull, when you already had all the necessary answers? And why assume the risks involved in "attempting the impossible task of being Catholic in creed and anti-Catholic in culture?" For you cannot be a possessor of truth and a pursuer of truth at one and the same time. The one is Catholic and the other is anti-Catholic. They are antithetical categories. Bull's exposition of this point appeared in the Jesuit periodical *Thought*. A better general statement of the intellectual isolation of the American priest could not be found:

> Here, at last, starting from that trait which no one who knows the Catholic mind can deny, which indeed its adversaries have scorned in it, its totality of view, as an attitude, a spontaneous direction, a thing taken for granted whenever it thinks at all, here we have the radically peculiar cast of the Catholic approach to learning and the objective without which its thinking is to itself unpalatable, of itself vain and pointless. It is the simple assumption that wisdom has been achieved by man, and that the humane use of the mind, the function proper to him as man, is contempla-

tion and not research. . . . In sum, then, research cannot be the primary object of a Catholic graduate school, because it is at war with the whole Catholic life of the mind.[242]

This conception of higher learning found its chief expression, as one might expect, in the philosophy classroom. There, problems, not of the student's own time or country, but problems carried over from ancient Greece or medieval Europe were proposed to the student in precisely arranged schemes. To these problems, definitions and premises were applied *a priori*. A series of syllogisms was then run through, after which one had a residue of conclusions which purported to be the answers to the problems. The cerebral huddle of professor and students was a centripetal event, all its intellectual processes incoming, none outgoing. The result was, in the words of John Courtney Murray, S.J., writing in 1949, to make the Catholic scholar "a self-enclosed spiritual monad in a secularist world." [243] Another result was to cause unnumbered priests to vilipend philosophy and consequently scholarship.

It is no consolation, in this connection, that a general spirit of anti-intellectualism was also running through American Protestantism after 1920, though for reasons in part directly counter to the rigidity and exclusivity of Catholic thought. Among Protestant clergymen a division occurred immediately after World War I along fundamentalist-modernist lines. Those clerics who took the fundamentalist position, rejecting the intellectualism and moral optimism of liberal theology, retreated into what Winthrop Hudson has called "a defensive, armor-clad system," and from there excoriated, in language worthy of *Pascendi*, all attempts by their modernist brothers to submit inherited orthodoxy to scientific test.[244] Protestant modernists, on the other hand, made their peace with the newer scientific thought and biblical studies; but the more they did so, confirming and approving the findings of supposedly objective scholarship, the more, paradoxically, were they regarded with indifference and even hostility by secular thinkers. That fundamentalist clerics should have been scorned by the secular establishment surprised no one, including the fundamentalists. But that modernists, or liberals, should turn out as targets of those whom they had befriended was a disillusioning experience, and one that should give pause to any contemporary Catholic clerics whose primary intent in initiating exchange with the intellectual community at large might be to curry secular favor and the questionable prestige that comes from such favor.

Having, it seemed, nothing specific to contribute to the world of thought from its own resources, modernist or liberal Protestantism disappeared gradually from the pages of the quarterly journals and literary monthlies, save as a target of the satirical jibes of H. L. Mencken or Sinclair Lewis. Hudson has pointed out that even as late as 1950, when "cultural" circles were becoming enamored once more of religion, the *Partisan Review's* symposium, "Religion and the Intellectuals," included only one representative out of twenty-nine who stood undeniably in the Protestant tradition; and the same historian added, "Such weighting would have been unthinkable and impossible as late as the second decade of the century. . . ." As for the Protestant minister, once his intellectual function became that of an echo, he disappeared rather suddenly from his predominant position on college faculties. "Throughout the nineteenth century," Hudson found, "the president of almost every important college and university was a clergyman, but by the fourth decade of the twentieth century no clergyman occupied the presidential chair of any leading institutuion of learning." [245]

While full restoration of intellectual status among the clergy would not come for a long while — indeed, has not come yet at the date of this writing — there were important movements toward reconstruction of an independent theological perspective, one that could speak with original wisdom to the American mind, beginning, one may estimate, from the publication in 1932 of Reinhold Niebuhr's *Moral Man and Immoral Society* and the arrival in the following year of Paul Tillich at Union Theological Seminary in New York. There is no question that by 1950 a theological renaissance had occurred. Commonly called neo-orthodoxy, it was a renaissance that was both fully aware of and contributory to what was happening in the general world of thought. One must at present question, however, whether that renaissance has spent its force, and whether the socially activist clergy of today has begun to lose the neo-orthodox sense of the transcendent, and to find itself more comfortably situated in the secularly oriented, socially relevant, "religionless Christianity" of modernist Protestantism.[246] Would such a recidivist clergy end by being once more an echo of, rather than a contributor to, the world of American thought? Such seems to be a legitimate speculation for the historian.

The Catholic clergy has also in these latter days enjoyed a certain intellectual renaissance. Called by no special name, its first faint beginnings can be traced to the work of certain seminal thinkers at the Catholic University of America in the field of applied moral theology, particularly in those areas that touched upon sociology and economics.

William J. Kerby, whose sociological training had been acquired at Louvain, deserves the title of founder of scientific social work among Catholics in the United States. Better known and of far greater influence nationally was John A. Ryan (1869–1945), who had been attracted to the moral aspects of economics by his professor, Thomas Bouquillon, and who first gained notice with his 1906 work, *A Living Wage*, which gave local meaning to the reform encyclical *Rerum novarum* of Leo XIII. In 1919, Ryan wrote the advanced draft of the "Bishops' Program of Social Reconstruction," a progressive document containing proposals which, though regarded by many at the time as radical, were eventually enacted into law. It was natural that Ryan's genius was directed along lines to ameliorate the economic conditions of the working class to which most of his Catholic compatriots belonged, but the social justice he promoted, in articles and speeches, in his capacity as member of federal boards during the New Deal years, and particularly as Director (1920–1945) of the Social Action Department of the National Catholic Welfare Conference, had beneficent effects in society far beyond the circle of his own communicants.[247]

Other clerics, too, were engaged in the advance of social justice theory and practice, among them Fathers Raymond A. McGowan, John O'Grady, John W. R. Maguire, C.S.V., William Bolger, C.S.C., and John P. Boland, all associates or disciples of Ryan; Bishops Joseph Schrembs of Toledo (1911–1921) and Cleveland (1921–1945) and Francis J. Haas of Grand Rapids (1943–1953); Father Peter E. Dietz in Cincinnati; and Father Charles E. Coughlin of Royal Oak, Michigan, whose radio oratory led him into politics and, eventually, into episcopal disfavor. In a cognate field Fathers Thomas E. Shields at the Catholic University of America and James A. Burns, C.S.C., at Holy Cross College in Washington, D.C., developed a Catholic theory of education specifically applicable to the American scene. At the Catholic University some advanced work was done by Fathers John M. Cooper in anthropology, Peter Guilday in American Catholic history, Thomas Verner Moore, O.S.B., in psychology, Franz Coeln and Heinrich Schumacher in scripture; like the work of Shields and Burns in education, however, their labors received little notice outside the Catholic community. Slightly more attention was earned by two accomplished Jesuits of the period, Edmund A. Walsh in foreign affairs at Georgetown, and Robert I. Gannon in liberal arts at Fordham.

Catholic theology and biblical studies also began to recover some of their pre-1907 vitality during the 1930's and 1940's. Old interests quickened, new subjects came under study, lively debates took place, new theological societies and publications began. The Catholic Biblical Association of America was founded at New York in 1936, and Edward P. Arbez, S.S., was elected president in the first general meeting which took place at St. Louis in the following year. Ten years later, in 1946, Fathers Joseph C. Fenton, Eugene M. Burke, C.S.P., Edmond D. Benard, and Francis J. Connell, C.SS.R., all associated with the *American Ecclesiastical Review,* took the lead in founding the Catholic Theological Society of America. Notable among the publications were the Jesuit-edited *Theological Studies,* begun at Woodstock in 1940 by William McGarry, and the *Catholic Biblical Quarterly,* of which Volume I, Number 1 appeared in January, 1939. *Theological Studies* was doubtless the first American Catholic periodical since 1908 that could claim to stand on the same plane with the old *New York Review.* Observing the highest canons of scholarship, its attention from the start was devoted to aspects of fundamental theology which took on unique color in the American situation. The first volume contained no less than three articles on ecumenism.[248] It was to this periodical that the Jesuits Gustave Weigel (1906–1964) and John Courtney Murray (1904–1966) probably the two most noted and influential theologians of the twentieth century American Church, contributed much of their ground-breaking work, Weigel in ecclesiology and ecumenical studies, Murray in the areas of Church-State relations, religious freedom, natural law in public life, and morality of warfare. There is no doubt that each had wide and salutary influence on the community of intellect outside his faith, as well as on the leadership within his faith: when United States bishops during the course of the Second Ecumenical Council of the Vatican (1962–1965) rose to speak in defense of the now-famous Declaration on Religious Liberty, drafted in great part by Murray, one of them commented to Bishop Robert E. Tracy of Baton Rouge, "The voices are the voices of United States bishops; but the thoughts are the thoughts of John Courtney Murray!" [249] Murray lived out his own definition of the Catholic intellectual as a "missionary" to the "thickening secularist intellectual and spiritual milieu."[250] The initial responsibility of such a missionary, he said, was

> . . . that of undertaking a comprehensive analysis of the present intellectual, cultural, and spiritual situation in its totality. If we are to interpret the world, as we must, even to itself, our first duty is to understand it, in detail, with full realism, under abnegation of the easy generalities with which the world is ordinarily denounced.[251]

Father Murray's words, written in 1949, demonstrate a truth that is not perhaps given the currency it deserves. The exultant flowering of thought, with its many and varied contacts with the secular and Protestant worlds, that has characterized much of the American priesthood since the proclamation of *aggiornamento* by Pope John XXIII in 1959, has not been an entirely sudden and unprepared-for event, but one whose coming was anticipated and nurtured over many years of time. One sees the shape of things to come in the back numbers of the *Catholic Biblical Quarterly, Theological Studies,* and in other serious publications such as *Worship,* a monthly with 10,000 subscribers, edited by Father Godfrey Diekmann, O.S.B., at St. John's University, Collegeville, Minnesota, in the interests of liturgical reform.[252] Although the American renaissance was years behind the scholarly advance of European Catholics, and most priests in this country were surprised — and some shocked — by what they read of European thought in Hans Küng's celebrated *The Council, Reform and Reunion,*[253] still it may be said that American priest-scholars contributed to the transition from *Pascendi* to *Aggiornamento,* and some succeeded, well before Vatican Council II, in opening the minds of their fellow clergy to the need of understanding in depth the life, culture, and science of the people among whom they lived.

Since 1962, the opening year of Vatican II, there has been a veritable explosion of scholarly activity in the American Catholic priesthood. In scripture, ecclesiology, moral theology and assorted other fields exciting new understandings have been discovered by an ever-increasing band of intelligent clergy. Graduate schools of theology have grown apace; priests have entered into ecumenical dialogue with Protestant and Jewish thinkers; numerous clergy have enrolled for courses in secular colleges and universities; bishops have taken refresher courses in theology at St. John's University in Collegeville, Fordham University, St. Louis University and elsewhere; diocesan and order priests alike have spent portions of their summers in institutes, workshops, seminars and study weeks; and certain dioceses, such as St. Petersburg in Florida, have provided since January, 1970, free time and funds for parish clergy to attend scholarly programs of their own choosing regularly each year. It seems to be the consensus among Catholic leaders today as the 1970's get underway that the Church in the United States should never again revert to the "separatism" espoused earlier in the century by Cardinal William O'Connell, Archbishop of Boston (1859–1944), or the "state of siege" which Father Joseph Clifford Fenton, editor of the *American Ecclesiastical Review* (1944–1960), thought was a perennial necessity on the grounds that Catholicism and modern culture were inevitably opposed.[254] The ideal contemporary priest, as conceived by Vatican II in the document with which we began this essay, is a priest involved in the thought as well as the action of the world around him. He is alert, aware and open to all things of the mind. He is able to tolerate uncertainty and to assign to its proper place what is tentative, provisional, or ambiguous. He uses his new elbow room creatively. Without losing his sacred or hieratic function, he strives to know and to contribute to the intellectual ferment of his times. In that endeavor he aims, of course, to possess more than the mere patina of learning. It is not enough to be a Stephen Fermoyle, hero of Henry Morton Robinson's novel, *The Cardinal*, who could trade witticisms on celestial navigation, dabble in political gossip, and play the German card game "Mühle." [255] Such dilletantism would only fashion a half-way covenant. What is needed, said the decree of Vatican Council II, is a man who understands what John Ireland meant when, seventy-six years before, he declared:

> This is an intellectual age. It worships intellect. By intellect, public opinion, the ruling power of the age, is formed. The Church herself will be judged by the standard of intellect. Catholics must excel in religious knowledge. . . . They must be in the forefront of intellectual movements of all kinds. The age will not take kindly to religious knowledge separated from secular knowledge.[256]

1. Walter M. Abbott, S.J., and Joseph Gallagher, eds., *The Documents of Vatican II* (New York: America Press, 1966), p. 450.

2. *Acta Apostolicis Sedis* 56 (1964), pp. 637 ff.

3. See John Tracy Ellis, *American Catholics and the Intellectual Life* (Chicago: Heritage Foundation, Inc., 1956), pp. 23 ff.

4. Edigio Vagnozzi, "Thoughts on the Catholic Intellectual," address delivered at Marquette University on June 3, 1961, published in *American Ecclesiastical Review* (hereafter cited as *AER*), LXVII (August, 1961), pp. 73–79.

5. Henry J. Browne mentions only one priest, John Courtney Murray, S.J., whose writings on the question of church and state have attracted much attention; in James Ward Smith and A. Leland Jamison, eds., *The Shaping of American Religion* (Princeton: Princeton University Press, 1961), I, p. 115. Ellis, *Intellectual Life*, likewise limits himself to Murray as a priest who has had impact on non-Catholic thought, p. 58.

6. See *ibid.* Cf. Thomas F. O'Dea, *American Catholic Dilemma: An Inquiry into the Intellectual Life* (New York: Mentor Omega, 1962).

7. See Philip Gleason, "Immigration and American Catholic Intellectual Life," *Review of Politics*, 26 (April, 1964), p. 156.

8. Joseph H. Fichter, *Priest and People* (New York: Sheed and Ward, 1965), p. 197.

9. John J. Meng, "American Thought: Contributions of Catholic Thought and Thinkers," *Bulletin*, National Catholic Educational Association, III (August 1956), p. 115. Also see John J. Kane, *Catholic-Protestant Conflicts in America* (Chicago: Regnery, 1955), Chapter IV, "The Case of: 'Priests vs. the People,' " pp. 49–69; and Walter J. Ong, S.J., *American Catholic Crossroads* (New York: Macmillan, 1959), p. 104.

10. Andrew M. Greeley, *The Hesitant Pilgrim* (New York: Sheed and Ward, 1966), Chapter 10, "Entering the Mainstream," pp. 141–161.

11. Daniel Callahan, *The Mind of the Catholic Layman* (New York: Scribners, 1963), pp. 126–128.

12. See Ellis, *Intellectual Life*; O'Dea, *Catholic Dilemma*; Greeley, *Hesitant Pilgrim*, p. 142.

13. This was suggested by O'Dea, *Catholic Dilemma*, Chapter III, "Reason and Faith," pp. 51–68.

14. See John J. McDermott, "The American Angle of Vision," *Cross Currents*, 15 (Winter, 1965), pp. 70–71. This article includes an excellent bibliography.

15. Herbert W. Schneider, *History of American Philosophy* (New York: Columbia University Press, 1946), vii.

16. Examples of this literature are Roger Shinn, ed., *The Search for Identity: Essays on the American Character* (New York: Harper & Row, 1964); Seymour Martin Lipset, *The First New Nation* (New York: Basic Books, 1963); Michael McGiffert, ed., *The Character of Americans* (Homewood, Ill.: The Dorsey Press, 1964).

17. See John Dewey, *Experience and Nature*, Rev. ed. (New York: Norton, 1929), p. 24; Alexis de Tocqueville, *Democracy in America*, ed. Phillips Bradley, 2 vols. (New York: Vintage Books, 1954); Robert C. Pollock, "Process and Experience: Dewey and American Philosophy," *Cross Currents*, IX (Fall, 1959), pp. 341–366; Robert K. Merton, "The Mosaic of the Behavioral Sciences," in Bernard Berelson, ed., *The Behavioral Sciences Today* (New York: Basic Books, 1963), pp. 247–272. On the point of novelty Daniel J. Boorstin has written: "In Europe discovering something new in the natural world required the concentration of a philosopher, the researches of a scholar, or the industry of an encyclopedist. In America it took effort to avoid novelty." *The Americans, The Colonial Experience* (New York: Random House, 1958), p. 163. Cautioning against an uncritical acceptance of uniquely American qualities, John Higham speaks of the "ambiguity of the American experience" and argues that "its complexity lies below the surface and therefore makes a special demand on the historical imagination." *The Reconstruction of American History* (New York: Humanities Press, 1962), p. 9.

18. This is the conclusion of Richard Hofstadter, *Anti-Intellectualism in American Life* (New York: Alfred A. Knopf, 1963), esp. pp. 24–51.

19. There is no satisfactory general history of Catholic immigration. The best statistical summary is still Gerald Shaughnessy, *Has the Immigrant Kept the Faith?* (New York: Macmillan, 1925). An excellent recent essay is Philip Gleason, "Immigration and American Catholic Intellectual Life," *The Review of Politics*, 26 (April, 1964), pp. 147–173. Other specialized studies of immigration with information related to religion are listed in Nelson R. Burr (in collaboration with the editors, James Ward Smith and A. Leland Jamison), *A Critical Bibliography of Religion in America*, Vol. IV, Parts 1 and 2, *Religion in American Life*, 4 vols. (Princeton: Princeton University Press, 1961), pp. 469–473.

20. The classic study of this nativist campaign is Ray Allen Billington, *The Protestant Crusade, 1800–1860: A Study of the Origins of American Nativism* (New

York: Macmillan, 1938). For the period after the Civil War see John Higham, *Strangers in the Land: Patterns of American Nativism, 1860–1925* (New Brunswick, N.J.: Rutgers University Press, 1955).

21. The Puritan Half-Way Covenant of 1657, accommodating the "covenant of grace" to the "covenant of work," can stand perhaps as the archtypical American solution of the tension between thought and action. See Perry Miller, *The New England Mind, From Colony to Province* (Cambridge: Harvard University Press, 1961), pp. 93–104. Cf. Merle Curti, *American Paradox, The Conflict of Thought and Action* (New Brunswick, N.J.: Rutgers University Press, 1956).

22. Alexis de Tocqueville, *Democracy in America*, I, p. 219. The nineteenth century priest in the main rejected evangelical Protestantism's identification of the course of American democracy with God's purpose. Certain prelates at the close of the century came close to stating this identification, however, notably Archbishop Ireland. The problem is studied in Dorothy Dohen, *Nationalism and American Catholicism* (New York: Sheed and Ward, 1967).

23. See Winthrop S. Hudson, *The Great Tradition of the American Churches* (New York: Harper & Row, 1963), pp. 218–220; John Dillenberger and Claude Welch, *Protestant Christianity* (New York: Charles Scribner's Sons, 1954), pp. 179–231.

24. Sidney E. Mead, "American Protestantism Since the Civil War. II. From Americanism to Christianity," in Richard M. Abrams and Lawrence W. Levine, eds., *The Shaping of Twentieth Century America* (Boston: Little, Brown and Co., 1965), pp. 93, 112–116. John Herman Randall, Jr., "The Churches and the Liberal Tradition," *Annals of the American Academy of Political and Social Science*, 256 (March, 1948), p. 150. Henry Steele Commager has described the consequences for Protestantism: "The church itself confessed to a steady secularization: as it invaded the social and economic fields, it retreated from the intellectual. Philosophy, which for over two centuries had been almost the exclusive property of the clergy, slipped quietly from their hands." *The American Mind: An Interpretation of American Thought and Character Since the 1880's* (New Haven: Yale University Press, 1960), p. 167.

25. Paul Tillich, *The Religious Situation*, tr. by H. Richard Niebuhr (New York: Meridian, Living Age Books, 1956), p. 182.

26. John Tracy Ellis, *Catholics in Colonial America* (Baltimore: Helicon Press, 1965), p. 445.

27. John Tracy Ellis, *Essays in Seminary Education* (Notre Dame: Fides Publishers, 1967), pp. 59–63.

28. Quoted in Peter Guilday, *The Life and Times of John Carroll* (New York: The Encyclopedia Press, 1922), p. 720. For names of some of the Irish clergy in this period see Thomas T. McAvoy, C.S.C., "The Irish Clergyman in the United States," *Records of the American Catholic Historical Society of Philadelphia* [hereafter cited as *RACHS*], LXXV (March, 1964 to December, 1964), p. 8.

29. Will Herberg, *Protestant-Catholic-Jew* (New York: Doubleday, 1960), pp. 146–147.

30. John Tracy Ellis, *The Life of James Cardinal Gibbons, Archbishop of Baltimore, 1834–1921*, 2 vols. (Milwaukee: Bruce, 1952), I, p. 376. For this episode see the entire Chapter IX, "Nationalities in Conflict." Cf. Colman J. Barry, O.S.B., *The Catholic Church and German Americans* (Milwaukee: Bruce, 1953), esp. pp. 77–84, 137–277.

31. See Leo F. Ruskowski, *French Émigré Priests in the United States, 1691–1815* (Washington, D.C.: The Catholic University of America Press, 1940); Charles G. Herbermann, *The Sulpicians in the United States* (New York: The Encyclopedia Press, 1916). Catholic immigration from France between the years 1815 and 1865 has been estimated at 137,417, with 9,668 Belgians, most of whom also spoke French. A number of Belgian priests served with distinction in the Midwest missions, notably Bishop Peter Lefevere (1804–1869) apostolic administrator of

Detroit, and Fathers Peter Kindekens in Detroit and Charles Nerinckx in Kentucky. Other national groups also brought clergy with them, especially after 1865, when large numbers of Catholics immigrated from eastern and southern Europe.

32. Ruskowski, *Émigré Priests*, p. 98.

33. *Ibid.*, p. 105; Theodore Maynard, *The Story of American Catholicism* (New York: Macmillan, 1941), p. 269.

34. J. Herman Schauinger, *Stephen T. Badin, Priest in the Wilderness* (Milwaukee: Bruce, 1956), p. 76.

35. *Ibid.*, p. 215 and p. 276.

36. Herbermann, *Sulpicians*, pp. 166–170. Other pioneer priests who were associated with the founding or early development of institutions of higher learning were the German Ferdinand Farmer (Steynmeyer), trustee of the College of Philadelphia in the 1780's; and the French Recollect John B. Causse, trustee of Franklin College at Lancaster, Pennsylvania, from 1787 to 1793; see John Gilmary Shea, *Life and Times of the Most Rev. John Carroll* (New York: John G. Shea, 1888), p. 279 and p. 295.

37. Ruskowski, *Émigré Priests*, pp. 109–111.

38. Celestine Joseph Nuesse, *The Social Thought of American Catholics, 1634–1829* (Washington, D.C.: The Catholic University of America Press, 1945), pp. 155–156. Irish-born Bishop John England (1786–1842) of Charleston questioned the degree to which the French clergy assimilated Catholic teaching to American principles and founded his own seminary at Charleston in 1822 rather than send students to the French, who "never can become American." England to Father Michael O'Connor, Charleston, February 25, 1835, quoted in Ellis, *Seminary Education*, p. 141.

39. *Ibid.*, 139.

40. Quoted in Columba E. Halsey, O.S.B., "The Life of Samuel Eccleston, Fifth Bishop of Baltimore, 1801–1851" (unpublished Master's thesis: The Catholic University of America, 1963), p. 20, p. 23.

41. See James F. Connelly, *The Visit of Archbishop Gaetano Bedini to the United States, June, 1853–February, 1854* (Roma: Libreria Editrice dell' Universita Gregoriana, 1960).

42. Richard Hofstadter, *Anti-Intellectualism*, p. 138.

43. Quoted in Colman J. Barry, O.S.B., "The German Catholic Immigrant," Thomas T. McAvoy, C.S.C., ed., *Roman Catholicism and the American Way of Life* (Notre Dame: University of Notre Dame Press, 1960), p. 192.

44. Gmeiner wrote under the title: *The Church and the Various Nationalities in the United States. Are German Catholics Unfairly Treated?* Cited in Barry, *German Americans*, pp. 77–80.

45. *The Question of Nationality in Its Relation to the Catholic Church in the United States.* Cited in Barry, *German Americans*, pp. 82–84.

46. The definitive study of the letter of Pope Leo XIII, *Testem benevolentiae*, and of the so-called "phantom heresy" which provoked it, is Thomas T. McAvoy, C.S.C., *The Americanist Heresy in Roman Catholicism, 1895–1900* (Notre Dame: University of Notre Dame Press, 1963). The historian of German Catholic immigration, Colman J. Barry, O.S.B., appears to regret the "too hasty Americanization" of the German population, and points to what contributions to American religious culture the Germans might have made in fields of liturgy, scripture, and arts and crafts had they been left to find their way into the mainstream at their own gait. "I personally think," he writes, "that such aspects of a Christian culture could have developed and received real impetus from immigrant groups like the Germans if they were not uprooted and shorn of their true identity so rapidly and completely." Barry, "German Catholic Immigrant," p. 203.

47. James F. Connelly, *Archbishop Gaetano Bedini*, p. 240.

48. Microfilm copy, University of Notre Dame Archives. Cited in Thomas T.

McAvoy, C.S.C., *A History of the Catholic Church in the United States* (Notre Dame: University of Notre Dame Press, 1969), p. 107.

49. James F. Connelly, *Archbishop Gaetano Bedini*, p. 242.

50. A recent and able study of Kenrick has been completed by John P. Marschall, C.S.V., "Francis Patrick Kenrick, 1851–1863: The Baltimore Years." (Unpublished doctoral dissertation: The Catholic University of America, 1965).

51. November 11, 1882.

52. This is the finding of Sister John Marie Reher, I.H.M., to whom the writer is grateful for this conclusion from her recent studies of McGlynn at Fordham University.

53. The best recent study of Varela is Joseph J. and Helen McCadden, *Father Varela, Torch Bearer from Cuba* (New York: United States Catholic Historical Society, 1969). Cf. Michael V. Gannon, *Rebel Bishop: The Life and Era of Augustin Verot* (Milwaukee: Bruce, 1964), p. 248 and n.

54. De Tocqueville, *Democracy in America*, I, p. 225.

55. "The Missions of Catholics in America," an address given in the Cathedral of Baltimore on November 10, 1889, and published in *John Ireland, The Church and Modern Society*, 2nd ed. (Chicago: D. H. McBride & Co., 1897), p. 81.

56. James F. Connelly, *Archbishop Gaetano Bedini*, p. 240.

57. William J. Kerby, *Prophets of the Better Hope* (Philadelphia: The Dolphin Press, 1937), pp. 8–9.

58. James F. Connelly, *Archbishop Gaetano Bedini*, p. 244. Cf. John Gilmary Shea, "The Catholic Church in American History," *The American Catholic Quarterly Review*, I (January, 1876), p. 163: "Among the clergy the science, learning and ability that might add laurels to the body are often kept unused by the severe toils of missionary life or by modest diffidence; and an occasional article in some magazine, unnoticed, and hence unappreciated, alone reveals what might be."

59. *Anti-Intellectualism*, 33.

60. Quoted in Ralph Henry Gabriel, *The Course of American Democratic Thought* (New York: Ronald Press, 1956), p. 69. On the cultural isolation of the Irish priest, Thomas T. McAvoy, C.S.C., has written: "Of all the non-English groups who have come in time to constitute the majority of American Catholicism, the Irish clergy have considered themselves the most American, yet have been most resistant to American literary and artistic ideas, presumably because the Irish were more keenly aware that American literary and artistic creations were from a Puritan milieu. Only the Germans had a stronger notion of the union between culture and religion because of the religious strife in the German lands. Unfortunately, because of the lack of a plentifully rich artistic production, the Irish cultural tradition in this country has been almost negative." McAvoy, "Irish Clergyman in the United States," p. 37.

61. Orestes A. Brownson, *Works*, ed. Henry F. Brownson, 20 vols. (Detroit: Henry F. Brownson, 1882–1887), XIV, p. 543.

62. Richard Hofstadter, *The Paranoid Style in American Politics* (New York: Alfred A. Knopf, 1965), p. 21.

63. See note 20.

64. (Baltimore: John Murphy Co., 1844.)

65. (Louisville: B. J. Webb and Brother, 1847.)

66. (Louisville: Webb, Gill and Levering, 1858.)

67. Spalding had the advantage of knowing connaturally that nineteenth century America was a non-intellectual society: "Kind persuasion goes much farther in this country than hard logic." He once wrote a friend, "The appeal to the heart is more effectual than that to the head." Spalding to Dr. W. N. Marshall, Baltimore, January 3, 1871; quoted in Sister Mary a'Kempis Corcoran, "American Catholic Opinion in Response to Freethought, 1865–1895" (unpublished Master's thesis, The Catholic University of America, 1952), p. 39. Cf. Adam A. Micek, S.T.L., *The Apologetics*

of Martin John Spalding (Washington, D.C.: The Catholic University of America Press, 1951), p. 20; John C. Reville, S.J., *The Church, Culture and Liberty* (New York: Joseph F. Wagner, Inc., 1923), x. Spalding's nephew and biographer, John Lancaster Spalding, said of *Miscellanea* that, "It would have been difficult to give to Americans a book better suited to the wants of the then existing state of the public mind," *The Life of the Most Reverend M. J. Spalding* (New York: The Christian Press Association Publishing Company, 1873), p. 189.

68. Kenrick to Mrs. Allen, Baltimore, December 4, 1861, quoted in Marschall, "Francis Patrick Kenrick," 180. *Vindication of the Catholic Church* was published in Baltimore by John Murphy, 1858.

69. *Brownson's Quarterly Review*, Second New York Series, IV (October 1859), p. 541. *The Book of Job and the Prophets* was published in Baltimore, by Kelly, Hedian and Pict, 1859.

70. See David J. O'Brien, "American Catholicism and the Diaspora," *Cross Currents*, 16 (Summer, 1966), pp. 312–315. Cf. Joseph J. McCadden, "Bishop Hughes versus The Public School Society of New York," *Catholic Historical Review*, L (July, 1964), pp. 188–207; Billington, *Protestant Crusade*, "The Catholic Church Blunders, 1850–1854," Chapter XII, pp. 289–321.

71. Isaac Hecker, "Dr. Brownson and Bishop Fitzpatrick," *Catholic World*, XLV (April, 1887), p. 1.

72. (New York: Appleton, 1855.)

73. For Hecker's life and career see Vincent F. Holden, C.S.P., *The Yankee Paul: Isaac Thomas Hecker* (Milwaukee: Bruce, 1958); Joseph McSorley, *Father Hecker and His Friends* (St. Louis: Herder, 1952); and Walter Elliott, *The Life of Father Hecker* (New York: Columbus Press, 1891).

74. Quoted in Holden, *The Yankee Paul*, p. 190.

75. "Present and Future Prospects of the Catholic Faith in the United States of America." Quoted in *ibid.*, p. 302. By this date Brownson was in thorough disagreement with Hecker's estimate of American spirituality, and said so: "There is scarcely a trait in the American character as practically developed that is not more or less hostile to Catholicity. Our people are imbued with a spirit of independence, an aversion to authority, a pride, an overweening conceit, as well as with a prejudice, that makes them revolt at the bare mention of the Church," *ibid.*, p. 324.

76. Ralph Henry Gabriel, *American Democratic Thought*, sees Hecker and Brownson as the first Catholics of importance to attempt to "harmonize Catholic doctrine and the American democratic faith," p. 58.

77. Quoted in James H. Moynihan, *The Life of Archbishop John Ireland* (New York: Harper & Brothers, 1953), p. 106.

78. Michael V. Gannon, *Rebel Bishop*, pp. 56–62.

79. Statement of the bishops attending the Ninth Provincial Council of Baltimore in 1858; Concilium Baltimorensis Provinciale IX, May 28, 1858, quoted in Frederick J. Swierlein, *Life and Letters of Bishop [Bernard J.] McQuaid* (Rochester: Art Print Shop, 1925), I, pp. 266–267.

80. James Hennesey, S.J., *The First Council of the Vatican: The American Experience* (New York: Herder and Herder, 1963), p. 329.

81. See Gannon, *Rebel Bishop*, pp. 220–221.

82. England to Father Michael O'Conner, Charleston, February 25, 1835, quoted in Guilday, *John England*, I, p. 481.

83. See Joannes D. Mansi, *Sacrorum Conciliorum nova et amplissima Collectio*, Vols. XLIX–LIII (Leipzig, 1923–1927), LIII, col. 499.

84. Ralph Henry Gabriel links Darwinism with the positivist philosophy of Auguste Comte as the leading formative force in American thought at this time: "The appearance of an aggressive humanism, a new religion of humanity immediately after the end of the Civil War is one of the most significant events in the history of American democratic thought. . . . When the anxieties of war relaxed,

there was a sudden impact of Darwinism upon Christian orthodoxy. . . . Comtean positivism affected American thought at the moment when Darwinism was challenging the old religious doctrines of the nature of man." *American Democratic Thought*, p. 173. Merle Curti agrees on the threat to Christian orthodoxy in this period: "The most striking event in the intellectual history of the last third of the nineteenth century was the blow dealt the historic doctrine of supernaturalism — the doctrine that a divine Creator stands above the laws of nature and intervenes directly in natural events and the affairs of men through miracles and the granting of grace — by new developments in the biological and physical sciences." *The Growth of American Democratic Thought*, 3rd ed. (New York: Harper & Row, 1964), p. 517. Henry Steele Commager writes: "Between them Darwin and Spencer exercised such sovereignty over America as George III never enjoyed." *The American Mind: An Interpretation of American Thought and Character Since the 1880's* (New Haven: Yale University Press, 1950), p. 87. Cf. Arthur M. Schlesinger, "A Critical Period in American Religion, 1857–1900," *Proceedings of the Massachusetts Historical Society*, LXIV (June, 1932), p. 525; Richard Hofstadter, *Social Darwinism in American Thought, 1860–1915* (Philadelphia: The University of Pennsylvania Press, 1944); Bert J. Loewenberg, "Darwinism Comes to America, 1859–1900," *Mississippi Valley Historical Review*, XXVIII (June, 1941), pp. 339–368.

85. The best study of American Catholic response is John L. Morrison, "A History of American Catholic Opinion on the Theory of Evolution, 1859–1950" (unpublished Ph.D. dissertation: University of Missouri, 1951). Less satisfactory is John Rickards Betts, "Darwinism, Evolution, and American Catholic Thought, 1860–1900," *Catholic Historical Review* [hereafter cited *CHR*], XLV (July, 1959), pp. 161–185. Morrison points out: "Strictly speaking, there has been no such entity as Catholic opinion on evolution. Rather there have been opinions, often contradictory, expressed by a great many Catholic writers, each speaking for himself and not for the Church. . . . As recently as 1945, when virtually all American scientists were evolutionists, Catholics were still being advised to wait and see;" p. 24.

86. *Evolution and Dogma* (Chicago: D.H. McBride & Co., 1896), p. 75.

87. *Works*, IX, p. 267.

88. "More About Darwinism," *Catholic World*, XVII (August, 1875), p. 641. It is not surprising that the philosophers of Darwinism posed a greater threat to Catholic churchmen than did the scientists of Darwinsim. Considered as a science, Darwinism could be handled dispassionately as an objectified challenge to the biblical origins of man, as then understood. On the philosophical level, however, Darwinism spawned an emotionally charged challenge called variously, "atheism," "agnosticism," "deism," "rationalism," "skepticism," and, with greatest frequency, "freethought." Here churchmen found the doctrines of faith under direct and deliberate assault, not only by the principal philosophers of the period, but more importantly, by popularizers of freethought such as Robert Green Ingersoll (1833–1899) and Benjamin Underwood (1839–1914). During the last quarter of the century a large number of clerical prize-fighters went forth to do battle with the exponents of freethought, notably the New York pastor, Henry A. Brann; the journalist Father Louis A. Lambert (1835–1910), whose refutation of Ingersoll, *Notes on Ingersoll* (1883), was one of the few Catholic apologetical works to win a favorable Protestant readership; James A. Corcoran, editor of the *American Catholic Quarterly Review*; Archbishop Patrick J. Ryan (1831–1911) of Philadelphia and Bishops Richard Gilmour (1824–1891) of Cleveland and Patrick N. Lynch (1817–1882) of Charleston. Unlike Protestantism the Catholic Church lost little of her following to the freethought movement. Samuel Eliot Morison and Commager credit this achievement to the Catholic attitude of "no compromise" of Christian philosophy with that of freethought and to the refusal of the clerics to "alter a jot or tittle" of Church dogma; *The Growth of the American Republic*, 2 vols. (New York: Oxford University Press, 1942), II, pp. 274–275. An able study of Catholic

apologetics in this period is Corcoran, "Response to Freethought." Cf. Sidney Warren, *American Freethought, 1860–1914* (New York: Columbia University Press, 1943); Edward A. White, *Science and Religion in American Thought: The Impact of Naturalism* (Stanford: Stanford University Press, 1952).

89. See Morrison, "Evolution," pp. 149–151.

90. Quoted in *ibid.*, p. 81, p. 89.

91. *Ibid.*, pp. 92–93. Mazella was later elevated to the cardinalate by Pope Leo XIII.

92. See Hofstadter, *Social Darwinism*, p. 16; Morrison, "Evolution," pp. 127–128.

93. "The Pastoral Letter of 1884" in Peter Guilday, ed., *The National Pastorals of the American Hierarchy (1792–1919)*, (Washington: National Catholic Welfare Council, 1923), p. 239.

94. Quoted in Morrison, "Evolution," p. 21.

95. "Christianity and Modern Science," *American Catholic Quarterly Review*, XIII (January, 1888), pp. 1–9.

96. See McAvoy, *Americanist Heresy*.

97. See the anonymous "Criticisms and Notes," *Ecclesiastical Review*, LXXIII (August, 1925), p. 210.

98. Rome, November 27, 1898. Quoted in Morrison, "Evolution," p. 233, fn. 100.

99. The entire episode is given in Ralph E. Weber, *Notre Dame's John Zahm, American Catholic Apologist and Educator* (Notre Dame: University of Notre Dame Press, 1961), 99–128.

100. Two noteworthy examples are Ellis, *Intellectual Life*, and O'Dea *Catholic Dilemma*. A volume of readings published in 1961 contains excerpts from forty-six books and articles on the question from the period 1955–1958 alone: Frank L. Christ and Gerard E. Sherry, eds., *American Catholicism and the Intellectual Ideal* (New York: Appleton-Century-Crofts, Inc., 1961).

101. United States Commissioner of Education, *Annual Report, 1870* (Washington, 1870), p. 418, quoted in John Tracy Ellis, *The Formative Years of The Catholic University of America* (Washington: American Catholic Historical Association, 1946), p. 18. See the entire Chapter I of Ellis, pp. 15–86.

102. "Shall We Have a University?" *American Catholic Quarterly Review*, I (April, 1876), p. 232.

103. Cf. Hofstadter, *Anti-Intellectualism*, pp. 33–34, and Ellis, *Formative Years*, pp. 22–26.

104. See John Henry Cardinal Newman, *The Idea of a University* (New York: Longmans, Green and Co., 1947), xxvii.

105. This is the opinion of Ellis, *Formative Years*, p. 26.

106. *Recollections of Seventy Years* (Boston: Houghton Mifflin Co., 1934), pp. 323–324.

107. Joseph Gorayeb, S.J., *The Life and Letters of Walter Drum, S.J.* (New York: The America Press, 1938), p. 33.

108. See O'Riordan's debate with Robert Seton in the *Freeman's Journal*, July 30, September 3, October 29, December 3, 1898.

109. "The Higher and Lower Education of the American Priesthood," *American Catholic Quarterly Review*, XV (January, 1890), p. 108.

110. "Vocations to the Priesthood," *American Catholic Quarterly Review*, V (January, 1880), p. 38.

111. The Milwaukee sermon, under the title "The Catholic Priesthood," is quoted in David F. Sweeney, O.F.M., *The Life of John Lancaster Spalding, First Bishop of Peoria, 1840–1916* (New York: Herder and Herder, 1965), pp. 136–138.

112. This sermon was published under the title "University Education" in *The Memorial Volume: A History of the Third Plenary Council of Baltimore* (Balti-

more: The Baltimore Publishing Company, 1855), pp. 87–101; quotations used here are from pp. 92–94.

113. See Ellis, *Formative Years*, pp. 81–82; Patrick H. Ahern, *The Catholic University of America, 1887–1896; the Rectorship of John J. Keane* (Washington: The Catholic University of America Press, 1948), p. 93, fn. 20.

114. See Daniel F. Reilly, *The School Controversy* (Washington, D.C.: The Catholic University of America Press, 1943); Robert D. Cross, *The Emergence of Liberal Catholicism in America* (Cambridge, Mass.: Harvard University Press, 1958), Chapter VII, "The Question of the Schools," pp. 130–145.

115. O'Gorman (1843–1921) was consecrated Bishop of Sioux Falls on April 19, 1896. Pace (1861–1938), a priest of the Diocese of St. Augustine, received the S.T.D. degree from Propaganda in Rome (1886) and the Ph.D. degree, *magna cum laude*, from the University of Leipzig (1891) where he studied under Wilhelm Wundt. When O'Gorman and Pace were engaged to teach at the Columbian Catholic Summer School in 1896, Bishop Sebastian G. Messmer of Green Bay, President of the school, attempted unsuccessfully to cancel the engagements, on the grounds that "the Catholic University and its Professors and Rector are not looked upon with favor by many of our Catholics;" Ahern, *Keane*, p. 174. The soundness of Pace's philosophy was questioned by Father Herman J. Heuser, conservative editor of the *Ecclesiastical Review*, who called Wundt, Pace's mentor at Leipzig, "one of most powerful agents for spreading materialistic doctrines in Germany;" *ibid.*, p. 175.

116. *Ibid.*, pp. 120 ff; Sweeney, *Spalding*, pp. 244–246. The dismissal was almost certainly the work of Cardinal Francesco Satolli, Apostolic Delegate to the United States (1893–1896).

117. *Our Seminaries: An Essay on Clerical Training* (New York: William H. Young and Company, 1897), pp. 250–252. The volume received an exceptionally favorable response from diocesan clergy and its criticisms touched off a lively public discussion in the pages of the *American Ecclesiastical Review* which lasted several years and attracted such pro-Smith contributors as Bishop McQuaid of Rochester. There were enough critics, however, to persuade Smith to publish a second edition in 1908 under the title, *The Training of a Priest: An Essay on Clerical Education, with a Reply to the Critics* (New York: Longmans, Green and Co.). Observing that, "The diocesan clergy praised it without stint, while dissenting from particular views," Smith dealt with the criticism leveled against the book by certain religious, that he had ignored the contributions of the religious orders. In writing, he explained in reply, he "had in mind a singular phenomenon, the rise of the diocesan priest in the American democracy to the important place which the religious priest occupies in the Old World. The brothers have changed places, a curious circumstance, which renders necessary the better training of the diocesan priest. . . . There is a stern necessity to remove from the diocesan priest the sense of inferiority, so long cherished by himself in the foolishness, and so thoughtfully sustained by the selfish among the religious communities," p. 398. He took note, too, of a typical German criticism, in *The Review* of St. Louis, which read: "All this fuss about being 'up to date,' 'not antiquated,' 'good enough for Europe but not for America,' 'American Church and American needs,' 'American boy and American priest,' 'even American theology and American asceticism' all this, we think, now more than ever, smells too strongly of Liberalism. . . . Moreover, we consider that too much condescension is given to the American boy. The youth of our country are the most inconstant and fickle-minded we hear of. They are made so by the atmosphere of Protestantism and infidelity in which they grow up," p. 349. To this criticism Smith replied: "The plan of saving the souls of Americans by making them or keeping them German or French sounds like a suitable theme for comic opera;" p. 350.

118. "The Mission of Catholics in America," a sermon preached on November 10, 1889 in the cathedral of Baltimore on the occasion of the 100th anniversary

of the establishment of the American hierarchy; published in Ireland, *Modern Society*, 74.

119. "The Church and the Age," a sermon preached on October 18, 1893 in the cathedral of Baltimore on the occasion of the 25th anniversary of the episcopal consecration of Cardinal Gibbons; in *ibid.*, p. 97.

120. James Cardinal Gibbons, *The Ambassador of Christ* (Baltimore: John Murphy & Co., 1896), p. 171.

121. See James F. Cleary, "Catholic Participation in the World's Parliament of Religions, Chicago, 1893," *CHR*, LV (January, 1970), pp. 585–609. For another account of the Parliament see John Henry Barrows, ed., *The World's Parliament of Religions*, 2 vols. (Chicago, 1893). Cf. Ahern, *Keane*, pp. 145–149.

122. Quoted in Barrows, ed., *World's Parliament*, I, pp. 16–17.

123. October 28, 1893; quoted in Ahern, *Keane*, p. 147.

124. *Leonis XIII Acta*, XV, pp. 323 ff., cited by *ibid.*, p. 149.

125. See Thomas T. McAvoy, "Bishop John Lancaster Spalding (1840–1916) and the Catholic Minority," *The Review of Politics*, XII (January, 1950), pp. 3–19. Archbishop John J. Glennon of St. Louis said of Spalding at the latter's golden sacerdotal jubilee, November 24, 1913, "I have no fear in placing Archbishop Spalding . . . as the one Catholic who has best understood the American mind. He has understood it because in all wherein it was best, it was his own. . . . And knowing it, he did not fear it; and because of the love of it, and because it was his duty, he would instruct and elevate it, he would Catholicize it." Quoted in Sweeney, *Spalding*, p. 366.

126. Encyclical *Testem benevolentiae*, January 22, 1899; quoted in John Tracy Ellis, *Documents of American Catholic History*, revised edition (Chicago: Henry Regnery Company, 1967), II, p. 546.

127. See McAvoy, *Americanist Heresy*, pp. 217–258.

128. McAvoy, *Catholic Church in the United States*, p. 220. For these reasons Richard Hofstadter could write: "The Progressive mind was preeminently a Protestant mind; and even though much of its strength was in the cities, it inherited the moral traditions of rural evangelical Protestantism." *The Age of Reform, from Bryan to F.D.R.* (New York: Knopf, 1955), p. 203.

129. See Robert J. North, S.J., "The American Scripture Century," *AER*, CL (May, 1964), pp. 322–323; John L. Murphy, "Seventy-five Years of Fundamental Theology in America, Part I," *AER*, CL (June, 1964), pp. 391–393.

130. A layman, Charles B. Herbermann, was editor in chief. Others on the organizing board of editors were Fathers Pace, Thomas J. Shahan, and John J. Wynne, S.J., and a second layman, Condé B. Pallen. Their formal work began at a meeting on January 11, 1905. The first volume appeared in March, 1907.

131. (New York: Macmillan, 1906.) See Francis L. Broderick, *Right Reverend New Dealer: John A. Ryan* (New York: Macmillan, 1963), pp. 27–75.

132. October 8, 1903.

133. Riordan to John J. Hughes, C.S.P., superior general, San Francisco, November 27, 1909; quoted in James Patrick Gaffey, "The Life of Patrick William Riordan, Second Archbishop of San Francisco, 1841–1914" (unpublished Ph.D. dissertation, The Catholic University of America, 1965), pp. 195–196. Moore went on to achieve a national and international reputation as a clinical psychologist at the Catholic University of America.

134. See Michael J. Murphy, "The Cornell Plan of Bishop Bernard J. McQuaid," *St. Meinrad Essays*, 12 (May, 1959), pp. 76–85. In educational matters the reputed "conservative" McQuaid promoted a genuinely progressive policy within his own diocese, as acknowledged by such "liberals" as Spalding, the Abbé Félix Klein, and Mother Seraphine Ireland, S.S.J., a sister of the Archbishop of St. Paul. See Gaffey, "Riordan," p. 517, n. 40. Within his own house some did not think he was progres-

sive enough, however, e.g., Edward J. Hanna, professor of dogmatic theology in St. Bernard's Seminary; *ibid.*, pp. 515–516.

135. San Francisco, July 24, 1906; quoted in *ibid.*, p. 185.

136. A description of Catholic life in New York at this time is given in John Talbot Smith, *The Catholic Church in New York*, 2 vols. (New York, 1905), II, pp. 449–459.

137. *AER*, XXIII (September, 1900), p. 234. Because of such comments it has been assumed popularly for many years that Gigot was a "modernist" and that he fell under a cloud after the condemnation of "Modernism" by Pope Pius X in 1907. There is no evidence, however, that either was the case. Gigot remained on the seminary faculty until his death on June 14, 1920.

138. See the interesting details of Ousanni's life and career in E. Harold Smith, "Recollections of the Aftermath," *Continuum*, 2 (Summer, 1965), pp. 236–237. Another distinguished Orientalist at this time was Father Eugene Xavier-Louis-Henri Hyvernat (1858–1941), who had come to the Catholic University of America in 1889.

139. Dyer to Driscoll, Baltimore, January 18, 1905, in the privately printed letter of Dyer, *To the Sulpicians of the United States* (Baltimore: St. Mary's Seminary, 1906), p. 15.

140. *Ibid.*, pp. 11–13. At first the review was to be called *The Apologist* or *The Apologetic Review*. Eventually, the editors decided on the *New York Review: A Journal of the Ancient Faith and Modern Thought*. Many years later, William L. Sullivan, a convinced modernist who left the Paulists and the Church in 1909, claimed a share of the credit for conceiving and founding the *Review*; see his *Under Orders: The Autobiography of William Laurence Sullivan* (New York: Richard R. Smith, 1944), pp. 105–108. In these same pages Sullivan describes the intellectual difficulties of Driscoll, Gigot, and Duffy, and remarks of Archbishop (later Cardinal) Farley that, although he was proud of the *Review*, "The poor Cardinal had not the least idea what these discussions in criticism were all about: and once in a while he dropped an inept remark concerning them, which his faculty transmitted to us with irreverent delight. We heard, however, of murmurs in opposition. A Canadian bishop, we were told, one day flung down a copy of the *Review* upon his table saying: 'I cannot get even a smell of orthodoxy from that thing.' "; p. 108.

141. Farley to Dyer, New York, March [n.d.] 1905; Dyer, *To the Sulpicians*, p. 54.

142. Dyer to Driscoll, Baltimore, January 18, 1905; *ibid.*, p. 16.

143. Dyer's account of Gigot's words to him in a meeting at Dunwoodie on January 13, 1906; *ibid.*, p. 69. The difficulties of censorship encountered by Gigot are recounted in pp. 4–21 and pp. 36–51.

144. Ibid., p. 58. The signatures to this letter were: James F. Driscoll, R[ichard] K. Wakeman, Francis E. Gigot, John R. Mahoney, and Timothy P. Holland. Holland joined not New York but his native diocese of Ogdensburg.

145. *Ibid.* Scattered through this collection of correspondence and commentary are petulant statements such as the following: "They could hardly have treated St. Sulpice and myself, her representative, with more contemptuous disregard . . . ; they have proceeded as though we did not exist, as though we had not a word to say about our own affairs; they decided upon and disposed of our interests, as though we were children or imbeciles, and they, our appointed guardians"; p. 123. Perhaps the only positive contribution of Dyer's work was to history, for it is thanks to his published compilation that we have the pertinent correspondence for the *New York Review* origins and for the withdrawal of the five faculty from St. Sulpice.

146. *Ibid.*, p. 104; also see pp. 53–58 and pp. 123–127. Cf. *The Catholic News* (New York), February 24, 1906.

147. Bruneau stayed at Baltimore one year, then went, in 1907, to St. John's Seminary in Brighton, Massachusetts. In 1909 he returned to St. Mary's in Baltimore

where he would stay, eventually becoming superior, until his death in 1933. His only serious published work after leaving Dunwoodie was a translation from English to French, with preface, of an 1865 study, *The Catholic Doctrine of the Atonement*, by Henry Nutcombe Oxenham (1829–1888), a leading figure in the Oxford Movement and convert to Catholicism, who left the Church briefly in the 1870's over the issue of infallibility. Bruneau's translation, *Histoire du Dogme de la Redemption: Essay [sic] historique et apologetique, avec une introduction sur le principe des développements théologiques* (Paris: Bloud, 1909), was roundly criticized in *La Civiltà cattolica*, I (January 27, 1910), pp. 331–337, where it was rejected for its "serious lack of critical history" and its "Protestant and rationalist prejudices." The papal Secretary of State directed Gibbons to make an investigation of Bruneau's teaching and writing, in consequence of which Bruneau's orthodoxy was successfully defended. See Ellis, *Gibbons*, II, pp. 475–476. Bruneau was never cited for "modernism" as such.

148. January 13 and February 3, 1906.

149. "To the Editor of the Boston Transcript," published in the Philadelphia *Catholic Times and Standard*, March 3, 1906.

150. John R. Slattery, "The Workings of Modernism," *The American Journal of Theology*, XIII (October, 1909), p. 571.

151. The writer is indebted for this information, and for copies of some of the pertinent documents concerning Driscoll and his colleagues, to Father Terrence F. X. O'Donnell, Church of St. Barnabas, Bronx, New York. The arrangement with Columbia University lasted from 1902 to 1925, when the privilege was revoked by the university's trustees because of many years of non-use: practically speaking, the connection was severed by Dunwoodie after the condemnation of modernism in 1907. A fellow student of Driscoll's at Paris, the French "Americanist" Abbé Felix Klein (1862–1953), professor in the Catholic Institute of Paris, paid a visit to Dunwoodie in 1904 and observed that the curriculum seemed "very well adapted to the present needs"; see Arthur J. Scanlan, *St. Joseph's Seminary, Dunwoodie, New York, 1896–1921* (New York: The United States Catholic Historical Society, 1922), p. 110.

152. Five of Loisy's books had earlier been placed on the Index of Prohibited Books, on December 17, 1903.

153. "Pascendi Dominici gregis," in Colman J. Barry, O.S.B., *Readings in Church History*, 3 vols. (Westminster, Md.: The Newman Press, 1965), III, pp. 112–113.

154. Quoted from *Pascendi* as translated in J. B. Lemius (Father John Fitzpatrick, tr.), *Catechism on Modernism: According to the Encyclical "Pascendi Dominici Gregis" of His Holiness, Pius X* (New York: Benziger Bros., 1908), p. 102. Father Joseph Lemius (1860–1923), an Oblate of Mary Immaculate, was a theologian who held various posts in the Roman curia. He may have been the principal author of the doctrinal part of the encyclical itself, according to evidence published last year by Alec R. Vidler, *A Variety of Catholic Modernists* (Cambridge: At the University Press, 1970), pp. 17–18.

155. *Ibid.*, pp. 102–103.

156. Certain of these documents are summarized in Ellis, *Seminary Education*, pp. 247–248.

157. Unsigned article, "Modernism in the Church in America," XXXVIII (January, 1908), pp. 1–3; Anthony Viéban, S.S., "Who Are the Modernists of the Encyclical?" XXXVIII (May, 1908), pp. 489–507; and Charles Warren Currier, C.SS.R. "Modernism in the Past Year, A Review," XXXIX (November, 1908), pp. 465–472; (December, 1908), pp. 618–627. The published books were J. B. Lemius, *Catechism on Modernism*; John Godrycz, *The Doctrine of Modernism and Its Refutation* (Philadelphia: John Joseph McVey, 1908); Norbert Jones, C.R.L., *Old Truths, Not Modernist Errors, Exposure of Modernism and Vindication of Its*

Condemnation by the Pope (New York: Benziger Bros., 1908); Thomas E. Judge (ed. and trans.), *The Encyclical of His Holiness Pius X on the Doctrines of the Modernists* (Chicago: n.p., 1908).

158. Attempts to identify the two movements in one way or another were made by Houtin, *L'Américanisme* (Paris, 1904); Dr. Anton Gisler, *Der Modernismus, Dargestellt und gewürdigt* (Einsiedeln, 1912); Jean Rivière, *Le Modernisme dans l'Eglise: Étude d'histoire réligieuse contemporaine* (Paris, 1929); Alec R. Vidler, *The Modernist Movement in the Roman Church: Its Origins and Outcome* (Cambridge, England: At The University Press, 1934); and more recently, Emmanuele Chiettini, O.F.M., "Americanismo," *Enciclopedia Cattolica* (Citta del Vaticano, 1948), I, p. 1056. A convincing rebuttal to this position is Thomas T. McAvoy, C.S.C., "Liberalism, Americanism, Modernism," *RACHS*, LXII (December, 1952), pp. 225–231.

159. XXXVIII (January, 1908), p. 2.

160. See above, fn. 158.

161. See above, fn. 157.

162. See his autobiography, *Under Orders*. Also see his *Letters to His Holiness Pope Pius X* (Chicago: Open Court Publishing Co., 1910), in which he describes defects in the Church and its ministers; and a partially autobiographical novel, *The Priest: A Tale of Modernism in New England* (Boston: Sherman, French and Co., 1911). A recent study of Sullivan appears in John Ratté, *Three Modernists: Alfred Loisy, George Tyrrell, William L. Sullivan* (New York: Sheed and Ward, 1967), pp. 259–336.

163. LXI (September 6, 1906), pp. 565–571.

164. XIII (October, 1909), pp. 555–574.

165. New York *Sun*, July 18, 1908.

166. July 19, 1908. Mulvey contributed one book review to the *New York Review*, on Francis G. Peabody, *Jesus Christ and the Social Question*, in *NYR*, II (May-June, 1907), pp. 796–798. Otherwise, he seems to have had little contact with other progessive centers of American Catholicism.

167. *Modernist Movement*, p. 213.

168. Quoted by Sullivan, *Letters to His Holiness*, xiii.

169. *Ibid.*, xvii–xviii.

170. See Currier, "Modernism in the Past Year: A Review," *Ecclesiastical Review*, XXXIX (December, 1908), pp. 618–619.

171. *Ibid.*, p. 619. Colman J. Barry, O.S.B., *The Catholic University of America, 1903–1909, The Rectorship of Denis J. O'Connell* (Washington: The Catholic University of America Press, 1950), p. 176.

172. This information was given to the writer by Father Terrence F. X. O'Donnell.

173. *NYR*, III, 2, 3 (September, October, November, December, 1907), iii. The advertisement at question was a half-page notice of *Through Scylla and Charybdis* and eight other books. A copy of this number of the *NYR* is in the Villanova University Library.

174. Archives of the Archdiocese of New York [hereafter cited AANY] Box I-11-K, Falconio to Farley, Washington, D.C. January 15, 1908. (The writer is grateful for the permission to use these archives given by Cardinal Terence J. Cooke, Archbishop of New York, and for the kind assistance rendered him in their use by Father Robert B. O'Connor, M.L.S., Librarian of St. Joseph's Seminary, Yonkers.) Falconio had earlier written to Cardinal Gerolamo Gotti, Prefect of the Propaganda, describing the *Review* as a periodical "which appears a little suspect of *Modernism;*" Falconio to Gotti, Washington, D.C., October 15, 1907, quoted in Gaffey, "Riordan," p. 524. Falconio was a naturalized American citizen, born in 1842 at Pescocostanzo, Italy, admitted to the Order of Friars Minor in Italy in 1860 (final vows, 1864), and ordained in Buffalo, New York by Bishop John Timon,

C.M., in 1866. After a varied career in New England during which he served as President of St. Bonaventure's College and Seminary, Allegheny, New York (1868–1869), administrator, chancellor, and vicar general of the Diocese of Harbor Grace (1871–1872), and missionary in New York and Connecticut (1882–1884), he returned to Italy in 1884 to become Provincial of the friars' Province of St. Bernardine. Consecrated bishop in 1892, he was appointed first Apostolic Delegate to Canada in 1899, and to the same post at Washington in 1902. He would be named a cardinal in 1911 and die at Rome in 1917. The "no favorable impression" at Rome may have been related to Falconio by Alexis Henri Lépicier, O.S.M. (1863–1936), a Servite professor at the Urban College of Propaganda who had publicly refuted three in a series of four articles in the *New York Review* on "The Human Knowledge of Christ," by Edward J. Hanna (1860–1944), professor of dogmatic theology at St. Bernard's Seminary, Rochester, New York: *NYR*, I (October-November, 1905), pp. 303–376; (December, 1905-January, 1906), pp. 425–436; and (February-March, 1906), pp. 597–615. Hanna's articles, which would later cause him much personal grief (see below), discussed the possible limitations of Christ's human knowledge, and opened to question the then common teaching that Christ as man enjoyed the beatific vision from birth. Lépecier, without mentioning Hanna by name, took copies of the *Review* into his classes, read excerpts from the Hanna articles, and, according to the reports of his students, commented that these were not the writings of professed enemies of the Church, but were writings found in a review published "Seminario Sancti Joseph Neo Eboracensis." See Gaffey, "Riordan," p. 525 and n; cf. Smith, "Recollections of the Aftermath," p. 234. Lépicier later published his lectures on the Hanna articles — this time mentioning the American by name — under the title, *De stabilitate et progressu dogmatis* (Rome, Typographia Editrix Romana, 1908). Since Lépicier was in communication with Falconio, it was perhaps the former's correspondence that led Falconio to make his charges against the *Review*.

175. AANY, Box I-11-K [all materials relating to the *Review* are grouped under this rubric in the archives], Farley to Falconio, New York, January 22, 1908 (copy).

176. AANY, Box I-11-K, John F. Brady to Falconio, New York, January 17, 1908 (copy).

177. *Under Orders*, p. 108.

178. Albert Houtin, *Histoire du modernisme catholique* (Paris: Chez l'auteur, 1913), p. 241. For Hanna see fn. 174, above. The Paulist McSorley, professor of dogmatic theology in St. Thomas College, Washington, D.C., was liberally oriented but hardly a modernist. Clifford (1859–1938), who contributed two articles and three book reviews to the *NYR*, had begun his sacerdotal career as a Jesuit. He attended City College and Fordham in his native New York City, entered the Society of Jesus in 1879, took further studies at Innsbruck and Louvain, and was ordained priest in 1898. He resigned from the Society in the following year, hoping for incardination into the Archdiocese of New York. Failing in that effort, he began a varied career that included teaching in Archbishop Ireland's St. Thomas College in St. Paul, Minnesota; the editorship of the Providence, Rhode Island, *Visitor*; parochial work in Bloomington and Morristown, New Jersey; teaching again, as professor of metaphysics and church history, in the Immaculate Conception Seminary of Seton Hall College, South Orange, New Jersey, which position he held in the eventful years 1907–1909; parochial work in Whippany, New Jersey; and, from 1913 to shortly before his death, lecturer on scholastic philosophy in the graduate school of Columbia University. Never in thought or sentiment a modernist, nonetheless Clifford appears to have fallen under suspicion. He was removed from his teaching position in 1909, ostensibly to conform with a decree of the Sacred Congregation of Religious (dated June 15, 1909) which prohibited ex-order priests from teaching or holding administrative positions in seminaries. However, *The Independent* of New York insinuated that he was removed because of modernism

(unsigned editorial, "Dunwoodie and Modernism," LXXVII (September 23, 1909), p. 716. And Father Terrence F. X. O'Donnell, to whom the present writer is indebted for information about Clifford, reports that some older priests in New Jersey wonder if the decree was used as a justification, and Clifford was in fact removed for reasons of safety. In any case, he deserves this lengthy mention as being one of the most gifted clerical minds of the decade. Father O'Donnell described him to the present writer as the exemplar of a priest interested in everything that was happening: "If something was new in Catholic thought, he would know about it. Ever an omnivorous reader, possessed of the memory of an eidetic, of a keen and penetrating mind, he also had the exquisite touch of a well bred gentleman. . . . His personal library was a treat for all who were privileged to view it. . . . It was no mean tribute to Fr. Clifford that President Nicholas Murray Butler of Columbia and Dr. Alexis Carrel of the Rockefeller Institute (both close personal friends of Clifford) took the time and trouble to go all the way to Morristown, N.J., to attend his funeral [see *New York Times*, December 8, 1938]."

179. AANY, Box I-12-K, Kennedy to Farley, Rome, December 26, 1907. The reference to Hanna concerns yet another article of the Rochester professor which was called into question by Roman authorities at the time Hanna was under consideration as coadjutor to Archbishop Riordan of San Francisco. His peculiar case, part of the modernism story, will be treated briefly later in the narrative. Msgr. Kennedy (1858–1917) was a native of Conshohocken, Pennsylvania. After ordination at Rome in 1887 he served successively as member of the faculty and Vice Rector of St. Charles Borromeo Seminary, Overbrook, until his appointment as rector of his alma mater, the North American College. He was promoted to titular archbishop in 1915. His correspondence in the AANY suggests that he was something of a gossip. Farley had other Roman sources of information, including William J. Ring, O.M.I., a convert, native of Ireland, who did missionary work in England, Canada, and the United States, and led Irish national pilgrimages to Lourdes and Rome. In Rome during the winter and spring of 1908, Ring wrote Farley: "I shall presume Your Grace's sanction to report anything of importance that may come under my notice with reference to the Encyclical, etc., for I imagine we are only at the beginning of a very serious controversy;" AANY, Box-I-11-R, February 22, 1908.

180. Genocchi was the exegete and consultor of the Pontifical Biblical Commission mentioned above in connection with Driscoll's lecture series at Dunwoodie. A man of pronounced liberal views, he used his influence to help friends during the anti-modernism reaction, and came under suspicion himself. Fogazzaro (1842–1911) was a layman and a novelist, best known in his own time for *Piccolo mondo antico* (1895). A sequel, *Il Santo* (1906), stressed the need for social, intellectual, and especially spiritual reform in the Church. It was quickly placed on the Index, which explains his pariah status in 1907. A recent study of Italian modernists is by Michele Ranchetti, *Cultura e riforma religiosa nella storia del modernismo* (Torino: Giulio Einaudi editore, 1963), pp. 91–183; this work has recently been published in English translation, *The Catholic Modernists: A Study of the Religious Reform Movement, 1864–1907* (Oxford University Press, 1969).

181. AANY, Box I-11-K, Falconio to Farley, Washington, D.C., January 15, 1908.

182. AANY, Box-11-K, Farley to Falconio, New York, January 22, 1908.

183. AANY, Box I-11-M, Mitty to Farley, Rome, January 19, 1908.

184. AANY, Box I-11-A, Albert to Farley, Rome, April 7, 1908.

185. AANY, Box I-11-R, Ryan to Farley, Rome, April 11, 1908.

186. AANY, Box I-11-S, Sheeran to Farley, Rome, April 12, 1908.

187. AANY, Box I-11-A, Albert to Farley, Rome, November 18, 1908.

188. AANY, Box 1-12-K, Kennedy to Farley, Rome, November 8, 1908. There is no record in the AANY of Farley's reply, if any. Cardinal Rafael Merry del Val

(1865–1930), of Spanish-English birth, was Papal Secretary of State (1903–1914).

189. AANY, Box I-12-H, Hughes to Farley, Washington, D.C., January 4, 1909.

190. See *The Catholic News* (New York), July 31, 1909. Slattery wrote of Driscoll's removal: "During the mid-summer vacation of this year, the Very Reverend Dr. Driscoll was removed from the rectorship of this diocesan seminary at Dunwoodie on direct orders from Rome. He was charged with being in touch with a censured priest"; "Workings of Modernism," p. 571. Cf. "Dunwoodie and Modernism" in *The Independent*, pp. 714–716, and Houtin, *Histoire du modernisme catholique*, p. 242, where he mentioned the switch and says of Chidwick: "dont le genre d'érudition ne pouvait porter ombrage a l'autorité suprême."

191. The alliance of Dunwoodie with Columbia would not be revoked formally until 1925, when the Columbia trustees cancelled the arrangement because of many years of non-use. The writer is again grateful to Father Terrence F. X. O'Donnell for a copy of the Minutes of the Trustees, 1924–1925, XLV, pp. 213–214, Report of the Committee on Education, Meeting of January 5, 1925. Chidwick was an alumnus of Manhatten College, ordained at St. Joseph's Seminary in Troy, New York. He served as an assistant at St. Stephen Parish, New York, and later as a chaplain in the United States Navy. He was cited for heroism on the occasion of the sinking of the battleship *Maine* in Havana harbor in 1898. In 1904 he became pastor of St. Ambrose and shortly afterwards was given the additional duties of police force chaplain.

192. See Smith, "Recollections of the Aftermath," p. 237.

193. The "bomb" to which Hales referred was the encyclical *Pascendi*; "The Americanist Controversy," *Month*, 31 (January, 1964), p. 36.

194. See above, fn. 174.

195. American Journal of Theology, X (January, 1906), pp. 175–184.

196. 15 volumes and Index (New York: The Encyclopedia Press, Inc., 1907–1914), I, pp. 61–66.

197. AANY, Box I-11-M, McQuaid to Farley, Rochester, February 2, 1908.

198. This communication, addressed to a "Monsignor Marini," is cited in Gaffey, "Patrick William Riordan," p. 522 and n. This unpublished dissertation and Robert F. McNamara, "Archbishop Hanna, Rochesterian," *Rochester History*, XXV (April, 1963), pp. 1–24, are the indispensable sources for the Hanna-Breen affair. The Gaffey work is documented. The AANY contains a letter in which McQuaid informed Farley: "When it became known that Dr. Breen was the professor at St. Bernard's who was Dr. Hanna's accuser at Rome, he handed in his resignation which met with immediate acceptance. No receding from the stand will be entertained for a moment, no matter what the pleading. I have shown unusual forebearance toward Breen, who is so self-conceited that he is unable to appreciate it." AANY, Box I-11-M, McQuaid to Farley, Rochester, N.Y., February 2, 1908. On Breen's later years see Benjamin J. Blied, "Rev. Andrew E. Breen, D.D., Priest, Professor, Author," *Salesianum*, XLVIII (October, 1953), pp. 172–179.

199. *Catholic Encyclopedia*, I, p. 61. Proposition forty-six of *Lamentabili* condemned the following: "In the primitive Church there was no concept of the reconciliation of the Christian sinner by the authority of the Church, but the Church by very slow degrees only grew accustomed to the concept"; *Acta Sanctae Sedis*, XL (1907), p. 475, quoted in Gaffey, "Riordan," p. 526, n. Bishop Kennedy, who could be relied upon to send the worst news to Farley, wrote the latter all the details surrounding the Roman uproar over Hanna's "unfortunate sentence"; AANY, Box I-12-K, Kennedy to Farley, Rome, January 20, 1908. "I assure you I am no alarmist," Kennedy stated, "but those writings have made a bad impression here . . ." In 1912 the "unfortunate sentence" was amended by a judicious entry in the *errata* of the *Catholic Encyclopedia*, XV, p. 776.

200. *NYR*, III (January–April, 1908), pp. 391–400, pp. 561–568. In a later article on "Penance" for the encyclopedia Hanna took pains to be conspicuously

orthodox, asserting that the Church from the earliest times believed in the power of absolution; *Catholic Encyclopedia*, XI (1911), p. 620. Also in the addenda of Vol. I of *CE* in the later editions.

201. Hanna was consecrated December 4, 1912, as auxiliary to Riordan. He succeeded the latter as archbishop in 1915, retired in 1935, and died at Rome in 1944.

202. See Barry, *The Rectorship of Denis J. O'Connell*, p. 231 n.

203. These events are described in *ibid.*, pp. 229–236; and in Ellis, *Gibbons*, II, pp. 171–182. They included a report dated November 22, 1908, of the University's committee of vigilance (Archbishop Ireland, chairman; Archbishops Farley and John J. Glennon of St. Louis; Bishop Matthew Harkins of Providence; and Denis O'Connell) stating that the University was free of any taint of modernism, but that there were doubts about Poels and his reluctance to accept certain decrees of the Biblical Commission.

204. Washington: n.p., 1910. According to Ellis, Cardinal Gibbons' position in the matter was that, after the "Americanism" debacle, "the university could not well stand to have its orthodoxy questioned again"; *Gibbons*, II, p. 181. A recent critical biography of Poels is Door J. Colsen, C.M., *Poels* (Roermond-Maaseik, J. J. Romen & Zonen, 1955); the Washington years are treated in pp. 162–207.

205. Francis E. Gigot, who wrote sixty-one articles for the *Catholic Encyclopedia* in the years 1907–1912, may be considered one Dunwoodie mind that did not cease activity. In the years between *Pascendi* and his death in 1920 he published three books, including one delicate study, *The Message of Moses and Modern Higher Criticism* (New York: Benziger Bros., 1915), and numerous monographs in the *Irish Theological Quarterly*.

206. *All Things Considered* (New York: John Lane Company, 1909), p. 213.

207. "Rightly Handling the Word of Truth," *AER*, III (December, 1930), p. 580.

208. Lemius, *Modernism*, p. 104, p. 106.

209. M. J. Ryan, "How Are We to Make Scholasticism Popular?" *AER*, XXXIX (September, 1908), p. 229, p. 233.

210. See James A. Magner, "Some Objectives in Seminary Training," *AER*, XXIV (November, 1935), p. 477.

211. Albert A. Power, S.J., *Plain Reasons for Being a Catholic* (New York: Frederick Pustet Co., 1929), pp. 115–116.

212. The title of a book, first published, conveniently, in 1907; see James J. Walsh, *The Thirteenth Greatest of Centuries* (New York: Fordham University Press, 1952). The present writer received a copy as a scholarship prize from St. Thomas Seminary, Bloomfield, Connecticut, in 1952. It seemed appropriate reading even then.

213. The final sentence of an oft-repeated passage of Thomas Babington, Lord Macaulay's review of Leopold van Ranke's *History of the Popes*, in "Revolutions of the Papacy," *Edinburgh Review*, LXXII (October, 1840), p. 228.

214. "Are Our Priests Intellectual?" *Homiletic and Pastoral Review* [hereafter cited as *Homiletic*], XXIII (September, 1923), p. 1293.

215. John L. Murphy, "The Seminary College Course," *AER*, XLV (October, 1966), p. 243.

216. "The Priest's Intellectual Arsenal," *Homiletic*, XXIII (August, 1923), p. 1126.

217. Perry Miller and Thomas H. Johnson, eds., *The Puritans*, 2 vols. (New York: Harper & Row, 1963), I, p. 24–25.

218. (Chicago: Willett, Clark & Colby, 1928), p. 227.

219. Is there an American Catholic priest, with the possible exception of John Courtney Murray about whom Arthur M. Schlesinger, Jr. might write an essay under a title similar to his "Theology and Politics from the Social Gospel to the Cold War: The Impact of Reinhold Niebuhr," in Cushing Strout, ed., *Intellectual History in America* (New York: Harper and Row, 1968), pp. 158–181? It is of interest, however, that when the present writer asked this question in a paper read

at the 1968 annual meeting of the American Catholic Historical Association, Protestant church historian Martin E. Marty responded: "The Catholic clergy ought not to be too modest. Reinhold Niebuhr is about the only such man that *we* can point to."

220. "By One of Them," "Are Our Priests Intellectual Men?" *Homiletic*, XXIII (June, 1923), p. 933.

221. J.J.E., "The Intellectual Standard of Our Priests," *Homiletic*, XXIV (October, 1923), pp. 70–72. A not untypical article in the *AER* during this period conceded that, "Practically, except in the case of the missionary priest, there are few professions that leave a man more spare time than the priesthood and this may be either a stepping stone or a stumbling block in the way of salvation." The solution for filling up the cleric's idle hours is given in the title of the article, by Edward B. Jordan, "Nature Study as a Hobby for Priests," LXII (June, 1920), pp. 657–667.

222. "Sacerdos," "Why Don't Our Young Priests Write?" *Homiletic*, XXIII (April, 1923), p. 686. Such writing as priests were doing at this time rarely reached beyond Catholic circles and indeed seems barely to have reached that far. A survey in 1928 of 100 laymen of good education and social standing revealed that most were unfamiliar with Catholic books and authors. Many, however, had read or purchased such works as Bruce Barton, *The Man Nobody Knows*, Will Durant, *The Story of Philosophy*, and Ralph Waldo Trine, *In Tune With the Infinite*. See S. A. Boldus, "Who Reads a Catholic Book?" *Catholic World*, CXXVII (September, 1928), pp. 714–716.

223. See, for example, "The Church and Science" in the celebrated answer book by Bertrand L. Conway, C.S.P., *The Question Box*, New Edition (New York: The Paulist Press, 1929), 114–116. Even John A. Zahm, C.S.C. was led to announce, triumphally, ". . . It would be less difficult, in the light of authentic history, to tell what the Church has not done for science than to state what she has done. To tell what the Church has done would be to write the history of every branch of science . . ."; *What the Church Has Done for Science* (Notre Dame, Indiana: "Ave Maria" Press, 1920), pp. 8–9. There is a perceptive article on this kind of literature in 1934 by John M. Cooper, "Christ and the Other Sheep, Our Human Cooperation in the Divine Work of Redemption," *AER*, X (May, 1934), pp. 449–461. A professor of anthropology in the Catholic University of America, Father Cooper marshalled facts and statistics that gave the lie to what he called "our unjustifiable scientific conceit." His article was also an extraordinary indictment for its time of the "hypocrisy" of American Catholics on the issues of Negro-white relations, poverty and social justice, birth control, honesty in government, and clean speech.

224. The interviews were conducted by Father Philip J. Murnion, of St. Gregory's Parish, New York City, as part of a study of the changing structure of the pastoral ministry from the 1920's to the present. It is a careful and thorough study, and the present writer is much indebted to Father Murnion for the use in this essay of his preliminary findings.

225. West Point had been proposed as a model for seminaries by the New Yorker, John Talbot Smith, in *Our Seminaries*, in 1897. He qualified the proposal somewhat in the 1908 sequel. *Training of a Priest*, where he put forward instead St. Bernard's Seminary in Rochester as "a model seminary which the whole world might study with profit"; p. 355.

226. Interviews conducted by Father Murnion; see note 224 above.

227. It is interesting to note that during this period no formal religion course was given in the six years of the minor seminary, save for a brief course in Bible history, and none was given in the first two years of major seminary except for an introduction to scripture. Furthermore, there was no spiritual director in the minor seminary. It would appear that, for the better part of a priest's education, the idea of a separate school for candidates was not based on the notion of giving them any special training in religious understanding.

228. Martin E. Marty, *The New Shape of American Religion* (New York: Harper Brothers, 1958), p. 74.

229. (Baltimore: John Murphy & Company, 1883).

230. (Baltimore: John Murphy & Company, 1896).

231. (New York: Benziger Brothers, 1903).

232. Tr. Thomas Byrne, (New York: Benziger Brothers, 1901).

233. (Boston: Marlier, Callaran & Company, 1900).

234. (New York: Longmans, Green and Co., 1907).

235. (New York: Longmans, Green and Co., 1896).

236. "Priests as Students and Book Lovers," *Homiletic*, XXIII (December, 1922), p. 254. Examples of these "ephemeral productions" were given by another priest, under the name "One of Them:" . . . They [priests] have daily secular newspapers in abundance. And in addition, the latest issues of *The Literary Digest, The Saturday Evening Post, The Red Book, The Smart Set, Judge, Life*, etc. — one or several of these are almost surely to be found encumbering the priest's desk, free from dust, and giving every indication that they are read from cover to cover"; "Are Our Priests Intellectual Men?" *ibid.*, XXIII (June, 1923), p. 932.

237. *Ambassador of Christ*, p. 173.

238. "Sacerdos," "Why Don't Our Young Priests Write?" *Homiletic*, XXIII (April, 1923), p. 689.

239. *Some Principles and Practices of the Spiritual Life*, pp. 244–245.

240. "Catholics and Science," *Commonweal*, 58 (August 28, 1953), pp. 509–514.

241. *Idea of a University*, xxvii.

242. "The Function of the Catholic Graduate School," *Thought*, XIII (September, 1938), pp. 364, 368, 378. In the same year, John A. O'Brien, still a voice in the wilderness, was saying that "present conditions in America render the need for Catholic scientists and research workers the need of the hour. . . . It too is a priestly ministry. . . ." John A. O'Brien, ed., *Catholics and Scholarship: A Symposium on the Development of Scholars* (Huntington, Indiana: Our Sunday Visitor, 1938), p. 16.

243. "Reversing the Secularist Drift," *Thought*, XXIV (March, 1949), p. 41. Walter J. Ong, S.J., spoke ten years later of the same phenomenon, in *American Catholic Crossroads: Religious — Secular Encounters in the Modern World* (New York: The Macmillan Co., 1959), esp. Chapter 5, "Research and American Catholic Education," pp. 91–117. Many clerical scholars, he said, are "intellectual retailers" who are "more given to compilation than to original discovery"; p. 103.

244. See Winthrop Hudson, *The Great Tradition of the American Churches* (New York: Harper Torchbooks, 1963), pp. 218–219.

245. *Ibid.*, pp. 196–197. Henry Steele Commager observed: "The church itself confessed to a steady secularization: as it invaded the social and economic fields, it retreated from the intellectual. Philosophy, which for over two centuries had been almost the exclusive property of the clergy, slipped quietly from their hands"; *American Mind*, p. 167. As late as 1961 it was the opinion of Peter L. Berger that "Protestantism has had little to say that would be of relevance to the mighty transformation through which American society has been passing"; *The Noise of Solemn Assemblies: Christian Commitment and the Religious Establishment in America* (Garden City, N.Y.: Doubleday & Co., 1961), p. 35.

246. "For a variety of reasons, this theological effort [neo-orthodoxy] has now run its course, and a new era has begun. The most potent cause of its demise was the continuing power of secularity in America's national consciousness, rendering the older 'Biblical' motifs, myths, and symbols which neo-orthodoxy sponsored almost meaningless to the laity, and arduous if not ultimately unreal to the preacher and the theologian who sought to work with them." Langdon Gilkey, "Social and Intellectual Sources of Contemporary Protestant Theology in America," *Daedalus*, 96 (Winter, 1967), pp. 82–83.

247. A scholarly biography of Ryan is Broderick, *John A. Ryan.*

248. J. P. Haran, S.J., "The Sacrament of Orders and the Ecumenical Movement" I (February, 1940), pp. 62–66; *Idem.*, "One Church and Reunion Movements," I (December, 1940), pp. 278 283; E. L. Murphy, S.J., "Church Unity and Protestant Missions," I (September, 1940), pp. 209–227.

249. Bishop Robert E. Tracy, *American Bishop at the Vatican Council* (New York: McGraw-Hill Book Company, 1966), p. 172.

250. Murray, "Secularist Drift," p. 41.

251. *Ibid.*, p. 37.

252. *Worship* began under the title *Orate Fratres* in 1925, edited by Virgil Michel, O.S.B.

253. (New York: Sheed and Ward, 1961).

254. See Joseph Clifford Fenton, "The Church and the State of Siege," *AER,* LX (January, 1945), pp. 54–63. "The Church, the City of God, has always been, and, until the end of time will be, beset by enemies. . . . She has always been perfectly correct in judging the mass of mankind outside the fold as hostile to her and to her interests," p. 63.

255. (New York: Simon and Schuster, 1950.)

256. *Modern Society*, I, p. 92. The sermon quoted was preached on November 10, 1889.

JOHN P. MARSCHALL

DIOCESAN AND RELIGIOUS CLERGY: THE HISTORY OF A RELATIONSHIP, 1789-1969

INTRODUCTION

The conciliar history of the Church reveals inner tensions coping with the relationship of the Church to the world on the one hand and with internal relationships on the other. The *Code of Canon Law*, promulgated in 1918, was a document devoted largely to those matters over which the Church had legal control, namely, internal affairs. Vatican Council II — following previous conciliar patterns — focused first on matters strictly ecclesiastical and then found itself under the scrutiny of the world when it began to consider such matters as religious liberty, ecumenism, and the relationship of the Church to non-Christian religions.

Submerged beneath the focus of publicity on these latter subjects was the perennially delicate question of the relationship of the diocesan and religious clergy. Like a scandal within the family, the internal ruptures between religious orders, bishops, and diocesan clergy had been matters discussed privately at rectories or in the common rooms of religious orders, but hostility, competition, and family embarrassment plainly were not matters digestible in public. During Vatican Council II, however, rumors were rife that the smaller congregations were going to be suppressed, or that the distinction between diocesan and religious clergy was being de-emphasized, or that religious orders and congregations were finally going to be allowed or forced to rid themselves of antiquarianism. A congeries of fear, hope, dismay, and uncertainty characterized the response of diocesan or religious priests who received the latest dispatch from a friend or *peritus* at Rome.

Religious bishops — whether to the right or left on other issues — rallied to support Dominican Cardinal Michael Browne's proposal that matters touching the international apostolate or "exemption" or the commission to preach remain unchanged. Three Jesuit missionary bishops, representing seventeen council fathers, battled to retain direct ties of religious groups with the Holy See and to resist closer dependence on the local ordinary. At the same time, Archbishop John C. Heenan of Westminster attacked the schema on the *Church in the Modern World*, because it was drafted by men in monasteries, seminaries, and universities who "hardly know the world as it really is." [1] Joseph T. McGucken, Archbishop of San Francisco, noted that most of those objecting to the schema on bishops were men who wished to reduce the control of liturgy and education by religious orders.[2] The Superior General of the Society of Mary, Joseph Buckley, S.M., spoke plainly to the issues that lay behind the simmering conflict between diocesan and religious clergy. He noted that disagreements between religious, bishops, and diocesan priests were a serious difficulty in the Church. He was quoted as saying:

> Bishops want to exercise a greater authority over the Religious in their diocese. Religious are worried about this. But we Religious might as well face up to the fact that some of our habits irritate the diocesan clergy; for example, our inclination to talk as if we were the only ones in the state of perfection.

"It is safe to say," Father Buckley added, "that Religious priests in active life are closer to diocesan priests than they are to contemplative religious." [3]

As in the past, synodal or conciliar statements have not been formulated in a vacuum. Written with tact, the decrees of the recent ecumenical council never explicitly called attention to disagreements and conflicts between diocesan and religious clergy; they reflected an earnest call to unity and cooperation.[4]

The task of this essay will be to provide some historical flesh for the conciliar pleas for unity by documenting the internal relationships of the American Catholic clergy over the past two centuries. The interactions under consideration will be those between religious congregations (or orders) and diocesan priests.[5] Integrating questions which might be raised at the outset are: "Have we advanced at all since the early days?" or "Are we less raucous but no more enlightened?"

The Ingredients of Controversy: A Historical Model

The history of the priesthood in the United States has been as stormy as the progress of the nation and the Church, but one might propose good-naturedly that it all began with the Jesuits. When on August 16, 1773, the Franciscan Pope Clement XIV capitulated to pressure from the Bourbon courts and suppressed the Society of Jesus, the latter's missionaries comprised the bulk of the clergy ministering to about fifteen or twenty thousand Catholics in the American colonies. In order to preserve their land holdings as income for future apostolic work, the ex-Jesuits formed a group called the "Corporation of the Roman Catholic Clergy." The first Bishop of Baltimore, John Carroll, had himself been a Jesuit and a member of the corporation, which agreed to provide an annuity of $1,000 for his support and that of his successors in the See of Baltimore. At Carroll's death in 1815, his successor, Leonard Neale (also a former Jesuit) gave to the newly restored Society of Jesus control and ownership of Georgetown College and eleven churches.[6]

Upon Neale's death in 1817, the former Sulpician Ambrose Maréchal was appointed Archbishop of Baltimore at a time when the Society of Jesus was in some financial difficulty. The archbishop quickly perceived that the Jesuits might discontinue their subsidy, and so he requested counsel from his friend John Cheverus, Bishop of Boston. Cheverus advised Maréchal to leave the matter to the conscience of the Jesuit superiors and to "live poor without murmurings, and without resentment. . . ."[7] This was not the kind of advice that Archbishop Maréchal was in a mood to accept. To his way of thinking it was not merely a question of finances but one of authority and jurisdiction. While the Jesuits were disputing the legality of the agreement between Archbishop Carroll and the clergy's Maryland corporation, Maréchal threatened to bring the case to civil court.

Meanwhile, the Jesuits decided to pay a reduced annuity of $560 for three years — a situation which Maréchal merely tolerated. In 1822 the matter was appealed to the Sacred Congregation de Propaganda Fide. Warmly articulated claims and counterclaims passed between Maréchal and the Jesuit Superior General, Aloysius Fortis, with the Jesuits threatening to remove all their men from the Province of Baltimore and the archbishop giving notice that he would resign his see if the dispute were not settled in his favor.[8] The Propaganda issued to the Jesuits a brief over the pope's signature demanding that they cede one of their major plantations, *Whitemarsh*, to Maréchal. The Jesuits produced arguments against this plan throughout 1823, just at a time when Pope Piux VII and his Secretary of State, Ercole Cardinal Consalvi, died.

Meanwhile, the Society of Jesus had approached the United States Secretary of State, John Quincy Adams, to protest the Roman brief as an act of interference by a foreign power in the civil affairs of the country.[9] After learning that the United States could not, at this time, resist such appeals, Maréchal informed Rome that he would accept $1,000 per year instead of the Jesuit plantation, denying the alleged poverty of the Jesuits, to whom he referred as "my lords" of the provincial clergy. In addition, Maréchal complained to his friend Joseph Cardinal Fesch that some of the Jesuits were continually appealing to their exempt status in order to remove themselves from his jurisdiction. He urged Fesch to prevail upon the Jesuit General to remove a few troublesome priests from the United States, and at the same time he encouraged the promotion of Father Benedict Fenwick, S.J., to the episcopacy so that he might be "contained" and peace thereby be restored to the archdiocese.[10]

In 1827 the Jesuits agreed to give the archbishop $800 as an annual stipend, and Maréchal accepted this sum on the condition that it would faithfully be paid to his successors in the See of Baltimore. During the next administration of James Whitfield, the Jesuits fought again and in 1829 lost the battle to suspend payment to the new archbishop.[11] The controversy was not completely settled until July of 1838 when Whitfield's successor, Samuel Eccleston, absolved the Jesuits of any further debt to himself or his successors by receiving $8,000 in a lump sum — about half of what was owed.[12] The continued friendly relations of the ex-Sulpician Eccleston and the American Jesuits ended the twenty-year controversy.

The Baltimore-Jesuit controversy reinforced in many a bishop's mind a lingering suspicion of the Society of Jesus and (by association) of any religious order or congregation.[13] Furthermore, the case set in relief the basic sources of disagreement which were to characterize the continued controversies between bishops and religious groups: (1) the prestige that would lend itself to recruiting seminarians in those dioceses where education was controlled by religious communities, and (2) the exempt status of religious orders, which affected the control of land, churches, and monies in particular dioceses.[14]

Although very few American bishops would have denied the absolute necessity of assistance from religious orders, there has been evidence of a distinct anti-religious feeling prevalent among many bishops and diocesan clergymen, as well as a corresponding attitude of superiority or detachment on the part of religious. The concomitant apprehensiveness or suspicion is known to exist by anyone working closely with those in positions of authority — particularly in those areas of the country where the pastoral life of the diocese depends on the assistance of religious groups and where the continued presence of the religious depends on the will of the bishop. Because of the obvious delicacy of such situations, the candid inter-relationships have become exceedingly difficult to document.

The Jesuits have dominated the American scene as intellectual leaders and by the sheer force of their numbers.[15] In addition, the Jesuits (more faithfully than other religious groups) have preserved and calendared their archival materials and permitted their own men as well as non-Jesuit historians to use these documents in their research.[16] Consequently, it would be an easy task — though historically inaccurate — to make the Jesuits the exclusive villains and heroes of this historical piece. It would be equally inaccurate to fail in acknowledging the existence of anti-Jesuit bias independent of other religious orders.

The Struggle for Jurisdiction and Control

The stipend controversy between the archbishops of Baltimore and the Jesuits encouraged the formation of factions sympathetic to one side or the other. One highly placed diocesan priest warned his friends in the Society that Archbishop James Whitfield was at least as much "an enemy of the Jesuits" as was his deceased predecessor Ambrose Maréchal. The priest urged the Jesuit superior to have the archbishop "admonished from Rome to free himself from his hatred for the Society. . . ."[17] And so it has gone. A little more than a decade after the settlement of the stipend controversy, the Maryland Provincial informed the Jesuit General of the unfavorable dispositions held by certain bishops toward religious orders.[18] And a few months later the same John Roothan was warned by Father Pierre De Smet that some bishops planned the "partial secularization" of religious.[19]

One incident that gave color and substance to these reports was the altercation that arose between the Jesuits and the Archbishop of New York, John Hughes. At stake were the archbishop's control of the property of St. John's College (later Fordham University) and the ownership of the Jesuit administered Church of St. Francis Xavier on 16th Street in Hughes' see city. Although the occasion of the conflict was finances, the nub of the problem was the bugbear of ecclesiastical jurisdiction.

The Jesuits charged that Hughes had deprived them of some of their land surrounding St. John's College, that he had gone back on his promise to give the Society a church, and that he had "restricted the spiritual ministry of the Society, by ordering the fathers not to hear the confessions of men, save in the regular confessionals in their church, which are always besieged by women." The Jesuits also secretly feared that St. Francis Xavier Church might be given to diocesan priests by Hughes' successor.[20] Hughes, on his part, countercharged that the Jesuits had agreed never to "claim the privilege of a mendicant order — should never make a collection or appeal to the faithful for alms — except with the previous knowledge and consent of the ordinary," but that they had violated this agreement.[21]

While the legal hassle between Hughes and the Jesuits continued from 1855 to 1860, the archbishop accused the Jesuits of working only with the pious rich, while the members of the Society, in turn, complained of having worked "without a word of appreciation or a penny of financial assistance from the diocese." [22] Hughes was not one to be swayed by this kind of whining, for to his way of thinking the contributions received from the parishoners of the Jesuit-administered church *were* diocesan monies.

The archbishop was a strong, self-confident, and autocratic leader. His control of the body of Irish-Americans and of the Archdiocese of New York is well known to church historians.[23] Hughes was the kind of man who would, according to Orestes Brownson, "suffer no man in my diocese that I cannot control." The archbishop was quoted as having said, "I will either put him down, or he shall put me down." [24] The Jesuits chose to fight the archbishop. They made their claims with rigidity and were met with inflexibility. When it was all over the Jesuits retired bruised and bleeding. They made a general apology for any question they had raised of the archbishop's veracity, candor, or honor. So after five years of heated exchanges, the Jesuits capitulated. Once the Society had tendered its obedience, Hughes agreed to sell the disputed property to them for $45,000. And before the archbishop died in 1864, he arranged for the title of St. Francis Xavier Church to be given to the Jesuits. The latter's surrender was evidently less an admission of fault than a deft maneuver in the art of the possible. The peace-maker in the story, Father John McElroy, used the only method which would placate the archbishop, namely, abject surrender. Good men fought, and what could not be achieved in war was won in peace.[25]

Some of the strongest anti-Jesuit sentiment was articulated at mid-century in St. Louis, where Archbishop Peter Richard Kenrick alleged excessive expense incurred in building the church on the campus of St. Louis University and criticized the Jesuits' lack of support for mission churches.[26] What is pertinent here is the feeling engendered by the controversy. Kenrick spoke of the Jesuits as those who expect the "shadow of a big name" to cover their defects and a group that possesses an "immense desire for praise." He also deplored their inordinate, unique *esprit* that caused them "to assume a position, both with respect to the Ordinaries and Secular clergy, which is anything but promotive [*sic*] of harmonious and united cooperation." He anticipated continued deterioration of relations with the Jesuits unless their exempt status was mitigated.[27] Again the exemption question of religious orders was the nub of the strife. Although Kenrick admitted his "high personal regard" for certain members of the Society, he charged that they constituted a "band apart" which sowed discord in the diocese. "Your influence is becoming too great," the archbishop was quoted as saying; "I ought to clip your wings." [28] This sentiment apparently came to include all religious.[29]

Several years later the Jesuit Bishop of Chicago, James Oliver Van de Velde, was involved in a dispute with the Archbishop of Baltimore. The altercation came about late in 1852 on the occasion of Van de Velde's visit to Rome with the decrees of the First Plenary Council of Baltimore. At that time, the midwestern bishop was seeking to be relieved of his onerous duties as Chicago's ordinary so that he might return to a common life among the Jesuits. Although Kenrick had publicly expressed the wish to have the city of Washington created a diocese distinct from Baltimore, Van de Velde took it upon himself to suggest to Pope Pius IX that the nation's capital be made a vicariate apostolic and that he (Van de Velde) be given episcopal jurisdiction in that territory. Van de Velde proposed to live with the Jesuits at Georgetown and use St. Patrick's Church as his pro-cathedral.[30]

The matter was complicated by the fact that although the Jesuits at one time had a claim on St. Patrick's Church, the property had reverted to its pastor, the Reverend William Matthews, who, in turn, had willed his property to the Archdiocese of Baltimore.[31] In his proposal to the pope, Van de Velde noted that Matthews was "dearly loved" by members of the Society of Jesus, and if Washington were cut off from the jurisdiction of Baltimore, the pastor would "dedicate all his goods to the new diocese." [32]

When Francis Patrick Kenrick, brother of the Archbishop of St. Louis, got wind of Van de Velde's suggestion, he moved quickly to have the whole matter squelched. Writing to Filippo Cardinal Fransoni, Prefect of the Propaganda, he objected to the appointment of anyone but a "proper bishop" for such a distinguished place. He also expressed the wish to place a bishop in Washington who was an outstanding native American.[33] There was no doubt in Kenrick's mind that Van de Velde's plan would place the capital of the nation in the hands of the Jesuits. "It would," he told his friend, Michael O'Connor, Bishop of Pittsburgh, "serve no purpose but the narrow views of the Society to the prejudice of the higher interest of the Church at large." If Van de Velde were given jurisdiction over the District of Columbia, Kenrick felt that "all would be absorbed by the Society" with the consequent difficulties of appointing a successor.[34]

The difficulties of the Kenrick brothers with Van de Velde and the Jesuits of St. Louis were matched many times afterwards as bishops and religious orders engaged in disputes over parochial rights. What was, on the surface, a difference of opinion concerning the "care of souls" often was complicated by financial concerns. One of the most colorful of these engagements occurred between the Jesuits and the Archbishop of San Francisco, Joseph S. Alemany, O.P. The two legal issues at stake were whether the Jesuits should be permitted to own the property of their college church (which served some of the laity not associated with the school), and whether their Marian sodality could be legitimately established in the city of San Francisco.[35] When, in 1863, Alemany removed the Jesuit church's quasi-parochial character, the Jesuits acceded at once, but the troubles did not end. The problem was not basically a legal one, and it could not be resolved by appealing to ancient privileges or to canon law governing episcopal authority.

What irked the San Francisco diocesan priests was that the Jesuit church was drawing many parishioners away from Sunday observance in the territorial churches. This was done, the diocesan men claimed, by enrolling men and women in a sodality whose indulgences could not be gained except by attendance at the Jesuit church. Finances were at the heart of the dispute. As Alemany put it to the Jesuit visitator: "There are other Churches in this city besides St. Ignatius, and they are much in debt, and are entitled to the support of their respective faithful; if the Jesuit Fathers wish to ignore this, no written agreements can satisfy me." [36]

Before acting against the Jesuit church, Alemany consulted almost a dozen of his priests in the area concerning their opinion of the "harmful" effects of Jesuit activities. Almost without exception the priests noted that the sodality and the attraction of indulgences alienated many people from their territorial churches. One objected to the blessing of babies and the sale of "Ignatius Water" in the Jesuit church. "It is my firm conviction," wrote another priest to Alemany, "that the element of meanness predominates in the means used by the Reverend Fathers to 'fill-up' their vast hall and alianate [*sic*] the Catholics of this city from their respective churches and pastors. . . ." [37] An important response to Alemany's query came from the Vicar General, James Croke, who in the opinion of certain Jesuits was the leader of the "attack" against them. In Croke's estimation, the members of the Society had succeeded in persuading many of the people of San Francisco that "Jesuit Fathers alone are the only truly devoted and zealous priests — that the seculars have neither the talents nor opportunities nor education to govern parishes or cure souls, and that many of them are endeavoring to serve two masters, God and Mammon." Croke stated that the Jesuits accused the secular priests of clubbing together to persecute the "meek and humble Fathers" and that the motive of this presecution was a "mean jealousy at their superior success in the holy ministry. . . ." [38]

Even after the archbishop had removed St. Ignatius Church from the rolls of "parish" institutions, the conflict dragged on until, in 1868, it was reported to Alemany that the Cardinal Prefect of the Propaganda was ready to rule in favor of the Society. [39] According to Alemany's informant, the Jesuits named the archbishop and certain diocesan priests as being anti-Jesuit. In these reports to Rome as well as in their apparently patronizing attitude which created so much hostility, the Jesuits could not be excused from a breach of charity or of good judgment.

The quarrel between the Archbishop of San Francisco and the Jesuits was closely watched by bishops throughout the country, but more intensely, perhaps, by Francis N. Blanchet, Archbishop of Oregon City. Blanchet's relationship with his priests — whether diocesan or religious — was so unhappy that he found himself under accusation to Pope Pius IX from his own men in 1851. In his replies to the Roman authorities, the archbishop was particularly defensive about his relationship with religious clergy. And in spite of the poor relations existing between himself and the Oblates of Mary Immaculate as well as the Jesuits, he took care to recognize the importance of religious orders in his archdiocese. [40] Blanchet, however, was determined to discover his informants. In the ensuing correspondence his authentic feelings toward religious as well as the issues of parochial jurisdiction, care of souls, finances, and the exemption question all came to the surface.

In a letter to the Oblate provincial superior, Charles Ricard, Blanchet supposed that the Oblates were at least one source of information to the Roman authorities, and he made it clear that he conceived their work in the archdiocese to be limited to a missionary apostolate among the Indians. [41] Three months later, Blanchet and his brother Augustin, Bishop of Nesqually, were absolved by the bishops of the

First Plenary Council of Baltimore of any guilt of charges brought against them "by certain religious societies in their dioceses." [42]

Francis Blanchet, however, continued to pursue the matter in a spirited fashion. In a lengthy letter to Pope Pius IX, he listed the charges brought against him and his brother by the clergy in the archdiocese. The items included: extending extremely harsh treatment of the diocesan clergy and above all of the religious clergy, obstructing the priestly ministry, contributing to a less fruitful missionary apostolate, being the archenemies of the Oblate Fathers, and accusing his priests of more interest in agriculture than in the care of souls. Indignantly, and at great length, the archbishop denied every charge.[43] On the following day he wrote to the Jesuit superior, Michel L. Accolti, and to the Oblate provincial asking if either had made charges against him to Rome. He further demanded to know why they had not so informed him, and he challenged them to provide him with evidence for the charges.[44]

Accolti and Ricard were both piqued by the archbishop's tone and by the implications of his rhetoric. Both denied that they had communicated any information except to their religious superiors. Rather, as Ricard pointed out, "everybody knows, and Your Grace ought not ignore the fact, that everyone knows that the secular clergy of Oregon addressed the complaints to Rome more than a year and a half ago; and that in a collective letter mention was made of antipathy against the regulars." [45] Ricard assumed that it was this letter from the diocesan clergy to which Blanchet was referring. He then enumerated in detail past difficulties between the Oblates and the archbishop. Ricard also recalled the promise made by Blanchet to the Oblates that they would be received into the archdiocese with the rights of common law, which the archbishop had undercut by attempting to obtain privileges opposed to that law. Ricard then hinted that, under the circumstances, it would be difficult for the Superior General to send more Oblates to the archdiocese. Several months later, Blanchet wrote to Cardinal Fransoni implicating the Oblates in the original report to Rome. He also noted that such groups made bishops "subject to judgment by their subjects." He then urged Fransoni to obstruct any attempt by the Oblates to leave the archdiocese!

Six years passed and Blanchet's relationship with the Jesuits and the Oblates had reached the point at which the archbishop could write to Alessandro Cardinal Barnabò: "The Jesuits and the Oblate Fathers cannot help me." [47] Later, Blanchet elaborated on the reasons for his discontent. He noted that the Oblates had been in Olympia for ten years without establishing one new mission for Indians or "whites," and that they had left the archdiocese to go to Victoria without consulting his brother, Augustin, the Bishop of Nesqually. "The good fathers," said Blanchet, "have lived and live together independent of the Bishops. . . ." He also complained that the Oblates had received 18,000 francs from the Society for the Propagation of the Faith, while each of the three bishops in the Northwest received less than that amount. He then accused the Jesuits and the Oblates of neglecting the Indians, suggested that the government could take better care of the natives, and finally asked the cardinal to send another order to replace the present missionaries.[48]

Under these circumstances, it is not surprising that the Jesuits joined the Oblates in an exodus from the Archdiocese of Oregon City. When asked to return to the Indian missions, both groups of religious refused. Blanchet sent another call for help to the Propaganda. When he noted that the religious as well as four diocesan priests had left the archdiocese, the cardinal prefect might have concluded that Blanchet had difficulty building any cooperative relationship with his priests.[49]

One matter that irked Archbishop Blanchet (and which was exacerbated by reports concerning Alemany's difficulties with the Jesuits) was the religious' interpretation of the vow of poverty. While claiming to be at the service of a particular diocese, religious congregations were using income from gifts received by reason of their work in that diocese for apostolic or internal purposes outside the diocese.[50] On the basis of his own experience and what he had heard was the "scandalous" rift between the Jesuits and Archbishop Alemany, Blanchet vented his own feelings in a long report to Cardinal Barnabò.

The Jesuits, he noted, manifested an excessive ambition, an attachment to their own pecuniary interests, an imprudent zeal, as well as a great lack of charity, humility, justice and religion. In fact, he charged, that "charity and justice is [*sic*] not to be found in religious orders." [51] With such a frame of mind it is difficult to understand his request only a few months earlier that the Jesuits open a college in Portland, even though he added that such a foundation be established under conditions to prevent the scandal of San Francisco and to insure "peace and harmony between the Regulars and the Seculars. . . ." [52]

During Archbishop Alemany's quarrel with the San Francisco Jesuits, Archbishop Blanchet, Bishops Modeste Demers of Vancouver Island, and Thaddeus Amat, C.M., of Monterey-Los Angeles, wrote reports to the Propaganda supporting Alemany's position. In view of the long accounts of their own trials with religious orders, these bishops might have confidently expected a decision from the Holy See giving them a wider jurisdiction over the religious in their respective dioceses. As it turned out, they were disappointed. For Rome upheld the traditional rights and privilges of the orders, whereby they were permitted to own "parochial" property and (in the case of the Jesuits) to maintain a nonterritorial church in conjunction with a college as well as a Marian sodality in the city of San Francisco.[53]

In summary, it can be said that although the Jesuits and Oblates held tenaciously to the rights and privileges accorded to them, their actions did little to smooth the ruffled feathers of diocesan clergy who viewed their attitude as alien to the total work of the diocese. On the other hand, the religious of the Far West and Northwest might have found themselves in the midst of complicated jurisdictional battles between bishops, if they had not retained autonomy under the Congregation of Religious.[54]

The religious' familiarity with their own history as well as subsequent events gave bishops and religious superiors a cause for carefully maintaining their independence. The Carmelite fathers, for example, were allowed by Bishop William McCloskey to take a "parish" at Paducah, Kentucky, in 1870, on the condition that they open a school. Although the bishop had promised title to the church land, he refused to give it to the Carmelites five years later, except on the incredible condition that the pastor leave the order and join the diocesan clergy.[55] The Carmelite superiors, on the other hand, reshuffled assignments in the same year, when one of their Kansan priests threatened "to give everything to the Bishop." [56]

The Tension of Ethnic Disparity

The interrelationship of diocesan and religious clergy in this country has been complicated by quarrels between religious orders themselves and by an unhealthy competition based on ethnic loyalties and interests. Divisions among religious orders reach back to the eighteenth-century struggles between the Jesuits, Capuchins, and Carmelites for control of the apostolate in the lower Mississippi Valley. Each group jealously guarded its jurisdiction over a particular mission, so that it eventually became necessary to cordon off the Illinois and Louisiana Territories into sections under the exclusive care of Capuchins, Jesuits, Carmelites, the Society of Foreign Missionaries of Paris, and priests of the Diocese of Quebec.[57]

The high feeling generated in this conflict had its origins in European ecclesiastical politics, but the spirit of the rivalry was carried over to the turn of the nineteenth century in this country as the former Jesuits dominated the Province of Baltimore. During the suppression of the Jesuits and after 1785, French diocesan priests and Sulpicians, as well as Irish Augustinians, Franciscans, and Dominicans were sent to the United States as missionaries. The appointment of Richard Luke Concannon, O.P., as first Bishop of New York and (after Concannon's death) John Connolly, O.P., as first resident Bishop of New York, and Michael Egan, O.F.M., as Bishop of Philadelphia in 1808, and of John England and Patrick Kelly as Bishops of Charleston and Richmond respectively in 1820 served as a beacon for other Irish clergy to come to this country. The French-born Ambrose Maréchal and his English-born successor, James Whitfield, had their own special difficulties with the influx of Irishmen.

Whitfield was almost paranoiac lest his confidential communiqués to Rome should reach "Irish ears." He expressed regret to his friend Nicholas Wiseman (then Rector of the English College, Rome) that "more Irish Bishops are added to our hierarchy, as I fear their increase in numbers will have power to have others of their countrymen nominated hereafter and bring over to this country a great number of Irish priests which I wish, with a few exceptions, they would all stay at home." [58]

Whitfield's hope was, of course, never realized. Irish bishops attracted Irish clergy to swell the ranks of the diocesan clergy so that by 1884 the Irish-born members of the episcopacy numbered twenty of the total seventy-two — only twenty-five of whom were American-born. The Germans comprised a larger percentage of the Catholic immigrant population in the 1880's, but they had only eight German-born bishops at the Third Plenary Council of Baltimore. What had happened in the preceding fifty years was that the influx of Irish clergy came to be closely tied with the native American clergy by reason of their common language. As other ethnic groups, like the Germans, began to make their presence felt, Irish and Americans manifested a kind of cultural exclusivity, which was its own special form of ecclesiastical nativism. As foreign-born religious priests assumed more and more the pastoral care of minority ethnic groups, while the incardinated English-speaking diocesan clergy continued to surpass in numbers the religious clergy, some of the ecclesiastical nativism came to be directed against foreign-born religious.

The Bohemia-born Redemptorist, John N. Neumann, was elevated to the See of Philadelphia in 1852. The German Benedictines had already established a foundation at Latrobe. And in 1853 rumors were abroad that the Bishop of Pittsburgh, Michael J. O'Connor, was to be replaced by a German and, possibly, a religious. The response of American priests to the unfamiliar customs of religious orders and of non-English-speaking clergy might be generalized from the emotive content of a statement from one Pennsylvania priest to another:

> . . .the Germans are putting their heads together, and are already busily at work to procure a German Bishop for Pittsburg — So we are to be germanized and Dutchified from one end of the State to the other — I deemed it a duty to communicate these probable surmises to you, as being the oldest, wisest, and most experienced head among us in hopes that you may derive some counteracting means to prevent so great an infliction.[59]

The German Jesuits of St. Louis had been equally critical. In one instance the local Jesuit provincial warned his Roman superior that the interests of the Society would suffer at the hand of Irish bishops. "Remember," he wrote to Father John Roothan, "that Msgr. [Peter R. Kenrick] is Irish and has a very dominant character. . . . Woe to Catholicism if the number of Irish bishops increases in the United States; schism will come from that. . . . The difficulties we have with Msgrs. Hughes, Purcell and Kenrick prove this. . . . A Kenrick will take from us what DuBourg and Rosati begged us to accept." [60] Father Pierre De Smet also expressed his certainty to Roothan that the majority of American bishops "have in mind the partial secularization of regular priests. . . ." [61]

The closest thing to schism occurring within the lifetime of the Jesuit superiors took place in 1858, when a group of American-born convert Redemptorists dissociated themselves from the heavily German parent group and formed the Congregation of St. Paul (or Paulists) under the leadership of Isaac Hecker. The basic cause of separation was a lack of sympathy on the part of the Redemptorist superiors for the establishment of an "American house" dedicated to the ministry among native Americans.[62] In addition, the fledgling group showed its own bias against the traditional style of religious life by insisting on the "voluntary principle" for its members rather than on the profession of formal vows of poverty, chastity, and obedience. The older form of religious life did not appear to these men to be an appropriate style of life for Americans.

Archbishop Hughes of New York exhibited a similar sentiment when, in 1848, he formally dissociated New York Catholics from what had been published as "the anxious wish of the Bishops, Priests, and laity of the United States to see an establishment of the Cistercian

Order founded in this country." [63] No doubt, Hughes' problems with the New York Jesuits, his unabashed Irish-American loyalties, and the understandable episcopal concern about mendicant religious orders all contributed to his prejudice against the Cistercians. Basically, however, it appeared that any anti-foreign bias held by bishops was incidental to the need they felt to guard against inroads on their jurisdiction.

When Michael O'Connor of Pittsburgh was faced with the establishment of a Benedictine monastery in his diocese, he reacted sharply to the concept as well as to the strong-willed German superior, Boniface Wimmer. O'Connor's point of view was that the foundation of an exempt monastery was not in keeping with modern times. Wimmer interpreted this attitude as a sign of the bishop's concern for his own authority and complained to King Ludwig I that the American bishops were "naturally mistrustful of every attempt to deprive them more or less of their unrestricted power, or to insure oneself against their arbitrariness." [64] The petty issues over which Wimmer and O'Connor disagreed are not particularly important. What is significant is the basic feeling shared by the respective parties toward the other. When, for example, St. Vincent's proposed to open a brewery, O'Connor expressed concern about how to deal with the matter in such a way as to "preserve his authority." [65] Wimmer, on his part, was not particularly disposed to give due respect to O'Connor, and he acted at times in total disregard of the local ordinary. [66]

The anti-foreign and anti-religious sentiment of many American clergy was epitomized in 1852 by Bishop O'Connor, who warned the Archbishop of Baltimore to "guard carefully against our feeble hierarchy being swamped by the number and influence of the religious orders which are not of natural growth in the country." As O'Connor explained, "They are rather organizations encouraged and blown into life by influences from abroad, who did not wish to work through the regular authorities, than [they are] the natural growth and expression of the piety of the country." Although the Bishop of Pittsburgh acknowledged the "piety" and "elements of good" within the orders, he judged that "if they become masters or coordinates, disorders may arise for which neither they nor we are prepared, and be a stumbling [sic] to each." As to the role of religious superiors in the deliberations of the First Plenary Council of Baltimore, O'Connor felt that it must be restricted to a consultative vote. "It strikes me," he told Kenrick, "that if they are to be admitted as deciding every thing with us on a perfect level, we might as well give them up at once our mitres and croziers. . . ." [67]

Recruitment of Bishops and Priests

In view of the quondam rivalries between religious congregations and some members of the American hierarchy, the adamant refusal of orders to allow their men to accept bishoprics was an unlikely but genuine source of abrasion. Although the American hierarchy was graced with some notable bishops who were members of religious groups, the Jesuits, Sulpicians, and Vincentians objected strenuously to the Holy See that their best men were being recruited for episcopal posts.[68] The Jesuits in particular were most obdurate in preventing their men from accepting a prelacy or any ecclesiastical honor. According to their rule, no such duty or dignity was to be accepted unless under an express command of obedience binding under pain of sin.[69] During the first half of the nineteenth century the number of educated and mature diocesan priests was too small to allow sufficient choice of worthy candidates, and the American hierarchy regularly called upon religious priests to fill episcopal posts.[70] During the second quarter of the nineteenth century, nine of the twenty-three bishops appointed in the Midwest were members of religious orders or congregations.[71] As the problem of recruiting *episcopabali* became less severe when the United States developed a numerically stronger native diocesan clergy, the American Jesuits and most other religious groups accepted the mitre largely for missionary territories outside of continental United States.

Associated with the flight from the mitre in the past century was the deep-seated rivalry between religious and diocesan clergy in attracting men for the priesthood. Shortly before 1850, the Bishop of Vincennes, Celestine de la Hailandière, complained to Rome that the Jesuits had been drawing his diocesan priests to their own Society and inducing them to flout his authority.[72] During the early stipend dispute with the Jesuits, Archbishop Whitfield had refused to allow one of his priests, John Lucas, to join the Society of Jesus because of its alleged loss of Ignatian spirit, and he was heard to say that the Jesuits "ought to be secularized." [73]

On the other hand, seventy years later the Archbishop of New York, Michael A. Corrigan, was in the position where he could be quoted as saying, "Sorry, but I never take in ex-order priests." [74] Behind the attitude of de la Hailandière, Whitfield, and Corrigan was the ever-present jurisdictional question of "who has control in this diocese?" Archbishop John B. Purcell had a like concern for the Diocese of Nashville, where Bishop Richard Miles, O.P., was nominating only Dominicans as his coadjutor. If the diocese received a regular succession of

Dominican ordinaries, Purcell feared that a secular bishop appointed to the see at some future time "would be like 'John Lackland.' " [75]

The ease with which the Jesuits — by reason of an ancient privilege granted by the Holy See — were able to recruit diocesan clergy into their ranks without permission of the bishop was a source of serious complaints from men like de la Hailandière, who revealed the evident breakdown between diocesan and religious groups when he ranked the interests of religious societies "far less important than those of the dioceses." [76] Even the mild-mannered Bishop of Louisville, Benedict Flaget, complained that his more talented priests wanted to leave the diocese to join the Jesuits. The heart of the problem for Flaget was that since the Society tried to staff colleges more than mission churches, they were virtually exempt from episcopal jurisdiction. [77] In response to the requests of these two bishops and the assembled hierarchy of the Sixth Provincial Council of Baltimore in 1846, the Holy See ruled that no diocesan priest ordained "for the missions" could enter a religious order without first obtaining written permission of the bishop. [78]

Unfortunately, conciliar decrees remained unenforcible dead letters when they ran contrary to powerful interest groups. The Redemptorist Provincial, Bernard Hafkenscheid, for example, openly defied the Propaganda's ruling by receiving a priest of the Diocese of Buffalo into the novitiate. His weak excuse for the action to Bishop John Timon, C.M., was the precedent of an old world tradition. Before Timon brought pressure to bear on the Redemptorists, Hafkenscheid returned the man to his diocese. [79]

The recruitment of a priest of the Archdiocese of Oregon City was the occasion for the development of an already strained relationship between Archbishop Blanchet and the Oblates of Mary Immaculate. On the occasion of the First Provincial Council of Oregon City in 1848, Bishop Modeste Demers of Vancouver Island proposed opening as many novitiates as possible on the condition that the religious societies "import their novices from Europe rather than accept secular priests which the Oregon bishops have procured at great expense." [80] Blanchet of Oregon City requested the Propaganda for the power to suspend the formation of religious novitiates until the moment when there would be a "sufficient core of native secular clergy to support and sustain the 'action' of the Bishop." [81] Two days later he requested the Holy See in vain for the power over the temporalities of secular and religious clergy lest there be what he termed a "continual conflict of authority." [82]

Problems did occur for the strong-minded archbishop of Oregon City. In 1848, the Oblates of Mary Immaculate received permission to come to the archdiocese, and the following year one of Blanchet's youngest priests, John F. Jayol, requested permission to enter the Oblate novitiate.[83] Blanchet did not directly answer the request but rather ordered Jayol to make a retreat to examine his vocation. After deciding to pursue his religious vocation, the priest was informed that his request had been denied and that he was to return to the archdiocese immediately.[84] Jayol refused to return; he finished his novitiate and professed his vows. Blanchet then ordered the priest to return to his post under penalty of interdict and "absolute and total suspension *ipso facto*" reserved to the archbishop himself.[85]

Roman sympathies apparently fell to the young priest. For, a short time later, when Blanchet found himself called upon by the Holy See to defend himself against accusations raised against him by his priests, he lamely explained concerning the Jayol affair that there never really was a suspension, since it was not received in a place falling within his jurisdiction.[86] It would seem that the Oblates violated the ruling of the Holy See in their response to the bishops of the Sixth Provincial Council of Baltimore, or that they should at least have appealed the matter to the Propaganda. It is not inconceivable, however, that Blanchet was aware of the irregularity of his suspension and that he merely wished to make an example of Jayol to his fellow diocesan priests. Neither the Oblates nor the archbishop seem to have been in a completely justifiable position.[87]

With a few notable exceptions it has been customary until the last decade for religious congregations and orders to train their own seminarians for the reason that overexposure to another religious order or to the diocesan seminarians might lead to a dilution of what was vaguely described as "the spirit of the order." It probably could be documented that almost all religious societies — except in times of extreme vocational stress — have not been inclined to accept students of other congregations or diocesan institutions within their ranks. It is still customary, for example, for Jesuits schooled in the old traditions to refer to each other as "Ours" and to non-Jesuits as "externs." [88] The same kind of exclusivism has been characteristic of many large diocesan seminaries in the past.[89] This sense of exclusivity has been balanced in part by the large number of religious priests who have helped to educate diocesan candidates for the priesthood. These men have not only exerted an edifying influence on the secular clergy but have also helped to provide a basis for mutual understanding and a sense of common sacerdotal apostolate.

An acute source of abrasion between the Society of Jesus and the Diocese of Helena until recent years concerned the recruitment of vocations. In July of 1931, the Reverend Joseph Piet, S.J., informed the Jesuit Provincial of the Oregon Province that the Bishop of Helena, George J. Finnegan, C.S.C., was obstructing the recruitment of young men into the Society. Finnegan demanded that all prospective postulants consult him personally before entering the Jesuits. The result of some of these visitations was that Finnegan often failed to send testimonials to the Society concerning interested recruits. Piet, however, encouraged the provincial, Walter F. Fitzgerald, to accept suitable candidates even without the usual testimonial letters.[90] Although Finnegan was himself a religious, he considered it his task to develop a native clergy in a diocese where the Jesuits had labored more than forty years before the diocese was established in 1884.[91] Bishop Finnegan informed the Jesuit superior that he expected cooperation from the Jesuits in encouraging diocesan vocations. But what pained Fitzgerald most of all "was the request for negative help of not soliciting vocations [for the Society], as though I had done so." [92] After Finnegan's death in 1932, the matter seems to have been quiescent during the brief episcopate of Ralph L. Hayes (1933–1935).

His successor, Joseph M. Gilmore, locked horns with the Jesuits on the subject of clerical vocations. The new Bishop of Helena objected to full scholarships being given for Gonzaga University in Spokane to "potential vocations" from the Helena diocesan college. Gilmore felt that the Jesuits were using their influence with young students of his diocese to obstruct his plans for developing a native clergy.[93] As a consequence, Bishop Gilmore imposed a set of conditions on all religious (in particular the Jesuits) who applied for faculties in the Diocese of Helena. The "Helena Promises," as they came to be called, read as follows:

> I hereby acknowledge the concession of the faculties of the Diocese of Helena which have been granted to me for the period ———————, under the following conditions:
>
> (1) That I shall confine my activities to the work for which I have been engaged, to wit:———————
>
> (2) That I shall not solicit students for any educational institution conducted by my religious community.
>
> (3) That I shall not solicit any young man or confer with the parents and guardians of any young man with a view of encouraging him to join the religious community to which I belong; that if any young man come to consult me about joining the religious

community to which I belong I shall insist without exception that he likewise consult with his confessor, pastor, and the Bishop of the Diocese.

(4) That the violation of any of the above conditions will '*ipso facto*' revoke the concession of faculties.[94]

The Jesuits considered the terms of the document unfair, since they looked upon their educational work as a genuine contribution to Catholicism in the entire diocese. The conditions became so intolerable that members of the Society or another group of religious began to interpret the words "solicit" and "students" in the strictest possible sense. For in 1953, the abused words were changed to "persuade" and "any young man," thus insuring the widest possible application. In the past decade, however, no such promises have been required of religious seeking faculties in the Diocese of Helena.[95]

More recently, a study of vocational recruitment practices authorized by the former Apostolic Delegate, Archbishop Egidio Vagnozzi, confirmed some of the thorny problems faced by religious congregations of men in the United States. The report characterized the realtionship of diocesan authorities to the vocational program of religious societies as "control," rather than cooperation.[96] The study revealed that 23.7 percent of the diocesan authorities excluded recruitment of religious unless the society also had a house in the diocese.[97] Foreign missionary societies, in particular, have suffered from the "no house, no recruitment" policy, because they usually do not have residences outside their mission fields. Of the 114 dioceses mentioned in the study's results, only four (all archdioceses, representing ten percent of the country's Catholic population) were reported as having "excellent programs." At the other extreme there were eighteen dioceses (representing 15.5 percent of the total Catholic population) in which it is currently impossible for religious societies to recruit at all or in which the arrangements are exceedingly unfavorable.

Religious societies experiencing poor relations with the diocesan authorities have responded that they are not permitted to "talk vocations" in diocesan schools or even to publish advertisements in the diocesan newspaper. One group reported, "The Bishop allows us in, but only if we promise not to wear our habit, not to tell who we are, and not to leave any literature." [98] The recruitment report was written in 1967 — two years after the assembled bishops at Vatican Council II had declared that religious congregations "have the right to spread knowledge of themselves by way of attracting vocations, and to seek out candidates as well." [99]

A few months before the Apostolic Delegate's recruitment report was made public, a situation arose in the Archdiocese of Detroit that showed the continued lack of communication between religious and diocesan institutions. Early in 1968, it was proposed to the Archdiocesan Synod that the minor seminary (Sacred Heart Seminary High School) "be used as a prep school for any student in the archdiocese who is contemplating entering a religious community of men." Eight vocational directors of religious societies in the diocese met on April 2, 1968, to express concern that local pastors and assistants were already encouraging boys to go to the archdiocesan seminary rather than join a religious congregation directly. The matter was taken up by the Vocations Committee of the Conference of Major Superiors of Men in May of 1968, and the problem was resolved in an equitable manner.[100] The combination of minor seminary facilities would seem to be a praiseworthy contribution to inter-group cooperation at a time of scarcity of vocations and money. What was deplorable in the Detroit situation was that a motion could be made in the synod without previous consultation with the religious congregations involved. On the other hand, the reaction of the vocation directors — though understandable — gave the impression of subdued panic in the face of impending disaster.

Since 1968, vocational directors of religious societies have had every reason to be concerned about increasing or stabilizing the recruitment rate. In 1849, religious accounted for about one-third of the total 1, 109 clergy in the United States.[101] Sixty years later in 1909, religious numbered 4,208 but formed only about twenty-five percent of the total clerical population.[102] In 1940 the number of religious again reached one-third of the total 33,912 clergy, and for the next quarter of a century the relative number of religious continued to rise. Between 1968 and 1969, however, the number of religious priests decreased by 184 and the diocesan clergy increased by only one priest out of 37,454. What was even more important for religious vocational directors to notice was the change in the number of seminarians. The diocesan students decreased thirteen percent while the religious seminarians decreased an alarming eighteen percent.[103] What remains to be seen is whether diocesan and religious superiors will choose to solve their vocational problems separately or in a cooperative fashion.

Participation in Policy Decisions

The lack of cooperation on an official level between diocesan and religious institutions has not been helped by the present posture of the

National Conference of Catholic Bishops *vis à vis* religious orders. Although in 1969 there were 22,166 religious priests out of a total 59,620 priestly population, no major religious superiors have been given a deliberative vote in the NCCB's proceedings, where national ecclesiastical problems are discussed and policy is determined. Even at Vatican Council II, superiors general of religious societies numbering more than 1,000 members had a vote in the deliberations, and in July of 1967, ten superiors general were elected to the World Synod of Bishops.[104] The only voice that religious orders and congregations have at the present time in the United States is the Conference of Major Superiors of Men, established in 1956 with more than 130 participating groups representing about 22,000 religious men. The only official tie between the religious superiors and the NCCB has been a liaison committee of one archbishop and four bishops, which was activated in January of 1968. Although the Conference of Major Superiors of Men will, in the revised code of canon law, be given official status as a "conference," the genuine power of the organization to assist in the decision-making process for the Church in the United States remains in doubt.

The disinterest or apathy of the American hierarchy toward the affairs of religious congregations might easily be explained by the consistent attempts by religious to maintain their independence. In any case, when sixty bishops were invited to attend a national meeting of major religious superiors in June of 1967, only ten accepted.[105] It was at this meeting that the Paulist Superior General, John F. Fitzgerald, informally requested the CMSM to investigate the dispute in which Bishop Thomas K. Gorman of Dallas had ordered the Paulist priests to leave the diocese where they had established a dynamic parish in the Dallas suburb of Richardson. Laymen of the parish had launched a campaign to retain the Paulists and had used the court of public opinion when they had no other recourse. Father Fitzgerald emphasized that although Bishop Gorman was fully within his rights to terminate his contract made with the Paulists in 1956, "he was ignoring what happened at Vatican II." When pursued for his opinion of the "real reason" for Bishop Gorman's action, Fitzgerald opined that the bishop "wanted to give this parish to one of his diocesan men." [106]

The issue was plainly one of episcopal jurisdiction. Archbishop John F. Dearden, who was present at the CMSM meeting, overruled any possibility of the case being adjudicated by the bishops-religious liaison committee. Newsmen reported him as saying that

canonically "we do not have this power." [107] Although Father Fitzgerald received a sympathetic hearing from the major superiors, "he
wasn't encouraged" to present any formal proposal to the group. As
a result, the CMSM resolutions committee reporting on the last day of
the conference made no reference to the Dallas case. And so the
CMSM and its liaison committee were impotent before the canonically
regulated power of a local bishop in matters of diocesan discipline.
There was no further recourse, and here the matter rested.

Religious order priests, on their part, have shown little interest in
the special problems of the diocesan clergy, such as retirement, security, salaries and other internal matters. Nor have the religious exercised
their right to join diocesan associations of priests. In 1967, in Chicago,
where the religious clergy working in the archdiocese numbered 1,197,
only 275 of them were dues-paying members of the association.[108]

Among the reasons given by religious for their lack of participation
in the Association of Chicago Priests (ACP) were the following: (1)
the Association was concerned with diocesan priests only; (2) it was
doubtful that an association with diocesan priests could add anything
to their lives; (3) religious lacked a permanent commitment to the
archdiocese due to the possibility of transfer by their superiors to
another place; and (4) the continued lack of communication on parish
policies between diocesan priests and the religious assisting in the
parishes was a confirmation that religious have been, are, and will
continue to be exploited as "cheap labor" by the diocesan men.[109]
Underlying the objections raised to joining the ACP was a sense of
futility on the part of the religious. It was felt that decisions made by
the Association could not easily break the bureaucratic red tape of
institutionalized religious life. The religious were also failing to recognize that the ACP was concerning itself with larger diocesan and
national problems. The disinterestedness of the vast majority of
religious — about one-half of the Chicago clergy — left the ACP without the leverage it was seeking to bring about archdiocesan policy
changes in matters of the liturgy, social action, and parochial experi-
mentation.

The recent representation of religious in diocesan associations and
priests' senates across the country has not been unlike that of Chicago.
Although there were 177 diocesan priests and 144 religious priests
serving the Diocese of Oakland in 1968, only four of the twenty-three
priests in the senate were religious.[110] In the Archdiocese of San
Francisco, the religious priests outnumbered the diocesan men 461 to
373, in 1968, and yet only four of the twenty-four priests in the elected

senate were religious.[111] A recent interim report of priests' senates and associations notes that "an overall average shows one representative for every fifteen diocesan priests and one for every sixty-six religious priests." [112] Whether the obvious inequality of representation in apportionment was due to the results of free at-large elections, or appointment of only a specified number of religious to the senate or association, or whether it was due to the lack of interest of the religious, is not clear. Whatever reason may be primary, it *is* clear from the interim report that religious are less involved in priests' organizations than are the diocesan clergy.[113]

The manner in which diocesan priests, elected senates and voluntary associations have recently emerged in the United States has been nothing short of "explosive." [114] The purpose of the priests' organizations has, in part, been to help solve one of the perennial problems in the American Church, namely, the delineation and exercise of priests' rights. In matters pertaining to diocesan policy or the appointment of bishops the clergy have had virtually no voice except for the election of the first Bishop of Baltimore in 1789. For the seventy years following, American priests chafed under what some considered to be the autocratic personalities of certain bishops. As one embittered priest remarked shortly before the First Plenary Council of Baltimore in 1852, "They [the bishops] might as well leave the priests [theologians] at home for all the weight they have." [115]

It was not unexpected that bishops faced with a recalcitrant priest have, in the past, sought to impose severe penalties on a man who obstructed ecclesiastical discipline in the Church's formative years in this country. In the second half of the nineteenth century a small group of prominent priests began working actively for a more effective voice in diocesan affairs.[116] It is not surprising that Archbishop Hughes — in view of his difficulties with the Jesuits — had forbidden any of his clergy to speak or write on the subject of clerical rights. It was the Reverend Thomas Heyden of Bedford, Pennsylvania, who championed the rights of priests during the 1850's. Heyden exercised his rhetoric on the foibles of the American hierarchy in well-timed letters to the Holy See, until the movement was picked up by the otherwise traditionalist editor of the New York *Freeman's Journal*, James A. McMaster.[117]

Religious do not appear to have taken an active role in the promotion of clerical rights. Religious priests charged with the care of souls were subject to the local ordinary in those matters specifically pertaining to their churches. But, as we have noted already, disputes arose over the privileges of exempt religious and the canonical distinction — if any — that obtained between a mission church controlled by any religious congregation and a city church staffed by diocesan clergy. As a missionary territory, the United States fell under the jurisdiction of the Congregation de Propaganda Fide until June 29, 1908, and therefore the universal canon law of the non-missionary countries did not always apply.[118]

Canonically speaking, the United States had no "parishes" and therefore no "pastors." Consequently, priests charged with the administration of a church had no tenure of office and were at the mercy of the local bishop who might or might not observe the decrees of plenary or provincial councils concerning such matters as the appointment of diocesan consultors. And the same bishops could invoke the penalty of suspension on a priest who had no effective court of appeal. The issue of clerical rights had its paradigm in the struggle by religious orders to maintain some autonomy from episcopal authority. Religious were able to use their superiors or the Sacred Congregation of Religious as a buffer between themselves and the local bishop. And this relative freedom of religious clergy was clearly a source of strife between the orders and the episcopacy and may have been a hidden cause of bitterness among diocesan priests.[119]

Throughout the past century, bishops continually warded off what they considered to be encroachments on their jurisdiction and authority. "If the Bishops are to be ruled by the Priests," wrote Bishop Michael Corrigan of Newark in 1877, "and must promote them to fat livings, according to the fancies of the latter, and cannot bring them to their senses save on conditions imposed, not by the Holy See, but by the culprits themselves, then the very idea of Episcopal Authority is lost, and all order in the Church of God is turned to chaos." [120]

The bishops chose to avoid the incipient "chaos" when they met at the Third Plenary Council of Baltimore in 1884. Several members of the hierarchy ironically invoked the model of government in religious orders to bolster their claims of independence from their consultors in such matters as the promulgation of a diocesan synod, election of a new consultor, division of a parish, and alienation of church property. Even the Benedictine Vicar Apostolic of Dakota, Isidore Robot, proposed that bishops ought not to be less free than an abbot in his monastery, who asks counsel and not consent from his priests.[121] The fourth deputation of theologians at the council was concerned largely with the affairs of religious — a matter not unconnected with the relationship of priests to bishops.

One member of the deputation, Bishop Bernard J. McQuaid of Rochester, had carefully followed the conflict of the English hierarchy and regulars, which ended in the settlement of their relationship by the Holy See in the Constitution, *Romanos Pontifices*, of May 8, 1881.[122] McQuaid's interests were those of his English colleagues, and he considered their *modus agendi* to be worthy of imitation for the American bishops.[123] Before the publication of *Romanos Pontifices*, McQuaid had feared any settlement in favor of the religious and wrote accordingly to Archbishop Corrigan:

> . . .it will be a bad day for the Church in America, if the Regulars carry the day in Rome.
>
> A priest in Toronto, an excellent and pious Frenchman, had charge of an Irish parish in Toronto. He had built a new church, schools, and parsonage. On New Year's Day, he announced to his congregation that all was paid for. A few days after he was informed that his parish was handed over to the Redemptorists, and that he might report to the Palace. If this priest were disposed to make trouble, he could carry his case to Rome and succeed. McMaster is loud in his praise of the Redemptorists who step in to oust the poor priest. It will not be long before the Archbp. and the Redemptorists will be at loggerheads.
>
> Once these good people get on the weak side of a bishop, the diocese loses and they gain. Fine promises are made only to be broken.[124]

Because the Holy See had already expressed its willingness to extend the provisions of *Romanos Pontifices* to the Universal Church, the legislation of the Third Plenary Council of Baltimore concerning religious was based primarily on that document.[125]

The "religious question" arose again during the period in which the American hierarchy awaited approval of its conciliar decrees by the Holy See. Of the two bishops commissioned by the hierarchy to carry the legislation to Rome, one was Joseph Gregory Dwenger, C.PP.S., Bishop of Fort Wayne. Several episcopal leaders feared that Dwenger and Bishop John Moore of St. Augustine, would not accurately represent the wishes of the majority. Bishop Richard Gilmour of Cleveland expressed the feelings of some of his colleagues when, in a letter to Cardinal Gibbons, he wrote: "Fort Wayne will not defend the Bishops against the Religious, &, as I see it, the Religious are but in the beginning of an absorbing move that, if not fully and vigorously stayed, will leave the future with trouble enough." Gilmour's concern was not merely with pressures of religious orders in the United States to maintain or increase their autonomy — especially in matters pertaining to ownership of property.[126] He also feared that the religious bishops, such as Martin Marty, O.S.B., of Dakota, would back Dwenger on the rights of religious. To Bishop McQuaid's way of thinking, however, it was the foreigners who were to be watched. "We have to dread Franzelin," he wrote, "more than any one else; he is German and Jesuit; his prejudices against us are very strong; he needs to be taught a lesson or two." [127] The element of nationality also colored McQuaid's opinion of the Bishop of Fort Wayne. "Don't trust Dwenger too much," he told Gilmour. "His skin, the marrow of his bones, his blood is Teutonic." [128]

The antipathy of McQuaid, Gilmour, and like-minded bishops toward religious was not simply a matter of personality conflict. Behind the scene was the very real concern to maintain centralized authority in the diocese. Although some bishops at the Third Plenary Council had proposed that ordinaries seek the consent of their consultors or irremovable rectors in order to lessen the bishop's responsibility (a position held by Dwenger of Fort Wayne), the majority followed the proposal of Archbishop Michael Heiss of Milwaukee that the word "counsel" be substituted for the word "consent" wherever it appeared in the conciliar documents.[129]

Neither the decrees of the Third Plenary Council of Baltimore, the apostolic constitution on religious, nor the promulgation of the code of canon law succeeded in removing the conflict between religious and diocesan institutions. Attempts to resolve differences have most often taken the form of an appeal to law or to ancient privilege. Adherence to law may, indeed, provide external order, but it provides no assurance of cooperative effort. Although little has been mentioned about finances — with the exception of the Baltimore-Jesuit stipend controversy — many of the conflicts arising since the Third Plenary Council of Baltimore have had money as their cause.

In 1890, the Reverend Charles Sigl, C.SS.R., led a party of six to a new establishment in Portland, Oregon. The Redemptorists found the diocesan clergy "a bit distant" and apparently ignorant of any arrangements made for the territory of the church to be administered by the religious. Although Archbishop William Gross (also a Redemptorist) was away when the small party arrived, they learned upon his return that their territory had been reduced on the more prosperous north side of the city. This had been done to silence the complaints of the diocesan clergy who wished to contain the religious in less affluent territory. As a result, the new parish was unable to survive due to lack of funds available in the curtailed boundaries.[130]

A similar situation obtained at the Blackfoot mission on Two Medicine River in Montana. Although the title to the mission church was in the hands of the Catholic Indian Bureau, the Jesuit administrators were expected to be responsible for debts incurred in remodeling, which had been required by Bishops Finnegan and Gilmore in the 1930's. A new brick church was built in 1938 and paid for by funds of the Marquette League — a Jesuit fund-raising organization for the missions. Due in part, however, to lack of funds, the mission had to be closed in September of 1940.[131]

Conclusion

As events, such as the above, become more contemporary, it is exceedingly difficult or inexpedient to document them. In the course of doing research for this essay, the author was informed of many incidents between religious and diocesan priests which he was advised to "bury." There have been stories of religious congregations sending men into parishes to seek out the wealthy for seminary burses. This has been done, on some occasions, with the knowledge that the local ordinary would not sanction the practice, but with the justification that it was the only way for the religious organization to pay for the education of seminarians who eventually would serve the parish. There is the well-known current practice of religious administering colleges and universities to establish alumni associations or clubs in large cities. Such organizations are formed to garner funds for the educational enterprise, but it is not always easy for the local clergy to understand how the need of the diocese is being served. There are instances of bishops blackballing a particular religious congregation from the diocese, of diocesan clergy who have systematically campaigned to remove religious from "plum" parishes or special assignments, of religious who have flaunted their academic degrees or otherwise cast aspersions on the competence of the diocesan clergy.

Some of these incidents — related both by religious, diocesan clergy, and bishops — may eventually be substantiated with critical apparatus. Still more will be lost with the memories of dying men. And still others will live on as part of the unwritten history of dioceses or religious orders — enlarged upon by fertile imaginations or truths half-told. Unfortunately, all too many instances of clerical conflict will be preserved in one form or another to feed the legacy of fraternal suspicion, narrow pride, or a myopic view of the priestly ministry, which have no place among Christians.

Mention has already been made of the debate on religious at Vatican Council II. At that time, Archbishop Eugene D'Souza of Bhopal, India, echoed a call for cooperation, noting that religious sometimes fear falling under a diocesan dictatorship. There is need, he said, for give and take; and to safeguard whatever interests religious might have beyond the care of souls, he urged that they be given a place on national episcopal conferences or on a permanent commission of bishops and superiors.[132] And the Marist Superior General, Joseph Buckley, called upon religious to recognize that "diocesan priests have their own sound spirituality," to acknowledge their common bonds in attempting to live the evangelical counsels, and to exhibit a manner of friendship rather than competition.[133] Perhaps what could not be achieved by legislation in an international council can be accomplished by mutual counsel, trust, and integrity.

LIST OF ABBREVIATIONS

AAB — Archives of the Archdiocese of Baltimore
AAPO — Archives of the Archdiocese of Portland in Oregon
AASL — Archives of the Archdiocese of St. Louis.
ADP — Archives of the Diocese of Pittsburgh
APF — Archives of the Congregation de Propaganda de Fide
ASJOP — Archives of the Society of Jesus: Oregon Province
MCUND — Manuscript Collection of the University of Notre Dame
ACHSP — Records of the American Catholic Historical Society of Philadelphia

1. Floyd Anderson, Ed., *Council Daybook: Vatican II, Session 3* (Washington: National Catholic Welfare Conference, 1965), pp. 23–25, 175.

2. *Ibid.*, p. 230.

3. Vincent A. Yzermans, Ed., *American Participation in the Second Vatican Council* (New York: Sheed & Ward, 1967), p. 437.

4. "Bishops' Pastoral Office in the Church," IV, pp. 33–35 in Walter M. Abbott, S.J., and Joseph Gallagher, Eds., *Documents of Vatican II* (New York: America Press, 1966), pp. 420–423; and "Ministry and Life of Priests," II, 8, *ibid.*, pp. 549–550.

5. Although there are distinctions in canon law between an "order," a "congregation," and a "society," all three terms will be used interchangeably unless otherwise specified.

6. Ronin John Murtha, O.S.B., *The Life of the Most Reverend Ambrose Maréchal, Third Archbishop of Baltimore, 1768–1828* (Ann Arbor: University Microfilms, 1965), pp. 243–245, 254.

7. Archives of the Archdiocese of Baltimore (hereafter, AAB): 14-I-24, Cheverus to Maréchal, Boston, July 15, 1818, *ibid.*, p. 253.

8. *Ibid.*, p. 255ff.

9. Archives of the English College, Baltimore Papers: 1–133, copy, Daniel Brent to Maréchal, October 20, 1824, ibid., p. 273.

10. Archives of the Congregation de Propaganda Fide (hereafter, APF): Congr. Amer. Cent. Vol. 8 (1823–1826), fols. 355r-356v, Maréchal to Fesch, Baltimore, November 4, 1824, *ibid.*, p. 275.

11. Matthew Leo Panczyk, "James Whitfield, Fourth Archbishop of Baltimore. The Episcopal Years: 1828–1834," *Records of the American Catholic Historical Society of Philadelphia* (hereafter, *Records ACHSP*), LXXVI (March, 1965), p. 37.

12. AAB: 27A-V-2, Eccleston to Mulledy, S.J., Georgetown, July 9, 1838, in Columba Halsey, O.S.B., "The Life of Samuel Eccleston, Fifth Archbishop of Baltimore, 1801–1851," in *Records ACHSP*, LXXVI, No. 3 (June, 1965), pp. 124–126.

13. The most recent evaluation of the stipend controversy has shown that all parties were not innocent of exaggeration, formal disobedience, or ignorance of United States civil law. The Jesuits were correct according to civil law in pursuing their rights, but they were less than loyal to the papal brief of 1822, which required them to make payment. On the other hand, the archbishops of Baltimore pursued a civilly untenable course of action in demanding their proper ecclesiastical jurisdiction over the Jesuits. Murtha, *op. cit.*, pp. 288ff.

14. Religious orders which had privileges of exemption from the authority of local bishops granted to them by the Holy See had some of these curtailed when the Code of Canon Law was promulgated in 1918. "Exempt" status, strictly speaking, was given only to those groups of men and women who professed solemn vows, such as Dominicans, Franciscans, Augustinians, Canons Regular, and Jesuits. Stanislaus Woywood, O.F.M., *A Practical Commentary on the Code of Canon Law* (New York: Joseph F. Wagner, Inc., 1957), c. 500, par. 378.

15. In 1785 the former Jesuits constituted the majority of the eastern clergy, and in 1968 they comprised almost 5,000 of the 22,350 religious priests in the United States. *Official Catholic Directory* (New York: P. J. Kenedy and Sons, 1968), General Summary, p. 1.

16. Although the author requested permission from six ordinaries in the Northwest to consult their archives in connection with this study, only one — Archbishop Robert F. Dwyer of Portland — granted unlimited access to official documents.

17. William Matthews, Administrator of the Diocese of Philadelphia, to Anthony Kohlmann, S.J., Washington, July 2, 1828, in Panczyk, *op. cit.*, p. 36.

18. Archives of the Society of Jesus, Rome: Maryland 8, 1, II, 14, Ignatius Brocard, S.J. to Frederick Roothan, June 8, 1849.

19. AASL: De Smet Letterbook, De Smet to Roothan, St. Louis, April 22, 1850.

20. Francis X. Curran, S.J., "Archbishop Hughes and the Jesuits," *Woodstock Letters*, LXXXXVII (Winter, 1968), 6, 20, 53.

21. *Ibid.*, p. 23. The problem of clerical begging by religious congregations was one that occupied the attention and confirmed the suspicions of bishops and diocesan priests who felt that religious priests were a threat to the diocesan income. Throughout the nineteenth century and well into the present century, strict and justifiable regulations have been imposed on religious organizations soliciting funds within a diocese. On the one hand, bogus priests have played the confidence game with unwitting Catholics, while *bona fide* religious societies dedicated to teaching have admittedly used parish funds as sources of revenue for existing religious foundations outside the diocese. Cf. AAB: Spalding & Gibbons Letterbook, p. 434, Martin J. Spalding to John B. Purcell, Baltimore, January 25, 1869. Also, Myron Judy, O.Carm., "Carmel Came. A History of the American Carmelite Province of the Most Pure Heart of Mary, 1864–1900," *The Sword*, XXIV (October, 1964), p. 75.

The Third Plenary Council of Baltimore advanced stringent warnings in 1884 to foreign bishops and religious superiors against permitting clerical beggars to come to any diocese for the purpose of collecting funds. Cf. *Acta et Decreta Concilii Plenarii Baltimorensis Tertii. A.D. MDCCCLXXXIV* (Baltimore: Joannis Murphy et Socilis, MDCCCLXXXVI), Tit. IX, Cap. V, par. 295. As recently as 1951, the President of the Catholic Church Extension Society was forced to deny funds to missionary bishops for the education of diocesan seminarians in part because of "the great begging campaign being carried on throughout the country by Religious Orders from all over the world, not to mention our own country. . . ." Archives of the Catholic Church Extension Society at Loyola University, Chicago: William D. O'Brien to Thomas K. Gorman, Chicago, March 16, 1951, (copy).

22. Curran, *op. cit.*, p. 39.

23. Henry J. Browne has written far and away the best biography of Hughes, but it still remains unpublished. The author wishes to thank Father Browne for the use of his important manuscript. Cf. also, John R. G. Hassard, *Life of the Most Reverend John Hughes, First Archbishop of New York* (New York: D. Appleton and Co., 1866).

24. "The Most Reverend John Hughes, D.D.," *Brownson's Quarterly Review*, Last Series II (1874), p. 84.

25. Curran, *op. cit., passim.*

26. John Rothensteiner, *History of the Archdiocese of St. Louis* (St. Louis: The Author, 1928), I, pp. 803ff.

27. "In your actual or approaching difficulties with some of the Jesuits," Kenrick wrote to James A. McMaster ,editor of the *Freeman's Journal* of New York, "you have and will have my sympathy, and the sympathy of everyone who does not wish to see the Press made a trumpet on which to proclaim the praises of those who appear to expect that the *magni nominis umbra* should cover every defect, and give importance to every success. It is to be regretted that the *laudis immensa cupido* should be found in religious men, justified, and, in some measure, sanctified by the conviction they appear to have, that whatever gathereth not with them scattereth, and that whatever is not for them, to the extent of their own views, is against them. I would gladly see the religious orders such as their sainted founders intended them to be; but the *esprit de corps* has, unfortunately, attained more than due preponderance in the working of the system, and has caused men, otherwise respectable, to assume a position, both with respect to the Ordinaries and Secular clergy, which is anything but promotive of harmonious and united cooperation. . . ; hence I believe that until some radical changes be made in the relation between the Bishops and the regular orders, we shall have the *rerum non hominum vitia* to deplore which in so many instances have resulted from this cause." Manuscript Collection of the University of Notre Dame (hereafter MCUND): Kenrick to McMaster, St. Louis, October 7, 1849 in an unpublished biography of Kenrick by Samuel J. Miller, courtesy of the Right Reverend John Tracy Ellis.

28. AASL: Jesuitica Missouri Province: John Elet, S.J., to John Roothan, S. St. Louis, January 14, 1850.

29. ". . . [Kenrick] finds fault with the increase of the sodality, the best thing ever done in S. Louis. He confessed however that thou [*sic*] opposed to us as regulars, he could not but respect us as individuals. . . ; he disliked the regulars principally because they were a cause of dissatissfaction [*sic*] to the secular clergy and were even at variance with them." AASL: DeSmet Letterbook, n.d., n.p. (probably Pierre Jean DeSmet, S.J., to James Oliver Van De Velde, S.J.) in Miller, *op. cit.*, p. 5.

30. APF: *Scr. orig.*, Vol 975, fol. 791r, Van de Velde to Pius IX, Rome, August 19, 1852.

31. APF: *Scr. rif. A.C.*, Vol 16, fol. 276v, Francis P. Kenrick to James O'Connor, Baltimore, October 2, 1852.

32. APF: *Scr. orig.*, Vol. 975, fol. 791r, Van de Velde to Pius IX, Rome, August 19, 1852.

33. APF: *Scr. orig.*, Vol. 977, fol. 541v, Baltimore, October 4, 1852.

34. APF: *Scr. rif. A.C.*, Vol. 16, fol. 267v, Kenrick to O'Connor (in Rome), Baltimore, October 2, 1852.

35. John Bernard McGloin, S.J., *California's First Archbishop: The Life of Joseph Sadoc Alemany, O.P., 1814–1888* (New York: Herder and Herder, 1966), pp. 192–202.

36. Alemany to Felix Sopranis, S.J., San Francisco, December 23, 1862, as cited *ibid.*, p. 203.

37. Michael King to Alemany, San Francisco, August 27, 1863, cited *ibid.*, p. 206.

38. Croke to Alemany, San Francisco, September 17, 1863, *ibid.*, p. 208.

39. Croke to Alemany, Doneraile, County Cork, Ireland, December 22, 1868, cited *ibid.*, p. 224.

40. Archives of the Archdiocese of Portland in Oregon (hereafter AAPO): Blanchet to Pius IX, Oregon City, January 27, 1851, in Letterbook I, p. 191.

41. AAPO: Blanchet to Ricard, Oregon City, February 18, 1852, *ibid.*, p. 221.

42. APF: *Scr. orig.*, Vol. 977, fol. 539r, "Minutes of the Council." Before the opening of the council, Archbishop Francis P. Kenrick had received notice from the Congregation de Propaganda Fide to head an investigation of charges brought against the Blanchet brothers by the Oblates that the ministry of the religious was being unduly limited. The mater was openly discussed at the council; and although no Oblates were present, Francis Blanchet produced letters indicating that the matter was settled between himself and the Oblates. Cf. APF: *Lettere*, Vol. 340, fols., 842v–843r, Barnabò to Kenrick, Rome, November 19, 1851 and *ibid.*

43. AAPO: Blanchet to Pius IX, Montreal, June 17, 1852, in Letterbook I, pp. 225–236. A similar letter was sent to Cardinal Fransoni in December of the same year, *ibid.*, p. 238.

44. AAPO: Blanchet to Accolti, Montreal, *ibid.*, p. 256; and Same to Ricard, Montreal, June 18, 1852, *ibid.*, pp. 256–257.

45. AAPO: Ricard to Blanchet, Olympia, August 14, 1852, *ibid.*, pp. 238–239.

46. AAPO: Blanchet to Fransoni, Oregon City, December 10, 1852, *ibid.*, p. 239.

47. AAPO: Oregon City, May 30, 1858, *ibid.*, pp. 309–311.

48. AAPO: Blanchet to Barnabò, Oregon City, November 5, 1859, *ibid.*, pp. 335–337.

49. AAPO: Blanchet to Barnabò, Oregon City, December 11, 1864, in *ibid.*, p. 453. In an attempt to establish the trustworthiness of Blanchet's written word, the author stumbled upon several open contradictions. One of these, in a context altogether different from the Oblate conflict, concerned his attitude toward the establishment of a settlers' government. On the one hand, he wrote in 1878 that he had never discouraged the early attempts of a settlers' government. On the other hand, in a memorial to George Simpson, head of the Hudson's Bay Company (which opposed the establishment of any local government), Blanchet accused the Protestant ministers of fomenting the cause of local government. In a word, wrote Blanchet, "our cause is that of the Honorable Company. . . ." Cf. Clarence B. Bagley (Ed.), *Early Catholic Missions in Old Oregon* (Seattle: Lowman and Hanford Company, 1932) I, 122; Sister Letitia Mary Lyons, *Francis Norbert Blanchet and the Founding of the Oregon Missions* (1838–1848). (Washington: Catholic University of America, 1940), pp. 56–57; and Ray Allen Billington, *Westward Expansion* (New York: The Macmillan Company, 1967), p. 529.

50. AAPO: Blanchet to Alemany, Oregon City, June 8, 1865, in Letterbook I, p. 478.

51. AAPO: Blanchet to Barnabò, Portland, May 25, 1866, *ibid.*, p. 501; also McGloin, *op. cit.*, p. 217.

52. AAPO: Blanchet to Rev. Nicholas Congiato, S.J., Portland, March 1, 1866, in Letterbook II, p. 171.

53. James Croke to Alemany, Doneraile, County Cork, Ireland, December 22, 1868, in McGloin, *op. cit.*, pp. 223–224. Cf. also AAPO: Blanchet to Alemany, Oregon City, June 8, 1865, in Letterbook I, p. 478.

54. Like the civil divisions of the Oregon Territory, the ecclesiastical lines of jurisdiction were in a confusing state. In 1846 Bishop Francis Blanchet had persuaded the Holy See to approve what proved to be a bizarre project, namely, the establishment in the Oregon wilderness — with few Catholics and almost no clergy — of an ecclesiastical province, which was second only to the all-embracing Province of Baltimore. A Jesuit missionary planning to build a mission church needed some insulation from jurisdictional changes, and the exempt status of the Society provided him with a form of self-sufficiency. During a forty-five year peroid, for example, the Flathead mission fell successively under the Diocese of St. Louis (to 1843), Oregon City Vicariate (to 1846), Walla Walla (to 1850), the Archdiocese of Oregon City, which administered Walla Walla (to 1853), Nesqually (to 1868), the Vicariate of Idaho (to 1883), the Vicariate of Montana (to 1884), and the Diocese of Helena thereafter. Robert Ignatius Burns, S.J., *The Jesuits and the Indian Wars of the Northwest* (New Haven: Yale University Press, 1966), p. 25.

55. Judy, *op. cit.*, pp. 70, 90.

56. Archives of the Carmelite Fathers, Rome: John (Cyrill) Knoll, O.Carm. to Savini (Superior General), n.p., June 18, 1870, in Judy, *op. cit.*, p. 88. A decade later, the Archbishop of Toronto refused to honor his predecessor's promise to give the Carmelites a parcel of land. During the controversy, the religious priests were denied the right to hear confessions, until they withdrew their property claims. The matter was settled by Archbishop Francesco Satolli in 1893, with the Carmelites purchasing the land at a reduced price. Archives of the Archdiocese of Toronto, Pius Mayer, O.Carm., to John Lynch, n. p., July 3, 1880, in Judy, *op. cit.*, p. 88; also, *ibid.*, pp. 115–122.

57. A survey of the interreligious disputes may be found in John Tracy Ellis, *Catholics in Colonial America* (Baltimore: Helicon Press, 1965), pp. 185–276. Jurisdictional conflicts between Jesuits and Capuchins are detailed in Claude L. Vogel, O.F.M., Cap., *The Capuchins in French Louisiana*, 1722–1766 (Washington: The Catholic University of America Press, 1928) and Jean Delanglez, S.J., *The French Jesuits in Lower Louisiana, 1700–1763* (Washington: The Catholic University of America Press, 1935).

58. Whitfield to Wiseman, Archives of the English College, Rome, Baltimore, June 6, 1833, in Panczyk, *op. cit.*, p. 42.

59. Archives of the Diocese of Pittsburgh (hereafter ADP): No. 680, James Bradley to Thomas Heyden, Newry, November 5, 1853.

60. AASL: Jesuitica Missouri Province, John Elet, S.J., to John Roothan, S.J., St. Louis, January 14, 1850.

61. *Ibid.*, De Smet Letterbook, St. Louis, April 22, 1850.

62. Vincent F. Holden, C.S.P., *The Yankee Paul, Isaac Thomas Hecker* (Milwaukee: The Bruce Company, 1958), pp. 205–413. For a variant interpretation of some of the facts, cf. John P. Marschall, "Kenrick and the Paulists: A Conflict of Structures and Personalities," *Church History*, XXXVIII (March, 1969), pp. 88–105.

63. New York *Freeman's Journal*, Saturday, October 14, 1848, copy in Manuscript Collection of the Catholic University of America (hereafter MCCUA): Hughes Papers, microfilm, reel 3.

64. Wimmer to Ludwig I, St. Vincent, Latrobe, February 13, 1852, in Colman J. Barry, O.S.B., *Worship and Work* (Collegeville: St. John's Abbey, 1956), p. 14.

65. AAB: 30-W-8, O'Connor to Francis P. Kenrick, Pittsburgh, April 2, 1852.

66. Archives of St. Paul's Outside the Walls, O'Connor to Bernard Smith, Pittsburgh, August 13, 1852, in Barry, *op. cit.*, p. 13. Wimmer's relationship to bishops is clarified in the following statement to Bishop Matthias Loras of Dubuque. ". . . a religious order stands in need of the confidence and benevolence of the Bishop, and in return a Bishop will earn a great deal of advantage from a well organized religious corporation; still there are regards for both of them that must be kept in view, which, Sir, I do not think hard, if you want to know the men, who would come to be your assistance in the vineyard of the Lord. Therefore I thought it necessary to speak frankly and to say what is our practice now and what may be our practice afterwards. *Nil nisi quod traditum est.* We enter only into the paths of our fathers of old. We are Germans, but not so obstinately as not to conform to the genius of the country if it be a good Catholic one; we have our countrymen, but not exclusively; we serve willingly the Bishops, whilst we try to observe our rule; and grant slowly the preference to other orders, already established here, but try not to be behind them." Archives of the Archdiocese of Dubuque, Wimmer to Loras, St. Vincent, Latrobe, February 8, 1856.

67. AAB: 30-W-9, O'Connor to Kenrick, Pittsburgh, April 18, 1852. O'Connor summarized his feelings by concluding: "Whereas dignities are so easily acquired as they are now in some orders, we may soon find them multiplying a little too fast. It is one thing to allow a person who has charge of an extensive and influential community in any country to take an important share in the lawmaking power. . . , and it is another to admit heads of pigmy bodies and dignitaries on paper who have or may have no intrinsic merit, nor back [*sic*], and be found after a few days amongst the dregs of their societies." An attitude toward cloistered or contemplative religious harbored by Hughes and O'Connor seems to have been shared by the first American Cardinal, John McCloskey of New York. When Maddalena and Costanza Bentivoglio arrived from Italy in 1875, they were rebuffed by McCloskey for pursuing the Poor Clare way of life which, from his pragmatic viewpoint, appeared alien to the spirit of the United States. Archives of the Monastery of St. Clare, Omaha, "Copy of the Chronicles. . . ," p. 62 in Henry W. Casper, S.J., *History of the Catholic Church in Nebraska*, Vol. II, *The Church on the Fading Frontier: 1864–1910* (Milwaukee: Bruce Publishing Company, 1966), p. 225.

68. One example among many may be found in AAB: 32B-C-6, James O. Van de Velde, S.J., to Francis P. Kenrick, Rome, September 1, 1852.

69. *Practica quaedam ad formulam scribendi* (Roma: apud Curiam Praepositi Generalis, 1948), p. 52. The author wishes to thank the Very Reverend James J. Hennesey, S.J., for this information.

70. APF: *Scr. rif. A.C.*, Vol. 11, fol. 634v–635r, Simon Bruté to the Propaganda, Rome, March 7, 1836. Also, Letter of the Third Provincial Council of Baltimore to Gregory XVI *ibid.: Scr. orig.*, Vol. 952 (1837, Part I), fol. 400v–401v, copy in MCUND.

71. Robert Frederick Trisco, *The Holy See and the Nascent Church in the Middle Western United States, 1826–1850* (Roma: Gregorian University Press, 1962), pp. 127–152.

72. APF: *Scr. rif. A.C.*, Vol. 14, fol. 112r–113r, in Trisco, *op. cit.*, p. 203.

73. Archives of Woodstock College: 209-T-2, William Beschter, S.J., to Francis Dzierozynski, S.J., Georgetown, May 8, 1829, in Panczyk, *op. cit.*, p. 36.

74. Interview with Mr. Schuyler Warren, July 30, 1963 by Terence O'Donnell, *American Modernists*. Unpublished M.A. thesis, (St. Joseph's Seminary, Dunwoodie, N.Y., 1963), Ch. 2, p. 11, fn. 2.

75. AAB: 31-D-28, Purcell to Francis Kenrick, Cincinnati, May 26, 1858.

76. APF: *Scr. rif. A.C.*, Vol. 14, fols. 112r–113r, de la Hailandière to the Propaganda, Rome, May 19, 1845, in Trisco, *op. cit.*, p. 203.

77. *Ibid.*, fols. 90r–v, in Trisco, *op. cit.*, p. 204.

78. APF: Acta, Vol. 209, fols. 438v, 440r, Ponenza of Cardinal Fransoni, De-

cember 7, 1846. The Sacred Congregation de Propaganda Fide reserved to itself the right to give its own opinion in special (presumably appealed) cases, for it evidently was interested in procuring European religious for the Church in the Middle West. Cf. Trisco, *ibid.*

79. Michael J. Curley, C.SS.R., *The Provincial Story: A History of the Baltimore Province of the Congregation of the Most Holy Redeemer* (New York: Redemptorist Fathers, 1963), p. 119.

80. Bertram F. Griffin, *The Provincial Councils of Portland in Oregon* (Rome: Pontificia Universitas Lateranensis, 1964), pp. 17–18.

81. AAPO: Blanchet to Giovanni Brunelli, Rome, May 6, 1846, in Letterbook I, p. 23e.

82. *Ibid.*, Same to Same, Rome, May 8, 1846, in Letterbook I, p. 23b.

83. AAPO: Charles Ricard, O.M.I., to Blanchet, St. Francis Xavier Mission, February 3, 1848, in Letterbook I, pp. 75–77.

84. AAPO: Blanchet to Jayol, Oregon City, February 26, 1849, and May 4, 1849, in Letterbook I, pp. 131 and 120 respectively.

85. AAPO: Blanchet to Jayol, Oregon City, August 18, 1850, in Letterbook I, p. 151a.

86. AAPO: Blanchet to Pius IX, Oregon City, January 27, 1851, in Letterbook I, p. 191.

87. Blanchet's handling of the Jayol suspension is similar to that of an ordinary in the 1960's, who called for the removal of a religious priest because of the latter's public promotion of a political candidate. After the priest's religious superior pleaded for a more humane treatment of the priest, whom he considered to be in good faith, the ordinary responded to the superior that he had acted as he did against the religious so that the matter could be dramatized forcibly to his confrères elsewhere in the territory. (Although this incident could be documented, the author has considered it in the best interest of the parties involved to retain their anonymity.

88. Cf, for example, Eugene J. Ahern, S.J., "The Society's Rules of Censorship," *Woodstock Letters*, LXXXXII (1963), pp. 383–394 and *passim*.

89. The Catholic University of America has long been one of the exceptions to this practice. In addition, seven religious seminaries in the Washington, D.C. area have recently formed themselves into a theological coalition, whereby each group would share many of its professors with students from other congregations. The new coalition is currently open to other religious and diocesan seminarians. Cf. also, ADP: 669a, Purcell to Michael J. O'Connor, Cincinnati, February 16, 1853, in which the Archbishop of Cincinnati explained his reasons for not accepting religious in his archdiocesan seminary. Concerning the Rosminian students, he said, "I was afraid of their chief."

90. Archives of the Society of Jesus, Oregon Province (hereafter ASJOP): Piet to Fitzgerald, San Jose, July 12, 1931.

91. Wilfred P. Schoenberg, S.J., *Jesuits in Montana* (Portland: The Oregon-Jesuit, 1960). Cf. also, ASJOP: Finnegan to Fitzgerald, Helena, July 2, 1931.

92. ASJOP: Fitzgerald to Finnegan, Spokane, July 3, 1931.

93. ASJOP: Gilmore to William G. Elliott, S.J., Helena, September 2, 1939.

94. ASJOP: n.d. (ca. 1939), typed copy.

95. Interview with the Rt. Rev. Joseph B. Oblinger, Chancellor, Diocese of Helena, by the author, June 7, 1969.

96. John W. Stafford, C.S.V., "Vocational Recruitment in Various Dioceses," Report to the Conference of Major Superiors of Men, June 14, 1968, p. 3. Questionnaires were sent to all religious orders and congregations in the United States. There was a return of 49.4 percent, which represented religious working in all twenty-nine archdioceses and eighty-seven of 113 dioceses — or 87.7 percent of the total Catholic population.

97. *Ibid.*, p. 3. "And for some reason not given, one diocese is reported to exclude a religious society if it *does* have a house in the diocese."

98. *Ibid.*, p. 5.

99. "Perfectae Caritatis," No. 24, October 28, 1965. Abbott-Gallagher, *op. cit.*, p. 481.

100. Very Reverend Nicholas Maestrini, P.I.M.E., to Reverend Boniface Wittenbrink, O.M.I., Detroit, April 3, 1968, copy in Manuscript Collection of the Clerics of St. Viator, Evanston, Vocations Committee, CMSM. The author wishes to thank Father Maestrini for permission to use materials from this letter.

101. *The Metropolitan Catholic Almanac for 1850* (Baltimore: Fielding Lucas Co., 1849), *passim.*

102. *Official Catholic Directory and Clergy List: 1909* (Milwaukee: Wiltzius & Co., 1919), *passim.*

103. *The Official Catholic Directory* (New York: P. J. Kenedy & Sons, 1968), General Summary; and *ibid.*, 1969.

104. Floyd Anderson (ed.), *Council Daybook: Vatican II. Sessions 1 & 2* (Washington: National Catholic Welfare Conference, 1965), p. 258. It might also be mentioned that although only the larger religious groups were represented at the council, some bishops were present who had less than ten diocesan priests.

105. Religious News Service, June 26, 1967.

106. *Ibid.*, June 23, 1967.

107. *Ibid.*, June 26, 1967.

108. 1,127 of the 1,419 diocesan priests were members of the Association of Chicago Priests as of December 11, 1967. *ACP Newsletter*, December 22, 1967, p. 3. A survey of the religious priests in the Archdiocese of Chicago revealed that 21 percent were engaged in full-time parish work and another 25 percent were providing part-time daily assistance to parishes. Cf. Fergus Lichteig, O.Carm.,: Unpublished report for the ACP Religious Order Committee, January 20, 1968.

109. Norman McPherson, S.S.S., and John P. Marschall, C.S.V., Unpublished report to the ACP Religious Order Committee, January 29, 1968.

110. Rt. Rev. John S. Cummins, Chancellor, Diocese of Oakland, to the author, Oakland, November 14, 1968. Cf. also, *Crux of the News, Extra*, January 5, 1968, p. 3.

111. Raymond G. Decker, Secretary of the Archdiocesan Senate, to the author, San Francisco, November 18, 1968.

112. Patrick M. McGeever, S.J., *Priest Organizations in the United States: An Interim Report.* Unpublished M.A. thesis. (Woodstock College, April, 1968), p. 9. The author wishes to thank the Reverend Mr. McGeever for permission to quote from his manuscript.

113. *Ibid.*, p. 9.

114. Official sanction for the establishment of diocesan senates was the *motu proprio* of Pope Paul VI, August 6, 1966. By the end of that year forty-five diocesan senates were functioning, and at the beginning of 1968 only twelve dioceses in the United States reported having no elected senate or voluntary association. *Crux of the News, op. cit.*

115. Manuscript Collection of Woodstock College, Diary of James Dolan, Pastor of St. Patrick Church, Baltimore, September 21, 1851.

116. ADP: No. 680, James Bradley to Thomas Heyden, Newry, November 5, 1853.

117. ADP: No. 776, John Hughes to Heyden, New York, August 31, 1858. Also, Sr. Mary Augustine Kwitchen, O.S.F., *James Alphonsus McMaster* (Washington: Catholic University of America Press, 1949), pp. 184–199.

118. Even after the Constitution *Sapienti Concilio* was promulgated in 1908, there was still no change in the status of parochial affairs. Until Pentecost of 1918,

the United States had neither parishes nor parish priests in the Tridentine acceptance of that term. Cf. Woywood, *op. cit.*, p. 184.

119. In a *Relatio* to the Roman authorities made in 1882 by George Conroy, Bishop of Ardagh and Ablegate to Canada, there is no mention of conflict between diocesan and religious clergy or between bishops and religious, although there is a considerable number of candid observations on the conflicts between diocesan clergy and bishops with some sharp suggestions for a change in the mode of choosing bishops, which would favor a more democratic and thorough process. APF: *Scr. rif. A.C.*, Vol. 36 (1882), fols. 195–217. The author wishes to thank the Very Reverend James Gaffey for the opportunity to study this document.

120. Archives of the Archdiocese of Newark: Drawer 25, copy, December 15, 1877, in Carl Derivaux Hinrichsen, "The Diocese of Newark: The Episcopacy of Michael Augustine Corrigan, 1873–1880," *Records ACHSP*, LXXVII, (March, 1966), 21. In another place and time, Corrigan confided to his diary that the "pernicious principle of priests choosing their own field of labor must be quietly put down." Archives of the Archdiocese of New York, Library Accounts, etc. Diary, 1872–1873, October 10, 1872, in Hinrichsen, *op. cit.*, p. 44, fn. 24.

121. Frederick J. Zwierlein, *The Life and Letters of Bishop McQuaid*, II (Rochester: The Art Print Shop, 1926), p. 313.

122. Cf., for example, J. G. Snead-Cox, *The Life of Cardinal Vaughan* (St. Louis: B. Herder, 1910), II, pp. 320–357.

123. Zwierlein, *op. cit.*, II, pp. 305–306.

124. *Ibid.*, II, p. 307, fn. 29.

125. *Acta et Decreta Concilii Plenarii Baltimorensis Tertii* (Baltimorae: Typis Joannis Murphy et Sociorum, MDCCCLXXXVI), Tit. II, Cap. IX, pp. 46–52.

126. Gilmour to Gibbons, Rome, March 21, 1885, in *ibid.*, p. 346.

127. McQuaid to Gilmour, in *ibid.*, p. 351.

128. *Ibid.*, p. 348, fn. 6.

129. *Ibid.*, p. 312.

130. Curley, *op. cit.*, pp. 219–220.

131. ASJPO: Walter J. Fitzgerald, S.J., to Amleto G. Cigognani, Portland, November 4, 1938; also, Wilfred P. Schoenberg, S.J., *A Chronicle: Of the Catholic History of the Pacific Northwest: 1743–1960.* Arranged after the manner of certain medieval chronicles and annotated with copious notes for further reference. (Portland: Gonzaga Preparatory School, 1962), p. 407.

132. September 22, 1964, in Anderson (Ed.), *Session 3, op. cit.*, p. 32.

133. November 11, 1964, Yzermans (Ed.), *op. cit.*, p. 437.

DAVID J. O'BRIEN

THE AMERICAN PRIEST AND SOCIAL ACTION

At the present time a crisis exists among Catholic priests throughout the world, a crisis that is deeply felt among priests in the United States. The media have for several years publicized the facts regarding clerical celibacy, vocational conflict, and vocal dissent among clergy and religious. James Kavanaugh's memoir, which juxtaposed a "modern priest" and his "outdated church," titillated the public and confirmed many stereotypes, but the book expressed in dramatic if exaggerated form the personal agony felt by a growing number of Catholic priests.[1] Only a minority have left the priesthood, but all suffer from the loss of a previously strongly-held sense of identity and purpose.[2] Father Emile Pin writes:

> The priest, it seems, no longer knows who he is. . . . The expectations of the faithful no longer give him a clear idea of what he should be and what he should do. Many priests feel that they are no longer of any use as priests.[3]

The very fact that priests and lay people raise these questions suggests the depths of the problem, for such self-consciousness usually emerges at moments of great personal stress. When such stress is widespread among a whole class of men, it provides considerable evidence of some profound historical changes in the whole context of their life and work. Today the church and the country are both involved in a historical upheaval which necessarily affects the life and work of ministers of the Gospel. As Cardinal Suhard emphasized almost a quarter of a century ago, the priest, called from men but sent to minister to them, must from the very nature of his vocation comprehend and evaluate the social and historical context within which he and his people work out their common destiny.[4]

In no area is this historical interpretation more necessary than in dealing with the topic "the priest and social action." Again and again the press reports the primacy of concern with social issues among discontented clergy. Yet rarely is that concern clarified by specific standards or clear goals. Instead the social criticism of post-conciliar Catholicism operates frequently in an atmosphere dominated by the theology of the Vatican Council but heedless of the political and social dynamics of American history and of the heritage of American Catholic social action.

That heritage is far from clear. For many years Catholics thought of social action mainly in terms of the "social problem" which was the consequence of the rise of an urban-industrial society, specifically the development of new social classes, the conflict between them and the simultaneous disaffection of large numbers of working people from the Catholic Church. These developments appeared to spring from forces apart from or even alien to the Church, so that they were frequently seen as threats to the Church's very existence, as in the socialist movement, or as constituting an arena for Christian missionary activity, as in the recurring efforts to regain the loyalty of the workers by identification with their struggle. The Church's social doctrine was a clearly defined body of teaching on the relation between economic, political and social life on the one hand and dogma and morals on the other, while social action constituted that work specifically addressed to "secular" affairs considered apart from the "sacred" world of sacramental, devotional and liturgical life.

Today, however, the meaning of social action is far more difficult to define. Of course, all the priest's work is social: that is, he defines his calling and organizes and directs his career in relation to other people and specific institutions. Even by the most narrow definition of priestly functions, celebration of the Mass and administration of the sacraments, the priest's activities are social, for they are carried out in a specific social setting and are meant to have a real impact on society, influencing the lives of the participants and, through them, the destiny of the entire human race. The real question at issue in discussing the priest and social action is not, then, whether the priest should engage in action aimed at changing society, but only what actions toward this end are particularly appropriate to him as priest. The answer to this question changes with changing needs. The pastor consecrated to the service of God's people must meet them where they are and he must adapt his time and energy to the demands of his particular pastoral responsibility.

To some extent, at least, the Vatican Council recognized this fact. Its document on "The Ministry and Life of Priests" was in part a theological reflection on the end of the "clerical era" in which the priest, separate and apart, sought to rule his flock in a paternalistic, even authoritarian, manner. Instead the spirit of the conciliar statement is one of fraternity, stressing the brotherhood of priests with their bishops and their people. Indeed, so sharp is the Council's emphasis on collaboration that it recalls Gustave Weigel's remark of the American priest that the priest was less the shepherd of the flock than the captain of the team.

More important, the Council broke through many of the old barriers separating religious and social life, clergy and layman, by emphasizing the common Christian vocation. "All men are called to belong to the new People of God," the Council Fathers stated, and all members of the Church have the "task of bringing all men to full union with Christ." In such a context, the spirit is one of service, of all Christians to the Church and of the Church to the world. Social responsibility and action are no longer seen as added to spiritual responsibilities but as intrinsic elements of Christian vocation. For the priest, the Vatican Council makes the point clearly:

> Because the human race today is joining more and more into a civic, economic and social unity, it is that much more necessary that priests, united in concern and effort, under the leadership of the bishops and Supreme Pontiff, wipe out every kind of division, so that the whole human race may be brought into the unity of the family of God.[5]

The ministry of preaching provides a dramatic example of the changes in attitude that now mark the priesthood in its social dimensions. Shortly before the turn of the century an American bishop advised priests in a widely used manual of pastoral theology that they should "never speak about local politics or the political parties of the country." "In Church our Catholic people seek rest from the noise and bustle of everyday life, from the discordant sounds of human strife and warring politics," he explained. "They come to church to free their minds from the disagreeable scenes of the world." [6] In contrast, the priest today often feels called to address himself to "the disagreeable scenes of the world" in order to move the hearts of his congregation; even more, he frequently feels called upon to act directly to bring about justice and peace. "His ministry of the word is not limited to preaching from the safe remove of the pulpit," a modern-day pastoral counsellor writes. "It also demands that he give his person to others, that his words become flesh." [7]

More and more priests live this reality, recognized by the Vatican Council, that if "priestly preaching. . . is to influence the mind of the listener more fruitfully, such preaching must present God's Word, not in general and abstract fashion only, but it must apply the perennial truths of the Gospel to the concrete circumstances of life." [8] To do this, it is necessary to know these circumstances, even to live among them, and to act in accord with the Gospel message, to practice what is preached. "I must carry my prayer beyond the Mass, and I must carry my prophecy beyond the pulpit," one active young priest said, and his thought is echoed in the actions of many of his colleagues.[9] In saying this, he was repeating what zealous observers of contemporary life have often noted, that the priest's role in a no-longer Christian society must be to carry the Gospel out of the churches and into the world. As Cardinal Suhard of Paris argued after World War II: "The apostles to the de-Christianized *melieux* find continually that if they are to announce the Good News they have first of all to live the same life as those around them, as Christ did who 'dwelt among us' and like Him, share their joys and sorrows, their hopes and disappointments, and stand squarely with the just aspirations of those around them." [10]

Social action, action in the world to combat injustice and inequality and to realize the Gospel's promise of peace, freedom and dignity, once regarded as a secondary responsibility of the priest, increasingly seems integral to his vocation. As a consequence the priest feels called to reassess his career, his style of life, and his allocation of time and energy between the traditional tasks as leader of a congregation and the newly-felt call to make of the whole world "one perfect offering to God the Father and a place fit for his sons to live in." [11]

As the American priest attempts to restructure a satisfying and efficacious career, both in his relation to his Church and to the broader human community both are to serve, he may find help by examining the development of Catholic social action in America. That development was shaped by three major factors. One was the body of official Church teachings on Catholic social action, contained in the great encyclicals of Popes Leo XIII, and Pius XI, and the pronouncements of the American hierarchy. The second factor was the life and work of the American Church, with its implicit priorities in allocating material and human resources. Finally, and of equal importance in shaping American Catholic social action, was the complex of attitudes and ideas held by informed and articulate Church leaders about that broader American society within which they and their fellow Catholics lived.

In a sense, the first was least important. Papal teachings provided legitimacy for Catholics who were actively concerned with social problems and served as a point of reference for judging American attitudes and practices. Moreover, they set a framework beyond which reformers were forbidden to go. Ultimately private property, while subject to limitations, enjoyed the status of a natural right. Catholic reformers could advocate government intervention in economic life, but they could not become socialists. Neither could they unequivocally assert the values of possessive individualism, strict social Darwinism, or complete *laissez-faire*. In other words, the encyclicals had greater influence for their negative checks on social thought and action than for their positive stimulation of reform. Moreover, they proved to be subject to widely differing interpretations, so that, while invariably expressing hope for a unified Catholic response to social problems, men could and did differ almost completely on the meaning and implementation of "social justice" or "a living wage." [12]

The second factor involved in the development of Catholic social action was the American context. The mobility, individualism, and preoccupation with material success and personal liberty characteristic of life in the United States contrasted sharply with the traditional values of Roman Catholicism. This apparent contradiction between Catholicism and Americanism dominated the nation's deep and enduring tradition of nativism and anti-Catholicism which, in turn, helped shape the development of Catholic social thought. One historian noted this conflict on the level of values and attitudes in the late nineteenth century:

> Much of the fumbling and inconsistency of American Catholic social thinking . . . arose from this conflict between the idea of progress with all it implied and the older concept of a fixed and mellowed social order. Most Catholics never abandoned the latter ideal completely, but the history of American Catholic social thought. . . is, in the main, the story of their attempt to fit it to social theories with which it was seemingly incompatible.[13]

Catholic social theory frequently became sidetracked by the effort to reconcile papal teachings and American values, manifesting the insecurity and the longing for honesty, integrity, and full commitment of the Catholic minority. "Although Catholic social work stemmed directly from the crying need to protect poor, helpless immigrants, other motives entered directly into its genesis and development," Aaron I. Abell wrote. "Then the core idea of Americanism, namely, the desire to win recruits from the non-Catholic population and to make the Church an integral and vitally important aspect of American civilization, was an ever present factor." [14]

Social action grows out of the context it is designed to influence. As Gustave Weigel once pointed out, American society was distinguished for the Catholic by the fact that his religion was not traditionally inherent in American culture.[15] Papal and European Catholic social thought, in contrast, developed in an historical setting which presupposed a social order in which Catholicism and the Church were integral elements. The day to day life of the European village from which so many Catholic immigrants came was suffused with religious symbols and ritual; official liturgy celebrated the rhythms of village life. The priest was apart from the people yet integral to the community; his role was clear to himself and others.

In the United States things were different. Men lived in large cities, cold and impersonal; they worked in factories dominated by the pace of the machine; their employment was subject to the whims of distant employers and to the inscrutable workings of the business cycle. Religious symbol and ritual were missing from most of their daily life unless they themselves supplied it, and what public ceremony did exist seemed alien and incomprehensible. The people reestablished many traditional customs in the isolation of the ghetto but always they were drawn out, to work, to secure a license, to learn the language, to insure their children's future. The priest's role changed too. On the one hand, his services to the congregation increased with their needs: he became interpreter, negotiator, and guide to many areas of life they found impossible to understand. Yet his influence declined, for while he could negotiate with outsiders, he could not control them, and they, the employers or the politicians, had their own objectives.

In the context of a European village social action, action to influence society, was unheard of, for society was given and taken for granted. In the nineteenth century European city social action became conceivable, but only in a historical context that suggested a method of mass organized action, a spirit of clerical control and domination, and an atmosphere of reaction. In a very real sense the leaders of the European Catholic social movement always believed that they were the carriers of the national tradition, battling for the preservation of old or endangered values and traditions, opposing modern and alien forces symbolized by the city and the factory. That spirit was present in America in the Populist movement, but here the endangered traditional values were those of rural Protestants who had no use for the Catholic immigrant. Indeed, for the rural fundamentalist the Church was both a sign of the old Europe from which America had escaped, and of the new urbanism that threatened to destroy it.

For American Catholics, then, social action was influenced by the fact that they were themselves outsiders, aspiring to belong and to be accepted. Social action had a defensive tone; it sought to preserve the loyalty of the Catholic people, refute the calumnies of the enemy, and demonstrate the compatibility, indeed the identity, of American and Catholic values. It was not revolutionary, for revolution would isolate the Catholic minority and open the floodgates to persecution. Neither was it conservative in the European sense, for the conservative image of the Church was the reason it was feared by the American democrat. Instead social action was part of an overall effort to establish "some middle way between the opposing perils of self-isolation and total absorption." [16] Here, as elsewhere, Catholics were flexible, pragmatic, reformist, liberal, in a word, American.

As long as the American Catholic Church lived as an immigrant Church in an alien land, its style and traditions in conflict with the general tenor of American life, social action for the clergy meant essentially ministering to the needs of the flock. Provision of religious services, assistance to people with personal problems, unceasing effort to reach out and encompass within the Church the hordes of newcomers daily appearing in the cities of the north and west, these were the essential forms of social action by the American clergy. For the nation as a whole the work of the Church and its priests in caring for the needy and alienated was an invaluable contribution, for few others had the concern or the resources to meet the pressing needs of the newcomers. Thus there was a great deal of truth in Cardinal Gibbons' conviction that "the more we extend the influence of the Christian religion, the more we will contribute to the stability of our political and social fabric." [17]

American Catholic social action, then, was primarily shaped by two sometimes conflicting forces: by the demands made on the Church to conform its values and ideals to those of American culture, demands increasingly assimilated and internalized by the Church and its leaders, and by the needs and aspirations of the Catholic people themselves. In the earliest days of our national history the small group of Catholics led by John Carroll was composed of prosperous and secure men of English origin who had settled in Maryland and Pennsylvania. Except for their religion, little set these men apart from their non-Catholic neighbors; heirs to a long tradition of ostracism and persecution, they welcomed the freedom of the new nation and desired nothing more than to remain quiet and inconspicuous. With anti-Catholic laws abolished and religious passions cooled, they felt no deep alienation from the culture and society around them. Even the many French priests and bishops who joined them were for the most part educated and refined men who represented a cultural and religious style widely admired by upper-class American Protestants. As a result the early Catholic minority "accepted all the essential elements of the English culture of America" and sympathized strongly with the sentiments of non-Catholics toward the very different Catholic immigrants gradually streaming into the seaboard cities.[18] In short, the early American Catholics were conformist in their social attitudes and deeply "anxious to convince their neighbors that they were not different from them except in creed." [19]

The cultural tradition of the early Anglo-Catholic minority remained extremely powerful in the American Church, exerting an influence far beyond its numbers.[20] Reinforced by noted converts like Orestes Brownson, Levi Sillman Ives, and James Roosevelt Bayley, the tradition was upheld by old Catholic families of Maryland and Kentucky, the most noticeable of whom were the Spaldings. Church leaders from abroad or from immigrant stock adopted much of that heritage, particularly its effort to moderate anti-Catholic feelings and win acceptance and respectability from the nation's dominant elite.

The priest of the early American Church accepted the pecularities of America, devoted himself to the spiritual welfare of his flock, and avoided unseemly controversy. "In American religion is a distinct sphere, in which the priest is sovereign, but out of which he takes care never to go," Alexis de Tocqueville noted, with the surprise one would expect from a man so familiar with the clergy's political role in post-revolutionary Europe.[21] The bishops of the nation took care to remind their priests of the differences, writing them in 1829: "From you the people expect instruction for the service of God, not suggestions as to the regulation of their own temporal concerns, with which you should avoid entanglement." [22]

Yet such a clear distinction between spiritual and temporal affairs is rarely possible, paricularly in a mission situation. America expanded rapidly and the Catholic population more than kept pace. Geographically the settlement of new territories meant the need for new dioceses of vast extent and for priests to reach the scattered people. At the same time the small stream of Catholic immigrants grew in the 1830's and 1840's to a tidal wave which threatened to engulf the settled Catholic minority and destroy its hard won freedom and respectability.

To preserve the faith of the western settlers beyond the reach of established churches and retain the loyalty of the hordes of poor, illiterate and foreign immigrants in the urban centers was a challenge which demanded the full dedication and attention of bishops and priests.

The first requirement was for laborers for the vineyard; the bishops were forced to rely on foreign born and trained clergy, many of whom came to America to escape scandal in Europe and caused their American superiors no end of trouble. The solution was to provide an adequate native clergy, trained by their bishops for disciplined service in the new world. Every national pastoral letter of the nineteenth century contained a plea for vocations, seminary support, and an exhortation of the clergy to exemplary behavior.

Equally important, the transformation of the Church by imigration placed severe strain upon the careful separation of spiritual and temporal concerns. The mission priest could hardly avoid involvement in the temporal affairs of his people, whether they were poor immigrants or western settlers. Enormous growth for the infant Church meant a preoccupation for the priest with practical problems and an activist temperament which excluded time for meditation and reflection. The result was that the drive to preserve the faith and to organize the Church on the frontier and in the city, a conservative objective often aimed at recreating apparently universal Catholic institutions, meant in practice adaptation to the demands of the American environment. Gabriel Richard, a pioneer priest in frontier Detroit, had no desire to meddle in the temporal lives of his people, but his pastoral zeal could hardly be confined to the sanctuary. The Bishop of Quebec, visiting Detroit in 1816, described Richard as a man "of an activity of which it is difficult to form an idea." He continued:

> Provided with newspapers, well informed on all political questions, ever ready to argue on religion when the occasion presents itself, and thoroughly learned in theology, he reaps his hay, gathers the fruit of his garden, manages a fishery fronting his lot, teaches mathematics to one young man, reading to another, devotes times to mental prayer, establishes a printing press confesses all his people, imports carding and spinning wheels and looms to teach the women of his parish how to work, leaves not a single act of his parochial register unwritten, invents an electric machine, goes on sick calls at a very great distance, writes letters to and receives others from all parts, preaches on every Sunday and holy day both lengthily and learnedly, enriches his library, spends whole nights without sleep, walks for whole days, loves to converse, teaches catechism to his parishoners, supports a girls' school under the management of a few female teachers of his own choosing, which he directs like a religious

community, whilst he gives lessons in plainsong to young boys assembled in a school he has founded, leads a most frugal life, and is in good health, as fresh and able, at the age of fifty, as one usually is at thirty.[23]

Add to this that Richard was a founder and vice president of the University of Michigan and the territory's delegate to Congress and the picture of a totally involved pastor is complete.

In the cities men of energy and enthusiasm found no less work to be done. At the end of the nineteenth century American Protestants created the "institutional church" in their effort to reach the urban masses, but years before Catholics had built the same kind of churches to solve their problems. First, churches were built to provide centers of worship; then devotional societies were established to sustain old world customs. When resources became available, parochial schools were built to educate the children in a setting conducive to the retention of the faith and often bringing the added benefit of reducing intergenerational conflict by keeping alive the memories, customs, and language of the old world. Charitable associations were formed to help the parish's poor; temperance societies to combat the evils of drink; societies for women and young men to provide some fellowship amid the drudgery of domestic life and the moral perils of the city. This wide range of parochial activity found its deepest source in the disruption of the migration experience which caused men to draw close to others like themselves. Through parish life these strangers in America could overcome their loneliness, assist one another, and rebuild the shattered bonds of community. The parish and, later, the national societies, in bringing men together, cemented their loyalty to the Church and, unless thwarted by ecclesiastical hostility, to the bishops as well. These associations thus became insuperable obstacles to Protestant proselytization and usually effective substitutes for such ethnic separatism as that represented by the Polish National Catholic Church. In similar fashion extra-parochial agencies — hospitals, orphanages, homes for wayward young men and lonely factory girls — counteracted the appeal of Protestant and nonsectarian institutions. Still, whatever the ecclesiastical benefits, the needs were real; the government did little or nothing to meet those needs and even the most disinterested and philanthropic non-Catholics devoted few resources to care for the newcomers. There was literally no one else to try to alleviate the suffering.

The result was the growth of the American parish which John

Talbot Smith called in 1905, "a complicated and useful machine, probably the highest achievement of the American priest." [24] Smith was perceptive, for, while the bishops' encouragement and the peoples' support were indispensable, it was the energy and idealism of the priests that shaped the history of the parish. The New York cathedral parish, for example, utilized the services of six priests to provide daily and Sunday masses, confessions on Friday and Saturday, special services and devotions constantly. One priest was always available for conferences and another for sick calls. In addition they directed schools with 1600 students and offered religious instruction to a much larger number, conducted a library and reading room, and oversaw the work of parish societies for men, women and young people and a host of devotional sodalities and leagues. [25]

Even more striking was the Church of St. James where Father Felix H. Farrelly presided over a tuition-free school of 1700 students, an industrial school providing free lunch and clothing as well as instruction for 200 destitute children, a twenty-one room mission house, a huge parish conference of the St. Vincent de Paul Society which annually spent $5,000 on poor relief and kept at least forty members constantly at work. Moreover 900 men were organized in parish temperance societies. Other parishes followed this example though few could match its performance. [26]

In short, the American priest was deeply involved in social action from the start. Henry J. Browne is more than justified in claiming that "the mission of the Catholic Church was almost from the outset conceived of as a social one." [27] This fantastic expenditure of men and resources to meet social as well as religious needs derived in the first instance not from a theory of the priest's role or from papal statements on social justice but from the deep commitment of bishops and priests to the care of their people. "The energies of the ordinary clergy were almost totally consumed in pastoral work," Thomas T. McAvoy has written, and this pastoral work was defined in the broadest terms of charity and service. [28] Whatever the regrettable effects of these priorities in terms of the delayed intellectual development of the American Church or the failure to develop a comprehensive self-awareness on the part of the clergy, the work and example of his nineteenth-century predecessors constitute an enduring and important legacy for the contemporary priest.

The enormous burden of work did inhibit the development of a critical Catholic perspective on American society. Deeply immersed in his work and strongly desiring acceptance in American society, the priest had to overcome the pervasive suspicion present even among some members of his congregation that the Catholic faith and Church were in conflict with American democracy. Accordingly the Church's leaders were inclined to praise the country and its institutions, not to criticize them. Moreover, whatever concern they may have felt over pressing national issues was submerged by the need to preserve the unity of the Church and to avoid giving its enemies ammunition for attack. Commenting on the failure of the hierarchy to speak out on slavery at the First Plenary Council of Baltimore in 1852, historian Peter Guilday wrote:

> Perhaps the outstanding proof of the wisdom of our prelates lies in their silence on the slavery question, then dividing political parties and the churches of other denominations into antagonistic groups which have never been wholly reconciled. . . . The prelates were face to face with problems of greater moment in their effort to keep abreast of the tide of immigration to our shores. No other church in the land, then as now, has realized the supreme need of keeping itself free from political questions; and no other Church has sympathized more profoundly with the basic American distrust of ecclesiastical interference in public life.[29]

However strongly the contemporary observer may disagree with this assessment, Guilday was undoubtedly correct in recognizing the preeminence of the bishops' concern with the Church and its people. Pressed by internal needs and by virulent external hostility in the pre-Civil War years, the hierarchy and most priests kept prudent silence and carefully adapted to shifts in national and sectional opinion.

Similar considerations continued to dominate policy in the late nineteenth century. When the social question was forced into the open by the violent labor upheavals of the 1870's and 1880's the Church responded cautiously. Association of Catholic workers with the Molly Maguires raised the danger that the Church would become identified in the public mind with labor radicalism. On the other hand, the Church's working class constituency prevented out and out rejection of protest and change. Accordingly, under the skillful leadership of Cardinal Gibbons, the hierarchy disavowed radicalism and affirmed its faith in the basic fairness of the American economic system and its leaders. At the same time the bishops defended the Knights of Labor against Vatican condemnation and granted the conservative trade unionism of the American Federation of Labor their tacit approval. Even the publication of *Rerum novarum* in 1891 raised no serious questions for the clergy or the bishops, most of whom honestly believed that the American system was beneficent and hardly merited the strictures that Leo XIII levelled against liberal capitalism.

Thus, in the very earliest days, American Catholic social thought on modern industrial problems developed a moderate, realistic tone that reflected the ambiguities of the Church's position in the United States. "As chiefly wage earning immigrants, American Catholics displayed many radical tendencies on the industrial front," Aaron Abell writes:

> This fact presented the Church with a double problem: how, on the one hand, to champion the cause of the poor without endangering the public interest or the common good, and, on the other, how to oppose Socialism without negating or ignoring the claims of social reform.[30]

Yet, continued labor violence and social polarization and the steady growth of American socialism after 1900 gave greater relevance to the Pope's warnings against radicalism, made explicit in his message to Americans in 1895:

> The scenes of violence which you witnessed last year in your country sufficiently admonish you that America too is threatened with the audacity and ferocity of the enemies of public order.[31]

Church leaders needed little admonition, for they had earlier recognized the danger and had moved steadily to address themselves to it. In the years before World War I they became more and more involved in the increasingly popular efforts for social reform, while at the same time deliberately working to discredit and destroy the infant socialist movement.[32]

Much Catholic effort for social reform was negatively anti-socialist, but it should be recognized that here too the motive was largely pastoral. In addition to a natural desire to affirm their respectability and their Americanism, the bishops and clergy were desirous of preserving the intimate ties that bound them to their people. As early as 1882 John Gilmary Shea had warned that the ranks of discontented workingmen were growing rapidly, and many of these laborers were Catholics. "The Church, if she is to retain her hold on them, must show them these dangers, and aid them in their lawful struggle, and sustain them in their trial." [33] Similar considerations figured largely in Cardinal Gibbons' defense of the Knights of Labor. Later, in 1904, William Stang, Bishop of Fall River, expressed the same concern:

"We know that, as priests, we are enshrined in the hearts of our Catholic working people, and that we are secure against the calumnies and vituperations of the rankest Socialist. It is our duty to preserve these intimate and sacred relations between people and priests." [34] Toward this end Stang wrote and lectured on the evils of Socialism while working actively to promote a Catholic movement for social reform. John A. Ryan, best known of Catholic social reformers, likewise stressed the pastoral responsibilities of the priest in the arena of social action. If the clergy were unable or unwilling "to understand, appreciate and sympathize directly with the aspirations of economic democracy," Ryan warned in 1909, "it will inevitably become more and more un-Christian, and pervert all too rapidly a larger and larger proportion of our Catholic population." [35]

Such efforts could find religious legitimacy in Leo XIII's encyclical, and they became increasingly acceptable to the native Protestant majority. In the early stages of industrial conflict, reformers had directed their attention to such moderate and popular solutions to social unrest as the temperance movement, designed to free the workers from the weakness which prevented him from improving his condition, and rural colonization, which would remove him from the oppression and temptations of urban life.[36] Bishop John Lancaster Spalding and Archbishop John Ireland, two of the more alert and socially conscious bishops, devoted considerable time and energy to both of these thoroughly respectable efforts at reform, and many priests joined them, particularly in the temperance movement which became organized in hundreds of parishes and many dioceses.

As the nation moved toward more direct assault on its problems after the Populist movement had spent its force in the free silver campaign of 1896, Catholic reformers, impatient with the moral uplift approach of the temperance crusade, found an increasingly sympathetic hearing. The German Central-Verein in fact discovered that social reform work rejuvenated the organization because of its attraction for the increasingly Americanized younger members of the German Catholic community.[37] While bishops and priests participated in social justice movements before World War I, they did so through laymen-led Catholic societies.[38] Moreover, as late as 1917, Father John A. Ryan could write that the number of bishops who had made any pronouncements on social issues could be counted on the fingers of one hand and the number of priests was not proportionately greater.[39]

Most clergymen remained deeply immersed in pastoral work; the carefully constructed parishes and societies of the nineteenth century were inundated by a new flood of immigrants after 1890 which reached huge proportions during the first decade of the twentieth century. The burden imposed by the "new immigration" on the parish priest and on Catholic relief and welfare agencies undoubtedly stimulated interest in the social justice and urban welfare phases of the progressive movement, but the burden of day to day work prevented priests from becoming actively involved. "As in the case of other immigrants," Father McAvoy writes, "the clergy had to devote most of their energies to the building of churches, orphanages and hospitals and to providing what instruction they could to keep their flock faithful to their Catholic principles and from engaging in the grosser forms of the general competition for wealth." [40] Moreover, the priest who wished to become involved frequently had to deal with a bishop who needed his services and regarded participation in organized social justice efforts, many of which were non-sectarian, with suspicion.[41]

In addition, churches, orphanages and schools imposed severe financial burdens upon pastors and bishops. Father Edward McGlynn, pastor of a very active parish in New York, recognized that the policy that gave priority to parochial schools carried with it the need to develop large parishes and to give inordinate attention to financial matters. He refused to build a school in his parish and with some of his friends argued for smaller parishes more easily adaptable to the needs of poor congregations.[42] At the peak of the progressive movement, Father Joseph Selinger, examining the contemporary situation of the nation and the Catholic people and the encylical of Leo XIII, concluded that it was the duty of parish priests "to do all in their power to work for social reform." The reason so few heeded the Pope's call to social action, Selinger felt, could be found in the manifold and expensive work of the parish. "Temporalities. . . so occupy them," he concluded, "that the care for these unduly detracts their attention from the pressing social problems." [43]

Selinger's explanation of the priest's failure to join in efforts for labor organization or legislative reform overstated the case. The very "temporalities" were evidence of the priest's concern with social problems; they simply restricted his attention in dealing with them to church agencies of relief and assistance, a restriction reinforced by the ethnocentrism of his flock and the evident requirements of the Church. "The desire of the immigrants to form communities similar to those they had left in Europe," said Oscar Handlin, "provided the Church with the zealous support which maintained its growth through the first quarter of the twentieth century." He continued:

All the ties of family, neighborhood, social and political loyalty, as well as faith, held these people together. In response to these, there appeared an array of social and religious institutions for men, women and children, all linked to the Church and each eliciting support by virtue of its appeal to both faith and group loyalty. The parish thus became the equivalent of the European village community.[44]

The confined, group oriented attitudes that this "ghetto mentality" nurtured were conducive to machine-style politics and to certain types of social legislation, but they were at odds with the moralistic temper of traditional liberal reform.

The highly Americanized Catholics, in tune with the dominant "Yankee-Protestant" reform spirit, could easily join in the progressive movement, but the typical Catholic of the city could support reform only through group action and association. His was at best a "bread and butter" liberalism which would not attain national recognition until the 1930's.[45] As a result, while deeply involved in charitable and welfare work, the Church and its priests were slow to develop the perspective that led to reform of the institutions responsible for social evils rather than alleviation of the suffering those evils entailed.

Catholic welfare agencies frequently dealt with social problems on a day to day basis, and the vast needs created by immigration, urban growth and industrial anarchy forced changes in this work in the early twentieth century. The priests had long been something of a benevolent jack-of-all-trades, but, as the problems of urban life multiplied and the resources of the church increased, it became possible and desireable to deal with the social work of the Catholic Church in more organized fashion. For years the priest could only deal with poverty, disease and destitution on a personal and *ad hoc* basis, but gradually it became clear that the resources of the church would have to be organized in a more systematic effort to alleviate suffering. Schools, orphanages, hospitals, nursing homes, boarding houses for working men and women, recreational facilities for the young, all became more and more organized after the turn of the century. Diocesan social action agencies coordinated fund raising, administration and social services as bishops sought to ease indebtedness and provide more systematic support for charitable and social work under their jurisdiction.

In the Archdiocese of Boston, William O'Connell found, upon succeeding John Williams as archbishop, that the myriad of social agencies were riddled with duplication, decaying facilities and intolerable debts. With assurance and deliberation O'Connell phased out unsupported programs, replaced pious but incompetent officials, centralized administration under his direction, and placed diocesan agencies on a sound financial footing. This experience was repeated in diocese after diocese as a new breed of talented administrators rose to episcopal office. The new National Conference of Catholic Charities (1910) lent its support to such movements and sought to convince Catholics of the need for trained professionals to supplement amateur volunteers in dealing with the mass of social problems heretofore handled by generous but untrained pastors and members of religious orders.[46]

One important corollary of these developments was the rise of the professional social worker and administrator to operate the new agencies. Devoting most of their time to administration and professional activity, frequently removed for many years from direct pastoral work, they pursued, as priests, careers that other men undertook as laymen. While initially many of the participants in this movement were laymen, diocesan centralization frequently meant in practice the utilization of priests in administrative posts. Indeed, the offices of the Archdiocese of New York after World War II had no laymen in its twenty-one member administrative staff and only thirty-three of its one hundred and fifty-eight specialized agencies were headed by laymen.[47]

Yet, not all priests participated; indeed, for the parish priest, matters he might have dealt with personally in previous years were now referred to professional marriage counsellors, charitable organizations and other specialized agencies of the diocese. Laymen retained an outlet for charitable work in the St. Vincent de Paul Society, whose work was coordinated under diocesan direction. While the laymen and the priest-professional had an enhanced social action role, that of the parish priest was now sharply circumscribed.

Implicit in the movement toward a more organized and scientific approach to social problems was a growing rejection of the notion that many of these problems were simply the result of personal weakness and sinfulness. Although many priests continued to adhere to such a view, the Church moved steadily towards an organized and sophisticated approach which at least implied that the environment of the industrial city was at fault, that there were, indeed, weaknesses in the American society. Nevertheless, while organized social action meant a recognition that society itself could cause poverty and suffering, most Catholic leaders remained concerned primarily with alleviating the results.

Fathers William J. Kerby, John A. Ryan and others who helped stimulate and guide the movement argued strongly for the need to deal with the causes of poverty which lay in the industrial system itself. They found support in the encyclical of Leo XIII, *Rerum novarum*, and could point to the leadership of European Catholics, particularly in Germany, in developing broad programs of social reform. But they were hampered by the fact that too few priests recognized the existence of real injustice, and fewer were willing to admit that America's system itself might be at fault. To have attacked the economic practices of the country would have risked censure by respectable Protestants and would have reopened the question, even in their own minds, of the compatibility of Catholic Christianity and American democracy.

More important, priests had not been prepared by background, training, or experience to understand the social and economic roots of poverty, to make informed judgment of the issues raised by reformers, or to lead their people toward a concerted attack on injustice. "There is scarcely any danger that the clergy of America will ever lose sympathy with the desire of the masses for industrial freedom and industrial opportunity," Father Ryan noted, "but there is a very real danger that their sympathy will not be equalled by their knowledge. The great majority of our clergy in the United States have not yet begun to study systematically or take more than superficial interest in the important social problems of the age and country." [48] To overcome this highly important roadblock to Catholic social action, Ryan, Kerby, Bishop Stang of Fall River and others began writing widely on Catholic social thought and on contemporary social issues. The *Catholic Charities Review*, founded in 1917, became an outlet for these writings and Kerby sought to incorporate educational programs for the clergy into the work of diocesan charitable organizations. [49] Equally important, the reformers fought strenuously for the introduction of the social sciences into the seminary curriculum. Arguing that the priest in training had to understand the society in which God's people were working out their salvation, that the social question was the single most important feature of twentieth-century life, and that the application of gospel teaching to modern conditions necessitated detailed knowledge of the facts of modern life and familiarity with the social theories and movement agitating society, the reformers pushed hard for educational reform. [50] Their effort to develop a broad knowledge of social problems on the part of all the clergy received added support from the increasing organization of Catholic charities, the growing respectability of reform and welfare work, the Church's fear of socialist influence, and the conviction that the traditional teachings of the Church, reinvigorated by *Rerum novarum*, offered solutions to the ills of the Catholic working-men and of the nation at large.

Thus social action had become by World War I not the work of a small group of reformers regarded by most Catholics with suspicion or hostility, but an acceptable means of fulfilling the priestly calling and, at the same time, vindicating the compatability of Catholicism and American values. Infused by a growing self-confidence and a note of triumphalism, the new message called for an active, energetic, clergy prepared to provide answers to all Americans: "The American priest, if he would be true to his calling as good shepherd, must use every legitimate means at his disposal to save society, to save America," Father George Schmidt wrote in 1919. He continued:

> The Catholic Church. . . alone can heal the cancerous wounds that must need sap the life blood of our republic. . . . The duty of the American priest will be to guard his workingmen against the snares of a false society that proposes to heal their wounds and right their wrongs. He must give them the only true remedy, that proposed by the Catholic Church.[51]

The priest who devoted his full energies to social reform occupied a precarious position nevertheless. If his work did not endanger the Church's unity or respectability, he could expect ecclesiastical toleration. If it did pose a threat, he could expect difficulty. Years earlier Father Edward McGlynn's concern for the poor in New York led him to advocate Henry George's single tax, which he felt would eliminate the causes of poverty from America and thus was "the economic expression of the Gospel." [52] When he actively supported George in the New York mayoralty election of 1886, he was suspended and ultimately excommunicated. McGlynn persisted in the advocacy of his views, and his friendships with well-placed bishops helped him to regain his priestly status. Other radicals were less fortunate. Fathers Thomas McGrady and Thomas Hagerty became involved with American socialism — Hagerty was a founder of the I.W.W. Both were repudiated by the Church and ended in bitter separation from it.[53] These men overstepped the boundaries of historical possibility in seeking to align their Church with social radicalism. Insecure and fearful of conflict and publicity, the bishops invariably turned on those who tried to involve her in radical, apparently un-American, action.

John A. Ryan noted in his autobiography that often it was a matter of style. Choosing his words carefully, phrasing his arguments for his audience, he won converts where other men received censure, even though his message was usually no less radical. From 1901 to 1919, when the nation itself embarked upon an era of reform, Ryan and other reform-minded priests gradually gained a hearing within the Church and enjoyed prestige and influence outside. Ryan's *A Living Wage* was a key document in the movement for minimum wage legislation, and he helped draft a model law in Minnesota.[54] While seeking to educate and organize the Catholic community, Ryan simultaneously was an active participant in numerous non-denominational reform organizations. Ryan was the leading Catholic progressive, but he was not alone. Increasingly, priests followed their concern about industrial conditions into the public arena. Edwin V. O'Hara, a young priest, drafted and later administered a model minimum wage law in Oregon. After World War I, O'Hara turned to problems of the countryside, organizing the National Catholic Rural Life Conference while serving as Bishop of Great Falls, Montana and later of Kansas City.[55] In San Francisco, Father Peter C. Yorke was a pioneer labor priest, backing the city's unions against open shop employers and joining other civic leaders in an effort to combat corruption in the unions and in government.[56]

Labor was the particular concern of Father Peter E. Dietz, who helped organize Catholic leaders of the American Federation of Labor while urging the Church to recognize and identify with labor's cause. As broadly involved as Ryan, Dietz was instrumental in the social reform work of the German Central-Verein and in the organization in 1901 of the American Federation of Catholic Societies, the latter a group that hoped to become the vehicle for a national program of social reform.[57]

These priests and others less well known established a pattern of clerical activism that seemed to open up new roles for the priest in a Church becoming more and more at home in America. The culmination of this movement came in 1919 with the publication of the "Bishops' Program of Social Reconstruction," a relatively radical series of proposals for social and industrial legislation published in the name of the American hierarchy. In the same year the bishops established a national organization, the National Catholic Welfare Council (later, Conference), with a Social Action Department headed by Ryan.

What distinguished Ryan, Dietz and Kerby from their predecessors and gave particular force to the Bishops' Program was the evident concern with reform rather than charity, with the causes of poverty rather than its symptoms. While the Church had been and continued to be preoccupied with caring for the immediate needs of its people, the reformers were urging their fellow Catholics to join other Americans to transform the nation's economic life, either through labor unions or social legislation, so that men would be able to care for their own and their familial needs. In 1919 it seemed for a moment that social reform had superseded social service.

Yet the burst of reform energy proved short lived, and in the 1920's the Church turned away from social reform. Few had ever felt as strongly as Ryan and Dietz the need for fundamental changes in the social order, and new conflicts between Catholics and Protestants over prohibition, the Ku Klux Klan and the candidacy of a Catholic, Alfred E. Smith, for the presidency drew Catholicism's leaders back to a concern with defense of the Church and its rights. Only with the great depression in the 1930's did large numbers of Catholics accept the need for serious social change, and only then did the challenge that Ryan and others had raised become an issue of general concern among American Catholics.

Indeed, in the 1930's for the first time the Church and its leaders became preoccupied with reform.[58] The sufferings of millions of unemployed, large numbers of whom were Catholics, the angry temper of farmers and the dispossessed, the apparent dangers of radicalism, the burdens experienced by Catholic Charities and indebted parishes and dioceses, the legislative activity of the New Deal administration of Franklin Roosevelt and the frenzied activity of the new labor unionism — all made social concern necessary and natural. Bishops, priests and laymen alike had to come to terms with the problems of an economically depressed America. Like other Americans, their confidence in the beneficence of America was severely shaken, so that they began to take seriously those sections of the papal encyclicals that condemned unrestrained liberal capitalism. The alternative was far from clear, as the "vocational group" proposals of Pope Pius XI's *Quadragesima Anno,* published in 1931, proved difficult to apply in the United States. Nevertheless, the more critical temper opened the Church to vigorous debate on social and political issues and provided the basis for a more realistic and honest self-evaluation. "Unquestionably the churches, including the Catholic Church in the United States, have been tied up too intimately with capitalism in the past," one bishop wrote, and this sentiment was widely shared.[59] The result was that pastoral energy was frequently directed away from parochial concern to active work to better the lot of all the poor and the oppressed and to help revise the institutional arrangements of American economic life.

Yet Catholic social reform remained within a framework set by the Church's experience in the United States, a framework of loyalty to the country and to the papal teachings; reform was dominated by the need to demonstrate that these dual loyalties were compatible. Within this framework, many hoped for the development of a unified Catholic social reform movement, but inevitable disagreement over the proper interpretation of papal teachings and correct understanding of American conditions inhibited such concerted action. Instead several approaches to Catholic social action emerged, each of which implied a somewhat different role for the priest. These models, developed in the 1930's, provided the major alternatives for clerical involvement in reform down to the revolutionary changes of the last decade.

One model was supplied by Father John A. Ryan, who argued throughout his career that the social problems with which Catholic agencies were concerned found their origins in the inequalities and failures of the American economic system. While he lent occasional support to other forms of social action, he concentrated his attention on politics and legislation as the major roads to reform. Ryan fought hard to win Catholic support for the New Deal, viewing its effort to establish governmental regulation of American industry and to enact legislation to protect men against its inequities and instability as according completely with Catholic social teachings.

Ryan's own career evidenced a style of clerical involvement that was unique. Because of his orientation toward politics, he tended to see honest, liberal political participation by laymen as the goal of the priest's efforts. He respected the work of other social activists and he welcomed efforts to develop strong lay organizations, but he devoted his attention to developing a realistic and generous political consciousness among clergy and laity alike. In dealing with priests he invariably stressed the need for them to be informed and aware of facts and issues, and of the Church's teachings, so that they would at least not obstruct efforts at organization and action and, at best, would lend to such efforts their own formal or informal support. There was no weakening of Ryan's energetic attempts to inform and enlighten the Catholic community, but the work of three decades left him less concerned with mobilizing Catholics in an organized Catholic social movement than with winning Catholic support for the political program of the New Deal.

More characteristic of clerical social action than Ryan's preoccupation with reform politics was involvement with the labor movement. As early as 1912, Father Dietz had sought with little success to win

Catholic support for the unions. Many social reformers, like Ryan, approved of unions in the abstract but were highly critical of the A.F. of L. The suffering of the depression led scores of priests to throw themselves into the effort to unionize the workers. Most industrial cities produced labor priests who combatted anti-union propaganda, helped in organizing drives and contributed to union morale during the long months of strikes and unemployment. Father Charles Owen Rice of Pittsburgh, for example, directed a local Catholic Worker house, organized the Catholic Radical Alliance to support the C.I.O. in the mills, and instructed workers in their duty to join the union. Bishops like Robert Lucey, Bernard Sheil and Edward Mooney similarly boosted the C.I.O. and argued forcefully that membership and responsible participation in a union was a requirement arising from the duty to implement social justice. Cincinnati's Archbishop John T. Nicholas assigned nineteen of his priests to labor work. Their actions legitimized the activity of the many priests who were active on the labor front, often in affiliation with the lay Association of Catholic Trade Unionists, an organization directed at encouraging active participation by Catholics in union affairs.[60]

Other priests established labor schools in which union men could study labor history, economics, parliamentary procedure, and collective bargaining techniques, as well as the social teachings of the Church. Still other priests served on government mediation and arbitration boards of a local, state and national level. Father Francis J. Haas of the Catholic University of America, who was active in all these programs, became one of the first appointees to President Roosevelt's Fair Employment Practices Committee during World War II.

Father Charles E. Coughlin, the famous radio priest from Royal Oak, Michigan, offered a third model of the social action priest. Beginning in 1930, Coughlin attracted a large following by attacking the evils of the economic system and demanding fundamental changes, notably in the area of currency and banking. The flamboyance and extremism of his involvement in the 1936 election and eventual lapse into anti-Semitic and anti-communist hysteria alienated most American Catholics and discredited political action as an appropriate activity for priests. Nevertheless, the nationalistic and anti-communist themes he developed remained powerful forces in the American Church, providing for many, in the post-war years, an alternative to social reform and a means to demonstrate their adherence to the creed of Americanism.[61] National isolationism and hatred of Communism drew many priests out of the confines of parish life into what they saw as an active social ministry. The pastoral concern of these men, fearful for the welfare of their Church and country, was no less honest or sincere than that of their moral liberal counterparts.

Yet another model was that of the Catholic who felt that it was necessary to preserve a distinct, separate Catholic culture, within which the faith could be nourished and preserved. Father Charles Bruehl, of Saint Charles Seminary in Philadelphia, wrote:

> If the purity of Catholic thinking and the integrity of Catholic practice are to be preserved, it is necessary to adopt measures against the social contagion emanating from our environment. We must, to the extent that it is possible, immunize our minds against the tainting and corrupting social atmosphere that surrounds us so closely and penetrates to our very souls.[62]

Such a point of view had always been identified with immigrant groups, particularly the German-Americans, who yearned to preserve the faith and culture of their native land. It was quite compatible with an energetic criticism of American social and economic practice. Catholic radicalism, indeed, found its roots in the sharp sense of conflict between Christianity and American life and often sought to build "the new society with the shell of the old" by withdrawal from factory and city, though always with the hope of redeeming the broader society.

Another approach to social reform, one with peculiar relevance for the clergy, was contained in the work of the Benedictine, Virgil Michel. Theologically sophisticated and socially concerned, Michel brought the vitality of the liturgical movement back from his European studies and gave it a strong social flavor. For Michel the priest's social role was to revitalize the liturgy in the spirit of the theology of the Mystical Body of Christ. He declared:

> It is not too much to say that the survival of true social human life will be achieved only under the inspiration of the liturgical life, since the specific divine purpose of the latter is to transform human nature after the mind of Christ and inspire it into a life replete like His love of God and man.[63]

The liturgy would then become a school of social action, drawing men to a sense of collective responsibility and common destiny which stood in marked contrast to the rampant individualism of American society. Imbued with the new spirit of Christian community, men would go forth to restore all things in Christ, to make the world reflect in its institutional life the solidarity and cooperation of the Mystical Body of Christ.

The liturgical movement found a ready response among the predominantly lay members of the radical Catholic Worker movement and it offered the reform-minded priest an outlet that was socially relevant and yet compatible with his traditional function in the Christian community. Together with the opportunities offered by the Catholic Worker houses and other social settlements for service to the poor, the liturgical movement remained until the 1960's a major concern of socially liberal priests.

Only a few priests like Paul Hanley Furfey of the Catholic University of America carried the vision that inspired Michel and the founders of the Catholic Worker into a truly radical critique of society and church. Furfey's vigorous denunciations of violence, racism and inequality in American society, and his telling criticisms of the American Church's implication in these defects, were highly unusual. Outspoken as a writer and critic, inspiring as a teacher, deeply involved in interracial and social justice programs in Washington, and actively promoting the reform of Catholic education and scholarship, Furfey was a neglected prophet whose message could reach only those whose disillusionment with America had gone farther than that of most Catholics until very recent years.[64]

Perhaps the most typical form of social action for priests was involvement in Catholic Action. As defined and elaborated during the pontificate of Pope Pius XI, Catholic Action was a highly organized effort to bring Catholics into the arena of social life as a force for reform. Officially, Catholic Action was "the participation of the laity in the apostolate of the hierarchy" aimed at restoring Christian practice to social life. Catholic Action required episcopal approbation and a priest as chaplain, but it was a lay movement, and its programs and tactics varied.

In the United States its foremost example on a national level was the Legion of Decency, whose record was mixed at best. More characteristic were the Chicago-based Catholic Action groups that grew in the late 1930's and during World War II, such as the Christian Family Movement and the Young Catholic Workers (an American affiliate of Canon Joseph Cardijn's famous *Jocists*), organizations given a good deal of freedom by certain bishops, guided by imaginative priests, and directed by enthusiastic laymen. In such organizations the socially conscious priest could find a half-way house, more free of bureaucratic responsibilities than his counterparts in Catholic charities, yet retaining a base in the parishes often lacking to the more radical or more independent reformers. European style Catholic Action controlled by the hierarchy, conflicted with the American dislike of clerical interference in secular affairs beyond such issues as birth control and pornography, but the less controlled Chicago movements appealed to the increasingly sophisticated Catholic middle class.[65]

As the United States entered World War II, support for organized labor and involvement in labor management disputes were the most characteristic mode of social action for priests. The Catholic Worker movement, soon to be sharply reduced in size as its pacifist position conflicted with the nation's rush to arms, was almost entirely a lay movement, though its moral impact on priests was very great. John Ryan's liberalism had great influence in raising important questions about American life and conditioning Catholics to the acceptance of liberal reform. His orientation toward political action, while it provided a rationale and legitimation for the Catholic impact on national politics, hardly provided a suitable outlet for clerical initiative, particularly after the unhappy experience with clerical political activity provided by the career of Father Coughlin.

The mainstream of social involvement for priests had to be found in action that was neither as radical in its implications as that of the Catholic Worker nor as political as that of John Ryan. It would have to be, then, in the area of voluntary organizations for social change, and few existed apart from the labor movement, which accordingly received an inordinate amount of attention from the Catholic press and from Ryan's successors at the N.C.W.C.

Monsignor Ryan died in 1945 but Fathers Raymond A. McGowan and George G. Higgins carried on his tradition of arousing concern for social evils and support for political programs and a realism derived from ecumenical and political contacts and experience. Both were more directly influenced by the encyclicals than Ryan had been and, as a result, they gave greater attention to organizing social action programs for Catholics and to aiding the labor movement. Actively combatting Catholic isolationism in foreign policy and growing suspicion of trade unionism and welfare legislation, they found themselves preoccupied with defending the gains of the New Deal years against mounting conservatism in the Church. In 1960, Monsignor Higgins pointed out that only one-fourth of the nation's seminarians received training in Catholic social teachings. Perhaps that fact explained why so much hostility developed toward trade unions, but equally important was the declining militance of labor itself.

Labor priests had supported organization, internal union democracy, and efforts to overthrow Communist leadership, and this work continued to demand attention in the post-war years. The recent involvement of the N.C.W.C.'s (now the United States Catholic Conference) Social Action Department in the effort to organize agricultural workers provides an illustration of the relevance of these traditional concerns. But labor action in earlier years had been part of an effort to build industrial democracy through provision for profit-sharing and eventual participation of workers in managerial decision-making, a goal which corresponded with the Church's concern that men should have the security and responsibility of property ownership. During World War II, the C.I.O. considered this goal in the so-called industry council plan, but the need to combat inflation, together with post-war prosperity, weakened union concern with such basic structural changes. As a result, despite the continuing efforts of Monsignor Higgins and others to revive interest in encyclical teachings on industrial organization, labor action became increasingly either simply a defense of gains achieved or an effort to incorporate unorganized workers into the existing union framework. However necessary such work, it no longer seemed to generate a moving vision of Christian social reform.[66]

Of course, there were other areas of voluntary organization than labor unions. In the late 1930's, Bishop Sheil joined a coalition that sponsored a broad-gauged effort to organize the stockyards area of Chicago. Unions, churches and social groups joined together to improve the neighborhood, combat crime and intergroup tensions, and battle for better city services. Led by Saul Alinsky and supported by the area's priests, the Back of the Yards Neighborhood Council became a model of future community organizations. Alinksy worked closely in his career as a professional organizer with church groups of every denomination and his type of community organization, which emphasized popular participation and self-help, was an attractive one to socially minded clergy.[67]

The rise of Black protest in the 1960's, together with renewed concern about the quality of urban life, would make the urban priest, or the "inner city vicar" as one priest in Rochester was called, the modern counterpart of yesterday's labor priest. Activism in this area meant a chance for useful work with government agencies, as clerical and Church involvement in the War on Poverty indicated. But it also meant sharp conflict with local government and with white residents, frequently Catholics, division in the local Church, and critical confrontation between members of the Catholic community. The priest of the 1930's who worked with the unions was usually on the side of working class Catholics against managers who were only rarely of his Church. The urban priest of the 1960's, however, is as frequently on the side of non-Catholics against local interest groups containing large numbers of his fellow Catholics. In this situation there is experienced a conflict between the priest's pastoral responsibilities to the poor, now no longer heavily Catholic, and his pastoral duties to his own parishioners and his superiors. To a great degree this is a new experience in a Church that became after World War II prosperous and middle class.[68]

The changes of the post-war years manifested a decline of old concerns with domestic and theological enemies. Instead, as Father Leo R. Ward, C.S.C., put it in 1959, "the Church is busy living her own creative life and living it with what must seem to outsiders as almost disconcerting confidence."[69] The major evidence of this vitality was to be found in Catholic Action, particularly in the Topsy-like growth of the Christian Family Movement, Young Catholic Workers, Young Catholic Students, Cana Conference for the engaged and the married, and Catholic Interracial Councils. Taking their lead from Chicago, these programs had priests as chaplains and counselors, but were lay-directed, blending the moderately liberal tone of the new Catholic middle class with loyalty to the Church and to the nation.

By the end of the 1950's the Catholic social action movement had entered upon dim days. Writing in *Social Order* in 1962, the Reverend Edward Duff, S.J. deplored the failure of Catholics to respond to *Mater et Magistra's* call to action to eliminate poverty and injustice. "Enjoying a tolerable order of economic justice and political freedom, the average Catholic is content," Duff wrote. "Indeed there is a danger that he may be identifying that culture, which he proudly calls 'the American way of life' with the Kingdom of God."[70] Duff's concern in 1962 came at the eye of the storm, when the Kennedy presidency had completed Catholicism's rise to full citizenship and before Vatican Council II, and the tragic events dating from November 22, 1963. Eight years later one can no longer believe that Catholics are by and large complacent, though Father Duff's concern for constructive social action remains central.

For many, Catholic social action proved a dead end. It failed to organize Catholics as a force for change, and what achievements it could claim resulted more from its identification with a viable cause than from its particular power or influence. Socially conscious, moderate Catholics had learned by the 1950's to work within government, the unions and the new community programs; they felt no need for a specifically Catholic organization. In the 1960's, the problems of the United States would become so severe as to destroy such complacency and expose the very foundations of men's identity, but whether specifically Catholic social action could provide a living vehicle for response was not at all clear.

The events of the last decade have undermined the models of social action developed before World War II. During the last ten years, the entire way in which Roman Catholics think about the church has been changing. "How Christians conceive of their relationship with the Church and, more fundamentally still, how they conceive of the nature and mission of the Church itself, affects every religious attitude which they have fashioned, consciously or unconsciously," Richard P. McBrien writes.[71] The way we think about the priest, his role and his mission, is dependent in large part upon the way we think about the Church. If the latter is thought of as a "perfect society" never in need of reform or development, if canon law supplies the key concepts for describing the Church, if the emphasis of churchmen is upon the need to preserve, defend and expand its institutional forms in order to maximize the possibility of men gaining the salvific graces the Church makes available, then the priest's functions are primarily ecclesiastical. He is supposed to win men to the Church, persuade them to be baptized, to attend services, hearken to his advice and accept the Church's discipline. Of course he may assist the poor, support labor unions, or fight discrimination, but always he seeks to spread the influence of the Church, to improve her image, to attract men to her banner, to motivate them to accept her leadership. The size, wealth and power of the Church become the criteria governing the priest's work, not as selfish ends, but as handy and reliable guides for assessing the spiritual well-being of a society and its people.

Without denying the continued existence of this attitude, it should be clear that the model on which it is based no longer is operative in the minds of most American Catholics. Their ideas about the Church have been shaken severely by the Council, so that the criteria for judging distinctively Christian action, to say nothing of distinctively priestly responsibility, have become subjects of very great dispute. In dealing with the laity, the Vatican Council II recognized and gave positive sanction to the *de facto* secularization of the life of the people:

> By their competence in secular fields and by their personal activity, elevated from within by the grace of Christ, let (the laity) labor

vigorously so that, by human labor, technical skill, and civic culture created goods may be perfected for the benefit of every last man. . . .[72]

In dealing with the clergy, however, the Council retained an explicit concern with order and structure, stressing the close collaboration of priests with their bishops in sanctifying and governing the church. Priests are seen as "prudent cooperators with the episcopal order, as well as its aids and instruments." Yet, elsewhere, the fathers repeat that "all the faithful of Christ of whatever rank and status are called to the fullness of Christian life and to the perfection of charity." And, in pursuing that common vocation, "Christians cannot yearn for anything more ardently than to serve the men of the modern world ever more generously and effectively." [73]

The Council's innovations altered significantly the emphasis on various elements of Christian life and held out an ideal of Christian vocation that contrasts sharply with the actual life of many priests in parishes or religious communities. His personal and professional dignity were vastly enhanced by the conciliar decrees, and his sights were raised beyond the confines of the orderly parish to a vision of the Kingdom of God striving to be born amid the complex of promise and desolation which mark our era. A priest could find his commitment renewed and invigorated by the Council; he could even find it transformed into something far more dynamic and ambitious than he had previously experienced.

While such a response was felt, and felt profoundly, by innumerable priests in this country, many immediately experienced the changes with a sense of impatience and frustration as they contrasted the new model of the Church and of the priesthood with the actual structure and atmosphere of parish life.[74] Caught in a conflict of loyalties to the institutional forms in which he had been trained and through which he had worked and his equally powerful desire for thorough professional training and for the freedom to identify with the cause of the poor, the oppressed and the desperate, the priest necessarily entered a period of anxiety and unrest.[75] Institutions change more slowly than the minds and hearts of their participants, so that, as Father Eugene Kennedy, M.M., puts it, "there is tension for the younger priests who have high personalist ideals because they find themselves somewhat frustrated by the still extant structure of a previous era." [76]

The Council and the revolutionary shift in emphasis in the Catholic understanding of the Church thus provided one major source of crisis for the Church and its ministers. The American priest had other causes for his anxiety. In the United States, the Council and the challenge it implicitly directed at the folk religion of the country came at a time when the national Church itself was undergoing tremendous changes. Throughout most of its history, the American Catholic Church has been primarily one of laborers and immigrants. Worldly success came slowly and as late as the 1930's most Catholics remained members of the working class, though significant numbers had risen to lower middle class rank. Regarded by their Protestant neighbors with suspicion because of their faith, they responded with a defiance and pride reinforced by the class structure. The fact that Catholic workingmen were immigrants or children of immigrants similarly reinforced their isolation but also supported their adherence to the faith.

The quarter century which preceded the Council, however, brought significant changes in the composition of the American Church. The G.I. Bill of Rights opened college education to millions of Catholics, promoting their ascendance from the ghetto to middle class suburbs. The C.I.O. unions brought improvements in income, living conditions and status to many Catholics who remained in the factories. Changes in national and international life reduced tensions between Catholics and others, gradually overcoming the minority consciousness so prominent in the Church in earlier years. Less and less did Catholics think of themselves as Irish, Italian and Poles; more and more they thought of themselves as Americans. The Church itself had been a melting pot, serving as the medium through which men moved from an ethnic to an American identity. A young, educated and self-confident laity increasingly challenged what seemed to them outmoded forms and practices. In the late 1950's, Donald Thorman, Andrew Greeley and others of the "new breed" called for the advent of what one of them called "a new generation: American and Catholic." [77] The election of John F. Kennedy symbolized and ratified these changes, demonstrating that the American Catholic was no longer a member of a despised and isolated minority, but a full-fledged participant in the American way of life, capable of rising to positions of power and influence, winning the respect of his neighbors on the basis of his talents and wealth, and assuming greater responsibility in all his affairs. Much of the program which these men proposed for the Church — vernacular liturgy, ratification of religious liberty, national autonomy and lay participation — was indeed adopted by the Council.

Yet these dramatic changes in the social structure and composition of the Church in the United States disturbed many, for they necessarily entailed a challenge to the style of the working class, immigrant Church. For no one was this more true than for the parish priest. In the immigrant Church the priest was often, as he had been in the village, the most educated man in the community. In a Protestant country he was the defender of his people against the attacks of nativists and bigots. He was their counselor and advisor, their mediator with the hostile American world. Industrialists who employed Catholic immigrants sought the priest's friendship, which often enabled him to alleviate the workers' grievances. The politician who desired immigrant votes found in the priest the surest link with the people, the means to gain their confidence and support. This in turn often allowed the priest to handle the legal difficulties and needs of his flock. His was a position of status and importance, attained through his service to his people. A young man who aspired to win the respect of his peers could find few better avenues to success than through the priesthood.

Nor did the priest's stature rest solely on his ability to preserve old world ties and mediate with the new society. Internally, too, he provided necessary services and exercised undisputed leadership. The priest administered the Church's sacraments and conducted her rituals; he supervised family life through the confessional and visitations; he administered the finances and property of the Church; he directed the moral formation of the young through parochial schools and catechism classes; he even influenced leisure pursuits through his control of parish associations.

In the years following the great depression, all of this changed. Old world ties became less important and in any case passed into the hands of educated, literate men who organized national societies which the priest could join but could not dominate. The children of the immigrants could themselves deal with American society and they could develop their own leadership in political parties and labor unions to negotiate on their behalf with other groups. A mobile population moving from place to place, receiving a college education, and subject to a wide variety of influences developed family patterns less and less subject to the influence of the priest. In times of crisis other professionals — psychiatrists, marriage counselors, doctors, social workers — easily assumed many of the priest's former advisory functions. Parochial schools remained and indeed flourished, and there was a steady increase in religious education programs, but it was difficult to find any significant differences in moral attitudes and behavior between those subject to their influence and those who were not. Mass communications, the spread of non-religious fraternal and social organizations, and the declining homogeneity of the parish, all drastically reduced the influence of the clergy over leisure pursuits. Church finances remained in his hands, but the priest found himself subject to pressures from above in the form of greater centralization of diocesan management and from below in the growing unwillingness of his middle class congregations to be permanently prevented from using their professional talents in managing the Church's finances and facilities. Only the sacraments and ritual remained wholly the prerogative of the priest, and his people, while they might desire changes, were content to leave these under his direction.

The effect of these changes on priests can be illustrated by reference to Catholic Action. On the one hand, the official character of Catholic Action seemed to imply that the chaplain was the agent of the bishop; his task was not only to guarantee orthodoxy but to insure conformity with diocesan policy. As one writer explained, "Catholic Action is participation by the laity in the hierarchical apostolate. . . . This is something obviously which cannot be assumed at will by those not in orders." [78] Yet there were many areas of life in which the priest could not carry on his work, and the pope had urged priests to recruit laymen to help in those areas in which they daily lived and worked. "The average priest, just because he is a priest and therefore separated from the rest of the community in its daily work, is precluded from carrying on the kind of apostolate required by the circumstances of our time," Stanley B. James wrote. By recruiting and training lay militants, who would "be to him as the hand is to the body," the priest could multiply his own effectiveness: "Whereas he formerly counted only as one in the arithmetic of heaven, he now counts as a thousand or more." [79]

Such an approach, which was in accord with Church teaching, was ill-suited to American conditions, particularly when the object of concern was not pornography but economic or racial justice. As Cardinal Gibbons had told Rome in 1886: "We find that, in our country the presence and explicit influence of the clergy would not be advisable where our citizens, without distinction of religious belief, come together in regard to their industrial interests alone." [80] What was true of labor unions seemed also true of many other areas of life. Raymond McGowan, John Ryan's assistant in the N.C.W.C. Social Action Department, believed strongly in the need for organized effort by Catholics to confront social issues. The National Catholic Social Action Conferences, held in 1938 and 1939 and renewed in the mid 1950's, were a step in the direction of unifying the work of social justice. While led by interested priests and bishops, such an effort seemed to Mc-

Gowan to depend ultimately on lay action. The work of his department, McGowan argued, and by implication the work of the priest, was simply to stimulate organization where it was lacking, encourage and guide work already under way, and educate Catholics to the need for reform.

Gradually this approach became dominant. Monsignor Reynold Hillenbrand in Chicago and Father Louis Putz at Notre Dame, among others, guided CFM and YCS–YCW in this direction. The priest was to teach and exemplify Catholic principles, train and form lay apostles, and act responsibly as a citizen, but he was to encourage and recognize the maturity of the laymen, being satisfied with the indirect influence of a teacher and model rather than the direct influence of· a leader. This approach found theological resources in the post war years in new theology of the laity that challenged the clericalism of earlier theories of Catholic Action.[81]

The new approach did not solve all the problems. It was never clear whether the chaplain was the agent of the bishop or of the group, to which constituency he should turn in moments of conflict. If his ordinary was generally permissive the problem might not become acute, but for those who worked under a bishop who concentrated on strong central control, the problem could be very real. Debates over the "official" or "unofficial" character of such organizations as the Catholic Interracial Council reflected this ambiguity. While the theory of lay independence and indirect clerical influence exerted an enormous impact in the development of Catholic social action, it by no means became an accepted consensus. Many bishops regarded CFM and similar organizations with distrust, and many priests preferred neat and tightly controlled organizations. "Since the apostolic function of the Catholic Church is an ordered work in which many men are privileged actively to participate, it is necessarily a work performed under definite direction," Father Joseph C. Fenton wrote. Acceptance of orders from above, he argued, was a crucial feature of priestly vocation: "In reality a diocesan priest works for Christ only when he fulfills, to the extent of his ability, the work to which his bishop has assigned him." [82]

Another problem was that of power. The pioneers of independent action and the lay apostolate were motivated in part by a desire to change the image of the Church which they believed was too frequently identified with internal authoritarianism and external power plays. Accordingly they urged laymen and lay organizations to accept responsibility in public affairs while insisting that they did not speak for the

Church. Bishops and priests on the other hand should avoid using their economic strength and their political power to influence public action on controversial issues. One problem with this approach was that it seemed to set severe limits to the priest's own political involvement, for if he ran for office, marched in a picket line or otherwise became directly involved, it seemed to mean that he had failed to train laymen to act in areas manifestly within their distinctive sphere. Moreover, such action seemed as well to confirm the stereotype of the Church's desire to use its members to protect and strengthen its political and social role. On the other hand, there were drawbacks to the liberal position. Obviously the Church did possess resources whose allocation was beyond lay control. When confronted with a social problem of massive dimensions, like racism, the question could arise, as it did in the 1960's, whether abstention and benevolent neutrality was an adequate policy for the Church, or whether she must throw her resources and her power behind movements for social change.

Involved here is a second problem, democracy in the Church. In arguing that the hierarchy and clergy should leave decisions in the public sphere to laymen, the advocates of the lay apostolate could easily find that the lay decision would not necessarily accord with papal teachings or the gospel message; again the race issue supplies illustration. All these are controversial issues that have come into the open in recent years; the point here is that the lay apostolate vision of Catholic Action contained no adequate resolution of the problems involved in defining the role of the priest in society. Rather it straddled these problems when it did not ignore them; in either case it was a position which, for the priest, hardly could withstand the shocks of the 1960's.[83]

The social changes of the post-war years, then, seemed to encourage the maturity of the layman and to confine the priest to sacerdotal functions that were supposed to inspire independent lay action. As Emile Pin, S.J., noted, however, such a stress on spiritual priestly functions presupposed a specific theology:

> Even when the priest was aware of his social impotence in the past, even when he realized his incompetence in the field of ethics, he could console himself with the performance of his vital functions. He might not contribute to the building up of the world by direct action or by spiritual counselling, but he would be able to save souls by administering the sacraments. Solidly grounded on the dogma of *ex opere operato*, he made every effort to see to it that the faithful would devote some time each week to their religious duties, no matter how much frivolity and materialism

infected their daily work. . . . Moreover, the confidence of the faithful helped to convince the priest that his work, however irrelevant in this world, surely had some usefulness for the world to come.[84]

Here the Vatican Council II caused the upheaval, for by changing much of the practice of the liturgy and reorienting its rationale towards the community, it suggested a trend that could easily result in questioning the need for the priest at all. Even when the question did not come up, the new stress on the Mass as a community celebration forced the priest's attention to the need to foster and develop the parish as a real community. Yet, the parish, no longer dominated by a single ethnic group of relatively similar education and social class, had become a heterogeneous collection of individuals from different backgrounds, with different interests and temperaments, sharply divided on social issues and on the moral and religious questions that the council raised. Far from fostering community, the liturgical changes, with their surrounding shifts in theological emphasis and their reorientation towards social concerns, frequently divided the superficial community of the territorial parish and left many a young priest, caught up in the fervor of the post-conciliar urge to reform, without a community or a constituency.

The Church in the 1960's, then, was passing through what historian Philip Gleason has called "the crisis of Americanization," the result of the assimilation of its people into the mainstream of American life. Gleason stated:

> Assimilation on the individual level has not only brought Catholics abreast of their fellow citizens in respect to social and economic status; it has also resulted in a new self conception for those who have adopted the attitudes and beliefs prevailing in secular society. These changes in the social composition and outlook of the group require a reshaping of Catholic institutions to bring them into line with the shifting configuration of the clientele whose needs they serve and whose values they symbolize and embody. A number of these institutional and ideological changes were already under way before Vatican II, but the loosening of traditional patterns set in motion by the Council has vastly accelerated the general tendency. All the old beliefs and patterns of action are called into question; all the old institutions must justify themselves afresh and demonstrate their relevance to the new situation.[85]

Here, then, are the two major sources of the present situation: the dramatic changes in the social composition of the Church in the United States, and the vast upheaval in attitudes and practices set in motion by Vatican Council II.

The blending of the changes in attitudes and style at home and the religious reforms of the Council should have been a source of satisfaction for the "new breed" laymen and even for the clergy. Any sense of accomplishment, however, was submerged by new issues and problems. In the wake of the Council, conflict developed throughout the Church; the Council had opened a hole in the dike of established power and the pent up waters of centuries threatened to pour through. Rome and the American bishops sought to preserve a middle ground, changing slowly and deliberately, avoiding the destruction of the old, hoping to find ways to preserve much of what they valued from the past. They were beset by the intransigent, who viewed the Council itself as a disaster and sought to repress the forces for change, to prevent erosion of the deposit of faith and the destruction of the Church herself. At the other extreme, younger Catholics in Western Europe and North America demanded immediate and radical renewal, whatever the cost. Birth control, clerical celibacy, the freedom of the faithful became issues that threatened to tear the Catholic community apart.

In the United States there were other and, in many ways, more serious events which threatened the process of creative adaptation following the Council. In 1960, Monsignor John Tracy Ellis, noting the new acceptance and maturity of American Catholics, had argued that "it is now asked of us that we learn to look beyond the narrow interests of our Catholic body to the interests of those around us. . . . What is demanded is a broader understanding of the society of which we are a part and the world in which we live." [86] That understanding in 1960 was a generally optimistic and progressive vision of an America which, while in need of greater attention to its unfinished business was, nevertheless, a nation whose fundamental decency and benevolence were taken for granted. This view of America, however natural to the now Americanized and prosperous Catholic, could hardly withstand the shocks of the decade to come.

The nation began to escalate to dramatic heights of destructiveness a war in southeast Asia which many regarded as unjust. The use of advanced military and para-military technology in an underdeveloped country brought frightening human destruction and posed a terrible challenge to the Christian conscience. At home the reality of racism, present from the nation's foundation, burst forth into the public consciousness as cities erupted and ghettos burned. Some of America's best leaders fell under assassins' guns. The political process increasingly seemed unresponsive to the needs of people and men were made aware of widespread physical and social decay that seemed to contradict the belief in American wealth and beneficence on which middle class Americans had been weaned. Polarization, of blacks and whites, of hawks and doves, of young and old, became characteristic of a nation that had prided itself on its stability, its consensus, its ability to resolve its "unfinished business" through rational, democratic processes. The Catholic crisis faded into the American crisis, and a new sense of urgency came to pervade the hearts of all decent men, whatever their political or religious views.[87]

Things did not work out as expected. The Church, which seemed to be freeing itself from the burden of the past in order to confront human problems openly and honestly, in the spirit of *Pacem in Terris* of 1963, seems now to many to be preoccupied with internal conflict, while the nation becomes more polarized, and more violent. Disillusionment and shock were perhaps inevitable, for the approach of American Catholics to the issues of reform had not prepared them for the collapse of so many things they had taken for granted. More than they recognized, their attitudes had been dominated by a determination, derived from their immigrant heritage, to reconcile once and for all, the claims of their Church and their nation. They had few doubts that a common Americanism provided a secure basis for cooperative efforts with others to promote the realization of goals at once Christian and American.

The old objective of a full American Catholicism was to be achieved by reforming Catholicism, for the American society seemed to need only a few minor adjustments. Kennedy's liberalism marked the limits of whatever Catholic Left existed a few years ago, aside from a few fringe groups of pacifists. Reform was ecclesiastical, designed to free the Catholic from the tensions which beset him by confirming his positive response to secular America, recognizing his dignity by structural democratic procedures and revitalizing his personal and community religious life by modernizing the liturgy.

The early liturgical reformers of the depression years had recognized the liturgy as a school of social justice, communicating a sense of human solidarity which would strengthen the drive for the Christian social reconstruction outlined in *Quadragesimo Anno.* Latter day liturgists paid lip service to the hopes for Christian social action flowing from the liturgy, but their real concern was with individual and group spirituality and, at best, secondarily related to social change. While many conciliar reforms were aimed at strengthening a sense of community in the Church, neither Vatican Council II nor most American reformers looked beyond liturgy and theology to the economic, social and political context within which such Christian community must take shape and develop. As a result, the hopes aroused were based on incomplete and weak foundations and failed to provide against the kind of awful contingencies which in fact have taken place in recent years.

Like other contemporary critics of large scale institutions, American Catholic reformers have been preoccupied with personal honesty and individual fulfillment, concerns particularly marked among the clergy. In reaction to the Church's long concern with its institutional strength and its corporate interests, many seem to regard renewal primarily as a liberation from the confining grasp of organization and law. This point of view is expressed in the longing for a non-institutional Church, a prophetic Christianity freed of the influence of nation, class, ethnic group or neighborhood.

In one of the most perceptive pieces to appear in recent years, John P. Sisk pointed to the twin dangers of the institution's "sweet dream of harmony" and the individual's "sweet dream of liberation." [88] Many bishops, priests and laymen, frightened by the ferment and consequent insecurity fostered by change, hold fast to the hope for an eventual restoration of consensus and unity — qualities deemed essential to the functioning of any institution and particularly necessary for the Church. The dream of liberation on the other hand is most marked among men long frustrated by the pressures of ecclesiastical conformity, but it infects as well many advocates of personalism, fired by high dedication and nourished by the shocked realization of the extent to which Catholicism has become encrusted with features having more to do with nationalism, class interest, or race consciousness than with the gospels.

Dorothy Dohen's muckraking portrayal of the super-patriotism of American Catholic bishops, whose identification with the national cause often contradicted the values they professed, is a good example of the shocked righteousness and critical honesty of younger American Catholic intellectuals. [89] Miss Dohen and dozens of others stand aghast at their Church's surrender to what Will Herberg called the "idolatrous new religion of Americanism." These young Catholics may have little else in common with Herberg or with the late Christopher Dawson, a long time critic of American religion, but they share with these older men a determination that the Christian religious values, however defined, come before national or class values.[90] Paraphrasing a popular question of a decade ago, they are Christians who happen to be Americans, rather than Americans who happen to be Catholics.

Their difficulty is that in the absence of meaningful community life in the Church it is hard to determine what being a Catholic or a Christian means. Thirty years ago Dorothy Day and Peter Maurin denounced Catholic acquiescence in American bourgeois culture in terms unmatched by today's radicals, but they were certain that they possessed a secure basis for building a truly Christian culture and society. By today's standards they were theologically conservative and they found in the liturgy a basis for community and a model of society, the Mystical Body of Christ.

Today's Catholics have been greatly influenced by the Catholic Worker's insistence on personal responsibility, but they are less able to regard the liturgy as central to their social and political concerns, even if many may find it crucial for their religious life. Equally important, they have been unable to transcend the polarization of the individual and the state which the Catholic Worker fostered by its hostility to welfare legislation and its doctrinaire pacifism. Maurin's personalism led him to dream of a liberation of the individual from the complexities of modern society. Today's young Catholics are unable to accept his simplification of the social problem, though they remain convinced of the relevance and utility of personalist categories, which they often transfer into a dream of liberation from an ambiguous and compromising Church.[91]

In the past the Americanist inheritance of Catholic intellectuals in the United States inhibited their attempt to define a Christian response to American society. The result was that the American church has failed to produce a creative leadership attuned, at once, to the needs of a Catholic people passing through a period of profound social change and to the demands of a revitalized Christianity. This weakness can be illustrated by contrasting the enthusiastic reception given by many to Harvey Cox's optimistic portrayal of middle class America, to which the Church was urged to direct its attention, and the demands for vaguely defined "basic," "fundamental," even "revolutionary" change which punctuate discussions of American society in the light of national violence. Such inconsistency and ambiguity is probably inevitable, given the rapidity and scope of changes affecting the Catholic community. But if the goal of a vital, reforming Church in a dynamic America is not to become a mockery, Catholic thinkers must attempt to discipline their personalism by a serious intellectual effort to understand American society, an effort at least as important as the theological speculation and liturgical tinkering that have so far received far greater attention.

Once such a stance is adopted, a role of major importance exists for the priest, who becomes in a sense, not merely a witness of opposition, but a prophetic agent of change. Father Herbert McCabe, O.P., for example, citing the Council statement that the priest is called to preach the gospel "to all men," argues that many of the problems of defining the priests' function arise from seeing the Church primarily as a community. "The Church is not first of all a community; it is first of all a movement within the community of mankind," McCabe writes. Christianity seeks change "to transform the institutional relations between men in order to better express the relationships which constitute them as human," and the priest is an agent of change, who is marked by his dedication to the revolutionary cause, the cause of realizing here the message of the gospel.[92]

Father McCabe's words may be an extreme statement of the case but the basic point is that the priest will have to go behind the facade of social upheaval and theological speculation to consider the whole context in its relation to Christ in order to find once again a distinctive role for himself. Again it was Cardinal Suhard who anticipated much of this:

> We can say that the first duty of a priest in the world is to be obsessed with the idea of making his work productive of good. Whatever be the mission entrusted to him. . . he must each evening, before God, set out on his desk or his poor table two maps of the parish. . . . Patiently and zealously he should compare, detail by detail, these two master plans. The old one will be that of the Church in the Christian community, with its acquired positions, its habitual practice. The other, that of the new society, with its swift expansion, its centers of spontaneous interest, its unexpected seethings. This priest, be he parish priest, curate, professor, or Catholic Action chaplain, should have no rest until the two plans overlay and the two coincide to become one City in truth and love. This man will spend every hour of the day and night in planning the City to come on the basis of the City that is.[93]

The radical priests who have emerged in America in recent years: Father James Groppi, Philip and Daniel Berrigan, the numerous participants in civil rights marches and draft board raids, and their counterparts in every diocese in this country, are men for whom the specifically priestly dimension of life has been subsumed into the Christian and human dimensions. Their search is less for the meaningful form of social action for the priest than for the proper form of action for the Christian man. In that sense they are truly radical, for they are grappling with the very roots of our contemporary situation.

In that search they have predecessors to whom they can look: Edward McGlynn, John A. Ryan, Virgil Michel, Paul Hanley Furfey, but those men, while they lived as priests in the midst of the world and took the Church to new frontiers, existed in more settled times. They never doubted the truth or value of their faith; they had few disagreements with the basic structures of the Church or the basic institutions of American life. The new radicals live in a revolutionary era in both Church and society, and, as a result, they feel forced to look for new styles of life simply to remain true to their Christian faith and their faith in humanity. In doing so they seem to many to have abandoned the true work of the priesthood, offering Mass and leading the community at worship. But surely the case can be made that in times of profound crisis the work of the Christian leader is to be out in the midst of men, joining them in the search for new ways of living, for new communities in which public worship and prayer will again be truly community celebrations.

The Church exists for all men; Pope John XXIII and Vatican Council II have made that clear. "The sorrow and anguish of the modern priest is to feel that the 'real world' exists and is being built without them, and that they are strangers to it . . . . the right proportions are reversed: whereas he should be seeking the lost sheep, in fact it is the lone sheep in the fold that occupies the greater part of their day." [94] The Church has broken down the walls between itself and the "real world" and has sought to correct the "proportions." The price is dissent and conflict; it may even be disappearance of the priesthood as a full time occupation, as Ivan Illich has predicted.[95] But the promise is the release of new energy and the formation of new commitments to service to God and man.

Surely the link between past and present is that pastoral concern that inspired Pope John to call the Vatican Council. It was the basis for the development of the institutions of American Catholicism, all of which were designed by decent and honest men concerned with the welfare of their people. Later the same pastoral motivation led men like John Ryan to urge reform of the nation's economic system so that it would serve the real needs of men. Labor priests, priests in the racial apostolate, priest pacifists and priest politicians, all were united to one another and to their less active colleagues by their common concern with the complete welfare, temporal and spiritual, of their fellow men. If that basic point is kept clearly in mind, men can recognize that, when the needs of people, once adequately served by a set of institutions, change in new historical situations, the truly concerned pastor will move quickly to meet them. The priest would serve the Church and all mankind, and he can do so, but only if he is prepared to accept as permanent a position on the cutting edge of sacred and secular, which means a life of permanent crisis, feeling always "ambiguity and uncertainty, moving constantly into the darkness with the light of the gospel." [96]

1. James Kavanaugh, *A Modern Priest Looks at His Outdated Church* (New York, 1967).

2. For documentary evidence of dissatisfaction and uncertainty, see Joseph H. Fichter, *America's Forgotten Priests — What They Are Saying* (New York, c. 1968).

3. Emile Pin, S.J., "The Priestly Function in Crisis," in Karl Rahner, S.J., ed., *The Identity of the Priest, Concilium,* Vol. XLIV (New York, 1969) pp. 46–47.

4. Emmanuel Cardinal Suhard, "Priests Among Men," in *The Church Today* (Chicago, c. 1953). pp. 217–344.

5. The quotations are taken from "The Dogmatic Constitution on the Church" in Walter M. Abbott, S.J., ed., *The Documents of Vatican II* (New York, 1966). successively pp. 30, 15, 55.

6. Rt. Rev. William Stang, *Pastoral Theology* (New York, 1867), p. 39.

7. Eugene C. Kennedy, M.M., *Comfort My People: The Pastoral Presence of the Church* (New York, 1968), p. 35.

8. "Decree on the Ministry and Life of Priests," in Abbott, *op. cit.,* pp. 5, 39–40.

9. Rev. Donald McIlvan, "The Troubled Priest: A *Commonweal* Symposium," *Commonweal,* LXXXVII (February 16, 1968), 594.

10. Suhard, "Growth or Decline?", in *The Church Today,* p. 149. It is well to note that the movement of worker-priests inspired by Suhard was suppressed because, in part, it appeared to jeopardize the spiritual life of its participants and the proper order and discipline of the church, a clear example of the sharp distinction between church and world which shaped Catholic thought. On the worker priests, see Bernard Wall, trans. *Priest and Worker: The Autobiography of Henri Perrin,* (New York, c. 1964).

11. Quentin Quesnell, "The Priesthood of the Future," in William H. Cleary, ed., *Hyphenated Priests — The Ministry of the Future* (Washington and Cleveland, 1969), p. 141.

12. This interpretation of Catholic social thought is developed at length in David J. O'Brien, *American Catholics and Social Reform: The New Deal Years,* (New

York, 1968). It is supported by many modern theologians; see in particular, Karl Rahner, *The Christian Commitment*, (New York, 1963), p. 7, 9–10.

13. James E. Roohan, "American Catholics and the Social Question," 1865–1900, Unpublished PhD. Thesis, Yale University, 1952, pp. 27–28.

14. Aaron I. Abell, *American Catholicism and Social Action*, (New York, 1960), p. 24.

15. Gustave Weigel, S.J., "An Introduction to American Catholicism" in Louis Putz, C.S.C., ed., *The Catholic Church: U.S.A.* (Chicago, 1965), pp. 3–20.

16. Philip Gleason, "The Crisis of Americanization" in Gleason, ed., *Contemporary Catholicism in the United States* (Notre Dame, 1969), p. 29.

17. James Cardinal Gibbons, *A Retrospect of Fifty Years*, II, (New York and Baltimore, 1916), 152. The statement was made in 1890.

18. Thomas T. McAvoy, C.S.C., "The Formation of the American Catholic Minority," *Review of Politics*, X (January, 1948), 13–34.

19. C. J. Nuesse, *The Social Thought of American Catholics*, 1634–1829, (Washington, 1945), p. 283.

20. This idea was developed in several articles by Father Thomas McAvoy, C.S.C. and provides a central theme of his *A History of the Catholic Church in the United States* (Notre Dame, 1969).

21. Alexis De Tocqueville, *Democracy in America*, Phillips Bradley, ed., quoted in John Tracy Ellis, ed., *Documents of American Catholic History*, I (Chicago, 1967), 235.

22. Peter Guilday, ed., *National Pastorals of the American Hierarchy* (Westminster, 1954), pp. 51–52.

23. The *Journal* of Joseph-Octave Plessis, Bishop of Quebec, 1816, reprinted in Ellis, *Documents, op. cit.*, 200.

24. John Talbot Smith, *The Catholic Church in New York*, II (New York and Boston, 1905), 470.

25. *Ibid.*, 438–439.

26. Abell, *op. cit.* pp. 30–31.

27. Henry J. Browne, "Catholicism in the United States" in James Ward Smith and A. Leland Jamison, ed., *The Shaping of American Religion* (Princeton, c. 1961) p. 87.

28. Thomas T. McAvoy, C.S.C., "The Irish Catholic Clergyman in the United States," American Catholic Historical Society of Philadelphia, *Records*, LXXV (March, 1964), p. 20.

29. Peter Guilday, *A History of the Councils of Baltimore*, (New York, 1932), p. 182.

30. Abell, *op. cit.*, preface, n.p.

31. Pope Leo XIII, *Longingua Oceani*, in Ellis, ed., *Documents* II, 509.

32. Abell, *op. cit.* chapter 5; Robert E. Doherty, "The American Socialist Party and the Catholic Church," 1901–1917, unpublished Ed. D. thesis, Teachers College, Columbia University, 1959; Henry F. Bedford, *Socialism and the Workers in Massachusetts 1886–1912* (Amherst, 1966), pp. 186–192, 214–215.

33. John Gilmary Shea, "Labor Discontent," *American Catholic Quarterly Review* VII (October, 1882), 712.

34. William Stang, "The Catholic Movement on Behalf of Social Reform," *American Ecclesiastical Review*, XXXVI (March, 1904), 258–278.

35. Quoted in Abell, *American Catholicism and Social Action*, p. 173.

36. Sr. Joan Bland, *Hibernian Crusade: The Story of the Catholic Total Abstinence Union of America*, (Washington, 1951); Mary E. Henthorne, BVM, *The Irish Catholic Colonization Association of the United States*, (Champagne, 1932); Roohan, *op. cit. passim.*

37. Philip Gleason, *The Conservative Reformers: German-American Catholics and the Social Order* (Notre Dame, 1968.).

38. Abell, *op. cit.* p. 173.

39. John A. Ryan, *The Church and Socialism and Other Essays*, (Washington, 1917), p. 159.

40. McAvoy, *op. cit.* p. 23.

41. Robert D. Cross, *The Emergence of Liberal Catholicism in America* (Cambridge, 1958), p. 107.

42. Henry J. Browne, "The Changing American Parish" in James O'Gara, ed., *The Postconciliar Parish* (New York, 1967), pp. 3–14.

43. Joseph Selinger, "Is Social Reform Work a Duty of the Parish Clergy?" *American Ecclesastical Review*, XLII (April, 1910) 453–458.

44. Oscar Handlin, "The Church and the Modern City," *Atlantic*, CCX (August, 1962), 103.

45. This interpretation draws heavily on the standard historiography of the twentieth-century reform. See in particular, Richard Hofstadter, *The Age of Reform* (New York, 1955); J. Joseph Hutmacher, "Urban Liberalism and the Age of Reform," *Mississippi Valley Historical Review*, XLIX (September, 1962), 231–241.

46. These developments can be traced in William J. Kerby, "The Catholic Charities of a City," *American Ecclesiastical Review*, XLVIII (June, 1913) 677–695; Charles P. Neill, "The Need for Trained Social Workers" (1914) in Aaron I. Abell, ed., *American Catholic Thought on Social Questions*, (Indianapolis and New York, 1968), pp. 277–285; Donald P. Gavin, *The National Conference of Catholic Charities*, (Milwaukee, 1962); and Robert F. Keegan, "Diocesan Organization in Charity" (1932) in Abell, *ibid.*, pp. 312–324.

47. Robert D. Cross, "Catholic Charities," *Atlantic* CCX (August 1962), p. 113.

48. John A. Ryan, "The Study of Social Problems in the Seminary," *American Ecclesiastical Review*, XXXIX (August, 1908), p. 117.

49. William J. Kerby, "The Catholic Charities of a City", *op. cit.* pp. 677–695.

50. See for example Francis W. Howard, "Social Science: An Aid to the Ministry," *American Ecclesiastical Review*, XII (April, 1895) 293–300; William J. Kerby, "Social Science as Part of Theological Study," in Abell, *op. cit.* pp. 265–276.

51. George T. Schmitt, *The American Priest* (New York, 1919), pp. 84–85.

52. Sylvester Malone, *Dr. Edward McGlynn* (New York, 1918), p. 4.

53. Robert Doherty, "The American Socialist Party and the Catholic Church, 1901–1917," Chapters 5, 6.

54. John A. Ryan, *Social Doctrine in Action*, (New York, 1941); *A Living Wage*, (New York, 1906) On Ryan's career see Francis L. Broderick, *Right Reverend New Dealer: John A. Ryan* (New York, 1963).

55. J. G. Shaw, *Edwin V. O'Hara: American Prelate* (New York, 1957.)

56. Bernard C. Cronin, *Father Yorke and the Labor Movement in San Francisco 1900–1910* (Washington, 1943).

57. Mary Harrita Fox, *Peter E. Dietz, Labor Priest* (Notre Dame, 1953); Henry J. Browne, "Peter E. Dietz, Pioneer Planner of Catholic Social Action," *Catholic Historical Review*, XXXIII (January, 1948), 448–456.

58. For a full discussion of the 1930's, see O'Brien, *op. cit.*, and George Q. Flynn, *American Catholics and the Roosevelt Presidency* (Lexington, 1968).

59. Bishop James A. Griffin, Springfield, Illinois to Francis Haas, September 7, 1933, Haas Papers, Catholic University of America.

60. James T. McNicholas, O.P., "Priests and Labor," *Catholic Mind*, XLIV (March, 1946), 158–159. On labor and the clergy see Abell, *American Catholicism and Social Action*, pp. 258–285; O'Brien, *American Catholics and Social Reform*, pp. 97–119; Paul Stroh, "The Catholic Clergy and American Labor Disputes," 1900–1939. Unpublished Ph. D thesis, Catholic University of America, 1939; Richard Ward, "The Role of the Association of Catholic Trade Unionists in the American Labor Movement," unpublished Ph.D. thesis, University of Michigan, 1952.

61. On Coughlin, see O'Brien, *op. cit.* Ch. 7; Charles Tull, *Father Coughlin and the New Deal* (Syracuse, 1965)

62. Charles Bruehl, "Influence of the Social Environment," *Central Blatt and Social Justice,* XXVIII (April, 1935), 3–4.

63. Virgil Michel, O.S.B., "Social Aspects of the Liturgy," *Catholic Action,* XVI (May, 1934), p. 11. On Michel, see Paul B. Marx, O.S.B., *Virgil Michel and the Liturgical Movement* (Collegeville, 1957).

64. Father Furfey's best known works are *Fire on the Earth* (New York, 1936); *This Way to Heaven* (Silver Springs, 1939); *The Respectable Murders* (New York, 1966) and *The Morality Gap* (New York, 1969).

65. On the early stages of Catholic Action and the contrast between European and American styles see O'Brien, *op. cit.,* pp. 182–185. For later development see the excellent anthologies of Louis Putz, C.S.C., *Catholic Church: U.S.A.,* cited above, and Leo R. Ward, C.S.C., *Catholic Life U.S.A.: Contemporary Lay Movements* (St. Louis, 1959).

66. On this subject, see in particular an interview with Monsignor Higgins in Donald McDonald, *Catholics in Conversation* (Philadelphia and New York, 1960), p. 121 *ff.* See also Abell, *op. cit.,* ch. 8.

67. Saul Alinsky, *Reveille for Radicals* (Chicago, 1946).

68. There is a growing literature on this subject. See in particular, Lyle E. Schaller, *Community Organization: Conflict and Reconciliation* (Nashville and New York, c. 1966).

69. Ward, *op. cit.,* p. 3.

70. Edward Duff, S.J., "Catholic Social Action in the American Environment," *Social Order* XII (September, 1962), 300–301.

71. Richard P. McBrien, *Do We Need the Church?* (New York, 1969), pp. 12–13.

72. Abbot, *op. cit.,* "Dogmatic Constitution on the Church," p. 63.

73. *Ibid.,* p. 67; "Pastoral Constitution on the Church and the Modern World," *Documents,* p. 307.

74. Rev. George Hafner: "In the Institutional Church, it's terribly difficult for a priest to have a sense of self-respect — when at the age of 45 he's supposed to be a leader, but still has to get permission to put more "coke" in the "coke" machine. And so he begins to wonder, aside from what it means to be a priest, if he can ever be a good man in this rigid, institutionalized structure. Before he can discover what it means to be a priest, I think he has to discover what it means to be a man." "The Troubled Priest," p. 583.

75. For an excellent treatment of the problem see John Tracy Ellis, "Whence Did they Come, These Uncertain Priests of the 1960's," *American Ecclesiastical Review,* CLXII (March, 1970 and April, 1970), 145–172, 234–248.

76. Kennedy, *op. cit.,* p. 11.

77. Michael Novak, *A New Generation: American and Catholic* (New York, 1964).

78. Stanley B. James, "The Priesthood in Catholic Action," *Homiletic and Pastoral Review,* XXXVIII (January, 1938), 356.

79. *Ibid.,* 361.

80. Memorial on Knights of Labor in Ellis, *Documents,* II, 449.

81. See as examples on this point, L. L. McReavy, "The Priest in Social Action," *Catholic Mind,* XLVII (February, 1949), 74–77; John F. Cronin, "The Priest and Social Action," *Catholic Mind,* XLIII (July, 1945), 424–430; Raymond McGowan, "Working for a New Social Order," *Catholic Action,* XLV (May, 1932), 22–23.

82. Joseph Clifford Fenton, *The Calling for the Diocesan Priest,* (Westminster, 1944), 57, 63.

83. These issues are discussed in Andrew Greeley, *The Catholic Experience* (New York, 1967), Chapter 8. Ed Marciniak, long a Catholic social actionist in Chicago, has written a biting critique of Catholic Action, in which too frequently

the clergy "pulled the strings" backstage: "The secular Christian is not an errand boy in the world for the clergy." He is even more strongly opposed to direct clerical involvement preferring to restrict the clergy to honest formation of lay apostles through their ecclesiastical functions perhaps on a part time basis while leaving the "secular Christian" with full responsibility for temporal affairs and for establishing democratic procedures for determining the Church's position on public issues. *Tomorrow's Christian* (Dayton, 1969).

84. Pin, *op. cit.*, p. 48.

85. Philip Gleason, "The Crisis of Americanization" in Gleason, ed., *Contemporary Catholicism in the United States* (Notre Dame, 1969), pp. 27–28.

86. John Tracy Ellis, "American Catholicism in 1960: An Historical Perspective,": in Ellis, *Perspectives on American Catholicism* (Baltimore, 1963), p. 57. Monsignor Ellis has himself reflected on the dramatic changes of the decade since that lecture. "The Church in Revolt: The Tumultuous Sixties," *Critic*, January-February, 1970. pp. 12–21.

87. See David J. O'Brien's "American Catholics in an Age of Crisis" *New City*, (November, 1967), pp. 4–9.

88. John P. Sisk, "The Sweet Dream of Liberation," *National Catholic Reporter*, August 31, 1966 and "The Sweet Dream of Harmony," *ibid.*, September 13, 1967.

89. Dorothy Dohem, *Nationalism and American Catholicism* (New York, 1967).

90. Will Herberg, *Protestant, Catholic, Jew* (New York, 1954); Christopher Dawson in *The Moral Curve* (New York, 1961).

91. On the Catholic Worker, see O'Brien, *op. cit.*, Chapter 8 and the forthcoming study by William Miller.

92. Herbert McCabe, O.P. "Priesthood and Revolution," in Donald Cutler, ed., *The Religious Situation: 1969* (Boston, 1969), pp. 980–992.

93. Suhard, *op. cit.*, p. 273.

94. *Ibid.*, p. 272.

95. Ivan Illich, "The Vanishing Clergyman," *The Critic*, June-July, 1967, pp. 18–27.

96. Kennedy, *op. cit.*, p. 43.

INDEX